CRITICAL SURVEY
OF
LONG FICTION

CRITICAL SURVEY
OF
LONG FICTION

English Language Series

REVISED EDITION
Dra-Hanl

3

Edited by
FRANK N. MAGILL

SALEM PRESS
Pasadena, California   Englewood Cliffs, New Jersey

SECOND PRINTING

Library of Congress Cataloging-in-Publication Data
Critical survey of long fiction. English language series/
edited by Frank N. Magill. — Rev. ed.
    p.   cm.
    Includes bibliographical references and index.
    1. English fiction—Dictionaries. 2. American
fiction—Dictionaries. 3. English fiction—
Bio-bibliography. 4. American fiction—
Bio-bibliography. 5. Novelists, English—
Biography—Dictionaries. 6. Novelists, American—
Biography—Dictionaries.
I. Magill, Frank Northen, 1907-   .
PR821.C7   1991
823.009′03—dc20   91-19694
ISBN 0-89356-825-2 (set)   CIP
ISBN 0-89356-828-7 (volume 3)

PRINTED IN THE UNITED STATES OF AMERICA

LIST OF AUTHORS IN VOLUME 3

CRITICAL SURVEY
OF
LONG FICTION

MARGARET DRABBLE

Born: Sheffield, England; June 5, 1939

Principal long fiction

A Summer Bird-Cage, 1963; *The Garrick Year*, 1964; *The Millstone*, 1965 (published in the United States as *Thank You All Very Much*); *Jerusalem the Golden*, 1967; *The Waterfall*, 1969; *The Needle's Eye*, 1972; *The Realms of Gold*, 1975; *The Ice Age*, 1977; *The Middle Ground*, 1980; *The Radiant Way*, 1987; *A Natural Curiosity*, 1989.

Other literary forms

Margaret Drabble has combined literary scholarship with her career as a novelist. She has edited a collection of critical essays about Thomas Hardy, *The Genius of Thomas Hardy* (1975), and has edited three of Jane Austen's lesser known works, *Lady Susan* (1974), *The Watsons* (1974), and *Sanditon* (1974). She has written biographies of William Wordsworth and Arnold Bennett and a literary travelogue of England, *A Writer's Britain: Landscape in Literature* (1979). Her edition of *The Oxford Companion to English Literature* was published in 1985 to great acclaim. Drabble has had a long-standing connection with drama and continues to write for the stage. Her works include *Bird of Paradise* (1969), a stage play; *A Touch of Love* (1969), a screenplay; and *Laura* (1964), a play for television.

Drabble has written a fair number of short stories, as yet uncollected, and only partially available to American audiences. These have been dismissed under the rubric of "women's magazine fiction," but Suzanne H. Mayer has recently suggested that they may be of value as clues to the genesis of Drabble's novels. Drabble has also written a book for children, *For Queen and Country: Britain in the Victorian Age* (1979).

Achievements

Drabble's novels charm and delight, but perhaps more significantly, they reward their readers with a distinctively modern woman's narrative voice and their unusual blend of Victorian and modern structures and concerns.

Although there seems to be critical consensus that Drabble has, as Bernard Bergonzi has said, "devised a genuinely new character and predicaments," the exact nature of this new voice and situation has not been precisely defined. Bergonzi sees the new character as an original blend of career woman and mother, yet Drabble's career woman begins to appear only in her eighth novel, *The Realms of Gold*. Her earlier, yet equally freshly portrayed heroines are often not mothers, as, for example, Sarah in *A Summer Bird-Cage*, or Clara in *Jerusalem the Golden*. Most of the mothers who precede Frances Wingate in *The Realms of Gold* can in no way be considered career women. Rose

Vassiliou in *The Needle's Eye* does not work; Rosamund Stacey in *Thank You All Very Much* works only sporadically to support her baby, and her job can hardly be considered a career.

Other critics have claimed that the new voice involves an unprecedented acquaintance with the maternal attitude toward children. This is the voice Erica Jong predicted would emerge once motherhood was no longer thought incompatible with literary artistry. In fact, only three Drabble novels can be said to contain this voice: *Thank You All Very Much*, *The Ice Age*, and *The Middle Ground*; yet all the novels seem to present something original in their female point of view.

Female characters have illuminated literature for more than a thousand years, but until recently they have appeared as secondary figures. The female has been present, but her point of view and voice have been lacking. Drabble seems to be able to evoke not only the female point of view but also the cadence of the female voice. Her ear for speech rhythms is exceptional, and each central female character has a distinct speech pattern and cadence. This is, of course, more intensely true in the first-person narratives of Drabble's earlier novels, but it is also true of her later novels in which the heroine's interior life is rendered by an omniscient narrator who mimes her speech in order to discuss her feelings and thoughts. Perhaps Drabble's artistry in portraying the sound of the female voice is among her most significant accomplishments: more simple and more complex than the evocation of a maternal career woman or of the mother-child bond.

Drabble has also begun to experiment with the return of the outspoken omniscient narrator. Drabble's rediscovery of an old literary technique seems timely rather than regressive. She does not embed the characters in the amber of the narrator's point of view, preventing them from dramatizing themselves. Drabble's omniscient narrator gives the reader a sense of place, a sense of location and history, without forcing the characters to bear the burden of carrying all that perception in their minds. It frees the characters to notice only what they perceive within the confines of their personalities, for there is a narrative voice to create the density of the social and physical scene.

The narrator's involvement in place and history has important thematic implications for Drabble's fiction. She departs from the prevalent modern emphasis on the centrality of the individual sensibility, reaching back instead to the tradition of two authors she admires, Arnold Bennett and George Eliot. She explores modern fragmentation as a function, to some extent, of human choice. She explores the consequences of choosing to submit to centrifugal forces as opposed to struggling against them in an effort to be true to one's roots.

This original blend of a deep concern for society's conventions and origins and an unusually sensitive evocation of the individual female sensibility gives Drabble's works their particular flavor.

Biography

Margaret Drabble was born into a family that at once reflects the breakup of old patterns and the power of conventions, which may account for her receptiveness to both aspects of modern England. Her parents, John Frederick Drabble and Kathleen Marie (Bloor) Drabble, were the first of their families to attend a university. The results of her parents' upward mobility were both creative and destructive. Her father became a barrister and then a judge; her mother suffered the dislocations which attend such rapid social changes. She became an atheist and thus estranged herself from her fundamentalist parents. Drabble says that her mother was released from the harshness of her religious training when, as a young woman, she read George Bernard Shaw. As she turned the pages she had a revelation that there was no God. "One could say," says Drabble, "that that was a revelation from God not to worry about him because it was going to drive her mad if she did." Drabble's mother has had to struggle against clinically diagnosed depression and has stabilized herself through drug therapy.

Drabble herself is the second of three daughters. Her sisters are Dr. Helen Langdon, a scholar, and Susan Duffy, a novelist, whose pen name is A. S. Byatt. She also has a brother, Richard J. B. Drabble. She attended a Quaker boarding school in York, The Mount School, and then read English at Cambridge, where she finished among the top of her class. In 1960, in the week that she finished at Cambridge, she married Clive Swift.

Swift was an aspiring actor who worked with the Royal Shakespeare Company. In the early years of their marriage, Drabble spent much of her time having three children, writing novels, and acting bit parts and understudying for the Royal Shakespeare Company. While she was writing *The Garrick Year*, she understudied Imogen in *Cymbeline*, played a fairy in *A Midsummer Night's Dream*, and had a bit part in *The Taming of the Shrew*.

Drabble separated from her husband in 1972; their divorce became final in 1975. In 1982, she married the biographer Michael Holroyd.

Analysis

Margaret Drabble's novels begin as female arias in the bel canto style, predominantly elaborate embellishments on a simple series of events relative only to the first-person narrator, events that reflect a brief but formative time in the narrator's life. The early novels deal with the lives of rather ordinary middle-class girls and, but for their sensitivity and subtlety of insight, come dangerously close to being considered women's magazine fiction. The later novels are more complex, exploring the delicate webs of social interconnections and covering longer periods of time in which the convergences of many lives upon one another effect subtle and not so subtle changes. Both the early and later novels express concern with finding the legitimate sources of growth and development.

Drabble's distinctive narrative voice is clear in her first novel. Sarah Bennett, a recent college graduate, is the protagonist of *A Summer Bird-Cage*, but figures mainly as a witness to her sister Louise's marriage. From her older sister's mistakes, Sarah learns about her own attitude toward the future. The novel begins as Sarah returns from Paris to attend Louise's marriage to Stephen Halifax, a boring, trendy, wealthy, satirical novelist. Louise is a stunning and exciting raven-haired beauty, yet Sarah cannot understand why she is marrying the bloodless Stephen Halifax. Sarah and her friends attempt to puzzle this out through the progress of the novel, especially as it becomes increasingly obvious that Louise has been having an affair with a very attractive actor, John Connell. In the end, Sarah learns directly from Louise what was obvious all the while: Louise married Stephen for his money. Rather than seeming anticlimactic, this knowledge solidifies Sarah's growing understanding of what fidelity and betrayal are about. Despite its socially sanctioned position, the marriage Louise has contracted is in fact adulterous because it is a betrayal of her heart and affections. The technical adultery is an act of faith.

Louise divorces Stephen to take her chances with John, and Sarah ends the novel with a forged bond of affection with Louise. Sarah is thus prepared for the return of her boyfriend, Francis, from America. Having observed Louise, Sarah realizes that fidelity to her vow to marry Francis is not as important as waiting to see if in fact their relationship has its roots in truth. Sarah will only marry if the action follows from an authentic feeling.

In her fourth novel, *Jerusalem the Golden*, Drabble experimented for the first time with omniscient narration, maintaining an ironic distance from her protagonist. Clara Maugham, a provincial girl from Northam, a small town in the north of England, is that young woman all too familiar in fiction, the woman whose capacities for development are greater than the opportunities presented by her narrow circumstances. In general, such a character is often created by writers who have escaped the clutches of small minds and tight social structures; an identity of author and character is usually suspected. The character becomes a vehicle through which the author gets back at the tormentors of his or her youth; the character finds dazzling fulfillment in the city.

Clara Maugham, then, comes out of this tradition, but does not lead the reader into the usual pitfalls. Drabble considers the problems of leaving one's roots for fuller possibilities. As impoverished as it may be, one's heritage provides the individual with a foothold in reality. Hence, the title of the novel is a mocking one: it alludes to the utopian dream that emerges from a hymn to which Clara is attracted as a schoolgirl:

> Jerusalem the Golden
> With Milk and Honey blest

Beneath thy contemplation
Sink heart and voice oppressed.
I know not, oh, I know not
What social joys are there
What radiance of glory
What light beyond compare.

For Clara, the mysteries of ecstasy counterpoint the threadbare, wretched, familiar world. For her there is nothing in between, and she leaves Northam only to find a sham Jerusalem in London.

Clara begins life believing that she is doomed to be as her mother is, a woman without hope who remarks that when she is dead the garbage man can cart her off. Mrs. Maugham is a jealous, inconsistent woman who verbally snipes at her neighbors behind her lace curtains because of their concern for their proprieties, and then she outdoes them in cheap ostentation. Rejecting such a life, Clara finds hope in literary images. Metaphors provide avenues of escape, as in the hymn. So too does a children's story that makes a deep impression on her, *The Two Weeds*. The story presents the choices of two weeds. One decides on longevity at the cost of a miserly conservation of its resources, growing "low and small and brown"; the other longs for intensity, the spectacular but short life, and puts its efforts into fabulous display. Each weed achieves its goal. The small, plain one survives, as it had hoped. The magnificent, attractive weed is plucked and dies happily at the bosom of a lovely girl. What impresses Clara about this story is the offer of any possibility other than the low road of mere survival. Little by little, Clara chooses the mysteries of ecstasy.

Clara has to make her way to these mysteries by rejecting a more moderate course, thus losing real opportunities to grow and succeed. Her intellect is widely despised by the good people of Northam, although it is valued by some of her teachers, who fight to attach her to their subjects. She is also revered by a boy named Walter Ash, who values culture and comes from a family tradition which stresses intellectual stimulation. Clara is cynical about her teachers' admiration; she does not value their esteem. She allows Walter to go out with her, but has little regard for him. She ultimately rejects him, thinking, "I shall get further if I'm pulled, I can't waste time going first."

This cryptic remark makes sense only in the light of her choices in London, to which she goes on scholarship to attend Queens College. By chance, she meets Clelia Denham at a poetry reading. This meeting drives her to an instinctual attachment to the girl and subsequently to her family, especially Clelia's brother Gabriel, with whom she has an affair. Although her attachments to the Denhams "pull her," and she does not need to "go first," it is questionable whether they take her anywhere. Indeed, the Denhams provide her the accoutrements of ecstasy. The life she leads with them, however, having torn herself away from her unsatisfactory family, is not one that she builds herself. It is one that envelops her in a "radiance of glory."

The Denhams are rich, and their money is old. Their family house is exquisitely done in tile, fireplaces, pictures, and mirrors: old, good things. Outside the house is a terraced garden that to Clara is the original Eden. The Denhams themselves are good-looking people who dress well and speak cleverly. Mrs. Denham is a writer known professionally as Candida Grey. Mr. Denham is a lawyer. Magnus, the oldest boy, is a rich capitalist. Gabriel is in television, and Clelia works in a chic art gallery.

To the detached eye, the Denham children seem smothered by this "good life." The oldest child, no longer living in the Denham house, has gone crazy. Clelia is startlingly infantile. She speaks in all situations as if to a close relative, never using tact or discretion. Although twenty-seven years old, she lives at home, seemingly unable to establish herself on her own as wife, mother, or career woman. The job she holds in the gallery is purely decorative, one she obtained through family connections, and on which she could never support herself. Her extremely chic room contains her childhood toys as part of the decor. Clara interprets their presence as part of Clelia's enviable sense of continuity with a happy childhood. Unfortunately for both Clelia and Clara, they are the sign of a childhood that has never ended.

Gabriel is married and lives with his wife and children in one of those fashionable sections of London that are emerging from slum conditions. He has a good job with Independent Television and makes a good salary. He and his wife, Phillipa, make stunning personal impressions. When Clara visits the couple, however, she is appalled to find that their home is in a state of chaos. The house is potentially as beautiful as others in the neighborhood which have been renovated, but nothing has been done to it. The floors are pitted and worn, the walls are badly in need of paint, the ancient wallpaper hangs in tatters, and the rooms are poorly lit. The kitchen is a war zone in which the litter of cracking plaster vies with expensive cooking equipment. Phillipa is unable to provide food for her family or any kind of supportive attention to the children. Gabriel is unable to organize a life of his own, so dependent is he on the glorious life of his mother and father's house. Gabriel becomes obsessively attracted to Clara and dreams of a ménage à trois between them and Clelia.

Magnus is an industrial mogul, a bachelor who becomes parasitically and emotionally attached to Gabriel's women. At first in love with Phillipa, when he senses the affair between Gabriel and Clara he begins an erotic flirtation with Clara. Clara gives herself over emotionally to all the Denhams, and sexually to the brothers Magnus and Gabriel. She feels little for them, or anyone, but the lust for inclusion in a beautiful life. She acts out increasingly more elaborate scenes with them, climaxed by a visit to Paris with Gabriel. During this journey, a flirtation between Clara and Magnus sends Gabriel back to the hotel where he and Clara are staying. Clara outdoes him by leaving him sleeping to miss his plane while she returns to London alone. Once there, she discovers that her mother is dying of cancer.

Clara visits her mother but there is no feeling between them. Returning to London, her connections to her childhood severed, she finds that the affair with the Denhams is just beginning. Despite the seemingly decisive break in Paris, Clara is now well into Denham games. Her future is to be composed of "Clelia, and Gabriel and she herself in shifting and ideal conjunctions." There is no mention of the development of her intellect or talents.

Clara, at last, contemplates her victory: her triumph over her mother's death, her triumph over her early life, her survival of all of it. "Even the mercy and kindness of destiny she would survive; they would not get her that way, they would not get her at all." These final words are fully ironic: Clara has not triumphed over anything. She is a victim of her own fear of life. Her evasion of a nebulous "them" is a type of paranoid delusion which amounts to a horror of life. Clara has been true to her need to expand, but false to what she is. The outcome is not a joyous one. She has achieved a perverse isolation in a bogus, sterile Jerusalem.

The same themes are explored in Drabble's next novel, *The Waterfall*. Though rendered in the first person by the central character, Jane Grey, *The Waterfall* is a highly ironic, fearfully complex exploration of the question which informs *A Summer Bird-Cage* and *Jerusalem the Golden*: To what must one be true? There is a vast variety of claims on one's fidelity, and these claims frequently pull in different directions. Shall one be true to one's family? One's religion? One's friends? One's heart? One's sexuality? One's intellect? Even from the simple personal perspective, Drabble arrives at an impasse from which the protagonist herself cannot reckon her obligations or even the main issue deserving of her attention.

Jane Grey begins her story giving birth, overwhelmed, that is, by her biology, shaped and determined by her gender, her flesh, her sexuality. This is confirmed by her statement to her husband, Malcolm, who has left her before the birth of their second child, "If I were drowning, I couldn't reach out a hand to save myself, so unwilling am I to set myself up against my fate."

Jane Grey is a woman who does not give allegiance to anything that requires conscious choice. She cannot sustain a marriage, a career, or any affiliation that calls for directed will. She is faithful only to what takes her, overwhelms her, leaving her no choice—her sexuality. Thus, she can be a mother, but not a wife. She can be a lover, but not a companion. The result is that she becomes the adulterous, almost incestuous lover of James, her cousin Lucy's husband. This comes about in a way that can be seen as nothing less than a betrayal of a number of social norms.

Because Jane has been deserted by Malcolm, Lucy and James alternate visits to assist her. Lucy, who has been like a sister to Jane, initiates these visits without Jane's request. Jane's breaking of her marriage vows and her betrayal of Lucy is not as uncomplicated as Louise's affair with John in *A Summer Bird-Cage*. Louise has violated nothing more than the law; Jane has violated the bonds of her heart, since Lucy has been so close to her, and the bonds of family and morality, as well as the bonds of law and ethics. Nevertheless, there is a fidelity in Jane's choice. She and James, whose name is deliberately the male reflection of hers, are, in being overwhelmed by each other, satisfying the deepest narcissistic sexuality in each other. It is, of course, true that in so doing they create social limbo for their mates and children, and for themselves.

Their adultery is discovered when they are in an automobile accident. James's car hits a brick, although he is driving carefully, as they begin a weekend outing together with Jane's children. The car turns over; only James is hurt, but he recovers almost fully. Jane and James continue with their ordinary life. Neither Malcolm nor Lucy exacts any payment from them. The lovers meet when they can. The novel ends with their only full weekend together after the accident. Jane and James climb the Goredale Scar, one of England's scenic wonders. They are there because someone described it so enthusiastically to Jane that it became her goal to see it herself. The Scar is the quintessential female sexual symbol, a cavernous cleft in the mountains, flushed by a waterfall and covered by a pubic growth of foliage. Drabble then sends the lovers back to their hotel room to drink Scotch inadvertently dusted by talcum powder, which leaves a bad taste in their mouths. They have been faithful in their own minds to a force validated by nature.

The Needle's Eye, regarded by many readers as Drabble's finest novel, takes its title from Jesus' proverbial words to a rich young man: "It is easier for a camel to go through the eye of a needle, than for a rich man to enter into the kingdom of God" (Matthew 19:24). At the center of the novel are Simon Camish, a barrister from a poor background who would seem to have regretfully gained the world at the expense of his soul, and Rose Bryanston Vassiliou, a rich young woman who compulsively divests herself of the benefits of her inheritance but is not fully enjoying her flight into the lower classes.

Rose, a pale, timid girl, had created a tabloid sensation by marrying out of her class. Her choice was the disreputable, seedy, sexy Christopher Vassiliou, son of Greek immigrants whose pragmatic financial dealings are not solidly within the boundaries of the law. Rose sought to escape from the evils of wealth through Christopher, one of the downtrodden. Much to her consternation, however, Christopher is not a "happy peasant." He detests poverty, legitimately, and associates it not with virtue but with humiliation and deprivation, both of which he has endured.

Christopher's dream is to make something of himself. This dream is only strengthened by the birth of their three children, for whom Christopher wants "only the best." He sees in Rose's war on wealth nothing but perverse self-destructiveness. His fury vents itself in physical abuse. Frail, pale Rose is equally adamant in the protection of her children's future. To her mind, "the best" means freedom from possessions. Again Rose and Christopher become figures of tabloid fantasy, this time in a dramatic divorce case.

Rose is working out her divorce settlement when she meets Simon. Simon is introduced to the reader on the same night that he is introduced to Rose; the reader first sees him in a store, buying liquor. Simon feels estranged from the lower-class types who frequent and staff the store. Soon thereafter, this isolation is established as a sharp discontinuity in Simon's life, for he has risen from these ranks. He has been pushed upward by a mother embarrassed by the meanness of her lower-class life and determined that her son will have what she never had. Ironically, the essential gap in his mother's life is also left unfilled in Simon's; that is, the need for warmth and affection. Simon tried to marry into an inheritance of warmth and wealth by his alliance with what he thought was a good-natured girl of the comfortable upper-middle class, Julie Phillips. Their marriage, however, only revealed her fear and insecurity, her essential coldness. What Simon had mistaken for warmth was merely superficial brightness, a by-product of the Phillips' affluence.

Rose and Simon have attempted to gain what each personally lacked through marriage, as if one could graft onto oneself a human capacity with a wedding ring: such marriages are doomed to failure. Also doomed has been Rose's attempt to meet human needs with "filthy lucre." She has given a huge portion of her inheritance to a schoolhouse in a lonely, little-known part of Africa. Within months, the school was demolished in the chaos of a civil war along with approximately one hundred children. Rose does not attempt to deny the futility of what she has done.

Simon and Rose strike up a professional acquaintance, casually, it seems, because Christopher has begun some devious maneuvers to get his children away from Rose. As he becomes increasingly involved in helping Rose, Simon realizes that he is in love with her. Rose reveals but a few of her feelings on this issue, but does indicate the joy she takes in his company. While Rose and Simon are chasing around after Christopher, who appears to be in the process of abducting the children and taking them out of England, Simon finally tells Rose that, were they at liberty, he would marry her. He blurts out this sentiment as they are walking in a woodland setting. The moment of his revelation finds them in sudden confrontation with a dead stoat, hanging grotesquely in front of them, a dried-up little corpse. According to the narrator, this is "a warning" to Simon and Rose.

The satisfaction that Rose and Simon might find together is based on their shared concern for their obligations and duties. To turn to each other, a temptation for both of them, would be a betrayal of the very basis of their attraction to each other, as it would necessitate shirking their responsibilities. It is the grace in them that understands commitments beyond the self. Understanding this, Simon and Rose remain friends; Christopher and Rose are reunited. Rose has achieved a modus vivendi with Christopher, who goes to work for her father. There is no fully articulated happiness, but a kind of integrity exists at the heart of Rose's and Simon's arrangement.

In the novel's final tableau, Rose is looking at a vandalized lion outside a second-rate British edifice called the Alexandra Palace. The lion's plaster head is broken, revealing a hollow inside. It has been spray-painted red with the name of a local gang, but Rose decides that she likes it. Although beginning life as an anonymous, mass-produced piece of kitsch, the lion has been worn into something unique: "it had weathered into identity. And this she hoped for every human soul." Rose's final wish accepts the uniqueness of life, the beauty of its mere being. She rejects the vision of a life that is continually being held up to an intellectual ideal, by which standards the lion, like her life, is an awful mess.

Drabble has said in an interview that, had she written *The Needle's Eye* after her husband left her, she might have altered Rose's destiny; perhaps she meant that Rose might have been sent off with Simon, after all. Perhaps these words reveal something of the personal Drabble, but they are a betrayal of the novel. The delicacy of Simon and Rose's poise in front of the dead stoat and the final image of the lion resist second thoughts.

Drabble has called *The Realms of Gold* her only comedy. It is the most elaborately plotted of her novels, and Drabble has observed that comedies are permitted such carefully structured plots. Perhaps Drabble defends her plot to excuse herself for pivoting the outcome of her story on the delay in the mail of a postcard, consciously parodying the tragic turn of William Shakespeare's *Romeo and Juliet* (1594-1596), when Romeo's letter from Friar Laurence is delayed. Unlike the passion of Romeo and Juliet, however, the passion of the lovers in *The Realms of Gold*, Frances Wingate and Karel Schmidt, is not "too swift, too unadvised." Frances and Karel are survivors, and it is for this reason that true love is possible.

The novel begins in a hotel room. Frances is on tour, lecturing about her discovery of an ancient city, Tizouk. One evening, in a fit of loneliness, she writes a postcard to Karel, whom she capriciously rejected six months previously. She now regrets her gesture. Impulsively, she writes on the card, "I miss you. I love you." Bothered when she receives no response to her card, she is ignorant of the fact that her card has not been delivered, having been mislaid by the European mail system. Frances is distraught, but carries on as mother to her four children, as a professional, and as a member of her family.

Karel, too, carries on, thinking hopelessly about Frances, his lost love, puzzled by her rejection of him, suffering at the hands of his deranged wife and his students at the polytechnic, where he is a lecturer in history. Both wife and students continually take advantage of Karel's patience and good nature, and he, not quite understanding why, allows them to victimize him.

Karel and Frances' professional interests, history and archaeology, bring to the novel the long view of continuity. This view is partially what sustains Karel and Frances, whose families cannot or will not support them. Karel has been cut off from his family by the horrors of history. He is Jewish, the only member of his immediate family to survive World War II. Frances, on the other hand, has a large family, but it is wracked with odd and self-destructive behavior: alcoholism, suicide, depression. Frances' family is composed of two estranged branches, isolated from each other by an ancient quarrel—that no one can remember—between two brothers. During the course of the novel, the branches are reconciled. The healing begins when Frances discovers her cousin David, of whom she has never before heard. She meets him professionally at a UNESCO conference in Adra.

The conference has taken Frances away from England at a particularly crucial time in the life of her family. In Tockley, in the English midlands, an old lady discovered dead of starvation turns out to be Frances' estranged great-aunt. As Frances' family is a prominent one, there is a scandal about this shocking neglect of a family member. Frances is called home from the conference and discovers another lost cousin, Janet Bird, the last person to see their great-aunt alive.

Meanwhile, Frances' cousin David is surprised at the conference by the arrival of Karel, who, finally receiving the delayed postcard, flies heedlessly to join Frances at the conference and must be escorted by David back to Tockley. The upshot of these and more complications is the marriage of Karel and Frances and the reunification of Frances' family.

Frances and Karel synthesize stability and freedom; their marriage triumphantly asserts the victory of human freedom through history, continuity, and culture. The horrors of history present in both the Nazi persecution of the Jews, Frances' blighted family history, and the evidence of child sacrifice which Frances has found in her ancient city Tizouk, do not lead to a rejection of continuity but to the passion to grow through it and outlive the evil it contains.

The major image of the novel incarnates the comic attitude necessary if one is to lay hands on that hard-won treasure known as life. Shortly before Frances had rejected Karel, causing the long separation that was to end in Tockley, Frances and Karel were enjoying a holiday together. Endeavoring to spend a pleasant day in the country, they had driven their car into the mud, resulting in the bespattering of their persons in a most unromantic way. In the midst of their predicament, they heard a strange, almost ominous sound. An investigation turned up hundreds of frogs simply honking away in a drainage pipe in a ditch. Frances and Karel were flooded with affection and amusement at this gratuitously joyous spectacle. The image of it never leaves them and becomes a sustaining force during their ordeal of separation. Perhaps this is Drabble's best image of a realistic optimism in a very flawed world, joy spontaneously uttered from a muddy ditch.

In *The Ice Age*, Drabble considers the problem of survival within a dying tradition. England is enduring an ice age: its social structure is collapsing. In a brilliantly dark vision, Drabble surveys the challenge this poses to personal resources.

As the novel begins, a reckless real estate speculator, Len Wincobank, is serving time in Scratby Open Prison for fraud. Len's technically innocent accomplice, Maureen Kirby, is wondering how to fit the pieces of her life back together again. A teenage girl, Jane Murray, daughter of an extremely beautiful former actress, Alison Murray, is on trial in the remote Communist country of Wallachia. Anthony Keating, a charming author of musical comedies turned real estate speculator, is recovering from a heart attack and the collapse of his financial empire.

All the characters are suffering through imprisonment in England. It is a time in which Max and Kitty Friedman are the victims of an IRA terrorist attack as they are having an anniversary dinner. England is plagued with degenerate youth, frightening in what it portends for the future. Jane Murray is an angry, shallow child, seemingly incapable of love or of true civility. Anthony Keating finds two young squatters on the empty floor of his former home. The girl is a heroin addict, pregnant and in labor. The boy is drunk and stoned, unable to summon assistance for the girl. Anthony's chance visit to his old house means that the girl will get to the hospital, but she will die and her baby will be born suffering from prenatal heroin addiction.

Through the gloom of England's dark night, Drabble feels her way toward dawn, steadfastly refusing to deny the value of principle because history is suffering temporarily from chaos. She paints a damning picture of a contemporary of Anthony, Mike Morgan, a comedian who pointlessly and viciously ridicules his audience because he mistakes a bad patch for the end of coherence. She also, however, defends the human being as a flexible, creative source of energy not be be trapped within rigidities of principle.

Alison Murray emerges as the polar opposite to Mike Morgan. She too is a doomed soul, because as England flails about, she has chosen the sterility of a noble perfection over the struggles of possibility. Alison's choice has been to devote herself to her brain-damaged daughter Molly rather than to her normal daughter, Jane. Molly can never develop and grow, despite Alison's martyrdom, and Jane is wild and sullen as a result of her displacement. Drabble shows that Alison's choice is at least as bad as Mike's, leading directly to her own misery and indirectly to Jane's self-imposed troubles in Wallachia. Alison's choice also leads indirectly to Anthony Keating's downfall.

Anthony, Alison's lover, goes to Wallachia to escort Jane home when the authorities suddenly decide to return her to England. A civil war erupts, randomly freeing Jane and trapping Anthony. He is mistaken for a British spy and remanded to a Siberian-style forced labor camp.

Between the extremes of Mike Morgan and Alison Murray lies the possibility of working one's way back to continuity by keeping the spirit free. The major examples of such survival in the novel are Maureen Kirby and Anthony Keating. Maureen is a lower-class girl, sexy rather than beautiful, who falls somewhat short of conventional morality. Hardly a person who eschews extremes, Maureen has been the partner of Len Wincobank in his whirlwind financial spree. She has also temporarily retreated into her own selfish, protected world when Len is imprisoned, but she is resilient. In a striking narrative device, Drabble looks into the future at the end of the novel, coolly summarizing the fates of her characters. Maureen is projected as a woman of the 1980's who ultimately marries well and becomes a model to young women. Her coarse-grained vitality and common sense lack the charm of Alison's elegant self-immolation, but it radiates the warmth of survival.

Anthony Keating, in his frozen Wallachian prison, the ice age of England made palpable, turns also toward life in the only way that is available to him. He becomes enthralled with watching birds, symbols of his spirit which, despite everything, remains untrammeled.

At the close of the novel, the state of the nation is given a good prognosis. It will recover, asserts the narrator. Anthony has come to terms. Len will surely go on to further development and a financial comeback. Maureen's trajectory is in ascent, but, asserts the narrator, Alison Murray will never recover. The doom of Alison Murray strongly suggests that her kind of retreat from possibility is the worst prison of all, subject to no reprieve or amelioration. Here Drabble seems to have found the limits of what critics have called her conservatism. Cutting off from one's roots to rise in the world brings peril, denying one's context in order to acquire more brings suffering; these may reveal the flaws in the liberal dream. The ultimate horror, however, would seem to be turning away from growth, regardless of the reason.

In her novels of the 1980's—*The Middle Ground*, *The Radiant Way*, and *A Natural Curiosity*—Drabble worked within the boundaries established in *The Realms of Gold* and *The Ice Age*. Featuring an intrusive narrator given to reflections on the nature of fiction and sometimes arch asides directed to the reader, all three of these novels center on well-educated, middle-aged characters of the upper-middle class whose domestic concerns are intertwined with larger social issues. In general, Drabble's novels of the 1980's met with a mixed critical reception. Some reviewers praised Drabble for her depiction of a beleaguered Britain under Margaret Thatcher. Others, however, saw a style hardening into mannerism and irrelevance. What is not in question is Drabble's ambition, as she has clearly sought to bring to the self-conscious late-twentieth century novel something of the scope and sweep of her great nineteenth century predecessors.

Martha Nochimson

Other major works

PLAYS: *Laura*, 1964; *Bird of Paradise*, 1969; *A Touch of Love*, 1969; *Isadora*, 1969 (with Melvyn Bragg and Clive Exton).

NONFICTION: *Wordsworth, Literature in Perspective*, 1966; *Arnold Bennett*, 1974; *A Writer's Britain: Landscape in Literature*, 1979.

CHILDREN'S LITERATURE: *For Queen and Country: Britain in the Victorian Age*, 1978.

EDITED TEXTS: *Lady Susan*, 1974; *The Watsons*, 1974; *Sandition*, 1974; *The Genius of Thomas Hardy*, 1975; *The Oxford Companion to English Literature*, 1985.

Bibliography

Creighton, Joanne V. *Margaret Drabble*. New York: Methuen, 1985. This slim volume begins with an introductory overview, followed by a chronological survey of Drabble's novels through *The Middle Ground*. Creighton argues that Drabble, with such contemporaries as John Fowles and Muriel Spark, has gradually changed her approach to fiction, "challenging the conventions and epistemological assumptions of traditional realistic fiction, perhaps in spite of herself." Includes notes and a bibliography.

Moran, Mary Hurley. *Margaret Drabble: Existing Within Structures*. Carbondale: Southern Illinois University Press, 1983. Discussing all of Drabble's novels through *The Middle Ground*, Moran organizes her analysis thematically rather than chronologically, so that the same novels are treated under different topical headings. Moran contends that Drabble's outlook is fundamentally fatalistic, that "the central concern of her fiction is human beings' lack of free will." Contains notes, a brief bibliography, and an index which includes the principal characters in Drabble's novels.

Myer, Valerie Grosvenor. *Margaret Drabble: Puritanism and Permissiveness*. London: Vision Press, 1974. Emphasizing Drabble's concern with the experience of women and her appeal to women readers, Myer's thematic study is divided into two parts. In the seven chapters of part 1, "The Reluctant Puritan," Myers builds on the premise that the "extended analysis of the puritan inheritance" is Drabble's "characteristic and unique contribution to the contemporary novel." In the four chapters that make up part 2, "The Artist," Myer discusses Drabble's conception of the artist and the role of the arts as reflected in her fiction. Treats only Drabble's first six novels, through *The Needle's Eye*.

Rose, Ellen Cronan. *The Novels of Margaret Drabble: Equivocal Figures*. Totowa, N.J.: Barnes & Noble Books, 1980. Rose's study seeks to "acknowledge and applaud [Drabble's] feminist vision and encourage her to give it freer rein in the future." Drabble's first three novels are discussed together in the opening chapter, while each of her next five novels (through *The Ice Age*) is given a separate chapter. Includes a list of works cited and endnotes for each chapter.

Sadler, Lynn Veach. *Margaret Drabble*. Boston: Twayne, 1986. Acknowledging that Drabble both "exasperates and delights" her, Sadler offers a balanced and readable appraisal. A very brief biographical sketch is followed by a chronological survey of Drabble's novels through *The Middle Ground*, with a coda on "Drabble's Reputation." Includes notes and an extensive bibliography, both primary and secondary; entries for secondary sources are annotated.

Schmidt, Dorey, ed. *Margaret Drabble: Golden Realms*. Edinburg, Tex.: Pan American University School of Humanities, 1982. A wide-ranging collection of essays on Drabble's fiction through *The Middle Ground*. Includes an interview with Drabble and an update (1977-1981) to the Drabble bibliography included in Robert J. Stanton's *A Bibliography of Modern British Novelists* (Troy, N.Y.: Whitson, 1978).

THEODORE DREISER

Born: Terre Haute, Indiana; August 27, 1871
Died: Hollywood, California; December 28, 1945

Principal long fiction
Sister Carrie, 1900; *Jennie Gerhardt*, 1911; *The Financier*, 1912, 1927; *The Titan*, 1914; *The "Genius,"* 1915; *An American Tragedy*, 1925; *The Bulwark*, 1946; *The Stoic*, 1947.

Other literary forms
The scope of Theodore Dreiser's literary accomplishment includes attempts in every major literary form, including autobiography and philosophy. His poetry is generally of poor quality; his plays have been produced on occasion, but drama was not his métier. His sketches, such as those included in *The Color of a Great City* (1923), are vivid and accurate, but seem to be only workmanlike vignettes which Dreiser developed for the practice or for later inclusion in one of his many novels. His short stories are, like the sketches, preparation for the novels, but the compression of scene, character, and idea necessary for the short story lend these pieces a life of their own, distinct from the monolithic qualities of the novels. Dreiser's philosophical works, such as *Hey, Rub-a-Dub-Dub!* (1920), and his autobiographical forays are the product of an obsession for explaining himself; the philosophy is often obscure and arcane and the autobiography is not always reliable. Dreiser's letters have been collected and offer further understanding of the man, as do the massive manuscript collections, which are the product of his tortuous composition and editing processes.

Achievements
The enigma that is Dreiser divides the critical world into two clearly identifiable camps—those who despise Dreiser and those who honor him just short of adulation—there is no middle ground. With the publication of *Sister Carrie* in 1900, Dreiser committed his literary force to opening the new ground of American naturalism. His heroes and heroines, his settings, his frank discussion, celebration, and humanization of sex, his clear dissection of the mechanistic brutality of American society—all were new and shocking to a reading public reared on genteel romances and adventure narratives. *Jennie Gerhardt*, the Cowperwood trilogy (at least the first two volumes), and *An American Tragedy* expand and clarify those themes introduced in *Sister Carrie*. Dreiser's genius was recognized and applauded by H. L. Mencken, who encouraged him, praised his works publicly, and was always a valued editorial confidant, but the general reaction to Dreiser has always been negative. He has been called a "crag of basalt," "solemn and ponderous" and "the world's

worst great writer," but his influence is evident in the works of Sherwood Anderson, Sinclair Lewis, Ernest Hemingway, and James T. Farrell, among others. Lewis refused the 1925 Pulitzer prize, which probably should have gone to Dreiser for *An American Tragedy*, and in 1930 took the Nobel Prize committee to task for choosing him as the first American Nobelist for literature instead of Dreiser. Dreiser's political and social activism during the long hiatus between *An American Tragedy* and *The Bulwark*, and his never-ending battle against censors and censorship, kept him in the public eye, and the failure of *The Bulwark* and *The Stoic* consigned him to years of neglect after his death. His technical and stylistic faults have often obscured his real value, but the effects of Dreiser's work are still rippling through American fiction. He was the first to point out the fragile vulnerability of the facade that was understood to be the American dream and to depict the awful but beautiful reality that supported the facade.

Biography

Theodore Herman Albert Dreiser was born in Terre Haute, Indiana, on August 27, 1871, into a family of German-Americans. His father, John Paul Dreiser, was a weaver by trade, and from the time of his entry into the United States (in 1846), he had worked westward in an attempt to establish himself. He induced Sarah Schanab (later shortened to Shnepp), the daughter of an Ohio Moravian, to elope with him and they settled near Fort Wayne. John Paul became the manager in a woolen mill and soon amassed enough funds to build his own mill in Sullivan, Indiana. In 1870, the year before Theodore's birth, the mill burned, John Paul was seriously injured, Sarah was cheated out of the family property by unscrupulous "yankee trickery," and the family was forced to move to Terre Haute, where Theodore was born the eleventh of twelve children, ten of whom survived to adulthood.

After the family misfortunes, John Paul never recovered physically and sank into a pattern of paternal despotism and narrow religious fervor, against which Theodore and the rest of the children could only express contempt and revolt and from which their only haven was the open, loving character of their mother.

In 1879, with the family teetering on the edge between poverty and penury, Sarah took Theodore and the youngest children to Vincennes, Indiana, and the girls stayed with John Paul in Terre Haute in an attempt to economize. There then followed a series of moves that took the two parts of the family, in succeeding moves, from Vincennes back to Sullivan, to Evansville to live with Theodore's brother Paul, who had succeeded in the vaudeville circuit, to Chicago, and finally to Warsaw, Indiana. This nomadic life could only deepen the destitution of the family and heighten the children's craving for the material part of life they never had. In 1887, after the move to Warsaw, sixteen-year-old Theodore announced that he was going back to Chicago; his mother, characteristically, gave him six dollars of her savings and her blessing, and Theodore went on his way back to the most wonderful city he had ever seen.

As a sixteen-year-old, alone in Chicago, Dreiser, like Carrie Meeber, could find only menial labor, first as a dishwasher, later working for a hardware company. In 1889, however, a former teacher who believed in his latent abilities encouraged him to enroll at Indiana University and subsidized his enrollment. After a year of frustrated attempts to break into the fraternity social life of Bloomington, Dreiser left Indiana University and returned to Chicago.

After another series of menial jobs, including driving a laundry delivery wagon, Dreiser managed to land a job with the Chicago *Globe* as a reporter. After a few months, he was invited to take a position on the St. Louis *Globe-Democrat* and *Republic* staff and he moved to St. Louis. In St. Louis, he covered the usual types of news events and met Sara (Sallie) White, to whom he found himself unaccountably attracted. In 1895, after brief periods on newspaper staffs in St. Louis, Toledo, Cleveland, and Pittsburgh, Dreiser took up residence in New York City. Even after his newspaper success in St. Louis and Chicago, however, Dreiser could only find free-lance work in New York City until his brother Paul, by then a successful songwriter and publisher, persuaded his publishers to make Dreiser the editor of their newly established music periodical, *Ev' ry Month*, for which he wrote monthly editorial columns. This forum for Dreiser's talents was the beginning of a long editorial career which led him to editorships of *Smith's Magazine*, *Broadway Magazine*, and editorial positions with Street and Smith and Butterick. During this period he published *Sister Carrie*, separated from his wife, Sallie White, whom he had married in 1898, saw his brother Paul die, began work on *Jennie Gerhardt*, and quit his position at Butterick's to avoid scandal and to devote his time to fiction.

After his publication of *Jennie Gerhardt*, Dreiser's career is the story of one laboriously prepared publication after another. Even at the end, he was working on *The Stoic*, the last of the Cowperwood trilogy, almost as if it were unfinished business. He died in Hollywood on December 28, 1945.

Analysis

Literary historians have shown, by identifying sources and characters, that Theodore Dreiser, even in his fiction, was a capable investigative reporter. His reliance on research for setting, character, and plot lines is evident in *The Financier* and *The Titan* and, most important, in *An American Tragedy*, but Dreiser was not bound by his investigative method. He went often to his own memories for material. Only when Dreiser combines autobiographical material with his research and reportage does his fiction come alive.

Dreiser's youth and early manhood prepared him for the themes he developed. His unstable home life; the dichotomy established between a loving, permissive mother and a narrow, bigoted, dogmatic, penurious father; abject poverty; and his own desires for affluence, acceptance, sexual satisfaction, and recognition were all parts of his fictional commonplace book. His sisters' sexual promiscuity was reflected in Carrie and Jennie, and his own frustrations and desires found voice in, among others, Clyde Griffiths. The character of Frank Cowperwood was shaped in Dreiser's lengthy research into the life of C. T. Yerkes, but Cowperwood was also the incarnation of everything that Dreiser wanted to be—handsome, powerful, accepted, wealthy, and capable. Dreiser projected his own dreams on characters such as Griffiths and Cowperwood only to show that human dreams are never ultimately fulfilled. No matter for what man (or woman) contested, "his feet are in the trap of circumstances; his eyes are on an illusion." Dreiser did not condemn the effort; he chronicled the fragile nature of the pursued and the pursuer.

The genesis of *Sister Carrie*, Dreiser's first novel, was as fantastic as its appearance in Victorian America. In Dreiser's own account, he started the novel at the insistence of his friend Arthur Henry and then only to appease him. In order to end Henry's wheedlings and annoyances, Dreiser sat down and wrote the title of the novel at the top of a page. With no idea of a program for the novel or who the basic characters were to be, Dreiser began the book which did more to change modern American fiction than any since.

The amatory adventures of Dreiser's sisters in Indiana and his own experiences in Chicago and in New York were the perfect materials for the story of a poor country girl who comes to the city to seek whatever she can find. The one thing she is certain of is that she does not wish to remain poor. With this kind of material, it is surprising that Dreiser escaped writing a maudlin tale of a fallen girl rescued at the end or an Algeresque tale of her rise from rags. *Sister Carrie* is neither of these. Carrie does rise, but she does so by the means of a male stepladder. She is not a simple gold digger; she is much more complex than that. Her goals are clothes, money, and fame, and the means by which she achieves them are relatively unimportant. More important, however, is that Carrie is a seeker and a lover. She cannot be satisfied. There must always be a new world to conquer, new goals to achieve. In New York, when she has finally acquired all that she has sought, Ames shows her that there is a world beyond the material—a world of literature and philosophy; it is an aesthetic world of which Carrie has not dreamed and which she recognizes as a new peak to conquer and a new level to achieve. There is a hint that this new level is more satisfying than any she has reached, just as Ames seems more interesting and satisfying than either of her previous lovers, Drouet and Hurstwood, but the novel ends with Carrie still contemplating her attack on this new world.

Carrie subordinates everything to her consuming ambition. She comes to understand the usefulness of sex, but she also understands the emotional commitment necessary to love, and she refuses to make that commitment. In the pursuit of the fullest expression and fulfillment of life she can achieve, human attachments are only transitory at best, and Drouet and Hurstwood are only means to an end for Carrie.

Drouet, the traveling salesman Carrie meets on the train to Chicago, becomes her first lover after she has had time to discover the frustration of joblessness and sweatshop employment and the despair of the poverty in which the relatives with whom she is staying live. Drouet ingratiates himself with Carrie by buying her dinner and then by slipping two ten-dollar bills into her hand. Not long thereafter, Drouet outfits a flat for her, and they set up housekeeping together. Drouet is, for Carrie, an escape. She does not love him, but his means are a source of amazement, and she recognizes that the relative opulence of his chambers and of the apartment he procures for her are the signs of that for which she is striving. She recognizes very early that Drouet is static, a deadend, but he is only an intermediary in her movement from poverty to affluence.

Hurstwood is the bartender and manager of a prominent Chicago tavern. As he watches Carrie perform in a cheap theatrical, he is smitten by her youth and her vitality. A middle-aged, married man, possessed of a virago of a wife, he is naturally attracted to Carrie. Carrie in turn recognizes the quality of Hurstwood's clothes, his style, and his bearing as distinct improvements on Drouet and makes it clear she will accept his advances. Hurstwood's wife uncovers the subsequent affair, a messy divorce threatens Hurstwood's stability and prestige in his job, fortuity brings him to embezzle ten thousand dollars from the bar safe, and he flees with Carrie first to Montreal and then to New York. Once in New York, the chronicle becomes the tale of Hurstwood's steady degeneration and Carrie's alternatively steady rise to stardom on the stage.

Hurstwood does not carry his status with him from Chicago to New York. In New York, he is merely another man who either cannot hold or cannot find a job. His funds are seriously depleted in the failure of an attempt to open his own saloon, and the more he fails the further he withdraws from life and from Carrie, until he becomes completely dependent on her. When Carrie leaves him because she cannot support both of them and buy the clothes necessary to her profession, he drifts deeper and deeper into New York's nether world until he commits suicide by turning on the gas in a Bowery flophouse. Typically, Carrie nevers knows or cares that Hurstwood is dead. If Drouet is a deadend, Hurstwood is a weak man trapped by circumstance and by his unwillingness or inability to cope with situations he recognizes as potentially disastrous. His liaison with Carrie is based on mutual attraction, but he is also enamored of his daily routine and of the prestige that accompanies it. Only when his wife threatens him with exposure is he forced to make the final commitment to Carrie and, eventually, to the gas jet.

Carrie's desertion of Hurstwood can be interpreted as cold and cruel, but she stays with him until it is clear that there is nothing anyone can do to save him. To try to save him would only mire her in his downward spiral. The counterpoint of Carrie's rise and Hurstwood's fall is the final irony of the novel. Carrie and Hurstwood reach their final disappointments in almost the same basic terms. Hurstwood dies tired of the struggle and Carrie realizes that she has finally arrived and there is nothing more to conquer or achieve. Only the promise of an aesthetic world beyond material affluence offers hope for Carrie, and that hope seems illusory. The ubiquitous rocking chair is the perfect symbol for *Sister Carrie*. It is an instrument that forever moves but never goes anywhere and never truly achieves anything. Carrie's every success is ultimately unsatisfying and every new horizon offers only a hollow promise.

Sister Carrie was stillborn in the first edition. Published but suppressed by the publisher, it did not reach the public until seven years later, when it was given to a new publisher. The novel contains the seeds of most of Dreiser's themes.

The protagonist of *Jennie Gerhardt*, Dreiser's second novel, is Carrie's natural sister or, perhaps, her alter ego. Jennie is also the product of Dreiser's early family life, of his sisters' fatal attraction to men and the natural result. When Dreiser turned to *Jennie Gerhardt* while still embroiled in the publication problems of *Sister Carrie*, he drew upon the events in the life of his sister Mame, who was seduced, abandoned, and ended up living successfully with another man in New York City. From this basic material, Dreiser created a girl much like Carrie in origin, who has the same desires for material ease, but who has none of the instincts Carrie possesses or who has the same instincts channeled into a different mode of expression.

Jennie Gerhardt is divided into two parts. In the first part, as the daughter of a poor washerwoman, Jennie is noticed by Senator Brander Matthews, another older man attracted by youth and vitality; he is kind, tips her heavily for delivering his laundry, and eventually seduces her. Matthews is, however, more than a stereotype. He has a real need for Jennie and a fatherly attachment to her. Jennie, who is more than the "fallen angel" as some have seen her, responds in kind. Surrounded by conventional morality and religious prohibitions, represented by Old Gerhardt and others, Jennie, unlike Carrie, has a desperate need to give in order to fulfill herself. Despite the veneer of indebtedness Jennie brings to her seduction by Matthews (he arranges the release of her brother from jail, among other things) there is a surprisingly wholesome atmosphere to the affair. Matthews is solicitous and protective and Jennie is loving and tender. When Jennie becomes pregnant, Matthews plans to marry her, put her parents in a more comfortable situation, and, in short, do the right thing. Matthews, however, dies, and Jennie gives birth to his illegitimate child; she is condemned by her parents and society, and her previous joy and prospects dissolve before her eyes.

Dreiser's portrayal of Jennie does not allow the reader to feel sorry for her. Vesta, Jennie's child, is not the product of sin, but the offspring of an all-suffering, all-giving earth mother. Dreiser's depiction of Jennie as a child of nature verifies this impression. Despite society and its narrow views, Jennie is not destroyed or even dismayed. She is delighted with her child and thus snatches her joy and fulfillment from a seeming disaster. As long as she can give, be it to child or lover, she is unassailable.

The second seduction occurs when the Gerhardts, except for Old Gerhardt, move to Cleveland at the behest of brother Bass and supposedly at his expense. Bass is expansive and generous for a while, but then begins to demand more and more until Jennie must take a position as a chambermaid at the Bracebridge house, where she meets Lester Kane. Once again, as with Brander Matthews, the seduction wears the facade of obligation—this time because Lester Kane helps the family when Old Gerhardt suffers debilitating burns, which deprive him of his glassblowing trade, his sole means of support. Lester has pursued Jennie and his help fosters the ensuing affair. Like the first seduction, however, the second is not the simple matter it seems.

Lester Kane is Dreiser's portrayal of the enlightened man—the man who has serious doubts about religion, morality, societal restrictions, and mores. He serves the basic needs of Jennie's character; he also understands his own needs for the devotion, care, and understanding which Jennie is able and willing to give. With his willingness to make a more-or-less permanent commitment to Jennie, he seems to be a match, but Lester also understands the restrictions of class that forbid him to marry Jennie and feels the strong pull of family duty, which requires that he play a vital part in shaping the family's considerable enterprises. Lester, then, is caught with Jennie, as Dreiser puts it, between the "upper and nether millstones of society."

When Jennie and Lester set up their clandestine apartment in Chicago, they are enormously happy until they are discovered by Lester's family; the newspapers make front-page news of the discovery, and Jennie reveals to Lester that she has hidden the existence of her daughter, Vesta, from him. Amazingly, Lester weathers all these shocks and even brings Vesta and Old Gerhardt to share the apartment with them, but Lester's "indiscretions" have allowed his less heroically inclined brother to take control of the family business, and when his father dies, his will decrees that Lester must make a choice. If he marries Jennie, he gets a pittance; if he leaves her, he gets a normal portion. At this point, Letty, an old flame of Lester—of the "right" class—surfaces, and Jennie, fully recognizing the mutual sacrifices she and Lester will have to make whether he leaves or stays, encourages him to leave her. Lester eventually marries Letty and claims his inheritance. Jennie sacrifices Lester and in rapid succession sees Old Gerhardt and Vesta die. Deprived of her family, she manufactures one by taking in orphans. The device is not satisfying and the worldly refinement she has assimilated in her life with Lester is not enough to succor her, yet she survives to be called to Lester's death bed. Lester tells her that he has never forgotten her and that he loves her still, and Jennie reciprocates. The scene brings together a man and a woman who have given away or had taken away everything they loved through no particular fault of their own.

Lester is a weak man, like Hurstwood, but unlike Hurstwood he does not give up, he is beaten until he can no longer resist. Unlike Carrie, Jennie is not brought to the point of emptiness by achievements, but by losses. Her nature has betrayed her, and when one sees her hidden in the church at Lester's funeral, unrecognized by his family, one senses the totality of her loss. One also senses, however, that she has emerged a spiritual victor. She seems to have grown more expansive and more generous with each loss. Her stature grows until she looms over the novel as the archetypal survivor. She has been bruised, battered, and pushed down, but she has not been destroyed. She cannot be destroyed so long as she can give.

In *The Financier*, the first of the three volumes of the Cowperwood *Trilogy of Desire*, which also includes *The Titan* and *The Stoic*, perhaps more than in any other of his works, Dreiser relied on research for character, setting, plot, and theme. The characters are not drawn from memories of his family or his beloved Chicago, at least not exclusively nor primarily; the themes are most clearly the result of Dreiser's enormous reading.

"*Genus Financierus Americanus*," or the great financial wizards of turn-of-the-century America, fascinated Dreiser, and in their world of amorality, power, money, and materialism, he saw the mechanism which led America. Frank Cowperwood is a fictional representation of Charles T. Yerkes, a relatively obscure name but one of the movers in American finance. Dreiser encountered Yerkes in Chicago and New York and watched his machinations from a reporter's and an editor's vantage. Yerkes was no worse or better than the Rockefellers or Goulds, but by the time Dreiser started the trilogy, Yerkes was dead and his career could be studied in its totality. In addition, Yerkes's career was extensively documented in newspaper accounts, a fact which facilitated Dreiser's research, and that career had the advantage of a wife and a mistress and the final breaking up of Yerkes's empire by his creditors—all of which fit nicely into Dreiser's plan. The failure by one of the "titans of industry" to leave an indelible mark on humanity or on his immediate surroundings is the key to Dreiser's "equation inevitable," a concept first clearly worked out in *The Financier*.

Dreiser's readings in Arthur Schopenhauer, Friedrich Nietzsche, Karl Marx, Herbert Spencer, Jacques Loeb, and others confirmed his idea that the strong are meant to fulfill their course, to alter the pattern of life, and to "be a Colossus and bestride the world." At the same time, other strong individuals or groups (the "masses" were a real but troublesome entity for Dreiser) appear with equal strength but opposite intentions specifically intended by nature to maintain an equilibrium—a sort of cosmic check and balance. For Dreiser, "no thing is fixed, all tendencies are permitted, apparently. Only a balance is maintained." All men, significant and insignificant, are tools of nature and all are, in some way, a part of the equation. From Cowperwood's youth, the equation is seen in action. His victory in a boyhood fight confirms his trust in strength and resolution (or the first lick), and the now-famous lobster/squid narrative clarifies his understanding of the operation of nature. If the squid is prey for the lobster and the lobster prey for man, then man must also be prey, but only to man. These early insights are borne out in Cowperwood's Philadelphia life.

Cowperwood's early successes and his dealings with Colonel Butler are built on his philosophy of prey, but they are also founded on his realization that form and substance are separate. In order to succeed, one must maintain the semblance of propriety while carrying on normal business, which is ruthless and unfeeling. When he is jailed, he does not consider it a defeat, only a setback. Cowperwood is basically a pragmatist who does what is necessary to please himself. Besides this pragmatic nature, however, Cowperwood has another side which seems anomalous in his quest for power.

The other side of Cowperwood is epitomized by his simultaneous lust for and pride in his women and his art collection. Often styled his quest for the beautiful, Cowperwood's desire for women and art, no matter which woman or which masterpiece, is still a facet of his acquisitive nature, but it is a facet which reflects the hidden recesses of his spirit. Inside the ruthless, conniving, buccaneering entrepreneur is a man seeking to outdo even nature by acquiring or controlling the best of her handiwork, but there is also a closely guarded, solidly confined sensibility. This artistic sensibility is confined because it is the antithesis of strength and power and because Cowperwood understands that if he yields to it, he will no longer be in control of his life, his fortune, and his world.

Morality has no relevance in Cowperwood's understanding of the equation. He and his desires are all that exist. His desires are completely carnal in relationships with women. Even with Aileen, who understands him best, there is only lust, never love, because love is a part of that hidden Cowperwood, which he knows he must suppress. The implication is that if he ever loved, Cowperwood would no longer be the financier, but would become simply human.

Aside from the development of the equation and its workings in Cowperwood's world, *The Financier* is a faintly realized novel when set against *Sister Carrie* or *An American Tragedy*. Cowperwood's motto, "I satisfy myself," is the prevailing motto and his failure to satisfy himself, his wife, his competitors, and anyone or anything, provides the answer to the motto's arrogance.

An American Tragedy is Dreiser's acknowledged masterpiece; of all his novels, it most successfully blends autobiography with the fruits of his painstaking research. In the work, Dreiser was interested in exposing the flaws in the seamless fabric of the American dream. He had seen the destructive nature of the untempered drive for success and he understood that such a drive was an unavoidable result of the social temperament of the times. He also understood that the victims of that destructive urge were those who strove not fully understanding why they struggled nor why they failed. Thus, his criticism is aimed at both those who struggle for an unattainable dream and at the society which urges them on and laughs when they fall. His research led Dreiser to the case of Chester Gillette and the narrative skeleton for *An American Tragedy*.

The events leading to Gillette's murder of Grace Brown in 1906 and the circumstances of his early life were amply documented in the sensational, yellow-press coverage of the Gillette trial, and they provide a circumstantial sketch of the events of Clyde Griffiths' life and times. Gillette and Griffiths also bear the marks of a common background with Dreiser. The poverty-stricken youth, the desire for success and material things, the sexual frustrations, and the attraction to beautiful, well-placed women are all parts of Dreiser's youth and young manhood. If one adds Dreiser's later unhappy marriage, his philandering, and his tense relationship with Helen Richardson, one has all the pieces that produced Dreiser's empathy for and attraction to Chester Gillette and, ultimately, Clyde Griffiths. Thus, in addition to the dramatic possibilities of the Gillette case, Dreiser felt a kinship with his protagonist which allowed him to portray him as a pitiable, arresting, trapped creature.

Clyde Griffiths, in Dreiser's vision, is trapped by forces over which he has little or no control. The "chemisms" of Clyde's life trap him: he no more has control over his desires for success, sex, and material goods than he has over the voice which urges him on during the accident/murder that kills Roberta. In short, Clyde has no control over the irresistible American dream. Writing of the Gillette case, Dreiser observes that Chester Gillette, if he had not committed murder, "was really doing the kind of thing which Americans should and would have said was the wise and moral thing to do" by trying to better his social standing through a good marriage. Gillette did, however, commit murder; Clyde Griffiths, on the other hand, intends to commit murder but loses his nerve in the boat with Roberta. When she falls into the water after he accidentally hits her with the camera, she drowns only because of Clyde's inaction. Faced with the decision to save her or not, Clyde cannot or will not make the decision, and his inaction damns him. The evidence against him is circumstantial at best and objective examination allows doubt as to his guilt. That doubt intensifies Clyde's entrapment. It is a trap of his own making, but the reader is never sure if he deserves his fate.

In the trial scenes and the events surrounding the trial, Dreiser shows all the external forces which work against Clyde to seal that fate. Political pressures on the defense attorneys and the prosecutors, the prejudice of the rural jury impaneled to try Clyde, the haste with which his wealthy cousins disavow him in order to save their social standing, and Clyde's own ineptitude as a liar form a second box around him, enclosing the first box of his own desires and failures.

Clyde's inevitable conviction and death sentence place him in the final box—his prison cell. This final enclosure is the ultimate circumstance over which Clyde has no control. There is no exit after the governor is convinced of Clyde's guilt by Clyde's mother and his clergyman. When Clyde is finally executed, his inexorable fall is complete.

Clyde's doom is sealed in his tawdry youth, first as a member of an itinerant evangelist's family, later in his work at the Green-Davidson, and ultimately in his fatal liaison with his wealthy Lycurgus cousins. He is not clever enough to help himself, is not wealthy enough to pay anyone to help him (especially during Roberta's pregnancy), and his "chemisms" drive him on in spite of his limitations. When he has his goal of wealth and success in sight, the only obstacle in his path, the pregnant Roberta, must be discarded at any cost without a thought of the consequences. His dreams are the driving force and those dreams are the product of forces over which he has not a shred of control. When he attempts to force his dreams to fruition, he further commits himself into the hands of those forces and they lead him to his death.

Clyde lacks Carrie's inherent sense for survival and success, Jennie's self-lessness and resilience, and Cowperwood's intelligence and wealth, but for all of that, he is a reflection of all of them and of the society in which they function. Clyde commits the crime and is punished, but Dreiser indicts all of society in Clyde's execution. Clyde's death sounds the knell for the romance of success and heralds the vacuum that takes its place. Clyde is not strong and falls; Cowperwood is strong and falls anyway. Carrie finds there is no fulfillment in success and feels the emptiness of her discovery; Jennie is beaten down again and again until she finds that she is living in a void which cannot be filled even with her abundant love. Thus, Clyde is not only the natural product of all these characters and of Dreiser's development but is also the symbol of Dreiser's world view: a relentless vision which permanently altered American literature.

Clarence O. Johnson

Other major works

SHORT FICTION: *Free and Other Stories*, 1918; *Chains: Lesser Novels and Stories*, 1927; *Fine Furniture*, 1930; *The Best Short Stories of Theodore Dreiser*, 1947 (Howard Fast, editor); *Best Short Stories*, 1956 (James T. Farrell, editor).

PLAYS: *Plays of the Natural and Supernatural*, 1916; *The Hand of the Potter: A Tragedy in Four Acts*, 1918.

POETRY: *Moods: Cadenced and Declaimed*, 1926, 1928; *The Aspirant*, 1929; *Epitaph: A Poem*, 1929.

NONFICTION: *A Traveler at Forty*, 1913; *A Hoosier Holiday*, 1916; *Twelve Men*, 1919; *Hey, Rub-a-Dub-Dub!*, 1920; *A Book About Myself*, 1922 (revised as *Newspaper Days*, 1931); *The Color of a Great City*, 1923; *My City*, 1929; *Dawn*, 1931; *Tragic America*, 1931; *America Is Worth Saving*, 1941; *Letters of Theodore Dreiser*, 1959; *Letters to Louise*, 1959; *American Diaries*, 1902-1926, 1982; *Selected Magazine Articles of Theodore Dreiser*, 1985.

Bibliography

Dudley, Dorothy. *Forgotten Frontiers: Dreiser and the Land of the Free.* 1932. Reprint. St. Clair Shores, Mich.: Scholarly Press, 1972. This refreshing volume allows the contemporary reader to view Dreiser's early career at a closer range than possible in more recent works. Still readable although lengthy, provides a detailed look at the early life, times, and literary career of Dreiser.

Elias, Robert H. *Theodore Dreiser: Apostle of Nature.* Ithaca, N.Y.: Cornell University Press, 1970. This emended edition by one of Dreiser's major critics provides a carefully written account of Dreiser's life and career. Of some value is a section of notes and a survey of early research and criticism that includes European, Russian, Japanese, and Indian scholarship.

Hakutani, Yoshinobu. *Young Dreiser: A Critical Study.* Madison, N.J.: Fairleigh Dickinson University Press, 1980. Finds Dreiser's early life the place to search for what is behind his later thoughts and literary production. Contends that Dreiser was not consciously influenced in his early works by French naturalism. Notes, a bibliography, and an index complete the work.

Hussman, Lawrence E. *Dreiser and His Fiction: A Twentieth-Century Question.* Philadelphia: University of Pennsylvania Press, 1983. Unlike some other influential studies of Dreiser's work, identifies in some of the novelist's childhood experiences the "seeds of certain intrinsically religious and moral ideas" that allow a reassessment of his work. This excellent study of his major novels contains notes and an index.

Moers, Ellen. *Two Dreisers.* New York: Viking Press, 1969. Explores the writing of two of Dreiser's masterpieces, *Sister Carrie* and *An American Tragedy.* An appendix comments on Dreiser's ancestry. Also contains a useful section of reference notes as well as an index.

Mookerjee, Rabindra N. *Theodore Dreiser: His Thought and Social Criticism.* Delhi, India: National, 1974. This lucid treatment of Dreiser traces his career chronologically, addressing formative influences and his emergence as a social critic. Relates Dreiser's view of a "tragic" America in the 1930's to his later movement toward religious faith. Helpful appendices, notes, a selected bibliography, and an index supplement the text.

Pizer, Donald. *Critical Essays on Theodore Dreiser.* Boston: G. K. Hall,

1981. This well-indexed collection of important Dreiser criticism contains both general essays and essays which treat major novels. Three phases of criticism are identified: one concerned with Dreiserian naturalism, one focusing on philosophical and political ideas, and one treating interpretation and establishing a base of knowledge about Dreiser himself.

LAWRENCE DURRELL

Born: Julundur, India; February 27, 1912
Died: Sommières, France; November 7, 1990

Principal long fiction

Pied Piper of Lovers, 1935; *Panic Spring*, 1937 (as Charles Norden); *The Black Book*, 1938; *Cefalû*, 1947 (republished as *The Dark Labyrinth*, 1958); *The Alexandria Quartet*, 1962 (includes *Justine*, 1957; *Balthazar*, 1958; *Mountolive*, 1958; *Clea*, 1960); *Tunc*, 1968; *Nunquam*, 1970; *The Avignon Quintet* (includes *Monsieur: Or, The Prince of Darkness*, 1974; *Livia: Or, Buried Alive*, 1978; *Constance: Or, Solitary Practices*, 1981; *Sebastian: Or, Ruling Passions*, 1983; *Quinx: Or, The Ripper's Tale*, 1985).

Other literary forms

Lawrence Durrell was a prolific writer in many genres. As a successful poet, he published many books, including *Ten Poems* (1932); *Bromo Bombastes* (1933); *Transition: Poems* (1934); *A Private Country* (1943); *Cities, Plains, and People* (1946); *On Seeming to Presume* (1948); *Deus Loci* (1950); *The Tree of Idleness and Other Poems* (1955); *Private Drafts* (1955); *Selected Poems* (1956); *The Ikons and Other Poems* (1966); *The Red Limbo Lingo* (1971); *Vega and Other Poems* (1973); and *Collected Poems 1931-1974* (1980). He wrote three plays in verse, *Sappho* (1950; produced 1959); *Acte* (1965; produced 1961), and *An Irish Faustus* (1963; produced 1966). He also published travel books such as *Prospero's Cell* (1945); *Reflections on a Marine Venus* (1953); *Bitter Lemons* (1957); *Sicilian Carousel* (1977); and *The Greek Islands* (1978); and humorous prose works mostly dealing with the diplomatic life, including *Esprit de Corps* (1957); *Stiff Upper Lip* (1958); and *Sauve Qui Peut* (1966). His essays and letters were published in *A Key to Modern British Poetry* (1952), *Art and Outrage* (1959), *Lawrence Durrell and Henry Miller: A Private Correspondence* (1963, George Wickes, editor), *Spirit of Place* (1969, Alan G. Thomas, editor). His publisher apparently persuaded him to identify one of his books, *White Eagles over Serbia* (1957), as being "for juveniles." He translated Greek poetry by C. P. Cavafy, George Seferis, and others, as well as *The Curious History of Pope Joan* (1954; revised as *Pope Joan: A Romantic Biography*, 1960) by Emmanuel Royidis. He published widely in periodicals as various as *Mademoiselle, Quarterly Review of Literature, New Statesman, T'ien Hsia Monthly of Shanghai*, and *Réalités*, and edited anthologies of poetry and collections of letters. He also spent some time working on the screenplay for the 1963 film *Cleopatra*. His last book, a nonfiction work entitled *Caesar's Vast Ghost: A Portrait of Provence*, appeared in 1990.

Achievements

Although Durrell was highly respected as a poet and travel writer, it is generally agreed that his greatest accomplishments were his *The Alexandria Quartet* and *The Avignon Quintet*. There is little doubt that Durrell's place in twentieth century literature rests on these extraordinary works. Throughout his career, Durrell had a sensuous, ornate, and lyrical style that sometimes degenerated into overwriting—a tendency to which he freely admitted. In his best books, however, the style reflected his Mediterranean surroundings of Greece, Egypt, or Provence, France. Influenced by Henry Miller but by no means an imitator of him, Durrell appealed to so-called literary tastes beginning with *The Black Book*. Yet the popularity of *The Alexandria Quartet* seems to be the result of the blend of an exceptional style with an exotic setting and characters, wit, and exciting plot elements such as murder, conspiracy, and unrequited love. *The Avignon Quintet* has these same elements and is no less a literary triumph for its lack of public acclaim.

Biography

Lawrence George Durrell was born in Julundur, India, on February 27, 1912, to Lawrence Samuel Durrell, an English engineer who built the Tata Iron and Steel Works, and Louise Florence "Dixie" Durrell, of Irish heritage. Both his parents' families had been in India for some time. When the boy was very young, the Durrells moved to Kurseong, near the Himalayas, so that the elder Durrell could accept a three-year contract on a mountain railway to Darjeeling. The sight of the mountains made a strong impression on the boy, so much so that he once described his childhood in a letter to Henry Miller as "a brief dream of Tibet." While in Darjeeling, he began his education at the College of St. Joseph and received the first encouragement for his writing from a Belgian priest, Father Joseph De Guylder.

At twelve, Durrell was sent to England with his brother Leslie "to get the hall-mark," as his father said, of a public school education. He attended St. Olave's and St. Saviour's Grammar School, where he developed his lifelong interest in Elizabethan writers, and later entered St. Edmund's School in Canterbury. Despite several attempts, he was never admitted to Cambridge University and would later write of his life in England, "That mean shabby little island . . . wrung my guts out of me and tried to destroy anything singular and unique in me."

The death of his father left Durrell with a small income, which he used to move to Bloomsbury in order to become a writer. During his Bloomsbury years, Durrell held a number of odd jobs, including jazz pianist and composer, race-car driver, and real estate agent. During this period, he also met his first wife, Nancy Myers, a student at the Slade School, with whom he ran a photo studio for a time. At nineteen, he met John Gawsworth in a café after fleeing from an upstairs window during a police raid on the Blue Peter Night Club, where Durrell was playing piano. Awed by Gawsworth's personal knowledge of many famous authors, he became his friend, and though they often disagreed on literary matters—Gawsworth was a very conservative poet who admired the literature of the 1890's and had little respect for W. H. Auden and Stephen Spender—Gawsworth helped him to get his first poems published. *Ten Poems* was published in 1932 under the pseudonym "Gaffer Peeslake" by Caduceus Press, founded by Durrell, his wife, and George Wilkinson.

Durrell began his first novel, *Pied Piper of Lovers*, while he and Nancy lived for a year in a Sussex cottage with George and Pam Wilkinson. After the Wilkinsons emigrated to Corfu, Durrell lived with his mother, sister, and two brothers in Bournemouth, where they received glowing letters from the Wilkinsons. Excited by the idea of the warm climate, Durrell left his novel under consideration at Cassell's and departed for Corfu. When the rest of his family followed a few weeks later, they bore the news that the book had been accepted, confirming Durrell in his notion to take up writing as a profession, though very few copies of the book would sell. The residence in Corfu had two important results for him. First, it began his long association with Greece, its poetry, and language; and second, he discovered *Tropic of Cancer* (1934) by Henry Miller.

The latter was probably the most significant development in the young Durrell's career. He wrote a letter of praise to Miller, who responded warmly, saying that the letter was the most intelligent he had yet received from a Briton about his book. By 1936, Durrell was clearly under the influence of Miller, apologizing for his second novel and engrossed in writing *The Black Book*. The next year, Durrell announced that he was the "first writer to be fertilized by H. M." and sent *The Black Book* to Miller, who paused in the writing of *Tropic of Capricorn* (1939) to type out (with Anaïs Nin) three copies to be sent to Herbert Read, T. S. Eliot, and Jack Kahane. Kahane published it in Paris, and Eliot endorsed it as "the first piece of work by a new English writer to give me any hope for the future of prose fiction." Durrell visited Paris, and Miller later visited Corfu, solidifying a friendship which would last until the latter's death, despite Durrell's forthright, often scathing, reviews of Miller's later works.

The war interrupted Durrell's idyllic life in Corfu. He moved to Athens in 1940, where he worked for the British Embassy, and then was posted to the Institute of English Studies in Kalamata. While in Athens he met George Katsimbalis and George Seferiades ("Seferis"), both of whom he would later translate. In 1941, he was forced to escape the Nazi invasion with Nancy and their daughter Penelope Berengaria in an old caique bound for Crete. From Crete, they went on to Egypt, where Durrell served as a foreign press service officer for the British Information Service. Nancy and Penelope spent the war in Palestine, and the marriage deteriorated, resulting in a divorce in 1947, when Durrell married Yvette Cohen, a dark-eyed Alexandrian woman who may have partly inspired the character of Justine.

Happy to escape from Egypt, Durrell lived for a time on Rhodes, then in Argentina and Yugoslavia, disliking both places. In the early 1950's, he left Yugoslavia for Cyprus, where he bought a home, taught school, and, during the developing civil war, became Public Relations Officer for the British government. His second marriage deteriorated early in his stay on Cyprus, but by 1956, he had completed *Justine*, the first novel of *The Alexandria Quartet*. Late that year, he moved on to Dorset with Claude Marie Vineenden, later to become his third wife, where he worked on *Bitter Lemons*, a book drawing on his experiences in Cyprus.

Financially exhausted, but unable to live away from the Mediterranean area for very long, Durrell and Claude began to look for a home in the Midi. Virtually overnight, he became a world-renowned author when *Justine*, *Bitter Lemons*, *White Eagles over Serbia*, and *Esprit de Corps* were published in 1957. He was translated into numerous foreign languages and could devote his entire time to writing. With his favored mode of work being intense days of some fourteen hours of writing, he allegedly produced *Justine* in four months, *Balthazar* in six weeks, *Mountolive* in twelve weeks, and *Clea* in eight.

For thirty years or so, Durrell lived a settled life in Provence, with occasional travel. On March 27, 1961, he and Claude were married, and in 1966, they moved into a larger house in Sommières to accommodate their guests, Claude's children by a previous marriage, Penelope, and their daughter Sappho-Jane. After a period of declining health, Claude died on New Year's Day, 1967. In 1973, Durrell married Ghislaine de Boysson, but by 1986 his fourth marriage was finished. The five novels of *The Avignon Quintet* appeared between 1974 and 1985 to mixed reviews, but there is no question that this thirteen-hundred-page sequence is a tour de force of the first order.

Lawrence Durrell died on November 7, 1990, at the age of seventy-eight in his home in Provence. His literary reputation, which rests chiefly on *The Alexandria Quartet*, is higher on the Continent and in the United States than in Great Britain.

Analysis

Lawrence Durrell's first novel, *Pied Piper of Lovers*, is a story of life among the Bohemians at Bloomsbury. It was sufficiently dismal to provoke a publisher to advise him to offer *Panic Spring* under the pseudonym of Charles Norden, so that the latter, a slightly better book, would not be associated with its predecessor. *Panic Spring* has been described as being influenced by, even imitative of, the works of Aldous Huxley; even as it was published, Durrell was writing an apology to Henry Miller for his "new and facile novel." In essence, Durrell's early career was characterized by a search for a paradigm or form for his talent, a search that ended with his discovery of *Tropic of Cancer*.

The impact of Miller's novel on the young Durrell was enormous. A comparison of his earlier works with his third novel, *The Black Book*, reveals a dramatic transformation. His creative impulses have been freed. As he described it in 1959, *The Black Book* is "a two-fisted attack on literature by a young man in the thirties," taking its aggressive intent from Miller's all-out assault on the literary establishment. The narrator, Lawrence Lucifer, recounts his experiences in a seedy London hotel from the perspective of his life on Corfu. In the hotel, he finds the diary of Herbert Gregory, which overlaps with his own experiences. There are numerous other characters and much obscurity as to the details of time and event. There is a great deal of erotic content, both homosexual and heterosexual, as the characters betray and cuckold one another. The novel's themes are revealed not through a carefully constructed plot but through a series of scenes, reminiscences, and vignettes.

Durrell later wrote in the 1959 Introduction to the second edition of *The Black Book*:

> With all its imperfections lying heavy on my head, I can't help being attached to it because in the writing of it I first heard the sound of my own voice, lame and halting, perhaps, but nevertheless my very own.

In it, the reader finds the first cry of Durrell's literary voice, his exotic characters, his sensual and sensuous prose, and his experiments with narrative time. When it was published, T. S. Eliot (among others) was perspicacious enough to recognize the voice of a major new talent. Had Durrell ended his career with *The Black Book*, it would most likely be forgotten. Burdened with an excessively baroque style, it is of interest chiefly because of its place in his career.

Cefalû, Durrell's next novel (reissued as *The Dark Labyrinth* after *Justine* had assured Durrell a place in twentieth century literature), can be viewed in much the same way as *The Black Book*. In it, he seems to be discovering himself, experimenting, finding the form and style which would achieve maturity in *The Alexandria Quartet*. One also sees a tugging away from Miller's influence—only a few years later, Durrell would write a scathing indictment of Miller's *Sexus* (1949)—and a reversion to the influence of Aldous Huxley that had been so apparent in *Panic Spring*. *The Dark Labyrinth* has extensive allegorical elements, reminiscent of Huxley: the characters are trapped in a labyrinth in Crete, and each finds in the maze that for which he or she has been looking. The book was written quickly—which is not unusual for Durrell—and seems rather derivative in structure, though the writing itself often attains his characteristic brilliance.

The four novels which compose *The Alexandria Quartet* are collectively one of the greatest achievements in the modern novel. Like many modern works, *The Alexandria Quartet* often seems to be about the creation of fiction. Darley, the narrator of *Justine* and *Balthazar*, is a novelist, as are two other characters. Diversity in point of view is regularly exploited through the use of diaries, letters, and recounted experiences. Truth becomes subjective and layered. The characters' knowledge is limited to what they perceive, and numerous questions are left unanswered.

The *Alexandria Quartet* is also an examination of love in the modern world as the characters pass through convoluted interrelationships. Sex and love, like art, become ways of glimpsing underlying truths, of developing one's knowledge of reality. Durrell has also stated that *The Alexandria Quartet* consists of four parts because he was attempting to produce a novelistic version of Albert Einstein's universe. Relativity (or subjectivity) thus appears as a justification for the exploitation of point of view, for the questionable reliability of narrators, and for an exploration of time and memory. Durrell, however, is careful, despite the modern and postmodern objectives of *The Alexandria Quartet*, to hang all the theory on a generous structure of narrative. There are a number of stories of betrayal, murder, love, devotion, and tragedy intertwined, and although they are elusive, they make the tetralogy accessible in a way that many "experimental" works are not, without compromising the artistic integrity of the work.

Finally, Durrell's extraordinary prose, his poetic, lyrical, and erotic use of language, elevates *The Alexandria Quartet* above most modern fiction, although this talent was manifest as early as *The Black Book*, provoking Miller to write "You are *the* master of the English language." Some critics have regarded Durrell's prose as excessive, overdone, a flamboyant collection of purple clichés and Victorian decadence. Yet, in each of his major works, and especially in *The Alexandria Quartet*, it is difficult to imagine a prose style without his deliberate rhythms and cadences that would be suitable to his themes and extraordinary settings.

The chief characters of *The Alexandria Quartet* may be loosely based upon people Durrell has known. Darley has a number of characteristics in common with the author: they are both novelists; three women (up to the writing of the novel) have played a major part in both their lives; and they have held similar jobs. Other resemblances between other characters and certain "real people" might be noted, but these would only contribute to the thematic question of how reality is transformed by experience, recollection, and novelization. The whole question adds another layer to the multiple levels among which the tetralogy moves.

Justine is one of the most haunting characters in the tetralogy. Born in Alexandria, she is a dark, beautiful Jewess with an intense sexuality and an obscure background. She runs the gamut of sexual pleasure and is seen from a variety of viewpoints, including the romanticized memories of Darley's love, the cynical stance of the novelist Pursewarden, and the *roman à clef* of her first husband, Arnauti. Though not really in love with Nessim Hosnani, a Copt, she marries the devoted Egyptian on the condition that he help her find her kidnaped child. Nessim becomes involved in gun-running into Palestine because of his hatred of the English. Narouz—Nessim's harelipped, violent, and earthy brother—becomes a force in the second and third volumes of the tetralogy. Balthazar, a physician, gives his name to the second volume, which he also partly narrates, though he is present throughout the books. A mystic homosexual, he seems to know most of the other characters' secrets, and his illuminations of Darley's perceptions provide new insights into the situations. Mountolive is a diplomat who has an affair with Leila Hosnani, Nessim's mother, who later contracts smallpox, loses her beauty, and engages in a lengthy correspondence with Mountolive, who falls in love with Pursewarden's blind sister, Liza.

Alexandria, with its convoluted intrigues, gradually wears away the English confidence of the diplomat as Nessim and others betray him as he investigates the circumstances of Pursewarden's suicide. Clea is a superstitious artist, beloved of Narouz, lover of Justine, Dr. Amaril, and eventually, Darley. With blonde hair and blue eyes, Clea's northern European beauty contrasts with Justine's Mediterranean beauty.

Even this short summary of the characters reveals the complexity of the story line of *The Alexandria Quartet*, and there are even more characters who play important roles: Scobie, the transvestite who becomes a saint; Cohen, who plots to liberate Palestine; Dr. Amaril, who loves the noseless Semira; Mnemjian, the dwarf barber; Pombal, involved in espionage; Capodistria of the great sexual prowess; and Toto de Brunel, who is murdered with a hatpin, probably by mistake. A complete list of characters would number more than a hundred.

Alexandria itself has often been discussed as playing a character-like role in the tetralogy. Like James Joyce's Dublin, Marcel Proust's Paris, and William Faulkner's Yoknapatawpha County, the landscape exhibits a crucial influence upon the characters, determining their behavior. Sometimes characters seem to be mere expressions of some element of the landscape, appearing and disappearing into the textures of Alexandrian life, just as the "reality" of Scobie is absorbed into the legend of "El Scob." Alexandria is mysterious, full of deception and treachery. There are always murderous undercurrents, such as when Justine suspects Nessim's plans to kill Darley at the duck shoot and when Toto is murdered at the masked ball, probably in Justine's place. Even Narouz's frustration at being unable to satisfy his love for Clea seems to explode out of his harpoon gun after his death, the accident nearly causing her to drown when her hand is staked to a sunken ship.

A brief discussion of *The Alexandria Quartet* can hardly do justice to the complexity of the work. With no ostensible intention of making a moral statement, Durrell's foremost intention was the creation of a work of art which reflected the relativistic sensibility of the modern world, yet he carefully maintained an absorbing plot to serve as a skeleton on which to flesh out his musings on love, sex, art, writing, memory, and time. Although Durrell celebrates life in a way many contemporary artists do not, *The Alexandria Quartet* also reveals ambiguities and darknesses. The tetralogy cannot be reduced to story, theme, or message. Its lush writing becomes a sensory experience of a world with overlapping, often conflicting layers of reality.

Tunc and *Nunquam*, the pair of novels which followed *The Alexandria Quartet*, have much in common with the tetralogy, despite the great difference in subject matter. Felix Charlock invents a computer, named Abel, which can recall or predict virtually anything. Charlock soon finds himself under contract to a huge conglomerate headed by Julian Merlin, a mysterious character who seems to control, through business connections, most of the people in the world. To join Merlin's is to be assured of comfort, but also to give up individual freedom. *Tunc* and *Nunquam* contain Durrell's usually rich selection of characters, including the neurotic Benedicta, Julian's sister; Iolanthe, a prostitute-become-movie-star; and Caradoc, a wordplaying architect.

In style, *Tunc* and *Nunquam* are similar to *The Alexandria Quartet*, despite the science-fiction mise-en-scène. When Merlin creates a robotic duplicate of Iolanthe, which can hallucinate eating and other bodily functions even though it does not do these things, Charlock comes to identify with the robot's quest for freedom, seeing in it his own struggle to remain an individual despite his absorption into Merlin's world. This thematic concern with individual freedom in the contemporary world does not play a large part in *The Alexandria Quartet*, but *Tunc* and *Nunquam* exhibit the tetralogy's themes of time, space, art, love, and sex, as well as a masterful use of language.

With the five novels that constitute *The Avignon Quintet* (*Monsieur: Or, The Prince of Darkness*; *Livia: Or, Buried Alive*; *Constance: Or, Solitary Practices*; *Sebastian: Or, Ruling Passions*; and *Quinx: Or, The Ripper's Tale*), Durrell recapitulates the themes of a lifetime with self-conscious exuberance, like a magician putting on his show for the last time. Shifts of viewpoint are kaleidoscopic in effect: bright, dazzling, patterned, but ambiguous as to meaning. He presents two novelists, Aubrey Blanford and Robin Sutcliffe, who explore the theme of novel-writing to a fare-thee-well. Durrell creates two different fates for each of these characters, as if his world suddenly split in two and his personae lived out opposing potentialities. Duality is rife in *The Avignon Quintet*, as one can see from the double titles of each novel.

There is one underlying idea, however, that permeates everything: entropy, the tendency for orderly systems to dissolve in anarchy and death. Taking the period from 1938 to 1945, with the whole of World War II occurring in *Constance*, Durrell shows entropy at work in Europe under the impact of Nazism, entropy in the failure of Western rationalism to stem the "death-drift" of society or individuals, and entropy in the breakdown of personality in the forms of insanity and suicide. Against entropy, Durrell poses the forces of love and art. Yet even these succumb to chaos and death.

As an author, Durrell is like the "Lord of Misrule," the comic king of festival, in *The Avignon Quintet*. His world is one in which social disorder reigns amid drinking and feasting. In fact, *The Avignon Quintet* describes celebrations and banquets frequently, often at the end of a novel, and often with something sinister at their cores. Durrell's comic tone and exuberance just barely conceal a deeply pessimistic outlook, like gallows humor.

The Provence town of Avignon is the geographical and spiritual center of the quintet. With its dual legacy, very much present in these novels, of having been the center of Catholicism and of the heretical Knights Templar in the Middle Ages, Avignon represents the opposing pulls of reason and mysticism, West and East, and life and death on the characters. Egypt stands for the East, for Gnostic mysticism (linked with the Templar heresy), and for death throughout *The Avignon Quintet*. Geneva is the site of safety and reason during World War II, an outpost of civilized Western values in an era turned savage and suicidal. Each locale—Avignon, Egypt, and Geneva—has its own distinct flavor and ambiguity, and each is fully realized artistically. Durrell's unique descriptive prose and his use of vignette and narrative event are matchless in creating the feel of place.

Most of the main characters are on a quest of sorts: some for love (Blanford, a novelist; Constance, a psychoanalyst; Chatto, a consul), some for sexual adventure (Livia, Prince Hassad), some for wealth (Lord Galen, Smirgel), some for revenge (Quatrefages, Mnemidis), and some for a sacrificial death at the hands of a Gnostic cult (Piers de Nogaret, Sebastian Affad). Several of these private quests are subsumed under one last, collective quest: the search for the lost Templar treasure, hidden centuries ago in a labyrinth of caves near the Roman aqueduct at Avignon, caves mined with explosives by Austrian sappers in the closing days of World War II. On a Friday the 13th, Blanford and Constance enter the caves, following a group of intoxicated revelers from a banquet at which Death has just appeared. The inconclusive end of this quest for treasure hints strongly that some poor fool set off the dynamite, sending *The Avignon Quintet* into the silence of extinction.

In the end, three aspects of life matter to Durrell: love as the means to truth, art as the mirror of truth, and a joyful acceptance of both life and earth as the final consummation of truth. By facing down entropy, his own and his world's, Durrell achieved a rare and disturbing kind of wisdom.

J. Madison Davis

Other major works
SHORT FICTION: *Esprit de Corps: Sketches from Diplomatic Life*, 1957; *Stiff*

Upper Lip: Life Among the Diplomats, 1958; *Sauve Qui Peut*, 1966; *The Best of Antrobus*, 1974; *Antrobus Complete*, 1985.

POETRY: *Quaint Fragment: Poems Written Between the Ages of Sixteen and Nineteen*, 1931; *Ten Poems*, 1932; *Bromo Bombastes*, 1933; *Transition: Poems*, 1934; *Proems: An Anthology of Poems*, 1938 (with others); *A Private Country*, 1943; *Cities, Plains, and People*, 1946; *Six Poems from the Greek of Sekilianos and Seferis*, 1946 (translation); *The King of Asine and Other Poems*, 1948 (translation); *On Seeming to Presume*, 1948; *Deus Loci*, 1950; *Private Drafts*, 1955; *The Tree of Idleness and Other Poems*, 1955; *Selected Poems*, 1956; *Collected Poems*, 1960; *Penguin Modern Poets 1*, 1962 (with Elizabeth Jennings and R. S. Thomas); *Beccaficio Le Becfigue*, 1963 (English; includes French translation by F. J. Temple); *Selected Poems 1935-63*, 1964; *The Ikons and Other Poems*, 1966; *The Red Limbo Lingo: A Poetry Notebook for 1968-70*, 1971; *On the Suchness of the Old Boy*, 1972; *Vega and Other Poems*, 1973; *Collected Poems 1931-1974*, 1980.

PLAYS: *Sappho*, 1950; *An Irish Faustus*, 1963; *Acte*, 1965.

NONFICTION: *Prospero's Cell*, 1945; *A Landmark Gone*, 1949; *A Key to Modern British Poetry*, 1952; *Reflections on a Marine Venus*, 1953; *The Curious History of Pope Joan*, 1954 (translation, revised as *Pope Joan: A Personal Biography*, 1960); *Bitter Lemons*, 1957; *Art and Outrage*, 1959; *Lawrence Durrell and Henry Miller: A Private Correspondence*, 1963 (George Wickes, editor); *Spirit of Place: Letters and Essays on Travel*, 1969 (Alan G. Thomas, editor); *The Big Supposer: Dialogues with Marc Alyn/Lawrence Durrell*, 1973; *Sicilian Carousel*, 1977; *The Greek Islands*, 1978; *Literary Lifelines: The Richard Aldington-Lawrence Durrell Correspondence*, 1981; *The Durrell-Miller Letters, 1935-1980*, 1988; *Caesar's Vast Ghost: A Portrait of Provence*, 1990.

CHILDREN'S LITERATURE: *White Eagles over Serbia*, 1957.

Bibliography

Adams, Robert M. *After Joyce: Studies in Fiction After "Ulysses."* New York: Oxford University Press, 1977. A look at modern and postmodern fiction, tracing James Joyce's influence from the 1920's through the mid-1970's. A bit sketchy and patronizing on Durrell.

Fraser, George S. *Lawrence Durrell*. London: Longman, 1970. A perceptive pamphlet-length study of Durrell's major literary output up to 1970, tracing the themes and plot of *The Alexandria Quartet* with admirable clarity. Contains a select bibliography.

Friedman, Alan W., ed. *Critical Essays on Lawrence Durrell*. Boston: G. K. Hall, 1987. A stimulating collection covering many aspects of Durrell's work. Concentrates on his important fiction, including *The Avignon Quintet*.

Moore, Harry T., ed. *The World of Lawrence Durrell*. Carbondale: Southern Illinois University Press, 1964. A landmark collection of early critical essays on Durrell by eminent scholars and writers, a reminiscence by Henry Miller, and letters to and from Durrell.

Pinchin, Jane LaGoudis. *Alexandria Still: Forster, Durrell, and Cavafy.* Princeton, N.J.: Princeton University Press, 1976. A study of how a seedy Egyptian port was transformed by three writers of genius, and by Durrell in particular, into a place of imagination, mystery, and romance. Includes a fine bibliography.

Weigel, John A. *Lawrence Durrell.* New York: Twayne, 1965. A balanced approach to the whole range of Durrell's writing, with a detailed examination of *The Alexandria Quartet* stressing theme, plot, character, and structure. Also contains an excellent bibliography with annotated secondary sources and background material.

MARIA EDGEWORTH

Born: Black Bourton, England; January 1, 1767
Died: Edgeworthstown, Ireland; May 22, 1849

Principal long fiction
Castle Rackrent, 1800; *Belinda*, 1801; *Leonora*, 1806; *Ennui*, 1809; *The Absentee*, 1812; *Vivian*, 1812; *Patronage*, 1814; *Harrington*, 1817; *Ormond*, 1817; *Helen*, 1834.

Other literary forms
Like a number of late eighteenth century and early nineteenth century authors, Maria Edgeworth did not intend to become a novelist, but began writing extended prose fiction as an outgrowth of other kinds of literary production. Her first works were children's tales, usually short and always with a clear and forcefully advanced didactic thesis—a few titles suggest the nature of the themes: "Lazy Laurence," "Waste not, Want not," "Forgive and Forget." Many of these stories were assembled under the titles *The Parent's Assistant: Or, Stories for Children* (1796, 1800) and *Moral Tales for Young People* (1801), the first of which encompassed six volumes, while the second filled five volumes.

These tales were written largely at the behest of Edgeworth's father, Richard Lovell Edgeworth, who was a deeply committed moralist and is still considered a notable figure in the history of education in England and Ireland. Both father and daughter collaborated on many of the stories, as they did on most of what Maria Edgeworth wrote. As a sort of commentary on the short fictions and certainly as an adjunct to them, the essays on education collected in *Essays on Practical Education* (1798) were designed to advance the liberal but moralistic theories on child-rearing that the elder Edgeworth had imbibed in part from Jean-Jacques Rousseau and had transmitted to his daughter. Richard Edgeworth's credentials for such a piece of writing were perhaps enhanced by the fact that he fathered no fewer than twenty-two children, with four wives.

Apart from further essays (again, chiefly written either in collaboration with her father or under his watchful eye) on education, morals, Ireland, and culture, Edgeworth's primary emphasis was on fiction, usually of novel length (her "novels" range in length from the quite short *Castle Rackrent*, merely one hundred pages, to *Belinda*, which extends to almost five hundred pages). The only other form she attempted—one in which, like many nineteenth century authors, she had no publishing success—was the drama. The plays were composed essentially for the pleasure of the family, as were the first drafts of the majority of the fictions; and the volume containing the best of them, *Comic Dramas, in Three Acts* (1817), is now almost universally unread.

Achievements

During her long lifetime, Edgeworth helped to make possible the Victorian novel. Reared with a rich background in the high achievements of Henry Fielding, Samuel Richardson, and Tobias Smollett, she began to write at a time when female novelists were just beginning to be accepted—a few of them, such as Fanny Burney and Elizabeth Inchbald, managing to attain some popularity. The novel of manners was the prevailing genre produced by these "lady writers." It had affinities with the lachrymose novel of sensibility (the classic example of which, *The Man of Feeling*, was penned in 1771 by a man, Henry Mackenzie), and the tight focus and excessively delicate feelings exhibited in this form limited its appeal and artistic possibilities. It lay to Jane Austen to instill clever and penetrating satire, along with a much greater sense of realism in regard to human behavior, and to Maria Edgeworth to extend its bounds of character depiction, to include persons of the lower classes, and to broaden its range: men are seen at the hunt, in private conference, and in all manner of vigorous activity unknown in Austen's fiction.

Edgeworth is, of course, bound to be compared with Austen, to the former's derogation; there can be no doubt that the latter is the greater novelist, from an artistic standpoint. This judgment should not blind the reader to Edgeworth's accomplishment. As P. N. Newby observes in *Maria Edgeworth* (1950), though "Jane Austen was so much the better novelist," yet "Maria Edgeworth may be the more important." Her significance rests chiefly on two achievements: she widened the scope of the "female" novel (the emphasis on female sensibility in her work is considerably less than in Austen's novels, though it can be detected); and, as Newby remarks, in her careful and detailed treatment of Ireland and its people, she "gave dignity to the regional subject and made the regional novel possible." Today, readers tend to take for granted the insightful historical works of, for example, Sir Walter Scott; they often do not realize that, had it not been for Edgeworth, Scott might not have attempted the monumental effort that he began in *Waverly* (1814), in whose Preface he gives Edgeworth full credit for inspiring him to essay the regional fiction in which his work became a landmark. It has also been claimed that such disparate figures as Stendhal and Ivan Turgenev were influenced by Edgeworth's sympathetic treatment of peasants. Some critics and literary historians have gone so far as to claim for her the title of the first intelligent sociological novelist in English literature. More than any author up to her time, Edgeworth revealed man as related to, and partially formed by, his environment.

Biography

January 1, 1767, is usually accepted as the birthdate of Maria Edgeworth; but, in *Maria Edgeworth: A Literary Biography* (1972), Marilyn Butler asserts that Maria herself "seems to have considered 1768 correct, and the Black

Bourton records on the whole support her." This is one of the few uncertainties in a life dedicated to family, friends, and literature. Edgeworth was born in England, the child of Richard Lovell Edgeworth (an Anglo-Irish gentleman with extensive estates in County Longford, about sixty miles from Dublin) and his first wife, Anna Maria Elers Edgeworth, who died when Maria was five years old. By all accounts, Maria got along well with her three siblings, two sisters and a brother (another child died before she was born), and with her father's next three wives and her seventeen half brothers and half sisters, most of whom she helped to rear. The general harmony in the Edgeworth household may be seen as all the more remarkable when one considers that Richard Edgeworth's last wife, Frances Anne Beaufort Edgeworth (with whose family Maria became quite friendly), was a year or two younger than her stepdaughter.

Much of this impressive concord can be credited to Richard Lovell Edgeworth, a man of enormous confidence and personal force. He took the not untypical eighteenth century view that, as the father in the household, he was the lord and master in a literal sense. Fortunately, he was a benevolent master. Although he believed firmly that he knew what was best for all his wives and children, what he believed to be best was their relatively free development, confined only by his sense of what was morally right and socially proper. Maria evidently accepted her father's guidance to the point of seeking and welcoming his advice. Richard Edgeworth had such confidence both in the good sense of his children and in his own principles of education, which were patterned after those of his eccentric friend, Thomas Day (author of the once-famous novel of education, *Sandford and Merton*, 1783-1789), that he informed his family of the reasons for nearly all of his decisions, and certainly for the important ones. The most important of these was his resolve to settle on his family estate in Ireland (he had been living in England for a number of years, having left Ireland about 1765; and Maria had visited Ireland only briefly, in 1773). One reason for the election to live in Ireland—Edgeworth could have afforded to stay in England, since he received rents from his Irish property—was that Richard Edgeworth was convinced by his reading and by the course of national affairs (one feature of which was the harsh economic treatment of Ireland because of the great expense incurred by England in its war with the American colonies) that Ireland could be one of the best and most productive areas in the British Empire.

To achieve the goal of proper estate management, a subject that was to engage the interest of Maria Edgeworth for the rest of her life, her father had to revolutionize the way in which his lands and tenants were cared for. The salient aspect of the change was a greater concern for genuine productivity and less for high rents. He was quite successful, partly because of the help of his adoring and sensible daughter. The estate and the family survived riots, famines, and the very real threat of a French invasion of Ireland during the

Napoleonic campaigns. From the time the Edgeworth family relocated to Edgeworthstown, in 1782, until her death, Maria Edgeworth lived in the family homestead—the constancy of her residence there being broken by only a few trips to England, France, and Scotland, and brief visits to other countries on the Continent. During these sojourns, she managed to become acquainted, largely through her father's influence, with some of the leading thinkers and artists of the day, notably Sir Walter Scott, with whom she formed a warm personal friendship and for whom she had a great admiration, which was reciprocated. Edgeworth was one of the first readers to recognize that the anonymously published *Waverly* was the work of "the Wizard of the North."

While visiting France in 1802, Edgeworth met the Chevalier Abraham Niclas Clewberg-Edelcrantz, a Swedish diplomat to whom she was introduced in Paris. For this somewhat shy, very small, not particularly attractive woman, the encounter was extraordinary. Edelcrantz was not handsome, and he was forty-six years old. On the positive side, he was very intelligent and quite well educated, a fact that appealed to Edgeworth. Although evidently astounded and pleased by Edelcrantz's proposal of marriage, she was wise enough to realize that his devotion to Sweden, which he could not think of leaving as his home, and hers to Ireland, were an absolute barrier to any happiness in such a union. Richard Edgeworth was apparently in favor of the marriage, but he did nothing to persuade Maria to accept the Swede, and he received her decision with equanimity.

Apart from helping her father to manage the estate—managing it herself almost single-handedly after his death, in 1817—and looking after the family, Edgeworth devoted herself almost exclusively to writing. Some of her novels began as very short tales written (usually on a slate, so that erasures and improvements could be made readily) for the entertainment of the younger members of the family circle. Richard Edgeworth, though, persuaded her to take her writing seriously. This she did for some fifty years, until shortly before her death in 1849, by which time she had become respected and, to a degree seldom achieved by a female author, famous.

Analysis

The novels of Maria Edgeworth are, to the modern reader, an odd combination of strengths and weaknesses. This phenomenon is not really very strange, given the times in which she lived and the progress of fiction-writing in the early nineteenth century. The work of all the novelists of that period may be considered strongly flawed and yet often unexpectedly effective (Sir Walter Scott is the obvious example, but the same might even be said of much of the work of Charles Dickens). What is perhaps more surprising is that Edgeworth herself was aware of the defects of her work. She knew, for example, that her writings were didactic to an often annoying degree. Her father, who had a great deal to do with her conviction that fiction should aim to elevate the morals of its readers, even comments on the fact in one of his Prefaces to her novels and claims that a severe attempt had been made to subdue the moralistic features. By modern standards, the attempts never fully succeeded in any of Edgeworth's novels.

One reason for the "failure" is simply the prevalence of the late eighteenth century belief that behavior can be modified by edifying reading and that character can be formed and, possibly more important, reformed by acts of the will. Those of Edgeworth's tales titled with the name of the central character, such as *Ormond*, *Belinda*, and *Vivian*, are thus the stories of how these young people come to terms with society and their responsibilities: in short, how they grow up to be worthy citizens. The concept itself is not ludicrous; literature is replete with studies of the ways in which young people come of age successfully. What is distressing in Edgeworth's "moral tales" (and those of many other writers of the era) are the improbable turns of plot such as those by which poor but honest people are suddenly discovered to be heirs to great properties, those believed to be orphans are revealed as the offspring of noble houses, and so forth. This sort of device has a long history in both fiction and drama, but it is especially dismaying in a work that is otherwise, and by clear intention, realistic. The distracting and hardly credible process by which Grace Nugent, in *The Absentee*, is proved legitimate, so that Lord Colambre can in good conscience marry her (the moral logic behind his reluctance to wed her, blameless as she is for the situation of her birth, may repel modern readers who are not familiar with the depth of the eighteenth century conviction concerning the influence of a flawed family background), is needlessly detailed. Such a device also intrudes on a story that is otherwise filled with convincing details about estate management (and mismanagement) in Ireland and fairly realistic studies of the lives of the common people.

Richard Edgeworth was blamed, perhaps unjustly, for the excess of didacticism in his daughter's novels (it is surely no accident that the only work lacking such material, *Castle Rackrent*, was her most popular title and is today her only novel still read); some of the tiresome passages of "uplifting" commentary do sound as if they came from his eloquent but ponderous pen, as in Belinda's comment in a letter, "Female wit sometimes depends on the beauty of its possessor for its reputation; and the reign of beauty is proverbially short, and fashion often capriciously deserts her favourites, even before nature withers their charms." To his credit, however, Richard Edgeworth is now known to have done a great deal to provide his daughter with ideas for stories and plot sequences. Perhaps the most important artistic flaw to which the younger Edgeworth pleaded guilty was a lack of invention, and critics over the decades have noticed that she depends to excess on details and facts, many of which she collected from her own family's records and memoirs. The rest she gathered by direct (and penetrating) observation, as in the realistic farm scenes in the Irish tales and the believable pictures of society gatherings in London and Paris. One of the most obvious indications of Edgeworth's failure to devise plots artfully is her reliance on the retrospective strategy of having a character reveal his or her background by telling it to another. Certainly, the review of her own life that Lady Delacour provides for Belinda is not without interest and is necessary to the story; yet it seems cumbersome, appearing as it does in two chapters that occupy more than thirty pages near the opening of the novel.

The two types of novels that Edgeworth wrote—the Irish tales and, as the title of one collection indicates, the *Tales of Fashionable Life* (1809-1812)— manifest the poles of her thematic interest. She believed, as did her father, that Ireland could benefit and even prosper from a more responsible aristocracy, landowners who lived on their property and saw that it was fairly and efficiently managed. In her three best Irish tales, *Castle Rackrent*, *The Absentee*, and *Ormond*, Edgeworth underlines the virtues of fair play with tenants, caution in dealing with hired estate managers (the wicked Nicholas Garraghty, in *The Absentee*, should be warning enough for any proprietor), and close attention to details of land and equipment. The years that Edgeworth spent aiding her father at Edgeworthstown bore impressive fruit in her grasp of the problems and difficulties faced by owners of large estates.

Because the sectarian, political, and economic problems that faced Ireland have tended to persist into the present, while the aspects of fashionable life have not, the "society" novels in Irish literature are almost unknown by the reading public today. In any case, Edgeworth was much more intellectually involved in the politics and social problems of her homeland than she was in the vagaries and evils of society life in big cities. Much as she believed that a great deal can be learned about the proper way to live one's life by observing society closely, she was personally never so involved in that topic as she was in such concerns as the injustices created by absentee landlords and the abuse of tenants by land agents hired by the absentees and given enormous power. Thus, while Belinda, Vivian, and Helen do hold some interest for the reader, their problems and challenges are dated. The modern reader has difficulty taking seriously the follies of Vivian, who manages to misjudge nearly everybody in the novel, leading to his not unexpected demise, which is sad but far from tragic. The peculiarities of King Corny in *Ormond*, however, as when it is revealed that he is elevating the roof of his large house so that he can construct attics under it, help to provide the reader with a more substantial grasp of the great power, the tendency toward eccentricity, and the frequent good-heartedness of Irish estate owners. Edgeworth usually dealt with events and conditions in the fairly recent past; as such, she can be considered a historical novelist. Her emphasis on what can be viewed as an international theme, however (the relationship between English, as well as Irish, characters and attitudes), is thought by many to be the most significant aspect of her novels. Critics have even suggested that her treatment of the topic prefigures the more detailed analyses by Henry James.

Edgeworth appeared on the literary scene at the best possible moment for her career and the future of the English novel. Her own records designate the amounts that she was paid by her publishers for each major work, and the list of payments is, by the standards of the time, impressive. For example, the minor novel *Patronage* earned Edgeworth 2,100 pounds, at that time an enormous sum. The influence that she had on the course of the historical and regional novel is proof of her little-known but vital contribution toward the development of the English novel.

In his Introduction to the Oxford English Novels edition of *Castle Rackrent* (1964), George Watson claims for this unusual book the distinction of being "the first regional novel in English, and perhaps in all Europe." Certainly, the work is a tour de force, all the more impressive because it was, by most accounts, achieved virtually by accident. Richard Edgeworth had on the estate a steward named John Langan. His opinions and mode of expression so struck Maria Edgeworth that she began to record his comments and became an able mimic of his dialect and turns of speech. Her letters to her father's sister, Mrs. Margaret Edgeworth Ruxton, one of her favorite correspondents, inspired this sympathetic lady to encourage her niece to develop the material into a story. Thus was born Maria Edgeworth's only substantial piece of fiction written during Richard Edgeworth's lifetime in whose composition he evidently did not play a part.

Edgeworth claimed that only the narrator was based on a real-life person, Langan; some scholars have suggested that one or two other characters might have been fashioned after people known to her. An example is the entertaining character, Sir Condy Rackrent, who may have been broadly patterned on Edgeworth's maternal grandfather. However great or small its basis in real life, the novel has the air of reality about it. The actions and the motivations ring true to life. *Castle Rackrent* is often praised for its lack of an obtrusive moral emphasis, but it would be a mistake to read the novel as having no message. The decline and fall of the Rackrent family is the story of irresponsibility and extravagance, an unfortunately common phenomenon in the history of Irish landowners.

The narrator, Thady Quirk, commonly called "honest Thady," tells the dismal but occasionally humorous tale of the several masters under whom he has served: Sir Patrick O'Shaughlin, who drinks himself to death early in the story; Sir Murtaugh Rackrent, who dies in a paroxysm of anger over a legalistic contretemps; Sir Kit Rackrent, who dies in a duel over the controversy stemming from his indecision regarding the choice of a new wife, when his first spouse seems on the point of death; and Sir Conolly Rackrent, whose narrative is longer than the tale of the first three owners of Castle Rackrent. Another innovative aspect of the novel besides the use of such an authentic narrator is the consistent employment of dialect. The text is not difficult to read, but many of the expressions are not easily comprehensible to a reader unfamiliar with the Irish speech and mores of that era. Wisely, Edgeworth—with her father's help—appended a glossary which explains, occasionally in needless detail, many of Thady's locutions and references. That Thady opens his memoir on a Monday morning might have little special significance unless the reader is informed by the glossary that "no great undertaking can be auspiciously commenced in Ireland on any morning but *Monday morning.*"

Perhaps the chief appeal of the work to the modern reader lies in the personality of Thady and in the folkways he embodies. On the first page, he tells of his "great coat," which poverty compels him to wear winter and summer but which is "very handy, as I never put my arms into the sleeves, (they are as good as new,) though come Holantide next, I've had it these seven years." The extraordinary loyalty of Thady to a family that seems not to deserve such fidelity is both exasperating and admirable. Thady is not, however, overcome with emotion when unfortunate circumstances arise. Though he cannot recall the drinking habits of Sir Patrick without the brief aside, "God bless him!," he speaks of a shocking event at the funeral with relative calm: "happy the man who could get but a sight of the hearse!—But who'd have thought it? Just as all was going on right, through his own town they were passing, when the body was seized for debt. . . ." Thady is moved enough to call the creditors "villains," but he swiftly moves on with his tale: "So, to be sure, the law must take its course—and little gain had the creditors for their pains." The old man spends more time on the legal implications of the seizure than on the event itself. This passage displays Edgeworth's understanding of the contentious element in the Irish personality and the formidable grasp of the law that even poorly educated people often had. Indeed, lawsuits and legal technicalities abound in Edgeworth's fiction.

Thady's almost eccentric equanimity and generous nature are further revealed when, after Sir Kit has gambled away virtually all the assets of the Rackrent estate, including the good will of his wealthy wife, the old retainer remarks, "the Castle Rackrent estate was all mortgaged, and bonds out against him, for he was never cured of his gaming tricks—but that was the only fault he had, God bless him!" Further, Thady seems untroubled by the confinement of Sir Kit's wife for seven years in her apartments (an incident based on the actual imprisonment of a Lady Cathcart, in 1745, who was kept locked up by her husband for a much longer period), apparently lost in admiration of the fierce temper of his master, which not only caused the drastic action but also discouraged anyone from asking him about it.

The first part of *Castle Rackrent* is entitled "An Hibernian Tale." It is indeed very "Hibernian," but no more so than the story of Sir Conolly Rackrent, whom Thady refers to as "ever my great favorite, and indeed the most universally beloved man I had ever seen or heard of." Condy's chief attractions are a good nature and a propensity to spend excessively. Both of these qualities contribute to the further impoverishment of the estate, a condition that he does little to alleviate. Even his marriage to the daughter of a wealthy landowner on a nearby estate (who promptly disinherits his offspring as soon as he learns of the wedding, thus frustrating even this halfhearted attempt to repair the Rackrent fortunes) is a matter of chance: Condy, who actually loves Thady's pretty but fortuneless grandniece, Judy M'Quirk, flips a coin to determine whether he will propose to Judy or the moneyed Isabella.

Despite the disinheritance, Sir Condy is fond of Isabella; when financial disaster looms, he attempts to provide her with a generous allotment in his will. The closing of the novel exposes another theme that may be derived from the plot. The villain who buys up Sir Condy's debts and brings on his personal ruin is Thady's own son, the self-serving Jason. Edgeworth possibly had in mind to make some point about the difference between the single-minded loyalty and honesty of the older generation and the selfish heartlessness of the younger. Even the attractive Judy, when Thady suggests that she might become the next mistress of Castle Rackrent (Isabella has had an accident from which Thady believes she will die), tells him there is no point in marrying a poor man; she has evidently set her sights on Jason, much to Thady's dismay.

Typically, the novel ends with a lawsuit. Lady Condy, after her husband's death from drinking, sues for the title to the estate. Thady does not know how the suit will end, and he seems not to care: "For my part, I'm tired wishing for any thing in this world, after all I've seen in it." With this touching close to what is considered Edgeworth's best novel, the reader may well believe that the author has provided the opportunity for a greater understanding of those elements of Irish culture and history that impelled her to devote a lifetime of study to them.

During Edgeworth's lifetime, *The Absentee* was probably her most influential work. The central problem addressed in the novel is that of the absentee landlords, who left the management of their often vast Irish estates in the hands of inept and frequently unscrupulous agents. These agents robbed the landlords as well as the tenants, but the indifferent landowners took little interest in the lands so long as the rents were paid on time. As Edgeworth makes eminently clear by the contrast between the sensible and benevolent Mr. Burke, one of Lord Clonbrony's agents, and the other, Nicholas Garraghty, who is scheming and dishonest, not all agents were bad; the trouble was that the owners had no accurate way of knowing, since they were almost never on the scene.

The hero of this novel, Lord Colambre, is the son of Lord and Lady Clonbrony; it is around this unbelievably virtuous and somewhat stuffy young man that the several subplots and themes are centered. Each subplot is designed to underline an obvious theme, and Colambre is a vital if artificial unifying element in a novel whose general absence of unity is disquieting.

The main plot line has to do with the Clonbronys, who live in London, because Lady Clonbrony believes that high society is indispensable to her happiness (typically, the other members of the "smart set" find her pretensions ridiculous; Edgeworth explores a number of opportunities to satirize the false values of such people). Lord Clonbrony would not mind returning to the family estate, and he realizes that remaining away may be ruinous, since he is already in considerable debt. Lord Colambre visits his father's lands in disguise, where he identifies the problem and recognizes the virtues and evils of the two agents. After vigorous efforts to repay his father's debts, he saves the situation and persuades his mother to return to Ireland. A related theme concerns the actions that Colambre will not take in order to pay the debts— chiefly, he will not marry for money, a time-honored method of acquiring funds in a short time. Edgeworth offers several illustrations of the folly of such a practice, though perhaps to the modern reader her emphasis on the legitimacy of the birth of Grace Nugent, Colambre's cousin, as a criterion for his proposing to her may seem artificial and even essentially immoral. Interestingly, when Miss Nugent (who has been unaware of the "disgrace") learns of the reason for Colambre's erstwhile restraint, she fully agrees that it would have been improper for him to offer marriage when her birth seemed under a cloud. Through an unlikely and tiresome concatenation of circumstances and accidents, the problem is solved: it is proved that Grace's birth was legitimate, and the marriage is approved, even by Lady Clonbrony, who for most of the story has been trying to persuade her son to wed the wealthy Miss Broadhurst.

The Absentee is filled with flat characters created in the heroic mold, most of whom befriend Colambre and impress him with a variety of sensible insights: the positive aspects of life in Ireland; the joys and satisfactions of the quiet country life (the O'Neill family, tenants on the Clonbrony estate, underline this point; they, too, are so honest and good-hearted as to be difficult to accept); the emptiness and falseness of "society"; and the great importance of taking responsibility and performing one's duty well. *The Absentee* emphasizes two aspects of Edgeworth's philosophy of life. She fully accepted the eighteenth century conviction that the class structure of society was inevitable and proper, and she wholeheartedly believed in the primacy of duty (a word iterated by her father as the chief element of a worthy life) as everyone's first responsibility. Thus, in *The Absentee* there is an interesting mingling of liberal attitudes toward the rights of the peasants and conservative views regarding the propriety of aristocratic privilege.

At the close of a long and complicated reticulation of plot lines, Edgeworth had the clever notion of ending the story simply and even humorously (there is an unfortunate paucity of humor in this novel) by completing the tale through the device of a letter written by an Irish coach-driver to his brother, who currently lives in England, telling him of the happy return of the Clonbronys to the estate, and the upcoming marriage of Colambre and Grace, and urging him to come back to Ireland, since "it's growing the fashion not to be an Absentee." *The Absentee* lacks the humor and directness of *Castle Rackrent*, but it makes its thematic points forcefully, and in Sir Terence O'Fay, Edgeworth has created a revealing, rounded portrait of an interesting Irish type: a good-natured wastrel who is no man's enemy but his own. His function in the plot is minimal, but he displays some of the most engaging features of the Irish personality.

Unlike *The Absentee*, whose title indicates that the subject is a general phenomenon, *Ormond*, as its title suggests, is about the development of a single individual. The novel is based on the view that a young person can change his character by learning from his experiences and exerting his will. Although Harry Ormond is not exactly Rousseau's "noble savage," he is clearly intended to be the image of an untutored, raw personality, full of fine possibilities that must be cultivated to be realized. During the long, complex advance of the story, this is just what happens.

The lad has been reared by an old friend of his father, who died in India, a minor aristocrat named Sir Ulick O'Shane, who believes that educating the boy would be a waste of time, since he is destined to be a poor dependent for life. The contrast between Harry Ormond and Ulick's own son, Marcus, a formally educated but weak and ineffective youth, is one of several that give the novel a sense of polarity: Ulick is contrasted with his cousin, Cornelius O'Shane, the King Corny who takes over the care of Harry when he is forced to leave Ulick's estate after a shooting incident; Dora O'Shane, the daughter of Corny, with whom for a while Harry believes himself to be in love, is seen as quite different from the modest and highly moral Florence Annaly, whom he does love and finally marries; and White Connal, Dora's first suitor, is, even by his name, contrasted with his brother, Black Connal, who ultimately is the man who marries Dora.

Harry Ormond is placed in the care of a succession of older men, and from each he learns things that help him grow into a responsible and sensitive man. Ulick teaches him some of the complexities of business and helps him to understand the difficulty of judging character in another; King Corny instructs him in the need for bold action and in the excellences to be found in the primitive personality; Dr. Cambray, a clergyman, starts Harry on his formal education; and, while staying with the Annaly family, Harry perceives the delights of a well-ordered life in a well-regulated family, something he has never experienced before.

The essence of the book, apart from Ormond's development into a mature person, is his ultimate winning of the girl he truly loves. His material dependence is easily (and, again, incredibly) solved by the discovery that his father has left him a fortune. His only real problem, then, is to pass a series of moral tests created by Edgeworth to prove that he is a worthy, responsible man.

The novel is marked by a number of traditional devices, such as the timeworn "While Sir Ulick is drinking his cup of cold coffee, we may look back a little into his family history," which is done for some six and a half pages. Frequent references to Ormond as "our hero" remind the reader that this is his story and that Harry is to be thought of as heroic, no matter what mistakes he makes (and he does blunder now and then, usually on the side of excessive credulity). The author does not hesitate to intrude into the story, to proclaim ignorance ("What he said, or what Florence answered, we do not know"), or to move the plot along with phrases such as "We now go on to," or "We now proceed to." *Ormond* is thus in many ways a traditional novel of the period, but it achieves a level of social criticism—of French society (a number of scenes are set in Paris) as well as of English and Irish ways—seldom found before William Makepeace Thackeray in the history of the English novel. This tale, unlike *The Absentee*, is also enlivened by humor.

Edgeworth's novels are unfortunately little read today, except by students of the English novel. Aside from plainly revealing the significant lines of tradition and transition from the eighteenth century to the nineteenth century novel, her work is enjoyable in itself. Nowhere else can one find such a lively and fairly balanced picture of the life and values found in the Ireland and England of the late Georgian period.

Fred B. McEwen

Other major works

SHORT FICTION: *The Parent's Assistant: Or, Stories for Children*, 1796 (3 volumes), 1800 (6 volumes); *Early Lessons: Harry and Lucy, I and II; Rosamond, I-III; Frank, I-IV and Other Stories*, 1801-1802 (with Richard Lovell Edgeworth); *Moral Tales for Young People*, 1801; *The Mental Thermometer*, 1801; *Popular Tales*, 1804; *The Modern Griselda*, 1805; *Tales of Fashionable Life*, 1809-1812; *Continuation of Early Lessons*, 1814; *Rosamond: A Sequel to Early Lessons*, 1821; *Frank: A Sequel to Frank in Early Lessons*, 1822; *Harry and Lucy Concluded*, 1825; *Tales and Miscellaneous Pieces*, 1825; *Gary Owen, and Poor Bob, the Chimney-Sweeper*, 1832; *Tales and Novels*, 1832-1833, 1848, 1857 (18 volumes), 1893 (10 volumes), 1893 (12 volumes); *Orlandino*, 1848; *Classic Tales*, 1883; *The Purple Jar and Other Stories*, 1931.

PLAYS: *Comic Dramas in Three Acts*, 1817; *Little Plays for Children*, 1827.

NONFICTION: *Letters for Literary Ladies*, 1795; *An Essay on the Noble Science of Self-Justification*, 1795; *Practical Education*, 1798 (also known as *Essays on Practical Education*, with Richard Lovell Edgeworth); *A Rational Primer*, 1799 (with Richard Lovell Edgeworth); *Essay on Irish Bulls*, 1802 (with Richard Lovell Edgeworth); *Essays on Professional Education*, 1809 (with Richard Lovell Edgeworth); *Readings on Poetry*, 1816 (with Richard

Lovell Edgeworth); *Memoirs of Richard Lovell Edgeworth Esq.*, 1820 (Vol. II); *Thoughts on Bores*, 1826; *A Memoir of Maria Edgeworth*, 1867 (Francis Edgeworth, editor); *Archibald Constable and His Literary Correspondents*, 1873; *The Life and Letters of Maria Edgeworth*, 1894 (Augustus J. Hare, editor); *Chosen Letters*, 1931 (F. V. Barry, editor); *Romilly-Edgeworth Letters*, 1813-1818, 1936 (Samuel H. Romilly, editor); *Letters from England*, 1813-1844, 1971 (Christina Colvin, editor).

TRANSLATION: *Adelaide and Theodore*, 1783.

Bibliography

Butler, Marilyn. *Maria Edgeworth: A Literary Biography*. Oxford, England: Clarendon Press, 1972. Does a good job of balancing Edgeworth's personal and working life. Her large family was very important to her and seems to have provided sources for her novels. Devotes much space to establish how her father, Richard Lovell Edgeworth, was a major influence in her life. Also focuses on Edgeworth's contemporary reputation, placing her as an important member of the literary milieu of her day. The bibliography and index are extensive. Includes three interesting appendices on her siblings and publication information regarding her novels.

Harden, O. Elizabeth McWhorter. *Maria Edgeworth*. Boston: Twayne, 1984. Attempts to dispel critical myths about Edgeworth, such as her father's negative influence over her, but does not always succeed. While trying to take an open-minded approach, Harden often treats Edgeworth and her contemporaries, such as Jane Austen, in highly conventional ways; for example, Harden's distinctions between Austen and Edgeworth in the last chapter are too simplistically polar. Provides a short biography and is divided into chapters based on Edgeworth's intended audiences, starting with children, moving to adolescents, and ending with adults, which is more useful than a purely chronological treatment. The bibliography is helpful given the limited number of works dealing with Edgeworth, even including chapters in books not specifically about her.

_____. *Maria Edgeworth's Art of Prose Fiction*. The Hague: Mouton, 1971. While this book treats Edgeworth's works simply, giving little more than plot summary and some approving comments for each novel, it is useful because it runs through her canon of fiction work by work, discussing them chronologically. The bibliography is good, including biographies, works containing important contemporary comments, mentions of Edgeworth in general works, contemporary reviews and notices, fiction technique studies, and general criticism and background. A good starting place for a study of Edgeworth.

Hurst, Michael. *Maria Edgeworth and the Public Scene: Intellect, Fine Feeling, and Landlordism in the Age of Reform*. Coral Gables, Fla.: University of Miami Press, 1969. Takes an interesting and fresh approach to Edgeworth, looking at her attitudes toward Irish reform in the early nineteenth century. Sees her as a moderate who wanted improvement for the lower classes of society but no fundamental change in the upper classes. Historically based and not especially literary, focusing on political events and Edgeworth's opinion of them. Since these events took place fairly late in her life, Edgeworth is seen as an older, possibly more political woman, and Hurst argues that since her father was dead, her opinions at this time were probably more fully her own than those during his life.

Newcomer, James. *Maria Edgeworth the Novelist.* Fort Worth: Texas Christian University Press, 1967. Newcomer sets out to correct what he sees as strong critical rejection of Edgeworth. Provides a thorough examination of her major novels, but tends to dismiss some on artistic grounds. Nevertheless, some of Newcomer's insights are valuable and illuminating, such as his theory that Thady Quirk of *Castle Rackrent* is at least disingenuous and perhaps even in league with his son Jason in the destruction of the Rackrents, an assertion that contradicts most views of Thady as a kindhearted but naïve old man. Also attempts to save Edgeworth from the charge of unrealistic portrayals of her society by comparing specific incidents in her novels with contemporary nonfiction accounts of conditions at the end of the eighteenth century.

GEORGE ELIOT
Mary Ann Evans

Born: Chilvers Coton, England; November 22, 1819
Died: London, England; December 22, 1880

Principal long fiction

Adam Bede, 1859; *The Mill on the Floss*, 1860; *Silas Marner*, 1861; *Romola*, 1862-1863; *Felix Holt, The Radical*, 1866; *Middlemarch*, 1871-1872; *Daniel Deronda*, 1876.

Other literary forms

George Eliot's three early stories, "The Sad Fortunes of the Reverend Barton," "Mr. Gilfil's Love Story," and "Janet's Repentance," originally published in *Blackwood's Magazine*, were collected as *Scenes of Clerical Life* in 1858. She wrote two other stories, "The Lifted Veil," also published in *Blackwood's Magazine* in 1859, and "Brother Jacob," published in *Cornhill* in 1864. *The Impressions of Theophrastus Such*, a miscellany of sketches and essays, was published in 1879. Eliot's poetry does not achieve the high quality of her prose. Most notable examples are *The Spanish Gypsy* (1868), a verse drama, and *The Legend of Jubal and Other Poems* (1874). Eliot wrote more than seventy periodical essays and reviews; the most comprehensive collection is Thomas Pinney's *Essays of George Eliot* (1963). Eliot translated David Friedrich Strauss's *Das Leben Jesu* as *The Life of Jesus Critically Examined* (1846) and Ludwig Feuerbach's *Das Wesen des Christenthums* as *The Essence of Christianity* (1854). Her translation of Benedictus de Spinoza's *Ethics* (1677) has never been published.

Achievements

Eliot's pivotal position in the history of the novel is attested to by some of the most distinguished English novelists. Reviewing *Middlemarch* in 1873, Henry James concluded, "It sets a limit, we think, to the development of the old-fashioned English novel"; and *Middlemarch* does, indeed, take what James calls the panoramic novel—"vast, swarming, deep-colored, crowded with episodes, with vivid images, with lurking master-strokes, with brilliant passages of expression," seeking to "reproduce the total sum of life in an English village"—to an unsurpassed level of achievement. Eliot was also an innovator. In the words of D. H. Lawrence, "It all started with George Eliot; it was she who put the action on the inside," thus giving impetus to the rise of the psychological novel, where the most significant actions derive from the motives of the characters rather than from external events. Eliot's work is, then, both the culmination of the panoramic Victorian novel as practiced by Charles Dickens and William Makepeace Thackeray and the beginning of the modern psychological novel as practiced by James, Lawrence, and many others.

More than anyone else, Eliot was responsible for making the novel, a genre which had traditionally been read primarily for entertainment, into a vehicle for the serious expression of ideas. Few novelists can equal Eliot's depth of intellect or breadth of learning. Deeply involved in the religious and philosophical ferment of her time, Eliot was probably the first major English novelist who did not subscribe, at least nominally, to the tenets of Christian theology. Nevertheless, her strong moral commitment, derived from her Evangelical Christian heritage, led her to conceive of the novel as an instrument for preaching a gospel of duty and self-renunciation.

Moral commitment alone, however, does not make a great novelist. In addition, Eliot's extraordinary psychological insight enabled her to create characters who rival in depth and complexity any in English or American fiction. Few novelists can equal her talents for chronicling tangled motives, intricate self-deceptions, or an anguished struggle toward a noble act. She creates a fictional world that combines, in a way unsurpassed in English fiction, a broad panorama of society and psychological insight into each character.

Biography

The woman known to countless readers as George Eliot—a name she did not use until she was nearly forty—was born on November 22, 1819, and christened Mary Ann Evans, the third child of Robert Evans and his second wife Christina Pearson. Evans, a man of extraordinary competence and unimpeachable integrity, worked as a general overseer of Arbury Hall, the seven-thousand-acre estate of the Newdigate family in Warwickshire. A shy and homely girl, Eliot excelled as a student in nearby boarding schools. Under the influence of a favorite teacher, Maria Lewis, the strict and conventional adherence to the Church of England which she learned from her parents acquired an overlay of pious Evangelicalism.

After her mother's death and her father's retirement, Eliot and her father moved to a new home outside Coventry. She soon established a close and lasting friendship with Charles and Cara Bray and Cara's sister Sara Hennell. Her conversations with the Brays, who were Unitarians and whose views of religion were more intellectual than those with which Eliot had been acquainted, accelerated the process of religious questioning that she had already experienced. At Bray's suggestion, she began to translate *Das Leben Jesu*, a key work of the German theologian David Friedrich Strauss. Strauss, by applying the methods of scientific research and criticism to the Bible, questioned the divinity of Christ. Eliot's work on this translation, published anonymously in 1846, completed the destruction of her religious orthodoxy.

Following the death of her father in 1849 and a brief stay in Switzerland,

Eliot moved to London, where she began to write for the *Westminster Review*. The fact that, while in Switzerland, she began to spell her name Marian suggests her awareness of a new and different life ahead of her.

Although the *Westminster Review* was nominally edited by John Chapman—a man with whom Eliot may have been romantically involved—Eliot assumed most of the responsibilities of editorship and was, especially after Chapman bought the periodical in January, 1852, virtual editor. Her work with the *Westminster Review* placed her near the center of the intellectual life of Victorian England and brought her into contact with many of the prominent thinkers of the time.

One of the persons whom Eliot met at this time was George Henry Lewes, who later became her common-law husband. A man of unusual versatility, Lewes had written novels, a blank verse tragedy, a history of philosophy, and many periodical articles on a variety of subjects. He was, with Thornton Leigh Hunt, coeditor of a weekly newspaper called *The Leader*.

Lewes, Hunt, and Lewes's wife Agnes subscribed to the notion that passions could not be restricted by social conventions; thus, when Agnes, after bearing Lewes four sons, delivered a fifth son who had been fathered by Hunt, Lewes quietly registered the child as his own. By the time Agnes bore a second child fathered by Hunt, however, Lewes no longer considered her his wife, although he continued to support her and to be on friendly terms with her and Hunt, with whom he continued to work on *The Leader*. Victorian laws made divorce virtually impossible and prohibitively expensive; the fact that Lewes had accepted Hunt's child as his own precluded his citing adultery as possible grounds.

Under the circumstances, Eliot and Lewes had the choice of living together in a common-law marriage or not living together at all. They chose the former, and on July 20, 1854, traveled to Germany as husband and wife. Eliot wrote to her friends to explain her new status and to ask that from henceforth they address her as Marian Lewes.

Although the couple had no children, their relationship was in many respects a model Victorian marriage. They lived happily together until Lewes's death in 1878; with their writing, they supported not only themselves but also Lewes's four sons and Agnes and her children by Hunt. Lewes's sons appeared to regard Eliot with great affection. In other respects, however, the irregularity of their relationship cut Eliot off from much of the social life of the time, since only the most courageous Victorian women dared risk their own respectability by calling on her. Eliot's family, especially her brother Isaac, also cut her off, condemning her relationship with Lewes as adulterous.

Encouraged by Lewes, Eliot published her first work of fiction, "The Sad Fortunes of the Reverend Amos Barton," in *Blackwood's Magazine* in January, 1857. Because Eliot wished to protect her standing as an editor and reviewer and because she feared that her unconventional marriage to Lewes would prejudice the reception of her fiction, she published under the pseudonym George Eliot. Encouraged by the favorable reception of these stories and protected by Lewes from adverse criticism, Eliot published her first full-length novel, *Adam Bede*, in 1859.

For the next two decades the chief events in Eliot's life were the publications of her novels—*The Mill on the Floss*, *Silas Marner*, *Romola*, *Felix Holt*, *Middlemarch*, and *Daniel Deronda*. Of these novels, only *Romola*, a meticulously researched historical novel set in fifteenth century Florence, was less than successful; the others won Eliot both an enthusiastic popular audience and critical recognition as the major English novelist of her time.

As the success of Eliot's novels and the continuing acceptance of Lewes's articles and books also brought considerable prosperity, the Leweses' life together was punctuated by trips to various parts of England and the Continent and by a series of moves to houses in more attractive parts of London. In November, 1878, only a few months after they moved to a long-sought-for house in the country, Lewes died.

Devastated by the loss of the emotional support that Lewes provided, on May 6, 1880, Eliot married John Cross, who, although twenty years younger than she, had long been a close friend and frequent visitor to the Lewes household. In the eyes of her sternly conventional brother Isaac, this marriage conferred respectability; he wrote to his sister for the first time since 1854 to offer his "sincere congratulations." Their marriage, though happy, was brief: Eliot died in December, 1880.

Analysis

Discussions of George Eliot's fiction are likely to begin by quoting Chapter 17 of *Adam Bede*, in which she makes one of the most persuasive statements of the creed of the realistic novelist to be found in nineteenth century literature. Indicating that she is seeking that "rare, precious quality of truthfulness that I delight in [in] many Dutch paintings," she goes on to state the need for "men ready to give the loving pains of a life to the faithful representing of commonplace things—men who see beauty in these commonplace things, and delight in showing how kindly the light of heaven falls on them." Through the truthful and sympathetic rendering of a fictional world no better than the actual one "in which we get up in the morning to do our daily work," novelists should win the reader's sympathy for "the real breathing men and women, who can be chilled by your indifference or injured by your prejudice, who can be cheered and helped onward by your fellow-feeling, your forbearance, your outspoken, brave justice." These statements suggest that Eliot conceived of fiction as a moral force, not because it is didactic in any narrow sense, but because it inculcates in the reader an attitude of sympathy for his fellow men, which in turn leads to everyday acts of justice and compassion that lighten the burden of the human lot. Fiction, then, performs one of the functions that is commonly associated with the church as a Christian community by reminding readers of Christ's second commandment, that they love their neighbors as themselves.

Indeed, although Eliot's belief in Christian theology waned when she was in her twenties, her devotion to the major elements of Christian morality as she understood them remained steadfast throughout her life and provided the moral framework for her fiction. Her practice as a novelist eventually goes beyond her statement in *Adam Bede* in both complexity and subtlety, but this statement remains as the foundation of her creed as a novelist.

As her career developed, Eliot's characters became complex moral paradigms that could serve her readers as both examples and warnings. The highest moral achievement of her characters is renunciation of their own claims to happiness in order to minister to the needs of others, sometimes less deserving, whose lives impinge on theirs. The act of renunciation involves acknowledgement of the claims of community and often provides a sense of continuity with the character's past or traditions. Conversely, the characters whom Eliot condemns most severely are those who evade their responsibilities by a process of self-delusion or self-indulgence, avoiding hard choices and hoping that chance will deliver them from the consequences of selfish actions. Characters are often moved toward renunciation by others who act as "messengers"—almost secularized angels—to guide them; their acts of renunciation and sense of community are often associated with the sacraments of baptism or communion. The process of egotistical self-indulgence, on the other hand, is often associated with a sexual relationship that is clearly inappropriate, although not necessarily illicit. Later in her career, Eliot treated the difficulty of finding an arena for purposeful life in the England of her time, but she never abandoned her intense commitment to individual moral responsibility.

Eliot's first full-length novel, *Adam Bede*, is built on two pairs of contrasting characters, one male and one female. Adam, a carpenter of consummate skill, is a model of rectitude and self-discipline whose only flaw is his intolerance of any weakness in others. Contrasting with Adam is Arthur Donnithorne, a well-intentioned young landowner whose moral weakness causes the principal catastrophe of the novel. There is a similar contrast between the two major female characters: Dinah Morris, a self-effacing Methodist preacher whose primary concern is doing what she can for others, and Hetty Sorrel, a young farm girl whose kittenish appeal conceals a hard core of egotism. The fact that both Adam and Arthur love Hetty intensifies the contrast between them. Adam, captivated by her charms, admires her as a paragon of femininity without ever perceiving her indifference to him. Arthur, without really intending to, takes advantage of Hetty's self-deluding dreams of being a wealthy landowner's wife to indulge in an affair with her. Frightened when she discovers that she is pregnant, Hetty runs away from home in a vain attempt to find Arthur, who has gone to rejoin his regiment. After her baby is born, she abandons it in a forest, where it dies of exposure. When she is arraigned for child murder, she appears hard and indifferent until Dinah moves her to repentance. Although Arthur succeeds in obtaining a pardon that saves Hetty from hanging, the young woman disappears from the story and, like the overwhelming majority of fallen women in Victorian fiction, dies. The somewhat improbable marriage of Adam and Dinah provides the happy ending that the contemporary audience expected.

The melodramatic aspects of *Adam Bede* tend to obscure, especially in summary, Eliot's primary concerns in the novel. Most conspicuously, the relationship between Arthur and Hetty is not simply a trite story of a sexual encounter between a wealthy young man and a simple farm girl; the sexual aspect of their relationship is less important than their self-delusion, self-indulgence, and egotism. Both characters embody moral issues that Eliot returned to again and again in her career: Arthur is attractive, likable, and well-intentioned, but he lacks both strength of purpose and self-knowledge. Intending to break off his relationship with Hetty, he finds himself contriving meetings with her; dreaming of being a model landowner, he comes near to destroying the happiness of his best tenants. Hetty's flaw is even more damaging: although she appears to be a creature of simple charm with the "beauty of young frisking things, round-limbed, gambolling, circumventing you by a false air of innocence," her egotism makes her indifferent to almost everything except her own beauty and her self-deluding dreams.

Similarly, Dinah's success in leading Hetty to repentance is a prototype of much more complex processes that occur in later novels, when characters who have greater potential for moral growth than Hetty are enabled to develop that potential. Dinah's willingness to take on responsibility for sympathetically ministering to the needs of people around her—a moral virtue Eliot lauds above all others—has to be learned by Adam, whose own stalwart rectitude causes him to scorn weakness in others. His success in learning sympathy is symbolized by his acceptance of a meal of bread and wine in an "upper room" the morning of Hetty's trial—one of several instances in Eliot's fiction where objects associated with a Christian sacrament are used to suggest the establishment of a sense of community.

Although it is a major achievement for a first novel, *Adam Bede* pales in comparison to Eliot's later fiction. Eliot's depiction of the self-deception and egotism of Arthur and Hetty looks ahead to the fuller development of this theme in later novels, but neither their characters nor their situation provides the opportunity for the depth of psychological insight Eliot shows later. Similarly, Arthur's last-minute rescue of Hetty from the very foot of the gallows is reminiscent of the clichés of nineteenth century melodrama and seems almost pointless in the light of Hetty's immediate disappearance from the story and her early death. The marriage of Adam and Dinah caters too obviously to the Victorian taste for this kind of conventional "happy ending" and seems inconsistent with the earlier description of Dinah. Adam himself is too idealized a character to be convincing.

Many minor characters, however, demonstrate Eliot's impressive gift for characterization. Mr. Irwine is the first of several Eliot clergymen who are virtuous but hardly spiritual; Mrs. Poyser's pungent sayings indicate Eliot's humor; and Adam's mother Lisbeth combines maternal love with grating querulousness and self-pity.

More than any of Eliot's other novels, *The Mill on the Floss*, her second novel, focuses on a single character—Maggie Tulliver. Considered one of Eliot's most complex creations, Maggie embodies both the tendency toward self-indulgence that Eliot condemns elsewhere and the earnest desire for moral achievement by renunciation of one's own happiness that is the hallmark of the characters of whom Eliot appears to approve most highly.

These conflicting tendencies in Maggie, although evident in the long childhood section of the novel, assume their full significance when Maggie begins a series of secret meetings with Philip Wakem, the crippled son of a lawyer whom Maggie's father regards as a mortal enemy. In some respects, these meetings are innocent enough: Philip and Maggie are both lonely, as Philip is set apart by his physical handicap and Maggie is isolated by her family's financial distresses, and their conversations provide them with companionship they find nowhere else. More significantly, however, Maggie's meetings with Philip are wrong in that they require her to deceive her family and because they would, if discovered, add to her father's already overflowing cup of grief and bitterness. Although the standard of conduct that Maggie is being asked to meet seems almost pointlessly rigid, Eliot makes it clear that Maggie errs by not meeting it. When Maggie's narrowly righteous brother Tom discovers the meetings and harshly puts a stop to them, even Maggie feels that the "sense of a deliverance from concealment was welcome at any cost."

Maggie's failure to meet the standards of conduct required of her has much more serious consequences when she allows herself to go away with Stephen Guest, a young man who is virtually engaged to her cousin Lucy. Although Maggie rejects Stephen's offer of marriage, their apparent elopement causes a scandal that prostrates Lucy and bitterly divides Maggie's family. Tom is especially adamant in condemning her.

Maggie is a character who is sometimes almost painful to read about, for she has too little self-discipline to avoid slipping into actions that she knows to be wrong and too sensitive a conscience not to feel acutely the consequences of her errors. The ideal of conduct that she longs for and ultimately achieves when she decides to reject Stephen's second proposal of marriage is expressed by passages marked in an old volume of St. Thomas à Kempis that is in a package of books given to Maggie in the depths of the Tullivers' poverty. Reading the words "Forsake thyself, resign thyself, and thou shall enjoy much inward peace," Maggie seems to see "a sudden vision" and feels this "direct communication of the human soul's belief and experience . . . as an unquestioned message."

Maggie is spared further conflict by the melodramatic conclusion of the novel. A flood gives her the opportunity to demonstrate her love for Tom by rescuing him from the mill. Maggie and Tom are briefly reconciled; then a floating mass of machinery bears down on their boat, drowning them both. Their epitaph—"In death they were not divided"—suggests a harmony that Maggie hungered for but seldom achieved in life.

The collision that results in the drowning of Maggie and Tom is, in fact, a kind of *deus ex machina* employed to achieve a resolution for Maggie that would be hard to envision otherwise. More intelligent and gifted than any of the other women in the novel, Maggie would hardly have found the fulfillment in marriage that appears to be the only resource for the women of the village, especially since marriage to Philip would have brought her into irreconcilable conflict with Tom and marriage to Stephen could only have been achieved at the cost of Lucy's happiness. Finally, since Maggie's sensitive compassion has conflicted with Tom's narrow dogmatism throughout the novel, it seems unlikely that their reconciliation could have been permanent. Even the renunciation she learns about in Thomas à Kempis seems to offer more a model of resignation than a pattern for a fruitful and fulfilling life. In the melodramatic ending, therefore, the issues raised by the novel finally remain unresolved.

As in *Adam Bede*, Eliot's brilliant creation of minor characters is one of the finest achievements of the novel. Especially noteworthy are the Dodson sisters, Maggie's aunts, who embody the common qualities of a proud and clannish family, and yet have traits which clearly distinguish them according to their age, degree of prosperity, and individual temperament.

Eliot's third and most perfectly constructed novel, *Silas Marner* embodies her complex moral vision with the precision of a diagram. Like *Adam Bede*, the novel is built on morally contrasting characters, but Silas Marner and Godfrey Cass reveal with much greater clarity than any of the characters in the earlier novel Eliot's concern with the moral patterns of renunciation and self-indulgence.

In a sort of prologue to the main action of the novel, Silas, a linen weaver who is a member of a pious religious sect in a large industrial city, is accused of stealing church funds by a close friend who actually stole the money. When a trial by lots sponsored by the sect declares Silas guilty, he loses faith in God and man and flees to a distant country village, where he isolates himself from the community and finds solace in constant weaving, like a "spinning insect."

Through years of weaving, Silas accumulates a hoard of gold coins which become the only object of his affections. When his gold is stolen by Godfrey Cass's irresponsible brother Dunstan, Silas is utterly devastated until Godfrey's daughter by a secret marriage toddles into his house after her mother dies of exposure and an overdose of laudanum. The presence of this child, whom Silas rears as his own, restores the contact with his fellow men that Silas had lost; Eliot compares the girl to the "white-winged angels" that "in old days . . . took men by the hand and led them away from the city of destruction."

Almost every act that Silas performs in relation to the loss of his gold and the rearing of the child takes on near-symbolic significance. His spontaneous turn to the men assembled at the village tavern when his gold is stolen and to the New Year's assemblage at the Cass house when he finds the child suggest an instinctive searching for community. His heeding the parish clerk's admonition not to accuse the innocent after his gold is stolen and his choice of his younger sister's "Bible name" of Hepzibah (shortened to Eppie) for the child suggest the reestablishment of ties to his past. Most particularly, his acceptance of lard cakes with I. H. S. pricked on them from his kindly neighbor Dolly Winthrop provides a secularized communion that suggests that ties between man and God may be replaced in importance by ties between man and man, as Eppie has replaced the white-winged angels of older days. It may also be significant that Silas spends Christmas in lonely isolation, while Eppie comes to his house on New Year's Eve.

Similarly, Godfrey embodies the consequences of a self-indulgent avoidance of one's responsibilities. Prevented by his secret marriage to the dissolute mother of Eppie from marrying Nancy Lammeter, he weakly trusts to chance, "the god of all men who follow their own devices instead of obeying a law they believe in," to somehow relieve him of the consequences of his actions. Godfrey has none of the malice of his younger brother Dunstan; nevertheless, his anxiety is so great that his "one terror" when Silas comes to his house with Eppie is that his wife might *not* be dead. He sees that the child is his, but fails to acknowledge her, salving his conscience by giving Silas a half-guinea when he finds that Silas has determined to keep her.

The chance that has relieved Godfrey of the consequences of his secret marriage eventually brings retribution. His marriage to Nancy is childless, and when Dunstan's body is discovered with Silas' long-lost gold, Godfrey finally tells Nancy that Eppie is his child. Their plan of relieving their childlessness by adopting Eppie comes to nothing when Eppie tells them that she can only think of Silas as her father. With poetic justice that even Godfrey recognizes, the man who admits that he "wanted to pass for childless once" will now "pass for childless against my wish."

Middlemarch is unquestionably Eliot's finest achievement as a novelist. Whereas *Silas Marner* presented the moral patterns of renunciation and self-indulgence with unparalleled clarity, *Middlemarch* explores them with profound subtlety and psychological insight. The vast scope of *Middlemarch*— it is more than twice the length of *Adam Bede* or *The Mill on the Floss*— gives Eliot room for a panoramic view of provincial life, and her focus on the upper-middle class and gentry gives her an opportunity to deal with characters whose experience is wider and whose motives are more sophisticated and complex than those of many of the characters in the early novels. In this "Study of Provincial Life," as the novel is subtitled, Eliot explores the familiar moral territory of renunciation and self-indulgence by developing four more or less distinct plot lines: the most important of these concern Dorothea Brooke and Tertius Lydgate, but Fred Vincy and Nicholas Bulstrode also claim a substantial amount of Eliot's attention.

This vast novel is unified not only by Eliot's moral concerns and by various cross-connections among the plot lines, but also by a pervasive theme of reform. The implied contrast between the climate for "far-resonant" action that existed when a "coherent social faith" allowed St. Theresa to find "her epos in the reform of a religious order" and the time of the novel, which ends "just after the Lords had thrown out the Reform Bill [of 1832]," suggests the difficulty of achieving meaningful action in the fragmented world of contemporary England. More than any previous novel, *Middlemarch* explores the moral achievements and failures of individuals against the background of an entire society, a society which does not provide many opportunities for people to put their best talents to use.

These issues are perhaps most fully embodied in Dorothea Brooke, a young heiress with "a nature altogether ardent, theoretic and intellectually consequent" who is "struggling in the bands of a narrow teaching, hemmed in by a social life which seemed nothing but a labyrinth of petty courses, a walled-in maze of small paths that led no whither." Seeking a way to give her life consequence and purpose, she marries Edward Casaubon, a dessicated pseudoscholar, whom she naïvely thinks of as a John Locke or a John Milton, a "winged messenger" who can guide her along the "grandest path." She soon discovers that Casaubon is not a great man, but a rather pathetic egotist, morbidly sensitive to real or imagined criticism of his work, pettishly jealous of Dorothea's friendship with his nephew Will Ladislaw, and incapable of offering her any real affection. She also learns that his projected work, grandly entitled a "Key to All Mythologies," is nothing but a monumental collection of trivia, already rendered obsolete by superior German scholarship. Nevertheless, Dorothea prepares to promise her husband, who is suffering from a "fatty degeneration of the heart," that she will continue his work after his death, a sacrifice from which she is saved by his timely demise.

Like Dorothea, Tertius Lydgate finds his ambitions for significant achievement frustrated by social pressures, but unlike Dorothea he adds to his difficulties by a tendency toward heedless self-indulgence. His well-intentioned plans for medical reform are jeopardized by his lack of sensitivity to the feelings of both patients and other practitioners and by his regrettable involvement with Nicholas Bulstrode, an unpopular but powerful leader in community affairs. More important, he shackles himself by marriage to Rosamond

Vincy, the beautiful and self-centered daughter of the mayor of Middlemarch. This marriage, which Lydgate slips into more or less intentionally, blights his hopes of success. He gets heavily into debt as both he and Rosamond carelessly incur expenses on the unconsidered assumption that they ought to live well. Rosamond, utterly unwilling to make any sacrifices, simply blames him for their problems.

These two plot lines come together when Dorothea, deeply moved by Lydgate's marital and financial problems and eager to clear him from blame in a scandal involving Bulstrode, offers to call on Rosamond. She finds Rosamond in what appears to be a compromising tête-à-tête with Will, whom she had come to love since Casaubon's death. Deeply distressed by what she assumes about Will's conduct, she nevertheless forces herself to "clutch [her] own pain" and think only of the "three lives whose contact with hers laid an obligation on her." Feeling "the largeness of the world and the manifold wakings of men to labour and endurance," she compels herself to make a second visit. She has some success in reconciling Rosamond to Lydgate and finds that Will's conduct was indeed blameless.

Although Dorothea's renunciation of herself has the unexpected result of opening the way for her marriage to Will, she never achieves her potential as a latter-day St. Theresa, "for the medium in which [her] ardent deeds took shape is forever gone" Her "full nature" spends itself "in channels which had no great name on earth" but which nonetheless bring benefits to her fellow men. Lydgate, who allowed himself to slip into marriage with the paralyzingly egotistical Rosamond, achieves financial success as a society doctor, but "always regarded himself as a failure; he had not done what he once meant to do."

The other two plot lines, although less important than those centering on Dorothea and Lydgate, afford Eliot opportunity to round out her study of provincial life. Fred Vincy, who is Rosamond's brother, overcomes his tendency to fritter away his money in casual pleasures when he realizes the distresses that his failure to pay a debt will cause the Garth family, who represented security for him, and recognizes that Mary Garth will not marry him unless he undertakes a worthwhile career. The plot line centering on Nicholas Bulstrode, although the least extensive of the four, contains some of Eliot's most perceptive explorations of self-delusion. Bulstrode, who had gathered a fortune dealing in stolen goods before coming to Middlemarch, aspires to leadership in the community as a banker and as an Evangelical Christian. Although he assiduously conceals his former life, he is no simple hypocrite, but an ambitious man who aims at "being an eminent Christian," capable of deluding himself even in his prayers. His lifetime habit of confusing his own desires with God's will comes to a climax when he allows his housekeeper to administer brandy to an alcoholic former associate who has been blackmailing him—a treatment which, although common at the time, has been forbidden by Lydgate. Only after the man dies does Bulstrode discover that the former associate has already revealed Bulstrode's long-guarded secrets in his drunken ramblings.

Although the principal themes of *Middlemarch* are developed primarily in the four major plot lines, the novel's extraordinary richness of minor characters is surely one of its outstanding features. Mr. Brooke, Dorothea's uncle, is one of Eliot's supreme comic creations, a man "of acquiescent temper, miscellaneous opinions, and uncertain vote." Caleb Garth, "one of those rare men who are rigid with themselves and indulgent to others," is a model of sturdy rectitude. Mrs. Bulstrode's loyal support of her guilty husband and her acceptance of "a new life in which she embraced humiliation" is one of Eliot's finest passages. The list could be continued almost at will, amply justifying the claim of the novel's subtitle to be a "study of provincial life."

The subtitle is also appropriate in that it calls attention to Eliot's recognition, more fully expressed in this novel than in any of the earlier ones, of the ways in which the circumstances of society limit her characters' options. Dorothea achieves the ideal of self-renunciation that earlier characters have striven for, but the conditions of her life prevent her from achieving her potential; Lydgate fails not only because of his ill-advised marriage, but also because the community views his eagerness to advance medical practice with suspicion and prejudice. Conditions of society, as well as moral flaws, frustrate the ambitions of even the worthiest characters.

Daniel Deronda, Eliot's final novel, emphasizes the search for purpose more than the ideal of renunciation. Eliot continues her examination of egotism and self-indulgence, but these themes are muted with pathos in the portrayal of Gwendolen Harleth. In subject matter, Eliot also takes another step or two up the social ladder, dealing in this novel with the wealthy upper-middle class and aristocracy.

The protagonist, Daniel Deronda, is such a paragon at the beginning of the novel that he has little need of the lessons in renunciation that Eliot's other protagonists must learn. Handsome, well-educated, and generously supported by Sir Hugo Mallinger, Deronda is only concerned with finding something purposeful to do with his life. His only burden is the assumption that he is Sir Hugo's illegitimate son. His discovery of a cause to which he can dedicate himself proceeds by easy stages. His rescue of Mirah, a Jewish singer who is preparing to drown herself, prompts his interest in Judaism. He succeeds in reuniting Mirah with her terminally ill brother Mordecai, a visionary Jewish mystic. When Mordecai sees Deronda from a bridge, which he describes as "a meeting place for spiritual messengers," he assumes that Deronda has been sent to bring him "my new life—my new self—who will live when this breath is all breathed out." Finally, Deronda discovers that he is actually the son of a distinguished Jewish singer who had asked Sir Hugo to bring him up as an Englishman. The discovery that he is Jewish enables him to marry Mirah, take up the torch from the dying Mordecai, and dedicate himself to the "restoration of a political existence to my people, giving them a national center, such as the English have." (In assigning this cause to Deronda, Eliot anticipated the Zionist movement by some twenty years and, indeed, gave powerful stimulus to the movement for the development of a Jewish national state.)

In Gwendolen Harleth, Eliot examines again the anatomy of egotism. Concerned only with her own comforts, Gwendolen rules imperiously over the household of her twice-widowed mother, Mrs. Davilow. Gwendolen's manifest dislike of men and her habit of sleeping in her mother's bedroom suggest sexual frigidity. Nevertheless, she is on the verge of marrying Henleigh Grandcourt, Sir Hugo's nephew and heir, when she discovers that Grandcourt has had four children by a mistress who deserted her own husband and whom Grandcourt still supports. An invitation to visit Germany with some family friends allows Gwendolen to evade a decision, but when her family loses its fortune, she decides on marriage rather than having her mother live in painfully reduced circumstances while she is forced to take the ignominious position of governess.

Gwendolen's motives in marriage are intriguingly mixed. To be sure, she is essentially egotistical and assumes that she will be able to control her husband. The family's dismal prospects after their catastrophic financial losses inevitably influence her. She is especially concerned for her mother, the one person for whom she feels genuine affection. Nevertheless, she also suffers an agony of guilt in her sense that her marriage has deprived Grandcourt's illegitimate children of any claim to his wealth.

Once they are married, the ruling hand is entirely Grandcourt's. Gwendolen bears his elegantly polite sadism with proud reserve, but is inwardly tormented by dread that her fear and hatred of her husband may drive her to some desperate act. When he drowns, perhaps because she fails to throw him a rope, she is overwhelmed with guilt. Desolated by the marriage of Deronda, whom she has turned to as a moral guide and mentor, she takes solace in Deronda's admonition that she "may live to be one of the best of women," although, as she adds in a final letter to Deronda, "I do not yet see how that can be."

Although Gwendolen's willingness to accept suffering scourges her egotism and brings her to a prospect of redemption that Rosamond Vincy glimpses only briefly, *Daniel Deronda* is in most ways Eliot's bleakest novel. An air of futility hangs like a pall over most of the characters; without a tradition of commitment to some place or purpose, they lack a future also. Mrs. Davilow moves from one rented house to another, and the estates passed down to Sir Hugo from the time of William the Conqueror will finally be inherited by Grandcourt's illegitimate son. Jewish characters such as Mirah's father and Deronda's mother wander over Europe, rejecting even an obligation to their own children. Only the dedication to art of Herr Kelsmer, a German musician, and the acceptance of Mordecai's dream of a national Jewish homeland by Deronda provide a sense of purpose of direction, and these vocations are ones from which most of the characters are inevitably excluded. Except in unusual cases, it appears that even the desire to renounce oneself may not be efficacious. The very circumstances of modern life work against moral achievement.

Erwin Hester

Other major works

SHORT FICTION: *Scenes of Clerical Life*, 1858.

POETRY: *The Spanish Gypsy*, 1868; *The Legend of Jubal and Other Poems*, 1874.

NONFICTION: *The Impressions of Theophrastus Such*, 1879; *Essays of George Eliot*, 1963 (Thomas Pinney, editor).

TRANSLATIONS: *The Life of Jesus Critically Examined*, 1846; *The Essence of Christianity*, 1854.

Bibliography
Beer, Gillian. *George Eliot*. Brighton, England: Harvester Press, 1986. One of a number of feminist readings of Eliot. Concentrates on her engagement with contemporary feminist issues in her fiction and the tensions between her life and her art set up by gender. Contains a full bibliography and an index.

Haight, Gordon. *George Eliot: A Biography*. New York: Oxford University Press, 1968. Still the basic biography of Mary Ann Evans, making full use of her letters. A very full index is provided.

Hardy, Barbara. *The Novels of George Eliot: A Study in Form*. London: Athone Press, 1959. This study has retained its revelance in the continuing discussion of Eliot's fiction, dealing particularly with attempts to shape tragedy out of fiction. Plot, characterization, setting, imagery, and voice are dealt with separately but then focused into a discussion of Eliot's construction of the moral individual.

Newton, K. M. *George Eliot: Romantic Humanist*. Totowa, N.J.: Barnes & Noble Books, 1981. This study of the philosophical structures of Eliot's novels seeks to evaluate how well she combines philosophical, moral, and artistic concerns. Indexed.

Pinion, F. B. *A George Eliot Companion*. Basingstoke, England: Macmillan, 1981. Not only is this volume a mine of information on Eliot's life and work; it also seeks to rehabilitate some of her neglected later fiction. Includes appendices and an index.

STANLEY ELKIN

Born: Brooklyn, New York; May 11, 1930

Principal long fiction

Boswell: A Modern Comedy, 1964; *A Bad Man*, 1967; *The Dick Gibson Show*, 1971; *The Franchiser*, 1976; *George Mills*, 1982; *The Magic Kingdom*, 1985; *The Rabbi of Lud*, 1987; *The Macguffin*, 1991.

Other literary forms

Stanley Elkin has published several collections of his short fiction, including *Criers and Kibitzers, Kibitzers and Criers* (1965), *Searches and Seizures* (1973), *The Living End* (1979), *Stanley Elkin's Greatest Hits* (1980), and *Early Elkin* (1985). *The Making of Ashenden* (1972) is a novella; Elkin has also written a filmscript, *The Six-Year-Old Man* (1968), and has edited several collections of short fiction. *Why I Live Where I Live*, a memoir, was published in 1983.

Achievements

Since their emergence in the mid-1960's, Elkin's novels and short fiction have been praised by critics as some of the best satirical writing in American literature. His novels tend to be darkly comedic performances of unusually articulate, marginal characters struggling to define themselves in a confusing and harsh modern world. His writing career has been generously acknowledged in the form of numerous grants and awards. In 1962, Elkin won the Longview Foundation Award, in 1965 the *Paris Review* prize, in 1966 a Guggenheim fellowship, in 1968 a Rockefeller fellowship, in 1971 a National Endowment for the Arts grant, in 1974 an American Academy grant, in 1980 a Rosenthal Foundation Award, in 1981 a *Sewanee Review* award, and in 1983 a National Book Critics Circle award.

Biography

Stanley Lawrence Elkin was born on May 11, 1930, in Brooklyn, New York. His father, a traveling salesman and noted storyteller, later moved to the Chicago area, where Elkin spent his early childhood. At the age of twenty-two, while enrolled at the University of Illinois at Urbana, Elkin married Joan Marion Jacobson, an aspiring young artist. Two years later, in 1955, he was enlisted into the United States Army, serving two years in the field of radio communications. After his tour of duty, Elkin and his wife spent some time in Europe, especially Rome and London, where he began writing what would later be his first novel, *Boswell*. Returning to the United States, Elkin resumed his studies at the University of Illinois at Urbana, continuing his graduate work in English and working for the student magazine, *Accent*, which published his first short story, "Among the Witnesses," in 1959.

Before receiving a Ph.D. from the University of Illinois at Urbana in 1961, Elkin took a position teaching English at Washington University in St. Louis, a post he has maintained since, with occasional stints as visiting lecturer at institutions such as Smith College, the University of California at Santa Barbara, the University of Wisconsin at Milwaukee, Yale University, and Boston University. Since 1983, he has held the title of Kling Professor of Modern Letters at Washington University.

Elkin and his wife have three children (a daughter and two sons) and live in St. Louis. Despite his suffering from multiple sclerosis, which was diagnosed in 1961, Elkin continues to write and teach, giving occasional readings and lectures across the country.

Analysis

Often erroneously categorized as a "black humorist," Stanley Elkin writes novels and short stories that bristle with a kind of modern satirical language and a blending of the ordinary and the bizarre which characterize much of the black humor which emerged in the 1960's. Yet unlike contemporaries such as Joseph Heller, J. P. Donleavy, and Kurt Vonnegut, Jr., Elkin does not produce works that are particularly pessimistic or given to excessive lamentations over the inadequacies of contemporary culture. The world Elkin depicts in his fiction is indeed bleak, desolate, and unforgiving, but Elkin's characters always seem to manage somehow, always seem to exhibit a certain kind of moral fortitude that enables them to persevere. It is Elkin's treatment of his characters that is perhaps the most striking element in his fiction, causing his work to stand apart from that of the black humorists. Unlike many of his contemporaries, Elkin does not disrespect the characters he satirizes, even when those characters have despicable traits or engage in criminal—even cruel—behavior. Too, his characters have the ability to make moral choices, a characteristic most protagonists in black humor lack. Yet despite his elaborate, artful characterizations, his fiction—because of his overpowering sophistication of style, his artful use of language and metaphor (far beyond the characters to which he typically ascribes the gift of language), and his lack of emphasis on plot—has been somewhat of an enigma to literary scholars who have struggled to understand the significance of his works and their place in the context of contemporary American literature.

His first novel, *Boswell*, centered on the protagonist James Boswell, conceived as a loose parody of the eighteenth century biographer who pursued the most eminent man in the London of his day, Samuel Johnson, eventually befriending him and writing his biography. Elkin's Boswell is also a pursuer of celebrities, but in twentieth century America, the task is more complicated—and the reasons for undertaking the task more pathological. Boswell is obsessed with death: the certainty of death and the prospect of having lived a meaningless life. In this regard, *Boswell* seems almost existential in nature. Yet unlike the earlier existential novelists, and unlike Elkin's contemporaries who often see life in the modern world as vacuous and absurd, Elkin pushes past this categorization, causing his protagonist to make a life-affirming gesture, to take from the confusion and chaos of modern life some organizing principle, or affirmative stance, that can overcome his oppressive feelings of meaninglessness. In Boswell's case, as he stands outside, unable to cross the police barrier in front of the hotel where celebrities are gathering at his own request, he finally comes to understand the inherent injustice of a world that gives special status, even immortal status, to certain individuals while others are left in meaningless obscurity. The novel ends with Boswell's uncharacteristically democratic gesture: he begins to shout opposition to these celebrities, choosing to remain an outsider just on the eve of his acceptance into their circle.

Boswell was received rather cautiously by critics and reviewers. Elkin's lack of plot—not much really "happens" in the novel—his intense, almost overwhelming rhetorical style, and his seemingly inconsistent juxtaposition of formal speech and street slang (often coming from the same character, in the same paragraph) caused several critics to denounce his work as too artificial, too self-conscious, and too uncontrolled. Peter J. Bailey, in defense of Elkin, has argued that the early characterizations of Elkin were unfair for a number of reasons. For one thing, Bailey argues, Elkin's literary antecedents were misunderstood. He was not trying to write realistic plot-based fiction and failing; instead, he was writing antirealistic, comedic novels of excess, very much like his contemporaries Thomas Pynchon, Robert Coover, and Donald Barthelme. The confusion, Bailey believes, comes about because other such novelists use language that is extravagant, rhetorically excessive, and comical. With Elkin, the language is the language one hears every day, the language of shopkeepers and grocers. This realistic speech in the midst of bizarre situations makes Elkin's work more insidious—and, Bailey argues, more effective.

Elkin's second novel, *A Bad Man*, continues what he began in *Boswell*. Like most of Elkin's novels, it focuses on a single protagonist who tells his own story, a protagonist who seeks to heal his disparate, chaotic life through a single profession, or obsession as the case may be. Leo Feldman, a department-store magnate, seeking a way to test his resolve, strength, and fortitude, has himself put into prison for doing his customers illegal favors. In prison, Feldman confronts the system, personified by the warden, and ultimately confronts Death itself in many guises, just as Boswell had done before him. The consummate salesman, Feldman is keenly aware of the art of selling himself, promoting the self, and he seeks to do this as he fights the warden and the system.

In his third novel, *The Dick Gibson Show*, Elkin turns to the world of radio broadcasting, a perfect medium for the depiction of the loner, the orphan (a characteristic of many Elkin protagonists), the marginal modern hero who lives isolated from others yet seeks a kind of renewal, a connection with an understanding, sympathetic "audience." The novel spans Gibson's career (which coincides with the introduction of radio as a mass medium). The format at which he excels is the talk show and, later, the telephone call-in shows that became popular in the 1960's. The callers telephone to articulate their despair, their feelings of inadequacy, and their inability to order their lives—feelings Gibson shares. Rather than succumb to these feelings however, Gibson uses his position as adviser to help himself overcome them. In the callers themselves he finds a substitute for the family he has spent his life seeking in vain.

The Franchiser, Elkin's fourth (and, some argue, his best) novel, was published in 1976. The protagonist, Ben Flesh, is yet another loner—a man living on the road in a late-model Cadillac opening franchises across the country—but a loner who feels at home anywhere in the United States. The opening sentence of the novel catalogs the various places to which he travels: wherever he is, "he feels he is home." Putting absolute faith in the newly emerged system of franchising, Flesh seeks to celebrate and homogenize the United States itself. For him the franchising system is the perfect democratic scheme, the means by which all Americans can participate. The novel ultimately shows the scheme to be misleading, but despite Flesh's setbacks— his businesses begin to fail, he is diagnosed with multiple sclerosis—the novel does not end in despair. Flesh recovers, and begins again, revealing an indomitable spirit, a certain moral fortitude that is characteristic of Elkin's heroes.

Elkin is perceived, even by those who look disparagingly at his fiction, as a master at the depiction of American popular culture, the world of hamburger joints, radio spots, and storefronts, the language of the jingle, shoptalk, and the hype of the sales floor. American consumer culture is Elkin's peculiar speciality, and his poetic treatment of it raises it almost to the level of myth. In Elkin's fifth novel, *George Mills*, he attempts to reveal the extent of these mythic proportions. The story of George Mills, a blue-collar worker in St. Louis, is depicted in the context of his ancestry: He comes from a long line of "working stiffs," beginning with a stableboy during the Fifth Crusade. It is as though George's bloodline had been cursed: each generation passes on a peculiar capacity to serve, each generation is destined to be followers, never leaders, and each generation is doomed to retain forever the hope that somehow God will come through in the end, that at the last minute something will happen to change their fate. The world of *George Mills* is a world where God is a trickster and a bully. Life is absurd, because what happens to people is merely God's trick, "God's fast one." Yet somehow Mills manages to retain his dignity, manages a kind of embrace of all those who are also the butt of God's jokes.

In *The Magic Kingdom*, Elkin carries the idea of life being God's practical joke to an even more poignant level. The novel probes the obsession of Eddy Bale, a Londoner who has recently lost his son to a terminal illness, to take a group of terminally ill children from their home in England to Disney World and the Magic Kingdom. The effort he expends to raise the money, make the travel arrangements, and orchestrate the medical needs of the children is enormous—his own personal battle against the inevitable. He hires a nurse, Mary Cottle, who is thirtyish, a self-imposed exile from romantic relationships because she is a disease carrier (every child born to her would be destined to be diseased and blind). Again the reader sees Elkin's dark vision of the world, a vision that critics justly compare to that of the nihilists, the black humorists. Yet Elkin's dark vision somehow refuses to remain dark. After losing a child during their week in Florida, and after making the arrangements for the body to be returned, Bale and Cottle end the novel in a frenzied sexual encounter that is, in an odd, perhaps perverted way, a gesture of renewal, a feeble attempt to repopulate the world, to replace the diseased children, even if they must be replaced with more diseased children.

The Rabbi of Lud explores Elkin's Jewish heritage: it concerns a rather cynical rabbi of Lud, New Jersey, by the name of Jerry Goldkorn. In the opening chapters, Elkin presents a series of descriptions that suggest his vision of the modern landscape: desolate, dirty, and reeking of death. The town's major feature, indeed its major business, is cemeteries and mortuaries. Lud, as Elkin describes it, is a closed system, a place he calls "thanatopsical," after the Greek word for death. It is the quintessential wasteland, T. S. Eliot's image that overwhelmed twentieth century fiction and poetry—the empty, spiritually defunct landscape of modern humanity. Rabbi Goldkorn is in a spiritual crisis, or rather a series of spiritual crises, involving his family and his career. He eventually moves to Alaska to be the rabbi of the Alaskan pipeline, a typically Elkian metaphor for the ultimately useless career.

Yet despite this rather forbidding depiction of modern life, and despite the trials that beset the rabbi, he is basically happy in his long-standing marriage to his wife, Shelley, and he enjoys his work—even finds it noble to a degree, despite the inevitability of its failure. The end of the novel characteristically reveals Elkin's refusal to paint a completely dismal picture of modern life. Obligated to deliver a eulogy for his friend Joan Cohen, Rabbi Goldkorn— after discussing the hopelessness of life and the inevitability of death— delivers a rather strange, visionary series of blessings that catalog the things in life there are to celebrate, small things such as eating fruit and smelling wood.

Again and again, Elkin shows his readers the resilience of the human spirit, the ability humans have to cope with the chaos of modern life, the meaninglessness of human values, and the entropy from which cultural systems suffer. The major characters in Elkin's novels, novellas, and collections of short fiction—James Boswell, Leo Feldman, Dick Gibson, Ben Flesh, George Mills, Eddy Bale, and Jerry Goldkorn—share the black humorist's understanding of the condition of modern culture, yet ultimately offer a constructive, if not ideal, response. All of his characters share a certain morality, a willingness to admit life's meaninglessness, but also a necessity of struggling against it with whatever strength they can muster. This almost dignified response in the face of life's inane absurdity is Elkin's particular legacy, and the measure by which his works are best understood.

Edward W. Huffstetler

Other major works

SHORT FICTION: *Criers and Kibitzers, Kibitzers and Criers*, 1965; *The Making of Ashenden*, 1972; *Searches and Seizures*, 1973; *The Living End*, 1979; *Stanley Elkin's Greatest Hits*, 1980; *Early Elkin*, 1985.

SCREENPLAY: *The Six-Year-Old Man*, 1968.

NONFICTION: *Why I Live Where I Live*, 1983.

Bibliography

Bailey, Peter J. *Reading Stanley Elkin*. Urbana: University of Illinois Press, 1985. One of the few book-length studies of Elkin's work. Bailey attempts to interpret Elkin's major novels in order to dispel misreadings of his work based on his association with black humorists. Seven chapters each discuss a separate theme or thematic element in Elkin's work. A comprehensive index follows.

Bargen, Doris G. *The Fiction of Stanley Elkin*. Frankfurt, Germany: Verlag Peter D. Lang, 1980. Bargen's work, the first book-length study of Elkin's work, examines his association with the literary movements of metafiction, black humor, American Jewish writers, and popular-culture novels. She concludes that Elkin's work is similar in some ways to all of these, but resists categorizing. Includes an extensive biography, an interview with the author, and a comprehensive bibliography and index.

Cohen, Sarah Blacher, ed. *Comic Relief: Humor in Contemporary American Literature*. Urbana: University of Illinois Press, 1978. Several authors pursue a discussion of the role of humor in the writers who emerged in the 1960's and 1970's, including Elkin. Aligns Elkin with black humorists and discusses their need to laugh at the absurdity of modern culture.

Olderman, Raymond M. *Beyond the Waste Land: The American Novel in the Nineteen Sixties*. New Haven, Conn.: Yale University Press, 1972. The first treatment of Elkin's work in the context of emerging authors of the 1960's. Discusses Elkin and others as repudiating the image of modern society as the "wasteland" depicted in Eliot's 1922 poem. Olderman sees a new kind of idealism, or hope, emerging in contemporary fiction.

Tanner, Tony. *City of Words: American Fiction 1950-1970*. New York: Harper & Row, 1971. Tanner discusses several tendencies among contemporary novelists. One is the obsession with the notion of entropy, that systems tend to break down, that somehow American culture is slowly dissipating. Another is the tendency to create lexiconical worlds—cities of words—to retreat to in the face of entropy. Tanner cites Elkin as a master of these cities of words, one who uses language as a buttress against a rather desolate vision of modern society.

Vinson, James, ed. *Contemporary Novelists*. 2d ed. New York: St. Martin's Press, 1976. This study is rather comprehensive and broad, including Elkin in an overview of writers from the 1960's and 1970's. The section that covers Elkin with the most clarity and thoroughness was written by David Demarest, Jr., and discusses Elkin's place among his contemporaries.

RALPH ELLISON

Born: Oklahoma City, Oklahoma; March 1, 1914

Principal long fiction
Invisible Man, 1952.

Other literary forms
Ralph Ellison's reputation rests primarily on *Invisible Man*, but *Shadow and Act* (1964), a collection of nonfiction prose, established him as a major force in the critical theory of pluralism and in Afro-American aesthetics. Arranged in three thematically unified sections, the essays, most of which appeared originally in journals such as *Antioch Review*, *Partisan Review*, and *The New Republic*, emphasize the importance of folk and popular (especially musical) contributions to the mainstream of American culture. Several of the essays from *Shadow and Act* are recognized as classics, notably "Richard Wright's Blues," "Change the Joke and Slip the Yoke," and "The World and the Jug." In addition, Ellison has published several excellent short stories, including "Flying Home" and "Did You Ever Dream Lucky?" At long intervals, several sections of his work-in-progress, a second novel, have appeared in periodicals. A new collection of essays, *Going to the Territory*, was published in 1986.

Achievements
Ellison occupies a central position in the development of Afro-American literature and of contemporary American fiction. Equally comfortable with the influences of Fyodor Dostoevski, Mark Twain, Louis Armstrong, Igor Stravinsky, James Joyce, and Richard Wright, Ellison was the first Afro-American writer to attain recognition as a full-fledged artist rather than as an intriguing exotic. Where Euro-American critics had previously, and unjustly, condescended to Afro-American writers such as Langston Hughes, Zora Neale Hurston, and Richard Wright, most granted Ellison the respect given Euro-American contemporaries such as Norman Mailer and Saul Bellow. A 1965 *Book World* poll identifying *Invisible Man* as the most distinguished postwar American novel simply verified a consensus already reflected in the recurrence of the metaphor of invisibility in countless works by both Euro-Americans and Afro-Americans during the 1950's and 1960's.

Within the Afro-American tradition itself, Ellison occupies a similarly prominent position, although his mainstream acceptance generates occasional reservations among some Afro-American critics, particularly those committed to cultural nationalism. A *Black World* poll, reflecting these reservations, identified Wright rather than Ellison as the most important black writer. The discrepancy stems in part from the critical image in the late 1960's of Ellison and James Baldwin as leading figures in an anti-Wright "universalist" movement in Afro-American culture, a movement that some critics viewed as a sell-out to Euro-American aesthetics. More recently, however, both Euro-American and Afro-American critics have recognized Ellison's synthesis of the oral traditions of black culture and the literary traditions of both his black and his white predecessors. The current consensus views Ellison as clearly more sympathetic than Wright to the Afro-American tradition. As a result, Ellison seems to have joined Wright as a major influence on younger Afro-American fiction writers such as James Alan McPherson, Leon Forrest, Toni Morrison, and David Bradley.

Ellison's most profound achievement, his synthesis of modernist aesthetics, American Romanticism, and Afro-American folk culture, embodies the aspirations of democratic pluralists such as Walt Whitman, Mark Twain, and Langston Hughes. His vernacular modernism has earned Ellison an international reputation while exerting a major influence on the contemporary mainstream. With a reputation resting almost entirely on his first novel, Ellison's career is among the most intriguing in American literary history.

Biography

Despite Ralph Waldo Ellison's steadfast denial of the autobiographical elements of *Invisible Man* and his insistence on the autonomy of the individual imagination, both the specific details and the general sensibility of his work clearly derive from his experience of growing up in a Southern family in Oklahoma City, attending college in Alabama, and residing in New York City during most of his adult life. Ellison's parents, whose decision to name their son after Ralph Waldo Emerson reflects their commitment to literacy and education, moved from South Carolina to the comparatively progressive Oklahoma capital several years before their son's birth. Reflecting on his childhood, which was characterized by economic hardship following his father's death in 1917, Ellison emphasizes the unusual psychological freedom provided by a social structure that allowed him to interact relatively freely with both whites and blacks. Encouraged by his mother Ida, who was active in socialist politics, Ellison developed a frontier sense of a world of limitless possibility rather than the more typically Southern vision of an environment filled with dangerous oppressive forces.

During his teenage years, Ellison developed a serious interest in music, both as a trumpet player and as a composer/conductor. Oklahoma City offered access both to formal classical training and to jazz, which was a major element of the city's nightlife. The combination of Euro-American and Afro-American influences appears to have played a major role in shaping Ellison's pluralistic sensibility. After he was graduated from high school in 1933, Ellison accepted a scholarship to the Tuskegee Institute, founded by Booker T. Washington, where he remained for three years, studying music and literature, until financial problems forced him to drop out. Although he originally planned to finish his studies, his subsequent relocation in New York City marked a permanent departure from the South.

Arriving in the North in 1936, Ellison established contacts with Afro-American literary figures, including Langston Hughes and Richard Wright, who encouraged him to develop his knowledge of both the Afro-American literary world and Euro-American modernism, especially that of T. S. Eliot and James Joyce. Never as deeply involved with leftist politics as Wright, Ellison nevertheless began developing his literary ideas in reviews and stories published in radical magazines such as *New Masses*. In 1938, Ellison, who had previously supported himself largely as a manual laborer, worked for the Federal Writers' Project, which assigned him to collect urban folklore, providing direct contact with Northern folk culture to complement his previous knowledge of Southern folkways. Ellison's short fiction began appearing in print in the late 1930's and early 1940's. After a short term as managing editor of *Negro Quarterly* in 1942, he briefly left New York, serving in the merchant marine from 1943 to 1945. Awarded a Rosenwald Fellowship to write a novel, Ellison returned to New York and married Fanny McConnell in 1946.

Invisible Man, which took Ellison nearly seven years to write, was published in 1952, bringing him nearly instantaneous recognition as a major young writer. The novel won the National Book Award in 1953, and its reputation has continued to grow. Since 1952, Ellison has taught at Bard College, Rutgers University, New York University, and other institutions. In addition, he has delivered public lectures, written essays, and worked on a second novel. Less inclined to direct political involvement than contemporaries such as Amiri Baraka and James Baldwin, Ellison participated in the civil rights movement in a relatively quiet manner. He nevertheless attracted political controversy during the rise of the Afro-American nationalist movements in the mid-1960's. Refusing to endorse any form of cultural or political separatism, Ellison was attacked as an aesthetic European and a political reactionary, especially after accepting appointments to the American Institute of Arts and Letters (1964) and to the National Council on the Arts and Humanities, acts which were interpreted as support for the Lyndon Johnson Administration's Vietnam policy. During the mid-1970's, however, these attacks abated as nationalist critics such as Larry Neal rose to Ellison's defense and a new generation of Afro-American writers turned to him for aesthetic inspiration. Retired from full-time teaching, during the 1980's Ellison continued to work on his second novel, which was delayed both by his own perfectionism and by events such as a house fire that destroyed part of the manuscript during the 1960's.

Analysis

A masterwork of American pluralism, Ralph Ellison's *Invisible Man* insists on the integrity of individual vocabulary and racial heritage while encouraging a radically democratic acceptance of diverse experiences. Ellison asserts this vision through the voice of an unnamed first-person narrator who is at once heir to the rich Afro-American oral culture and a self-conscious artist who, like T. S. Eliot and James Joyce, exploits the full potential of his written medium. Intimating the potential cooperation between folk and artistic consciousness, Ellison confronts the pressures which discourage both individual integrity and cultural pluralism. The narrator of *Invisible Man* introduces Ellison's central metaphor for the situation of the individual in Western culture in the first paragraph: "I am invisible, understand, simply because people refuse to see me." As the novel develops, Ellison extends this metaphor: Just as a man can be rendered invisible by the willful failure of others to acknowledge his presence, so by taking refuge in the seductive but ultimately specious security of socially acceptable roles, he can fail to see *himself*, fail to define his own identity. Ellison envisions the escape from this dilemma as a multifaceted quest demanding heightened social, psychological, and cultural awareness.

The style of *Invisible Man* reflects both the complexity of the problem and Ellison's pluralistic ideal. Drawing on sources such as the blindness motif from *King Lear* (1605), the underground man motif from Fyodor Dostoevski, and the complex stereotyping of Richard Wright's *Native Son* (1940), Ellison carefully balances the realistic and the symbolic dimensions of *Invisible Man*. In many ways a classic *Künstlerroman*, the main body of the novel traces the protagonist from his childhood in the deep South through a brief stay at college and then to the North, where he confronts the American economic, political, and racial systems. This movement parallels what Robert B. Stepto in *From Behind the Veil* (1979) calls the "narrative of ascent," a constituting pattern of Afro-American culture. With roots in the fugitive slave narratives of the nineteenth century, the narrative of ascent follows its protagonist from physical or psychological bondage in the South through a sequence of symbolic confrontations with social structures to a limited freedom, usually in the North.

This freedom demands from the protagonist a "literacy" that enables him to create and understand both written and social experiences in the terms of the dominant Euro-American culture. Merging the narrative of ascent with the *Künstlerroman*, which also culminates with the hero's mastery of literacy (seen in creative terms), *Invisible Man* focuses on writing as an act of both personal and cultural significance. Similarly, Ellison employs what Stepto calls the "narrative of immersion" to stress the realistic sources and implications of his hero's imaginative development. The narrative of immersion returns the "literate" hero to an understanding of the culture he symbolically left behind during the ascent. Incorporating this pattern in *Invisible Man*, Ellison emphasizes the protagonist's links with the Afro-American community and the rich folk traditions that provide him with much of his sensibility and establish his potential as a conscious artist.

The overall structure of *Invisible Man*, however, involves cyclical as well as directional patterns. Framing the main body with a prologue and epilogue set in an underground burrow, Ellison emphasizes the novel's symbolic dimension. Safely removed from direct participation in his social environment, the invisible man reassesses the literacy gained through his ascent, ponders his immersion in the cultural art forms of spirituals, blues, and jazz, and finally attempts to forge a pluralistic vision transforming these constitutive elements. The prologue and epilogue also evoke the heroic patterns and archetypal cycles described by Joseph Campbell in *Hero with a Thousand Faces* (1968). After undergoing tests of his spiritual and physical qualities, the hero of Campbell's "monomyth"—usually a person of mysterious birth who receives aid from a cryptic helper—gains a reward, usually of a symbolic nature involving the union of opposites. Overcoming forces that would deprive him of the reward, the hero returns to transform the life of his community through application of the knowledge connected with the symbolic reward. To some degree, the narratives of ascent and immersion recast this heroic cycle in specifically Afro-American terms: the protagonist first leaves, then returns to his community bearing a knowledge of Euro-American society potentially capable of motivating a group ascent. While it emphasizes the cyclic nature of the protagonist's quest, the frame of *Invisible Man* simultaneously subverts the heroic pattern by removing him from his community. The protagonist promises a return, but the implications of the return for the life of the community remain ambiguous.

This ambiguity superficially connects Ellison's novel with the classic American romance that Richard Chase characterizes in *The American Novel and Its Tradition* (1957) as incapable of reconciling symbolic perceptions with social realities. The connection, however, reflects Ellison's awareness of the problem more than his acceptance of the irresolution. Although the invisible man's underground burrow recalls the isolation of the heroes of the American romance, he promises a rebirth that is at once mythic, psychological, and social:

> The hibernation is over. I must shake off my old skin and come up for breath. . . . And I suppose it's damn well time. Even hibernations can be overdone, come to think of it. Perhaps that's my greatest social crime, I've overstayed my hibernation, since there's a possibility that even an invisible man has a socially responsible role to play.

Despite the qualifications typical of Ellison's style, the invisible man clearly intends to return to the social world rather than lighting out for the territories of symbolic freedom.

The invisible man's ultimate conception of the form of this return develops out of two interrelated progressions, one social and the other psychological.

The social pattern, essentially that of the narrative of ascent, closely reflects the historical experience of the Afro-American community as it shifts from rural Southern to urban Northern settings. Starting in the deep South, the invisible man first experiences invisibility as a result of casual but vicious racial oppression. His unwilling participation in the "battle royal" underscores the psychological and physical humiliation visited upon Southern blacks. Ostensibly present to deliver a speech to a white community group, the invisible man is instead forced to engage in a massive free-for-all with other blacks, to scramble for money on an electrified rug, and to confront a naked white dancer who, like the boys, has been rendered invisible by the white men's blindness. Escaping his hometown to attend a black college, the invisible man again experiences humiliation when he violates the unstated rules of the Southern system—this time imposed by blacks rather than whites—by showing the college's liberal Northern benefactor, Mr. Norton, the poverty of the black community. As a result, the black college president, Dr. Bledsoe, expels the invisible man. Having experienced invisibility in relation to both blacks and whites and still essentially illiterate in social terms, the invisible man travels north, following the countless Southern blacks involved in the "Great Migration."

Arriving in New York, the invisible man first feels a sense of exhilaration resulting from the absence of overt Southern pressures. Ellison reveals the emptiness of this freedom, however, stressing the indirect and insidious nature of social power in the North. The invisible man's experience at Liberty Paints, clearly intended as a parable of Afro-American involvement in the American economic system, emphasizes the underlying similarity of Northern and Southern social structures. On arrival at Liberty Paints, the invisible man is assigned to mix a white paint used for government monuments. Labeled "optic white," the grayish paint turns white only when the invisible man adds a drop of black liquid. The scene suggests the relationship between government and industry, which relies on black labor. More important, however, it points to the underlying source of racial blindness/invisibility: the white need for a black "other" to support a sense of identity. White becomes white only when compared to black.

The symbolic indirection of the scene encourages the reader, like the invisible man, to realize that social oppression in the North operates less directly than that in the South; government buildings replace rednecks at the battle royal. Unable to mix the paint properly, a desirable "failure" intimating his future as a subversive artist, the invisible man discovers that the underlying structure of the economic system differs little from that of slavery. The invisible man's second job at Liberty Paints is to assist Lucius Brockway, an old man who supervises the operations of the basement machinery on which the factory depends. Essentially a slave to the modern owner/master Mr. Sparland, Brockway, like the good darkies of the Plantation Tradition, takes pride in his master and will fight to maintain his own servitude. Brockway's hatred of the invisible man, whom he perceives as a threat to his position, leads to a physical struggle culminating in an explosion caused by neglect of the machinery. Ellison's multifaceted allegory suggests a vicious circle in which blacks uphold an economic system that supports the political system that keeps blacks fighting to protect their neoslavery. The forms alter but the battle royal continues. The image of the final explosion from the basement warns against passive acceptance of the social structure that sows the seeds of its own destruction.

Although the implications of this allegory in some ways parallel the Marxist analysis of capitalist culture, Ellison creates a much more complex political vision when the invisible man moves to Harlem following his release from the hospital after the explosion. The political alternatives available in Harlem range from the Marxism of the "Brotherhood" (loosely based on the American Communist party of the late 1930's) to the black nationalism of Ras the Exhorter (loosely based on Marcus Garvey's Pan-Africanist movement of the 1920's). The Brotherhood promises complete equality for blacks and at first encourages the invisible man to develop the oratorical talent ridiculed at the battle royal. As his effectiveness increases, however, the invisible man finds the Brotherhood demanding that his speeches conform to its "scientific analysis" of the black community's needs. When he fails to fall in line, the leadership of the Brotherhood orders the invisible man to leave Harlem and turn his attention to the "woman question." Without the invisible man's ability to place radical politics in the emotional context of Afro-American culture, the Brotherhood's Harlem branch flounders. Recalled to Harlem, the invisible man witnesses the death of Tod Clifton, a talented co-worker driven to despair by his perception that the Brotherhood amounts to little more than a new version of the power structure underlying both Liberty Paints and the battle royal. Clearly a double for the invisible man, Clifton leaves the organization and dies in a suicidal confrontation with a white policeman. Just before Clifton's death, the invisible man sees him selling Sambo dolls, a symbolic comment on the fact that blacks involved in leftist politics in some sense remain stereotyped slaves dancing at the demand of unseen masters.

Separating himself from the Brotherhood after delivering an extremely unscientific funeral sermon, the invisible man finds few political options. Ras's black nationalism exploits the emotions the Brotherhood denies. Ultimately, however, Ras demands that his followers submit to an analogous over-simplification of their human reality. Where the Brotherhood elevates the scientific and rational, Ras focuses entirely on the emotional commitment to blackness. Neither alternative recognizes the complexity of either the political situation or the individual psyche; both reinforce the invisible man's feelings of invisibility by refusing to see basic aspects of his character. As he did in the Liberty Paints scene, Ellison emphasizes the destructive, perhaps apocalyptic, potential of this encompassing blindness. A riot breaks out in Harlem, and the invisible man watches as DuPree, an apolitical Harlem resident recalling a number of Afro-American folk heroes, determines to burn down his own tenement, preferring to start again from scratch rather than even attempting to work for social change within the existing framework. Unable to accept the realistic implications of such action apart from its symbolic justification, the invisible man, pursued by Ras, who seems intent on destroying the very blackness he praises, tumbles into the underground burrow. Separated from the social structures, which have changed their facade but not their nature, the invisible man begins the arduous process of reconstructing his vision of America while symbolically subverting the social system by stealing electricity to light the 1,369 light bulbs on the walls of the burrow and to power the record players blasting out the pluralistic jazz of Louis Armstrong.

As his frequent allusions to Armstrong indicate, Ellison by no means excludes the positive aspects from his portrayal of the Afro-American social experience. The invisible man reacts strongly to the spirituals he hears at college, the blues-story of Trueblood, the singing of Mary Rambro after she takes him in off the streets of Harlem. Similarly, he recognizes the strength wrested from resistance and suffering, a strength asserted by the broken link of chain saved by Brother Tarp.

These figures, however, have relatively little power to alter the encompassing social system. They assume their full significance in relation to the second major progression in *Invisible Man*, that focusing on the narrator's psychological development. As he gradually gains an understanding of the social forces that oppress him, the invisible man simultaneously discovers the complexity of his own personality. Throughout the central narrative, he accepts various definitions of himself, mostly from external sources. Ultimately, however, all definitions that demand he repress or deny aspects of himself simply reinforce his sense of invisibility. Only by abandoning limiting definitions altogether, Ellison implies, can the invisible man attain the psychological integrity necessary for any effective social action.

Ellison emphasizes the insufficiency of limiting definitions in the prologue when the invisible man has a dream-vision while listening to an Armstrong record. After descending through four symbolically rich levels of the dream, the invisible man hears a sermon on the "Blackness of Blackness," which recasts the "Whiteness of the Whale" chapter from *Moby Dick* (1851). The sermon begins with a cascade of apparent contradictions, forcing the invisible man to question his comfortable assumptions concerning the nature of freedom, hatred, and love. No simple resolution emerges from the sermon, other than an insistence on the essentially ambiguous nature of experience. The dream-vision culminates in the protagonist's confrontation with the mulatto sons of an old black woman torn between love and hatred for their father. Although their own heritage merges the "opposites" of white and black, the sons act in accord with social definitions and repudiate their white father, an act that unconsciously but unavoidably repudiates a large part of themselves. The hostile sons, the confused old woman, and the preacher who delivers the sermon embody aspects of the narrator's own complexity. When one of the sons tells the invisible man to stop asking his mother disturbing questions, his words sound a *leitmotiv* for the novel: "Next time you got questions like that ask yourself."

Before he can ask, or even locate, himself, however, the invisible man must directly experience the problems generated by a fragmented sense of self and a reliance on others. Frequently, he accepts external definitions, internalizing the fragmentation dominating his social context. For example, he accepts a letter of introduction from Bledsoe on the assumption that it testifies to his ability. Instead, it creates an image of him as a slightly dangerous rebel. By delivering the letters to potential employers, the invisible man participates directly in his own oppression. Similarly, he accepts a new name from the Brotherhood, again revealing his willingness to simplify himself in an attempt to gain social acceptance from the educational, economic, and political systems. As long as he accepts external definitions, the invisible man lacks the essential element of literacy: an understanding of the relationship between context and self.

His reluctance to reject the external definitions and attain literacy reflects both a tendency to see social experience as more "real" than psychological experience and a fear that the abandonment of definitions will lead to total chaos. The invisible man's meeting with Trueblood, a sharecropper and blues singer who has fathered a child by his own daughter, highlights this fear. Watching Mr. Norton's fascination with Trueblood, the invisible man perceives that even the dominant members of the Euro-American society feel stifled by the restrictions of "respectability." Ellison refuses to abandon all social codes, portraying Trueblood in part as a hustler whose behavior reinforces white stereotypes concerning black immorality. If Trueblood's acceptance of his situation (and of his human complexity) seems in part heroic, it is a heroism grounded in victimization. Nevertheless, the invisible man eventually experiments with repudiation of all strict definitions when, after his disillusionment with the Brotherhood, he adopts the identity of Rinehart, a protean street figure who combines the roles of pimp and preacher, shifting identities with context. After a brief period of exhilaration, the invisible man discovers that "Rinehart's" very fluidity guarantees that he will remain locked within social definitions. Far from increasing his freedom at any moment, his multiplicity forces him to act in whatever role his "audience" casts him. Ellison stresses the serious consequences of this lack of center when the invisible man nearly becomes involved in a knife fight with Brother Maceo, a friend who sees only the Rinehartian exterior. The persona of "Rinehart," then, helps increase the invisible man's sense of possibility, but lacks the internal coherence necessary for psychological, and perhaps even physical, survival.

Ellison rejects both acceptance of external definitions and abandonment of all definitions as viable means of attaining literacy. Ultimately, he endorses the full recognition and measured acceptance of the experience, historical and personal, that shapes the individual. In addition, he recommends the careful use of masks as a survival strategy in the social world. The crucial problem with this approach, derived in large part from Afro-American folk culture, involves the difficulty of maintaining the distinction between external mask and internal identity. As Bledsoe demonstrates, a protective mask threatens to implicate the wearer in the very system he attempts to manipulate.

Before confronting these intricacies, however, the invisible man must accept his Afro-American heritage, the primary imperative of the narrative of immersion. Initially, he attempts to repudiate or to distance himself from the aspects of the heritage associated with stereotyped roles. He shatters and attempts to throw away the "darky bank" he finds in his room at Mary Rambro's. His failure to lose the pieces of the bank reflects Ellison's conviction that the stereotypes, major aspects of the Afro-American social experience, cannot simply be ignored or forgotten. As an element shaping individual consciousness, they must be incorporated into, without being allowed to dominate, the integrated individual identity. Symbolically, in a scene in which the invisible man meets a yam vendor shortly after his arrival in Harlem, Ellison warns that one's racial heritage alone cannot provide a full sense of identity. After first recoiling from yams as a stereotypic Southern food, the invisible man eats one, sparking a momentary epiphany of racial pride. When he indulges the feelings and buys another yam, however, he finds it frost-bitten at the center.

The invisible man's heritage, placed in proper perspective, provides the crucial hints concerning social literacy and psychological identity that allow him to come provisionally to terms with his environment. Speaking on his deathbed, the invisible man's grandfather offers cryptic advice which lies near the essence of Ellison's overall vision: "Live with your head in the lion's mouth. I want you to overcome 'em with yeses, undermine 'em with grins, agree 'em to death and destruction, let 'em swoller you till they vomit or bust wide open." Similarly, an ostensibly insane veteran echoes the grandfather's advice, adding an explicit endorsement of the Machiavellian potential of masking:

Play the game, but don't believe in it—that much you owe yourself. Even if it lands you in a strait jacket or a padded cell. Play the game, but play it your own way—part of the time at least. Play the game, but raise the ante, my boy. Learn how it operates, learn how *you* operate. . . . that game has been analyzed, put down in books. But down here they've forgotten to take care of the books and that's your opportunity. You're hidden right out in the open—that is, you would be if you only realized it. They wouldn't see you because they don't expect you to know anything.

The vet understands the "game" of Euro-American culture, while the grandfather directly expresses the internally focused wisdom of the Afro-American community.

The invisible man's quest leads him to a synthesis between these forms of literacy in his ultimate pluralistic vision. Although he at first fails to comprehend the subversive potential of his position, the invisible man gradually learns the rules of the game and accepts the necessity of the indirect action recommended by his grandfather. Following his escape into the underground burrow, he contemplates his grandfather's advice from a position of increased experience and self-knowledge. Contemplating his own individual situation in relation to the surrounding society, he concludes that his grandfather "*must* have meant the principle, that we were to affirm the principle on which the country was built but not the men." Extending this affirmation to the psychological level, the invisible man embraces the internal complexity he has previously repressed or denied: "So it is that now I denounce and defend, or feel prepared to defend. I condemn and affirm, say no and say yes, say yes and say no. I denounce because though implicated and partially responsible, I have been hurt to the point of abysmal pain, hurt to the point of invisibility. And I defend because in spite of all I find that I love. In order to get some of it down I *have* to love."

"Getting some of it down," then, emerges as the crucial link between Ellison's social and psychological visions. In order to play a socially responsible role—and to transform the words "social responsibility" from the segregationist catch phrase used by the man at the battle royal into a term responding to Louis Armstrong's artistic call for change—the invisible man forges from his complex experience a pluralistic art that subverts the social lion by taking its principles seriously. The artist becomes a revolutionary wearing a mask. Ellison's revolution seeks to realize a pluralist ideal, a true democracy recognizing the complex experience and human potential of every individual. Far from presenting his protagonist as a member of an intrinsically superior cultural elite, Ellison underscores his shared humanity in the concluding line: "Who knows but that, on the lower frequencies, I speak for you?" Manipulating the aesthetic and social rules of the Euro-American "game," Ellison sticks his head in the lion's mouth, asserting a blackness of blackness fully as ambiguous, as individual, and as rich as the whiteness of Herman Melville's whale.

Craig Werner

Other major works

NONFICTION: *The Writer's Experience*, 1964 (with Karl Shapiro); *Shadow and Act*, 1964; *Going to the Territory*, 1986.

Bibliography

Benston, Kimberly, ed. *Speaking for You: The Vision of Ralph Ellison*. Washington, D.C.: Howard University Press, 1987. A useful resource of responses to Ellison's fiction and essays. Also includes an extensive bibliography of his writings.

Bloom, Harold, ed. *Ralph Ellison*. New York: Chelsea House, 1986. A good collection of essays on Ellison's writings, with an introduction by Bloom.

Nadel, Alan. *Invisible Criticism: Ralph Ellison and the American Canon*. Iowa City: University of Iowa Press, 1988. A look at Ellison's place in the study of American literature.

O'Meally, Robert G. *The Craft of Ralph Ellison*. Cambridge, Mass.: Harvard University Press, 1980. Traces Ellison's development as a writer and includes considerations of his fiction published after *Invisible Man*. Since 1960, sections of his novel-in-progress have appeared in a variety of publications.

_____, ed. *New Essays on "Invisible Man."* New York: Cambridge University Press, 1988. A collection of essays which includes many responses to questions raised by earlier critics.

Trimmer, Joseph F., ed. *A Casebook on Ralph Ellison's "Invisible Man."* New York: Thomas Y. Crowell, 1972. An invaluable aid to students and teachers, this volume is a collection of social and literary background material useful for understanding the traditions that inform *Invisible Man*. Also contains critical essays.

LOUISE ERDRICH

Born: Little Falls, Minnesota; July 6, 1954

Principal long fiction
Love Medicine, 1984; *The Beet Queen*, 1986; *Tracks*, 1988; *The Crown of Columbus*, 1991 (with Michael Dorris).

Other literary forms
Jacklight (1984) and *Baptism of Desire* (1989) are books of poetry (along with a few folktales) which present vivid North Dakota vignettes, as well as personal reflections on Louise Erdrich's relationships to her husband and children.

Achievements
A poet and poetic novelist, Erdrich has drawn on her Chippewa and German-immigrant heritage to create a wide-ranging chronicle of Indian and white experience in twentieth century North Dakota. Since she began to publish her fiction and poetry in the early 1980's, her works have garnered high critical praise, and her three novels have been best-sellers as well. *Love Medicine*, Erdrich's first novel, won the National Book Critics Circle Award in 1984, and three of the stories gathered in that book were also honored: "The World's Greatest Fishermen" won the five-thousand-dollar first prize in the 1982 Nelson Algren fiction competition, "Scales" appeared in *Best American Short Stories, 1983* (1983), and "Saint Marie" was chosen for *Prize Stories 1985: The O. Henry Awards* (1985). Two of the stories included in the novel *Tracks* also appeared in honorary anthologies: "Fleur" in *Prize Stories 1987: The O. Henry Awards* (1987) and "Snares" in *Best American Short Stories, 1988* (1988).

Erdrich's works often focus on the struggle of Chippewa Indians for personal, familial, and cultural survival. Yet her treatment of white and mixed-blood characters also reveals an empathic understanding of the ways in which North Dakota people of all races long for closer connection with other people and the land.

Biography
Louise Erdrich grew up in Wahpeton, a small town in southeastern North Dakota. Her father, Ralph Erdrich, is a German immigrant who taught in Wahpeton at the Indian boarding school. Her mother, Rita Journeau Erdrich, is a three-quarters Chippewa who also worked at the school. Erdrich's mixed religious and cultural background provided a rich foundation for her later poetry and fiction.

Erdrich earned two degrees in creative writing, a B.A. from Dartmouth College in 1976 and an M.A. from The Johns Hopkins University in 1979. In 1981, she was married to Michael Dorris, a professor of anthropology and head of the Native American Studies Program at Dartmouth.

Erdrich and Dorris have devoted their lives to ambitious family, literary, and humanitarian goals. Like Erdrich, Dorris is three-eighths Indian, and years before his marriage to Erdrich he had adopted three Indian infants from Midwestern reservations. Dorris and Erdrich have produced three more children and are rearing their family in an eighteenth century farmhouse in Cornish, New Hampshire. Erdrich and her husband have said that they collaborate on virtually all the works that either one publishes—whether fiction, poetry, or nonfiction. Thus Erdrich acknowledges Dorris' important contribution to all of her fiction; similarly, she collaborated with him on his first novel, *A Yellow Raft in Blue Water* (1987), and on his study of fetal alcohol syndrome (FAS), *The Broken Cord* (1989). Erdrich and Dorris have donated money and campaigned for legislation to combat FAS, which afflicts the lives of many Indian children born to alcoholic mothers.

Analysis

In a 1985 essay entitled "Where I Ought to Be: A Writer's Sense of Place," Louise Erdrich states that the essence of her writing emerges from her attachment to her North Dakota locale. The ways in which Erdrich has brought this region to literary life have been favorably compared by critics to the methods and style of William Faulkner, who created the mythical Yoknapatawpha County out of his rich sense of rural Mississippi. Like Faulkner, Erdrich has created a gallery of diverse characters spanning several generations; she also uses multiple points of view and shifting time frames. Erdrich's fiction further resembles Faulkner's in that the experience of her characters includes a broad spectrum of experience "from the mundane to the miraculous," as one critic put it. Erdrich's stories generally begin with a realistic base of ordinary people, settings, and actions. As her tales develop, however, these people become involved in events and perceptions that strike the reader as quite extraordinary—as exaggerated or heightened in ways that may seem deluded or mystical, grotesque or magical, comic or tragic, or some strange mixture of these. Thus one critic has described Erdrich as "a sorceress with language" whose lyrical style intensifies some of the most memorable scenes in contemporary American fiction.

Erdrich's first novel, *Love Medicine*, spans the years 1934-1984 in presenting members of five Chippewa and mixed-blood families, all struggling in different ways to attain a sense of belonging through love, religion, home, and family. The novel includes fourteen interwoven stories; though the title refers specifically to traditional Indian magic in one story, in a broader sense "love medicine" refers to the different kinds of spiritual power that enable Erdrich's

Chippewa and mixed-blood characters to transcend—however momentarily—the grim circumstances of their lives. Trapped on their shrinking reservation by racism and poverty, plagued by alcoholism, disintegrating families, and violence, some of Erdrich's characters nevertheless discover a form of "love medicine" that helps to sustain them.

The opening story, "The World's Greatest Fishermen," begins with an episode of "love medicine" corrupted and thwarted. Though June Kashpaw was once a woman of striking beauty and feisty spirit, by 1981 she has sunk to the level of picking up men in an oil boomtown. Unfortunately, June fails in her last attempts to attain two goals that other characters will also seek throughout the novel: love and home. Yet though she appears only briefly in this and one other story, June Kashpaw is a central character in the novel, for she embodies the potential power of spirit and love in ways that impress and haunt the other characters.

Part 2 of "The World's Greatest Fishermen" introduces many of the other major characters of *Love Medicine*, as June's relatives gather several months after her death. On the one hand, several characters seem sympathetic because of their closeness to June and their kind treatment of one another. Albertine Johnson, who narrates the story and remembers her Aunt June lovingly, has gone through a wild phase of her own and is now a nursing student. Eli Kashpaw, Albertine's granduncle, who was largely responsible for rearing June, is a tough and sharp-minded old man who has maintained a traditional Chippewa existence as a hunter and fisherman. Lipsha Morrissey, who, though he seems not to know it, is June's illegitimate son, is a sensitive, self-educated young man who acts warmly toward Albertine. In contrast to these characters are others who are flawed or unsympathetic when seen through the eyes of Albertine, who would like to feel that her family is pulling together after June's death. These less sympathetic characters include Zelda and Aurelia (Albertine's gossipy mother and aunt), Nector Kashpaw (Albertine's senile grandfather), and Gordon Kashpaw (the husband whom June left, a hapless drunk). Worst of all is June's legitimate son King, a volatile bully. King's horrifying acts of violence—abusing his wife Lynette, battering his new car, and smashing the pies prepared for the family dinner— leave Albertine with a dismayed sense of a family in shambles.

Love Medicine then shifts back in time from 1981, and its thirteen remaining stories proceed in chronological order from 1934 to 1984. "Saint Marie" concerns a poor white girl, Marie Lazarre, who in 1934 enters Sacred Heart Convent and embarks on a violent love-hate relationship with Sister Leopolda. In "Wild Geese," also set in 1934, Nector Kashpaw is infatuated with Lulu Nanapush, but his affections swerve unexpectedly when he encounters Marie Lazarre on the road outside her convent. By 1948, the time of "The Beads," Marie has married Nector, had three children (Aurelia, Zelda, and Gordie), and agreed to rear her niece June. Nector, however, is drinking and philandering, and June, after almost committing suicide in a children's hanging game, leaves to be brought up by Eli in the woods. "Lulu's Boys," set in 1957, reveals that the amorous Lulu Lamartine (née Nanapush) had married Henry Lamartine but bore eight sons by different fathers. Meanwhile, in "The Plunge of the Brave," also set in 1957, Nector recalls the development of his five-year affair with Lulu, and tries to leave his wife Marie for her, but the result is that he accidentally burns Lulu's house to the ground.

The offspring of these Kashpaws and Lamartines also have their problems in later *Love Medicine* stories. In "The Bridge," set in 1973, Albertine runs away from home and becomes the lover of Henry Lamartine, Jr., one of Lulu's sons, a troubled Vietnam veteran. "The Red Convertible," set in 1974, also involves Henry, Jr., as Lyman Lamartine tries unsuccessfully to bring his brother out of the dark personality changes that Vietnam has wrought in him. On a lighter note, "Scales," set in 1980, is a hilarious account of the romance between Dot Adare, an obese white clerk at a truck weighing station, and Gerry Nanapush, one of Lulu's sons who is a most unusual convict: enormously fat, amazingly expert at escaping from jail, but totally inept at avoiding capture. "A Crown of Thorns," which overlaps the time of "The World's Greatest Fishermen" in 1981, traces the harrowing and bizarre decline of Gordie Kashpaw into alcoholism after June's death.

Though in these earlier *Love Medicine* stories the positive powers of love and spirit are more often frustrated than fulfilled, in the last three stories several characters achieve breakthroughs that bring members of the different families together in moving and hopeful ways. In "Love Medicine," set in 1982, Lipsha Morrissey reaches out lovingly to his grandmother Marie and to the ghosts of Nector and June. In "The Good Tears," set in 1983, Lulu undergoes a serious eye operation and is cared for by Marie, who forgives her for being Nector's longtime extramarital lover. Finally, in "Crossing the Water," set in 1984, Lipsha helps his father, Gerry Nanapush, escape to Canada and comes to appreciate the rich heritage of love, spirit, and wiliness that he has inherited from his diverse patchwork of Chippewa relatives—especially from his grandmother Lulu, his aunt Marie, and his parents, June and Gerry.

In *The Beet Queen*, her second novel, Erdrich shifts her main focus from the Indian to the European-immigrant side of her background, and she creates in impressive detail the mythical town of Argus (modeled on Wahpeton, where she was reared, but located closer to the Chippewa reservation) in the years 1932-1972.

The opening scene of *The Beet Queen*, "The Branch," dramatizes two contrasting approaches to life that many characters will enact throughout the novel. On a cold spring day in 1932, two orphans, Mary and Karl Adare, arrive by freight train in Argus. As they seek the way to the butcher shop owned by their Aunt Fritzie and Uncle Pete Kozka, Mary "trudge[s] solidly forward," while Karl stops to embrace a tree that already has its spring blossoms. When they are attacked by a dog, Mary runs ahead, continuing her search for the butcher shop, while Karl runs back to hop the train once again. As the archetypal plodder of the novel, Mary continues to "trudge solidly forward" throughout; she is careful, determined, and self-reliant in pursuit of her goals. On the other hand, Karl is the principal dreamer—impressionable, prone to escapist impulses, and dependent on others to catch him when he falls.

The Adare family history shows how Karl is following a pattern set by his mother, Adelaide, while Mary grows in reaction against this pattern. Like Karl, Adelaide is physically beautiful but self-indulgent and impulsive. Driven to desperation by her hard luck in the early years of the Depression, Adelaide startles a fairground crowd by abandoning her three children (Mary, Karl, and an unnamed newborn son) to fly away with the Great Omar, an airplane stunt pilot.

In Argus, Mary tangles with yet another beautiful, self-centered dreamer: her cousin Sita Kozka, who resents the attention that her parents, Pete and Fritzie, and her best friend, Celestine James, pay to Mary. Yet Mary prevails and carves a solid niche for herself among Pete, Fritzie, and Celestine, who, like Mary, believe in a strong work ethic and lack Sita's pretentious airs.

A number of episodes gratify the reader with triumphs for Mary and comeuppances for the less sympathetic characters Karl, Adelaide, and Sita. Mary becomes famous for a miracle at her school (she falls and cracks the ice in the image of Jesus), gains Celestine as a close friend, and in time becomes manager of the Kozka butcher shop. By contrast, Karl becomes a drifter who finds only sordid momentary pleasure in his numerous affairs. Meanwhile, Adelaide marries Omar and settles in Florida, but she becomes moody and subject to violent rages. Similarly, Sita fails in her vainglorious attempts to become a model and to establish a fashionable French restaurant; she escapes her first marriage through divorce and becomes insane and suicidal during her second.

Yet even as Erdrich charts the strange and sometimes grotesque downfalls of her flighty characters, she develops her more sympathetic ones in ways that suggest that the opposite approach to life does not guarantee happiness either. Mary fails in her attempt to attract Russell Kashpaw (the Chippewa half-brother of Celestine), and she develops into an exotically dressed eccentric who is obsessed with predicting the future and controlling others. Like Mary, Celestine James and Wallace Pfef are hardworking and successful in business, but their loneliness drives each of them to an ill-advised affair with Karl, and he causes each of them considerable grief. In addition, the union of Celestine and Karl results in the birth of Dot Adare (who grows up to be the ill-tempered lover of Gerry Nanapush in the *Love Medicine* story "Scales"); since Celestine, Mary, and Wallace all spoil the child, Dot turns out, in Wallace's words, to have "all of her family's worst qualities." As a teenager,

Dot herself comes to grief when she is mortified to learn that Wallace has rigged the election for Queen of the Argus Beet Festival so that she, an unpopular and ludicrously unlikely candidate, will win.

Yet in addition to the defeats and disappointments that all the characters bear, Erdrich also dramatizes the joy that they derive from life. The compensations of family and friendship—ephemeral and vulnerable as these may be—prove to be significant for all the characters at various times in the story, particularly at the end. The irrepressible vitality of these people, troublesome as they often are to one another, keeps the reader involved and entertained throughout the novel.

Erdrich's third novel, *Tracks*, is her most concentrated, intense, and mystical. It is the shortest (at 226 pages, compared to 272 for *Love Medicine* and 338 for *The Beet Queen*), covers a time span of only twelve years, and alternates between only two first-person narrators. This compression serves the story well, for the human stakes are high. At first, and periodically throughout the novel, the Chippewa characters fear for their very survival, as smallpox, tuberculosis, severe winters, starvation, and feuds with mixed-blood families bring them close to extinction. Later in the novel, government taxes and political chicanery threaten the Chippewas' ownership of their family homesteads. In response, Erdrich's Chippewa characters use all the powers at their command—including the traditional mystical powers of the old ways—to try to survive and maintain their control over the land.

Nanapush, one of the novel's two narrators, is an old Chippewa whom Erdrich names for the trickster rabbit in tribal mythology who repeatedly delivers the Chippewas from threatening monsters. In *Tracks*, Erdrich's Nanapush often does credit to his mythological model by wielding the trickster rabbit's powers of deliverance, wiliness, and humor. He saves Fleur Pillager, a seventeen-year-old girl who is the last of the Pillager clan, from starvation. Later he delivers young Eli Kashpaw from the sufferings of love by advising him how to win Fleur's heart. Also, Nanapush is instrumental in saving the extended family that forms around Fleur, Eli, and himself. This family grows to five when Fleur gives birth to a daughter, Lulu, and Eli's mother, Margaret Kashpaw, becomes Nanapush's bedmate. As these five come close to starvation, Nanapush sends Eli out to hunt an elk; in one of the most extraordinary passages of the novel, Nanapush summons a power vision of Eli hunting that the old man imagines is guiding Eli to the kill. Nanapush also demonstrates the humor associated with his mythological model in his wry tone as a narrator, his sharp wit in conversation, and the tricks that he plays on his family's mixed-blood antagonists: the Pukwans, Morrisseys, and Lazarres.

Foremost among these antagonists is the novel's other narrator, Pauline Pukwan. A "skinny big-nosed girl with staring eyes," Pauline circulates in Argus from the Kozkas' butcher shop to the Sacred Heart Convent, and on the reservation from the Nanapush-Pillager-Kashpaw group to the Morrissey and Lazarre clans. At first attracted to Fleur by the beauty and sexual power that she herself lacks, Pauline later takes an envious revenge by concocting a love potion that seems to drive Fleur's husband, Eli, and Sophie Morrissey to become lovers. Ironically, though one side of her believes in a Catholic denial of her body, Pauline later gives birth out of wedlock to a girl named Marie, and at the end of her narrative Pauline enters the convent to become Sister Leopolda—the cruel nun who later torments her own daughter, Marie Lazarre, in *Love Medicine*.

Though Erdrich clearly feels passionately about the sufferings visited on her Chippewa characters in *Tracks*, she treats this politically charged material with her usual disciplined restraint. Her dispassionate, deadpan use of first-person narrators (never broken by authorial commentary) matches the understated, stoic attitude that Nanapush adopts toward the numerous waves of hardship and betrayal that the Chippewas must endure.

If in some ways *Tracks* seems to conclude with a feeling of fragmentation and defeat, in other ways it strikes positive notes of solidarity and survival, especially when considered in relation to *Love Medicine* and *The Beet Queen*. Fleur disappears, leaving her husband and daughter, but Nanapush uses his wiliness to become tribal chairman and then to retrieve Lulu from a distant boarding school. At the end, the reader is reminded that Nanapush has addressed his entire narrative to Lulu: the old man hopes that his story will convince Lulu to embrace the memory of Fleur, "the one you will not call mother." Further, the reader familiar with *Love Medicine* will realize how this young girl, who becomes Lulu Lamartine, carries on the supernaturally powerful sexuality of her mother Fleur and the wily talent for survival of Nanapush, the old man who gave her his name and reared her.

If Louise Erdrich had been born two hundred years earlier, she might have become a traditional Chippewa storyteller, whose tales would have reminded her listeners of their unchanging relationship to the land and to the mythic and legendary characters who inhabited it. Now several generations removed from such a stable and undamaged culture, Erdrich nevertheless creates a richly neotribal view of people and place. Her novels testify to the profound interrelatedness of her characters—Indian and white, contemporaries and ancestors—both with one another and with their North Dakota homeland.

Terry L. Andrews

Other major works

POETRY: *Jacklight*, 1984; *Baptism of Desire*, 1989.

Bibliography

Bly, Robert. "Another World Breaks Through." *The New York Times Book Review* 92 (August 21, 1986): 2. This review of *The Beet Queen* by a notable American poet includes a suggestive discussion of Erdrich's style.

Erdrich, Louise. "Where I Ought to Be: A Writer's Sense of Place." *The New York Times Book Review* 91 (July 28, 1985): 1, 23-24. In this invaluable essay, Erdrich discusses her roots and sense of purpose as a writer. She describes contemporary American society as a nomadic culture that is in danger of losing its humanity, and argues that writers should cultivate an exhaustively detailed sense of a specific place, no matter how trivial and vulgar some of the cultural details of that place may seem.

Strouse, Jean. "In the Heart of the Heartland." *The New York Times Book Review* 94 (October 2, 1988): 1, 41-42. Strouse's positive review of *Tracks* discusses Erdrich's work in the context of other regional American writers. She also draws a fruitful analogy between the "tracking" performed by the characters and that accomplished by the author in the act of writing.

Towers, Robert. "Roughing It." *The New York Review of Books* 35 (November 19, 1988): 40-41. In this negative review of *Tracks*, Towers provocatively develops his opinion—shared by some other critics—that in comparison with her earlier two novels, Erdrich's writing in *Tracks* has become too melodramatic and overcharged.

Wickenden, Dorothy. "Off the Reservation." *The New Republic* 195 (October 6, 1986): 46-48. This mixed review of *The Beet Queen* presents useful analysis of the novel's characters and stylistic effects, and it raises the issue—also voiced by other critics—of whether Erdrich relies too heavily on sensational incidents and a contrived ending, rather than on careful development of plot and characters.

JAMES T. FARRELL

Born: Chicago, Illinois; Feburary 27, 1904
Died: New York, New York; August 22, 1979

Principal long fiction

Young Lonigan: A Boyhood in Chicago Streets, 1932; *Gas-House McGinty*, 1933; *The Young Manhood of Studs Lonigan*, 1934; *Judgment Day*, 1935; *Studs Lonigan: A Trilogy*, 1935; *A World I Never Made*, 1936; *No Star Is Lost*, 1938; *Tommy Gallagher's Crusade*, 1939; *Father and Son*, 1940; *Ellen Rogers*, 1941; *My Days of Anger*, 1943; *Bernard Clare*, 1946; *The Road Between*, 1949; *This Man and This Woman*, 1951; *Yet Other Waters*, 1952; *The Face of Time*, 1953; *Boarding House Blues*, 1961; *The Silence of History*, 1963; *What Time Collects*, 1964; *When Time Was Born*, 1966; *Lonely for the Future*, 1966; *New Year's Eve/1929*, 1967; *A Brand New Life*, 1968; *Judith*, 1969; *Invisible Swords*, 1971; *The Dunne Family*, 1976; *The Death of Nora Ryan*, 1978.

Other literary forms

James T. Farrell began his career, as so many other novelists have done, by writing short stories, and his more than two hundred tales are an integral part of the vast world he portrays. Most of his stories have been gathered in collections such as *Calico Shoes and Other Stories* (1934) and *$1,000 Dollars a Week and Other Stories* (1942), but there are several stories and manuscript works that remain unpublished. His poetry, collected by Farrell himself in a 1965 edition, seems to be the product of early and late speculations—the early poetry probably coming from the period of *Studs Lonigan* and the later poetry seemingly produced during the early 1960's when he was beginning his "second career" with *A Universe of Time*, an unfinished multicycled series of novels, stories, and poems. All the poetry is uneven in quality and, despite some remarkable effects, is not memorable. Farrell also published volumes of literary criticism, cultural criticism, and essays on a wide range of subjects. *The Mowbray Family* (1940), a play written with Hortense Alden Farrell, is a dramatic treatment of the same material which he treats brilliantly in his fiction. The drama, however, lacks the vitality of his novels and seems lifeless alongside a work such as *My Days of Anger*. His letters remain to be collected, and his biography has yet to be completed.

Achievements

Farrell's career encompassed many diverse literary movements and trends. He was active to the end of a long life, publishing his last novel in the year before his death, and any final assessment of his achievements would be premature. Nevertheless, on the evidence of his three major complete works, the *Studs Lonigan* trilogy, the Danny O'Neill series (or the O'Neill-O'Flaherty series, as Farrell preferred to call it), and the Bernard Carr trilogy, Farrell presented urban America and the people who sprang from it with a brutal candor rarely equalled in American literature.

His youth, spent in Irish-Catholic, lower- and middle-class Chicago, gave him the milieu from which a whole society could be examined and explained. His career began with his conscious decision to quit a steady job and become a writer and survived despite indifference, shock, bad reviews, prejudice, and ignorance. Farrell's social activism led him into and out of Marxist circles, sustained him through attacks by the Marxist critics who accused him of abandoning the cause, and gave him the focus necessary to show Americans an entire society that survived and prospered in spite of its environment.

Farrell never achieved great popularity; his style was considered too flat and brusque, his language profane, and his methods inartistic. His fiction was considered basically plotless or merely photographic, and he was condemned, especially by the Marxists, for failing to be didactic. In recent years, however, the scope of his urban vision has been recognized; Farrell's fictional world has the breadth of conception associated with greatness and has been compared favorably to that of William Faulkner. Much like Theodore Dreiser, whom he admired, Farrell went his own way when it was extremely unpopular to do so, and his impact on modern fiction remains to be assessed.

Biography

James Thomas Farrell was born on February 27, 1904, in Chicago, where he lived continuously, except for a short sojourn in New York City during the 1920's, until 1931. The son of a family of Irish teamsters and domestics, he was the product of a curious dual life-style in his youth. One of fifteen children, Farrell was taken, when he was three, to live with his maternal grandparents as the result of his own family's impoverished condition. His grandparents, John and Julia Daly, were of the same poor, hard-working stock as his father and mother, but they were somewhat more financially stable and lived a different, more affluent life. The difference in these two families was important in Farrell's development.

Living with the Dalys, Farrell found himself in a neighborhood of modern brick buildings which were a sharp contrast to the poor, wooden-shack neighborhood where his parents lived with the rest of their children. The personal confusion and divisions of loyalties caused by this unusual arrangement were only a part of Farrell's childhood problems. Living in one household and coming from another made Farrell the center of many family tensions and involved him in most of the family's disagreements.

Farrell entered Corpus Christi Parochial Grammar School in 1911, and through the course of his education was a loner and a dreamer. He became an excellent athlete, taking seven letters in sports at St. Cyril High School.

He attended St. Cyril after giving up early plans to attend a seminary in preparation to become a priest. He excelled in his studies and was active on the St. Cyril *Oriflamme*, the school's monthly magazine, in addition to being an active member of the high school fraternity, Alpha Eta Beta. He was desperately in need of acceptance, but his classmates sensed that he was different and his social incapacity was another influence on his later life.

After high school, Farrell went to work full time for the Amalgamated Express Company, where he had worked summers while in school. After nearly two years with the express company, Farrell felt trapped by the routine and, in 1924, enrolled in night classes at De Paul University as a pre-law student. He first encountered political and economic theory there and first read Theodore Dreiser. The financial and mental strain eventually became too much for Farrell, and he left De Paul and the express company in 1925. He then took a job as a gas station attendant for the Sinclair Oil and Refining Company and saved part of his wages for tuition at the University of Chicago.

In eight quarters at the University, completed between 1925 and 1929, Farrell became a voracious reader, enjoyed an intellectual awakening which has been compared to Herman Melville's similar awakening in the 1840's, and discovered that he wanted to become a writer. In 1927, he dropped out of school and hitchhiked to New York City, determined to make it as a writer. He returned to Chicago in 1928, reentered the University, and began to write, placing critical articles and book reviews in campus publications and in Chicago and New York newspapers. By 1929, he had sold his first story, "Slob," to a little magazine, and his career was launched.

Farrell and Dorothy Patricia Butler were secretly married in 1931. (Farrell was to divorce Dorothy later, marry the actress Hortense Alden, whom he also divorced, and remarry Dorothy in 1955.) Also in 1931, Farrell and Dorothy sailed for France immediately after their wedding. In France, Farrell discovered that he had little in common with the American expatriates in Paris and that he had important admirers and supporters such as Samuel Putnam, James Henle, and Ezra Pound. The publication of *Young Lonigan* and *Gas-House McGinty* by the Vanguard Press during this period established Farrell as a writer and confirmed his faith in his vision. He began to publish a great number of short stories, and by the time the Farrells returned to New York in 1932, his conceptions for the entire *Studs Lonigan* trilogy and the first Danny O'Neill novel, *A World I Never Made*, were outlined. He was prepared to become an integral part of American literary history. His contribution to American letters included stormy confrontations with Marxist critics and novelists and a staunch defense of the integrity of art and the artist as opposed to the socialist demands that fiction, and all art, serve the party.

The 1930's were the end of the personal experiences that Farrell used as the material for his major fiction; the *Studs Lonigan* trilogy, the Danny O'Neill series, and the Bernard Carr trilogy are all drawn from the same well; in describing that world, Farrell was determined to "shake the sack of reality" until it was empty. In 1957, he completed his original life plan for twenty-five volumes which were to be "panels of one work" and had begun a second lifework, called *A Universe of Time*, of which he had published seven volumes, (*The Silence of History*, *What Time Collects*, *When Time Was Born*, *Lonely for the Future*, *A Brand New Life*, *Judith*, and *Invisible Swords*). Farrell died in New York on August 22, 1979, before this lifework was complete.

Analysis

An understanding of James T. Farrell and his work on the basis of one novel or even as many as three individual novels is impossible. Farrell's vision was panoramic, however limited his subject matter may have been, and cannot be understood except in terms of large, homogenous blocks of fiction. He did not write exclusively of Chicago or of Irish-Catholics, but it was on this home "turf" that he most effectively showed the effects of indifference and disintegration on an independent, stubborn, often ignorant, urban subculture. He was at once appalled by and attracted to the spectacle of an entire people being strangled by the city and by their own incapacity to understand their position, and he was most successful when he embodied the society in the life and times of an archetypal individual.

Farrell's three major, complete works total eleven novels; each of the eleven creates another panel in the same essential experience. While the *Studs Lonigan* trilogy, the five novels of the O'Neill-O'Flaherty series, and the Bernard Carr trilogy have different protagonists, they all share a common impulse and reflect Farrell's almost fanatical obsession with time, society, and the individual's response to both. Studs Lonigan, Danny O'Neill, and Bernard Carr are extensions or facets of Farrell's primal character, pitted against a hostile urban environment.

The *Studs Lonigan* trilogy, arguably Farrell's best and certainly his best-known work, is the story of the development and deterioration not only of the title character, but also of the Depression-era, Irish-Catholic Chicago society from which he springs. In the fifteen-year span of *Young Lonigan*, *The Young Manhood of Studs Lonigan*, and *Judgment Day*, Farrell shows the total physical, moral, and spiritual degeneration of Studs Lonigan.

Studs is doomed from the moment he appears just prior to his graduation from grammar school. His announcement that he is "kissin' the old dump goodbye tonight" is ominously portentous. He drops out of high school, goes to work for his father, a painting contractor, and becomes a member and leading light of the gang that hangs out in Charlie Bathcellar's poolroom. The association with the gang is Studs's life—everything else is "plain crap." Through a swirl of "alky," "gang-shags," "craps," and "can-houses," Studs fights to prove himself to be the "real stuff" and ultimately finds himself a frail, thirty-year-old shell of the vigorous youth he once was. The physical ruin of Studs Lonigan, however, is only the result of larger deficiencies.

Studs is a sensitive, moral being who consciously rejects his innate morality as a weakness. He blindly accepts his Catholic upbringing without believing it. There is never a present for Studs Lonigan—there is only a future and a past. In *Young Lonigan*, the future is the vision of Studs standing triumphantly astride the fireplug at 58th and Prairie proclaiming his ascendancy to the brotherhood of the gang. The past is his rejection of juvenile harassment he suffered as the result of his one moment of ecstasy with Lucy Scanlan in Washington Park. He proclaims himself the "real stuff" and flees from human emotions and the potentialities of those experiences with Lucy.

Studs consistently refuses to allow his emotional sensitivity to mature. The spiritual stagnation which results confines him to dreams of future aggrandizement or of past glories. The future dies, and Studs is left with memories of his degeneracy. His affair with Catherin Banahan awakens new sensibilities in Studs, but he is unable to nurture them, and they die stillborn. His heart attack at the beach, his dehumanizing odyssey through the business offices of Chicago looking for work, his shockingly prurient behavior at the burlesque show, and his final delirium are simply the payment of accounts receivable.

As Studs dies, his world is dying with him. His father's bank has collapsed, the mortgage on his building is due, Studs's fiancée is pregnant, and the gang has generally dispersed. These are not the causes of Studs's failures, however; they are reflections of that failure. Studs is the product and the producer. He is not a blind victim of his environment. He makes conscious choices—all bad. He is bankrupt of all the impulses which could save him. He batters and abuses his body, he strangles his emotions, and he clings to the stultifying spirituality of a provincial Catholicism. As Lucy Scanlan dances through his final delirium and his family abuses his pregnant fiancée, Studs Lonigan's dying body becomes the prevailing metaphor for the empty world it created, abused, and in which it suffered.

Danny O'Neill, of the O'Neill-O'Flaherty series, is the product of the same environment, but recognizes that he controls his destiny in spite of overbearing environmental pressures and, by the end of the series, seems on the verge of success. If he succeeds, he does so because he refuses to fall into the trap that Studs builds for himself, and he thus escapes into the larger world that Studs never knows. In the five novels of the series, *A World I Never Made*, *No Star Is Lost*, *Father and Son*, *My Days of Anger*, and *The Face of Time*, Danny not only escapes the strictures of environment but also sloughs off the psychological and spiritual bondage of family and religion and creates his own freedom.

Farrell's most clearly autobiographical work, the O'Neill-O'Flaherty series, portrays Danny's growth from 1909 to 1927—from a five-year-old child to a man breaking from college and Chicago. Unlike the *Studs Lonigan* trilogy, the O'Neill series portrays a larger world and more diverse elements of that world. While the Lonigan trilogy is dependent on the portrayal of its central character for action and meaning, Danny's story introduces more people and more settings and thus illustrates one of the major differences between Studs and Danny. Whereas Studs demands his personal image as a loner but actually depends heavily upon his gang as a prop, Danny begins as an atypical child— the result of his life in a bifurcated family much like Farrell's own—and learns the hypocrisy of the accepted values around him, which prompts him to formulate and depend on his own personal values.

The process by which Danny reaches this understanding is the contorted progress of a hybrid adolescence. Born to Jim and Lizz O'Neill, a poor, working-class Irish couple, he is taken to live with his grandparents, of the lace-curtain Irish variety, because his parents cannot support their already large family. He is accepted wholeheartedly by his grandmother, and he accepts her as a surrogate mother, but he has problems rationalizing his relatively opulent life while his natural siblings are dying of typhoid and neglect. He also refuses, violently, to return to his natural parents, to the poverty in which they live, and to the oppressive Roman Catholicism that his mother practices.

The tensions forged between the two families are the stuff of which Danny is made, but he is also affected by the lonely, drunken promiscuity of his Aunt Peg, the decorous commercialism of his Uncle Al, and the maternal tyranny of his grandmother, Mary O'Flaherty. Danny grows up alone in a world which he has difficulty understanding and which seems to engulf but reject him summarily. He is not a clear member of either of the families that are the heart of the story, he is rejected by Studs Lonigan's gang because of his youth and because he is considered a neighborhood "goof," and he cannot find the love he desperately seeks. Only late in the series does he understand Jim, his father, and come to accept him for what he is, a hard-working, decent, poor, Irish laborer, who loves his children desperately enough to thrust them into a better world than he can make for them.

By the time Danny understands his father, Jim is dying, Danny has discovered the importance of books, he has had a hint of love through a college affair, and he has realized that education may be his key to a broader world. In the course of his intellectual discoveries at the University of Chicago, he has rejected religion and become something of a socialist. He has also discovered that New York City is the hub of the world, and, after quitting his job and dropping out of college in order to pursue his dream, seems on the verge of simultaneously discovering himself and success by migrating to New York.

The O'Neill series, then, comes full circle—from Chicago back to Chicago both actually and metaphorically; the distinction is unimportant. For all his effort to escape what he views as mindless and oppressive, Danny finally seems to understand that his basic character is still that of the poor, hard-working, Irishman that, with all its flaws, is at least pitiable rather than repugnant. As Danny prepares to escape from Chicago, he escapes with a fuller appreciation and self-preserving understanding of his heritage and an ability to progress beyond his previous angry rejections. He does not give up his new certainties, particularly in relation to the Church and religion (he has become an avowed atheist), but he displays a tolerance and acceptance of himself and his culture that are the foreground of promised success.

Bernard Carr seems to take up the story where Danny leaves it. The trilogy of *Bernard Clare* (Farrell changed the name to Carr in the second novel after a man named Bernard Clare brought libel proceedings against him), *The Road Between*, and *Yet Other Waters*, is Farrell's attempt to represent the lives of a generation of artists in New York during the Depression era and in the circles of politically radical activism.

The trilogy, for the first time in Farrell's fiction, is largely set in New York. Bernard's life in New York, however, is highlighted with periodic flashbacks of Chicago; thus Farrell's integrity of vision is preserved, and Bernard's lower-class origins are discovered. Bernard is the last member of Farrell's Irish-Catholic trinity—he is the embodiment of the whole man whom Studs could not become and Danny might well have become had his story been continued.

Bernard's New York is a world of struggling artists and Communists. In the early New York years, Bernard becomes involved with Communists and then rejects them as being little more than a gang—brutes who demand mindless adherence to the party propaganda, no matter what that adherence does to artistic integrity and vitality. He also recognizes that the dogma of Communism is akin to that of Roman Catholicism—that they are both crutches for weak men.

Bernard's marriage introduces him to family life, the wonder of birth and rearing a child, and is the spur in his attempt to recover and understand his family and his heritage. During all of these events, Bernard is achieving a limited success from his writing, and by the end of the trilogy he has brought all the pieces together and has found himself, his vocation, and an enlightened ability to see life for what it is and make the most of it.

The Bernard Carr trilogy does not carry the impact of the Lonigan saga, but the diffusion necessary to present Bernard's story precludes the grim concentration necessary to portray Studs and his life. The world expands for Danny and Bernard, and that expansion naturally admits the people, ideas, ideals, and philosophies which are the components of an expanded sensibility.

The dovetailing of the experiences and environments of his three major characters is what ultimately makes Farrell's work live. Their stories make up a tapestry which mirrors the world from which they sprang and rivals it for true pathos and vitality.

Clarence O. Johnson

Other major works

SHORT FICTION: *Calico Shoes and Other Stories*, 1934; *Guillotine Party and Other Stories*, 1935; *Can All This Grandeur Perish? and Other Stories*, 1937; *The Short Stories of James T. Farrell*, 1937; *$1,000 a Week and Other Stories*, 1942; *Fifteen Selected Stories*, 1943; *To Whom It May Concern and Other Stories*, 1944; *When Boyhood Dreams Come True*, 1946; *The Life Adventurous and Other Stories*, 1947; *A Hell of a Good Time*, 1948; *An American Dream Girl*, 1950; *French Girls Are Vicious and Other Stories*, 1955; *An Omnibus of Short Stories*, 1956; *A Dangerous Woman and Other Stories*, 1957; *Saturday Night and Other Stories*, 1958; *Side Street and Other Stories*, 1961; *Sound of a City*, 1962; *Childhood Is Not Forever*, 1969; *Judith and Other Stories*, 1973; *Olive and Mary Anne*, 1977.

PLAYS: *The Mowbray Family*, 1940 (with Hortense Alden Farrell); *A Lesson in History*, 1944.

POETRY: *The Collected Poems of James T. Farrell*, 1965.

NONFICTION: *A Note on Literary Criticism*, 1936; *The League of Frightened Philistines and Other Papers*, 1945; *The Fate of Writing in America*, 1946; *Literature and Morality*, 1947; *The Name Is Fogarty: Private Papers on Public Matters*, 1950; *Reflections at Fifty and Other Essays*, 1954; *My Baseball Diary*, 1957; *It Has Come To Pass*, 1958; *On Irish Themes*, 1982.

Bibliography

Bogardus, Ralph F., and Fred Hobson. *Literature at the Barricades: The American Writer in the 1930s*. Tuscaloosa: University of Alabama Press, 1982. This three-part work on American writers of the 1930's includes two essays on Farrell. The essay by Donald Pizer shows how *Studs Lonigan* incorporates the attitudes toward character and experience associated with the 1930's. A reprint of a 1939 essay by Farrell himself provides a convincing description of the 1930's writer.

Branch, Edgar M. *James T. Farrell*. New York: Twayne, 1971. After tracing Farrell's "plebeian origin," Branch discusses major works including the *Studs Lonigan* trilogy, the *O'Neill-O'Flaherty* series, and the Bernard Carr trilogy. Essays on other works including the cycle of *A Universe of Time* follow. A chronology, notes, a selected bibliography, and an index complete the work.

Butler, Robert James. "Parks, Parties, and Pragmatism: Time and Setting in James T. Farrell's Major Novels." *Essays in Literature* 10 (Fall, 1983): 241-254. Argues that Farrell's trilogies depict a "uniform and coherent fictive world." Identifies time and setting as two important ways in which Farrell unified his major novels: time as a "temporal equilibrium," parks as high points, and parties as nadirs. Refutes the "amorphous monster" reputation of the novels.

Pizer, Donald. *Twentieth-Century American Literary Naturalism: An Inter-

pretation. Carbondale: Southern Illinois University Press, 1982. This fine book opens with an essay on Farrell's *Studs Lonigan* trilogy, declared to be "the archetypal thirties novel." Cites techniques such as indirect discourse and stream of consciousness as contributing to the novels' success. Notes, bibliography, and an index are included.

Wald, Alan M. *James T. Farrell: The Revolutionary Socialist Years*. New York: New York University Press, 1978. After a chronology and an introduction, follows Farrell's literary career from its emergence in the 1920's through the mid-1970's. Presents Farrell as a prolific and successful revolutionary novelist. Contains a section of illustrations in addition to notes, a bibliography, and an index.

J. G. FARRELL

Born: Liverpool, England; January 23, 1935
Died: Bantry Bay, Ireland; August 12, 1979

Principal long fiction

A Man from Elsewhere, 1963; *The Lung*, 1965; *A Girl in the Head*, 1967; *Troubles*, 1970; *The Siege of Krishnapur*, 1973; *The Singapore Grip*, 1978; *The Hill Station: An Unfinished Novel*, 1981.

Other literary forms

J. G. Farrell's perceptive and entertaining account of his 1971 visit to India, posthumously titled "Indian Diary," is appended to *The Hill Station*, an unfinished novel published after Farrell's death. He is known primarily for his novels.

Achievements

In the main, Farrell's early efforts—*A Man From Elsewhere*, *The Lung*, and *A Girl in the Head*—fail to display the power, intricacy, and inventiveness that characterize his fourth book, *Troubles*, and the rest of his completed fiction. Set in rural Ireland between the years 1919 and 1921—a period of bloody civil war—*Troubles* earned for Farrell the Geoffrey Faber Memorial Prize and signaled his interest in producing carefully documented and closely detailed historical fiction. Farrell's fifth novel, *The Siege of Krishnapur*, takes place in India in 1857, when protest of the British presence in that country suddenly grew violent and widespread. *The Siege of Krishnapur* was awarded Britain's prestigious Booker Prize and convinced many critics that Farrell, not yet forty, was fast on his way to a spectacular career. Set during the 1930's in what was then British Malaya, Farrell's sixth book, *The Singapore Grip*, was generally less enthusiastically received than *The Siege of Krishnapur*. Tragically, Farrell's life was cut short when, in 1979, he drowned in waters off Ireland's southern coast. Still, on the basis of his later work, Farrell must be considered a highly original talent and can be ranked among the finest historical novelists of his generation.

Biography

Though born in Liverpool, James Gordon Farrell had strong family ties to Ireland, which he visited regularly as a child and adolescent. After completing his public-school training at Rossall, in Lancashire, Farrell worked briefly as a fire fighter along a NATO defense line in the Canadian Arctic. In 1956, during his first term at Oxford, Farrell contracted polio, which left his chest and shoulder muscles permanently weakened. After taking his degree in 1960, Farrell taught in France and traveled to both Africa and the United

States but spent the bulk of the following decade living in London, where he formed friendships with many fellow writers and developed the highly disciplined work habits that enabled him to produce a series of increasingly lengthy and complex novels.

In the early 1970's, in the wake of the considerable critical and financial success of *The Siege of Krishnapur*, Farrell traveled throughout Asia, where he conducted extensive research for *The Singapore Grip*. In April, 1979, Farrell moved into an old farmhouse on the Sheep's Head Peninsula of Bantry Bay in Ireland's County Cork. Here, while fishing close to his house, Farrell fell from a rock and—according to witnesses—was quickly swept out to sea.

Analysis

J. G. Farrell was essentially a realist, whose most accomplished works draw upon extensive historical research and are both carefully crafted and meticulously detailed. In each of his historical novels, Farrell focuses on various outposts of British colonialism that are under attack and, by implication, in decline. Often, these works bluntly ridicule the cultural codes and biases that made the British empire possible; indeed, they tend to ridicule narrow-mindedness of any kind and suggest, implicitly, that no religion or ideology can convincingly account for the existence of man. Much of Farrell's fiction focuses on the seeming randomness of human life, on the least attractive attributes—particularly on the brutality and the greed—that are part of human nature. Its tone, moreover, is frequently sardonic and aloof—but by no means misanthropic. Instead, as Farrell's friend and fellow novelist Margaret Drabble has observed, "Farrell combined a sense of the pointless absurdity of man with a real and increasing compassion for characters caught up in decay and confusion."

Farrell's first book, *A Man from Elsewhere*, is set in France and focuses largely on a journalist named Sayer, who seeks to expose a former Communist alleged to have dealt too intimately with the Nazis during World War II. In his second novel, *The Lung*, Farrell's principal figure is Martin Sands, a young man confined to an iron lung and in love with Marigold, his stepdaughter and nurse. *A Girl in the Head*, Farrell's third novel, depicts the romantic difficulties of Boris Slattery, a Polish count living in the English resort town of Maidenhair. These novels are certainly not without merit: They contain some fine tragicomic moments, and they feature characters such as Slattery who, in some scenes, come convincingly alive. Farrell's early novels, however, are ponderously paced; they tend to reveal the self-consciousness of a beginning writer who is trying hard to be original and clever but failing to conceal his debt to other authors. In *A Girl in the Head*, for example, it is not difficult to detect the presence of Iris Murdoch, whose celebrated first novel, *Under the Net* (1954), similarly and more successfully combines a disaffected young hero and a supporting cast of eccentrics with serious philosophical themes and, throughout, a charmingly whimsical tone.

The far better *Troubles* is set in the Irish coastal town of Kilnalough and covers the years between 1919 and 1921—a period in which militant Irish nationalists were beginning to employ violence more frequently as a means of freeing their country from British control. The book's central figure, Major Brendan Archer, is a veteran of World War I who comes to Kilnalough's huge Majestic Hotel, where his fiancée, Angela Spenser, resides with her father, Edward, a jingoistic, increasingly unbalanced man who owns the hotel and must work hard to keep it running. The Majestic is—like the British Empire itself—an aging, sprawling structure in a slow but certain state of decay. The Majestic is dusty, gloomy, and filled with odd, elderly guests; in its lobby, one hears the constant ticking of an ancient pendulum clock.

Unlike the protagonists in Farrell's earlier novels, the Major is neither intellectually nor artistically inclined. He is, in fact, a rather bland figure who enjoys reading serialized adventure stories and who has without reflection absorbed most of the prejudices of his nation and his class. Though not a religious man, he regards with particular prejudice and suspicion the tenets and practices of Roman Catholicism. He also takes for granted the notion that Irish Catholics are still simply too irrational and unruly to be trusted with the task of governing themselves. The Irish Republican movement, he unthinkingly assumes, "was merely an excuse for trouble-makers moved more by self-interest than patriotism." Still, Archer is so well-rounded that he cannot be dismissed as a mere bigot and an utterly unsympathetic character. The Major, Farrell makes clear, has been keenly disappointed both in life and in love; as a veteran of trench warfare, he has been on close terms with hunger, fear, and death. Early in *Troubles*, the Major—fresh from war—is shown attending a tea party and causing some discomfort among his fellow guests because of the intensity with which he studies their heads, arms, and legs: "He was thinking: 'How firm and solid they look, but how easily they come away from the body!' And the tea in his cup tasted like bile."

Troubles does contain many comical characterizations and scenes, including a failed sexual interlude which features a pair of fumbling young men and a set of naïvely flirtatious twins and which balances with a stunning deftness the pathetic and the ribald. Most of *Troubles*, however, focuses bluntly on the brevity of life, on the sobering reality of change and decay. The Majestic, for example, literally crumbles bit by bit throughout the novel: It becomes overrun with weeds and rats and—at the novel's close—burns to the ground after being shelled by Irish rebels. Images of skulls and skeletons abound; the silent, mysterious Angela quietly suffers from leukemia and suddenly dies. Meanwhile, not far from the hotel—and, Farrell keeps noting, throughout much of the rest of the world—men continue to slaughter men with brutal gusto. Indeed, by alluding frequently to newspaper accounts of the world's never-ending wars and riots, Farrell not only lends an element of authenticity to his work but also underlines the point that, unfortunately, bloody "troubles" fester wherever men gather; because human beings are territorial and animalistic, they will invariably fail in their attempts to construct a serene and civilized world.

The theme of human brutality is even stronger in *The Siege of Krishnapur*. This work shows the effect of the Sepoy Rebellion of 1857 on some of the English men and women who were then helping rule India in the name of the British-owned East India Company. The novel's principal character, Mr. Hopkins—"the Collector," or chief administrator, at the British outpost at Krishnapur—is a sober, optimistic man who early in the work proclaims his belief that the perfection of mankind will surely be achieved through "Faith, Science, Respectability, Geology, Mechanical Invention, Ventilation, and the Rotation of Crops." Another principal character is George Fleury, a young, melancholic, rather overly sensitive Englishman who is fond of Romantic poetry and no longer certain of the tenets of orthodox Christianity. Fleury—a recognizable Victorian "type," like all the principal characters in *The Siege of Krishnapur*—must then suffer the fulsome proselytism of the Reverend Mr. Hampton, a boorish Anglican clergyman identified throughout the novel as "the Padre."

The early chapters of *The Siege of Krishnapur* portray well-settled British in a world of poetry readings and cricket matches, of elegant meals served by obsequious native servants who, in some cases, must bear with a smile the insulting nicknames that their masters have bestowed upon them. As the remainder of the novel reveals, however, that cozy, very Victorian world is utterly shattered when mutinous Indian soldiers—or "sepoys"—begin an attack on the British compound at Krishnapur that drags on for months and that results not only in countless Indian and English casualties but also—for the English—severe shortages of ammunition and food. Eventually, the survivors find themselves filthy, disease-ridden, rag-clad, and so famished that they willingly devour their horses and prey upon bugs. In the end, they are saved by British reinforcements, but by then, as one of their rescuers observes, they look less like gentlemen and gentlewomen than the pathetic untouchables whom they once automatically scorned.

The Siege of Krishnapur is full of extremely well-paced, graphically described battle scenes. Like *Troubles*, and like Alfred, Lord Tennyson's *In Memoriam* (1850)—perhaps the greatest and most representative poetical work of the Victorian era—*The Siege of Krishnapur* also frequently addresses the most basic of philosophical questions: Does God exist? What is the true nature of man? Is there a divine plan that can account for the ruthlessness of nature and the universality of human pain? In several amusingly constructed scenes, Farrell portrays the Padre arguing at length in favor of the existence of a Supreme Intelligence and offering as proof dozens of such ingeniously practical phenomena as the eel's eyes, the boar's tusks, and the bee's proboscis. Like *Troubles*, however, *The Siege of Krishnapur* focuses principally on a world of nature that is, in Tennyson's famous phrase, "red in tooth and claw"; it conveys strongly the impression that the god or gods who designed the world now seem quite uninterested in its day-to-day operation. It suggests that the margin between civilization and barbarism is frighteningly narrow, and that, moreover, the codes and biases by which men and women order their lives are not only arbitrary but also often bizarre. Indeed, at the conclusion of *The Siege of Krishnapur*, the Collector, older and more cynical and back in England, asserts bluntly that "culture is a sham. It's a cosmetic painted on life by rich people to conceal its ugliness."

The Singapore Grip, Farrell's final completed novel, is a particularly lengthy work that, some critics have suggested, occasionally bogs down under the weight of too many characters and documentary details. Set entirely in Singapore, *The Singapore Grip* focuses principally on the years just prior to December, 1941, when all of British Malaya was rapidly overrun by the Japanese. Its principal characters are related to a large British rubber company run by Walter Blackett, who takes for granted the invincibility of British power in the Pacific and so—like other Britons portrayed in the book—fails to comprehend the seriousness of the Japanese threat. Blackett, who is described as having hairy "bristles" that run up and down his back, is probably too much the stereotypical big-business tycoon: He is aggressive, envious, calculating. Far more appealing is Brendan Archer, who is retired from the military but who, as in *Troubles*, retains the title "the Major." Some of the most poignant scenes in *The Singapore Grip* show Archer "fixed in his habits, apparently suspended in his celibacy like a chicken in aspic" and living out his remaining days in modest quarters in Singapore, surrounded by old, bleary-eyed dogs he no longer likes, but—out of a continuing sense of obligation—continues to board.

The Singapore Grip makes clear that Farrell likes the Major not only for his pluck and respect for duty but also for the many quirks he has accumulated over the years. Indeed, as in *Troubles* and *The Siege of Krishnapur*, Farrell in *The Singapore Grip* reveals a continuing fondness for harmless eccentrics—and underdogs—of all sorts. By focusing extensively on Blackett and his operations, however, Farrell also makes obvious his continuing disdain for cultural chauvinism and the blundering pursuit of profit at any cost. By filling *The Singapore Grip* with vivid, unsettling scenes of war, Farrell also once again indicates his belief that the study of human history is essentially the study of brutality and folly, that only by self-deception can one insist on the universality of human goodness and the inevitability of a saner, more harmonious world.

Brian Murray

Bibliography

Binns, Ronald. *J. G. Farrell*. London: Methuen, 1986. This first full-length study of Farrell traces the development of the idiosyncratic Anglo-Irish novelist's career. Emphasizes Farrell's three novels of the British Empire (*Troubles, The Siege of Krishnapur, and the Singapore Grip*), considered one of the most ambitious literary projects of a British novelist in recent years.

_____. "The Novelist as Historian." *Critical Quarterly* 21 (Summer, 1979): 70-72. Discusses *The Singapore Grip*, the last of Farrell's novels about the decline of the British Empire, as well as his other two novels on the subject. Binns considers this "trilogy" a "remarkable achievement." An appreciative piece, clear and insightful.

Blamires, Harry, ed. *A Guide to Twentieth Century Literature in English*. New York: Methuen, 1983. The entry on Farrell describes his early novels as dabbling in "the bizarre and the grotesque." Praises *The Siege of Krishnapur* and *The Singapore Grip*, however, for their "meticulously researched" emphasis on the rhythms of everyday life against political upheaval.

Bradbury, Malcolm, and David Palmer, eds. *The Contemporary English Novel*. London: Edward Arnold, 1979. Discusses Farrell in the context of historical fiction, but emphasizes his concern with human individual lives. Calls *The Singapore Grip* a "very fine novel." An informative and valuable piece of criticism on Farrell.

Halio, Jay L., ed. *British Novelists Since 1960*. Vol. 14 in *Dictionary of Literary Biography*. Detroit: Gale Research, 1983. In addition to biographical information, contains critical commentary on Farrell's work and discussions of Farrell's early novels, which are largely dismissed. Gives more attention to the three Empire novels, in particular *The Singapore Grip*, which is not only an accurate account of the British collapse in Malaysia, but also a statement about normality in social and political collapse.

Wilson, A. N. "An Unfinished Life." *Spectator* (April 15, 1981): 20-21. In the main an admiring piece, in which Wilson acknowledges Farrell as an "outstanding novelist of his generation," but Wilson also sees flaws in Farrell's three Empire novels. Gives particular praise to Farrell's "Indian Diary" of 1971, which he says embodies the "satire and wistful good-naturedness of J. G. Farrell's best writing."

WILLIAM FAULKNER

Born: New Albany, Mississippi; September 25, 1897
Died: Oxford, Mississippi; July 6, 1962

Principal long fiction

Soldiers' Pay, 1926; *Mosquitoes*, 1927; *Sartoris*, 1929; *The Sound and the Fury*, 1929; *As I Lay Dying*, 1930; *Sanctuary*, 1931; *Light in August*, 1932; *Pylon*, 1935; *Absalom, Absalom!*, 1936; *The Unvanquished*, 1938; *The Wild Palms*, 1939; *The Hamlet*, 1940; *Go Down, Moses*, 1942; *Intruder in the Dust*, 1948; *Requiem for a Nun*, 1951; *A Fable*, 1954; *The Town*, 1957; *The Mansion*, 1959; *The Reivers*, 1962; *Flags in the Dust*, 1973 (original version of *Sartoris*).

Other literary forms

William Faulkner published two volumes of poetry and several volumes of short stories. Most of his best stories appear in *Knight's Gambit* (1949), *Collected Short Stories of William Faulkner* (1950), and the posthumous *Uncollected Stories of William Faulkner* (1979). His early journalistic and prose pieces have been collected and published as have his interviews and a number of his letters. Recent years have seen the publication of several interesting minor works, including a fairy tale, *The Wishing Tree* (1964), and a romantic fable, *Mayday* (1976). New Faulkner material is steadily seeing print, much of it in the annual Faulkner number of *Mississippi Quarterly*. Scholars are making public more information on Faulkner's screenwriting in Hollywood, where he collaborated on such major successes as *To Have and to Have Not* (1944) and *The Big Sleep* (1946). Several of his works have been adapted for television and film; notably successful were film adaptations of *Intruder in the Dust* and *The Reivers*.

Achievements

When Faulkner received the Nobel Prize in Literature in 1949, he completed an emergence from comparative obscurity that had begun three years before. In 1946, when nearly all of Faulkner's books were out of print, Malcolm Cowley published *The Portable Faulkner*. Cowley's introduction and arrangement made clear "the scope and force and interdependence" of Faulkner's oeuvre up to 1945.

Even in 1945, Faulkner was reasonably well known to the readers of popular magazines, his stories having appeared with F. Scott Fitzgerald's and Ernest Hemingway's in publications such as the *Saturday Evening Post*, *Scribner's Magazine*, *Harper's Magazine*, and *The American Mercury*. Despite his success in selling short stories and as a Hollywood screenwriter, Faulkner's novels, except for the notorious *Sanctuary*, had little commercial success until after Cowley's volume and the Nobel Prize. The notoriety of *Sanctuary*, widely reviewed as salacious, brought him to the attention of the film industry; it was his screenwriting which sustained him financially during the years of comparative neglect when he produced the series of powerful novels which constitute one of the major achievements of world fiction. His first novel to appear after Cowley's volume, *Intruder in the Dust*, was filmed in Faulkner's hometown, Oxford, Mississippi, and released in 1949.

After the Nobel Prize, honors came steadily. He was made a member of the French Legion of Honor, received two National Book Awards for *A Fable* and *Collected Short Stories of William Faulkner*, and received two Pulitzer Prizes for *A Fable* and *The Reivers*. He traveled around the world for the United States State Department in 1954. During 1957, he was writer-in-residence at the University of Virginia. Recognition and financial security, while gratifying, neither diminished nor increased his output. He continued writing until his death.

Faulkner has achieved the status of a world author. His works have been painstakingly translated into many languages. Perhaps more critical books and articles have been written about him in recent times than about any other writer with the exception of William Shakespeare. Critics and scholars from all over the world have contributed to the commentary. Faulkner's achievement has been compared favorably with that of Henry James, Honoré de Balzac, and Charles Dickens; many critics regard him as the preeminent novelist of the twentieth century.

Biography

William Cuthbert Faulkner was born in New Albany, Mississippi, on September 25, 1897. His ancestors had emigrated from Scotland in the eighteenth century. Faulkner's great-grandfather, William Clark Falkner, was a colonel in the Civil War, wrote *The White Rose of Memphis* (1881) a popular romance, and provided a model for the patriarch of the Sartoris clan in *The Unvanquished*. Faulkner's family was very important to him. The oldest son of Maud and Murry Falkner, William Cuthbert later became the head of the family. He took this responsibility seriously, struggling most of his life to care for those whom, whether by blood or moral commitment, he considered members of his family. In 1924, he changed the spelling of his family name to Faulkner.

Faulkner discovered his storytelling gifts as a child, but his writing career did not really begin until after his brief training for the Royal Air Force in Canada, shortly before the World War I Armistice in 1918. He attended the University of Mississippi for one year, worked at odd jobs, and published a volume of poetry, *The Marble Faun* (1924). He took writing more seriously, with encouragement from Sherwood Anderson, while living in New Orleans in 1925. The influence of Anderson, especially his "The Book of the Grotesque" from *Winesburg, Ohio* (1919), seems to pervade Faulkner's work. During his apprenticeship he spent several months traveling in Europe. Out of his experiences in New Orleans and Europe came a number of journalistic sketches, most dealing with New Orleans, and a group of short stories set in Europe.

The early novels are interesting, but Faulkner began to show his powers as a prose stylist and as a creator of psychologically deep and interesting characters in *Sartoris*, which he had originally written as *Flags in the Dust*. Beginning with *The Sound and the Fury* and up through *Go Down, Moses*, Faulkner wrote the major novels and stories of his Yoknapatawpha series. Of the ten novels he published in these thirteen years, five are generally considered to be masterpieces: *The Sound and the Fury*, *As I Lay Dying*, *Light in August*, *Absalom, Absalom!*, and *Go Down, Moses*. At least two others, *Sanctuary* and *The Hamlet*, are widely studied and admired. The entire series of novels set in the mythical Yoknapatawpha County, Faulkner's "little postage stamp of native soil," is sometimes considered as a great work in its own right, especially when all of the Snopes trilogy (*The Hamlet*, *The Town*, *The Mansion*) is included with the above named masterpieces. Stories from his two collections of the 1929 to 1942 period regularly appear in anthologies; "Old Man" and "The Bear," which are parts of *The Wild Palms* and *Go Down, Moses*, are perhaps his best-known novellas.

Faulkner's personal life was difficult and has provoked much critical interest in tracing relationships between his life and his work. The family-arranged and unhappy marriage to Estelle Oldham in 1929 ended in divorce. Both Faulkner and his wife were subject to alcoholism; he carried on a virtually continuous struggle against debt, resentful and unhappy over the necessity of working in Hollywood in order to keep his family solvent. Though Faulkner was a fiercely loyal husband and father, he was also capable of philandering.

Faulkner preferred to work at home in Mississippi. Still, he traveled a great deal, first for education, later to deal with publishers and to work in Hollywood, and finally as a goodwill ambassador for the United States. He met and formed acquaintances with several important contemporaries, notably Nathanael West, Sherwood Anderson, and Howard Hawkes.

Faulkner died of a heart attack on July 6, 1962, after entering the hospital to deal with one of his periodic drinking bouts.

Analysis

When William Faulkner accepted the Nobel Prize in December, 1950, he made a speech which has become a justly famous statement of his perception of the modern world and of his particular place in it. In the address, Faulkner speaks of the modern tragedy of the spirit, the threat of instant physical annihilation, which seems to overshadow "the problems of the human heart in conflict with itself." He argues that all fiction should be universal and spiritually significant, "a pillar" to help mankind "endure and prevail." Literature can be such a pillar if it deals with "the old verities and truths of the heart, the universal truths lacking which any story is ephemeral and doomed—love and honor and pity and pride and compassion and sacrifice."

All of Faulkner's greatest works were written before the first explosion of the atomic bomb, yet in all of them there is an awareness of the threat of annihilation of which the bomb may be only a symptom: a kind of spiritual annihilation. Lewis P. Simpson argues that Faulkner, like the greatest of his contemporaries, dramatizes in most of his novels some version of the central problem of modern man in the West, how to respond to the recognition that man has no certain knowledge of a stable transcendent power which assures the meaning of human history. Panthea Broughton makes this view of Faulkner more concrete: in Faulkner's world, characters struggle to find or make meaning, exposing themselves in various ways to the danger of spiritual self-destruction, of losing their own souls in the effort to find a way of living in a universe which does not provide meaning.

The immense quantity of critical commentary on Faulkner provides several satisfying ways of viewing and ordering the central concerns of his novels. While the way into Faulkner suggested by Simpson and Broughton is only one of many, it seems particularly helpful to the reader who wishes to begin thinking about Faulkner's whole literary career. Broughton demonstrates that the Faulknerian universe is characterized essentially by motion. Human beings need meaning; they need to impose patterns on the motion of life. Out of this need spring human capacities for mature moral freedom as well as for tragic destructiveness. Closely related to this pattern that Broughton sees in Faulkner's stories are his tireless experimentation with form and his characteristic style.

In his essay in *William Faulkner: Three Decades of Criticism* (1960), Conrad Aiken notes the similarities between Faulkner's characteristic style and that of Henry James. The comparison is apt in some ways, for both in their greatest novels seem especially concerned with capturing in the sentence the complexity of experience and of reflection on experience. As Walter Slatoff, in the same volume, and others have shown, Faulkner seems especially drawn to paradox and oxymorons, kinds of verbal juxtaposition particularly suited to conveying the tension between the motion of life and the human need for pattern. Once one notices these aspects of Faulkner's style in a complex novel such as *Absalom, Absalom!*, in which Faulkner's characteristic style finds its ideal subject, much that initially seems obscure becomes clearer.

Faulkner seems to have found most instructive the "loose" forms characteristic of the Victorian panoramic novel as it was developed, for example, by his favorite author, Charles Dickens. Faulkner's novels generally contain juxtapositions of attitudes, narrative lines, voices, modes of representation, and emotional tones. His more radical and probably less successful experiments in this vein include the alternation of chapters from two quite separate stories in *The Wild Palms* and the alternation of fictionalized historical narrative with dramatic acts in *Requiem for a Nun*, a kind of sequel to *Sanctuary*. *Light in August* is his most successful work in this direction. Somewhat less radical and more successful experiments involved the incorporation of previously published stories into "collections" and sustained narratives in such a way as to produce the unity of a novel. Parts of *The Unvanquished*, the Snopes Trilogy, and *A Fable* have led dual lives as stories and as parts of novels. *Go Down, Moses* is probably the most successful experiment in this direction. Faulkner was particularly interested in the juxtaposition of voices. His career as a novelist blossomed when he juxtaposed the voices and, therefore, the points of view of several characters in *The Sound and the Fury* and *As I Lay Dying*. In *Absalom, Absalom!*, the juxtaposition of voices also becomes the placing together of narrative lines, comparable episodes, points of view, modes of narration, attitudes, and emotional tones. This one novel brings together everything of which Faulkner was capable, demonstrating a technical virtuosity which in some ways is the fruit of the entire tradition of the novel. *Absalom, Absalom!* also realizes to some extent a special potential of Faulkner's interest in juxtaposition, the conception of his Yoknapatawpha novels as a saga that displays a unity of its own.

The technique of juxtaposition, like Faulkner's characteristic style, reflects his concern with the problems of living meaningfully within the apparently meaningless flow of time. Because life will not stand still or even move consistently according to patterns of meaning, it becomes necessary to use multiple points of view to avoid the complete falsification of his subject. Juxtaposition, the multileveled and open-ended sentence, and the oxymoronic style heighten the reader's awareness of the fluidity of the "reality" which the text attempts to portray. Faulkner's most tragic characters are those who feel driven to impose so rigid a pattern upon their lives and on the lives of others as to invite destruction from the overwhelming forces of motion and change. These characters experience the heart in conflict with itself as the simultaneous need for living motion and meaningful pattern.

The Sound and the Fury is divided into four parts to which an appendix was added later. Faulkner repeated in interviews that the novel began as a short story which grew into the first section. He then found that the point of view he had chosen did not tell the whole story even though it closely approximated the flow of events before a nonjudgmental consciousness. Gradually, Faulkner found himself retelling the story four and, finally, five times. The effect of reading these juxtapositions may be described as similar to that of putting together a puzzle, the whole of which cannot be seen until the last piece is in place. Like several of Faulkner's novels, notably *Absalom, Absalom!*, *The Sound and the Fury* is not fully comprehendable upon a single reading. The first reading provides a general idea of the whole with subsequent readings allowing one to fill in the details and to see ever more deeply into this moving narrative.

The novel concerns the tragic dissolution of the Compson family. The decline dates decisively from the marriage of Candace (Caddy), the only daughter of Jason Compson III and Caroline Bascomb. Caddy's marriage is not the sole cause of the family's decline; rather, it becomes symbolic of a complex of internal and external forces that come to bear on this Mississippi family early in the twentieth century. Caddy becomes pregnant by Dalton Ames, a romantic, heroic, and apparently devoted outsider. Her mother then seeks out Sydney Herbert Head as a respectable husband for her. After the marriage, Herbert finds he has been gulled and divorces Caddy. These events deprive all the Compson men of their center of meaning. Quentin, the oldest son who loves Caddy not as a sister but as a woman, commits suicide. Jason III drinks himself to death, having lost the children upon whom his meaning depended. Jason IV seeks petty and impotent revenge on Caddy's daughter, also named Quentin, because he believes the failure of Caddy's marriage has deprived him of a chance to get ahead. Benjy, the severely retarded youngest brother, suffers the absence of the only real mother he ever had. Control of the family passes to Jason IV, and the family ceases finally to be a place where love is sustained, becoming instead, despite the efforts of the heroic and loving black servant, Dilsey, a battleground of petty scheming, hatred, and revenge.

This general picture emerges from the internal monologues of Benjy, Quentin (male), and Jason IV, from a third-person narrative centering on Dilsey and Jason IV, and from the final appendix. Each of the four main sections is set on a particular day: Benjy's section on his thirty-third birthday, Easter Saturday, 1928; Jason's on Good Friday; and Dilsey's (the fourth section) on Easter Sunday of the same year. Quentin's section is on the day of his suicide, June 2, 1910. As the portrait of the family's decline emerges from these juxtaposed sections, their tragic significance becomes apparent.

Benjamin Compson's internal monologue consists of images, most of which are memories. At the center of his memory and of his stunted life is Caddy, whose "hair was like fire" and who "smelled like trees." Every experience of Benjy, which evokes these images or which resembles any experience he has had with Caddy, automatically triggers his memory. As a result, Benjy lives in a blending together of past and present in which memory and present experience are virtually indistinguishable. The spring of his suffering is that for him the experience of losing Caddy is continuous; the memory of her presence is perfect and the experience of her absence is constant.

This section proceeds by a series of juxtapositions which place Benjy's present, deprived condition starkly beside the richness of his memory. Though the pattern is difficult to see at first, repeated readings show that Faulkner works in this section primarily by pairing certain events: the funeral of Damuddy (Caroline's mother and Benjy's grandmother) and Caddy's wedding with all the attendant suggestions of meaning; Caddy with her boyfriends on the porch swing and Quentin (female) with her boyfriends; Benjy at the gate waiting for Caddy to come home from school one Christmas and Benjy waiting at the gate on the day Jason IV leaves it open. This last event, part of Jason's spitefulness against Caddy, leads to Benjy's castration after he grabs a school girl to ask about Caddy, though he cannot speak. Among the many pairings, the most pathetic appears at the end of the section. Benjy remembers his family long ago:

> Her hair was like fire, and little points of fire were in her eyes, and I went and Father lifted me into the chair too, and Caddy held me. She smelled like trees.
>   *She smelled like trees. In the corner it was dark, but I could see the window. I squatted there, holding the slipper. I couldn't see it, but my hands saw it.*

The contrast between the firelight of the library, with its mirror and the loving people and the now barren and dark library with only one of Caddy's wedding slippers reveals much of the mood, the meaning, and the effectiveness of technique in Benjy's section.

Quentin's section also proceeds largely by the juxtaposition of memory and present experience. Quentin's memories are triggered by present events and he is sometimes unable to distinguish between memory and external reality. He commits suicide at the end of his first year at Harvard. As he carries out his plans to drown himself, he is caught up in various events which repeat aspects of his loss of Caddy, the last being a picnic with some college classmates during which he remembers his abortive attempt to be the brother who avenges a wronged sister. This memory is simultaneous with and is repeated in a fight with Gerald Bland, the kind of womanizer Quentin wishes Dalton Ames was.

Perhaps the major irony of Quentin's suicide is that the state of being which he desires is in many ways like the state in which his youngest brother suffers. Quentin wishes to be free of time, to end all motion. He gives as a motive his fear that grief over the loss of Caddy will attenuate, for when grief is gone, his sister will have become meaningless and his life utterly empty. Yet his grief, of which every event reminds him, is unbearable. He wishes to keep Caddy as she was and to deny the repetitions which force him to remember her loss. Though he sees such a transcendent state in many images in his world, he can only *imagine* himself in that state, for it is impossible in life. Suicide seems his only alternative. In death, he can at least shirk everything, he can at least escape the *again* which to him is a sadder word than *was*.

Quentin's relationship with Caddy is highly problematic. One fairly simple way of understanding how his sister becomes so important to him that he must commit suicide when she marries is to observe Quentin's and Caddy's relationship with their parents: Jason III does not love Caroline. She believes that he has come to resent the fact that her family is socially inferior. In reality, she is a selfish and stupid woman who is completely inadequate as a mother and wife. Her husband is unable to deal with her. His growing unhappiness and cynicism magnify her weakness. The result is that these children have no real parents, and the responsibility falls on the gifted Caddy. Despite her extraordinary capacity, Caddy is a girl. When she grows into a woman, she must inevitably betray the brothers who depend on her love. Even when she is with them, she cannot love them as an adult would; she cannot teach them to give. Her gifts lead her to another who is also capable of passion, Dalton Ames. This affair exaggerates the meaning of the betrayal by heightening the inadequacy of the family, including Quentin, to meet Caddy's needs. Caddy's sense of her parents' failure is captured in her memory of a picture in a book which made her think of her parents as keeping her from the light. Quentin needs Caddy not only as a mother, a source of pure affection, but also as a center of meaning. She embodies all the forms and traditions to which Quentin clings to escape the despair his father teaches him. Losing her, he loses his life.

Jason's section of the novel is much easier to read, for his interior life is more or less in the present. He neither desires nor even conceives of any transcendent reality; he desires power above all things, even money, though he is well aware that money is, in his world, the superior means to power. He delights in the power to be cruel, to make others fear him, yet he is remarkably impotent. His impotence stems from his inability to imagine in others any motives different from his own. In these respects, his character, as well as the mode in which it is presented, recall the jealous monk in Robert Browning's "Soliloquy of the Spanish Cloister." Jason's interior monologue is the only one of the three which has all the marks of being spoken. It is as if Jason were two people, one constantly explaining and justifying himself to the other.

Jason tells primarily about his troubles bringing up Caddy's daughter, Quentin. The girl has been left in the care of the family while the divorced Caddy makes her way in the world. Quentin becomes the central instrument of Jason's revenge against Caddy for the failure of her marriage and the disappointment of his hope. Jason is so fixed on his need to exercise cruel power that he is unable to restrain himself sufficiently to keep the situation stable. He drives Quentin out of the family, losing the monthly checks from Caddy which he has been appropriating, the hoard he has collected in part from this theft, and the one person on whom he can effectively take his revenge.

"I've seed de first en de last," says Dilsey. She refers to the beginning and the end of the doom of the Compson family, to Caddy's wedding and Quentin's elopement. Each of these events suggests more meanings than can be detailed here, but the importance of Dilsey's section is that she sees a pattern of human meaning in the events which threaten an end to meaning for so many. Her part in these events has been a heroic struggle to bind the family together with her love and care, a doomed but not a meaningless struggle, for she can still see pattern, order, meaning in all of it. The events of Easter morning, in which Dilsey figures, suggest that at least one source of that power to mean and to love is her community at the black church service, a community which, in the contemplation of the Christian symbols of transcendence, attains an experience of communion which partakes of the eternal even though it is temporary. Dilsey's church is a model of the family and her experience there is not unlike Benjy's experience in Caddy's arms on Father's lap before the library fire. The Compson family has somehow lost this experience. As the appendix suggests, all of the Compsons, except perhaps for Benjy, are damned, for they have all, in various ways, come to see themselves as "dolls stuffed with sawdust."

The Sound and the Fury is in part an exploration of the loss of the Christian world view. Temple and Popeye in *Sanctuary* respond in ways similar to Jason's. Addie in *As I Lay Dying* and Horace Benbow in *Sanctuary* play parts similar to Quentin's: Benbow attempts to prove the truth of the traditional view he has inherited from his family and class, the view that "God is a gentleman" and that Providence takes an active hand in human affairs. He is disastrously and blindly wrong and apparently suffers the loss of his faith. Addie Bundren's attempt to impose order on her world seems even more disastrous because Faulkner centers attention on the suffering she causes her family.

Addie Bundren wants and fails to find a kind of transcendent communion with some other being. When she realizes the inevitable impermanence of such communion, she plans revenge against the people who have failed her, especially her husband, Anse. She makes him promise that he will bury her with her relations in Jefferson. This simple promise is a subtle revenge because it binds Anse with words for which he has too much respect and it becomes a terrible vengeance when Anse comes to fulfill that promise. Addie believes that a word is "a shape to fill a lack." By this she means that the communion she feels when she is pregnant with her firstborn is an essential experience for which words are unnecessary and inadequate. Not only are words inadequate to this experience, but they are also symbols of separation from this experience. At one point Addie reflects, ". . . I would think how words go straight up in a thin line, quick and harmless, and how terribly doing goes along the earth." By making Anse "promise his word," Addie forces him to attempt a union of saying and doing, an attempt which sends her entire family on a grotesque and tortured journey along the earth.

Addie imposes a verbal pattern on her family in revenge because pregnancy and passion are temporary. Each pregnancy ends in separation. Her one love affair is with the Reverend Whitfield, whom she describes as "the dark land talking the voiceless speech." When this affair ends in the birth of Jewel, her third son, her despair is complete. The promise she extracts from Anse elicits a catastrophic juggernaut, for she dies at the beginning of a storm which floods the area, making the wagon journey to Jefferson next to impossible.

The novel is presented in a series of monologues similar in depth and intensity to Quentin's in *The Sound and the Fury*. As the narrative emerges from these monologues so do the internal relationships of the family. The reader becomes intensely aware of the feelings and the needs of each family member. Anse is driven not only by his promise but also by the desire to regain the dignity he believes he loses by having no teeth. A sedentary man, he has needed this prod to set him in motion. He eventually returns, not only with teeth and dignity, but with several other new possessions as well, including a new wife. Cash, the oldest son, is the family's repository of technical skill. Almost without questioning, he solves the material problems of the journey. In crossing the flooded river, he breaks his leg, yet he finishes the journey in incredible pain. Darl, the son Addie has rejected, is the most sensitive of her children. He is seemingly capable of a kind of communion that might have fulfilled her, for he seems able to read minds and to know of events he does not see. He opposes the journey at every significant point, understanding that it is Addie's revenge and that it threatens to tear apart the family. Anse finally commits Darl to a mental hospital in order to escape financial responsibility for a barn which Darl ignites in an attempt to burn Addie and end the journey.

Jewel, product of the Whitfield affair, though he is barely articulate, comes to seem the living embodiment of Addie's wordless will to revenge. He saves the coffin from the flood when the wagon overturns in the river and from the fire in the barn. He sacrifices his much prized pony in trade to replace the mules lost in the river crossing. Dewey Dell, the only daughter, is desperate to reach Jefferson where she believes she can get an abortion. She shares Darl's sensitivity and hates it because it makes her feel naked and vulnerable. She violently assists in the capture of Darl for she is glad to be rid of the kind of communion Addie so deeply desired. Vardaman, the youngest son, suffers loss. Drawn along on the journey by promises of bananas and a view of a toy train, he registers all the family's pain: the loss of a mother, the dislocations of the journey, the humiliation as Addie begins to smell, the shiftless poverty of Anse, the sufferings of the brothers, the vulnerability of Dewey Dell and, finally, the loss of Darl. Because the unity of the family is his identity, he suffers a kind of dismemberment.

This brief glimpse hardly conveys the richness and power of this novel. Still it should make clear that part of the novel's meaning derives from Addie's attempt to impose a rigid pattern upon a significant part of her family's life and the extreme suffering her success brings about. While Addie responds to her perception of the impermanence of transcendent communion by forcing a pattern on her family, Temple Drake responds to society's failure to give her life some order by yielding fully to impulse.

Popeye and Temple in *Sanctuary* are lost children, victims of their moment in history, in that they are without souls. Their culture has failed to give them reasons for doing one thing rather than another. They do not have the natural acquisitiveness of Jason IV and the Snopeses, nor do they have a motive such as revenge to give direction to their lives. Popeye wears the mask of a gangster, though the mask slips occasionally. It is the role itself which gives Popeye substance and makes him appear somewhat like a normal human being. He also has a vague desire which he expresses in his abduction of Temple Drake. He desires to join the human community, to live a meaningful life. Just as he imitates gangsters in order to take possession of some identity, he also imitates the acts of men who reveal themselves to be under the power of a strong motive. He tries to desire and to possess Temple Drake because other men desire her. He fails even to desire her and apparently, as a result of this failure, he gives up his life. He has money, says the narrator, but there is nothing to buy with it.

Temple is perhaps the most fully developed example in early Faulkner of a character who simply flows, who seeks no meanings at all, but merely acts out her impulses. When she is abducted by Popeye, she is freed of the social restraints which have never been made important to her. Nothing in her experience has taught her to internalize social restraints as communal values. She is virtually without values, virtually unable to make moral choices; freed of external restraint, she seeks pointless and ultimately unsatisfying gratification of whatever impulses come to the fore. She becomes capable of killing in order to achieve sexual satisfaction. In her final act in the novel, she pointlessly condemns an innocent man to death as she begins to adopt Popeye's failed strategy, assuming a role to pass the time.

In Temple one sees that the utter surrender to motion is no solution to the search for meaning in Faulkner's world. Neither surrender nor rigid resistance to the flow of events will suffice. Faulkner's heroes, like Dilsey, are generally those who are able to find a balance between what Broughton calls the abstract and the actual, a balance which seems to answer the cry of the heart and to make loving possible. Faulkner's novels suggest that the modern tragedy of a lack of soul, of spiritual annihilation, results from some decisive break in the process by which one generation teaches the next how to love.

The central juxtaposition in *Light in August* is between Lena Grove and Joe Christmas. Lena Grove, scandalously pregnant and deserted by Lucas Burch, alias Joe Brown, walks the dirt roads of Alabama, Mississippi, and finally Tennessee in tranquil search of a husband. She is a center of peace and faith and fertility, though all around her may be waste and catastrophe. She is like the peaceful center of Herman Melville's Grand Armada on the outer circles of which the stricken whales murder one another. Byron Bunch, who loves her at first sight even though she is nine months pregnant, tells his friend, the Reverend Gail Hightower, that Lena seems to have two persons inside her, one who *knows* that Lucas Burch is a scoundrel who will never marry her, and another who *believes* that God will see to it that her family will be together when the child is born. God somehow keeps these two persons within Lena from meeting and comparing notes.

When the child is born, there is a family indeed, for Lena seems to attract all the help she needs. Byron is camped outside her door. Gail is convenient to deliver the child. Joe Christmas' grandparents are present, reliving a past moment which promises them some small redemption. Even Lucas Burch makes a brief appearance before leaving the field open to Byron. Lena's tranquil faith, her trust in the world and its people, and her submission to her natural being make her into a kind of Faulknerian heroine. She is capable of finding meaning for herself in the flow of life, and this meaning attracts and vitalizes others. The images used to describe her are filled with the paradoxes of stillness in motion. This attitude gives her power, not a power that she often consciously uses, but still a real power to draw recluses such as Byron and Gail out of spiritual death and into the flow of living.

While Lena moves peacefully through the book, seeking a husband and bearing a child, Joe Christmas careens through the last days of his life, the culmination of more than thirty years of bigoted education. Joe's life story is the center of a novel which is composed largely of condensed biographies. Of the major characters, only Byron and Lena have relatively obscure pasts. Gail, Joanna Burden, and Joe are presented as the end products of three generations in their respective families. Even Percy Grimm, a relatively minor character, receives a fairly full biography. Each of these lives contrasts starkly with the life of Lena and, eventually, with Lena and Byron's relationship. Gail, Joanna, Joe, and Percy are, in the words of Gail, "lost children among the cold and terrible stars." They are the children of a generation that saw its world crumble and that adopted fanatic versions of Calvinism mixed with an inherited racism in order to resist the flow of history with its threat of meaninglessness. They are products of the failure of love. While Lena, miraculously immunized against lovelessness, is capable of accepting the world and its lawful motion as her home, most of the other major characters resist and reject the world, living in alienation.

Joe's life reveals the sources and meanings of resistance and alienation. The story of his life comes in several blocks. After learning that Joe has murdered Joanna, the reader is plunged deeply into the suffering consciousness of the murderer during the twenty-four hours preceding the crime. Joe is seen as a driven man: he seems to be under the control of the voices which speak inside him, and he is unaware of the loving, caressing voices in his natural environment. This glimpse into his consciousness reveals ambivalent attitudes toward his racial background, a hatred of the feminine, a sense that Joanna has somehow betrayed him by praying over him, and a sense of being an abandoned child who wants to be able to say with conviction, "God loves me, too." The middle section of the novel separates into strands the inner voices that drive Joe to murder which, in his culture, is a suicide.

In an orphanage at age five, Joe accidentally provokes the dietician into speeding his placement with a family. His adoptive father, the Calvinist fanatic Simon McEachern, teaches Joe the skills of resistance to nature. He learns to cultivate a rocklike will and an indomitable body. He learns to relate to people impersonally. He grows up not only without love but also in resistance to love: to be a man is not to love. McEachern derives his hatred of the world from his Calvinist theology, while Joe learns to resist the world in defense of his selfhood. Joe is not a Calvinist; he resists the content of McEachern's teachings by mastering its forms. Inside Joe, the voice perhaps first awakened by a girl who mothered him in the orphanage continues to speak. Joe continues to desire to love, to belong, and ultimately to be free of the voices which drive him.

Of the forms Joe's rebellion against his culture takes, those involving sex and race seem most significant. Joe's desire to love and be loved is revealed and betrayed in his adolescent affair with Bobbie Allen, a local prostitute, a relationship which paradoxically combines intimacy with impersonality. In his adult life, his rebellion often takes the form of asserting his presumed black blood. In doing so, he provokes a ritual reaction which becomes the dominant pattern in his life, the pattern that is worked out in full when he kills Joanna and suffers the consequences.

His affair with Joanna, his life and death in Jefferson, Mississippi, replay the patterns of his life in their full significance, bringing him again to the moment of rebellious protest in which he faces an authority figure in the fullness of his identity and strikes out in murderous self-defense. Joe and Joanna are virtually doubles. They proceed through tortured and perverse phases of sexual relations until they reach a kind of purged state of near normality, a point at which both seem seriously able to contemplate marriage, children, a normal human life. When Joanna enters menopause, however, she is unable simply to accept the natural flow of time. Her "sins" with Joe lose their meaning if they do not lead to marriage, motherhood, and "normal" feminine fulfillment. She reverts to her inherited Calvinism and racism, changing from Joe's double to McEachern's double. Betrayed herself, she betrays Joe, trying to form into a piece of her sick world. Joe responds to this change as he responded to McEachern's attempt to cast him into Hell.

During Joe's flight from the pursuing Jefferson authorities, he comes closer than ever before to the peace, freedom, and love he has desired. In his disorientation and physical suffering, for the first time in his life, he feels unity with the natural world. He partakes of "the peace and unhaste and quiet" that are characteristic of Lena's experience because for the first time he is really free of the compulsive voices of his culture, free to feel at home in his world.

Contrasted to this experience is the story of Joe's first five years as told to

Gail by Joe's fanatical grandfather, Doc Hines, and by his grandmother. Doc Hines sees himself as the agent of a Calvinist deity avenging the lust after worldly pleasure symbolized by femininity and the inferior race ("God's abomination upon the earth"). Against these disembodied "voices of the land," Joe emerges as somewhat ambiguously victorious in his death. Joe's death is inevitable. Even though he seems to have found freedom from the internal compulsions which have driven him to self-destruction, he cannot escape the consequences of his actions in the world. He can only accept. The way in which Joe accepts the consequences of his acts suggests for him a kind of heroic status.

Joe's death is inevitable because he has set in motion a deeply embedded social ritual, a fateful machine which cannot stop until it has completed its movement. The community's heritage of Calvinism and racism has produced that ritual machine. In a desperate need to assert control over the flow of history, the culture has embraced the Calvinist denial of all things in this world which might turn one's attention from God.

Among other elements which contribute to the view of Joe as a hero is his effect on Gail. Gail has been on the edges of all the events of these days in Jefferson. He has had several opportunities to mitigate suffering, but he has, on the whole, failed to act. He is afraid to leave his sanctuary in order to help those he could really help. Joe appears at Gail's door, moments before dying, like an avenging god to strike Gail down in a kind of judgment, even as Gail confesses part of his sin. Finally, Joe dies in Gail's house, another sacrifice to the very kinds of rituals and legalisms which Gail has used to buy what he calls peace, the right to sit unmolested in his house dreaming of his grandfather's absurdly heroic death. Gail learns from this experience. He goes on to make, to himself at least, a full confession of his sins. He faces the fact that what he has wanted, a sterile stasis in a dead past moment, was selfish, that this desire has led him to bring about his wife's death, to welcome being ostracized by the town, ultimately to serve his small need at the cost of abandoning those he promised to serve when he became a minister.

The juxtaposition of lives tragically ruined by a heritage of racism and fanatical Calvinism with Lena's life creates an unforgettable and moving work. One of the easily overlooked effects of the whole is the impression it gives of a community whose heart is basically good, which responds, albeit sometimes grudgingly, with sympathy to those in need and with kindness to those in trouble. Lena brings out this side of the community. On the lunatic fringe of the community are those who express the deep compulsions which thrive in the insecurity of modern life. Joe is brought up to evoke this underside of the community which it would like to forget. They are not to forget. The images of horror pass from one generation to the next. The uncertainties of life, especially in a world which seems to have lost the easy comfort of religious consensus, continue to produce personalities such as those of Doc Hines and

Percy Grimm, who cannot deal with or bear an indifferent universe. Their rigid imposition of abstraction upon the flow of life forces them ever backward to the legalism of their secret rituals. Society is tragically in the grip of the past despite its great desire to be finally free of these compulsions.

Absalom, Absalom! juxtaposes differing accounts of the same events. In *The Sound and the Fury*, Faulkner thought of himself as trying to tell the whole story and finding that he had to multiply points of view in order to do so. In *Absalom, Absalom!*, as Gary Stonum argues, "the labor of representation is . . . made a part of the text." The story is only partly known; it is a collection of facts, not all of which are certain, which seem to those who know them profoundly and stubbornly meaningful. The various characters who try their formulae for bringing those facts together into a meaningful whole are the historians of the novel. Faulkner has written a novel about writing novels, about giving meaning to the flow of events. *Absalom, Absalom!* dramatizes so effectively the processes and obstacles to creating a satisfying structure for events and offers such an ideal wedding of structure, content, technique, and style, that many critics regard it as Faulkner's greatest achievement. With *The Sound and the Fury* this novel shares characters from the Compson family and a degree of difficulty which may require multiple readings.

The central concern of the narrative is the life of Thomas Sutpen and his family. Sutpen has appeared out of nowhere to build a vast plantation near Jefferson, Mississippi, in the early nineteenth century. Apparently without much wealth, he nevertheless puts together the greatest establishment in the area, marries Ellen Coldfield, a highly respectable though not a wealthy woman, and fathers two children by her. When Sutpen's son, Henry, goes to college, he meets and befriends Charles Bon. Charles and Sutpen's daughter, Judith, fall in love and plan to marry. For no apparent reason Sutpen forbids the marriage and Henry leaves his home with Charles. During the Civil War, Ellen dies. Near the end of the war, Henry and Charles appear one day at the plantation, Sutpen's Hundred, and Henry kills Charles. After the war, Sutpen becomes engaged to Rosa Coldfield, Ellen's much younger sister, but that engagement is suddenly broken off. A few years later, Sutpen fathers a daughter with Milly Jones, the teenage daughter of his handyman, Wash Jones. When Sutpen refuses to marry Milly, Jones kills him. Then Sutpen's daughter, Judith, and his slave daughter, Clytie, live together and, somewhat mysteriously, care for the descendants of Charles Bon by his "marriage" to an octoroon.

Though not all the known facts, these constitute the outline of the story as it is generally known in Jefferson. The major mysteries stand out in this outline. Why did Sutpen forbid the marriage? Why did Henry side with Charles and then kill him? Why did Rosa agree to marry Sutpen and then refuse? Why did Sutpen get a squatter's daughter pregnant and abandon her, bringing about his own death? Why did Judith take responsibility for Bon's family? These are the questions to which Rosa Coldfield, Jason Compson III and his father General Compson, and Quentin Compson and his Harvard roommate Shreve McCannon address themselves. A rough chapter outline will give an idea of the novel's structure while suggesting how the various accounts interrelate.

The setting in Chapters 1 through 5 is day one of time present, early September, 1909, before Quentin Compson leaves for Harvard. (1) Afternoon, Rosa tells Quentin about Sutpen in summary, painting him as a destructive demon of heroic proportions. (2) Evening, Jason III repeats his father's description of how Sutpen built his empire of one hundred square miles and married Ellen. (3) Evening, Jason III gives the public version, with some inside information, of Rosa's relationship with Sutpen, centering on her involvement with the Judith-Charles relationship and her eventual refusal to marry Sutpen. (4) Evening, Jason attempts to explain why Sutpen forbade the marriage and why Henry killed Charles. He argues that Bon intended to keep his octoroon mistress/wife when he married Judith. Jason offers this explanation as plausible but does not really feel it is adequate. (5) Later that same evening, Rosa tries to explain why she refused to marry Sutpen, giving her own version of how she came to be on the scene and describing the death of Bon and its effect on the family. She ends this part by revealing her belief that the Sutpen mansion contains some secret which she intends to discover that evening.

Chapters 6 through 9 are set in day two of time present, January of 1910; Quentin and Shreve spend an evening in their Harvard dormitory working out their version of the Sutpen story. (6) Quentin has a letter saying that Rosa is dead. The story is recapitulated with more details coming to light and completing the story of the Sutpen line in outline. (7) Quentin and Shreve concentrate on Sutpen's youth, retelling his story up to his death in the light of information Quentin received directly from his grandfather. (8) The boys work out the story of Charles Bon's and Henry Sutpen's relationship, constructing a new answer to the question of why Henry killed Charles. Not only was Charles Henry's half brother, but he also had black blood. (9) Quentin recalls his trip with Rosa to Sutpen's house on the September night and his brief meeting with the returned Henry. They finish Jason III's letter and contemplate the whole story.

The novel's climax comes in Chapter 8 when Shreve and Quentin construct their explanation. They "discover" through intense imaginative identification with Henry and Charles a meaning latent in the facts they have gathered. Their discovery implies that Sutpen prevented the marriage and alienated Henry by revealing that Charles and Henry were half brothers. The substance of their discovery is that the first wife whom Sutpen put aside, the mother of Charles, was a mulatto. Sutpen reserves this information as his trump card in case Henry comes to accept an incestuous marriage. Only this revelation could have brought Henry to kill Charles rather than allow him to marry Judith. The means by which the boys arrive at this conclusion reveal much about the meanings of the novel. Not least among these meanings is the revelation of a sickness at the "prime foundation" of the South, the sickness of a planter society that prevents one from loving one's own children.

There is no way for the boys to *prove* this solution. Their discovery is above all an imaginative act, yet it has the ring of truth. No one who is alive, except Henry, knows what passed between Sutpen and Henry in the conversations which broke off the marriage and led to the murder, and Henry tells no one before his own death. The truth is utterly hidden in the past. The materials which make up this truth are fragmentary, scattered in distance, time, and memory. Only through the most laborious process do Quentin and Shreve gather the facts together from the narratives of their elders and a few documents. Informants such as Rosa and Jason III are Sherwood Anderson grotesques; they have chosen simple truths to which they make all their experiences conform. Rosa's portrait of Sutpen grows almost entirely out of Sutpen's proposal that they produce a child before they marry. Jason III's portrait of Charles Bon is an idealized self-portrait. Even eyewitnesses such as General Compson and Rosa have faulty memories and biased points of view. In the world of this novel, the truth is difficult to know because the facts on which it is based are hard to assemble.

When the facts are assembled, they are even harder to explain. Jason realizes that he has "just the words, the symbols, the shapes themselves." Quentin and Shreve are able to explain, not because they find the facts, but because they use their imaginations so effectively as to find themselves in the tent with Sutpen and Henry in 1865 and in the camp when Charles tells Henry that even though they are brothers, Charles is the "nigger" who is going to marry his sister. Quentin and Shreve have felt Thomas Sutpen's motives, his reasons for opposing the marriage. They have felt Charles's reasons for insisting on the marriage and Henry's victimization as an instrument of his father. They have entered into the heart's blood, the central symbolic image of the novel, the symbol of the old verities which touch the heart and to which the heart holds as truth. Sutpen's honor is embodied in the design that will crumble if he accepts Charles as his son or allows the marriage. The love of sons for fathers and of brothers for sisters becomes a tragic trap within that design. If love, honor, courage, compassion, and pride are found at the center of these inexplicable events, then the boys have discovered "what must be true." As Cass Edmonds says to young Ike McCaslin in *Go Down, Moses*, "what the heart holds to becomes truth, as far as we know truth."

In order for Quentin and Shreve to complete this act of imagination, they must come to understand Sutpen more fully than anyone does. The key to understanding Sutpen comes in Chapter 6, when Quentin repeats what he has learned from General Compson, to whom Sutpen has confided much of his life story. Sutpen is the child of an independent mountain family who have fallen on hard times and have become tenant farmers. His ambition springs into being on the day he discovers that in the eyes of the plantation owner's black doorman he is insignificant "white trash." On that day, he determines to right this injustice by becoming a planter himself. He dreams that when he is a planter, he will not turn away the boy messenger from his door. He becomes a planter in Haiti, then abandons everything to go to Mississippi. Having built a second plantation there and begun his dynasty again, he sacrifices his son to cancel the son by the first marriage. As General Compson sees it, Sutpen's great weakness is his innocence. Sutpen is never able to understand how history betrays him. By becoming a planter, Sutpen inevitably adopts the material forms which determine the morality of the planter, and he lacks the imagination to circumvent those forms. In fact, Sutpen is so literal, rigid, and puritanical in his adoption of the design that he becomes a grotesque of a planter. The messenger boy who comes to his door is his own mulatto son, yet Sutpen can only turn away without even so much as an "I know you are my son though I cannot say so publicly."

Sutpen's innocence and the rigidity of his design account for many of the mysteries of his life. As General Compson says, Sutpen seems to think of morality, even of life as a whole, as like a cake; if one includes the ingredients and follows the recipe, only cake can result. Supten's design is so abstract that he is utterly blind to the feelings of others. He fails to anticipate Rosa's probable reaction to the second proposal. He never thinks of how Wash will react to his treatment of Milly. He never expects that Charles Bon will be the boy at his door. When Sutpen tells his story to General Compson, he is seeking the missing ingredient which has twice prevented him from completing his design and his revenge. Sutpen's boyhood experience has cut him off from the truth of the heart. He has, instead, rigidly grasped a single truth and has made it into a falsehood in his Olympian effort to make the world conform to the shape of that truth.

Because of Sutpen's failure, many children stand before doors which they cannot pass. Only an act of sympathetic imagination can get one past the symbolic doors of this novel, but most of the children are so victimized that they are incapable of imaginative sympathy. Even Quentin would not be able to pass his door, the subjects of incest and a sister's honor, without help from Shreve. Without Quentin's passion and knowledge, Shreve would never have seen the door. Their brotherhood is a key "ingredient" in their imaginative power.

Many significant elements of this complex novel must remain untouched in any brief analysis. One other aspect of the novel, however, is of particular interest: in *Absalom, Absalom!*, Faulkner suggests the possibility of seeing the Yoknapatawpha novels as a saga, a unified group of works from which another level of significance emerges. He chooses to end *Absalom, Absalom!* with a map of Yoknapatawpha County. This map locates the events of all the preceding Yoknapatawpha novels and some that were not yet written, though the relevant Snopes stories had appeared in magazines. Reintroducing the Compson family also suggests that Faulkner was thinking of a unity among his novels in addition to the unity of the individual works. It seems especially significant that Shreve McCannon, an outsider, neither a Compson nor a Southerner nor an American, makes the final imaginative leap which inspirits Sutpen's story with the heart's truth. In this way, that truth flows out of its narrow regional circumstances to a world which shares in the same heart's blood. With *Absalom, Absalom!*, Faulkner may have seen more clearly than before how his novels could be pillars to help men "endure and prevail" by reminding them of those "old verities," the central motives which bind mankind and the Yoknapatawpha novels together.

In *Go Down, Moses*, Faulkner juxtaposes two sides of the McCaslin family. This contrast comes to center on Lucas Beauchamp, a black descendant, and Isaac McCaslin, a white descendant of L. Q. C. McCaslin, the founder of the McCaslin plantation. Although the novel divides roughly in two and has the appearance of a collection of stories, it is unified as an explanation of the opening phrases which summarize Isaac's life. Ike is distinguished by his refusals to inherit the family plantation or to own any other land because he belives the earth belongs to no man, by his love for the woods, and by the fact that though he has married and is uncle to half a county, he has no children.

"Was," "The Fire and the Hearth," and "Pantaloon in Black" deal with the Black McCaslins primarily. Taken together, these stories dramatize the suffering of basically good people, black and white, as they struggle to make and preserve their marriages and to honor their blood ties despite the barrier of racism.

"Was" tells how Tomey's Turl and Tennie arrange their marriage. Turl and Tennie are slaves on neighboring plantations in the days when such farms were half a day's travel apart. In this comic interlude, remembered from before Isaac's birth, Hubert Beauchamp, owner of the neighboring farm, tries without success to marry his sister, Sophonsiba, to Isaac's father, Buck McCaslin. It becomes clear that the plot to land Buck is a cooperative effort among the slave couple and the Beauchamps. The plot ends with a poker game in which Buck's twin, Uncle Buddy, nearly outmaneuvers Hubert. That Turl is the dealer convinces Hubert to settle for the advantages he has gained rather than chance losing everything to Buddy. Buck escapes for the time being, though he eventually marries Sophonsiba, and Tennie and Turl achieve their marriage. These two marriages generate the two main characters of the novel, Lucas and Isaac. From this point of view the tale is funny and almost heartwarming, but it has a tragic undertones, for Turl, it turns out, is half brother to the twins. Even though Buck and Buddy are reluctant and enlightened slaveholders, they try to prevent their brother's marriage and must be tricked into permitting it.

This barrier of race which separates brothers and threatens marriages is the center of "The Fire and the Hearth." This long story dramatizes two pairs of conflicts. In the present, Lucas Beauchamp discovers a gold piece buried on Roth Edmonds's plantation. The Edmonds have become inheritors of the McCaslin land because of Isaac's repudiation. In his mad search for "the rest of the gold," Lucas becomes a barrier to the marriage of his daughter with George Wilkins, a rival moonshiner. To get rid of Wilkins, Lucas uses the very racist rituals which have caused himself suffering before; he appeals to Roth's paternalistic dominance of his black tenants. This conflict reminds Lucas of his previous conflict with Roth's father, Zack. In this conflict, Zack and Lucas, who were reared as brothers, nearly kill each other because as a black, Lucas cannot simply believe Zack's statement that though he had the opportunity, he has not cuckolded Lucas.

The second present conflict arises when Lucas's wife, Mollie, decides she will divorce her husband because he has become obsessed with finding gold. When she announces this plan to Roth, Roth remembers his own relationship with Lucas and Mollie, especially that Mollie is the only mother he ever had. His childhood memories prominently include the shame he felt when racism came between him and his "family." Now, when he most needs to, he cannot talk with them heart to heart.

In "Was" and "The Fire and the Hearth," the wall of racism divides lovers, brothers, parents, and children. All suffer because what their hearts yearn for is forbidden by their racial experience. Familial love is blocked by racism. "Pantaloon in Black" completes this picture of tragic suffering with a powerful image of what whites, especially, lose by inherited racist attitudes. Rider and Mannie, tenants on Edmonds land, love passionately. When Mannie dies, Rider cannot contain his grief. He moves magnificently toward a complex love-death. Juxtaposed to this image is the marriage of a local deputy which contains no passion or compassion. They live separate lives, the wife's emotional needs satisfied by card parties and motion pictures. Their brief discussion of Rider's grief and death reveals that because they are unable to see their black brothers as human, they are cut off from imagining their feelings, cut off from sympathy and, finally, cut off from their own humanity.

"The Old People," "The Bear," and "Delta Autumn" tell the story of Isaac: of his education for life in the woods, his consecration to that life, the resulting decision to repudiate his inheritance and the consequence of that decision, including his wife's refusal to bear his children.

Isaac's education begins with Sam Fathers. Sam contains the blood of all three races which share in the founding of America. In him the wilderness ideal of brotherhood is made visible. On the other hand, Sam contains the sins of the Indians who sold land not theirs to sell and then went on to buy and sell men, including Sam, who was sold a slave by his own father. Sam is the last of the old people and, therefore, figures in both the origins and the victimizations of the races. When Isaac perceives these meanings in Sam's life, his spontaneous response is, "Let him go!" But this Mosaic wish is futile, Ike is told. There is no simple cage which can be unlocked to free Sam. From that moment, Ike tries to discover some effective way to set some of God's lowly people free.

By means of the stories of the old people, Sam teaches Ike that, in the wilderness, all men are guests on the earth. In the wilderness, the hunt becomes a ritual by which man, in taking the gifts of the land for his sustenance, participates in the immortal life processes of the cosmos. Here even the barriers between life and death lack significance. Opposed to this view is the civilization represented by the divided fields outside the wall of the big woods. In this outer world, land ownership divides the haves and the have-nots. Conceiving of the land as dead matter to be bought and sold leads to conceiving of people as beasts to be bought and sold. Ike comes to see this decline in humanity in his own family history as contained in the ledgers of the plantation commissary.

In Part IV of "The Bear," having seen the death of Old Ben, the bear which stands for the life of the old wilderness, Ike explains to his older cousin, Cass Edmonds, why he will not accept his inheritance, the McCaslin plantation. Though quite complex, his argument is mainly that if owning land leads directly to the exploitation of God's lowly people, then refusing to own the land may help end such exploitation. He takes on the responsibility of attempting to realize in civilization the values of the wilderness to which he has consecrated himself. Among the reasons for his choice is the pattern he sees in his family history.

His grandfather, L. Q. C. McCaslin, seems almost incomprehensible to Ike because he bought a beautiful slave, fathered a daughter on her and then fathered a son, Tomey's Turl, on that daughter. To Ike, these acts represent the worst of the violations which arise from arrogant proprietorship. In his grandfather's will, in the subsequent actions of Buck and Buddy in freeing slaves, in the Civil War and in his own education, Ike sees a pattern which leads him to think his family may have a responsibility to help bring an end to these wrongs. By repudiating his inheritance, he hopes humbly to participate in making love possible between the races.

Critics disagree about whether readers are to see Ike as heroic in the tradition of saintliness or as a fool who hides his light under a bushel by refusing to risk the exercise of power in behalf of his beliefs. While Ike does not fall into Sutpen's trap, largely because he conceives of his mission as acting for others rather than for himself, he may choose too passive a means to his end. It may be that Faulkner intended a suspension between these alternatives which would heighten the tragic dimensions of moral choice in the complex welter of human events. It is difficult to fault Ike's motives or his perception of the situation, but when assessing the effectivenes of his actions, one finds roughly equal evidence for and against his choice.

In "Delta Autumn," Ike is a respected teacher. He speaks with a wisdom and authority which command attention if not full understanding from his companions and which speak directly to Roth Edmonds' shame at his inability to marry the mulatto woman he loves and to claim his son by her. While Ike has nothing of which to be ashamed, his refusal of the land has helped to corrupt the weaker Roth. Ike has known that he would probably never see the amelioration for which he has worked and, more than any of his companions, Ike understands that something sacred, which he can call God, comes into being when people love one another. Nevertheless, he must suffer seeing the sins of his grandfather mirrored by Roth, for Roth's mistress is a descendant of Tomey's Turl. Ike must tell that woman to accept the repudiation of her love, and he must accept her accusation that he knows nothing about love. Whether Ike is a saint or a fool seems endlessly arguable. That he is to some extent aware of this dilemma may be part of the tragic significance of his life. He cannot learn whether his example will contribute to ending the shame of denied love which results from racism and which perpetuates it. He can only believe.

"Go Down, Moses," the last story, reemphasizes the desire for spiritual unity between the races and the apparently insuperable barriers which remain. Mollie Beauchamp's grandson, Samuel Worsham Beauchamp, is executed for murdering a Chicago policeman. Sam is the opposite of Sam Fathers. He is the youngest son, sold into the slavery of making money too fast which devalues human life. Mollie's grieving chant that Roth Edmonds sold her Benjamin into Egypt echoes the imagined grief of the biblical Jacob whom his sons claim will die if they return from Egypt without their youngest brother. Roth has taken responsibility for this young relation and then has repudiated him. Mollie's accusation is fundamentally correct. The sympathetic but paternalistic white community of Jefferson cannot see this connection and so, despite its good heart, it cannot cross the barrier between races and truly enter into Mollie's grief. Gavin Stevens, the community's representative, feels driven from the scene of grief before the fire on the hearth by the intense passion of Mollie's grieving. Ike's sacrifice has changed nothing yet, but whether it was a bad choice remains hard to decide.

Faulkner wrote many fine novels which cannot be discussed here. The Snopes Trilogy and *The Reivers* are often included among his masterpieces, in part because they reveal especially well Faulkner's great but sometimes overlooked comic gifts.

Faulkner's reputation has grown steadily since his Nobel Prize. Some critics are ready to argue that he is America's greatest novelist. They base their claim on the power of his novels to fascinate a generation of readers, to provoke serious and profound discussion about the modern human condition while engaging significant emotions, and to give the pleasures of all great storytelling, the pleasures of seeing, knowing, believing in and caring for characters like oneself at crucial moments in their lives. The quantity and quality of his work as well as the worthy unity of purpose which emerges from analysis of his career tend to confirm the highest estimate of Faulkner's accomplishment.

Terry Heller

Other major works

SHORT FICTION: *These 13*, 1931; *Doctor Martino and Other Stories*, 1934; *The Portable Faulkner*, 1946, 1967; *Knight's Gambit*, 1949; *Collected Short Stories of William Faulkner*, 1950; *Big Woods*, 1955; *Three Famous Short Novels*, 1958; *Uncollected Stories of William Faulkner*, 1979.

SCREENPLAYS: *Today We Live*, 1933; *To Have and Have Not*, 1945; *The Big Sleep*, 1946; *Faulkner's MGM Screenplays*, 1982.

POETRY: *The Marble Faun*, 1924; *A Green Bough*, 1933.

NONFICTION: *New Orleans Sketches*, 1958; *Faulkner in the University*, 1959; *Faulkner at West Point*, 1964; *Essays, Speeches and Public Letters*, 1965; *The Faulkner-Cowley File: Letters and Memories, 1944-1962*, 1966 (Malcolm Cowley, editor); *Lion in the Garden*, 1968; *Selected Letters*, 1977.

MISCELLANEOUS: *The Faulkner Reader*, 1954; *William Faulkner: Early Prose and Poetry*, 1962; *The Wishing Tree*, 1964; *Mayday*, 1976.

Bibliography

Blotner, Joseph. *Faulkner: A Biography*. 2 vols. New York: Random House, 1974. Once criticized for being too detailed (the two-volume edition is some two thousand pages) this biography begins before Faulkner's birth with ancestors such as William Clark Falkner, author of *The White Rose of Memphis*, and traces the writer's career from a precocious poet to America's preeminent novelist.

Brodhead, Richard H., ed. *Faulkner: New Perspectives*. Englewood Cliffs, N.J.: Prentice-Hall, 1983. One volume in the Twentieth Century Views series under the general editorship of Maynard Mack, offering nearly a dozen essays by a variety of Faulkner scholars. Among them are Irving Howe's "Faulkner and the Negroes," first published in the early 1950's, and Cleanth Brooks's "Vision of Good and Evil" from Samuel E. Balentine's *The Hidden God* (Oxford, England: Oxford University Press, 1983). Contains a select bibliography.

Cox, Leland H., ed. *William Faulkner: Biographical and Reference Guide*. Detroit: Gale Research, 1982.

_____. *William Faulkner: Critical Collection*. Detroit: Gale Research, 1982. These companion volumes constitute a handy reference to most of Faulkner's work. The first is a reader's guide which provides a long biographical essay, cross-referenced by many standard sources. Next come fifteen "critical introductions" to the novels and short stories, each with plot summaries and critical commentary particularly useful to the student reader. A three-page chronology of the events of Faulkner's life is attached. The second volume contains a short potpourri, with Faulkner's "Statements," a *Paris Review* interview, and an essay on Mississippi for *Holiday* magazine among them. The bulk of the book is an essay and excerpt collection with contributions by a number of critics including Olga Vickery, Michael Millgate, and Warren Beck. Includes a list of works by Faulkner including Hollywood screenplays.

Kinney, Arthur F. *Critical Essays on William Faulkner: The Compson Family*. Boston: G. K. Hall, 1982. In addition to an informative introduction by the editor and material by the author himself, this volume contains a section of contemporary reviews, including some from abroad, and one of critical essays and excerpts called "Understanding the Compsons," which is devoted to *The Sound and the Fury*.

Vickery, Olga W. *The Novels of William Faulkner*. Baton Rouge: Louisiana State University Press, 1959. This volume, with its comprehensive treatment of the novels, has established itself as a classic, a *terminus a quo* for later citicism. The chapter on *The Sound and the Fury*, providing an analysis of the relation between theme and structure in the book, remains relevant today despite intensive study of the topic.

Volpe, Edmond L. *A Reader's Guide to William Faulkner*. New York: Noonday Press, 1964. While many books and articles have contributed to clearing up the murkiest spots in Faulkner, the beginning student or general reader will applaud this volume. In addition to analysis of structure, themes, and characters, offers critical discussion of the novels in an appendix providing "chronologies of scenes, paraphrase of scene fragments put in chronological order, and guides to scene shifts."

GABRIEL FIELDING
Alan Gabriel Barnsley

Born: Hexham, England; March 25, 1916
Died: Bellevue, Washington; November 27, 1986

Principal long fiction

Brotherly Love, 1954; *In the Time of Greenbloom*, 1957; *Eight Days*, 1958; *Through Streets Broad and Narrow*, 1960; *The Birthday King*, 1962; *Gentlemen in Their Season*, 1966; *Pretty Doll Houses*, 1979; *The Women of Guinea Lane*, 1986.

Other literary forms

Gabriel Fielding's literary reputation rests primarily on his prose, but his early work was in poetry, published in two collections, *The Frog Prince and Other Poems* (1952) and *XXVIII Poems* (1955), neither of which matches his prose in quality or critical acclaim. He also published two books of short stories—*Collected Short Stories* (1971) and *New Queens for Old: A Novella and Nine Stories* (1972)—which are substantial enough in literary quality and theme to form a significant part of Fielding's canon.

Achievements

By 1963 Fielding had established the reputation which was maintained, but never enhanced, by his later work. Some critics view Fielding as a Catholic writer, comparable with Graham Greene, Evelyn Waugh, and Muriel Spark, concerned with social and moral issues from a specifically Catholic point of view; this aspect of his work was duly recognized in his being awarded the St. Thomas Moore Association Gold Medal in 1963 and the National Catholic Book Award in 1964. Other critics, however, see him as a writer belonging to the school of European existentialist writers, sharing their philosophic worldview; this second estimate was expressed in the W. H. Smith Literary Award, which Fielding received in 1963.

Biography

Alan Gabriel Barnsley was born in Hexham, Northumberland, Great Britain, on March 25, 1916, the fifth of six children of an Anglican vicar. After going to school at St. Edward's, Oxford, he took a B.A. at Trinity College, Dublin, and from there went to St. George's Hospital, London, from which he was graduated with a medical degree in 1941. He immediately started his war service in the Royal Army Medical Corps, continuing his service until demobilization in 1946. After the war, he was in general medical practice in Maidstone, Kent, until 1966, part of his duties being those of Medical Officer for Maidstone Prison, the experience of which contributed significantly to several of his novels. He did not start writing seriously until his middle thirties, and in 1966, when he considered his literary career to be established, he left the medical profession to become, first, Author in Residence and then Professor of English at Washington State University, Pullman, a position which he held until retirement. Fielding died in Bellevue, Washington, on November 27, 1986.

Analysis

In the context of British novelists of the twentieth century, Gabriel Fielding presents some characteristics that distinguish his work sharply from that of the mainstream novelist and at the same time place him firmly in a tradition that, in fact, goes back to the realistic social novel of Daniel Defoe. Fielding's distinctiveness lies in a steadiness and explicitness of worldview and ethical philosophy which raise his novels well above mere stories or entertainments; his identification with British literary tradition reveals itself in the spell he casts as a storyteller whose characters, plots, and settings have the dramatic quality of those found in the works of Thomas Hardy and Charles Dickens, striking the reader's mind like reality itself and haunting the memory forever. The result of what is, for a British novelist, an unusual combination of philosophic outlook and intensity of fictional realization is an integrated creativity that expresses the writer's unified sensibility of spirit and mind and that evokes within the reader an intense and often uncomfortable urge to reassess his or her own preoccupations and prejudices, yet whose effect is ultimately cathartic.

Fielding's major novels—*In the Time of Greenbloom*, *The Birthday King*, and *Gentlemen in Their Season*—pursue and explore a theme which is more frequently found in the European novel than the British: that of individual responsibility in an irrational world. Each of the three novels has a different "world" as its setting—a middle-class English county, Nazi Germany, and postwar liberal London—but the dilemmas of decision and action that face the protagonists in each novel are of the same kind. The novels' settings reflect the stages of Fielding's own life: country vicarage and Oxford, wartime military service, and postwar intellectual life in London. In many ways one feels that the novels represent a working-out in fiction of the writer's own perplexities, which were not resolved until his emigration to the United States, to the more primal setting of eastern Washington and the Moscow Mountains, where it is clear that Fielding found a peace and joy of life, and a professional satisfaction, which had eluded him in England.

The autobiographical element of Fielding's work is seen most clearly in the four novels concerning the Blaydon family. The family name itself is a well-known Northumbrian place-name, while the chronicles of John Blaydon—spanning childhood in *Brotherly Love*, adolescence in *In the Time of Greenbloom*, adulthood and medical studies in *Through Streets Broad and Narrow*, and wartime medical service in *The Women of Guinea Lane*—reflect the early progress of Fielding's own life. Of the three Blaydon novels, *In the Time of Greenbloom* is the most striking, in its presentation of a guilt-ridden and domineering adult society bent on finding sin in the young. In the novel, twelve-year-old John Blaydon is wrongly blamed for the death of his friend Victoria Blount, who has been murdered by a hiker in a cave. He is made the scapegoat for an adult crime, and he is ready to acquiesce in the guilt forced on him by the adult world when he is saved by the ministrations of Horab Greenbloom, an eccentric Jewish Oxford undergraduate who applies to John's sense of guilt a bracing dose of Wittgensteinian positivism and Sartrean existentialism. Greenbloom's therapeutic interest is that of one scapegoat for another, and his remedy is to make John see that the empty, abstract categories of the adult moral scheme lead ultimately to personal irresponsibility and inevitable pangs of guilt which must be transferred to the innocent and vulnerable for punishment.

The theme of blame, and the accompanying figure of the scapegoat, had initially been explored in *Brotherly Love*, in which John observes and chronicles the moral demolition of his older brother, David, by his domineering mother, who forces him to become a priest, thereby perverting David's natural creative talents into sordid sexual encounters and alcoholism. In this earlier novel, the adult world is only too successful in transferring its empty notions of duty, faith, sin, and shame to the adolescent, but there is no suggestion of an alternative, redemptive way. *In the Time of Greenbloom* offers hope for redemption in the magus figure of Greenbloom through his resolute opposition to spurious objective abstraction and his insistence that John must make his own moral decisions and not accept those offered by his elders. (In this and in several other respects, Fielding anticipates the concerns and solutions offered in Robertson Davies' *The Deptford Trilogy*.)

The theme of guilt, blame, and the scapegoat principle is one that preoccupies Fielding in all of his major novels, but nowhere does it achieve more compelling realization than in *The Birthday King*, which elevates and generalizes John's suffering in a northern English county to the agony of a whole race in wartime Nazi Germany. The novel chronicles the rise and fall of Nazi Germany through the lives of two Jewish brothers, Alfried and Ruprecht Waitzmann, who are directors of a large industrial group and thus somewhat protected from liquidation by the Nazis. The contrasting responses of the two brothers to the dictatorship of Adolf Hitler represent the twin facts of Jewishness and of humans as a whole in reaction to mindless oppression. Alfried, as a rather self-indulgently pious man, innocent yet provocative, opts for the untidiness of life, represented by the dirty, smelly goat in the Kommandant's garden. His rejection of the hygienic bureaucracy and simple slogans of the Nazis causes him to be imprisoned and tortured in an attempted "cure" of his wayward individuality, and he thus becomes the scapegoat, despised by his friends more than by the Nazis (for whom he actually lightens the burden of guilt). Ruprecht, on the other hand, represents the alternative path: survival at any cost. He is an opportunist and a schemer, preserving the family business by betraying Alfried and running his factories on forced labor for the Nazi regime.

The novel explores the consequences of the brothers' different choices—sacrifice and survival—each of which has been made with existential authenticity, both in their different ways morally "right." Alfried's response, with its mystical innocence and awkward honesty, is that of the child who rejects the adult world of organized belief and consequent absurd moral simplifications. Ruprecht's response is just as true to his own shrewd, aggressive, and lucky nature in a world in which he sees Germany as one gigantic concentration camp in which the only possible choice is for survival. The kind of choice each brother makes is less important than the fact that each actually makes a conscious choice freely, rather than choosing to join the bored sleepwalkers: the camp Kommandant, his puritanical wife, and the aristocratic remnants of old Germany, such as von Hoffbach and von Boehling, who applaud the new Wagnerian romanticism of the Third Reich while sneering at the inferior social status of the Nazi party upstarts. For Fielding, the only corrective to the mind-numbing boredom represented by Nazi Germany is the exercise of free will in subjective decision.

Boredom provides the focus of *Gentlemen in Their Season* as well, but Fielding narrows his scope to marriage in the postwar, liberated world. In many ways, this novel is more complex than the earlier and, arguably, better novels in that issues are less clear-cut and the possibility of authentic decision is consequently much reduced. Moreover, the setting and characters, in their familiarity and ordinariness, are uncomfortably close to the reader, who is unable to distance himself from the action as he is in *In the Time of Greenbloom* and *The Birthday King*. The plot of *Gentlemen in Their Season* concerns two middle-aged, middle-class liberal intellectuals, Randall Coles and Bernard Presage, whose marriages, to an assertive humanist and a rather religiose Catholic, respectively, have stagnated to the point of artificiality, which takes the form of clever parties, esoteric intellectualism, mutual criticism, and automatic churchgoing. Each man drifts into a pointless affair, with tragic consequences for a third party, Hotchkiss, whose simple Christian faith in monogamy has already led to his imprisonment for the manslaughter of his wife's lover, who escapes from prison to confront her current lover, Coles, and to force him to practice the morality that he preaches as director of religious programming for the British Broadcasting Corporation (BBC). In impulsive reaction, and horrified at having to make a simple act of faith in front of Hotchkiss, Coles betrays him to the police, who kill him in their attempted arrest.

This novel, probably the blackest, most ironic and comic of all of Fielding's novels, reduces the sleepwalking quality of a whole nation in *The Birthday King* to the level of ordinary, casual, and unthinking behavior of men whose abstract conceptions of what modern marriage should be make them indecisive, vacillating, and morally irresponsible, while they continue to justify their behavior on intellectualized principles remote from the concerns of real life. Hotchkiss, by breaking out of prison and confronting Coles, makes the only authentic decision in the whole course of events, and by consciously being an agent, rather than a victim to whom things lamely happen, he forces action on the part of others and thus, in his self-sacrifice, atones for the sins of his intellectual and social superiors.

The central concern in all of Fielding's major novels is the moral necessity for human action in the fullest sense of deliberate, self-aware decisiveness in a society that is largely content to go along with the crowd, to rationalize behavior in terms of social, political, religious, and intellectual abstractions. The actions that result from such decisiveness may, in fact, lead to the protagonist's becoming the scapegoat for society's somnambulistic and self-justifying atrocities but ultimately awaken the sleepwalkers for a while, dazzling people into self-awareness by their enormity. Although this theme is existential, it is a Catholic existentialism, reconciling the principles most fundamental to Christian faith with the natural, human, subjective conscience, and promoting will as a necessary accompaniment to belief. Adult institutions of class, politics, and church may, and for most do, substitute slogans for principles and apologetics for action, but the blame lies not in the institutions themselves but in society's slavish and easy acquiescence in the precepts which demand least exercise of will.

The starkness of Fielding's theme associates his work most closely with European preoccupations, constantly reminding the reader of figures such as Jean-Paul Sartre, Albert Camus, Hermann Hesse, and Günter Grass. The only British writer who shares these preoccupations is Graham Greene, whose continentalism makes most British critics, who are more comfortable with what might be called the cardigan-and-post-office kind of novel, suspicious of the underlying philosophic concerns of his fiction. The poor critical response in Great Britain to Fielding's work arises, one imagines, from a similar fear of philosophic depth.

Despite the philosophic significance of Fielding's novels, they are works of literature, not of philosophy. What elevates Fielding beyond the level of mere "messenger," didacticist, or programmatic writer is the other face of his work: the elevation of narrative over precept, of imagery and language over naked theme. His novels are by no means mere illustrative allegories of ready-made themes, but explorations in narrative which lead, perhaps to the surprise of the writer, to inevitable philosophic conclusions. It is the power and richness of plot, character, and language, and the concreteness of setting that put Fielding in the grand tradition of the English novel with Dickens, the

Brontës, and Hardy, making his novels compelling and memorable in themselves, not merely as vehicles of Catholic-existentialist thought. The elemental images of purifying water and oppressive earth, the institutional images of the prison, the school, the hospital, and the bureaucratic machinery, together with the evocative associations of proper names ("Badger," "Toad," "Greenbloom," "Hubertus," and "Presage") interweave with one another and with settings rich in symbolism (the cave where Victoria is murdered, the Anglo-Catholic church with its dead image of Christ, the deserted swimming pool where Ruprecht and Carin make love, the camp of forced workers, Alfried's punishment cell, and Hotchkiss' prison cell), creating a text of such richness as to transcend its constituent parts and to enter the reader's consciousness like reality itself. The texture of Fielding's language is that of the best dramatic poetry: Images, allusions, and references, in the vigorous expression of quite ordinary speech, cluster and weave to engender a depth and breadth of experience which triggers unconscious associations supporting the reader's conscious interpretation of plot and character to produce a wholly new, vital, and often disturbing sensibility.

Frederick Bowers

Other major works
SHORT FICTION: *Collected Short Stories*, 1971; *New Queens for Old: A Novella and Nine Stories*, 1972.
POETRY: *The Frog Prince and Other Poems*, 1952; *XXVIII Poems*, 1955.

Bibliography
Bloom, Harold ed. *Twentieth Century British Literature*. Vol. 2. New York: Chelsea House, 1986. The entry on Fielding lists his works up to his novel *Pretty Doll Houses*. Reprinted here is an interview with Fielding from 1967, entitled "The Longing for Spring," which provides much useful information on the author and his work up until the mid-1960's.
Bowers, Frederick. "Gabriel Fielding." In *Contemporary Novelists*, edited by James Vinson. London: St. James Press, 1976. Appraises Fielding in the light of his growing reputation as a major novelist with commentary on three of his novels: *In the Time of Greenbloom, The Birthday King*, and *Gentlemen in Their Season*. An appreciative essay that cites his novels as "good dramatic poetry."
_____. "Gabriel Fielding's *The Birthday King*." *The Queen's Quarterly* 74 (Spring, 1967): 148-158. Explores the themes of guilt, innocence, and personal responsibility in this novel, comparing the work to existentialists Albert Camus and Jean-Paul Sartre.
_____. "The Unity of Fielding's *Greenbloom*." Review of *In the Time of Greenbloom*, by Gabriel Fielding. *Renascence* 18 (Spring, 1966): 147-

155. A favorable review, in which Bowers claims that the novel is of "major importance and worth in theme and execution." Comments on the existentialist nature of the novel, comparing it to the philosophy of Soren Kierkegaard, and on the scapegoat theme in this work.

HENRY FIELDING

Born: Sharpham Park, Somersetshire, England; April 22, 1707
Died: Lisbon, Portugal; October 8, 1754

Principal long fiction

An Apology for the Life of Mrs. Shamela Andrews, 1741; *The History of the Adventures of Joseph Andrews, and of His Friend Mr. Abraham Adams*, 1742; *The History of the Life of the Late Mr. Jonathan Wild the Great*, 1743, 1754; *The History of Tom Jones, a Foundling*, 1749; *Amelia*, 1751.

Other literary forms

Henry Fielding's literary output, besides his novels, can be categorized in three groups: plays; pamphlets and miscellaneous items; and journals. In addition, the publication of his three-volume *Miscellanies* (1743) by subscription brought together a number of previously published items, as well as new works, including the first version of *The History of the Life of the Late Jonathan Wild the Great* commonly known as *Jonathan Wild*, and an unfinished prose work, "A Journey from This World to the Next."

Fielding's dramatic works, many presented with great success at either of London's Little Theatre in the Haymarket, or the Drury Lane Theatre, include ballad opera, farce, full-length comedy, and adaptations of classical and French drama. Most are overtly political in theme. Because of their contemporary subject matter, few have survived as viable stage presentations, although *The Covent-Garden Tragedy* (1732) was presented by The Old Vic in London as recently as 1968. Fielding also wrote a number of prologues, epilogues, and monologues performed in conjuction with other dramatic pieces.

The pamphlets and miscellaneous items which are currently attributed to Fielding, excluding those for which he merely wrote introductions or epilogues, are: "The Masquerade" (1728), a poem; *The Military History of Charles XII King of Sweden* (1740), a translation; "Of True Greatness" (1741) a poem; "The Opposition: A Vision" (1741), a poem; "The Vernoniad" (1741), a poem; "The Female Husband" (1746); "Ovid's Art of Love Paraphrased" (1747); "A True State of the Case of Bosavern Penlez" (1749); "An Enquiry into the Causes of the Late Increase in Robbers" (1751); "Examples of the Interposition of Providence in the Detection and Punishment of Murder" (1752); "A Proposal for Making an Effectual Provision for the Poor" (1753); "A Clear State of the Case of Elizabeth Canning" (1753); *The Journal of a Voyage to Lisbon*, published posthumously (1755).

Fielding edited and made major contributions to four journals: *The Champion* (November 15, 1739-June 1741; the journal continued publication without Fielding until 1742); *The True Patriot* (November 5, 1745-June 17, 1746); *Jacobite's Journal* (December 5, 1747-November 5, 1748); *The Covent-Garden*

Journal (January 4-November 25, 1752).

Achievements

Fielding's lasting achievements in prose fiction—in contrast to his passing fame as an essayist, dramatist, and judge—result from his development of critical theory and from his aesthetic success in the novels themselves. In the Preface to *The History of the Adventures of Joseph Andrews, and of His Friend Mr. Abraham Adams*, more commonly known as *Joseph Andrews*, Fielding establishes a serious critical basis for the novel as a genre and describes in detail the elements of comic realism; in *Joseph Andrews* and *The History of Tom Jones, a Foundling*, popularly known as *Tom Jones*, he provides full realizations of this theory. These novels define the ground rules of form that would be followed, to varying degrees, by Jane Austen, William Makepeace Thackeray, George Eliot, Thomas Hardy, James Joyce, and D. H. Lawrence, and they also speak to countless readers across many generations. Both, in fact, were translated into successful films (*Tom Jones*, 1963, *Joseph Andrews*, 1978).

The historical importance of the "Preface" results from both the seriousness with which it treats the formal qualities of the novel (at the time a fledgling and barely respectable genre) and the precision with which it defines the characteristics of the genre, the "comic epic-poem in prose." Fielding places *Joseph Andrews* in particular and the comic novel in general squarely in the tradition of classical literature and coherently argues its differences from the romance and the burlesque. He also provides analogies between the comic novel and the visual arts. Thus Fielding leads the reader to share his conception that the comic novel is an aesthetically valid form with its roots in classical tradition, and a form peculiarly suited to the attitudes and values of its own age.

With his background in theater and journalism, Fielding could move easily through a wide range of forms and rhetorical techniques in his fiction, from direct parody of Samuel Richardson in *An Apology for the Life of Mrs. Shamela Andrews*, to ironic inversion of the great man's biography in *Jonathan Wild*, to adaptation of classical structure (Vergil's *Aeneid*, c. 29-19 B.C.) in *Amelia*. The two major constants in these works are the attempt to define a good, moral life, built on benevolence and honor, and a concern for finding the best way to present that definition to the reader. Thus the moral and the technique can never be separated in Fielding's works.

Joseph Andrews and *Tom Jones* bring together these two impulses in Fielding's most organically structured, brilliantly characterized, and masterfully narrated works. These novels vividly capture the diversity of experience in the physical world and the underlying benevolence of natural order, embodying them in a rich array of the ridiculous in human behavior. Fielding combines a positive assertion of the strength of goodness and benevolence (demonstrated by the structure and plot of the novels) with the sharp thrusts of the satirist's attack upon the hypocrisy and vanity of individual characters. These elements are held together by the voice of the narrator—witty, urbane, charming—who serves as moral guide through the novels and the world. Thus, beyond the comic merits of each of the individual novels lies a collective sense of universal moral good. The voice of the narrator conveys to the reader the truth of that goodness.

Although the novels were popular in his own day, Fielding's contemporaries thought of him more as playwright-turned-judge than as novelist. This may have been the result of the low esteem in which the novel itself was held, as well as of Fielding's brilliant successes in these other fields. These varied successes have in common a zest for the exploration of the breadth and variety of life—a joy in living—that finds its most articulate and permanent expression in the major novels.

Today Fielding is universally acknowledged as a major figure in the development of the novel, although there is still niggling about whether he or Richardson is the "father" of the British novel. Ian Watt, for example, claims that Richardson's development of "formal realism" is more significant than Fielding's comic realism. Other critics, notably Martin Battestin, have demonstrated that Fielding's broader, more humane moral vision, embodied in classical structure and expressed through a self-conscious narrator, is the germ from which the richness and variety of the British novel grows. This disagreement ultimately comes down to personal taste, and there will always be Richardson and Fielding partisans to keep the controversy alive. There is no argument, however, that of their type—the novel of comic realism—no fiction has yet surpassed *Joseph Andrews* or *Tom Jones*.

Biography

Henry Fielding was born April 22, 1707, in Sharpham Park, Somersetshire, to Edmund and Sarah Fielding. His father, an adventurer, gambler, and swaggerer, was a sharp contrast to the quiet, conservative, traditional gentry of his mother's family, the Goulds. In 1710, the family moved to Dorset, where Fielding and his younger brother and three sisters (including the future novelist, Sarah Fielding) would spend most of their childhood on a small estate and farm given to Mrs. Fielding by her father, Sir Henry Gould.

The death of Fielding's mother in April, 1718, ended this idyllic life. Litigation over the estate created a series of family battles that raged for several decades. In 1719, Fielding was sent to Eton College, partly because the Goulds wanted him influenced as little as possible by his father, who had resumed his "wild" life in London, and partly because he disliked his father's new, Catholic wife. Remaining at Eton until 1724 or 1725, Fielding made many friends, including George Lyttleton and William Pitt. At Eton he began his study of classical literature, a profound influence on his literary career.

Few details are known of Fielding's life during the several years after Eton. He spent a good deal of time with the Goulds in Salisbury, but also led a hectic, boisterous life in London, spending much time at the theater, where the popular masquerades and burlesques influenced him greatly. His visits to the theater stimulated him to try his own hand at comedy, and in February, 1728, *Love in Several Masques*, based on his own romantic adventures of the previous year, was performed at Drury Lane.

In March, 1728, Fielding enrolled in the Faculty of Letters at the University of Leyden (Netherlands), where he pursued his interest in the classics. In August, 1729, at the age of twenty-two, he returned to London without completing his degree.

It is clear from his literary output in the 1730's that Fielding was intensely involved in theatrical life. From 1730 through 1737 he authored at least nineteen different dramatic works (as well as presenting revivals and new productions of revised works), most with political themes, at both the Little Theatre in the Haymarket and the Drury Lane. In addition to writing ballad opera, full-length comedies, translations, and parodies, Fielding was also producing, revising the plays of other writers, and managing theater business. He also formed a new, important friendship with the artist William Hogarth.

His theatrical career came to an abrupt halt (although a few more plays appeared in the 1740's) with the passage of the Licensing Act of 1737 which resulted in the closing of many theaters. Fielding's political satire offended Prime Minister Sir Robert Walpole and had been part of the motivation for the government's desire to control and censor the theaters.

In addition to this theatrical activity with its political commentary, Fielding found time from 1733 to 1734 to court and marry Charlotte Cradock of Salisbury. Charlotte's mother died in 1735, leaving the entire estate to the Fieldings and alleviating many of the financial problems caused by the legal disputes over the estate in Dorset. The couple moved from London to East Stour the same year, although Fielding regularly visited London, because he was manager, artistic director, and controller-in-chief of the Little Theatre. Their first child, Charlotte, was born April 17, 1736; and later they would have two additional children.

Fielding's relentless energy (and desire to add to his income) compelled him to begin a new career in late 1737, whereupon he began to study law at the Middle Temple. He became a barrister on June 20, 1740, and spent the next several years in the Western Circuit. During this service he became friends with Ralph Allen of Bath. He remained active in the practice of justice, as attorney and magistrate, until he left England in 1754.

Fielding continued to involve himself in political controversy, even while studying law. He edited, under pseudonyms, *The Champion*, an opposition newspaper issued three times a week, directed against Prime Minister Walpole (a favorite subject of Fielding's satire). Later he would edit *The True Patriot* in support of the government during the threat of the Jacobite Rising, *Jacobite's Journal*, and *The Covent-Garden Journal*.

From theater to law to journalism—Fielding had already charged through three careers when the first installment of Richardson's *Pamela* appeared on November 6, 1740. Deeply disturbed by the artificiality of the novel's epistolary technique, and appalled by its perversion of moral values, Fielding quickly responded with *An Apology for the Life of Mrs. Shamela Andrews*, often referred to as *Shamela*, an "Antidote" to *Pamela*. Although published anonymously, Fieldling's authorship was apparent and created ill-feelings between the two authors that would last most of their lives.

The success of *Shamela* encouraged Fielding to try his hand at a more sustained satire, which eventually grew into *Joseph Andrews*. In 1743 he published, by subscription, the *Miscellanies*, a collection of previously published works, and two new ones: an unfinished story, "A Journey from This World to the Next," and the first version of *Jonathan Wild*.

Although the mid-1740's brought Fielding fame, success, and money, his personal life was beset with pain. He suffered continually from gout, and Charlotte died in November, 1744. In the following year he became involved in the propaganda battles over the Jacobite Rising. On November 27, 1747, he married his wife's former maid, Mary Daniel, and some sense of peace and order was restored to his private life. They would have five children.

While forming new personal ties and continuing strong involvement in political issues, Fielding was preparing his masterwork, *Tom Jones*. He also took oath as Justice of the Peace for Westminster and Middlesex, London, in 1748, and opened an employment agency and estate brokerage with his brother in 1749. His last novel, *Amelia*, was not well-received, disappointing those readers who were expecting another *Tom Jones*.

The early 1750's saw Fielding's health continue to decline, although he remained active in his judgeship, producing a number of pamphlets on various legal questions. In June of 1754, his friends convinced him to sail to Lisbon, Portugal, where the climate might improve his health. He died there on October 8, 1754, and is buried in the British Cemetery outside of Lisbon. *The Journal of a Voyage to Lisbon*, his last work, was published one year after his death.

Analysis

Analysis and criticism of Henry Fielding's fiction have traditionally centered on the moral values in the novels, the aesthetic structure in which they are placed, and the relationship between the two. In this view, Fielding as moralist takes precedence over Fielding as artist, since the aesthetic structure is determined by the moral. Each of the novels is judged by the extent to which it finds the appropriate form for its moral vision. The relative failure of *Amelia*, for example, may be Fielding's lack of faith in his own moral vision. The happy ending, promulgated by the *deus ex machina* of the good magistrate, is hardly consistent with the dire effects of urban moral decay that have been at work upon the Booths throughout the novel. Fielding's own moral development and changes in outlook also need to be considered in this view. The reader must examine the sources of Fielding's moral vision in the latitudinarian sermons of the day, as well as the changes in his attitudes as he examined in greater detail eighteenth century urban life, and as he moved in literature from *Joseph Andrews* to *Amelia*, and in life from the theater to the bench of justice.

As is clear from the Preface to *Joseph Andrews*, however, Fielding was equally interested in the aesthetics of his fiction. Indeed, each of the novels, even from the first parody, *Shamela*, conveys not only a moral message but a literary experiment to find the strongest method for expressing that message to the largest reading public. This concern is evident in the basic plot structure, characterization, language, and role of the narrator. Each novel attempts to reach the widest audience possible with its moral thesis. Although each differs in the way in which Fielding attempts this, they all have in common the sense that the *how* of the story is as important as the *what*. The novels are experiments in the methods of moral education—for the reader as well as for the characters.

This concern for the best artistic way to teach a moral lesson was hardly new with Fielding. His classical education and interests, as well as the immediate human response gained from theater audiences during his playwriting days, surely led him to see that fiction must delight as well as instruct. Fielding's novels are both exempla of this goal (in their emphasis on incidents of plot and broad range of characterization) and serious discussions of the method by which to achieve it (primarily through structure and through narrative commentary).

The direct stimulation for Fielding's career as novelist was the publication of Samuel Richardson's *Pamela*, a novel that disturbed Fielding both by its artistic ineptitude and by its moral vacuousness. Fielding was as concerned with the public reaction to *Pamela* as he was with its author's methods. That the reading public could be so easily misled by *Pamela*'s morals disturbed Fielding deeply, and the success of that novel led him to ponder what better ways were available for reaching the public with his own moral thesis. His response to *Pamela* was both moral (he revealed the true state of Pamela/Shamela's values) and aesthetic (he exposed the artificiality of "writing to the moment").

Sermons and homilies, while effective in church (and certainly sources of Fielding's moral philosophy) were not the stuff of prose fiction; neither was the epistolary presentation of "virtue rewarded" of *Pamela* (nor the "objectively" amoral tone of Daniel Defoe's *The Fortunes and Misfortunes of the Famous Moll Flanders*, 1722). Fielding sought a literary method for combining moral vision and literary pleasure that would be appropriate to the rapidly urbanizing and secular society of the mid-eighteenth century. To find that method he ranged through direct parody, irony, satire, author-narrator intrusion, and moral exemplum. Even those works, such as *Jonathan Wild* and *Amelia*, which are not entirely successful, live because of the vitality of Fielding's experimental methods. In *Joseph Andrews* and *Tom Jones*, he found the way to reach his audience most effectively.

Fielding's informing moral values, embodied in the central characters of the novels (Joseph Andrews, Parson Adams, Tom Jones, Squire Allworthy, Mr. Harrison) can be summarized, as Martin Battestin has ably done, as Charity, Prudence, and Providence. Fielding held an optimistic faith in the perfectability of humanity and the potential for the betterment of society, based on the essential goodness of human nature. These three values must work together. In the novels, the hero's worth is determined by the way in which he interacts with other people (charity), within the limits of social institutions designed to provide order (prudence). His reward is a life full of God's plenty (providence). God's providence has created a world of abundance and plenitude; man's prudence and charity can guarantee its survival and growth. Both Joseph Andrews and Tom Jones learn the proper combination of prudence and charity. They learn to use their innate inclination toward goodness within a social system that insures order. To succeed, however, they must overcome obstacles provided by the characters who, through vanity and hypocrisy, distort God's providence. Thus, Fielding's moral vision, while optimistic, is hardly blind to the realities of the world. *Jonathan Wild*, with its basic rhetorical distinction between "good" and "great," and *Amelia*, with its narrative structured around the ill effects of doing good, most strongly reflect Fielding's doubts about the practicality of his beliefs.

These ideas can be easily schematized, but the scheme belies the human complexity through which they are expressed in the novels. Tom Jones is no paragon of virtue, but must learn, at great physical pain and spiritual risk, how to combine charity and prudence. Even Squire Allworthy, as Sheldon Sacks emphasized in *Fiction and the Shape of Belief* (1964), is a "fallible" paragon. These ideas do not come from a single source, but are derived from a combination of sources, rooted in Fielding's classical education; the political, religious, and literary movements of his own time; and his own experience as dramatist, journalist, and magistrate.

Fielding's familiarity with the classics, begun at Eton and continued at the University of Leyden, is revealed in many ways: through language (the use of epic simile and epic conventions in *Joseph Andrews*), through plot (the symmetry of design in *Tom Jones*), through theme (the importance of moderation in all the novels), and through structure (the relationship of *Amelia* to Vergil's *Aeneid*, c. 29-19 B.C.). The Preface to *Joseph Andrews* makes explicit how much Fielding saw in common between his own work and classical literature. His belief in the benevolent order of the world, especially illustrated by country living, such as at Squire Allworthy's estate (Paradise Hall), is deeply rooted in the pastoral tradition of classical literature.

These classicial elements are combined with the beliefs of the latitudinarian homilists of the seventeenth and eighteenth centuries, who stressed the perfectibility of mankind in the world through good deeds (charity) and good heart (benevolence).

While Fielding's thematic concerns may be rooted in classical and Christian thought, his literary technique has sources that are more complex, deriving from his education, his own experience in the theater, the influence of Richardson's *Pamela*. It is difficult to separate each of these sources, for the novels work them into unified and original statements. Indeed, *Joseph Andrews*, the novel most closely related to classical sources, is also deeply imbued with the sense of latitudinarian thought in its criticism of the clergy, and satire of Richardson in its plot and moral vision.

The London in which Fielding spent most of his life was a world of literary and political ferment, an age of factionalism in the arts, with the Tory wits (Swift, Pope, John Gay, John Arbuthnot) allied against Colley Cibber, the poet laureate and self-proclaimed literary spokesman for the British Isles. Swift's *Gulliver's Travels* (1726) and Gay's *The Beggar's Opera* (1728) had recently appeared; both were influential in forming Fielding's literary methods: the first with its emphasis on sharp political satire, the second with the creation of a new literary form, the ballad opera. The ballad opera set new lyrics, expressing contemporary political and social satire, to well-known music. Fielding was to find his greatest theatrical success in this genre, and was to carry over to his fiction, especially *Jonathan Wild*, its emphasis on London low life and its excesses of language.

It was a time, also, of great political controversy, with the ongoing conflicts between the Tories and Jacobites about the questions of religion and succession. Prime Minister Walpole's politics of expediency was a ripe subject for satire. Fielding's career as journalist began as a direct response to political issues, and significant portions of *Joseph Andrews* and *Tom Jones*, as well as *Jonathan Wild*, deal with political issues.

These various sources, influences, and beliefs are molded into coherent works of art through Fielding's narrative technique. It is through the role of the narrator that he most clearly and successfully experiments in the methods of teaching a moral lesson. Starting with the voice of direct literary parody in *Shamela* and moving through the varied structures and voices of the other novels, Fielding's art leads in many directions, but it always leads to his ultimate concern for finding the best way to teach the clearest moral lesson. In *Tom Jones* he finds the most appropriate method to demonstrate that the world is a beautiful place if man will live by charity and prudence.

The key to understanding how *Shamela* expresses Fielding's concern with both the moral thesis and the aesthetic form of fiction is contained in the introductory letters between Parsons Tickletext and Oliver. Oliver is dismayed at Tickletext's exuberant praise of *Pamela* and at the novel's public reception and popularity. The clergy, in particular, have been citing it as a work worthy to be read with the Scriptures. He contends that the text of *Shamela*, which he encloses, reveals the "true" story of Pamela's adventures and puts them in their proper moral perspective. By reading Oliver's version, Tickletext will correct his own misconceptions; by reading *Shamela* (under the guidance of the prefatory letters), the public will laugh at *Pamela* and perceive the perversity of its moral thesis.

Shamela began, of course, simply as a parody of Richardson's novel, and, in abbreviated form, carries through the narrative of the attempted seduction of the young serving girl by the squire, and her attempts to assert her virtue through chastity or marriage. Fielding makes direct hits at Richardson's weakest points: his two main targets are the epistolary technique of "writing to the moment" and the moral thesis of "virtue rewarded" by pounds and pence (and marriage).

Fielding parodies the epistolary technique by carrying it to its most illogical extreme: Richardson's technical failure is not the choice of epistolary form, but his insistence on its adherence to external reality. Shamela writes her letters at the very same moment she is being attacked in bed by Squire Booby. While feigning sleep she writes: "You see I write in the present tense." The inconsistency of Pamela's shift from letters to journal form when she is abducted is shown through Fielding's retention of the letter form throughout the story, no matter what the obstacles for sending and receiving them. He also compounds the criticism of Richardson by including a number of correspondents besides Shamela (her mother, Henrietta Maria Honora Andrews, Mrs. Jewkes, Parson Williams), and including various complications, such as letters within letters within letters.

Fielding retains the essential characters and key scenes from *Pamela*, such as Mr. B's hiding in the closet before the attempted seduction, Pamela's attempted suicide at the pond, and Parson Williams' interference. For each character and scene Fielding adopts Richardson's penchant for minute descriptive detail and intense character response to the event; he also parodies the method and seriousness of the original by revealing the motives of the characters.

The revealing of motives is also Fielding's primary way of attacking the prurience of Richardson's presentation, as well as the moral thesis behind it. He debunks the "punctillo" (decorum) of the central character. Shamela's false modesty ("I thought once of making a little fortune by my person. I now intend to make a great one by my virtue") mocks Pamela's pride in her chastity; the main difference between them is Shamela's recognition and acceptance of the mercenary motives behind her behavior and Pamela's blindness to her own motivation. Richardson never examines the reliability of Pamela's motivations, although he describes her thoughts in detail. Fielding allows Shamela to glory in both her ability to dupe the eager Squire Booby and her mercenary motives for doing so. The reader may, as Parson Oliver wants Tickletext to do, easily condemn Shamela for a villain but never for a hypocrite.

Fielding also attacks Richardson's refusal to describe the sexual attributes of his characters or to admit the intensity of their sexual desires, particularly in the case of Pamela herself. Pamela always hints and suggests—and, Fielding claims, wallows in her suggestiveness. Fielding not only describes the sexual aspects directly, but exaggerates and reduces them to a comic level, hardly to be taken sensually or seriously. *Shamela* quickly, fully, and ruthlessly anni-hilates the moral thesis of "virtue rewarded" through this direct exaggeration. Fielding does not, however, in his role as parodist, suggest an alternative to *Pamela*'s moral thesis; he is content, for the time, with exposing its flaws.

This first foray into fiction served for Fielding a testing ground for some of the rhetorical techniques he used in later works, especially the emphasis on satiric inversion. These inversions appear in his reversal of sexual roles in *Joseph Andrews*, the reversal of rhetoric in the "good" and "great" in *Jonathan Wild*, and the reversal of goodness of motive and evil of effect in *Amelia*. Fielding's concern to find a rhetorical method for presenting a moral thesis was confined in *Shamela* to the limited aims and goals of parody. He had such success with the method (after all, he had his apprenticeship in the satiric comedy of the theater), that he began his next novel on the same model.

Like *Shamela*, *Joseph Andrews* began as a parody of *Pamela*. In his second novel, Fielding reverses the gender of the central character and traces Joseph's attempts to retain his chastity and virtue while being pursued by Lady Booby. This method of inversion creates new possibilities, not only for satirizing Richardson's work, but for commenting on the sexual morality of the time in a more positive way than in *Shamela*. The most cursory reading reveals how quickly Fielding grew tired of parody and how *Joseph Andrews* moved beyond its inspiration and its forerunner. Even the choice of direct narration rather than epistolary form indicates Fielding's unwillingness to tie himself to his model.

Most readers agree that the entrance of Parson Adams, Joseph's guide, companion, and partner in misery, turns the novel from simple parody into complex fiction. Adams takes center stage as both comic butt, preserving Joseph's role as hero, and moral guide, preserving Joseph's role as innocent.

Adams' contribution is also part of Fielding's conscious search for the best way to convey his moral thesis. The narrative refers continually to sermons, given in the pulpit or being carried by Adams to be published in London. These sermons are generally ineffectual or contradicted by the behavior of the clergy who pronounce them. Just as experience and the moral example of Adams' life are better teachers for Joseph than sermons—what could be a more effective lesson than the way he is treated by the coach passengers after he is robbed, beaten, and stripped?—so literary example has more power for Fielding and the reader. Adams' constant companion, his copy of Aeschylus, is further testament to Fielding's growing faith in his exemplary power of literature as moral guide. In *Joseph Andrews*, narrative art takes precedence over both parody and sermon.

Fielding's concern for method as well as meaning is given its most formal discussion in the Preface. The historical importance of this document results from both the seriousness with which it treats the formal qualities of the novel and the precision with which it defines the characteristics of the genre, the "comic epic-poem in prose." The seriousness is established through the careful logic and organization of the argument and through the parallels drawn between the new genre and classical literature (the lost comic epic supposedly written by Homer) and modern painting (Michelangelo Caravaggio and William Hogarth).

Fielding differentiates the comic epic-poem in prose from contemporary romances such as *Pamela*. The new form is more extended and comprehensive in action, contains a much larger variety of incidents, and treats a greater variety of characters. Unlike the serious romance, the new form is less solemn in subject matter, treats characters of lower rank, and presents the ludicrous rather than the sublime. The comic, opposed to the burlesque, arises solely from the observation of nature, and has its source in the discovery of the "ridiculous" in human nature. The ridiculous always springs from the affectations of vanity and hypocrisy.

Within the novel itself, the narrator will continue the discussion of literary issues in the introductory chapters to each of the first three of four books: "of writing lives in general," "Of divisions in authors," and "in praise of biography." These discussions, although sometimes more facetious than serious, do carry through the direction of the opening sentence of the novel: "examples work more forcibly on the mind than precepts." Additionally, this narrative commentary allows Fielding to assume the role of reader's companion and guide that he develops more fully in *Tom Jones*.

While the Preface takes its cue from classical tradition, it is misleading to assume that *Joseph Andrews* is merely an updating of classical technique and ideas. Even more than *Shamela*, this novel brings together Fielding's dissatisfaction with Richardson's moral thesis and his support of latitudinarian attitudes toward benevolence and charity. Here, too, Fielding begins his definition of the "good" man in modern Christian terms. Joseph redefines the place of chastity and honor in male sexuality; Parson Adams exemplifies the benevolence all men should display; Mrs. Tow-wowse, Trulliber, and Peter Pounce, among others, illustrate the vanity and hypocrisy of the world.

The structure of the novel is episodic, combining the earthly journey and escapades of the hero with suggestions of the Christian pilgrimage in John Bunyan's *The Pilgrim's Progress* (1678-1684). Fielding was still experimenting with form and felt at liberty to digress from his structure with interpolated tales or to depend on coincidence to bring the novel to its conclusion. The immediate moral effect sometimes seems more important than the consistency of rhetorical structure. These are, however, minor lapses in Fielding's progression toward unifying moral thesis and aesthetic structure.

In *Jonathan Wild*, Fielding seems to have abandoned temporarily the progression from the moral statement of parody and sermon to the aesthetic statement of literary example. *Jonathan Wild* was first published in the year immediately following *Joseph Andrews* (revised in 1754), and there is evidence to indicate that the work was actually written before *Joseph Andrews*. This is a reasonable assumption, since *Jonathan Wild* is more didactic in its method and more negative in its moral vision. It looks back toward *Shamela* rather than ahead to *Tom Jones*.

Jonathan Wild is less a novel, even as Fielding discusses the form in the Preface to *Joseph Andrews*, than a polemic. Critic Northrop Frye's term, "anatomy," may be the most appropriate label for the work. Like other anatomies—Sir Thomas More's *Utopia* (1516), Swift's *Gulliver's Travels*, and Samuel Johnson's *The History of Rasselas, Prince of Abyssinia*, (1759)—it emphasizes ideas over narrative. It is more moral fable than novel, and more fiction than historical biography, altering history to fit the moral vision.

More important, it was Fielding's experiment in moving the moral lesson of the tale away from the narrative (with its emphasis on incident and character) and into the rhetoric of the narrator (with its emphasis on language). Fielding attempted to use language as the primary carrier of his moral thesis. Although this experiment failed—manipulation of language, alone, would not do—it gave him the confidence to develop the role of the narrative voice in its proper perspective in *Tom Jones*.

Fielding freely adapted the facts of Wild's life, which were well-known to the general public. He chose those incidents from Wild's criminal career and punishment that would serve his moral purpose and he added his own fictional characters, the victims of Wild's "greatness," expecially the Heartfrees. Within the structure of the inverted biography of the "great" man, Fielding satirizes the basic concepts of middle-class society. He differentiates between "greatness" and "goodness," terms often used synonymously in the eighteenth century. The success of the novel depends on the reader's acceptance and understanding of this rhetorical inversion.

"Goodness," characterized by the Heartfrees, reiterates the ideals of behavior emphasized in *Joseph Andrews*: benevolence, honor, honesty, and charity, felt through the heart. "Greatness," personified in Wild, results in cunning and courage, characteristics of the will. The action of the novel revolves around the ironic reversal of these terms. Although Wild's actions speak for themselves, the ironic voice of the narrator constantly directs the reader's response.

Parts of *Jonathan Wild* are brilliantly satiric, but the work as a whole does not speak to modern readers. Fielding abandoned the anatomy form after this experiment, recognizing that the voice of the narrator alone cannot carry the moral thesis of a novel in a convincing way. In *Jonathan Wild*, he carried to an extreme the role of the narrator as moral guide that he experimented with in *Joseph Andrews*. In *Tom Jones*, he found the precise balance: the moral voice of the narrator controlling the reader's reaction through language and the literary examples of plot and character.

In *Tom Jones*, Fielding moved beyond the limited aims of each of his previous works into a more comprehensive moral and aesthetic vision. No longer bound by the need to attack Richardson nor the attempt to define a specific fictional form, such as the moral fable or the comic epic-poem in prose, Fielding dramatized the positive values of the good man in a carefully structured narrative held together by the guiding voice of the narrator. This narrator unifies in a consistent pattern Fielding's concern for both the truthfulness of his moral vision and the best way to reach the widest audience.

The structure of *Tom Jones*, like that of *Joseph Andrews*, is based on the secularization of the spiritual pilgrimage. Tom must journey from his equivocal position as foundling on the country estate of Squire Allworthy (Paradise Hall) to moral independence in the hellish city of London. He must learn to understand and control his life. When he learns this lesson, he will return to the country to enjoy the plenitude of Paradise regained that providence allows him. He must temper his natural, impetuous charity with the prudence that comes from recognition of his own role in the larger social structure. In precise terms, he must learn to control his animal appetites in order to win the love of Sophia Western and the approval of Allworthy. This lesson is rewarded not only by his gaining these two goals, but by his gaining the knowledge of his parentage and his rightful place in society. He is no longer a "foundling."

Unlike the episodic journey of *Joseph Andrews*, *Tom Jones* adapts the classical symmetry of the epic in a more conscious and precise way. The novel is divided into eighteen books. Some of the books, such as I and IV, cover long periods of time and are presented in summary form, with the narrator clearly present; others cover only a few days or hours, with the narrator conspicuously absent and the presentation primarily scenic. The length of each book is determined by the importance of the subject, not the length of time covered.

The books are arranged in a symmetrical pattern. The first half of the novel takes Tom from his mysterious birth to his adventures in the Inn at Upton; the second half takes him from Upton to London and the discovery of his parentage. Books I through VI are set in Somerset at Squire Allworthy's estate and culminate with Tom's affair with Molly. Books VII through XII are set on the road to Upton, at the Inn, and on the road from Upton to London; the two central books detail the adventures at the Inn and Tom's affair with Mrs. Waters. Books XIII through XVIII take Tom to London and begin with his affair with Lady Bellaston.

Within this pattern, Fielding demonstrates his moral thesis, the education of a "good man," in a number of ways: through the narrative (Tom's behavior continually lowers his moral worth in society); through characters (the contrasting pairs of Tom and Blifil, Allworthy and Western, Square and Thwackum, Molly and Lady Bellaston); and through the voice of the narrator.

Fielding extends the role of the narrator in *Tom Jones*, as teller of the tale, as moral guide, and as literary commentator and critic. Each of these voices was heard in *Joseph Andrews*, but here they come together in a unique narrative persona. Adopting the role of the stagecoach traveler, the narrator speaks directly to his fellow passengers, the readers. He is free to digress and comment whenever he feels appropriate, and there is, therefore, no need for the long interpolated tales such as appeared in *Joseph Andrews*.

To remind his readers that the purpose of fiction is aesthetic as well as moral, the narrator often comments on literary topics: "Of the Serious in Writing, and for What Purpose it is introduced"; "A wonderful long chapter concerning the Marvelous"; "Containing Instructions very necessary to be perused by modern Critics." Taken together, these passages provide a guide to Fielding's literary theory as complete as the Preface to *Joseph Andrews*.

Although in *Tom Jones* Fielding still schematically associates characters with particular moral values, the range of characters is wider than in his previous novels. Even a minor character, such as Black George, has a life beyond his moral purpose as representative of hypocrisy and self-servingness.

Most important, *Tom Jones* demonstrates Fielding's skill in combining his moral vision with aesthetic form in a way that is most pleasureable to the reader. The reader learns how to live the good Christian life because Tom learns that lesson. Far more effective than parody, sermon, or moral exemplum, the combination of narrative voice and literary example of plot and character is Fielding's greatest legacy to the novel.

Lawrence F. Laban

Other major works

PLAYS: *Love in Several Masques*, 1728; *The Author's Farce,* 1730, 1734; *The Temple Beau*, 1730; *Tom Thumb: A Tragedy*, 1730 (revised as *The Tragedy of Tragedies: Or, The Life and Death of Tom Thumb the Great*, 1731); *Rape upon Rape: Or, The Justice Caught in His Own Trap*, 1730 (also known as *The Coffee-House Politician*); *The Letter-Writers: Or, A New Way to Keep a Wife at Home*, 1731; *The Welsh Opera: Or, The Grey Mare the Better Horse*, 1731 (revised as *The Genuine Grub-Street Opera*); *The Covent-Garden Trag-*

edy, 1732; *The Mock Doctor: Or, The Dumb Lady Cur'd*, 1732; *The Modern Husband*, 1732; *The Miser*, 1733; *Don Quiote in England*, 1734; *The Intriguing Chambermaid*, 1734; *An Old Man Taught Wisdom: Or, The Virgin Unmask'd*, 1735; *Pasquin*, 1736; *Tumble-Down Dick:Or, Phaeton in the Suds*, 1736; *The Historical Register for the Year 1736*, 1737; *Eurydice*, 1737; *Miss Lucy in Town*, 1742 (with David Garrick); *Plutus, the God of Riches*, 1742 (with William Young); *The Wedding-Day*, 1743.

NONFICTION: *The Journal of a Voyage to Lisbon*, 1755.

TRANSLATION: *The Military History of Charles XII King of Sweden*, 1740.

MISCELLANEOUS: *Miscellanies*, 1743 (3 volumes).

Bibliography

Battestin, Martin C. *The Moral Basis of Fielding's Art: A Study of Joseph Andrews*. Middletown, Conn.: Wesleyan University Press, 1959. An important study arguing that in *Joseph Andrews* Fielding presents an allegory of the conflict between vanity and true Christian morality. Like John Bunyan's *The Pilgrim's Progress*, the novel traces the movement from the sinful city to the redemptive countryside. Sees the story of Mr. Wilson not as a digression but as a central expression of the novel's theme.

Battestin, Martin C., with Ruthe R. Battestin. *Henry Fielding: A Life*. London: Routledge, 1989. *The Sunday Times* voted this work one of the four best biographies of the year. Based on fourteen years' research, this detailed biography replaces Wilbur L. Cross's *The History of Henry Fielding* (1918, New York: Russell & Russell, 1945) as the definitive life. Includes a useful bibliography of Fielding's writings.

Johnson, Maurice. *Fielding's Art of Fiction: Eleven Essays on "Shamela," "Joseph Andrews," "Tom Jones," and "Amelia."* Philadelphia: University of Pennsylvania Press, 1961. Johnson writes in his introduction, "I want to suggest how, in his fiction, Fielding attempted vigorously and cheerfully to define the good life, within the severe limitations set by Fortune, society, and man's own errant nature" (pages 16-17). These eleven pieces provide a good critical survey of Fielding's fiction.

Rogers, Pat. *Henry Fielding: A Biography*. New York: Charles Scribner's Sons, 1979. A lively, short biography for the general reader or beginning student. Offers little critical analysis of the works. Nicely illustrated.

Sacks, Sheldon. *Fiction and the Shape of Belief*. Berkeley: University of California Press, 1964. Posits three categories of fiction: satire, apologue, and novel. Argues that, because Fielding uses characters to demonstrate his moral stance, his works are novels, but that his various digressions, providing more overt moral lessons, are apologues.

Stoler, John A., and Richard D. Fulton. *Henry Fielding: An Annotated Bibliography of Twentieth-Century Criticism, 1900-1977*. New York: Garland, 1980. After listing a number of major Fielding bibliographies and various editions of his works, this bibliography provides a comprehensive, annotated list of secondary works. Arrangement is by title, so students seeking material on a specific work, such as *Tom Jones*, can quickly find what they need.

Watt, Ian. *The Rise of the Novel: Studies in Defoe, Richardson, and Fielding.* Berkeley: University of California Press, 1957. While praising Fielding's "wise assessment of life," Watt believes that Fielding's novelistic techniques reject verisimilitude for the sake of the moral. Hence, Watt sees Fielding's approach as a fictional dead end. Contains some useful observations about Fielding's plots and language.

F. SCOTT FITZGERALD

Born: St. Paul, Minnesota; September 24, 1896
Died: Hollywood, California; December 21, 1940

Principal long fiction

This Side of Paradise, 1920; *The Beautiful and Damned*, 1922; *The Great Gatsby*, 1925; *Tender Is the Night*, 1934; *The Last Tycoon*, 1941.

Other literary forms

Charles Scribner's Sons published nine books by F. Scott Fitzgerald during Fitzgerald's lifetime. In addition to the first four novels, there were four volumes of short stories, *Flappers and Philosophers* (1920), *Tales of the Jazz Age* (1922), *All the Sad Young Men* (1926), and *Taps at Reveille* (1935); and one play, *The Vegetable: Or, From President to Postman* (1923). The story collections published by Charles Scribner's Sons contained fewer than a third of the 165 stories that appeared in major periodicals during his lifetime; now, virtually all of Fitzgerald's stories are available in hardcover collections. Fitzgerald also wrote essays and autobiographical pieces, many of which appeared in the late 1930's in *Esquire* and are now collected, among other places, in *The Crack-Up* (1945). Fitzgerald's Hollywood writing consisted mainly of collaborative efforts on scripts for films such as *Gone with the Wind* and *Infidelity*, although during his life and since his death there have been various screen adaptations of his novels and stories. In recent years, Fitzgerald's notebooks, scrapbooks, and letters have been published, and the record of his literary achievement is now nearly complete.

Achievements

Curiously, Fitzgerald has appealed to two diverse audiences since the beginning of his career: the popular magazine audience and the elite of the literary establishment. His work appeared regularly in the 1920's and 1930's in such mass circulation magazines as the *Saturday Evening Post, Hearst's, International, Collier's,* and *Redbook*. The readers of these magazines came to ask for Fitzgerald's flapper stories by name, expecting to find in them rich, young, and glamorous heroes and heroines involved in exciting adventures. Popular magazines in the 1920's billed Fitzgerald stories on the cover, often using them inside as lead stories. Long after Fitzgerald lost the knack of writing the kind of popular stories that made him famous as the creator of the flapper in fiction and as the poet laureate of the jazz age, magazine headnotes to his stories identified him as such. Those who recognized the more serious side of his talent as it was evidenced particularly in his best stories and novels included Edmund Wilson, George Jean Nathan, H. L. Mencken, Gertrude Stein, Edith Wharton, and T. S. Eliot, who offered criticism as well as praise. Fitzgerald was generous with advice to other writers, most notably to Ring Lardner, Ernest Hemingway, and Thomas Wolfe; but also to struggling unknowns, who wrote to him asking advice and got it.

Many of Fitzgerald's critical opinions went into the public domain when he published his Crack-up essays in *Esquire* in the late 1930's, his dark night of the soul. Regarded by some in Fitzgerald's time as self-pitying, these essays are now often anthologized and widely quoted for the ideas and theories about literature and life that they contain. At the time of his death, Fitzgerald seemed nearly forgotten by his popular readers and greatly neglected by literary critics. After his death and the posthumous publication of his incomplete *The Last Tycoon*, a Fitzgerald revival, still in progress, began. With this revival, Fitzgerald's reputation as a novelist (principally on the strength of *The Great Gatsby* and *Tender Is the Night*), short-story writer, and essayist has been solidly established.

Biography

Francis Scott Key Fitzgerald was born in St. Paul, Minnesota, on September 24, 1896. His mother's side of the family (the McQuillan side) was what Fitzgerald referred to as "straight 1850 potato famine Irish," but by the time of his maternal grandfather's death at the age of forty-four, the McQuillan fortune, earned in the grocery business, was in excess of $300,000. Fitzgerald's father was a poor but well-bred descendant of the old Maryland Scott and Key families. Always an ineffectual businessman, Edward Fitzgerald had met Mary McQuillan when he had come to St. Paul to open a wicker furniture business, which shortly went out of business. In search of a job by which he could support the family, Edward Fitzgerald moved his family from St. Paul to Buffalo, New York, in 1898—then to Syracuse and back to Buffalo. When Fitzgerald was eleven, the family returned to St. Paul and the security of the McQuillan wealth.

With McQuillan money Fitzgerald was sent for two painfully lonely years to private school, the Newman School in Hackensack, New Jersey. Discovering there a flair for writing musical comedy, Fitzgerald decided that he would attend Princeton, whose Triangle Club produced a musical comedy each year. At Princeton, Fitzgerald compensated for his feelings of social inferiority by excelling in the thing he did best, writing for the Triangle Club and the *Nassau Literary Magazine*. During a Christmas vacation spent in St. Paul, Fitzgerald met Ginevra King, a wealthy Chicago debutante whose initial acceptance of Fitzgerald was a supreme social triumph; her later rejection of him became one of the most devastating blows of his life. He kept her letters, which he had typed and bound and which ran to over two hundred pages, until his death.

In 1917, Fitzgerald left Princeton without a degree, accepted a commission in the army, and wrote the first draft of what was to become his first novel,

This Side of Paradise. During the summer of 1918, Fitzgerald met Zelda Sayre while he was stationed near Montgomery, Alabama; and having recently received word of Ginevra King's engagement, he fell in love with Zelda. Zelda, however, although willing to become engaged to Fitzgerald, did not finally agree to marry him until he could demonstrate his ability to support her. Fitzgerald returned to New York, worked for an advertising firm, and revised his novel, including in it details from his courtship with Zelda. When Charles Scribner's Sons agreed in September, 1919, to publish the novel, Fitzgerald was able to claim Zelda, and they were married in April of the following year.

The first two years of their marriage were marked by wild parties, the self-destructive mood of which formed the basis for some of the scenes in Fitzgerald's second novel, *The Beautiful and Damned*. After a trip to Europe, the Fitzgeralds returned first to St. Paul and then to Great Neck, New York, where they lived among the Astors and Vanderbilts while Fitzgerald accumulated material that would figure in *The Great Gatsby*.

In the decade that followed the publication of that novel, the Fitzgeralds lived, among other places, on the French Riviera, which would provide the background for *Tender Is the Night*. Zelda headed toward a mental collapse, a fictionalized version of which appears in the novel; Fitzgerald sank into alcoholism. In 1930, Zelda was institutionalized for treatment of her mental condition. The rest of Fitzgerald's life was spent writing stories and screenplays that would pay for her treatment, both in and out of institutions. In 1937, Fitzgerald went to Hollywood, met Sheila Graham, worked under contract for M-G-M, and accumulated material for his last novel, while Zelda remained in the East. Fitzgerald died of a heart attack on December 21, 1940, while working on his unfinished novel, *The Last Tycoon*.

Analysis

"The test of a first-rate intelligence," F. Scott Fitzgerald remarked in the late 1930's, "is the ability to hold two opposed ideas in the mind at the same time, and still retain the ability to function." At his best—in *The Great Gatsby*, in parts of *Tender Is the Night*, in the unfinished *The Last Tycoon*, and in parts of his first two novels, *This Side of Paradise* and *The Beautiful and Damned*—Fitzgerald demonstrates the kind of intelligence he describes, an intelligence characterized by the aesthetic principle of "double vision." An understanding of this phrase (coined and first applied to Fitzgerald's art by Malcolm Cowley) is central to any discussion of Fitzgerald's novels. "Double vision" denotes two ways of seeing. It implies the tension involved when Fitzgerald sets things in opposition such that the reader can, on the one hand, sensually experience the event about which Fitzgerald is writing, immersing himself emotionally in it, and yet at the same time retain the objectivity to stand back and intellectually criticize it. The foundation of double vision is polarity—the setting of extremes against each other; the result in a novel is dramatic tension. By following the changes in Fitzgerald's narrative technique from *This Side of Paradise* to *The Beautiful and Damned* to *The Great Gatsby* and finally into *Tender Is the Night*, one can trace the growth of his double vision, which is, in effect, to study his development as a literary artist.

The major themes of Fitzgerald's novels derive from the resolution of tension when one idea (usually embodied in a character) triumphs over another. Amory Blaine, the protagonist of Fitzgerald's first novel, *This Side of Paradise*, is a questing hero armed with youth, intelligence, and good looks. Anthony Patch in *The Beautiful and Damned* has a multimillionaire grandfather, a beautiful wife, and youth. Jay Gatsby in *The Great Gatsby* possesses power, newly made money, and good looks. Finally, Dick Diver in *Tender Is the Night* has a medical degree, an overabundance of charm, and a wealthy wife. The common denominators here are the subjects with which Fitzgerald deals in all of his novels: youth, physical beauty, wealth, and potential or "romantic readiness"—all of which are ideals to Fitzgerald. Set against these subjects are their polar opposites: age, ugliness, poverty, squandered potential. Such conflict and resulting tension is, of course, the stuff of which all fiction is made. With Fitzgerald's characters, however, partly because of the themes with which he deals and partly because of his skillful handling of point of view, the choices are rarely as obvious or as clear-cut to the main characters at the time as they may be to a detached observer, or as they may seem in retrospect to have been. Daisy, for example, so enchants Gatsby and the reader who identifies with him that only in retrospect (if at all) or through the detached observer, Nick, does it become clear that she and the other careless, moneyed people in the novel are villains of the highest order. It is Fitzgerald's main gift that he can draw the reader into a web of emotional attachment to a character, as he does to Daisy through Gatsby, while simultaneously allowing him to inspect the complexity of the web, as he does through Nick. That is what Fitzgerald's double vision at its best is finally about.

For the origins of Fitzgerald's double vision, it is helpful to look at several ingredients of his early life, particularly at those facets of it which presented him with the polarities and ambiguities that would later furnish the subjects and themes of his art. "In a house below the average on a block above the average" is the way that Fitzgerald described his boyhood home. A block above the average, indeed. At the end of the "block" on Summit Avenue in St. Paul lived James J. Hill, the multimillionaire empire-builder referred to by Gatsby's father in the last chapter of *The Great Gatsby*. The Fitzgerald family, however, nearly in sight of such wealth, lived moderately on the interest from his mother's inheritance, taking pains not to disturb the capital; for Fitzgerald's father, in spite of his idealistic gentility and an ancestral line that linked him to the Maryland Scott and Key families, was unable to hold a good job. One of Fitzgerald's most devastating memories was of his father's loss of a job with Proctor and Gamble, which left the older Fitzgerald, then beyond middle age, broken and defeated. When Fitzgerald was sent East to boarding school and then to Princeton, it was with his mother's money, less than a generation earned, and with considerably less of it than stood behind most of his classmates. Early, then, Fitzgerald, a child with sensitivity, intelligence, and good looks—qualities possessed by most of his heroes and heroines—was impressed with the importance of money, at least to the life-style of the moneyed class. Yet Fitzgerald's participation in that life-style, like that of many of his fictional creations, was limited by something beyond his control: the fixed income of his family. In addition, he watched his father, an idealist unable to compete in a materialistic world, defeated.

With this kind of early life, Fitzgerald was prepared, or more accurately left totally unprepared, for the series of events in his life which formed the basis of much of his later fiction. Two of these stand out: his romantic attachment to Ginevra King, a wealthy Chicago debutante who in his words "ended up by throwing me over with the most supreme boredom and indifference"; and his relationship with Zelda Sayre, who broke their engagement (because Fitzgerald was neither rich enough nor famous enough for her) before finally marrying him after his first novel was accepted for publication by Charles Scribner's Sons. Fitzgerald emphasizes the importance of the Ginevra King episode in particular and of biographical material in general in his essay "One Hundred False Starts": "We have two or three great and moving experiences in our lives. . . . Then we learn our trade, well or less well, and we tell our two or three stories—each time in a new disguise—maybe ten times, maybe a hundred, as long as people will listen." The subjects and themes from those experiences formed what Fitzgerald called "my material."

Through Ginevra King, Fitzgerald saw the opportunity to be accepted into the wealth that the King family represented. Her father, however, did not conceal his "poor boys shouldn't think of marrying rich girls" attitude, recorded in Fitzgerald's notebooks, and when Fitzgerald was "thrown over" in favor of an acceptable suitor with money and social position, he saw the rejection not only as a personal one but also as evidence that the emergence of an upper caste in American society had rendered the American dream an empty promise. Curiously though, Fitzgerald's infatuation with wealth and the wealthy, symbolized by the Kings, stayed with him for the rest of his life. As he wrote to his daughter in the late 1930's on the eve of seeing Ginevra King for the first time since she had rejected him nearly twenty years earlier, "She was the first girl I ever loved and I have faithfully avoided seeing her up to this moment to keep that illusion perfect." It was this experience, then, coupled with the near-loss of Zelda and their subsequent, complex relationship that would provide his "material." Fitzgerald also describes an attitude which grows out of these experiences of enchantment and loss and which he identifies variously as his "solid gold bar" or his "stamp": "Taking things hard—from Ginevra to Joe Mank. That's the stamp that goes into my books so that people can read it blind like Braille."

Writing in 1938 about the subject matter of his first novel, Fitzgerald alludes to its origins in his experience: "In 'This Side of Paradise' I wrote about a love affair that was still bleeding as fresh as the skin wound on a haemophile." The love affair that he refers to is his relationship with Ginevra King, and it is but one of many episodes from Fitzgerald's life—his courtship with Zelda is another—that are loosely tied together in *This Side of Paradise* to form a *Bildungsroman*. Unlike the novel of "selected incident," the *Bildungsroman* is a novel of "saturation"—that is, a novel in which the hero takes on experiences until he reaches a saturation point; by virtue of his coming to this point he reaches a higher level of self-awareness. In *This Side of Paradise*, Amory Blaine, the hero and thinly veiled Fitzgerald persona, reaches this point when, at the end of the novel, he rejects all of the values that have been instilled in him, embraces socialism, and yells to the world, "I know myself . . . but that is all."

The route which Amory follows to arrive at this pinnacle of self-knowledge is more a meandering process of trial and error than it is a systematic journey with a clearly defined purpose. His mother, whom Amory quaintly calls by her first name, Beatrice, and whom he relates to as a peer, instills in Amory an egotism (almost unbearable to his own peers as well as to the reader) and a respect for wealth and social position. These qualities make Amory an object of ridicule when he goes away to an eastern boarding school. His years at St. Regis are spent in isolation, and there he finally makes the emotional break with his mother that frees the "fundammental Amory" to become, in Fitzgerald's words, a "personage." The landmarks of this becoming process are, for the most part, encounters with individuals who teach Amory about himself: "The Romantic Egotist," as he is referred to in Book One of the novel, is too solipsistic to go beyond himself even at the end of the novel. After learning from these individuals, Amory either leaves or is left by them. From Clara, a cousin whose beauty and intelligence he admires, he learns that he follows his imagination too freely; he learns from his affair with Rosalind, who almost marries him but refuses because Amory lacks the money to support her, that money determines the direction of love. Through Monsignor Darcy, he learns that the Church of Rome is too confining for him; and from half a dozen of his classmates at Princeton, he discovers the restlessness and rebelliousness that lead him to reject all that he had been brought up to believe, reaching out toward socialism as one of the few gods he has not tried.

The reader will perhaps wonder how Amory, whose path has zig-zagged through many experiences, none of which has brought him closely in contact with socialism, has arrived at a point of almost evangelical, anticapitalistic zeal. It is worth noting, however, that, in addition to its interest to literary historians as an example of the *Bildungsroman*, *This Side of Paradise* also has value to social historians as an enlightening account of jazz age manners and morals. One contemporary observer labeled the novel "a gesture of indefinite revolt," a comment intended as a criticism of the novel's lack of focus. The social historian, however, would see the phrase as a key to the novel's value, which view would cast Amory in the role of spokesman for the vague rebelliousness of the "lost generation," a generation, in Amory's words, "grown up to find all gods dead, all wars fought, all faiths in man shaken." As Malcolm Cowley has noted, "More than any other writer of these times, Fitzgerald had the sense of living in history. He tried hard to catch the color of every passing year, its distinctive slang, its dance steps, its songs . . . its favorite quarterbacks, and the sort of clothes and emotions its people wore." John O'Hara, for one, recalls the impact of *This Side of Paradise* on his generation: "A little matter of twenty-five years ago I, along with half a million other men and women between fifteen and thirty, fell in love with a book. . . . I took the book to bed with me, and I still do, which is more than I can say of any girl I knew in 1920." By Fitzgerald's own account, the novel made him something of an "oracle" to his college readers, and largely on the strength of *This Side of Paradise*, Fitzgerald became the unofficial poet laureate of the jazz age.

Yet, for those interested in Fitzgerald's development as a novelist, the value of *This Side of Paradise* goes beyond its worth as a novel of growth or its importance as a social document. In it are contained early versions in rough form of most of the novels that Fitzgerald later wrote. By the time of its completion, Fitzgerald's major subjects were cast and marked with his "stamp": "taking things hard." Amory "takes hard" the breakup with the young, wealthy, and beautiful Isabel, modeled on Ginevra King. Amory "takes hard" his rejection by Rosalind by going on an extended drunk, similar to Fizgerald's response when Zelda refused to marry him until he demonstrated that he could support her. Event after event in the novel shows Fitzgerald, through Amory, "taking hard" the absence of wealth, the loss of youth, and the ephermerality of beauty. Even in the characterization of Amory, who is born moneyed and aristocratic, Fitzgerald seems to be creating his ideal conception of himself, much the way Gatsby later springs from his own platonic conception of himself. With his subject matter, his themes, and his distinctive stamp already formed, Fitzgerald needed only to find a point of view by which he could distance himself, more than he had through Amory, from his material. He had yet, as T. S. Eliot would have phrased it, to find an "objective correlative," which is to say that he had not yet acquired the double vision so evident in *The Great Gatsby*.

Although *The Beautiful and Damned*, Fitzgerald's second novel, is usually considered his weakest, largely because of its improbable and melodramatic ending, there is evidence in it of Fitzgerald's growth as a writer. Unlike *This Side of Paradise*, which is a subjective rendering through a thinly disguised persona and which includes nearly everything from Fitzgerald's life and work through 1920 (one critic called it "the collected works of F. Scott Fitzgerald"), *The Beautiful and Damned* moved toward the novel of selected incident. Written in the third person, it shows Fitzgerald dealing in a more objective fashion with biographical material that was close to him, in this instance the early married life of the Fitzgeralds. Whereas *This Side of Paradise* was largely a retrospecive, nostalgic recounting of Fitzgerald's recently lost youth, *The Beautiful and Damned* projects imaginatively into the future of a life based on the belief that nothing is worth doing.

In spite of the differences between the two novels, however, particularly in narrative perspective, it is clear that the characters and subjects in *The Beautiful and Damned* are logical extensions, more objectively rendered, of those introduced in *This Side of Paradise*, making the former a sequel, in a sense, to the latter. With slight modifications, Anthony Patch, the hero of *The Beautiful and Damned*, is Amory Blaine grown older and more cynical. Add to Amory a heritage that links him to Anthony Comstock, a mother and father who died in his youth, a multimillionaire grandfather, and half a dozen years, and the result is a reasonable facsimile of Anthony. To Amory's Rosalind (a composite of Ginevra King and Zelda), add a few years, a "coast-to-coast reputation for irresponsibility and beauty," and a bit more cleverness, and the result is strikingly similar to Gloria Gilbert, the heroine of *The Beautiful and Damned*, who will, unlike Rosalind, marry the hero.

When Fitzgerald created Rosalind, of course, Zelda had for the time rejected him. Her reappearance in *The Beautiful and Damned* as the hero's wife reflects Fitzgerald's change in fortune, since he and Zelda had been married for two years when *The Beautiful and Damned* was published. Their life together provided the basis for many of the experiences in the novel, and there is good reason to believe that the mutual self-destructiveness evident on nearly every page of the novel reflects Fitzgerald's fears of what he and Zelda might do to each other and to themselves. In *This Side of Paradise* Amory knows himself, "but that is all." Anthony carries this knowledge two years into the future and cynically applies it to life: he will prove that life is meaningless and that "there's nothing I can do that's worth doing." His task is to demonstrate that it is possible for an American to be gracefully idle. Gloria's goal is to avoid responsibility forever, which was essentially Rosalind's goal in *This Side of Paradise*. The kind of life that Gloria and Anthony desire is dependent on the possession of wealth, of which Anthony has promise through the estate of his grandfather, a virtual guarantee until the social-reformer grandfather happens into one of the Patches' parties and disinherits Anthony.

The novel could logically end there, but it does not. Instead, its long conclusion leads the reader through a maze of melodramatic circumstances and improbabilities. Gloria and Anthony contest the will and, with dwindling funds, sink into despair and self-destructiveness. Gloria auditions for a part in a motion picture and is told that she is too old for the part; Anthony remains drunk, tries unsuccessfully to borrow money from friends, and finally gets into a senseless fight with the film producer who has given Gloria the news that she is too old for the part she wants. On the day of the trial that will determine whether the will is to be broken, Anthony loses his mind and is capable only of babbling incoherently when Gloria brings him the news that they are rich.

The major flaw in the novel is this long, melodramatic ending and the thematic conclusions it presents. On the one hand, Fitzgerald posits the theory that life is meaningless, yet Anthony's life is given meaning by his quest for money, not to mention that the philosophy itself can be practiced only when there is enough money to support it. Certainly Gloria, who is sane and happy at the novel's end, does not seem much impressed by life's meaninglessness, and the reader is left with the feeling that Anthony, when the advantages that his inheritance can offer him are evident, will recover from his "on-cue" flight into insanity. The effect of the ending is to leave the reader with the impression that Fitzgerald had not thought the theme carefully through; or, as Edmund Wilson hints, that Fitzgerald himself had not taken the ideas in either of his first two novels seriously:

> In college he had supposed that the thing to do was to write biographical novels with a burst of energy toward the close; since his advent into the literary world, he has discovered that another genre has recently come into favor: the kind which makes much of tragedy and what Mencken has called "the meaninglessness of life."

The greater truth suggested by Wilson here is that through 1922 Fitzgerald was writing, in part, what he thought he should write. With the completion of *The Beautiful and Damned*, his apprenticeship was over, and with an artistic leap he moved into his own as an original prose stylist, writing in *The Great Gatsby* what Eliot called "the first step that American fiction has taken since Henry James."

For Amory Blaine in *This Side of Paradise*, there are four golden moments, as many perhaps as there are new and exciting women to meet; for Anthony Patch in *The Beautiful and Damned*, the moment is his meeting with Gloria Gilbert. For Jay Gatsby, the golden moment is the time when "his unutterable vision" meets Daisy's "perishable breath." For Fitzgerald, the artistic golden moment was the creation of *The Great Gatsby*. Critics have marveled that the author of *This Side of Paradise* and *The Beautiful and Damned* could in less than two years after the publication of the latter produce a novel of the stature of *The Great Gatsby*. As should be clear by now, the writer of *This*

Side of Paradise did not blossom overnight into the author of *The Great Gatsby*. The process by which Fitzgerald came to create *The Great Gatsby* is a logical one. From the beginning of his career as a novelist, Fitzgerald stayed with the subjects and themes that he knew well and that were close to him: wealth, youth, and beauty. What did change between the creation of *This Side of Paradise* and *The Great Gatsby* was Fitzgerald's perspective on his material and his ability to objectify his attitudes toward it. In 1925, Fitzgerald was more than five years removed from his affair with Ginevra King, which gave him the distance to be Nick Carraway, the novel's "objective" narrator. Yet he was also near enough in memory that he could recall, even relive, the seductiveness of her world; that is, he was still able to be the romantic hero, Jay Gatsby. In effect, he had reached the pivotal point in his life that allowed him to see clearly through the eyes of both Gatsby and Nick; for the time of the creation of *The Great Gatsby*, he possessed double vision.

The success of the novel depends on Fitzgerald's ability to transfer to the reader the same kind of vision that he himself had: the ability to believe in the possibilities of several opposite ideas at various levels of abstraction. On the most concrete level, the reader must believe that Gatsby will and will not win Daisy, the novel's heroine and symbol of the American ideal. On a more general level, he must believe that anyone in America, through hard work and perseverance, can and cannot gain access to the best that America has to offer. Until Daisy's final rejection of Gatsby in the penultimate chapter of the novel, the reader can, indeed, believe in both alternatives because he has seen them both from the perspective of Gatsby (who believes) and from the point of view of Nick (who wants to believe but intellectually cannot).

The central scene in *The Great Gatsby* nicely illustrates how Fitzgerald is able to present his material in such a way as to create dramatic tension through the use of double vision. This scene, which occupies the first part of Chapter Five, is built around the reunion of Gatsby and Daisy after a five-year separation. The years, for Gatsby, have been devoted to the obsessive pursuit of wealth, which he wants only because he belives it will win Daisy for him. Daisy, who has married Tom Buchanan, seems to have given little thought to Gatsby since her marriage. The moment of their reunion, then, means everything to Gatsby and very little to Daisy, except as a diversion from the luxurious idling of her daily existence. In this meeting scene, as Gatsby stands nervously talking to Daisy and Nick, Fitzgerald calls the reader's attention to a defunct clock on Nick's mantlepiece. When Gatsby leans against the mantle, the clock teeters on the edge, deciding finally not to fall. The three stare at the floor as if the clock has, in fact, shattered to pieces in front of them. Gatsby apologizes and Nick replies, "It's an old clock."

On the level of plot, this scene is the dramatic high point of the novel; the first four chapters have been devoted to preparing the reader for it. The image of Daisy's desirability as she is seen through Nick's eyes in Chapter One has been followed with an image at the chapter's end of Gatsby standing, arms outstretched, toward the green light across the bay at the end of Daisy's dock; the image of the emptiness of the Buchanans' world in Chapter One has been followed with the image in Chapter Two of the valley of ashes, a huge dumping ground in which lives the mistress of Daisy's husband Tom; the open public gathering of Gatsby's lavish parties in Chapter Three has been set against the mysterious privacy of Gatsby's life. All of these scenes have come to the reader through the central intelligence, Nick, who has learned from Jordan Baker a truth that, at this point, only Gatsby, Jordan, and Nick know: Gatsby wants to turn time backward and renew his relationship with Daisy as if the five years since he has seen her have not gone by. Nick, Daisy's cousin and Gatsby's neighbor, is the natural link that will reconnect Daisy and Gatsby. To the tension inherent in the reunion itself, then, is added the ambivalence of Nick, who, on the one hand, despises Gatsby's gaudiness but admires his romantic readiness; and who is captivated by Daisy's charm but also, by the time of the meeting in Chapter Five, contemptuous of her moral emptiness.

On coming into the meeting scene, the reader is interested, first on the level of plot, to see whether Gatsby and Daisy can renew their love of five years before. In addition, he is interested in the reaction of Nick, on whose moral and intellectual judgment he has come to depend. At a deeper level, he is ready for the confrontation of abstract ideas that will occur in the clock scene. The clock itself, a focal point of the room in which Gatsby and Daisy meet, represents the past time that Gatsby wants to repeat in order to recapture Daisy's love for him. That this clock, which has stopped at some past moment, can be suspended on a mantlepiece in front of them affirms the possibility of bringing the past into the present. Yet, the fact that they all envision the clock shattered on the floor suggests that all three are aware of the fragility of this past moment brought into the present. The fact that the clock does not work hints at the underlying flaw in Gatsby's dream of a relationship with Daisy.

The scene is a foreshadowing of what the rest of the novel will present dramatically: the brief and intense renewal of a courtship that takes place behind the closed doors of Gatsby's mansion, a courtship that will end abruptly behind the closed doors of a Plaza Hotel room after a confrontation between Gatsby and Tom, convinces Daisy finally to reject Gatsby. The death of Myrtle, Tom's mistress; Gatsby's murder by Myrtle's husband; Daisy and Tom's "vacation" until the confusion dies down; Gatsby's funeral, whose arrangements are handled by Nick—all follow with an unquestionable inevitability in the last two chapters of the novel. Nick alone is left to tell the story of the dreamer whose dreams were corrupted by the "foul dust" that floated in their wake and of the reckless rich who "smashed up things and people and then retreated back into their vast carelessness, or whatever it was that kept them together, and let other people clean up the mess they had made."

At this end-point, the reader will recall the ominous foreshadowing of the broken clock: Gatsby cannot, as Nick has told him, repeat the past. He cannot have Daisy, because as Nick knows, "poor guys shouldn't think of marrying rich girls." Gatsby cannot have what he imagined to be the best America had to offer, which Nick realizes is *not* Daisy. Yet, the fault does not lie in Gatsby's capacity to dream, only in "the foul dust" which floated in the wake of his dreams—a belief in the money-god, for example—which makes him mistake a counterfeit (Daisy) for the true romantic vision. "No—Gatsby turned out all right at the end," Nick says in a kind of preface to the novel, a statement which keeps Fitzgerald's double vision intact in spite of Gatsby's loss of Daisy and his life. At the highest level of abstraction, the novel suggests that an idealist unwilling to compromise can and cannot survive in a materialistic world, an ambivalent point of view that Fitzgerald held until his death. No longer did he need to write what he thought he should write; he was writing from the vantage point of one who saw that he had endowed the world of Ginevra King with a sanctity it did not deserve. Part of him, like Gatsby, died with the realization. The other part, like Nick, lived on to make sense of what he had lost and to find a better dream.

For the nine years that followed the publication of *The Great Gatsby* (sometimes referred to as "the barren years"), Fitzgerald published no novels. During the first five of these years, the Fitzgeralds made four trips to Europe, where they met Ernest Hemingway in 1925 and where they lived for a time on the French Riviera, near Gerald and Sara Murphy, prototypes for Dick and Nicole Diver in Fitzgerald's last complete novel, *Tender Is the Night*. In 1930, Zelda had her first mental breakdown and was hospitalized in Switzerland. Two years later she had a second one. For Fitzgerald, the years from 1930 to 1933 were years during which he was compelled to write short stories for popular magazines, primarily the *Saturday Evening Post*, to enable Zelda to be treated in expensive mental institutions. All of the years were devoted to developing a perspective on his experiences: his feelings about Zelda's affair with a French aviator, Edouard Jozan; his own retaliatory relationship with a young film star, Lois Moran; his attraction to the life-style of the Murphys; Zelda's mental illness; his own alcoholism and emotional bankruptcy. He carried the perspective he gained through seventeen complete drafts, fully documented by Matthew J. Bruccoli in *The Composition of Tender Is the Night* (1963), to its completion in his novel.

Partly because it attempts to bring together so many subjects, partly because it deals with so complex a theme as the decline of Western civilization, and partly because of its experimentation with multiple points of view, *Tender Is the Night* is usually regarded as Fitzgerald's most ambitious novel. The story line of the novel is straightforward and has the recognizable Fitzgerald stamp. Its hero, Dick Diver, is a gifted young American in Europe who studies psychiatry with Sigmund Freud, writes a textbook for psychiatrists, marries a wealthy American mental patient, and over a period of years makes her well, while sinking himself into an emotional and physical decline that leads him away from Europe to wander aimlessly in an obscure part of upper New York state. The plot rendered chronologically can be represented as two *v*'s placed point-to-point to form an *X*. The lower *v* is Dick's story, which follows him from a relatively low social and economic position to a high one as a doctor and scientist and back again to the low point of emotional bankruptcy. The story of his wife Nicole can be represented by the upper *v*, since Nicole starts life in America's upper class, falls into mental illness (caused by an incestuous relationship with her father), and then rises again to a height of stability and self-sufficiency.

Fitzgerald, however, does not choose to tell the story in chronological sequence, electing instead to focus first on Dick Diver at the high point of his career, following him through his training in a flashback, and ending the novel with his collapse into anonymity. Nicole's story, secondary to Dick's, is woven into that of Dick's decline, with the implication that she has helped to speed it along. Nor does Fitzgerald select for the novel a single focus of narration, as he does in *The Great Gatsby*. Instead, Book One of the novel shows Dick in June and July of 1925 at the high point of his life, just before the beginning of his decline, from the viewpoint of Rosemary Hoyt, an innocent eighteen-year-old film star whose innocence Dick will finally betray at his low point by making love to her. Book Two contains four chronological shifts covering more than a decade, beginning in 1917, and is presented variously from Dick's and then Nicole's perspective. Book Three brings the story forward one and a half years from the close of Book Two to Dick's departure from the Riviera and Nicole's marriage to Tommy Barban, and it is from the point of view of the survivor, Nicole.

The complicated shifts in viewpoint and chronological sequence are grounded in the complexity of Fitzgerald's purposes. First, he is attempting to document both the external and internal forces which bring about the decline of a gifted individiual. In Dick Diver's case, the inward flaw is rooted in an excess of charm and in a self-destructive need to be used, which the reader can best see from Dick's own perspective. From without, Nicole's money weakens his resistance and serves as a catalyst for the breaking down of his will power, a process more clearly observable in the sections from Nicole's point of view. The value of seeing Dick at a high point early in Book One through Rosemary's eyes is that it emphasizes how attractive and desirable he could be; by contrast, the fact of his emotional bankruptcy at the end of the novel gains power. Fitzgerald, however, is also attempting to equate Dick's decline with the decline of Western society, a subject that had come to him primarily through his reading of Oswald Spengler's *The Decline of the West* (1918-1922). As Fitzgerald wrote to Maxwell Perkins: "I read him the same summer I was writing *The Great Gatsby* and I don't think I ever quite recovered from him." The moral invalids of the international set, who gather on "the little prayer rug of a beach" in *Tender Is the Night*, are, like the characters in Eliot's wasteland, hopelessly cut off from the regenerative powers of nature. There is evidence that even Nicole, whose strength seems assured at the novel's end, may soon be in danger of being overcome by Barban, whose name hints at the barbarian takeover of Western culture predicted by Spengler.

At first glance, *Tender Is the Night* may appear far removed in theme and narrative technique from *The Great Gatsby*, even farther from the two apprenticeship novels, *This Side of Paradise* and *The Beautiful and Damned*. Yet, it does not represent a radical departure from what would seem a predictable pattern of Fitzgerald's growth as a novelist. In *Tender Is the Night*, as in all of his earlier work, Fitzgerald remains close to biographical material, particularly in his drawing on actual people for fictional characters and parts of composite characters. Dick and Nicole Diver are patterned, in part, on Gerald and Sara Murphy, whose "living well" Fitzgerald admired and to whom he dedicated the novel. The Divers are, of course, also the Fitzgeralds, plagued in the 1930's by mental illness and emotional bankruptcy. Similarly, Rosemary Hoyt, whose innocent and admiring viewpoint sets up the first book of the novel, is patterned after the young actress Lois Moran, and Tommy Barban is a fictional representation of Zelda's aviator, Jozan. Also, in drawing on subjects and themes that had characterized even his earliest work, especially wealth and its corrosive influence, Fitzgerald was extending his past concerns from as far back as *This Side of Paradise* into the present: most notably in Baby Warren in *Tender Is the Night*, who callously "buys" Nicole a doctor. Finally, the multiple viewpoint of the novel is a logical extension of the narrator-observer in *The Great Gatsby*, an attempt to carry objectivity even further than he does in that novel. Only perhaps in his reaching into historical prophecy does Fitzgerald go beyond his earlier concerns. Yet even *The Great Gatsby*, which Nick calls "a story of the West," appears on one level to address the moral decay of society on an international level. What *Tender Is the Night* finally reflects, then, is a novelist who has gained philosophical insight and technical skill and has added them onto the existing foundation of his craftsmanship.

Fitzgerald's achievements rest on three obsessions which characterized him as an artist and as a man. The first of these was "his material." It included the subjects of youth, wealth, and beauty and was an outgrowth of his social background. The second was his "solid gold bar" or his "stamp," which he defined as "taking things hard," an attitude which grew out of his background and was partly rooted in his feelings of social inferiority. The third was his "double vision," an artistic perspective that remained his goal until the end. This double vision matured as he gained objectivity toward his material. With these cornerstones, Fitzgerald constructed a set of novels which document the development of one of the most complex and fascinating literary personalities of modern times; which chronicle a time of unparalleled frivolity and subsequent national despondency in America; and which speak with authenticity about an international wasteland almost beyond reclaiming. "The evidence is in," wrote Stephen Vincent Benét regarding the body of Fitzgerald's work in a review of the incomplete *The Last Tycoon*. "This is not a legend, this is a reputation—and seen in perspective, it may well be one of the most secure reputations of our time."

Bryant Mangum

Other major works

SHORT FICTION: *Flappers and Philosophers*, 1920; *Tales of the Jazz Age*, 1922; *All the Sad Young Men*, 1926; *Taps at Reveille*, 1935; *The Stories of F. Scott Fitzgerald*, 1951; *Babylon Revisited and Other Stories*, 1960; *The Pat Hobby Stories*, 1962; *The Apprentice Fiction of F. Scott Fitzgerald, 1907-1917*, 1965; *The Basil and Josephine Stories*, 1973; *Bits of Paradise*, 1974; *The Price Was High: The Last Uncollected Stories of F. Scott Fitzgerald*, 1979.

PLAY: *The Vegetable: Or, From President to Postman*, 1923.

NONFICTION: *The Crack-Up*, 1945; *The Letters of F. Scott Fitzgerald*, 1963; *Letters to His Daughter*, 1965; *Thoughtbook of Francis Scott Fitzgerald*, 1965; *Dear Scott/Dear Max: The Fitzgerald-Perkins Correspondence*, 1971; *As Ever, Scott Fitzgerald*, 1972; *F. Scott Fitzgerald's Ledger*, 1972; *The Notebooks of F. Scott Fitzgerald*, 1978.

MISCELLANEOUS: *Afternoon of an Author: A Selection of Uncollected Stories and Essays*, 1958.

Bibliography

Bloom, Harold, ed. *F. Scott Fitzgerald*. New York: Chelsea House, 1985. A short but important collection of critical essays, this book provides an introductory overview of Fitzgerald scholarship (5 pages), plus readings from a variety of perspectives on his fiction (208 pages).

Bruccoli, Matthew J., ed. *New Essays on "The Great Gatsby."* Cambridge, England: Cambridge University Press, 1985. This short but important collection includes an introductory overview (14 pages) of scholarship, plus interpretive essays on Fitzgerald's best-known novel (120 pages).

_____. *Some Sort of Epic Grandeur*. New York: Harcourt Brace Jovanovich, 1981. In this outstanding biography, a major Fitzgerald scholar argues that Fitzgerald's divided spirit, not his life-style, distracted him from writing. Claims that Fitzgerald both loved and hated the privileged class that was the subject of his fiction (624 pages).

Eble, Kenneth. *F. Scott Fitzgerald*. New York: Twayne, 1963. A clearly written critical biography, this book traces Fitzgerald's development from youth through a "Final Assessment," which surveys scholarship on his texts.

Gervais, Ronald J. "The Socialist and the Silk Stockings: Fitzgerald's Double Allegiance." *Mosaic* 15 (June, 1982): 79-82. This useful article explores the tension of Fitzgerald's use of individualism and his Marxist inclinations. Some biographical data is provided.

Lee, A. Robert, ed. *Scott Fitzgerald: The Promises of Life*. New York: St. Martin's Press, 1989. An excellent collection of essays by Fitzgerald scholars, this book includes an introduction that surveys scholarship on the texts. Topics include Fitzgerald's treatment of women, his notion of the decline of the West, his "ethics and ethnicity," and his use of "distortions" of the imagination (220 pages).

SHELBY FOOTE

Born: Greenville, Mississippi; November 17, 1916

Principal long fiction

Tournament, 1949; *Follow Me Down*, 1950; *Love in a Dry Season*, 1951; *Shiloh*, 1952; *Jordan County: A Landscape in Narrative*, 1954; *Three Novels*, 1964 (contains the previously published *Follow Me Down*, *Jordan County*, and *Love in a Dry Season*); *September September*, 1978.

Other literary forms

Shelby Foote began his writing career with poetry. According to James E. Kibler's bibliography, Foote wrote a total of twenty-seven poems; twenty-two of them were published in his high school newspaper, *The Pica*, and they included such titles as "Embers" (November, 1932), "A Judas Tree" (April, 1933), "Nightfall" (September, 1933), "Judas Iscariot" (November, 1933), "Her Knight Comes Riding" (January, 1934), "The Ugly Duckling to the Princess (On the Styx)" (February, 1935), and "the Revenge of the Browbeaten Wife" (February, 1935). Of the remaining poems, four were published in *The Oxford Magazine*, an independent magazine published in Oxford, Mississippi; the final poem, "Prescription," was published in *The Carolina Magazine*, the University of North Carolina's literary magazine. Foote later admitted, however, that he was more attracted to prose than to poetry, that he thought prose rhythms were more interesting than poetic rhythms, and that the novelist was superior to the poet; consequently, he abandoned poetry for prose writing.

Foote has also written a number of short stories; all of his early stories appeared in *The Carolina Magazine*, including such titles as "The Good Pilgrim: A Fury Is Calmed," "Sad Hiatus: A Short Story," "The Old Man That Sold Peanuts in New Orleans," "The Village Killers: A Story," "The Primrose Hill: A Short Story," "A Tale Untitled," and "Bristol's Gargoyle." *Saturday Evening Post* published "Flood Burial," which eventually became an incident in *Tournament*; *Saturday Evening Post* also published "Tell Them Good-by," a shorter version of what was eventually entitled "Ride Out." Portions of *Shiloh* appeared in *Blue Book Magazine* and in *Esquire*. In 1957, Foote edited a book of short stories entitled *The Night Before Chancellorsville and Other Civil War Stories*, which included a legitimate shorter version of Foote's "Pillar of Fire." Because he favored the novel over the short story, however, he abandoned the latter form.

As writer-in-residence at the University of Virginia, Memphis State University, and Hollins College, Foote has lectured extensively on such subjects as the Civil War, Freshman English, Creative Writing, the novelist as play-wright, Jane Austen's novels, T. S. Eliot's poetry, Ernest Hemingway's short stories, Henry James's *The Portrait of a Lady* (1881), and William Faulkner's works. Foote's Memphis State lectures are all on tape, but his lectures at Hollins College were neither recorded nor published.

While writer-in-residence at the Arena Stage Theater in Washington, D.C., Foote wrote one three-act play entitled *Jordan County: A Landscape in the Round*, adapted from his novel *Jordan County*. Directed by Mel Shapiro, it was performed only once, on June 15, 1964, and has not been published. According to one critic, the only surviving texts are mimeographed script copies kept in the Arena Stage's files.

Besides his major novels, Foote's most imposing and critically acclaimed work is his three-volume *The Civil War: A Narrative* (1958, 1963, 1974). More than a million and a half words in length, Foote's account of the Civil War took twenty years to complete; as he humorously remarked in one of the bibliographical notes, it took him "five times longer to write the war than the participants to fight it." Intensely interested in history, Foote believes that the historian and the novelist are interested in "the same truth," yet they attempt to reach it by different means. Although he does not believe that historians should distort truth, he advises them not only to read the novels of the period they are studying but also to learn the novelists' and poets' techniques.

Acclaimed by reputable and demanding critics, Foote's *The Civil War* combines the research and methods of the historian with the techniques and art of the novelist. His Civil War narrative employs various literary techniques: the protagonist (the South) versus the antagonist (the Union), with each force embodied in its leaders, Jefferson Davis and Abraham Lincoln; the in-depth development of its major and minor characters; the scenes rendered as a novelist would depict them; the alternation of scene and summary; a novelist's feel for the texture of language. Because of its scope and power, *The Civil War* has been labeled "one of the finest histories ever fashioned by an American," "one of the most thorough histories of the Civil War yet done," and "a major achievement in the literature of the Civil War."

Achievements
Perhaps Foote's most notable achievement is that he won great distinction both as a novelist and as a historian. In recognition of Foote's talent and dedication to literature, special issues of the *Mississippi Quarterly* (1971) and *Delta* (1977), a French publication, were devoted entirely to his works.

The Guggenheim Memorial Foundation granted Foote a Guggenheim Fellowship in 1957, 1959, and 1960, and in his "Bibliographical Note" to the second volume of *The Civil War*, he thanked the Foundation for the extended fellowship which "made possible the buying of books and bread." In 1963, he was awarded a Ford Foundation Grant.

Biography

Shelby Foote was born in Greenville, Mississippi, on November 17, 1916, to Shelby Dade and Lillian Rosenstock. His father was a prominent Greenville businessman. His grandfather, Huger Lee Foote, an early planter near Greenville, was the model for Hugh Bart, the protagonist of *Tournament*. Foote's great-grandfather had been a cavalry officer at Shiloh, and another ancestor, Isaac Shelby, had been one of Kentucky's earlier governors and had fought in the Battle of Kings Mountain.

Foote attended grammar and high school in Greenville. When he was about twelve years old, he read *David Copperfield* (1849-1850), which made him realize that reading would be "worth a grown man's time," but he freely admits that neither he nor his family had a literary background. The Foote household did possess, however, the Harvard Classics, Stoddard's Lectures, and current novels by writers such as Rex Beach, Vina del Mar, Percy Marks, and "lots of others mercifully forgotten." One of Foote's best friends in Greenville was Walker Percy, later to become a distinguished novelist himself. Percy was being reared by his uncle, William Alexander Percy, who had a tremendous influence on Foote's reading and eventual interest in literature. Foote recalls that there were literally thousands of books in the Percy house and says that if the Percys had not moved to Greenville he might not have developed an interest in literary things. Very early, William Percy recommended that Foote read what he regarded as the three great modern novels— Marcel Proust's *Remembrance of Things Past* (1913-1927), James Joyce's *Ulysses* (1922), and Thomas Mann's *The Magic Mountain* (1924)—all three of which Foote read in about a six-week period; and Foote soon became an intense reader.

While in high school Foote began writing poetry but soon turned from poetry to prose. After he was graduated from high school, he enrolled in the University of North Carolina at Chapel Hill. Even though he was impressed with the large university library, he soon realized that he did not want a college degree, and about halfway through his first quarter, he dropped all of the subjects he did not like. He remained on the campus and would sneak into undergraduate and even graduate courses which interested him. He particularly enjoyed medieval history, philosophy, and courses in the novel, but, ironically, he did not take creative writing. From 1935 to 1937, he worked on *The Carolina Magazine*, the university's literary publication, in which he published book reviews, poetry, and short stories.

When the Germans invaded Poland in September, 1939, Foote joined the Mississippi National Guard. He wrote *Tournament* in 1939 and submitted the manuscript to Alfred A. Knopf, but it was politely rejected by one of the editors, who informed Foote that, even though several other editors had liked it, *Tournament* was so experimental that it would not sell. The editor did suggest, however, that Foote put this first novel away and write another one, which they would be glad to print.

In 1940, Foote's National Guard unit was activated, and as an artillery sergeant, he marched off to Camp Blanding in Mississippi and then to World War II. He was eventually promoted to captain and then was discharged because he left his post in Northern Ireland to visit his girlfriend in Belfast (she eventually became his first wife). During the fall and winter of 1944, he worked as an Associated Press reporter in New York. On his days off he again began reading, often rereading those books he had enjoyed as an adolescent.

From January to November, 1945, he was in the combat intelligence branch of the Marine Corps. In the postwar years he was a construction worker, a radio copywriter, and a reporter for Hodding Carter's *Delta Democrat-Times*; Carter later said that Foote missed numerous assignments because he was busy writing fiction. Late in 1945, Foote took out the *Tournament* manuscript, reread it, and began a revision; as he himself admitted, it had been influenced too heavily by Joyce, Thomas Wolfe, and various other writers. *Tournament* was published in 1949, and Foote was touted as a "young creative writer of unusual talent." This first novel established Foote's fictional landscape; in *Tournament* and subsequent novels, Washington County and Greenville, Mississippi, become the fictional Jordan County and Bristol, Mississippi. With history as a backdrop, the novel introduced certain motifs which Foote's future narratives would examine: the transition from the old to the new South, the crisis of manhood, and the basic loneliness of man.

Following the publication of *Tournament*, Foote began a great creative period, publishing *Follow Me Down*, *Love in a Dry Season*, *Shiloh*, and *Jordan County* in quick succession. With the exception of *Shiloh*, all of these novels are about the changing "life-away" in the South and around Bristol and Jordan County. After the publication of *Jordan County*, Foote moved to Memphis, Tennessee, and in 1954 he began writing his monumental *The Civil War*, which would require three volumes and twenty years to complete.

In 1956, Foote married Gwyn Rainer of Memphis; they have two children, Margaret Shelby Foote and Huger Lee Foote. In April, 1956, Foote wrote "The Down Slope," a Civil War tale about Mosby's Rangers, which Stanley Kubrick wanted to produce as a film. Although Kubrick had film options for "The Down Slope" and *Love in a Dry Season*, neither was made into a film because, as Foote remarked, his main characters are usually observers who do very little and who do not express what they are thinking in conversation with others. These qualities, says Foote, do not translate into good films.

In November, 1963, Foote was the writer-in-residence at the University of Virginia, where he lectured about his methods of writing historical narrative. From 1963 to 1964, he was playwright-in-residence at the Arena Stage Theatre in Washington, D.C., where he adapted "Rain Down Home," "A Marriage Portion," and "The Freedom Kick"—three stories from *Jordan County*—into a three-act play entitled *Jordan County: A Landscape in the Round*.

Foote moved his family to the Alabama coast in 1964 but ran afoul of the Ku Klux Klan because of his stand on racial equality. After repeated threats, he moved his family back to Memphis. From 1966 to 1967, he was writer-in-residence at Memphis State University, and during the spring term of 1968, he held the same position at Hollins College, where he taught a course in the modern novel and gave lectures. After this latter stint, he confessed that he would not want to do it again, because the college campus was the "worst place on God's earth for a creative writer"; the exchanges, he said, sap the writer's creativity instead of stimulating it. In the summer of 1976, he was one of the guest speakers at the University of Mississippi's annual Faulkner Conference. In 1978, Foote published *September September*.

Past the age of seventy Foote remained active in historical circles; in 1987, for example, he published a short article in *American Heritage*. In that same year, Random House issued a paperback version of *The Civil War*, to renewed critical acclaim.

Analysis

Shelby Foote's *The Civil War* and his six novels are based on three elements: a sense of history, a sense of place, and a sense of change. Foote's sense of history is not that of the antiquarian; rather, he is preoccupied with the historical roots of present conditions. As a novelist, he has sought to "thicken the present" in his narratives by bringing out the historical background. In *Tournament*, for example, Foote concentrates on the historical background of Jordan County and Bristol—the settling of the area in the 1820's, the Civil War, and World War I. *Love in a Dry Season* spans the period from the 1920's to World War II. The historical background for *September September* is the integration crisis at Little Rock Central High School.

Foote's sense of place is distinctly Southern. As William Faulkner created his mythical Yoknapatawpha County and Jefferson, Mississippi, so Foote has created his mythical Jordan County and Bristol, Mississippi, which he has peopled with blacks and whites, rich and poor, old and young. Like Faulkner's saga, Foote's series of novels includes recurring characters; a major character in one novel may be mentioned only in passing in another. *Tournament*, *Follow Me Down*, *Love in a Dry Season*, and *Jordan County* all take place in Bristol in Jordan County, and even though *September September* takes place in Memphis, four of the main characters are from Bristol. In novel after novel, then, Foote highlights the history of his South as it was first settled in the early 1800's, as it began to flourish and prosper, as it was torn and scarred by the Civil War, as it was decimated by the yellow fever epidemic, and as it changed in the ensuing decades.

In a critical comment, Foote grouped novelists into two categories. The first decides to write about a "situation in which a man does so-and-so"; the second decides to write about a "man who does so-and-so," which is followed by the situation. Foote believes that for a good writer, the *man* must come before the *situation*. Foote's interest in history and his rich sense of place are both subservient to his preoccupation with moral action, with men and women making choices, especially under the pressure of change.

Foote's themes arise logically from his analysis of history, place, and change. Beginning with *Tournament*, one of his major themes is man's loneliness. Man is utterly alone, says Foote, in orgasm, in nausea, and in dying. Human beings must accept loneliness as a fact of life, attempting to achieve contact without expecting to lose their essential solitude. Another recurring theme in Foote's works is the crisis of manhood. Rooted in the romantic antebellum South, this concept of masculinity involves a complex code which governs every aspect of a man's life.

Foote readily acknowledged that his first novel, *Tournament*, was written when he was "sort of thrashing around in the wilds of the English language." *Tournament* foreshadows Foote's interest in history, place, and change and introduces his themes of loneliness and masculinity. At the center of the story is the rise and fall of Hugh Bart. Structurally, the events are framed by a type of prologue and epilogue, both of which are entitled "Asa," who is Bart's grandson and who, because he really never knew his grandfather, begins piecing together facts and details. Bart's rise and legend begin when he is elected to a four-year term as sheriff of Issawamba County, Mississippi; the climax of his rise is his restoring of Solitaire Plantation and his acceptance among the wealthy planters. Bart's fall begins with his son's refusal to accept the responsibility of his heritage and culminates when Bart sells Solitaire, leaves the horses and the land, and moves to "the buildings and sidewalks and people."

Foote's sense of history and place are evident in the plot line of *Tournament*. Once Bart purchases Solitaire Plantation, the actions center on Jordan County and Bristol. History figures prominently in the plot, as Foote gives an in-depth account of Isaac Jameson's cotton empire, carved out of the Mississippi wilderness and later destroyed during the Civil War. Symbolically, the fall of the Jamesons and the destruction of Solitaire not only parallel the fall and destruction of the old South but also parallel the fall and destruction of Bart's dream: Just as the Jamesons' way of life faded with a new era, so too will Bart's.

The changes that doom Bart are not directly related to the Civil War or any other particular historic event but rather are indigenous to the times. Bart's first son, Hugh, is expected to assume management of the plantation. Instead, he withdraws from the University of Mississippi after his freshman year, fails at managing Solitaire, and is fired from another job. Even Hugh's accidental death in a 1917 army camp is symbolic of Bart's doomed way of life. Other forces contributing to Bart's fall are his daughter Florence's lesbianism and his daughter-in-law's promiscuity.

Along with the railroads, automobiles, and cinema palaces comes the new world of business and finance, and this ruthless greed for money is something Bart does not understand. He feels antagonistic toward those who make their livelihoods merely by manipulating money. The ruthlessness of such men is emphasized when Lawrence Tilden refuses to extend the due date on Abraham Wisten's loan, which results in Wisten's suicide. Ironically, too, Bart loses $250,000, the money he got from selling Solitaire, when he deposits it in the Commercial National Bank in Memphis and the bank fails. Foote's emphasis on how such changes mark an end to an era is nowhere more symbolic or poignant than in Bart's funeral procession. "It had to be horse-drawn" was Bart's command, and so the horse-drawn black hearse is followed by the people in their automobiles.

Foote's *Tournament* also explores the Southern tradition of masculinity; the title suggests the medieval sense of honor, a code of conduct befitting gentlemen. Bart is elected sheriff because of his excellent marksmanship, and his skills in both trap shooting and hunting win him acceptance among the planter aristocracy. Bart's courage is also a mark of his masculinity. This courage is evidenced when he single-handedly crashes through a barricaded cabin door and blows the head off the fugitive, and when he attempts to intervene in the gunfight between Cassendale Tarfeller and Downs Macready. Bart's business ethics are evident in his indignation toward Tilden's mercenary treatment of Wisten.

Finally, *Tournament* analyzes the theme of loneliness. The closing sentences in the Asa sections emphasize the basic loneliness of Bart's life. In the prologue, Asa says that the one conviction that he has learned from Bart's life is that "each man, even when pressed closest by other men in their scramble for the things they offer one another with so little grace, is profoundly alone." In his closing section, Asa quotes Bart's dying words: "I'm in the dark, alone." Loneliness thus frames Bart's life and death, even though Bart had achieved some kind of contact with the people in his life.

According to Foote, *Follow Me Down* was influenced by Robert Browning's *The Ring and the Book* (1868-1869) and by two of Faulkner's novels, *The Sound and the Fury* (1929) and *As I Lay Dying* (1930). *Follow Me Down* was also influenced by Ernest Hemingway, from whom Foote claims to have learned about the "terrific ambiguity of life"; Foote equates the irony and pity in *Follow Me Down* with the pity and irony in *The Sun Also Rises* (1926). Considered by some critics to be Foote's most striking novel, *Follow Me Down* is about the adulterous affair between Luther Eustis, a fifty-one-year-old Solitaire tenant farmer, and Beulah Joyner, a twenty-year-old girl. Their affair ends tragically when Luther hears strange voices ordering him to kill Beulah; he drowns her and weighs her body down with two concrete revetment blocks, a crime for which he is sentenced to life in prison at Parchman.

Structurally, this is one of Foote's most interesting novels in that the entire narration is composed of nine monologues. Beulah's monologue is the center of the novel and is framed by two monologues by Luther. Preceding these are monologues by the circuit court clerk, the newspaper reporter, and a deaf-mute; following Beulah's and Luther's monologues are ones by Luther's wife, the lawyer, and the turnkey at the jail. Foote has said that this technique was an experiment which enabled him to "examine a crime of passion by moving into it and then out of it." The beginning monologues become increasingly more personal, climaxing with Beulah's; then the monologues again move to the impersonal, ending with that of the turnkey, Roscoe Jeffcoat. Each character becomes individualized in his narration, and various details of the crime are seen from different points of view. Foote later used variations of this technique in *Shiloh* and *September September*.

In *Follow Me Down*, as in *Tournament*, Foote concentrates on the South in transition from traditional Southern morality to modern sexuality. This conflict is skillfully and symbolically initiated when Foote describes the disruption of Brother Jimson's prayer meeting four different times by an automobile carrying three soldiers and two women, one of whom is Beulah. The harsh intrusion of the modern world is symbolized by the automobile, which, with horn blaring and engine roaring, scatters dust on the worshipers. The conflict between tradition and modernism is even more apparent when Jimson bodily hurls each of the soldiers into the bushes. The tragic and damning implication of this conflict is typified in the adulterous affair between Luther, who represents traditional religion, and Beulah, who represents modern sexuality. Instead of dealing guardedly with sexuality as he did in *Tournament*, Foote relates the perverse details of both Beulah's and her mother's past.

The major theme in *Follow Me Down* is again the basic loneliness of man. As Parker Nowell, Luther's lawyer, prepares his defense, he suddenly realizes that the "biographies" of Luther, Mrs. Pitts, and Beulah are actually "histories of inadequacy, the failure of Love." At the same time, he recognizes this condition in his own life; his wife has left him for another man. He concludes: "Love has failed us. We are essentially, irrevocably alone. . . . Love has failed us in this century."

Perhaps Foote's most widely read novel, *Love in a Dry Season* has been ranked with *Follow Me Down*, and one critic even compares its tone to that of F. Scott Fitzgerald's best work. Indeed, Jeff and Amy Carruthers are reminiscent of Tom and Daisy Buchanan in *The Great Gatsby* (1925), but Foote's novel is unquestionably his own. The plot is an intricate weaving of the stories of the Barcrofts, Jeff and Amy Carruthers, and Harley Drew.

In *Love in a Dry Season*, Foote is once more concerned with history and place as background for his narrative. The center of action is again in Bristol, with side treks to Memphis, Winston-Salem, North Carolina, and Europe. Historically, it is Bristol in a period of transition, from the 1920's to World

War II. The Barcroft section, which opens the novel, is a historical measuring stick by which Foote deals with the further erosion of Southern values and traditions. Though Major Malcolm Barcroft is in the mold of Jameson or Bart, he does not equal their stature. He imitates the old order in his conduct and demeanor, but he does not quite succeed because he is between two eras and a part of neither. He was too young for the Civil War and never saw action in the Spanish-American War; he marries into money instead of wrenching his fortune from the Mississippi wilderness; his son dislikes hunting and horses and is killed in a hunting accident; his daughters never marry, so there will be no Barcroft dynasty.

Jeff and Amy Carruthers and Harley Drew highlight the changes that have come to the South and Jordan County in the 1920's. Amy is the only one who has Bristol roots, but she was orphaned as a child and went to live in North Carolina, so her roots are not very deep. She becomes very promiscuous, a sign of the age, and thus becomes another character representing modern sexuality. Jeff is an outlander from Winston-Salem, and his family wealth comes, not from growing tobacco, but rather from manufacturing it; the emphasis on manufacturing underscores the rise of business and finance in the South with which Foote had dealt in *Tournament*. The wealth from manufacturing contrasts with the wealth the earlier Southern planters received from working the land. Moreover, the new wealth turns people such as Josh Carruthers into petty and vindictive figures. Even Amy and Jeff's marriage is symptomatic of the times; their marriage is a constant round of quarreling and physical violence. Amy's promiscuity and Jeff's voyeurism become grotesque and self-defeating. When he is blinded in an automobile accident, Jeff's voyeurism becomes even more grotesque because he can no longer watch; as he complains, "It's no fun in the dark."

Another interesting character is Harley Drew, another outlander whose business ethics and morals are completely self-serving. For him, women are to be used either for his own sexual gratification (his assignations with hotel whores) or for advancing him socially and financially (his methodical courting of Amanda Barcroft). Drew is, moreover, an extension of the unscrupulous businessman such as Josh Carruthers and Lawrence Tilden; Tilden hires Drew for his bank and they work well together. Conducted in other towns and later in the Briartree mansion with Jeff downstairs, Amy and Drew's adulteries mark the nadir of morality in Jordan County. In his characterization of Jeff, Amy, and Drew, Foote depicts the new Southern generation whose values and morals are confused. Since they are so corrupt, indeed even comical, they are incapable of significant tragic action.

As the title implies, *Love in a Dry Season* is primarily about the failure of love. Like the characters' values and dreams, love has become distorted and devoid of meaning. Major Barcroft's narrow-eyed views of love make him domineering and ridiculous. Harley Drew's courtship of Amanda is based on personal gain instead of love, and his affair with Amy is couched in lust. Amy and Jeff's marriage contains no love at all. Equally important in the novel is the theme of masculinity or lack of it. Neither Drew nor Jeff conducts himself as their earlier counterparts would have. The duel between Cass Tarfeller and Downs Macready in *Tournament* seems senseless, yet Cass acts properly for a man whose daughter has been violated. Jeff's attempted murder of Drew is a parody of the duel, as well as being an ineffectual attempt at manhood.

Among the influences on his next novel, *Shiloh*, Foote includes the works of Leo Tolstoy, Stendahl, and Stephen Crane. Acclaimed by critics as a "brilliant book" and the "nearest thing of its kind to Crane's *The Red Badge of Courage* (1895)," *Shiloh* uses the multiple viewpoints previously used in *Follow Me Down* and later used in *September September*. *Shiloh* is composed of seven chapters; with the exception of the first and last chapters, which are narrated by Lieutenant Palmer Metcalfe, the chapters alternate between Union and Confederate narrators. The preparations for the battle in the first two chapters, the actual movement into the battle in chapter 3 followed by details of the battle, and the moving out of the battle in the last chapter echo a progression somewhat similar to that in *Follow Me Down*.

Unlike his other works, Foote's *Shiloh* does not take place in Jordan County. Even though some of the combatants are from Mississippi, Foote's aim is not to emphasize his mythical county but rather to deal with a particularly bloody battle which presaged the defeat of the South and the end of the old order. Lieutenant Metcalfe embodies these concepts, especially when he helps plan a perfect battle strategy on paper, and when he recalls the words of his father and of the Union general William Tecumseh Sherman. His father has foretold the defeat of the South because of its "incurable romanticism and misplaced chivalry," while Sherman has observed that the North has industry while the South has only "spirit and determination."

The crisis of manhood is the major theme of Shiloh, because war is a crucible that tests men's mettle. Both Southern and Northern soldiers are quick to praise courageous and ferocious actions on either side. Sergeant Jefferson Polly, for example, feels ashamed for the six thousand Yankee soldiers he sees who have fled from battle and are skulking under the river bluff; he then recalls the bravery of the Yankees who fought in the Hornets Nest and whom he praises as being "as brave as any men." In *Shiloh*, the epitome of Southern masculinity is General Forrest, who is inspiring and courageous, the "first cavalryman of his time." Typical of Forrest's courage is the incident in which he leads a charge and finds himself surrounded by enemy troops but cuts and slashes his way to freedom. When Jeff Carruthers, Harley Drew, and Rufus Hutton are compared with Forrest, one can readily see the decline of the South.

Jordan County is a collection of short stories which, like Joyce's *Dubliners* (1914), Sherwood Anderson's *Winesburg, Ohio* (1919), and Faulkner's *Go*

Down, Moses (1942), should be read as a novel. Termed a history in reverse, *Jordan County* begins with "Rain Down Home," set in the post-World War II era, and ends with "The Sacred Mound," set in the 1700's.

"Rain Down Home" is primarily about the effects of change and the lack of love. Pauly Green, a World War II veteran, returns to Bristol and exclaims: "They changed it on me while my back was turned." As he wanders through Bristol he notes these changes, and he also attempts conversations with people. He talks with a waitress in a café, a little girl, and an old man in Wingate Park, but he encounters indifference at every turn. Symbolically, his odyssey through Bristol and his attempts at conversation are based on the initial question he asks the waitress: "Why doesnt [sic] everybody love each other?" Later in the conversation with the old derelict, Pauly says that he wants to live in the world but that he does not understand why people cannot be happy, and he adds, "Not cant [sic]: wont [sic]." Completely frustrated by the lack of love and communication in a changed Bristol, all Pauly can do is shoot up the Greek café; the subsequent headlines label him a "deranged veteran."

"Ride Out" has been widely praised for its artistic excellence and for its tragic rendering of the ambiguities of life. Beginning in Bristol, it moves to New York and then back to Bristol. The story captures the flavor of the jazz age; its main character is Duff Conway, a Bristol black who learns to play the cornet in reform school and rises to become a famous jazz musician in New York, where he gets tuberculosis. He returns to Bristol, where he falls in love with Julia Kinship, who has a "capacity for cruelty" and who uses Duff until someone better comes along. Chance Jackson, a gambler from Oxford, furnishes the violence Julia demands. Duff shoots Jackson and is electrocuted for the murder. The decline of traditional Southern values is vividly imaged in this final confrontation, in which the notion of manhood has been violently perverted. Foote appears to endorse Duff's simple explanation to Harry Van, his New York friend: "Going off like that I lost touch with everything I was born to be with. . . . I ought to stayed home where I belonged."

"A Marriage Portion" is set in the 1920's and is narrated by a married woman. She talks about dating, marriage, and wedded life. During her narration, certain facts emerge which relate to Foote's themes. She and her husband are confined in a loveless marriage (the failure of love); the husband is unstable and an alcoholic (the fall from greatness and heroic action); she had wanted him to "tame" her, but she is obviously the stronger of the two (the emasculation of the male).

"Child by Fever" is more a novella than a short story. As part of Foote's history in reverse, its time span includes the historical background of the Sturgis and Wingate families and focuses primarily on Hector Sturgis' life from 1878 to 1911. Spoiled and pampered by his grandmother, Esther Wingate, Hector is another example of the emasculated and ineffectual male.

Two incidents are crucial in developing this idea. First, as a boy Hector reacts violently to the taunts of his classmates but becomes physically sickened by his actions. Second, he marries Ella Lowry, whose extramarital affairs anger him so that he slaps her, but when she urges him to hit her again, he can only weep. His death is not even tragic because he is incapable of decisive action; he commits suicide after continually blaming himself for Ella's death, even though she and her lover were accidentally asphyxiated while making love.

"The Freedom Kick" examines the change that freedom entails for the blacks. When the narrator's father is roughed up by a black policeman, his mother wants to sue the town of Bristol. From his retrospective viewpoint, the narrator explains that his father's scuffle and his mother's actions were indicative of the confused times. The carpetbaggers were talking about freedom, for example, and the Ku Klux Klan was night-riding and burning crosses.

"Pillar of Fire" is the only story in the collection to deal directly with the Civil War. The plot details the Jameson history—the carving of an empire out of the wilderness and the destruction of the Solitaire mansion by a Union detachment. The destruction of Solitaire symbolizes the defeat and destruction of the South and the dissolution of the planter aristocracy and the old Southern way of life. The pity and irony of both defeats climaxes in the description of Isaac Jameson, who, alone, aged, and partially paralyzed, can only sit in a chair in the yard and watch the pillar of fire.

The last story, "The Sacred Mound," takes place in the Province of Mississippi in 1797. It is in the form of a court-recorded deposition made by a Choctaw Indian, Chisahahoma, whose Christian name is John Postoak. He relates the murders of Lancelot Fink and a man identified only as Tyree. Captured by the Indians, these two trappers suffer bloody deaths. Tyree's heart is cut out and shown to him before he dies; Lancelot Fink's sexual organs are cut off and thrown at his feet, and he dies "badly, still crying for mercy when he was far beyond it." Tyree's stoical death contrasts with Fink's, and the deaths relate to Foote's theme of masculinity. In addition, this story deals with civilizations in transition. Just as the coming of the white settlers foretells the end of the Choctaw civilization, so too will changes in later historical eras bring an end to traditional Southern life-styles.

September September is set in Memphis, Tennessee, in 1957. Podjo Harris, Rufus Hutton, and Reeny Perdew—who all live in Bristol—have come to Memphis to kidnap a black boy, Teddy Kinship, son of Eben Kinship and grandson of the wealthy Theo Wiggins. Timing the kidnaping to coincide with the integration crisis at Little Rock Central High School, Podjo and Rufus successfully kidnap the boy and get the sixty thousand dollars in ransom money. Jealous and angry because Reeny prefers Podjo to him, Rufus double crosses Podjo, takes all of the ransom money except for a thousand dollars, and is killed in an automobile accident.

The backdrop of the integration crisis in Little Rock highlights the changes that have evolved through the centuries in Foote's fictional world. As a successful and wealthy Beale Street businessman, Wiggins typifies the rise of some blacks. The impending violence in Little Rock indicates that such transitional periods bring extremes of both good and evil. Ironically, the potential violence from the white community is the basis of the threat Podjo and Rufus use to intimidate Eben and Theo.

The transient lives of the characters of *September September* is symbolic of the shift from the small towns of the South to the sprawling cities. As these people desert their Southern heritage and as they are caught up in modernism, their dreams and ambitions shrink to a pitiable level. Podjo's dream is to be a big winner in Las Vegas; Reeny's dream is to come "powing out of cakes"; and Rufus wants fame and a new automobile. Eben's dreams are of his family's secure future, which contrasts with the ephemeral and hedonistic goals of the other three characters. Part of the novel's irony is that Eben is the only one who succeeds in his endeavors. He has courage enough to confront Theo about a higher salary and a house of his own.

An enduring author both particularizes and universalizes his own fictional world. Like Faulkner, Foote has created an imaginary corner of Mississippi, a fictional place which comes to seem as real as the house next door. Such an achievement is possible only in a cycle of novels, in which generations pass and familiar characters come and go. Like Faulkner, although on a much smaller scale, Foote has achieved in his cycle of novels something of the density and complexity of real life, and it is for that achievement that his fiction will be remembered.

Edward C. Reilly

Other major works

PLAY: *Jordan County: A Landscape in the Round*, 1964.

NONFICTION: *The Civil War: A Narrative, Fort Sumter to Perryville*, 1958; *The Civil War: A Narrative, Fredericksburg to Meridian*, 1963; *The Civil War: A Narrative, Red River to Appomattox*, 1974; *Conversations with Shelby Foote*, 1989.

ANTHOLOGY: *The Night Before Chancellorsville and Other Civil War Stories*, 1957.

Bibliography

Foote, Shelby. Interview by Evans Harrington. *Mississippi Quarterly* 24 (Fall, 1971): 349-377. Much more revealing and helpful than most interviews with contemporary writers. Foote speaks perceptively from his house in Memphis in June, 1968, about the American literary scene at the time and the influences on his own work.

Landess, Thomas H. "Southern History and Manhood: Major Themes in the Works of Shelby Foote." *Mississippi Quarterly* 24 (Fall, 1971): 321-347. Studies a single theme in Foote's novels, stories, and the two volumes of *The Civil War: A Narrative* published at that time. Realizing that society has forgotten "how to behave" he has created in his work an "antimyth" designed to correct the myth of the South "which has been religiously merchandised to the nation as a whole."

Rubin, Louis D., ed. *The History of Southern Literature*. Baton Rouge: Louisiana State University Press, 1985. This comprehensive literary history of the South contains a brief chapter on Foote by Robert L. Phillips providing short summaries of his novels starting with *Tournament*, set in the month and year that Arkansas governor Orval Faubus attempted to stop integration of the Little Rock Central High School by standing in the doorway.

Vauthier, Simone. "The Symmetrical Design: The Structural Patterns of *Love in a Dry Season*." *Mississippi Quarterly* 24 (Fall, 1971): 379-403. An extremely complicated analysis of "narrative and structural pattern" involving "two basic narrative structures" in the novel. While the mathematical nature of the essay (involving a host of pretentious terms such as "triadic relationships" and "ternary patterns") may be too ingenious to convince, other less arcane observations are often insightful.

White, Helen, and Redding S. Sugg, Jr. *Shelby Foote*. Boston: Twayne, 1982. The first full-length study of Foote as both a literary figure and a historian. Begins with a history of the Mississippi Delta, Foote's country "with its rich soil that created a wealthy plantation class" and "increased Southern intransigency" in the years preceding the Civil War. While largely descriptive in its concept, this book does provide analytical and critical insights. A chronology and helpful bibliography are attached.

FORD MADOX FORD
Ford Madox Hueffer

Born: Merton, England; December 17, 1873
Died: Deauville, France; June 26, 1939

Principal long fiction

The Shifting of the Fire, 1892; *The Inheritors*, 1901 (with Joseph Conrad); *Romance*, 1903 (with Joseph Conrad); *The Benefactor*, 1905; *The Fifth Queen*, 1906; *Privy Seal*, 1907; *An English Girl*, 1907; *The Fifth Queen Crowned*, 1908; *Mr. Apollo*, 1908; *The "Half Moon,"* 1909; *A Call*, 1910; *The Portrait*, 1910; *The Simple Life Limited*, 1911; *Ladies Whose Bright Eyes*, 1911; *The Panel*, 1912; *The New Humpty-Dumpty*, 1912; *Mr. Fleight*, 1913; *The Young Lovell*, 1913 (also known as *Ring for Nancy*); *The Good Soldier*, 1915; *The Marsden Case*, 1923; *The Nature of a Crime*, 1924 (*published serially*, 1909; with Joseph Conrad); *Some Do Not*, 1924; *No More Parades*, 1925; *A Man Could Stand Up*, 1926; *The Last Post*, 1928; *A Little Less Than Gods*, 1928; *No Enemy*, 1929; *When the Wicked Man*, 1931; *The Rash Act*, 1933; *Henry for Hugh*, 1934; *Vive le Roy*, 1936; *Parade's End*, 1950 (includes *Some Do Not, No More Parades, A Man Could Stand Up, The Last Post*).

Other literary forms

Ford Madox Ford was an extremely prolific author, working in virtually every literary form. His children's stories and fairy tales include *The Brown Owl* (1892); *The Feather* (1892); *The Queen Who Flew* (1894); *Christina's Fairy Book* (1906); and the pantomime *Mister Bosphorus and the Muses* (1923). His volumes of poetry include *The Questions at the Well* (1893, as Fenil Haig); *Poems for Pictures* (1900); *The Face of the Night* (1904); *From Inland and Other Poems* (1907); *High Germany* (1911); *Collected Poems* (1913); *On Heaven* (1918); *A House* (1921); *New Poems* (1927); and *Collected Poems* (1936). Ford, who is acknowledged with Joseph Conrad as coauthor of the novels *The Inheritors* and *Romance*, may have had some hand in the composition of a number of Conrad's other works during the decade from 1898 to 1908. Ford's biographical, autobiographical, and critical works include *Ford Madox Brown* (1896); *Rossetti* (1902); *Hans Holbein, the Younger* (1905); *The Pre-Raphaelite Brotherhood* (1907); *Ancient Lights* (1911); *The Critical Attitude* (1911); *Henry James* (1913); *Thus to Revisit* (1921); *Joseph Conrad: A Personal Remembrance* (1924); *The English Novel* (1929); *Return to Yesterday* (1931); *It Was the Nightingale* (1933); and *Mightier Than the Sword* (1938). During the last years of his life, Ford served as professor of comparative literature at Olivet College in Michigan and prepared his final book, a massive critical history of world literature, *The March of Literature* (1938). His history and travel books include *The Cinque Ports* (1900); *Zeppelin*

Nights (1916); *Provence* (1935); and *Great Trade Route* (1937). Collections of essays include *The Soul of London* (1905); *The Heart of the Country* (1906); *The Spirit of the People* (1907); *Women and Men* (1923); *A Mirror to France* (1926); *New York Is Not America* (1927); and *New York Essays* (1927). Several volumes Ford classified simply as propaganda, including *When Blood Is Their Argument* (1915) and *Between St. Dennis and St. George* (1915). Ford also edited *The English Review* and later *the transatlantic review* and wrote much ephemeral journalism.

Achievements

It is generally agreed that Ford's *The Good Soldier* is one of the master-pieces of modernism, a major experimental novel of enormous historical and artistic interest. His tetralogy *Parade's End*, composed of *Some Do Not, No More Parades, A Man Could Stand Up*, and *The Last Post*, is also a key work in the modernist revolution, more massive than *The Good Soldier*, more sweeping in its treatment of historical change, but less daring in its formal innovations. After these five novels, there is a considerable drop in the quality of Ford's remaining fiction. The historical trilogy concerning Henry VIII (*The Fifth Queen, Privy Seal*, and *The Fifth Queen Crowned*) is cited by some critics as meriting serious reading. Scattered among his many volumes, works such as *A Call* reward the reader with surprisingly high quality, but most of the lesser books are all too obviously potboilers.

Ford was equally at home in the English, French, and German languages, and he contributed to the cosmopolitan and polyglot texture of European modernism. As an editor of influential literary magazines, he recognized and encouraged many writers who have since become famous. His collaboration with Joseph Conrad in the 1890's corresponded with Conrad's most productive artistic period, but whether Conrad's achievements were stimulated by Ford's collaboration or accomplished in spite of Ford's intrusion is still under debate. Ford also exercised a considerable influence on Ezra Pound during Pound's early London years. Later, after World War I, Ford was associated with all the prominent writers of the Parisian Left Bank: James Joyce, Ernest Hemingway, Jean Rhys, and others.

Ford's achievement then, was as a man of letters whose diverse contributions to modern literature—particularly as an editor and as a champion of modernist writers—far transcended his not inconsiderable legacy as a novelist.

Biography

Ford Madox Hermann Hueffer was born in what is now London on December 17, 1873; he was named for his maternal grandfather, the pre-Raphaelite painter Ford Madox Brown (1821-1893). Brown had two daughters: the elder married William Michael Rossetti (brother to the poet Dante Gabriel Rossetti); the younger daughter, Catherine, married the German journalist Francis Heuffer, music critic for the London *Times*, who wrote many books and had a serious scholarly interest in Richard Wagner, Arthur Schopenhauer, and Provençal poetry. Ford was born to this couple and grew up in an intellectual hothouse of painters, musicians, artists, and writers with advanced ideas. His family expected him to be a genius, which led him to acquire, early in his life, a sense of inadequacy and failure. Ford tended later to falsify information in his biography and to have difficulty separating reality from fantasy in his recollections. He attended the coeducational Praetorius School in Folkestone, apparently an institution with very modern ideas of education. One of his schoolmates there was Elsie Martindale, a young woman whom he married against her parents' wishes in 1894. Perhaps this elopement by the impetuous young lovers shows Ford's tendency to play out in reality the conventions of courtly love, a subject of intense study by Ford's father and a preoccupation of the author himself in all his fiction, evident even in his final book, the critical survey *The March of Literature*. Ford and Elsie did not, however, find passionate love a practical way to attain long-term happiness or stability.

In September, 1898, Edward Garnett introduced Ford to Joseph Conrad, now recognized as one of the greatest English-language novelists, even though his native tongue was Polish. Ford, like Conrad, was multilingual, and, at least to some degree, he helped Conrad with the niceties of the English idiom. The two would often write in French, then translate the work into English. By the spring of 1909, however, Ford and Conrad had quarreled and were never again closely associated. They acknowledged that they collaborated on *The Inheritors* and *Romance*, although Ford must have had at least some slight hand in many of Conrad's fictions written between 1898 and 1909. In fairness, the reader should note that Ford, too, must have had his ideas and his style permanently shaped to some degree by his collaboration with the older, more worldly-wise master, Conrad.

Conrad had married an Englishwoman, Jessie George, in 1896, and he lived in a settled and respectable way with her until his death in 1924. At least in part, Conrad's breach with Ford stemmed from Jessie's dislike for what she regarded as Ford's ever more outrageous sexual behavior. In 1903, Ford had an affair with his wife's sister, Mary Martindale. Throughout his fiction, Ford replays similar real-life issues of passion, adultery, and their tawdry consequences. Thomas C. Moser in *The Life in the Fiction of Ford Madox Ford* (1980) maintains that Ford's writing follows a cyclical pattern, with each outburst of creativity triggered by the introduction of a new love into his life: Elsie Martindale, Mary Martindale, Arthur Marwood, Violet Hunt, Brigit Patmore, Jean Rhys, Stella Bowen, and Janice Biala. Moser's thesis is a bit too neat to be completely convincing, but its outline suggests the generally messy personal life that Ford must have been living while writing his voluminous works.

Analysis

From his association with Conrad, his study of Henry James and of the rise of the English novel, and his knowledge of French literature, Ford Madox Ford developed his notion of *literary impressionism*, which is central to an understanding of his masterpiece, *The Good Solider*. Ford's clearest statement of his theory of literary impressionism is found in *Joseph Conrad: A Personal Remembrance*. Literary impressionism, Ford says, is a revolt against the commonplace nineteenth century novel, or "nuvvle," as he calls it. The impressionist novel should not be a narration or report, but a rendering of impressions. Rather than following a linear plot, giving one event after another as they occur, the impressionist novel enters the mind of a storyteller and follows his associated ideas in a tangled stream of consciousness, so that vivid image becomes juxtaposed to vivid image, skipping across space and time in a collage of memory and imagination. The impressionist novel takes as its subject an *affair*, some shocking event which has already happened, and proceeds in concentric rings of growing complication as the storyteller cogitates. The focus of the novel is internal rather than external. The reader must focus on the storyteller's mental processes rather than on the events themselves. The impressionist novel is limited to the mind of the storyteller, and so is finally solipsistic. The novel refers to itself, so that the reader can never "get out of" the storyteller's limited mentality and judge whether he is reliable or unreliable, perhaps merely a madman telling a tale which has no connection whatever to reality. Limited and unreliable narration, time-shifts, fragmentation of details torn from the context in which they occur, verbal collages of such fragments in configurations produced by the narrator's association of ideas, defamiliarization of the commonplace—all these are characteristics of Ford's best work.

The traditional nineteenth century English novel depended on the convention of the linear plot. The process of reading from page one to the end of the text was generally assumed to correspond to the passage of time as one event followed another in the story, so that the hero might be born on page one, go to school on page fifty, commit adultery or consider committing adultery on page one hundred, and meet his just reward in the concluding pages of the book. In *The Good Soldier*, Ford Madox Ford rejected this linear structure and substituted for it the "affair": a shocking set of events has already occurred before the book begins, and the narrator weaves back and forth in his memories related to the affair. Gradually, in concentric circles of understanding, the reader learns the complicated situation underlying the superficial first impressions he may have formed. The drama of the story shifts from the events of the tale to the process of the telling; such stories necessarily contrast first appearances with deeper "realities" revealed in the narration.

The Good Soldier concerns two married couples: Arthur Dowell (the narrator) and his wife Florence (Hurlbird) Dowell and Edward Ashburnham and his wife Leonora (Powys) Ashburnham. The events of the story take place between August, 1904, and August, 1913, a nine-year period throughout most of which the two couples are the best of friends, living the life of the leisured rich at European spas, in elegant, cultivated idleness. There is an elegiac tone to this work, reflecting the autumn sunshine of the Edwardian era and a way of life which would be brutally wiped out with the outbreak of World War I.

The texture of the novel invites the reader to consider the conflict between appearance and reality. For most of the nine-year period of the action, Arthur Dowell believes that his wife is suffering from a heart ailment which confines her travels and requires her to be shut in her room under peculiar circumstances from time to time. He subsequently learns, however, that her heart is sound and that these arrangements are necessary to allow her to commit adultery, first with a young man named Jimmy and later with Edward Ashburnham himself. Dowell imagines Ashburnham to be a model husband, only gradually learning that he has engaged in a series of affairs and that his wife does not speak to him except when required to do so in public. This novel is like a hall of mirrors, and any statement by the narrator must be doubted.

Because readers are accustomed to novels with linear plots, the novel is more easily understood if the plot is rearranged into the customary linear sequence of events. Edward Ashburnham is from an ancient Anglican landholding family who owns the estate, Branshaw Teleragh. As the novel opens, he has recently returned from serving as a military officer in India and arrives at the health spa, Bad Nauheim, in Germany, where he meets the Dowells for the first time. Although he appears to be brave, sentimental, and heroic, like the knights in ancient romances, the reader learns that he has been involved in a series of unfortunate affairs with women. His parents arranged his marriage to Leonora Powys, a Catholic girl, convent-educated, whose impoverished family had an estate in Ireland. Religious and temperamental differences soon cause their marriage to cool. While riding in a third-class carriage, Edward tries in a blundering way to comfort a servant girl and is arrested for sexual misbehavior in what is called the Kilsyte case. This misadventure leads him for the first time in his life to consider himself capable of bad conduct. His next affair involves a short-lived passion for a Spanish dancer, La Dolciquita, who demands cash for spending a week with him at Antibes. Reckless gambling at the casino, combined with the direct expenses of La Dolciquita's passion, substantially deplete Edward's inherited fortune. His wife, Leonora, makes herself the guardian of his estate and sets out to recover their financial losses. She demands that he take a military post in India for eight years and doles out his spending money carefully while squeezing his tenants and lands back in England for as much profit as possible.

In India, Edward finds his next woman, Mrs. Basil, whose husband, a brother-officer, allows the affair to continue in order to blackmail Edward. Eventually, Mrs. Basil's husband is transferred to Africa so that she can no longer stay with Edward. Edward then makes an alliance with Mrs. Maidan, also the wife of a junior officer. Mrs. Maidan has a heart condition and accompanies the Ashburnhams to Bad Nauheim for treatment. On the day that the Dowells and the Ashburnhams first meet, Leonora Ashburnham has found Mrs. Maidan coming out of Edward's bedroom in the hotel. Enraged, Leonora has slapped her and, in doing so, entangled her bracelet in Mrs. Maidan's hair. Florence Dowell, in the hall, sees them struggling there and comes to help. Leonora lamely explains that she has accidentally caught her bracelet in Mrs. Maidan's hair, and Florence helps them get untangled, as the sobbing Mrs. Maidan runs to her room. That evening, Leonora Ashburnham insists on sitting at the Dowells' dinner table in the hotel so as to prevent any gossip about that day's events in the hallway. Mrs. Maidan soon commits suicide, leaving Edward free to form a liaison with Florence Dowell herself.

Edward's ward, Nancy Rufford, is being educated in the same convent where Leonora went to school. As Nancy grows to a mature woman, Edward becomes attracted to her, but he is caught in the conflict between love and honor. He desires Nancy, but he is honor-bound not to violate his sacred trust to protect her. After Florence Dowell learns of Edward's affection for Nancy (along with some other distressing developments), she too commits suicide. Edward remains firm, however, and refuses to take advantage of his ward or corrupt her, even when she openly offers herself to him. He arranges for her to be sent to her father in Ceylon. On her voyage there, she cables from Brindisi a cheerful note implying that she feels no sorrow about leaving him. Edward then commits suicide with a penknife, and Nancy goes insane when she hears of his death. His widow, Leonora, marries a rabbitlike neighbor, Rodney Bayham, while Arthur Dowell is left as the proprietor of the Branshaw Teleragh estate, where he nurses the insane Nancy Rufford.

From the exterior, to those who know him only slightly, Edward Ashburnham appears almost superhumanly noble, the ideal of the British country gentleman and good soldier. If the reader believes all that is alleged about him, he is quite the contrary, a raging stallion, recklessly ruining every female he meets. The superficial goodness is merely a veneer masking his corruption. All the other characters, as well, have two sides. Florence Dowell, the respectable wife, has had an affair before her marriage to Arthur with the despicable Jimmy and may have married simply to get back to her lover in Europe. She certainly does not hesitate to become Edward Ashburnham's mistress and commits suicide when she learns in a double-barrelled blow that Edward is attracted to Nancy Rufford and that the man in whose house she committed adultery with Jimmy is now talking with her husband in Bad Nauheim. Leonora is purposeful in trying to manage her husband's estate economically, but she is cruel and unloving. The reader can easily imagine that her husband would be driven to seek other company. Arthur Dowell, the narrator himself, is stupid, lazy, and piggish.

Since the story is told entirely from the point of view of Arthur Dowell, and since his is a limited intelligence, the reader can never entirely trust his narration as reliable. Dowell may assert on one page that a character is noble, yet show the reader in a hundred ways that the character is despicable. The reader is caught in the web of Dowell's mind. Clearly, Dowell sometimes does not tell the "truth"; but since the total work is fiction, the reader is not simply confronted with a conflict between appearance and reality but with the status of competing fictions. Is Edward a noble knight or a despicable roué? The story evaporates into the impressions in Dowell's mind. What Dowell thinks or believes *is* the truth at that moment in the fiction. It could be seriously argued that Edward, Leonora, and Florence have no external "reality" at all, that they are simply the imaginings of the sickly Dowell as he tells or dreams his story. This approach may shock readers of conventional fiction, who are accustomed to reading a novel as if the characters were real people, yet all characters in every fiction are simply projections of the author's creative imagination.

Ford's massive tetralogy, *Parade's End*, consists of four separate novels: *Some Do Not*; *No More Parades*; *A Man Could Stand Up*; and *The Last Post*. The main theme of these works repeats a major concern of *The Good Soldier*, the destruction of the Tory gentleman. Edward Ashburnham in *The Good Soldier* belongs to the same class as Christopher Tietjens, the protagonist of *Parade's End*. Both are said to have been modeled on Ford's friend Arthur Marwood, who collaborated with Ford in publishing *The English Review*. Ashburnham is the landowner of Branshaw Teleragh, whereas Tietjen's family owns the Groby estate. Both feel an obligation to their dependants and take seriously their stewardship over the land. Both are highly altruistic in certain areas, but are tormented by the conflict between their sexual impulses and what is considered proper or honorable behavior. They are Tory gentlemen, landowning, relaxed in manner, Anglican in religion, physically vigorous, classically educated, generous, virile, and possessed of a world view in which man's place in the universe is clearly defined. Such men are assailed on all sides by women, by modern commercial industry, by Catholics and Jews, by Fascists and Communists, and finally by the internal contradictions of their own characters. World War I smashed that class of Tory landholding gentlefolk once and for all, in an externalization of that internal battle.

Because the books are a kind of verbal collage, creating a palimpsest of memory and imagination, weaving backward and forward through the minds of characters who are frequently under stress and incapable of reporting events without distorting them, the linear plot of the tetralogy is difficult to summarize. The first novel, *Some Do Not*, opens with Christopher Tietjen's traveling in a railway carriage. His destination, unknown to him at the time, is the future world, the wasteland created by World War I and the destruction of the comfortable Tory universe into which he was born. His wife, Sylvia, has a child of whom he is perhaps not the true father, and she has run away with another man to Europe. Christopher meets an attractive young woman named Valentine Wannop. In the course of the tetralogy, Valentine replaces Sylvia as Tietjen's mate. The war, when it breaks out, is a terrifying expression of the conflict already implied in the mind of Christopher. In *No More Parades*, Christopher sees the men on the battlefield harassed by infidelity at home. The combat scenes in the next volume, *A Man Could Stand Up*, include ones in which Christopher is buried in a collapsed trench under fire, fights desperately to free his companions, and then is demoted for having a dirty uniform. At the end of this book, Valentine and Christopher come together in a nightmare party celebrating the end of the war. The final volume in the tetralogy, *The Last Post*, is composed of a series of dramatic monologues in which the reader learns that the estate has passed to other hands and that the Groby elm, signifying the Tietjens' ownership of the land, has been cut down.

Ezra Pound suggested that Ford's contribution to modern literature could be measured less by reference to any given works than by "the tradition of his intelligence." While most of Ford's many novels have been consigned to oblivion, *The Good Soldier* and *Parade's End* testify to his manifold gifts as a man of letters and as a godfather to the modernists.

Todd K. Bender

Other major works

POETRY: *The Questions at the Well*, 1893 (as Fenil Haig); *Poems for Pictures*, 1900; *The Face of the Night*, 1904; *From Inland and Other Poems*, 1907; *Songs from London*, 1910; *High Germany*, 1911; *Collected Poems*, 1913; *Antwerp*, 1915; *On Heaven, and Poems Written on Active Service*, 1918; *A House*, 1921; *New Poems*, 1927; *Collected Poems*, 1936.

NONFICTION: *Ford Madox Brown*, 1896; *The Cinque Ports*, 1900; *Rossetti*, 1902; *The Soul of London*, 1905; *Hans Holbein, the Younger*, 1905; *The Heart of the Country*, 1906; *The Pre-Raphaelite Brotherhood*, 1907; *The Spirit of the People*, 1907; *Ancient Lights*, 1911; *The Critical Attitude*, 1911; *Henry James*, 1913; *When Blood Is Their Argument*, 1915; *Between St. Dennis and St. George*, 1915; *Zeppelin Nights*, 1916; *Thus to Revisit*, 1921; *Women and Men*, 1923; *Joseph Conrad: A Personal Remembrance*, 1924; *A Mirror to France*, 1926; *New York Is Not America*, 1927; *New York Essays*, 1927; *No Enemy*, 1929; *The English Novel*, 1929; *Return to Yesterday*, 1931; *It Was the Nightingale*, 1933; *Provence*, 1935; *Great Trade Route*, 1937; *Mightier Than the Sword*, 1938; *The March of Literature*, 1938.

CHILDREN'S LITERATURE: *The Brown Owl*, 1891; *The Feather*, 1892; *The Queen Who Flew*, 1894; *Christina's Fairy Book*, 1906; *Mister Bosphorus and the Muses*, 1923.

Bibliography

Cassell, Richard A., ed. *Critical Essays on Ford Madox Ford*. Boston: G. K. Hall, 1987. In his introduction, Cassell reviews Ford criticism, which he believes becomes more laudatory and perceptive after 1939. Though there are essays dealing with Ford's romances, poetry, and social criticism, the bulk of the book focuses on *The Good Soldier* and *Parade's End*. Also valuable are contributions by literary figures such as Graham Greene, Ezra Pound, and Conrad Aiken. Well indexed.

_____. *Ford Madox Ford: A Study of His Novels*. Baltimore: The Johns Hopkins University Press, 1961. The first three chapters (biography, aesthetics, literary theory) are followed by close readings not only of the major works (*The Good Soldier, Parades's End*) but also of neglected minor fictional works, particularly *Ladies Whose Bright Eyes, The Rash Act*, and *Henry for Hugh*. Also includes helpful discussions of Joseph Conrad's and Henry James's influence on Ford.

Green, Robert. *Ford Madox Ford: Prose and Politics*. Cambridge, England: Cambridge University Press, 1981. Unlike earlier studies which applied New Criticism to Ford's work, places Ford within his historical context and identifies his political beliefs. Asserts that Ford drew no firm line between fiction and nonfiction, treating such works as *Ancient Lights* and *Henry James* as important in themselves and as glossing over Ford's major fiction, *The Good Soldier* and *Parade's End*. Also contains a chronological bibliography of his work as well as an extensive yet selected bibliography of Ford criticism.

Huntley, H. Robert. *The Alien Protagonist of Ford Madox Ford*. Chapel Hill: University of North Carolina Press, 1970. Focuses on the Ford protagonist, typically a man whose alien temperament and ethics produce a conflict with his society. After extensive treatments of neglected novels (*An English Girl, A Call, The Fifth Queen*), concludes with an entire chapter devoted to *The Good Soldier*, which is discussed in terms of Ford's historical theories.

Leer, Norman. *The Limited Hero in the Novels of Ford Madox Ford*. East Lansing: Michigan State University Press, 1966. After defining "heroism" in Ford's thought, Leer discusses the early novels and the ineffectual hero before an extended analysis of *The Good Soldier* and *Parade's End*. Leer sees a decline in Ford's post-1929 fiction, but praises Ford's travel books of the same period. A first-rate bibliography of secondary sources is also included.

Lid, R. W. *Ford Madox Ford: The Essence of His Art*. Berkeley: University of California Press, 1964. Claims that Ford was both a germinal and transitional figure whose early work culminated in his two masterpieces, *The Good Soldier* and *Parade's End*, after which he "merely" defined and refined his sense of the past. The analysis of these two works is supplemented by an excellent bibliography of *The Good Soldier* and *Parade's End*.

MacShane, Frank, ed. *Ford Madox Ford: The Critical Heritage*. London: Routledge & Kegan Paul, 1972. An invaluable collection of reviews and responses, gleaned from literary journals, to Ford's fiction and poetry. Includes an 1892 unsigned review of *The Shifting of the Fire*, as well as essays by such literary greats as Theodore Dreiser, Arnold Bennett, Ezra Pound, Conrad Aiken, Christina Rossetti, H. L. Mencken, Graham Greene, and Robert Lowell. There are reviews of individual novels, essays on controversies in which Ford was embroiled, and general studies of Ford's art.

RICHARD FORD

Born: Jackson, Mississippi; February 16, 1944

Principal long fiction

A Piece of My Heart, 1976; *The Ultimate Good Luck*, 1981; *The Sports-writer*, 1986; *Wildlife*, 1990.

Other literary forms

Rock Springs (1987) brings together short stories that previously appeared in *Esquire*, *Antaeus*, *The New Yorker*, *Granta*, and *TriQuarterly*. Richard Ford has written screenplays, including an adaptation of his novel *Wildlife*, and a play, *American Tropical*, which was performed by the Louisville's Actors Theater in 1983.

Achievements

Ford has received increasingly high critical praise ever since *The Sports-writer*, which was generally regarded as one of the best novels of 1986. His short-story collection *Rock Springs* received accolades from many of North America's major reviewers. Ford's novels mark a return of the Southern writer and a high point for "neorealist" or minimalist fiction. As such, they combine the symbolic and psychological depth of William Faulkner with the blunt, forceful prose of Ernest Hemingway, two writers whom Ford has acknowledged as being primary influences. Ford's evocation of a transient, displaced America is rendered with a deceptive simplicity that itself acts as counterpoint and comment on the complexity of postmodern American society.

Biography

Richard Ford was the only son of Parker Carrol, a salesman, and Edna (Akin), a housewife. Ford spent his youth in Jackson, Mississippi, but after his father's nonfatal heart attack in 1952, Ford lived part of each year at his grandparents' hotel in Little Rock, Arkansas. As a teenager in Mississippi, Ford had several minor scrapes with the law. His father had another heart attack and died in Ford's arms in 1960.

Ford entered college at Michigan State University in 1962 to study hotel management. While there he met his future wife, Kristina Hensley, in 1964. They were married in 1968; Kristina eventually earned a Ph.D. in urban planning. Ford gave up hotel management for English, and was graduated with a B.A. in 1966. He began and abandoned a law degree, then pursued a master of fine arts degree in fiction writing (awarded 1970) at the University of California at Irvine, where he studied under E. L. Doctorow. In 1970 he applied himself to becoming a full-time writer, attempting, without success, to publish short stories. The following year he began work on his first novel, *A Piece of My Heart.*

Ford has held teaching positions at the University of Michigan, Williams College, and Princeton University. Ford and his wife's life reflects the transience that is one of the major themes of his writings: in just over twenty years of marriage, they had lived in twelve houses. Avid hunters and anglers, they have no children.

Analysis

Richard Ford's novels have been called neorealist and minimalist, and, although Ford disavows a connection to the minimalist school of writing, a deceptive simplicity of style does mark his novels. In response to the clutter of contemporary America, Ford has retreated into a spare vision in which each image in his stripped-down prose resounds beyond itself. In the same fashion, the simple relationships of family and friendship that form the nexus of his narratives imply larger complexities. Ford often writes in the first person, and his central protagonists tend to be the marginalized: observers, outsiders, people carried away by circumstances. The mood of his novels is often one of impermanence, and this finds its analogue in the bleak, large, often featureless landscapes of the South and the Midwest that Ford favors. Characters move across these landscapes, through relationships, through livelihoods, with a casualness that demonstrates at once the potential and the rootless condition of twentieth century life.

In Ford's first novel, *A Piece of My Heart,* two men, Robard Hewes and Sam Newel, arrive on an uncharted island in the Mississippi River peopled only by Mark Lamb, his wife, and their black servent, Landrieu. Hewes arrives to take a short-term job running poachers off the island. He has come to nearby Helena, Arkansas, to take up an old relationship with his cousin, Buena, now married to an industrial-league baseball player named W. W. That relationship is threatened by the possible jealousy of W. W. and the manic sexuality of Buena. Newel, a Southerner now living in Chicago, arrives at the prompting of his lover, Beebe Henley, a stewardess and granddaughter to Mrs. Lamb. One month from completing his requirements for a law degree, Newel is emotionally unbalanced, and Henley suggests a rest on the island. Newel is haunted by memories of his youth, memories that revolve around the grotesque and absurd: a midget film star, a pair of lesbians in a motel room, an electrocution.

The novel oscillates between the story of Hewes and Newel, and these characters are in many ways mirror images or complements of each other: both displaced Southerners, they are driven by contradictory passions. On a symbolic level, Hewes is the body and Newel the mind; together, they are the spiritually troubled and physically corrupt South. The island on which they meet their fates is uncharted and lies between the states of Mississippi and Arkansas: like Joseph Conrad's Congo, it is a metaphoric destination, the human condition, the allegorical South. All the characters on the island are bound by their inability to escape the forces that have isolated them. Thus they go to their fates with sheeplike acceptance, a fact reflected in the game Ford plays with their names: Lamb, H*ewes*, N*ewe*l. The island becomes, for the two main characters, not an escape or a place of homecoming, but a crucible for the forces that have shaped, and will destroy, both them and the culture they represent.

Having satisfied his lust, Hewes seems bent on escape. He takes Buena to a motel and there recoils from her insistent, and perhaps perverse, sexuality. His rejection prompts her to turn on him and call on her husband for vengeance. Hewes runs back to the island, but, though he escapes W. W., he cannot escape the retarded boy who guards the boat and who himself may be a symbol of the incestuous coupling in which Hewes has been engaging. Newel cannot escape the absurd and the contingent, and he witnesses the comically maladroit death of Lamb while the two are fishing together. Of all the novel's characters, Lamb comes the closest to the cantankerous and colorful Southerners of Faulkner, and his death may mark the passing of the Southern individualist. Newel lies to Mrs. Lamb about Lamb's last words, apparently too embarrassed to repeat their absurd banality.

The novel begins and ends with the image of the retarded boy on the riverbank with the gun in his hand. If this image summarizes Ford's view of the South, the other image patterns of the novel reflect the contingency of American life as a whole. Beebe Henley's job moves her to different corners of the globe almost every day. Newel's luggage disappears. When Hewes and Newel cross the river to the island, Newel sees a deer, swimming across the river, suddenly pulled under the water by a powerful force, never to rise again. Nothing is permanent or reliable; Ford's characters fight their personal battles on uncharted land surrounded by the constant flow of the river that most signifies the South, but that also, in its power and treachery, represents the larger America.

Contingency and displacement become synonymous with violence and deceit in Ford's next novel. In *The Ultimate Good Luck*, Harry Quinn, an alienated Vietnam veteran, is asked by his former lover Rae to help free her brother, Sonny, from a jail in Oaxaca, Mexico, where he is serving a sentence for drug smuggling. Quinn makes arrangements to free Sonny through bribery with the help of a local lawyer, Bernhardt, but matters become complicated. Sonny's superiors believe that Sonny stole some of the drugs he was carrying and hid them before he was arrested. Oaxaca itself is under terrorist siege and is filled with police. Bernhardt's allegiance and motives are inscrutable. Quinn is terrorized by Deats, an "enforcer" working for Sonny's superiors. Unsuspected layers of power unfold, often in conjunction with arbitrary violence.

Indeed, the novel is dominated by images of violence and chance. The contingency that dominated *A Piece of My Heart* here is marked for higher stakes. With a flat, tough prose reminiscent of Dashiell Hammett's, Ford presents a *film noir* world of threat and hidden danger. The novel opens with a scene of violence and casual sexuality: Quinn meets an Italian tourist and takes her to a Mexican boxing match that is especially vicious. This casual encounter is indicative of Quinn's life: in flashback the reader discovers that Quinn first met Rae, by chance, at a dog-racing track; he has pursued jobs, such as game warden, that have brought him close to violence. As the novel unfolds, these chance encounters and acts of violence become less controllable. Quinn sees three American girls vanish during their vacation. He and Rae see a family of tourists killed by a terrorist bomb as they stand in front of an ice-cream store; Sonny is attacked and mutilated in jail; Deats binds Quinn and threatens him with a scorpion. Even Quinn's own body, hardened by war and decorated with tattoos, betrays him in a fit of dysentery. Oaxaca becomes a nightmare landscape of violence and confusion, closer to Quinn's Vietnam experience than "the world." Like the island of the first novel, Oaxaca becomes a crucible of the forces that drive the characters, a metaphoric landscape of their souls.

The plot is resolved by death. Sonny is killed in jail, Bernhardt is gunned down, and Quinn ends his search in a shootout with strangers. Although Quinn takes some pride in his accomplishment, his survival is simply the ultimate good luck, another chance in a series of gambles.

The Sportswriter was Ford's most well received novel, though it may be his least typical. Told in the first person by Frank Bascombe, a thirty-eight-year-old short-story writer turned sportswriter, the novel details Bascombe's adventures over an Easter weekend, beginning with an annual pilgrimage, with his former wife (referred to only as X), to the grave of his first son, who died at age eight of Reye's disease. It was that death that had led to Bascombe's divorce and what he calls his period of "dreaminess," actually a form of detachment or emotional numbness. Over the course of the Easter weekend, Bascombe flies with his lover, Vicki Arcenault, to Detroit, where he interviews a paraplegic former football hero, Herb Wallagher. Cutting the trip short, they return home to Haddam, New Jersey. Bascombe visits the home of Vicki's parents on Easter Sunday, but the visit is interrupted by a call from X: Walter Luckett, a member of the Divorced Men's Club, a casual society to which Bascombe belongs, has committed suicide. Before returning to Haddam, Bascombe fights with Vicki. Bascombe eventually takes a late train into Manhattan to visit his office, something he does not normally do. There a chance encounter with a new female writer sparks what will become an affair. In the epilogue, Bascombe is in Florida, waiting for a young Dartmouth woman to visit. He seems to have overcome grieving for his son, and he may be on the verge of writing fiction once more.

Detached, ironic, and cerebral, Bascombe looks for solace in the mundane and regular: he keeps up the appearances, if not the reality, of a suburban husband and father; he revels in the petty regularities of Haddam; he studies the regularized and "safe" world of professional sports. At these pursuits he is successful, but his adherence to routine and detail itself becomes part of his dreaminess, his detachment. Unable, or unwilling, to extend himself emotionally, he remains aloof from Walter Luckett's grief over a brief homosexual affair, he rejects the vision of the crippled former athlete he interviews, and he ultimately quarrels and breaks with Vicki. His failure to continue writing fiction is an analogue of his inability to connect emotionally, and the novel itself, this fictional memoir, may be a movement back toward a regularized life.

Wildlife is told as a memoir. Set in 1960 when Joe, the narrator, is sixteen years old (Ford's own age in 1960), the novel details the breakdown of the marriage of Jerry and Jeanette, Joe's parents. The family had recently moved to Grand Falls, Montana, where Jerry works as a golf professional. When he is fired because of a misunderstanding, Jerry signs on to fight the forest fires that rage in the hills outside the town. That sudden decision sends Jeanette into a short affair with a well-to-do local man named Warren Miller. The bulk of the novel is a re-creation of the events of those three days, told with stark simplicity. Joe, like the child protagonists of Ford's short stories, seems caught in the emotional detachment that was precipitated by the marriage breakdown and forced to re-create the situation with the dispassion that has marked his subsequent life. The result is a hesitant accumulation of detail and dialogue, as the retelling of the events becomes a cathartic event for Joe.

The novel is dominated by the image of fire. There are the fires that burn in the foothills and that capture the father's imagination. It seems they cannot be extinguished; they burn through the winter, ignoring the natural seasons, and they come to stand for the unpredictable and confusing in the human experience. When Jerry leaves to fight these fires, he sets off a metaphorical fire in his wife, a yearning for passion and completeness that she attempts, unsuccessfully, to fulfill with the affair. When Jerry returns and discovers the adultery, he drives to Warren Miller's house and attempts to burn it down with a bottle of gasoline. That fire, like the mother's adultery, burns itself out and leaves behind recriminations and guilt. Ultimately ineffective, both of these fires succeed only in scarring the psychic landscape of the characters who set them.

The most starkly realistic of Ford's novels, and the closest to minimalist in its style, this novel received mixed reviews. Some critics have found in the simplicity of its prose a poetic intensity (particularly in the descriptions of the forest fire and Jerry's attempt to burn down the house); others have found that the stark dialogue threatens to push the novel in to banality. In tone and style, *Wildlife* is certainly more reminiscent of Ford's short stories than of his other novels.

Paul Budra

Other major works
SHORT FICTION: *Rock Springs*, 1987.
PLAY: *American Tropical*, 1983.

Bibliography

Ford, Richard. Interview by Kay Bonetti. *Missouri Review* 10 (Fall, 1987): 71-96. An excellent and intensive interview in which Ford, with character-istic candor, discusses his life and writing influences. An essential article.

_____. "The Three Kings: Hemingway, Faulkner, and Fitzgerald." *Es-quire* 100 (December, 1983): 577-587. In this article Ford frankly discusses his own formation as a writer and the influences of Ernest Hemingway, William Faulkner, and F. Scott Fitzgerald on his writing and consciousness. An essential article for understanding Ford's literary self-consciousness.

Gold, Victor. "The Far Side of Yoknapatawpha County." *National Review* 28 (November, 1976): 1240-1241. One of the first reviews to acknowledge Ford as a promising novelist, this reading of *A Piece of My Heart* compares him, especially in the use of symbolism and treatment of the South, to Faulkner. Although short, this review touches on most of the major symbol patterns in the novel.

Manguel, Alberto. "America's Best Novelist." *Saturday Night* 105 (July/August, 1990): 60-61. This review of *Wildlife* examines Ford's decision to recount the complexity of American society in a style that is simple almost to a fault. Though not a long article, it does manage to isolate the distinc-tive qualities of Ford's prose and argue for his place at the head of his generation of American writers.

Schroth, Raymond A. "America's Moral Landscape in the Fiction of Richard Ford." *The Christian Century* 106 (March, 1989): 227-230. Primarily a discussion of *The Sportswriter*, with some mention of *The Ultimate Good Luck* and *Rock Springs*, this article provides a general discussion of Ford as a distinctively American writer. Schroth's intelligent analysis of *The Sports-writer* leads him to compare Ford with such writers as William Dean Howell and Frank O'Connor. A good introduction to Ford's work.

E. M. FORSTER

Born: London, England; January 1, 1879
Died: Coventry, England; June 7, 1970

Principal long fiction

Where Angels Fear to Tread, 1905; *The Longest Journey*, 1907; *A Room with a View*, 1908; *Howards End*, 1910; *A Passage to India*, 1924; *Maurice*, 1971.

Other literary forms

In addition to his novels, E. M. Forster wrote short stories, travel books, biographies, essays, and criticism. A number of these works, as well as his novels, have already appeared in the standard Abinger Edition, in progress. *The Celestial Omnibus and Other Stories* (1911) includes his frequently anthologized story "The Road from Colonus" and five other stories written in a fantastic vein which is found much less frequently in his novels. *Aspects of the Novel* (1927) remains one of the most widely read discussions of that genre, while the essays of *Abinger Harvest—A Miscellany* (1936) and *Two Cheers for Democracy* (1951) have also found many receptive readers. In *Marianne Thornton: A Domestic Biography, 1797-1887* (1956) Forster recalls his great-aunt, a woman whose long life plunged him into the social history of a milieu going back to the closing years of the eighteenth century. A useful description of Forster's uncollected writings by George H. Thomson may be found in *Aspects of E. M. Forster* (1969), a *Festschrift* honoring the author on his ninetieth birthday. In the same volume, Benjamin Britten recounts one more Forster achievement: the libretto he coauthored with Eric Crozier for Britten's opera *Billy Budd* (1951).

Achievements

Forster will continue to stand a little apart from other major novelists of this century. Because he made it difficult to decide by which standards his work should be judged, assessing it fairly presents problems. Unlike many of his Bloomsbury friends, he did not rebel against the Victorians or their literary habits; neither did he embrace the literary trends of his own time with any great enthusiasm. He lamented the encroachment of a commercial culture, but he did not war on the modern world. Although he composed a set of lectures on the novel, its plural title, *Aspects of the Novel*, anticipates his refusal to develop therein any single theory of the form in which he distinguished himself. On the one hand, his work is impossible to pigeonhole; on the other hand, his half dozen novels do not entitle him to a lonely eminence overshadowing his most able contemporaries.

Readers of the novel will not lose sight of Forster, however, because the very ambiguities and inconsistencies which frustrate efforts to find a niche for him continue to intrigue critics. Forster lived long enough to see his reputation fade and then rebound strongly. He had gained critical acclaim while still in his twenties, written a masterpiece in mid-life, and published no fiction for nearly two decades before Lionel Trilling's *E. M. Forster* (1943) swung critical attention back to him. Since that time, a formidable body of books and articles dealing with Forster has risen, and many aspects of his work have been studied in great detail. While incapable of putting Forster in a specific place, his critics agree overwhelmingly that he deserves a place of honor among English novelists.

Forster's critics, fortunately, do not hold his unusually protracted silence against him. The author's failure to write a novel in the final forty-six years of his life has been explained in various ways—for example by noting that instead of exercising his talents in succession, husbanding his resources, exhausting one mode before moving to another, Forster put all of himself into the first six novels and then ceased at an age when many novelists are just reaching their prime. Whatever the reason for his early retirement from a literary form successfully practiced by so many older writers, he furnished his critics no occasion to regret the decline of his powers.

Those powers yielded fiction marked by a blend of qualities—intelligence, wit, sensitivity, compassion, and ever-alert moral imagination—that few other writers can match. No doubt, many readers begin *A Passage to India* in the line of duty—for it has attained the rank of "classic"—but they are likely to complete it, and then begin the earlier ones, out of a desire to know better a man who could write so movingly and yet so tough-mindedly about the climate created by racial and religious prejudice. Few such readers are disappointed, for while the earlier novels are less fine, the distance between *Where Angels Fear to Tread* and *A Passage to India* is not nearly so great as that between the apprentice and masterworks of most writers. Even if his final novel is, as one critic puts it, "Forster's sole claim upon posterity," those who delve into his other works will continue to reap rewards in proportion to the attention they bestow on them, for neither wit nor wisdom is ever far away.

The critical consensus is that Forster's most successful mode is comic irony, and his name is often coupled with those of Jane Austen and George Meredith, whose test for comedy—"that it shall awaken thoughtful laughter"—Forster passes with flying colors. Critics invariably hasten to point out that Forster refused to confine himself to this mode; in the midst of deploring these deviations from high comedy, they find in Forster's odd blends of comedy, melodrama, fantasy, lyricism, and tragedy a distinctiveness they would not willingly relinquish.

Biography
Edward Morgan Forster lived a long but rather uneventful life. Born on

New Year's Day, 1879, he was reared by his possessive mother and worshipful great-aunt (whose biography he later wrote) after the death of his father from tuberculosis before Forster had turned two. Happy, protected, and dominated by women in his early years, he suffered painfully the transition to the masculine, athletically oriented Tonbridge School—later the model for Sawston School in *The Longest Journey*. After a more congenial four years, 1897 to 1901, at King's College, Cambridge, he took a second-class degree. In the next few years, he wrote seriously, traveled in Italy and Greece, tutored the children of a German countess, and also indulged in walking tours of his native land.

His first novel, *Where Angels Fear to Tread*, much of which is set in Italy, received favorable reviews in 1905, and Forster produced three more novels in the next five years, of which *A Room with a View* drew also on his Italian experience, while *The Longest Journey* and *Howards End* both reflect his keen delight in the English countryside. Thereafter, having attained a considerable reputation a a novelist, he slowed his pace. He began, but could not finish, a novel called *Arctic Summer*; completed a novel about homosexuality, his own orientation, which he knew to be unpublishable; and brought out a volume of short stories. Among his many friends he numbered Leonard and Virginia Woolf, as well as others of the Bloomsbury group, of which, however, he was never more than a fringe member. World War I found him in Egypt as a Red Cross worker. Although he disliked Egypt, his life there led to the writing of two nonfiction books.

Forster had first visited India in 1912, but his second sojourn there as personal secretary to the Maharaja of Dewas gave him the opportunity to observe the political and social life closely enough to inspire him to write another novel. *A Passage to India*, which appeared in 1924, increased his fame and led to an invitation to deliver the Clark Lectures at Trinity College, Cambridge, in 1927, published later that year as *Aspects of the Novel*. Although he continued to write for several more decades, he published no more novels. Forster received a number of honors, culminating in the Order of Merit, presented to him on his ninetieth birthday. He died in June of 1970.

Analysis

E. M. Forster's most systematic exposition of the novelist's art, *Aspects of the Novel*, is no key to his own practice. Written three years after the publication of *A Passage to India*, the work surveys neither his achievement nor intentions. While full of the insights, charm, and homely but colorful metaphors which also distinguish Virginia Woolf's *Common Reader* volumes (1925, 1932), the book is an enthusiast's, rather than a working writer's, view of the novel, as if Forster were already distancing himself from the form which earned him his fame as a writer.

A lecture given twenty years later by Lionel Trilling, who had already published his book on Forster, gives a better sense of Forster's achievement. In "Manners, Morals, and the Novel," later published in *The Liberal Imagination* (1950), Trilling explains the novel as the writer's response to the modern world's besetting sin of snobbery, which he defines as "pride in status without pride in function." Europeans, and perhaps especially the English, familiar with snobbery as a manifestation of class structure, require less explanation than do Americans of the novel's relation to snobbery. The central tradition of the English novel from Henry Fielding through Jane Austen, Charles Dickens, William Makepeace Thackeray, and George Meredith—and indeed English comedy as far back as Geoffrey Chaucer's *The Canterbury Tales* (1387-1400)—stands as evidence.

In Forster's time, however, that tradition was being modified. For one thing, the greatest English novelists at work during Forster's formative years were a wealthy American expatriate and a retired Polish mariner. No one as sensitive as Forster could escape the influence of Henry James and Joseph Conrad, but these men made curious heirs to Dickens and Thackeray and George Eliot. James, while intensely interested in the textures of society, focused his attention on the relations between the English (and Continental) leisure class and those American travelers that Mark Twain had christened "innocents abroad," thus limiting his social scrutiny, in Forster's opinion, to the narrow perceptions of a few wealthy idlers. Conrad diverged even more sharply from the path of previous English novelists, for he neither understood nor cared to understand any level of English society. A man of his temperament and interest might be imagined as a literary force in the mid-century United States of Nathaniel Hawthorne's *The Scarlet Letter* (1850) and Herman Melville's *Moby Dick* (1851), but not in the England of Thackeray's *Vanity Fair* (1847-1848) and Dickens' *Bleak House* (1852-1853). Nevertheless, Conrad was more in tune with his own literary milieu than Meredith, who at the end of the century reigned as the grand old man of English letters, and Conrad's work, like that of James, diverted the creative energy of many of the new century's novelists into new channels.

Of native English novelists still regarded as substantial, the most active at the time of Forster's entry into the field were Arnold Bennett, H. G. Wells, and John Galsworthy—all men born in the 1860's and all inheritors of the native tradition of the novel, albeit on a somewhat reduced scale. The next generation of novelists, born slightly after Forster in the 1880's, included Woolf, James Joyce, and D. H. Lawrence, all of whom published their initial works after Forster has already written five of his six novels. This latter group obviously belongs to a new literary dispensation. Society and its network of snobbery, though still significant, have receded into the background, and the conflicts of the protagonists are waged at a more personal, intimate, sometimes semiconscious level. Clearly the work of psychologists such as Sigmund Freud and Henry James's brother William influenced these later writers and drove them to develop literary techniques adequate to the task of a more truly psychological novel.

Forster, as has been suggested, stands in the middle. A friend of Virginia Woolf and in her mind, certainly, no part of the decaying tradition she trounced so severely in her essay "Mr. Bennett and Mrs. Brown," Forster nevertheless anticipated few of the technical innovations of the novelists who reached their maturity after World War I. His last novel stands with the post-Freudian achievements. *Howards End*, his most ambitious novel, is in most respects a novel of the old school. It is denser, symbolically richer, than the characteristic work of Bennett, Wells, and Galsworthy, but the same might be said of *Bleak House*, written more than half a century earlier.

Only around the time of Forster's birth did novelists begin to insist on the novel as an art form and write theoretical defenses of it. Meredith delivered a lecture on "The Idea of Comedy and the Uses of the Comic Spirit" (1877), which, though mentioning Miguel de Cervantes and Fielding, has more to say of Aristophanes and Molière; Henry James's essay "The Art of Fiction" appeared in 1884. By the century's end, novelists had achieved respectability, and Conrad could soberly echo Longinus: "Art is long and life is short, and success is very far off."

Such new expressions of the novelist's kinship with poet and playwright did not end the nineteenth century habit of producing loose, baggy narratives in a diversity of modes, punctuated by their author's abrupt changes of direction, interpolated moral essays, and episodes introduced for no better reason than a hunch that readers, who cared nothing for artistic integrity, would enjoy them. Stock literary devices that storytellers had accumulated over the centuries—bizarre coincidences, thoroughly improbable recognition scenes thrust into "realistic" contexts, the bundling forth of long-lost (often supposedly deceased) personages in the interests of a happy or surprising denouement, all devices that twentieth century novels would shun—still flourished in Forster's youth, and he used many of them unashamedly.

If Forster's moment in literary history partly explains his wavering between Victorian and modern canons, his skeptical, eclectic temperament must also be cited. His astute analyses of the morals and manners of society involved him in comedy, tragedy, romance, and fantasy—the sort of "God's plenty" that the supposedly neoclassical John Dryden admired in Chaucer and Ben Jonson in William Shakespeare. Such men would write any sort of work and take up with any sort of character. Forster was similarly indiscriminate. His veneration for Leo Tolstoy's *War and Peace* (1865-1869), though "such an untidy book," betrays his Englishman's weakness in believing that God's plenty would overcome the artist's scruples.

Of course Forster's novels are not so long as *War and Peace* or the Victorian ones that readers worked their way through in installments spread over many months. Compared to the seamless garments of Woolf or even the longer works of Joyce and William Faulkner (both of whom exhibit an un-English type of variety but also an astonishing coherence), Forster's juxtapositions of sharply contrasting modes invite criticism by readers who take in his works in two or three successive evenings. Thus, while Forster does not belong with Wells and Galsworthy, neither does he quite keep company with the greatest of his slightly younger contemporaries, for he loved too much the variety and freedom that most earlier English novelists permitted themselves.

Nevertheless, his motto for *Howards End*—"Only connect"—applies to his work generally. If he does not always make the artistic connections, his consistent theme is the necessity of making moral connections with fellow humans, of struggling against the class divisions which so many Englishmen, including a number of his fellow novelists, took for granted. In his novels, prudence is invariably on the side of those who, like Henry Wilcox in *Howards End* and Ronnie Heaslop in *A Passage to India*, resist the breakdown of social barriers; but courage, generosity, friendship, and sympathy are found among Forster's liberal opponents of snobbery. In the world of Forster's novels, the closed class is always sterile and corrupt.

Forster's eclecticism, his versatility, his refusal to ignore the claims either of heart or head make the reading of his novels an ambiguous but rich experience. Never, though, does he seem like a mere exhibitionist. Rather, his openness to life's variety amounts to a perpetual invitation to the participation of alert and open-minded readers. He is far less afraid of a gaucherie than of a missed opportunity to "connect."

Forster's shortest and most tightly focused novel is *Where Angels Fear to Tread*. A young man named Philip Herriton is commissioned by his mother and sister Harriet to bring back from Italy the infant son of Lilia Carella, the widow of another of Mrs. Herriton's sons. Within a year after marrying Gino Carella, the aimless son of a small-town dentist, Lilia died giving birth to a son. Aided by Harriet and by Caroline Abbott, who as Lilia's traveling companion had been able to do nothing to ward off the offensive marriage, Philip finds Gino resistant to Mrs. Herriton's pocketbook and ultimately becomes involved in a shabby kidnaping venture engineered by Harriet—a venture that ends with the accidental death of the child. On the way home, Philip finds himself drawn emotionally to Caroline, who reveals that she too has fallen in love with Gino. In the common effort to minister to the pitifully unregenerate Harriet, however, Philip and Caroline become friends.

Thus summarized, the novel bears some resemblance to one by James. Forster enjoys contrasting Anglo-Saxon and Italian mores, and he shares James's fascinated horror over the machinations and intrigues of sophisticated schemers. He may have owed the idea of centering the story on a somewhat detached emissary to James, whose novel *The Ambassadors* (1903) appeared shortly before Forster began work on his own book.

Forster's handling of his material, however, differs substantially from

James's. He cannot resist scathing treatment of the characters whose company he expects his readers to keep and with whom they are to sympathize. Harriet, appalled by Italy's uncleanliness, carries a bottle of ammonia in her trunk, but Forster has it "burst over her prayer-book, so that purple patches appeared on all her clothes." Prayer brings out the worst in many of Forster's characters, an exception being Caroline, who is able to pray in the church in Gino's hometown, "where a prayer to God is thought none the worse of because it comes next to a pleasant word to a neighbor." For Philip to develop neighborliness is a struggle. Not only is he much less experienced and resourceful than Strether or any other Jamesian ambassador, he is also decidedly unattractive: callow, priggish, and cowardly. Caroline's assessment of him in the final chapter, though tardily arrived at, is accurate enough: "You're without passion; you look on life as a spectacle, you don't enter it; you only find it funny or beautiful." By the time he hears this, however, Philip has learned what neither his mother nor his sister ever suspects: that the son of an Italian dentist can love his child more than wealth, that he is capable of trust and friendship, that he can be not merely angered but also hurt by a betrayal. Philip has also felt enough by this time to be hurt by Caroline's words.

Though selfish and short-sighted, Gino is without the treachery of a Jamesian Italian such as Giovanelli in *Daisy Miller* (1879). Indeed, Forster makes him morally superior to the Herriton women. Fixing on a domestic vignette of a sort impossible in any well-appointed English household (or in a James novel, for that matter)—Gino bathing his infant son—Forster draws Caroline into helping him and lets Philip come upon them so engaged, "to all intents and purposes, the Virgin and Child, with Donor." Forster's heroes tend to idealize people who are only behaving a little better than expected, but the capacity to idealize is a symptom of their regeneration.

Harriet tricks Philip into the kidnaping; he discovers the ruse only after the baby has died and his own arm has been broken in a carriage accident. He returns to confess the transgression, only to have the grief-stricken Gino cruelly twist his broken arm and then nearly choke him to death before Caroline appears to stop him. In a typically Forsterian piece of symbolism, she persuades Gino and Philip together to drink the milk that had been poured for the child. In a pattern that Forster repeats in later novels, Philip, though excessive in his estimate of Caroline's goodness, is nevertheless "saved" by it. Salvation is at least partly illusion, but such an illusion serves him better than the cynicism that Philip has spent his youth imbibing.

Like Philip, Rickie Elliot of *The Longest Journey* is frail and aesthetic. In addition, a deformed foot which he has inherited from his father marks him as different from his Cambridge classmates. At the beginning of the novel, both his father, whom he despised, and his beloved mother are dead; his father's sister, Mrs. Failing, is his closest relative. On her Wiltshire estate lives a young man, Stephen Wonham, an illegitimate half-brother to Rickie.

Rude, truculent, undiscriminating in his choice of companions, and more or less a habitual drunkard, Stephen also proves loyal and almost pathetically trusting. The relationship between the two brothers forms the core of the novel.

The title of the book, from Percy Bysshe Shelley's poem *Epipsychidion* (1821), alludes to the folly of denying the rest of the world for the sake of "a mistress or a friend," with whom, in consequence, one must "the dreariest and longest journey go." In the midst of mulling over the poem, Rickie ironically decides to take his journey with Agnes Pembroke, a girl whose first lover, a strapping athlete, has died suddenly of a football injury. Death, it may be noted, always strikes with unexpected suddenness in Forster's novels. The marriage disgusts Rickie's closest friend, Stewart Ansell, and Rickie himself comes soon enough to regret it. Discouraged by Agnes and her elder brother Herbert from pursuing a career as a writer, Rickie takes a teaching post at Sawston School, where Herbert is a master. By a strange coincidence, a maladjusted boy at the school writes a letter to Stephen Wonham, among other total strangers, asking Stephen to "pray for him." Agnes's practical mind senses trouble if Stephen appears at the school, but mercifully the boy withdraws before Stephen can carry out an offer to come visit him. Rickie, while not fond of Stephen, is willing for him to receive his aunt's property when she dies; not so Agnes. When Mrs. Failing sends the troublesome Stephen packing, he decides to visit Sawston and inform Rickie of their relationship—which Rickie already knows.

Outside the school, Stephen meets Stewart Ansell, on hand to verify for himself the death of his friend's spirit in his loveless union with the Pembrokes, and, after receiving an insult, knocks him down. Before Stephen can see Rickie, Agnes intercepts him and offers him the money she is sure he wants in return for leaving Sawston and sparing Rickie the embarrassment of acknowledging him. Stunned and stung, the utterly unmercenary Stephen leaves, but Ansell, won over not only by Stephen's fist but also by his principles, breaks into the Sawston dining hall during Sunday dinner and, in front of masters, students, and all, rebukes Rickie for turning away his own brother in the latter's deepest distress. As the assemblage gapes, Ansell reveals what he has correctly intuited: that Stephen is not the son of Rickie's father, as Rickie had supposed, but of his beloved mother. At this news Rickie faints.

Although wildly improbable, the scene has an electric intensity about it. Ansell, with all the clumsy insistence of a true egalitarian and all the insight of a true friend, has, while mistakenly charging Rickie with complicity in Agnes's treachery, stripped away the hypocrisy behind which the couple has hidden. There is about this revelation something of the quality of the recognition scene of a tragedy such as Sophocles' *Oedipus Tyrannus* (c. 429), with Rickie the lame protagonist faced with the consequences of his disastrous marriage and of his unjust assumption about his father, as well as of his denial of his brother.

From the time Rickie listened mutely to his classmates' discussion of whether the cow in the field was "there" if no one was present to perceive her, he has searched unavailingly for reality. He has misinterpreted his love for Agnes as real, watched his son—inevitably deformed like his father and himself—die in infancy, and seen his attempt at a schoolmaster's life tumble. Now he tries, none too successfully, to effect a reconciliation with his brother. He leaves Agnes and the school and tries to rekindle the flame of his short-story writing. When Stephen disappoints him on a visit to Mrs. Failing by breaking a promise not to drink, Rickie concludes that people are not "real." Finding Stephen sprawled drunkenly across the tracks at a railroad crossing, Rickie finds the strength to move him from the path of an oncoming train— but not the strength to save himself.

Rickie's aunt and brother-in-law, incapable of seeing his rescue of Stephen as worthwhile, see him as a failure whose life is mercifully over. Stephen, who is no thinker, is not so sure. In the final chapter, he feels himself to be in some sense the future of England, for he is now the father of a girl who bears the name of his and Rickie's mother. Dimly, he acknowledges that his salvation is from Rickie.

Not only does *The Longest Journey* run to melodrama, but it also incorporates some rather tedious moralizing, both on the part of Mrs. Failing and in an interpolated essay by Forster which forms the whole twenty-eighth chapter (although the chapter is a short one). Probably the greatest burden, however, is the one Stephen Wonham is forced to carry. First of all, he is the disreputable relative who knocks people down and falls down drunk himself. He serves a contrasting and complementary purpose as a kind of spiritual extension of Rickie, particularly after Rickie, recognizing him as his mother's son, begins to invest him with her excellencies, as recollected. In the final chapter, Stephen becomes the consciousness of the novel itself.

Without Stephen, however, Forster's brilliant portrait of Rickie is not only incomplete but also depressing, for Rickie dies, sad to say, murmuring agreement with Mrs. Failing's antihumanist convictions that "we do not live for anything great" and that "people are not important at all." Stephen exists and procreates and retains the idea of greatness to prove Rickie wrong.

Forster sends his principals off to Italy again in *A Room with a View*. The room in question is one which Lucy Honeychurch and her elder cousin Charlotte Bartlett do not enjoy at the beginning of their stay in a Florentian hotel but which two other travelers, the elderly Mr. Emerson and his son George, are more than willing to exchange for the one that furnishes the ladies with only a disappointing view of the courtyard. Characteristic of Forster's well-bred characters, they lose sight of Emerson's generosity in their horror at the directness and bluntness of his offer, for he has interrupted their conversation at dinner before other guests: "I have a view, I have a view." Having defied the convention that forbids hasty and undue familiarity with a stranger, Mr. Emerson must be certified by an English clergyman, after which the ladies somewhat stiffly accept the view. Mr. Emerson, of course, has throughout the novel a "view" which the cousins, who hate the darkness but blanch at openness, achieve only with difficulty.

Soon an unexpected adventure literally throws Lucy and George Emerson more closely together. While enthusiastically and uncritically buying photographs of Italian masterpieces, Lucy witnesses a stabbing in a public square. She faints; George catches her and, after throwing her blood-spattered photographs into the River Arno, conducts her away gently. Later, Lucy puzzles over the affair and comes to the conclusion that, despite his kind intentions, George Emerson is devoid of "chivalry."

When circumstances throw them together again, George impulsively kisses Lucy. Such behavior drives Lucy and Charlotte to Rome, where they meet Cecil Vyse. He is propriety itself, never once offering to kiss Lucy, and back in England Lucy and Vyse become engaged. By coincidence, Vyse has met the Emersons and introduces them to the neighborhood where Lucy and her mother live. Though well-intentioned, Vyse is one of Forster's snobs. He is also a drab lover, and when Lucy finally tastes one of his unsatisfactory kisses, she is thrown into a panic by the prospect of another meeting with George. They meet again, and George kisses her again, with the result that Lucy deems George impossible and Vyse intolerable and breaks her engagement to the latter with the resolve never to marry anyone.

Clearly Forster is on a different, more wholeheartedly comic, course in this novel, and the denouement fulfills the tradition of romantic comedy, the inevitable marriage of Lucy and George being brought about through the ministrations of a lady who casts off her role as an apparently irredeemable snob—cousin Charlotte. What Forster says of the Honeychurch house, Windy Corner, might almost be said of the novel: "One might laugh at the house, but one never shuddered." Despite the play of Forster's wit throughout the novel and the sympathy he extends to a girl as silly as Lucy, the reader does shudder occasionally. Two murders, the real one Lucy sees and a supposed one, interrupt the proceedings. The latter is a rumor, bruited about by a clergyman named Eager, that Mr. Emerson has murdered his wife. The charge is baseless and seems to have been injected to deepen Emerson's character as a man of sorrows. The real death is even more gratuitous—unless it is meant to validate George Emerson's seriousness and dependability.

Events lead Lucy into a series of lies which she supposes to be little white ones but which threaten general unhappiness until Mr. Emerson, whom she has led to believe that she still intends to marry Vyse, induces heart's truth and persuades her to marry George. The novel ends with the honeymooners back in Florence speculating on Charlotte's motive in bringing about Lucy's climactic meeting with Mr. Emerson. They conclude that "she fought us on the surface, and yet she hoped."

Mr. Emerson in two respects at least echoes the writer of the same name. He is convinced of the importance of discovering Nature, and he is apostle of self-trust. A good man, he grows tedious after the initial chapter, functioning finally as his son's advocate. George himself never quite comes into focus, and the reader is forced to accept on faith Charlotte's change of heart. The lightest of Forster's novels, *A Room with a View*, had it been lighter yet and avoided the rather heavy-handed symbolism of the "view" and the dark, might not have turned out the weakest of the five novels Forster published in his lifetime.

Howards End, Forster's most ambitious novel, recounts the adventures of two sisters, Margaret and Helen Schlegel, after two encounters with people not of their quiet, cultivated London set. At the beginning Helen has, while a guest at the country home of the Wilcoxes, a family the Schlegels had met while traveling abroad, become engaged—at least in her own mind—to one of the Wilcox sons, Paul. Her visit and engagement end awkwardly when her aunt whisks her back to London. The second incident grows out of Helen's inadvertently taking home from the theater the umbrella of a bank clerk named Leonard Bast. Standing "at the extreme verge of gentility," Leonard wishes to approach closer. The idealistic Schlegels appreciate the impulse and strike up an acquaintance. Meanwhile, the Wilcox connection is reestablished when the Wilcoxes rent a flat across from the house where the Schlegels, including younger brother Tibby, live, and Margaret, the oldest Schlegel, comes to know Mrs. Wilcox.

A quiet, even dull woman, Ruth Wilcox is an utterly charitable person who conveys to Margaret "the idea of greatness." Her husband Henry, a prosperous businessman, and the three Wilcox children—young adults like Helen and Tibby—radiate energy, good humor, and physical health but lack wit, grace, and any sense of beauty. Suddenly, a quarter of the way through the novel, Ruth Wilcox dies.

In marrying Henry Wilcox, Margaret proves very nearly as improvident as Lilia Herriton or Rickie Elliot. The two have little in common, and before long a series of fortuitous events shakes their precarious union. As a result of offhand bad advice from Henry, duly passed on by the Schlegel sisters, Leonard Bast loses his job. Leonard makes a pilgrimage to Oniton, that one of several Wilcox estates on which Henry and Margaret are living. Unfortunately, Leonard chooses to bring along his unbecoming common-law wife, who turns out to be a former mistress of Henry Wilcox. When Henry angrily turns the Basts away, the conscience-stricken Helen insists on trying to compensate Bast. Like Stephen Wonham, he indignantly refuses her money. The impulsive and emotionally overwrought Helen refuses to abandon him. Later Helen disappears into Germany for a time; on her return Margaret discovers that she has conceived a son by Leonard.

When Margaret relays to her husband Helen's request that she be permitted to stay at the unused Howards End for one night, he indignantly refuses, and Margaret realizes that Henry, the betrayer of his own first wife, is unrepentant in his maintenance of a moral double standard. One tragic scene remains. Leonard appears at Howards End to beg forgiveness for sinning with Helen, Charles Wilcox (Henry's other son) totally misunderstands the intruder's motive and strikes him down with the flat of a sword, and Leonard's weak heart gives way. Charles is convicted of manslaughter, and at the end, Margaret, Helen and her child, and the broken-spirited Henry are living together at Howards End.

The reader will have noted similarities to Forster's first two published novels—the melodrama, the improbable coincidences, the often awkward modulations between comic and tragic tone, and so on. The pattern of events in *Howards End*, on the other hand, is both more richly and less intrusively symbolic. As many critics have observed, this is a novel about England, written in the uneasy pre-World War I years of growing antagonism between Germany and England. Forster permits himself a series of meditations on, paeans of praise to, his native isle in the manner of John of Gaunt's "This blessed plot, this earth, this realm, this England" speech in *Richard II* (1595-1596). At the same time, Forster clearly intimates that England is also the Wilcoxes—insular in their outlook, stolid in their prejudices, merciless in their advocacy of the class structure. The Schlegel sisters spring from a German father and revere German Romantic culture. Chapter 5 of the novel celebrates their (and Forster's) extraordinary sensitivity to Ludwig van Beethoven, it being after a performance of the *Fifth Symphony* that Helen takes Leonard's umbrella.

Margaret also loves England, typified by Howards End, which is no ancient seat of the Wilcoxes but a property which had belonged to Mrs. Wilcox herself, even though she sometimes seems to be amid alien corn there. England, Forster seems to say, needs to unite the best in its Wilcoxes, its providers and healthy consumers of material goods, with the Schlegel principle, expressed in the love of art and civilized discussion. By themselves the Schlegels are ineffectual. They can only watch helplessly as commercial development dooms their London house. After Helen has been carried away by her feeling for Leonard's plight, she flees to her father's ancestral home but cannot live there. Only at Howards End can she live securely and watch her child grow up.

As a symbol for England and for the possibilities of a balanced life, Howards End might seem to have some deficiencies. It is lacking in beauty and tradition. It has become the seat of a philistine family, for even the saintly Ruth demonstrates no artistic interest more highly developed than a fondness for flowers and for a certain adjacent meadow in the early morning. On her first visit to Howards End, Helen Schlegel sees more of nature's beauties than any of the

Wilcoxes, preoccupied with croquet, tennis, and "calisthenic exercises on a machine that is tacked on to a greengage-tree," ever perceive.

The agent who renders Howards End truly habitable is an uneducated farm woman who refuses to accept her "place." When Margaret first visits Howards End, where, it is thought, they will *not* make their home, she finds Miss Avery there. The old woman, who for a second mistakes Margaret for the first Mrs. Wilcox, has taken it upon herself to guard the empty house. Her presumptuousness, which in the past has taken the form of wedding gifts to both Henry's daughter and daughter-in-law—gaucheries the Wilcoxes are quick to condemn—extends shortly thereafter to unpacking the Schlegel books and other personal belongings, which have been stored there following the expiration of the lease on the London house. After ranging the Schlegel library in bookcases and arranging the Schlegel furniture to suit herself, the woman declines to accept even polite criticism: "You think that you won't come back to live here, Mrs. Wilcox, but you will."

Thus it is an intuitive country person who joins the half-foreign Schlegel culture to the native Wilcox stock. Miss Avery also sends over a country boy, Tom, after Helen and Margaret, in defiance of Henry, spend a night together at Howards End. "Please, I am the milk," says Tom, speaking more truth than he knows. As in *Where Angels Fear to Tread*, the milk is spiritual as well as physical nourishment. Peopled with such life-affirming folk, Howards End becomes a sustaining place, an embodiment of what English life might yet be if the deepening disorder of 1910 is somehow averted. Finally won over to permitting Helen to reside there—and thus at least tacitly acknowledging his own fornication—Henry decrees that at his death the property will pass to Margaret; Ruth Wilcox herself had wanted to give it to her.

The motto of *Howards End* is "Only connect." In the house, "the prose and passion" of life, the Wilcox and Schlegel principles, are joined through the ministrations of another of Forster's characters willing to defy the class system in the interests of a nobler order.

The central symbol of *Howards End* is hay. Ruth Wilcox is first observed "smelling hay," a product that the naturally fertile estate produces in abundance. The rest of the Wilcoxes, Miss Avery at one point observes maliciously, all suffer from hay fever. Forster uses the hay very much as Walt Whitman, whom he occasionally quotes and from whom he appropriated the title of his final novel, uses the grass: to suggest life, sustenance, hope, democracy. At the end of the novel, the chastened Henry's case of hay fever seems to have subsided when Helen, her baby, and Tom burst in from the meadow, with Helen exclaiming, "It'll be such a crop of hay as never!"

Written a few years after *Howards End*, *Maurice* did not see print until the year following Forster's death. In a later "terminal note" to this novel of a homosexual, Forster observed a change in the public's reaction to this subject from one of "ignorance and terror" at the time he wrote it to "familiarity and contempt" in his old age, so he continued to withhold the work. Maurice Hall also defies the class system, for his sexual partner is a gamekeeper on a college classmate's estate. Given the rigid penal code of the time, the novel is also about criminality.

Aside from his sexual orientation, Maurice resembles his creator very little, being rather ordinary in intellect, little drawn to the arts, and rather robust physically. Whereas Rickie Elliot had been effeminate, his deformed foot a symbolic impediment to satisfactory heterosexuality, Maurice seems quite "normal" to his friends. His college friend Clive Durham, leaning somewhat to homosexuality in college, ironically changes after an illness and a trip to Greece, and marries. The Durhams are gentlefolk, though somewhat reduced, and Maurice has gotten on well with them, but Clive's marriage drives a wedge between them. After indulging in, and apparently escaping from, a furtive but passionate affair with Alec Scudder, their gamekeeper, Maurice suffers a blackmail threat from his former lover, but in the end Alec proves true, and instead of emigrating with whatever conscience money he might have extracted, Alec returns to the Durham estate, where, in the boathouse, the two come together again. At the end, Maurice's revelation to the conventionally horrified Clive leaves the latter trying "to devise some method of concealing the truth from Anne"—his wife.

Maurice demonstrates Forster's conviction that the desire for loving human relations is proof against the snobbery of all social classes. Although it could not be printed when it was written, the novel now seems more dated than Forster's other works, perhaps because its style is plain and drab. It obviously suffers from its lack of a contemporary audience, although Forster showed it to Lytton Strachey and received some constructive advice. Significantly, when Oliver Stallybrass, the editor of the Abinger Edition of Forster's works, assembled his favorite quotations from Forster, he could find nothing in *Maurice* worth including.

Although Forster committed himself wholeheartedly to friendship, it cannot be called the central theme of any of his novels until *A Passage to India*. The friendship of Rickie Elliot and Stewart Ansell, while vital to the former's development and self-discovery, is subordinated to the theme of brotherhood, in its familial sense, and Rickie can find no basis for friendship with Stephen. The incipient friendship of Margaret Schlegel and Ruth Wilcox is aborted by the latter's death. *A Passage to India*, while treating of brotherhood in its largest sense, is at heart a novel of friendship and its possibilities in the context of a racially and religiously fragmented society.

Beginning with the visit to India of the mother and fiancée of Ronnie Heaslop, the young colonial magistrate, and the complications of their encounters with a few educated natives, the narrative comes to focus on the friendship that as a consequence waxes and wanes between the English schoolmaster Cyril Fielding and the young Muslim Dr. Aziz. Forster dedicated the book to another Anglo-Indian friendship: his own with Syed Ross Masood, who first knew Forster as his tutor in Latin prior to Masood's entrance to Oxford in 1906, and who provided the impetus for Forster's own initial passage to India a few years later. Since Anglo-Indian prejudice was one of the loquacious Masood's favorite subjects, Forster understood it well by the time he came to write the novel. Indeed, his friendship with Masood demonstrated the possibility of such a relationship surviving the strains imposed on it by one partner's determination to pull no punches in discussing it.

Aziz, accused by Ronnie's fiancée Adela Quested of assaulting, or at least offending her (for she remains vague about the matter throughout), in a cave they are exploring, is a less masterful and self-confident figure than Masood, and the reader knows all along that there must be some mistake. Adela has seen how Ronnie's Indian service has exacerbated the weaker aspects of his character and has broken off their engagement, but she is not, as Aziz affects to believe, a love-starved female—at least not in the crude sense Aziz intends.

Forster draws an unforgettable picture of the tensions between the colonial rulers and the Indian professional class. The most idealistic Englishmen, it seems, succumb to the prevailing intolerance. It is an effort to consider the natives as human, as when Ronnie, told by his mother, Mrs. Moore, of her meeting with a young doctor, replies: "I know of no young doctor in Chandrapore," though once he learns that his mother has actually been consorting with a Muslim, he identifies him readily enough.

An exception to the rule is Fielding, already over forty when he came to India and a continuing believer in "a globe of men who are trying to reach one another." When Aziz's trial divides the community more openly and dangerously than usual, Fielding supports the young doctor—a move that assures the enmity of the English without guaranteeing the affection of the skeptical Indians. After Adela withdraws her charges against Aziz, the intimacy between the two men reaches its height; almost immediately, however, they quarrel over Aziz's determination to make his tormentor pay damages.

Fielding cannot persuade Aziz to show mercy, but Mrs. Moore can, even though she has left the country before the trial and in fact has died on her return passage. For the sake of the mother of the detested man whom Aziz still believes Adela will marry, he spares the young woman, knowing that the English will interpret this decision as an indication of guilt. With Adela finally gone, Aziz mistakenly assumes that Fielding, now contemplating a visit to England, intends to marry her himself. When the friends meet again two years later, the old frankness and intimacy has been shattered. Although Fielding has married, his bride is the daughter of Mrs. Moore.

The final chapter is a particularly excellent one. As Aziz and Fielding ride horses together, the former vowing that they can be friends but only after the Indians "drive every blasted Englishman into the sea," the horses swerve apart, as if to counter Fielding's objection. Religion, land, people, not even animals want the friendship now. It is difficult to escape the conclusion that under imperial conditions no rapprochement is possible.

Much of the interest in this novel has centered on Mrs. Moore, a rather querulous old woman with a role not much larger than Mrs. Wilcox's in *Howards End*. Although she joins the roster of Forster's admirable characters who defy the taboos that divide people, she refuses to involve herself in the Aziz trial. Nevertheless, the Indians make a legend out of her and invest her with numinous powers. Critics have tended to regard her as a more successful character than Mrs. Wilcox. Part of the explanation may lie in Forster's decision to allow the reader to see her not only at first hand but also through the eyes of the Indians. If their view of Mrs. Moore is partly illusion, the illusion itself—like the more familiar illusions of the English—becomes itself a part of the truth of the situation. It is one of Forster's virtues that he knows and communicates the often conflicting values and attitudes of native Indians.

Nor is the Indian version of Mrs. Moore completely illusory, for in addition to her openness and candor, Mrs. Moore in one respect surpasses all the Europeans, even the gentle Fielding. She loves and respects life, especially unfamiliar life. It is illuminating to contrast her attitude with that of two incidental characters—missionaries who live among the people and never come to the whites' club. They measure up to their calling very well for Forster clergymen, allowing that God has room in his mansions for all men. On the subject of animals they are not so sure; Mr. Sorley, the more liberal of the two, opts for monkeys but stumbles over wasps. Mrs. Moore, more alert to the native birds and animals than she is to many people, is even sympathetic to a wasp ("Pretty dear") that has flown into the house. It is doubtless significant that the wasp is very different from the European type. Long after she is gone, Professor Godbole, Aziz's Hindu friend, remembers her in connection with the wasp. Love of humble forms of life, which the other Westerners in the novel notice only as irritations if at all, is for the Indians of Forster's *A Passage to India* a reliable indication of spirituality.

The sensitivity of Mrs. Moore and the good will of Fielding seem like frail counterweights to the prevailing cynicism and prejudice which stifle the necessarily furtive social initiatives of well-intentioned victims such as Aziz. If these flawed but genuine human beings have little impact on the morally bankrupt society in which they move, they have for more than half a century heartened readers of like aspirations.

Robert P. Ellis

Other major works

SHORT FICTION: *The Celestial Omnibus and Other Stories*, 1911; *The Eternal Moment and Other Stories*, 1928; *The Collected Tales of E. M. Forster*, 1947; *The Life to Come and Other Stories*, 1972; *Arctic Summer and Other Fiction*, 1980.

PLAY: *Billy Budd*, 1951 (libretto, with Eric Crozier).

NONFICTION: *Alexandria: A History and a Guide*, 1922; *Pharos and Pharillon*, 1923; *Aspects of the Novel*, 1927; *Goldsworthy Lowes Dickinson*, 1934; *Abinger Harvest—A Miscellany*, 1936; *Virginia Woolf*, 1942; *Development of English Prose Between 1918 and 1939*, 1945; *Two Cheers for Democracy*, 1951; *The Hill of Devi*, 1953; *Marianne Thornton: A Domestic Biography, 1797-1887*, 1956; *Commonplace Book*, 1978.

Bibliography

Beer, J. B. *The Achievement of E. M. Forster*. London: Chatto & Windus, 1962. Although heavy on plot summary, this cogent discourse is valuable for its discussion of Forster's "comedy, moral seriousness, and imaginative passion." Discusses the novels and short stories and sees Forster as a romantic writer, an heir of William Blake, Samuel Taylor Coleridge, Percy Bysshe Shelley, Ludwig von Beethoven, and Richard Wagner, and as a symbolist. The book is indexed and includes selective primary/secondary bibliographies.

Crews, Frederick J. *E. M. Forster: The Perils of Humanism*. Princeton, N.J.: Princeton University Press, 1962. This comprehensive, readable introduction to Forster's novels and short stories argues that, although Forster's mind is anchored in liberalism, he is always aware of the liberal tradition's weaknesses. Claims that "his artistic growth runs parallel to his disappointments with humanism." Although he is agnostic and anti-Christian, Forster's "books are religious in their concern with the meaning of life" and the virtues of private freedom, diversity, personal relationships, sincerity, art, and sensitivity to the natural world and its traditions. Indexed.

Furbank, P. N. *E. M. Forster: A Life*. London: Secker & Warburg, 1978. This major biographical study written by another famous novelist is readable and perceptive in its analyses of the novels, short stories, and criticism. Finds pertinent influences on Forster's writing in his childhood, adolescent, and early adult years. An index is included.

Gransden, K. W. *E. M. Forster*. 1962. 2d ed. New York: Grove Press, 1970. This insightful study summarizes Forster's career, the influences of Samuel Butler, George Meredith, and Jane Austen, and his novels and short fiction. Included is a postscript to the 1970 revised edition which celebrates Forster's tenacious hold on his readers as well as selective primary/secondary bibliographies and an index.

McConkey, James. *The Novels of E. M. Forster*. Hamden, Conn.: Archon Books, 1957. This historically important study looks forward to the 1960's emphasis on textual and philosophical criticism of Forster's writings. Analyzes the author's use of point of view, fantasy, images, symbols, and rhythms and demonstrates that both the transcendent and the physical worlds are always present in Forster. Selective primary and secondary bibliographies and an index conclude the book.

Trilling, Lionel. *E. M. Forster.* Norfolk, Conn.: New Directions, 1943. This is one of the most important, most influential assessments of Forster ever written. Trilling's discussion of Forster and the liberal imagination went far to influence a revival of interest in the work. Considers Forster's novels, short fiction, and criticism to show that his work is to be explained in terms of his emphasis upon the disastrous effects of "the undeveloped heart." An index is included.

JOHN FOWLES

Born: Leigh-on-Sea, England; March 31, 1926

Principal long fiction

The Collector, 1963; *The Magus,* 1965, 1977; *The French Lieutenant's Woman,* 1969; *The Ebony Tower,* 1974; *Daniel Martin,* 1977; *Mantissa,* 1982; *A Maggot,* 1985.

Other literary forms

In addition to his novels, John Fowles has written philosophy, essays for scholarly and popular audiences, criticism, poetry, and short fiction. He has also translated several other writers into English. *The Aristos: A Self-Portrait in Ideas,* first published in 1964 and later revised in 1966 and 1968, is his philosophical "self-portrait in ideas." Patterned after writings of Heraclitus, the fifth century B.C. Greek philosopher, it reflects Fowles's philosophical stance, outlining many of the views which Fowles expresses more fully and artistically in his fiction. His collected poetry is published in *Poems* (1973); much of it reflects his period of residence in Greece, the major setting for *The Magus.* His longer nonfiction pieces reflect his love for and interest in nature: *Shipwreck* (1977), a text to accompany the photographs of shipwrecks along the English coast near Fowles's home; *Islands* (1978), about the Scilly Islands off the English coast, but more about the nature of islands as a metaphor for literature and the writer; *The Tree* (1980), an extension of the same theme with emphasis on the tree as representative of all nature; and *The Enigma of Stonehenge* (1980), a further extension of nature to encompass the mystery of a sacred place. All of these themes find definition and elaboration in his fiction. Fowles's only collection of short fiction, *The Ebony Tower,* includes a novella from which the title is taken, three short stories, and a translation of a medieval romance with a "Personal Note" that comments on its relation to his fiction. The collection, entitled *Variations* in manuscript, also reflects Fowles's central themes in the longer fiction.

Achievements

Fowles's place in literary history is difficult to assess. At this point in his career, he has established an excellent reputation as a writer of serious fiction, one who will continue to be read. He continues to receive the notice of numerous critics; more than a dozen books have been published about him. Fowles, however, is no "ivory tower" author; he enjoys a wide readership, and several of his novels have been made into motion pictures, including *The Collector, The Magus,* and *The French Lieutenant's Woman.* Readers can expect to find in Fowles's works a good story with a passionate love interest, complex characters, a healthy smattering of philosophy, all presented within the context of the plot. Critics can slice away multiple layers to get at the wheels-within-wheels of meaning on existential, historical, philosophical, psychological, and myriad other levels.

Because Fowles rarely tells the same story in the same way, genre is a topic of much discussion among his critics. His fiction reflects not only his experimentation with genre, but also his questioning of authorial voice, the continuum of time, moments out of time, split viewpoint, a story without an ending, a story with a choice of endings, and still another with a revised ending. Despite such experimentation, most of the novels are in many ways quite old-fashioned, reflecting the ancient boy-meets-girl, boy-loses-girl, boy-seeks-to-find-girl-again-and-in-so-doing-finds-himself quest motif that characterizes so much fiction. They are fairly straightforward "good reads" without the dizzying experimentation of a James Joyce to make them virtually inaccessible to all but the most diligent reader. On any level, Fowles is enjoyable, and what reserves him a place among memorable writers is that he is discoverable, again and again.

Biography

John Fowles was born in Leigh-on-Sea, Essex, England, on March 31, 1926, to Robert and Gladys Richards Fowles. During World War II, his family was evacuated to the more remote village of Ippeplen, South Devon, and it was there that Fowles discovered the beauty of the country of Devonshire, his "English Garden of Eden" that figures so prominently in other guises in his fiction. During that same period, he was a student at the exclusive Bedford School, where he studied German and French literature, eventually rising to the stature of head boy, a position of great power over the other boys in the school. It was there that he got his first taste of literature, which he loved, and power, which he despised. The knowledge of both was influential in his own writing.

From Bedford, he went into military service, spending six months at the University of Edinburgh and completing training as a lieutenant in the merchant marine just as the war was ending. Following the war, he continued his education in German and more particularly French literature at New College, Oxford University; he was graduated in 1950 with a B.A. with honors. His fiction owes many debts to his study of French literature, particularly his interest in existentialism as espoused by Jean-Paul Sartre and Albert Camus and his knowledge of the Celtic romance, from which stems his expressed belief that all literature has its roots in the theme of the quest.

Upon graduation, Fowles taught English at the University of Poitiers. After a year at Poitiers, he took a job teaching English to Greek boys on the island of Spetsai in the Aegean Sea. The school, the island, the aura of Greece, and the thoughts of the young teacher became the material for *The Magus*, his first novel (although not published first). It was also on Spetsai that he met Elizabeth Whitton, whom he married three years later. For Fowles, Greece was the land of myth, the other world, the place of the quest. Leaving Greece, Fowles suffered the loss of another Eden, but that loss inspired him to write. While writing, he continued to teach in and around London until the publication of *The Collector* in 1963, the success of which enabled him to leave teaching and devote himself full time to writing. The following year, he published *The Aristos* and in 1965 he finally published *The Magus*, twelve years after its conception.

A year later, he and Elizabeth moved to Lyme Regis in Dorset, a small seaside town away from London where they have continued to live. First living on a rundown farm, the Fowleses later moved to an eighteenth century house overlooking Lyme Bay. The dairy, the house, and the town of Lyme figure prominently in his third novel, *The French Lieutenant's Woman*, a work that established his international reputation. Following its success were his *Poems, The Ebony Tower, Daniel Martin*, the revised version of *The Magus*, *Mantissa*, and *A Maggot*.

Fowles's love of nature is evident in his writing as well as his life, especially in such nonfiction works as *Islands* and *The Tree*. At his home in Lyme Regis, he oversees a large, wild garden overlooking Lyme Bay, in which he fosters the natural development of the flora, passions that have not died since boyhood. One that has died, however, is the collection of living things. Once a collector of butterflies, like his character Frederick Clegg in *The Collector*, Fowles now abhors such activities. Rather, he collects Victorian postcards and antique china, reads voluminously, goes to London infrequently, and shares a very private life with his wife, who is his best critic. It was a life he very much enjoyed until he suffered a mild stroke in early 1988. Although the stroke caused no permanent damage, it left him depressed by the sudden specter of death and by a resulting loss of creative energies.

Analysis

John Fowles's fiction has one theme: the quest of his protagonists for self-knowledge. Such a quest is not easy in the modern world because, as many other modern authors have shown, the contemporary quester is cut off from the traditions and rituals of the past that gave men a purpose and sense of direction. Still, desiring the freedom of individual choice which requires an understanding of self, the Fowlesian protagonist moves through the pattern of the quest as best he can.

Following the tradition of the quest theme found in the medieval romance, which Fowles sees as central to his and all of Western fiction, the quester embarks on the journey in response to a call to adventure. Because the quester is in a state of longing for the adventure, oftentimes not recognized as such by him, he readily responds to the call. The call takes him across a threshold into another world, the land of myth. For Fowles's questers, this other world is always described as a remote, out-of-the-way place, often lush and primeval. In this place the quester meets the usual dragons, which, in modern terms, are presented as a series of challenges that he must overcome if he is to proceed.

Guided by the figure of the wise old man who has gone before him and can show the way, the quester gradually acquires self-knowledge, which brings freedom of choice. For Fowles's heroes, this choice always centers around the acceptance of a woman. If the quester has attained self-knowledge, he is able to choose the woman—that is, to know and experience love, signifying wholeness. Then, he must make the crossing back into the real world and continue to live and choose freely, given the understanding the quest has provided.

What separates the journey of the Fowlesian hero from the journey of the medieval hero is that much of it has become internalized. Where the quester of old did actual battle with dragons, monsters, and mysterious knights, the modern quester is far removed from such obvious obstacles. He cannot see the enemy in front of him, since it is often within him, keeping him frozen in a state of inertia that prevents him from questing. The modern journey, then, can be seen in psychological terms; while the events are externalized, the results are measured by the growth of the protagonist toward wholeness or self-knowledge. Thus, as Joseph Campbell describes in *The Hero with a Thousand Faces* (1949), "The problem is . . . nothing if not that of making it possible for men and women to come to full human maturity through the conditions of contemporary life."

Each of Fowles's protagonist/heroes follows the pattern of the mythic quest. Each journeys to a strange land (the unconscious): the Greek island of Phraxos and Conchis' more secret domain for Nicholas Urfe, the isolated countryside house for Frederick Clegg, the primitive Undercliff of Lyme Regis for Charles Smithson, the hidden manor in the forests of Brittany for David Williams, the lost landscape of his youth and the journey up the Nile for Daniel Martin, the interior space of the mind of Miles Green, and the ancient landscape of Stonehenge plus the mystery of the cave for Bartholomew and Rebecca. Each undergoes a series of trials (the warring aspects of his personality) intended to bring him to a state of self-consciousness. With the exception of Clegg, whose story represents the antiquest, each has the aid of a guide (the mythical wise old man): Conchis for Nicholas, Dr. Grogan for Charles, Breasley for David Williams; Professor Kirnberger, Georg Lukács, a Rembrandt self-portrait, and others for Daniel Martin; the various manifestations of the muse for Miles Green; and Holy Mother Wisdom for Bartholomew and Rebecca. Each has an encounter with a woman (representative of "the other half" needed for wholeness): Alison for Nicholas, Miranda for Frederick, Sarah for Charles, the "Mouse" for David, Jane for Daniel, Erato for Miles, Holy

Mother Wisdom for Bartholomew, and Bartholomew for Rebecca. The ability of the quester to calm or assimilate the warring aspects within him, to come to an understanding of himself, and as a result reach out to the experience of love with the woman, represents the degree of growth of each.

Feeling strongly that his fiction must be used as "a method of propagating [his] views of life" to bring a vision of cosmic order out of modern chaos, Fowles sees himself on a journey to accomplish this task. An examination of his fiction reveals the way in which he tackles the task, providing his readers with a description of the journey that they, too, can take.

The Magus was Fowles's first novel (although it was published after *The Collector*) and it remains his most popular. Fowles himself was so intrigued by the novel that he spent twelve years writing it, and even after publication, produced a revised version in 1977 because he was dissatisfied with parts of it. While some critics see changes between the original and the revision, there is little substantive difference between the two books beyond the addition of more explicit sexual scenes and the elaboration of several sections; thus the discussion of one suffices for the other.

The story derives from Fowles's period of teaching in Greece, and its protagonist, Nicholas Urfe, is much like Fowles in temperament and situation. As is often the case with Fowles, his fiction describes protagonists of the same age and temperament as himself at the time of his writing; thus an examination of the corpus reveals a maturing hero as well as a maturing author. In this first novel, Nicholas is twenty-five, Oxford-educated, attracted to existentialism, and bored with life. He is the typical Fowlesian protagonist, well-born and bred, aimless, and ripe for the quest.

Discontented with his teaching job in England, he, like Fowles, jumps at the opportunity to teach in Greece. His subconscious desire is for a "new land, a new race, a new language," which the quest will provide. Just before going, he meets Alison, who is to become the important woman in his life, although it takes many pages and much questing through the labyrinth of self-knowledge on Phraxos for Nicholas to realize this. Alison, as the intuitive female, the feeling side Nicholas needs for wholeness, recognizes the importance of their relationship from the beginning, while Nicholas, representing reason, does not. In discussing the elements of the quest that bring Nicholas to an understanding and acceptance of the feeling side of himself which allows him to experience love, one can chart the pattern of the quest which Fowles presents in variations in all his fiction.

On Phraxos, Nicholas responds to the call to adventure embodied in the voice of a girl, the song of a bird, and some passages of poetry, especially four lines from T. S. Eliot: "We shall not cease from exploration/ And the end of all our exploring/ Will be to arrive where we started/ And know the place for the first time." These lines state the mystery of the journey that awaits him: to quest outside so as to come back to himself with understanding.

Put another way, it is the yearning in man for the return to the harmony of the Garden of Eden. It is, as well, the thesis of *Four Quartets* (1943), which solves for Eliot the problem of the wasteland. Finally, it is the concept that motivates almost all of Fowles's questers, beginning with Nicholas.

Crossing the threshold beyond the *Salle d'Attente*, or Waiting Room, to the domain of myth at Bournai, Nicholas meets Conchis, his guide through the quest. Under Conchis' tutelage, Nicholas' "discoveries" begin. Nicholas understands that something significant is about to happen, that it is somehow linked to Alison, and that it restores his desire to live. Conchis exposes Nicholas to a series of experiences to teach and test him. Some he describes for Nicholas; others make Nicholas an observer; and still others give him an active, sometimes frightening role. In all, whether he is repulsed, fascinated, or puzzled, Nicholas wants more, allowing himself to be led deeper and deeper into the mysteries. These culminate in the trial scene, during which Nicholas is examined, his personality dissected, his person humiliated. Finally, he is put to the test of his ability to choose. Longing to punish Lily/Julie, the personification of woman Nicholas romantically and unrealistically longs for, he is given the opportunity at the end of the trial to flog her. His understanding that his freedom of choice gives him the power to resist the predictable, to go against the dictates of reason alone and follow the voice of the unconscious, signifies that he has become one of the "elect." Nicholas emerges from the underground chamber reborn into a higher state of consciousness. He must then make the return crossing into the real world.

To begin the return journey, he is given a glimpse of Alison, although he has been led to believe that she has committed suicide. Realizing that she is alive and that she offers him "a mirror that did not lie" in her "constant reality," he understands that the remainder of the quest must be toward a reunion with Alison. Apparently, however, he is not yet worthy of her, being dominated still by the ratiocinative side of himself, that part that seeks to unravel logically the mystery that Conchis presents. Thus, on his return to London he is put through additional tests until one day, completely unsuspecting of her arrival, he sees Alison again and follows her to Regents Park for their reunion.

Signifying the experience of the Garden of Eden when man and woman existed in wholeness, the park provides an appropriate setting for their reunion. Echoing lines from Eliot, Nicholas has arrived where he started. Now he must prove that he is worthy of Alison, that he can accept the love she once offered freely but that he must win her just as Orpheus attempted to win Eurydice from the dead. Becoming his own magus, he acts out a drama of his own making, challenging Alison to meet him at Paddington Station, where their journey together will begin. Unlike Orpheus, who was unsuccessful in bringing Eurydice from the dead, Nicholas has the confidence gained in his quest to leave Alison and not look back, knowing that she will be at the train station to meet him. While there is some question among critics as to whether Nicholas and Alison do meet and continue their journey together, Fowles has indicated that "Alison is the woman he will first try to love." Certainly, in either case it is the element of mystery that is important, not whether Nicholas wins this particular woman. The significance is in his yearning for her, demonstrating that he has learned to accept and give love, that he has journeyed toward wholeness.

What makes such a journey significant for the reader is that he or she can partake of the experience as an insider, not as an outsider. This results from the narrative technique Fowles employs. In Fowles's first-person narrative, Nicholas reveals only what he knows at any particular point on his journey; thus the reader sees only what Nicholas sees. Not able to see with any more sophistication than Nicholas the twistings and turnings of Conchis' "godgame," the reader must do exactly what Nicholas does: try to unravel the mystery in its literal sense rather than understand the "mystery" in its sacred sense. Believing every rational explanation Nicholas posits, one learns as he learns. As his own magus, Nicholas leads the reader into the mystery he was led into, not spoiling one's sense of discovery as his was not spoiled, and providing one with the experience of the journey as he experienced it. Of course, behind Nicholas is the master magus Fowles, whose design is to lead each reader to his own essential mysteries. The technique provides an immediacy that allows each reader to take the journey toward his own self-discovery; the novel provides a paradigm by which the mystery of Fowles's other novels can be deciphered.

The Collector, in sharp contrast to *The Magus*, presents the other side of the coin, sounding a warning. Here the protagonist is the antihero, his captured lady, the heroine. She goes on the journey he is incapable of taking, which, in his incapacity to understand her or himself, he aborts.

Frederick Clegg, the protagonist, shares many similarities with Nicholas of *The Magus*. Each is orphaned, in his twenties, and aimless. Each forms an attachment to a blond, gray-eyed woman, and each goes to a remote land in which the relationship with this woman is explored. Each is given the opportunity to become a quester in that land, and each tells a first-person narrative of the experience. In each, the narrative structure is circular, such that the novel arrives where it started.

The major difference, of course, is that Nicholas journeys toward wholeness; Clegg, while given the same opportunities, does not. The reason for Clegg's failure lies in the fact that he cannot understand the mythic signals; thus, he cannot move beyond his present confused state. The novel begins and ends in psychic darkness; the hero does not grow or develop. Yet, while Clegg remains unchanged, the captive Miranda, trapped as Clegg's prisoner, undergoes a transforming experience that puts her on the path of the quest Clegg is unable to take. The tragedy is not so much Clegg's lack of growth as it is the futility of Miranda's growth in view of the fact that she cannot apply in the real world the lessons learned in her quest. She is incapable even of having any beneficial effect on her captor.

Part of the problem between Miranda and Clegg lies in the differences in their cultural backgrounds. Miranda has the background of a typical Fowlesian quester in terms of education and social standing; Clegg's, however, is atypical in his lower-class roots and lack of education. Part of the thesis of this novel is the clash between these two as representative of the clash between the "Many" and the "Few," which Fowles describes in detail in *The Aristos*. The novel, presented as a divided narrative told first by Clegg and then by Miranda, depicts in its very structure the division between Miranda and Clegg that cannot be bridged.

The first problem for Clegg as a quester is that he captures the object of his quest, keeping her prisoner in a hidden cellar. In psychological terms, Miranda, the feeling side of Clegg, is kept in the cellar "down there," which disallows the possibility of union. Clegg remains a divided man, living above in the house, with Miranda imprisoned below. Miranda, however, discovers that her "tomb" becomes a "womb" in which she grows in self-consciousness and understanding. Thus, the quest centers on her and the antiquest centers on Clegg.

As a butterfly collector, Clegg sees Miranda as his prize acquisition. He hopes that she will come to love him as he thinks he loves her, but what he really prizes is her beauty, which he has hoped to capture and keep as he would a butterfly's. When she begins to turn ugly in her vitality and lack of conformity to his preconceived notions of her, she falls off the pedestal on which he has placed her, and he then feels no compunction about forcing her to pose for nude photographs.

Clegg's problems are many. On a social level, he identifies too closely with what he sees as the judgment of the middle class against his lower-class background. On a psychological level, he is possessed by images from his past, the negative influences of his aunt, and his upbringing. His sexual fears and feelings of personal inadequacy combine to lock him into his own psychological prison in the same way that he locks Miranda in hers. Trapped in his internal prison, the outward presence of Miranda remains just that, outside of himself, and he cannot benefit from her proximity. She, however, while externally imprisoned by Clegg, is not prevented from making the inward journey toward self-discovery. At the same time, there is within Clegg, although deeply buried, a desire to break away and move onto the mythic path, and Miranda sees that aspect of him, his essential innocence, which has caused him to be attracted to her in the first place. Nevertheless, it is too deeply buried for Miranda to extract, and his power over her becomes his obsession. When he blurts out, "I love you. It's driven me mad," he indicates the problem he faces. Love is madness when it takes the form of possession, and Clegg is possessed by his feelings in the same way that he possesses Miranda. As Miranda asserts her individuality and Clegg becomes repulsed by her, he is able to shift blame for her death to her as a direct consequence of her actions.

While Clegg learns nothing from his experience and uses his narrative to vindicate himself, Miranda uses her narrative to describe her growing understanding and sense of self-discovery, aborted by her illness and subsequent death. After her death, Clegg cleans out the cellar, restoring it to its original state before Miranda's arrival. This circular structure, returning the reader to the empty cellar, echoes the circular structure of *The Magus*, except that Clegg has learned nothing from his experience, and Nicholas has learned everything. It is not that Nicholas is essentially good and Clegg essentially bad; rather, it is that Clegg cannot respond to the good within him, rendered inert by the warring aspects of his personality. Clegg's failure to respond to the elements of the quest is, in some respects, more tragic than Miranda's death, because he must continue his death-in-life existence, moving in ever-decreasing circles, never profiting or growing from the experience of life. In his next conquest, he will not aim so high; this time it will not be for love but for "the interest of the thing."

Reflecting the bleakness of Clegg's situation, the novel is filled with images of darkness. The pattern of *The Collector* is away from the light toward the darkness. Miranda's dying becomes a struggle against "the black and the black and the black" and her last words to Clegg—"the sun"—are a grim reminder of the struggle between them: the age-old struggle of the forces of light against those of darkness. Miranda's movement in the novel is upward toward light, life, and understanding; Clegg's is one of helpless descent toward darkness, evil, and psychic death.

With *The French Lieutenant's Woman*, Fowles returns to the theme of the successful quest. Here the quester is Charles Smithson, much like Nicholas in social standing and education. The important differences between the novels are that *The French Lieutenant's Woman* is set in Victorian England and that Charles, in his thirties, a decade older than Nicholas, reflects the older viewpoint of the author. Like Nicholas, his twentieth century counterpart, Charles is representative of his age and class. Also like Nicholas, Charles is somewhat bored with his circumstances, despite the fact that he is finally taking the proper course of marriage to the proper lady, Ernestina. Not nearly so aware of his boredom as is Nicholas, Charles is nevertheless immediately attracted to Sarah upon their first meeting, sensing instantly that she is not like other women. Meeting her again in Ware Commons and its more secret Undercliff, Charles finds in this "other world" the mythic encounter for which he unconsciously yearns. A seeker after fossils, he subconsciously fears his own extinction in the receding waters of the Victorian age, a gentleman left behind in the face of the rising tide of the Industrial Revolution.

Sarah, having recognized her uniqueness in a world of conformity, relishes her position apart from others, particularly in its ability to give her a freedom other women do not possess. As the French lieutenant's woman (a euphemism for whore), she is outside society's bonds. Capitalizing on her position, she has already begun her own quest when she meets Charles; thus, she leads him to his own path for the journey. Ernestina represents the known, the predictable, the respectable; Sarah, the opposite: the unknown, the mysterious, the forbidden. Torn between the two choices, Charles eventually comes to know himself well enough to be able to make the more hazardous choice, the one more fraught with danger, yet far more likely to lead to wholeness.

The feeling and reasoning aspects of Charles's psyche war within him. Seeking advice from Dr. Grogan, he gets the proper scientific viewpoint of Sarah and is prescribed the proper course of action: return to Ernestina. One side of Charles, the rational, longs to do so; the other side, the feeling, cannot. Thus, after much wrestling with the problem, Charles chooses Sarah, breaks his engagement to Ernestina, and returns to Sarah for what he thinks will be the beginning of their beautiful life in exile together—only to find her gone. At this point, Charles's real journey begins. Sarah has brought him to the point of resisting the predictable and recognizing his feeling side; he must now learn to live alone with such newfound knowledge.

Such a choice is not a simple one, and the reader must choose as well, for there are three "endings" in the novel. The first is not really an ending, as it comes in the middle of the book. In it, Charles rejects Sarah, marries Ernestina and lives, as it were, happily ever after. One knows, if only by the number of pages remaining in the book, that this is not really the ending; it is merely Victorian convention, which the author-god Fowles quickly steps in to tell the reader is not the actual ending. Thus, the reader passes through another hundred pages before he comes to another choice of endings, these more realistic.

The first is happy; the second is not. The endings themselves indicate the evolutionary process that Charles as well as the novel takes; for if one includes the hypothetical early ending, one moves from the traditional Victorian view to the emancipated view of Charles's and Sarah's union to the final existential view of the cruelty of freedom which denies Charles the happy ending. Fowles wanted his readers to accept the last ending as the right choice, but feared that they would opt for the happy ending; he was pleased when they did not.

In the first ending, the gap between Charles and Sarah is bridged through the intercession of Lalage, the child born of their one sexual encounter. The assertion that "the rock of ages can never be anything but love" offers the reader a placebo that does not effect a cure for the novel's dilemma. Fowles then enters, turns the clock back, and sets the wheels in motion for the next ending. In this one, the author-god Fowles drives off, leaving Sarah and Charles to work out their fate alone in much the same way that Conchis absconds from the "godgame" when Nicholas and Alison are reunited in *The*

Magus. In both cases, Fowles is trying to demonstrate that the freedom of choice resides with the individual, not with the "author." Since Sarah fears marriage for its potential denial of her hard-won freedom and sense of individuality, she cannot accept Charles's offer to marry, nor can he accept hers of friendship in some lesser relationship. Sarah then gives Charles no choice but to leave, and in his leaving he is released from his bonds to the past, experiencing a new freedom: "It was as if he found himself reborn, though with all his adult faculties and memories." Like Nicholas in *The Magus*, the important point is not whether he wins this particular woman but that he has learned to know himself and to love another. This is what sets him apart as an individual, saves him from extinction, and propels him into the modern age.

Intending to name his collection of short works *Variations* because of its reflection of various themes and genres presented in his longer fiction, Fowles changed the name to *The Ebony Tower* (after the title novella) when first readers thought the original title too obscure. Anyone familiar with Fowles's themes, however, immediately sees their variations in this collection. The volume contains the title novella, followed by a "Personal Note," followed by Fowles's translation of Marie de France's medieval romance *Eliduc* (c. 1150-1175), followed by three short stories: "Poor Koko," "The Enigma," and "The Cloud." In his "Personal Note," Fowles explains the inclusion of the medieval romance, relating it first to "The Ebony Tower," more generally to all of his fiction, and finally to fiction in general.

The title story describes a quester who inadvertently stumbles into the realm of myth only to find that he cannot rise to the challenge of the quest and is therefore ejected from the mythic landscape. The other three stories are all centered on enigmas or mysteries of modern life. These mysteries arise because "mystery" in the sacred sense no longer appears valid in modern man's existence. The movement of the stories is generally downward toward darkness, modern man being depicted as less and less able to take the journey of self-discovery because he is trapped in the wasteland of contemporary existence. Thus, the variations in these stories present aspects of the less-than-successful quest.

David Williams of "The Ebony Tower" leaves his comfortable home and life-style in England and enters the forests of Brittany, the land of the medieval romance, to face an encounter with Henry Breasley, a famous (and infamous) painter. Because David is a painter himself, he is interested in the journey from an artist's perspective; he does not anticipate the mythic encounter that awaits him in this "other" world. Within this other world, Breasley attacks the "architectonic" nature of David's work in its abstraction, in contrast to Breasley's art, which has been called "mysterious," "archetypal," and "Celtic." In defaming David's art for its rigidity and lack of feeling, Breasley serves as a guide to David. David also finds the essential woman here in the figure of

Diana, "The Mouse." The two characters offer him the potential of becoming a quester. The story represents the forsaken opportunity and its aftermath.

David's problem, like that of Nicholas and Charles at the beginning of their quests, is that he is so caught up with the rational that he cannot understand the emotional, in others or in himself. To all that he finds bewildering, he tries to attach a rational explanation. When finally confronted with pure emotion in his meeting with Diana in the Edenic garden, he hesitates, fatally pausing to consider rationally what his course of action should be. In that moment, he loses the possibility of responding to his innermost feelings, failing to unite with the woman who represents his feeling side; as a result, he is evicted from the mythic landscape.

Caught between two women, his wife and Diana, David cannot love either. His situation is in sharp contrast to that of Eliduc, who also encounters two women, and can love both. For Eliduc, love is a connecting force; for David, a dividing force. Thus, when David leaves the Brittany manor, he runs over an object in the road, which turns out to be a weasel. Here the weasel is dead with no hope of being restored to life. In *Eliduc*, love restores the weasel to life.

The rest of the story is David's rationalization of his failure. Like Clegg of *The Collector*, David first recognizes his failure but knows that he will soon forget the "wound" he has suffered and the knowledge of his failure. Already the mythic encounter seems far away. By the time he arrives in Paris, he is able to tell his wife that he has "survived." Had David succeeded in his quest, he would have done far more than survive: he would have lived.

The remaining stories in the collection are connected to the title story by the theme of lost opportunities. In "Poor Koko" the narrator, a writer, is robbed by a young thief who burns his only possession of value, his manuscript on Thomas Love Peacock. The story is the writer's attempt to understand the seemingly meaningless actions of the thief, which he finally comes to realize extend from the breakdown in communication between them. On a larger scale, the clash between the boy and the old man is the clash between generations, between a world in which language is meaningful and one in which it is empty.

In the succeeding story, "The Enigma," a mystery of a different kind is presented: the disappearance of John Marcus Fielding, member of parliament, and the subsequent investigation by Sergeant Jennings. The first mystery focuses on the reason behind the disappearance of Fielding, whose body is never discovered and whose motive is never revealed. What is hinted at by Isobel Dodgson, the former girl friend of Fielding's son and the last person to have seen Fielding before he disappeared, is that Fielding absconded from life because it offered no mystery; thus he provided his own by disappearing.

The second and more engaging mystery is seen in the developing relationship between Jennings and Isobel. While theirs is not of the dimensions of the relationship between Charles and Sarah, Nicholas and Alison, or even David and Diana, since they are not on the mythic journey, it is nevertheless interesting because it provides a sense of mystery. In a world that motivates a Fielding to walk out, it will have to suffice.

The last story, "The Cloud," is probably the most mysterious in the literal sense, although it describes a world most lacking in mystery in the sacred or mythic sense. The setting is a picnic with two men, Peter and Paul, and two women, sisters, Annabel and Catherine. While the setting describes an idyllic day, one senses from the outset that this is not paradise, because the women are lying in the sun, "stretched as if biered," an image of death that pervades the story. Catherine has apparently suffered the loss of a loved one, presumably her husband, and is in deep depression. She seems unable to make the crossing back into the world. Language does not serve as a bridge, and her feelings elicit no depth of response from the others. Thus, by the end of the story, she enters a myth of her own making, which is described in the story she invents for her niece about the princess abandoned by her prince. Catherine remains behind, unbeknown to the others when they leave the woods, and the reader is left with the assumption that she commits suicide, symbolized by the presence of the dark clouds rolling over the scene. Thus, the dark image of the ebony tower in the first story is replaced by the dark cloud in the last, and the reader has come full circle once again.

Having described aspects of the failed quest in *The Ebony Tower*, Fowles once again returns to the theme of the successful quest in *Daniel Martin*. This time the quester is a mature man in his forties, as was the author at the time of the novel's composition, and this time Fowles is able to write the happy ending that had eluded him in his other fiction. The first sentence of the novel contains its thesis and the summation of Fowles's philosophy: "WHOLE SIGHT OR ALL THE REST IS DESOLATION." Like the questers in *The Magus* and *The French Lieutenant's Woman*, Daniel Martin must take the mythic journey to learn the meaning of whole sight and to change his world from a place of desolation to one of fulfillment.

While the first sentence of the novel states the thesis, the epigraph states the problem: "The crisis consists precisely in the fact that the old is dying and the new cannot be born; in this interregnum a great variety of morbid symptoms appears." Trapped in the wasteland of contemporary existence, Daniel experiences "morbid symptoms" in his failure to feel deeply and to be connected to a meaningful past. It is the movement of the novel from the crisis to whole sight that constitutes the quest.

The call to adventure comes with a phone call announcing the impending death of Anthony, an old friend. In going to England to be at his friend's bedside, he returns to the land of his youth and to the time when love was real. That love was with Jane, who later married Anthony, forcing both Daniel and Jane to bury their true feelings for each other. With Anthony's death,

Daniel is once again faced with the dilemma of his own happiness and the role that Jane can play in it. At the same time, Daniel is wrestling with the problem of his desire to write a novel; subsequently, as the story unfolds, Daniel's novel unfolds, such that at the completion of the story one also has the completion of Daniel's novel, the demonstrable product of his successful quest.

Moving in and out of time, the novel skips from Daniel's boyhood to his present life in Hollywood with Jenny, a young film actress, to his memories of happy days at Oxford, and to his continuing relationship with Jane in the present. It also has several narrative points of view: Daniel tells certain sections, the omniscient author tells others, and still others are told by Jenny.

Daniel is aided on his journey by several wise old men: among them, Otto Kirnberger, the professor he and Jane meet on their trip up the Nile; and the Hungarian Marxist literary critic Georg Lukács, whose writings explain Daniel's choices as a writer. Daniel also describes several Edenic settings which he calls the experience of the "*bonne vaux.*" Remembrance of these experiences at Thorncombe, at Tsankawi, and at Kitchener's Island reinforce his desire to bring them more fully into his life; thus he quests on.

Realizing that the essential element of the quest is his ability to express his love for Jane, he worries that he will be rejected by her. Jane, less certain of her ability to choose her own future, tries to retreat from his declaration of love, telling him that she sees love as a prison. Jane is not yet ready to accept Daniel, but they journey on together, this time to Palmyra, a once-beautiful but now desolate and remote outpost. In this wasteland, they experience the renewal of love. The catalyst comes in the form of a sound, "a whimpering, an unhappiness from the very beginning of existence." The sound is that of a litter of forlorn puppies, followed by another sound from their bedraggled mother, who tries to protect her puppies by acting as a decoy to distract the couple. The scene propels Jane out of her own wasteland into an enactment of a private ritual. Burying her wedding ring in the sand, she symbolically severs herself from her restrictive past to connect with the present and Daniel.

On his return to England, Daniel then severs himself from his remaining past by rejecting Jenny, recognizing all the while the importance of compassion in his relations with her and others. Following their last meeting, he enters a nearby church and is confronted with a living picture of all that he has learned: the famous late Rembrandt self-portrait. In this vision of compassion and whole sight, Daniel sees how far he has come and where the path into the future will lead. In Daniel's experience of the happy ending, the reader sees also a beginning. Thus, the last sentence of the novel one reads becomes the first sentence of the novel that Daniel will write. Again the experience is a circle, arriving where it started, with the circle expanding as it does in *The Magus* and in *The French Lieutenant's Woman*.

The movement of Fowles's fiction through *Daniel Martin* suggested the completion of a cycle: from a statement of the thesis in *The Magus*, to a statement of its opposite in *The Collector*, to an examination of the thesis from a different historical perspective in *The French Lieutenant's Woman*, to variations in *The Ebony Tower*, and to arrival at the long-sought happy ending in *Daniel Martin*. One could easily anticipate that the next novel would be very different, and so it was. *Mantissa*, which Fowles defines in a footnote, is a term meaning "an addition of comparatively small importance, especially to a literary effort or discourse." The novel's critical reception was mixed, some critics applauding the obvious departure from Fowles's customary style and others deploring its seeming frivolousness. Fowles contends that it should be taken as "mantissa," a kind of lark on his part. In it, he explores the role of creativity and freedom for the author, expressed through his protagonist Miles Green, as he wakes up to find himself an amnesiac in a hospital. The action of the novel, although it appears to have numerous characters entering and leaving the hospital, is really taking place in the protagonist's head, with the various characters representing manifestations of the muse Erato. The debate between muse and author gives Fowles the opportunity to turn the essential question of "freedom to choose," which he makes the object of the quest for his protagonists in his novels, the object of the quest for the author/ protagonist in this one. It also gives Fowles the opportunity to poke fun at the literary-critical approaches of the day, especially deconstruction. Finally, it gives Fowles the perfect opportunity to write graphically about sexual en- counter, which he claims is one of the reasons he revised *The Magus:* to correct a "past failure of nerve."

In his next novel, *A Maggot*, he again chooses a title that requires explana- tion, his use of the term being in the obsolete sense of "whim or quirk." He goes on to explain in his prologue that he was obsessed with a theme arising out of an image from his unconscious of an unknown party of riders on horseback, and his desire was to capture this "remnant of a lost myth." This same obsession with an image is what led to the writing of The French Lieutenant's Woman, the historical novel set in the nineteenth century. In *A Maggot* the temporal setting is the eighteenth century, and, as in *The French Lieutenant's Woman*, the struggle of a man and a woman to break out of their trapped existence is once again the focus. The man is Bartholomew, the son of a wealthy lord, and the woman is a prostitute named Fanny whose real name is Rebecca Lee. Bartholomew leads Rebecca into the quest, but he disappears, and the remainder of the novel becomes a search for the truth behind the events leading to his disappearance. To conduct this investigation, Bartholomew's father hires the lawyer Henry Ayscough, and the form of the novel shifts from third-person omniscient to first-person depositions, as Ays- cough locates and questions everyone connected with the journey leading to the mysterious disappearance of Bartholomew. Everyone has a different view of the event, none of which Ayscough finds convincing. His desire for the truth is based on a belief that there is a rational, logical explanation; yet, despite the thoroughness of his inquiries, he cannot come up with one, finally concluding, without the evidence to prove it, that it must have been a murder.

The crux of the problem lies in his statement to Rebecca, "There are two truths, mistress. One that a person believes is truth; and one that is truth incontestible. We will credit you with the first, but the second is what we seek." Rebecca's belief, that Bartholomew has been transported by a maggot-shaped spaceship to June Eternal and that she has been reborn into a new life, frees her to break out of the trap of her existence by founding what will become the Shaker Movement, which the daughter to whom she gives birth at the end of the novel will take to America. The mystery of Bartholomew's disappearance is never solved, and the reader is left to decide where the truth lies. For Rebecca, the central quester, the truth she experienced in the cave gives her the freedom to choose a new life, which is the object of the quest.

Carol M. Barnum

Other major works

POETRY: *Poems*, 1973.

NONFICTION: *The Aristos: A Self-Portrait in Ideas*, 1964; *Shipwreck*, 1974; *Islands*, 1978; *The Tree*, 1980, *The Enigma of Stonehenge*, 1980 (with Barry Brukoff); *A Brief History of Lyme*, 1981.

Bibliography

Barnum, Carol M. *The Fiction of John Fowles: A Myth for Our Time*. Greenwood, Fla.: Penkevill, 1988. Discusses six novels and the short-story collection from the point of view of the quest motif, which unites the seemingly disparate approaches of the fiction under a central theme. Includes notes, index, and a subdivided bibliography.

Huffaker, Robert. *John Fowles*. Boston: Twayne, 1980. A good overview and introduction to Fowles, including chronology through 1980. Discusses fiction through *Daniel Martin*, focusing on the theme of naturalism. Includes notes, selected bibliography, and index.

Loveday, Simon. *The Romances of John Fowles*. New York: St. Martin's Press, 1985. Includes a chronology through 1983 plus an introductory chapter on the author's life and work. Discusses the fiction through *Daniel Martin*, with a concluding chapter that places Fowles in the romance tradition. Notes, subdivided bibliography, and index.

Onega, Susana. *Form and Meaning in the Novels of John Fowles*. Ann Arbor: University of Michigan Press, 1989. Treats the novels, but not the short-story collection *The Ebony Tower*, as related by the recurring theme of human freedom, in relation to both the self and society. Includes the transcript of a public interview with Fowles. Notes, bibliography, and index.

Palmer, William J., ed. "Special Issue: John Fowles." *Modern Fiction Studies* 31 (Spring, 1985). An excellent collection of essays on the fiction through *Daniel Martin*, plus an interview and a good, selected bibliography, subdivided by individual works, as well as general essays and interviews.

Pifer, Ellen, ed. *Critical Essays on John Fowles*. Boston: G. K. Hall, 1986. A collection of essays previously published elsewhere in journals. A good introduction by the editor is followed by essays organized under two themes: the unity of Fowles's fiction and discussions of individual works. Coverage through *Mantissa*. Includes notes and an index.

Tarbox, Katherine. *The Art of John Fowles*. Athens: University of Georgia Press, 1988. Discusses the novels through *A Maggot* with emphasis on Fowles's dictum to "see whole." Does not include a chapter on *The Ebony Tower*. The last chapter is an interview with the author. Notes, subdivided bibliography, and index.

HAROLD FREDERIC

Born: Utica, New York; August 19, 1856
Died: Henley on Thames, England; October 19, 1898

Principal long fiction

Seth's Brother's Wife: A Study of Life in the Greater New York, 1887; *In the Valley*, 1890; *The Lawton Girl*, 1890; *The Return of the O'Mahony*, 1892; *The Copperhead*, 1893; *Mrs. Albert Grundy: Observations in Philistia*, 1896; *The Damnation of Theron Ware*, 1896; *March Hares*, 1896 (as George Forth); *Gloria Mundi*, 1898; *The Market Place*, 1899.

Other literary forms

Harold Frederic was a journalist by profession so it is no surprise that he wrote a considerable amount of nonfiction. A large portion of his copy for *The New York Times* was essayistic and well-researched and developed. Extended pieces also appeared regularly in English and American magazines. Two sizable groups of dispatches were brought out in book format, *The Young Emperor William II of Germany: A Study in Character Development on a Throne* (1891) and *The New Exodus: A Study of Israel in Russia* (1892). The first of these is not a notable work, despite the fact that its subject became one of the crucial figures of the early twentieth century; and despite the fact that, like almost all of Frederic's fiction, it is a character study. The second work, however—a series of reports on pogroms under Czar Alexander III— was so effective that Frederic became persona non grata in Russia. One is tempted to add to his list of nonfiction the novel *Mrs. Albert Grundy*, a book that hangs by a narrative thread and is precisely what its subtitle proclaims: *Observations in Philistia*, that is, satirical sketches of the London bourgeoisie.

Also not surprising for a journalist, Frederic tried his hand at short fiction. His output ranges from poorly written juvenile beginnings to very readable stories about Ireland, to a number of short novels and short stories about the Civil War. These latter pieces are his best; they are collected in variously arranged editions and attracted the attention of writers such as Stephen Crane. In them, Frederic examines the effect of the war on the people at home in central New York through insightful and striking situations, and through a skillful handling of description, dialogue, and point of view.

Achievements

Writing a "Preface to a Uniform Edition" for Scribner's 1897 edition of his Civil War stories, *In the Sixties*, Frederic remarks about the upstate New York places and people in his fiction that "no exact counterparts exist for them in real life, and no map of the district has as yet been drawn, even in my own mind." This statement was written at a time when Frederic had left his American fiction behind and turned his attention to English matters; the journalist who desired fame as a serious writer did not wish to be taken for someone who merely transcribed the personal experiences of his youth. Although Frederic's fiction is almost evenly divided between American subject matter on the one hand and English and Irish on the other, the influence of America is felt even in the non-American works, and Frederic's acknowledged masterpiece, *The Damnation of Theron Ware*, is thoroughly American.

Thomas F. O'Donnell has argued that Frederic is upstate New York's greatest writer since James Fenimore Cooper. In his regional novels, Frederic studies politics (*Seth's Brother's Wife*), history (*In the Valley*), socioeconomics (*The Lawton Girl*), and religion (*The Damnation of Theron Ware*), and thus gives a comprehensive view of his part of the world. Just as Gustave Flaubert anchors his sweeping presentation of human passions in *Madame Bovary* (1857) in the Caux, a rural district of Normandy which easily matches the provinciality of the Mohawk Valley, so, too, does Frederic derive the Jamesian solidity of specification so central to the art of the novel from the authoritatively detailed depiction of his native region.

Although his first model was the successful popular French combination of Erckmann-Chatrian, Frederic grew into a major writer because of his keen observation (sharpened by his reportorial work), his Howellsian sympathy with the common man, and above all, his Hawthornian understanding of the truth of the human heart and the complexity of the American Adam. Hence, Frederic is partly a realist, like Flaubert, and partly a romancer, like Nathaniel Hawthorne, but also, like both of these, a writer with universal themes that are embedded in regional actuality. Were it not for his premature death, he might well have duplicated the achievement of his American fiction with his English fiction. As it is, his reputation will stand on his American works.

Biography

Harold Frederic was born on August 19, 1856, in Utica, a small city of then about twenty thousand, situated in the picturesque Mohawk Valley of upstate New York. His family tree reached far back into colonial times to Dutch and German farmers and artisans, and he could proudly point out that all four of his great-grandfathers had fought in the Revolutionary War. When Frederic was only a year and a half old, his father died in a train derailment; his mother, however, was energetic and capable and kept the family above water until she remarried. She was a somewhat severe woman, not given to spoiling her children, and Frederic always remembered the early morning chores he had to do in the family milk and wood businesses before setting out for school. He also remembered the Methodist upbringing he received and the unseemly bickerings among the parishioners of his neighborhood church.

Like many children at the time, Frederic did not receive extensive schooling and was graduated from Utica's Advanced School at the age of fourteen. For the next two years, he worked for local photographers, slowly progressing from errand-boy to retoucher. He then tried his luck in Boston, dabbling in art and working for a photographer, but in 1875, he returned to Utica and changed his career by becoming a proofreader for the town's Republican morning paper, shortly afterward switching to its Democratic afternoon counterpart. By this time, Utica had almost doubled its population and had become a political center of the first order, giving the state a governor in Horatio Seymour and the country two senators in Roscoe Conkling and Francis Kernan (it would later add a vice-president in James Sherman). Frederic became a firm Democrat and took a lively interest in politics. He soon became a reporter for his paper and also began writing fiction; it was sentimental and imitative beginner's work, but enough of it was published to encourage him.

The centennial celebration of the Battle of Oriskany in 1877 proved to be an intellectual milestone in Frederic's life. He helped prepare the occasion, convinced that the battle had been a turning point of the war and not merely a minor skirmish away from the major battlefields. As he listened to Horatio Seymour's call for a greater awareness on the part of the living of their proud and important history, Frederic resolved to write a historical novel that would give the Mohawk Valley its due and its present inhabitants the historical connectedness Seymour demanded. The regionalist Harold Frederic had come into being, even though *In the Valley* was not published until 1890, respectively and affectionately dedicated to the memory of the late governor.

That fall, Frederic married his neighbor Grace Williams. At that point, he was able to support a family because of his financial success at the *Observer*, becoming news editor in 1879 and editor in 1880, a seasoned and successful journalist before he turned twenty-four. During that time, Frederic's Methodism was softened through his friendship with Father Terry, an accomplished Irish Catholic priest with a modern and unorthodox outlook who introduced him to Utica's growing Irish community. For the rest of his life, Frederic would be a champion of the Irish, and he paid literary tribute to Father Terry and his circle of friends a few years later in his finest novel.

In 1882, Frederic took another step ahead in his career in becoming editor of the *Evening Journal* in Albany, the state capital. Barely settled in town, the Democratic editor made his Republican paper bolt the party line, thereby helping Grover Cleveland become governor. Cleveland appreciated the support and took a genuine liking to the young newspaperman. Frederic was even bolder—and quite prophetic—the following year when he wrote that Cleveland ought to run for President. In early 1884, the paper changed ownership, and Frederic lost his job. Helped by the recommendation of Cleveland's chief lieutenant, he secured a position as foreign correspondent with *The New York Times* and sailed for England with his wife and their two daughters.

Frederic's position with the respected American paper and a letter of introduction from Governor Cleveland soon established him in London. A daring tour of cholera-stricken Southern France made him a celebrity, and Cleveland's accession to the presidency made Frederic a person of importance. He was admitted to a number of London clubs, where he met many of England's political leaders, the men behind Irish home rule, and the foremost intellectuals, artists, and writers of the day. In this milieu, being only a newspaper correspondent was not satisfactory to Frederic; he set about his literary career with great determination and energy, hoping to become financially independent of journalism and famous as well.

From 1887 on, Frederic's novels appeared in rapid succession, and while they brought him considerable contemporary reputation (*The Damnation of Theron Ware* was a sensation on both sides of the Atlantic), they did not bring him financial independence. That would have been hard to do even if the sales had been bigger, since Frederic enjoyed a comfortable life-style and had a growing family to support. In fact, he had to support two families, for in 1890, he met and fell in love with Kate Lyon, a fellow upstate New Yorker, openly established a second household, and subsequently had three children with her. For some time, Harold and Grace Frederic had been drifting apart. While he split his time between his two families, it was Kate's place that became the center of his intellectual and artistic life, and it was there, for example, that he entertained his friend Stephen Crane.

Financial necessities put a great strain on Frederic. Between his continuing journalistic work (which he carried out thoroughly and faithfully and which involved several extended trips to the Continent), his writing (for which he continued to educate himself by reading widely), his club life, and his family life (including return visits to America and to his beloved Mohawk Valley as well as vacations in Ireland), he simply wore himself out. Of imposing physique, he drew upon his strength so recklessly that he suffered a stroke in August, 1898, from which he never recovered. Kate Lyon's resistance to doctors and her trust in a Christian Science healer led to a widely publicized manslaughter trial after Frederic's death on October 19; eventually, the defendants were acquitted. Heavily in debt, Frederic had left his family in such financial trouble that friends took up a collection. Five months later, Grace died of cancer. In 1901, the ashes of Harold and Grace Frederic were brought home to their native valley.

Analysis

Harold Frederic was not one of those writers who bursts upon the scene with a *magnum opus* and then fades from view; rather, his writing steadily improved from *Seth's Brother's Wife* to his masterpiece, *The Damnation of Theron Ware*. Ever since the Oriskany Centennial, Frederic's ambition had been the writing of *In the Valley* as the great American historical novel. The preparation for this book was so slow and painstaking that it took years, as well as the experience of writing *Seth's Brother's Wife* first, to complete the Revolutionary War novel. *In the Valley* interprets the Revolutionary War as more of a struggle between the democratic American farmers and the would-be aristocratic American landed gentry than as a conflict between crown and colony. It gives a stirring description of the Battle of Oriskany, but its plot is trite, pitting the sturdy Douw Mauverensen against the slick Philip Cross as political opponents and rivals for the same woman.

In his uniform edition Preface, Frederic states that he firmly controlled everything in *Seth's Brother's Wife* and *In the Valley*, but that in *The Lawton Girl*, "the people took matters into their own hands quite from the start." More than one great novelist has insisted that in truly great fiction, the author does not prescribe to his characters but rather allows them to unfold as they themselves demand, integrating them into the whole. *The Lawton Girl* is a respectable book, despite some plot and character contrivances, for the longer rope Frederic had learned to give to his characters and for his continuing ability to ground his work in regional authenticity.

Before *The Damnation of Theron Ware* appeared, Frederic had published *The Return of the O'Mahony*, a playful work that expresses his strong interest in Ireland and Irish home rule. Even in this pleasant book, there is, as Austin Briggs and others have noted, the abiding sense of a past that conditions the present, a theme familiar from Nathaniel Hawthorne's *The House of the Seven Gables* (1851). *March Hares* (published under the pseudonym of George Forth), is a comedy of mistaken identities in a make-believe world. These light works were followed by the weightier novels *Gloria Mundi* and *The Market Place*. *Gloria Mundi* is essentially concerned with an investigation of the English aristocracy, which Frederic shows as a hollow, outdated remnant of medieval caste structure. This major theme is accompanied by a variety of probing social observations, at the end of which stands the insight of the new Duke of Glastonbury: "A man is only a man after all. He did not make this world, and he cannot do with it what he likes. . . . There will be many men after me. If one or two of them says of me that I worked hard to do well, and that I left things a trifle better than I found them, then what more can I desire?"

This distillation of Frederic's ultimate philosophy of life is evident as early as Seth Fairchild, but it is not a view shared by Theron Ware or the central figure of *The Market Place*, Joel Stormont Thorpe. Ware has visions of greatness and power; Thorpe is the most ruthless and most successful of financiers and prepares by way of sham philanthropy to go into politics and rule England. Frederic's final assessment of people in this world is therefore a very balanced and realistic one: one would like to have the Seth Fairchilds without the Theron Wares and the Stormont Thorpes, but the wish is not going to make those who want to do with the world what they like desist or disappear. The present will always have to find its own way against the past and will always in turn become the next present's past: so passes the glory of the world, and so also does the world go on and on in continuous struggle between good and evil.

Seth's Brother's Wife has all the strengths and weaknesses of a respectable first novel, but only recently have critics taken it as something more than a mixture of realistic regionalism and sentimental melodrama. Its very title is confusing, since Seth Fairchild, not Isabel is the book's main character, since personal integrity rather than amatory complication constitutes the book's principal theme, and since—as the subtitle, *A Study of Life in the Greater New York*, signals—the book's compass reaches well beyond the three people mentioned in the title. Set in the Mohawk Valley region in the early 1880's, *Seth's Brother's Wife* is the familiar story of a young country lad who goes to town, experiences sometimes severe growing pains, but in the end prevails because of his basic personal decency and his values, which, though tested to the breaking point, hold and are therefore rewarded. Frederic called the novel a romance, and one does well to see it in a line of American stories of initiation that begins, if not with Benjamin Franklin's *The Autobiography* (1791), then with Charles Brockden Brown's *Arthur Mervyn* (1799-1800), and reaches Frederic by way of Nathaniel Hawthorne.

One of three brothers, Seth comes from a farming family whose fortunes have been declining. His brother John is editor of the local paper; his other brother, Albert, who is college-educated, is a successful New York City lawyer, and comes home to establish residence and a political base for his bid to be a congressman. Albert finds Seth a job with the area's leading daily; reminiscent of Frederic's own career, Seth eventually becomes editor and is instrumental in the paper's bolting from its traditional political adherence. Seth finds himself opposing his brother, to whom he owes his position in the first place, and supporting his friend Richard Ansdell, a principled reform candidate who has done much for Seth's intellectual and moral growth.

In a powerful sequence of chapters all set during the same night, the ruthless Albert corners the well-meaning but immature Seth. Seth has fallen under the spell of Albert's young, neglected, city-bred wife, Isabel, and although he never fully succumbs to the temptation, Seth feels the sting of Albert's attack on his political purity: How hypocritical that Seth stand on ethics in politics when he was about to make love to his brother's wife. As Albert leaves to discuss with his henchman, Milton Squires, a scheme of buying the nomination, Seth stumbles out into the darkness conscious of his weakness and foolishness, finds his old love Annie, and proposes to her on the spot in order to save himself from himself.

The nominating convention is ruled by the area's political boss, Abe Beekman. Beekman rebuffs Albert's attempt to buy him off (he is in politics for the fun, not the money) and decides to have Ansdell nominated. When news of Albert's death arrives, Beekman turns into the driving force behind the investigation, and after many melodramatic plot complications—including a suspicion that Seth took revenge on his brother—all ends well: Squires is convicted of murdering Albert to get the buy-off money; Seth is united with Annie; Isabel leaves the uncongenial countryside and goes to Washington where, in a pointed undercutting of the validity of happy endings, she will marry Ansdell.

A plot summary of this action-packed book is inadequate to clarify Frederic's major concerns and accomplishments. The conflict between city and country, which is so essential to Arthur Mervyn's initiation, is developed here with forceful realism and admirable balance. Life on the farm is dispiriting, squalid drudgery amid often incredibly vulgar exemplars of humankind, but it is also the smell of blossoms in the orchard and the rustle of autumn leaves underfoot and the taste of fresh cider. Life in the city means not only new cultural and intellectual dimensions but also the distraction of the beer hall and, down the dark alley, the depths of prostitution. In politics, honesty and expediency are played against each other without a facile conclusion; most important, Beekman is no saint and Ansdall no new founding father.

Frederic manages to make none of the major characters a one-dimensional stereotype: the good ones have enough weakness (even Annie does), and the bad ones (even Isabel) have enough strengths to forbid easy and schematic moralizing. Seth is the case in point. The youngest, handsomest, and most promising of the brothers, he is also the most sluggish and the most foolish, almost the proverbial fairy-tale late bloomer. His temporary infatuation with Isabel makes him say things about his sweetheart Annie that are as contemptible as Theron Ware's thoughts and comments about his wife at a similar juncture, but unlike Ware, Seth—with some help from John and Annie and even from Albert—catches himself in time. His ability—which is lacking in Albert, in Ware, and in Arthur Mervyn—to realize that he has been as "weak as water"—is his saving grace and the book's chief moral; there is no bedrock in this world other than the hard-won decency of one's own character. That may not be the basis of which the American dream is made, Frederic seems to say, but it is much more than its sobering simplicity might at first suggest, and after all, the only way to life in this imperfect world.

Whatever differences of opinion literary critics have had over the years concerning Frederic's novels, they have been unanimous in designating *The Damnation of Theron Ware* as his masterpiece, and they have generally accorded it a high rank in American literature. The book is so complex, ironic, and ambiguous that no unified critical interpretation has emerged; among the best readings are those of John Henry Raleigh, Stanton Garner, and Austin Briggs, nor can one afford to overlook Edmund Wilson's caution that no truly great novel was ever built on the humiliation of its hero.

The novel opens on the closing session of the annual conference of Central

New York's Methodist Episcopal Church. With leisure and deliberation, Frederic sketches the decline of Methodism in the faces of its ministers. Successively, the deterioration of sterling qualities of devotion, honesty, and simplicity is visible in the faces of the younger generations of ministers, with those of the most recently ordained reverends showing almost no trace of them. This verdict, however, is not confined to the clergy. For most of the parishioners, true worship has long since given way to elbowing for social position within the congregation. It is in this spirit that the standing-room-only crowd listens to the eagerly awaited announcement by the bishop of the ministerial assignments for the upcoming period of service.

The well-to-do and socially ambitious Tecumseh congregation, having housed the conference in style in its fine and new facilities, is bent upon adding to its glory by adorning itself with an "attractive and fashionable preacher." On the basis of the sermons delivered at the conference, the congregation's choice is the Reverend Theron Ware, a young minister who has made a study of pulpit oratory, and whom Frederic describes as a "tall, slender young man with the broad white brow, thoughtful eyes, and features moulded into that regularity of strength which used to characterize the American Senatorial type. Ware and his wife, Alice, are quietly informed that they are Tecumseh's choice, but to the bitter disappointment of the couple and the uncharitable outrage of the congregation, the district's plum is awarded to an uncharismatic older pastor. Even here, it is evident that among Theron's and Alice's personal qualities, the spiritual ones are not strongly developed.

Theron is assigned to Octavius, a town twice as large as their previous one, Tyre, and much larger than his first entirely rural post. Like Seth Fairchild, Theron Ware is a country-bred young man who, because of his better than average intellectual abilities, leaves the farm to move on to bigger and presumably better things; like Seth, he—at least initially—neither glorifies nor condemns his country background, and again like Seth, he marries the loveliest and most refined country girl around. Their first year in Tyre is filled with all the radiance of a new life together, until they discover that they are heavily in debt, a discovery which forces them into a joyless attempt at mere survival for the remainder of their time there, and from which they are miraculously released by a gift from Abram Beekman, who had figured so imposingly in *Seth's Brother's Wife*.

The Octavius congregation is old-fashioned in a mean way, believing in "straight-out, flat-footed hell," no milk on Sundays, and no flowery bonnets in church. Theron's first meeting with the trustees is a bitter revelation; the very names of their leaders, Pierce and Winch, suggest the tortures of the Inquisition. Theron rejects their attempt to reduce his already skimpy salary but sacrifices Alice's bonnet without a fight (though not long afterward, he buys himself a new shining hat). To improve his finances, he decides to write a book on Abraham, the Old Testament patriarch. Cogitating about it on a walk, he by chance witnesses the last rites of a Catholic Church upon an Irish workman who has fallen from a tree to his death. The elaborate Latin ceremony with its sonorous, bell-like invocations deeply impresses Theron, as do the priest, Father Forbes, and the organist, the striking Celia Madden. The workman's fall prefigures Theron's own, but it is some time before Frederic's careful structure becomes evident.

The chance acquaintance leads to other meetings between Theron and Celia and Theron and Forbes, entirely destroying Theron's narrowly preconceived notions of the Irish and of Catholicism. His first visit with the urbane and educated priest turns into an eye-opener for Theron: Forbes dismisses Theron's fundamentalist notions of Abraham with a brief survey of modern scholarship on the subject; he discourses learnedly on "this Christ-myth of ours"; he admits to exercising pastoral functions without troubling himself or his congregation overly about fine points of doctrine. Similarly, Forbes's agnostic friend, Dr. Ledsmar, impresses Theron with his scientific learning and the easy authority of his judgments on art, science, and religion. Celia Madden, finally, captivates Theron's emotional side with her sophisticated looks, her self-assured behavior, and her musical proficiency. In their several ways, the lives of these three are firmly grounded in traditions against which Theron's country background and seminary education appear painfully paltry.

The threesome has opened up a new world for Theron, a world that he fervently desires to comprehend and enter. What he calls his "illumination" (Frederic uses light imagery in many key scenes and gave the English edition the title *Illuminations*) is really intoxication: what for others might be light is for him heady wine against which he proves helpless. In his urge to foist himself upon the three, he attempts the sort of manipulation that has made him a slick preacher, substituting public relations techniques for substance. When he condemns everything his life has been, including his wife, Forbes, Ledsmar, and Celia all turn away from him. Forbes—who, despite his latitudinarianism, would never think of maligning his Church—is shocked by Theron's defamation of his congregation and of his Episcopalian roots. Ledsmar, who among other things conducts inhumane scientific experiments, resents Theron's prying into a possible liaison between Forbes and Celia, abruptly terminates their meeting, and gives Theron's name to an evil-looking lizard in his collection. Celia's case is more complicated; in a memorable scene, she practically seduces Theron with her enchanting personality, her bewitching playing of Frédéric Chopin, and her quasi-Arnoldian Hellenism. At a meeting in the forest, she permits the fawning, craven minister to kiss her lightly, a kiss which she later explains as a good-bye, but one which Theron takes quite the other way. Whatever Theron's considerable shortcomings, Celia does play with fire, and it is fitting that Frederic has her apologize in *The Market Place* for the extravagant ways of her youth.

The more Theron is enamored of Celia, the more he hardens himself against

Alice (appropriately, Celia is not only a short form of the name of the patron saint of sacred music but also a classy anagram of "Alice"). Alice in turn has been receiving the innocent, chiefly horticultural attentions of the church's junior trustee. Theron, who rationalizes away his own infidelity, suspects Alice and Gorringe and draws self-justification from the situation. His downward progress is rapid and complete, not only through Celia but also through Sister Soulsby, a professional fund-raiser employed by the trustees to void the church debt. She fixes Theron's strained relations with his congregation, but requires of him the casting of an immoral, fraudulent vote with his erstwhile nemesis Pierce.

Theron Ware lacks entirely that which saves Seth Fairchild: the ability to be honest with himself, to admit his weakness, to recognize his complicity with evil, and to be grateful for his wife's love. Celia really dismisses Theron for the wrong reason when she tells him that he is "a bore"; much more to the point is the indictment by her brother Michael, who, on his deathbed, gives Theron the ringing "damnation" speech that warrants the book's American title. It is to Sister Soulsby's credit that she puts the fallen Theron Ware together again, sending him (and Alice) to Seattle to go into the real-estate business. Much has been made of that ending; some critics take it to mean that a chastened Theron will begin a new and—more fitting for him—secular life, whereas others see in his political vision at the very end (he sees himself as a United States senator) the continuation of his failure to understand anything about himself. Perhaps one may tolerate immorality more readily in politicians than in clergymen, and perhaps Frederic does not use irony when he describes Theron's features as senatorial in the beginning, but one must also remember that boss Beekman is a rather decent fellow after all, a man whose outstanding characteristic in *Seth's Brother's Wife* is his ability to size up people and whose counsel to Theron to quit the ministry and go into law instead, Theron unfortunately and condescendingly disregards.

Much, too, has been made of Theron Ware as a Faust figure. This is surely a libel on Johann Wolfgang von Goethe's *Faust* (1790) at least. Critics also go too far when they insist that Theron is a fallen Adam. Theron never quests like Faust, and he is never innocent to begin with; his is a myth several numbers smaller than theirs. Conversely, not enough has been made of the money side of Theron Ware. He lives beyond his means and goes into debt in Tyre; he trades his wife's flowery hat off against a sidewalk repair bill; he glories in visions of Celia's wealth; he plays the big spender in New York after "inadvertently" having brought along the church collection. More than any other myth, Frederic's fable is surely about that aberration in the American makeup which accounts for the "In God We Trust" stamped on the quarter dollar.

As in *Seth's Brother's Wife*, so in *The Damnation of Theron Ware*: Frederic makes no one entirely good and no one entirely bad. For the longest time, he manages to make the reader sympathize with Theron. It is only when Theron turns viciously and deviously against his own wife that he is truly damned.

Frederic produced in *Seth's Brother's Wife* a solid first novel. Its strength lies in its authenticity of place, people, and dialect; its weakness in its insistence on a cloak-and-dagger plot, which at times overshadows the basic theme of growth of character. In *The Damnation of Theron Ware*, Frederic achieves a powerful blending of regional ambience and psychological penetration of character, only slightly marred by an occasional touch of melodrama.

Frank Bergmann

Other major works

SHORT FICTION: *The Copperhead and Other Stories of the North During the American War*, 1894; *Marsena and Other Stories of the Wartime*, 1894; *In the Sixties*, 1897; *The Deserter and Other Stories: A Book of Two Wars*, 1898; *Stories of York State*, 1966 (Thomas F. O'Donnell, editor).

NONFICTION: *The Young Emperor William II of Germany: A Study in Character Development on a Throne*, 1891; *The New Exodus: A Study of Israel in Russia*, 1892.

Bibliography

Briggs, Austin, Jr. *The Novels of Harold Frederic*. Ithaca, N.Y.: Cornell University Press, 1969. A thorough study of Frederic's novels, this book is mostly literary criticism, with a chapter on each of the major novels, a bibliography, and an index. The frontispiece is a pencil sketch of Frederic drawn by Briggs himself.

Fortenberry, George E., Stanton Garner, and Robert H. Woodward, eds. *The Correspondence of Harold Frederic*. Fort Worth: Texas Christian University Press, 1977. The only primary source of Frederic's papers available to most students, this collection includes all of his known letters, photographic facsimiles, a calendar of correspondence, a chronology of his life and writings, an index, and a photograph of Frederic.

Garner, Stanton. *Harold Frederic*. Minneapolis: University of Minnesota Press, 1969. This short pamphlet (45 pages) is a good general introduction, touching on biography and major works, but has no room for details. The bibliography is not as thorough as those available in the other works.

O'Donnell, Thomas F., and Hoyt C. Franchere. *Harold Frederic*. New York: Twayne, 1961. The first book-length study of Frederic, this book is valuable for its annotated bibliography, a chronology of his life and writings, and an index. After a chapter of biography, proceeds to address each of Frederic's novels in a separate section, including a full chapter on *The Damnation of Theron Ware*.

O'Donnell, Thomas F., Stanton Garner, and Robert H. Woodward, eds. *A Bibliography of Writings by and About Harold Frederic*. Boston: G. K. Hall, 1975. The most complete listing of material on Frederic, this bibliography is the place for all students of Frederic to begin their research. Lists all of his works and articles and books, both popular and scholarly, about his works.

WILLIAM GADDIS

Born: New York, New York; December 29, 1922

Principal long fiction

The Recognitions, 1955; *JR*, 1975; *Carpenter's Gothic*, 1985.

Other literary forms

William Gaddis' literary reputation is based upon his novels; in the 1980's, though, he contributed a number of essays and short stories to major magazines.

Achievements

Gaddis' work is convoluted, confusing, and difficult, qualities that have led some readers to criticize it. His work is also sophisticated, multilayered, and technically innovative, qualities that have led other readers to consider Gaddis as one of the most important writers since World War II, and certainly one of the least appreciated and understood. Considering the complexities of his fiction, it is not surprising that the earliest reviews of *The Recognitions* were unenthusiastic. Although they gave Gaddis credit for his extensive knowledge of religion and aesthetics, of art, myth, and philosophy, they criticized the absence of clear chronology, the diffuseness of so many intersecting subplots and characters, the large number of references, and the supposed formlessness.

In the decade following the publication of *The Recognitions*, very little was written about this allusive novel or its elusive author. Readers had difficulties with the book, and Gaddis did nothing to explain it. Few copies of the original edition were ever sold and the novel went out of print. In 1962, Meridian published a paperback edition under its policy to make available neglected but important literary works. Gradually, *The Recognitions* became an underground classic although it again went out of circulation. Not until 1970 did another paperback edition appear. Throughout the precarious life of this novel, Gaddis has probably been the person least surprised by its uncertain reception and reader resistance. During a party scene in *The Recognitions*, a poet questions a literary critic about a book he is carrying: "You reading that?" The critic answers, "No, I'm just reviewing it . . . all I need is the jacket blurb."

Gaddis' accomplishments began to receive greater attention in the late 1960's and early 1970's, during which time he was at work on his second monumental novel, *JR*. Between 1955 and 1970, only a single article on him appeared in the United States, but in the 1970's momentum started to build. The first doctoral dissertation on Gaddis was published in 1971, providing valuable information on *The Recognitions* and basic facts about Gaddis' life.

The year 1982 saw the publication of new essays in a special issue of the *Review of Contemporary Fiction*, as well as a full-length guide by Steven Moore to *The Recognitions* and a prestigious MacArthur Prize fellowship.

Although *JR* may be even more difficult than Gaddis' first novel, it met with a more positive reception. Critics pointed to its imposing length, diffuse form, and lack of traditional narrative devices, but they believed that it was a novel which could not be ignored by people seriously interested in the future of literature. Reviewers included John Gardner, George Steiner, Earl Miner, and George Stade, further evidence of Gaddis' growing reputation. Gaddis' winning the 1976 National Book Award in fiction for *JR* confirmed his success. Indeed, Gaddis responded by publishing his third novel only a decade later, down from the twenty years between his first two efforts. *Carpenter's Gothic* was widely hailed for its bitter yet readable satire of ethical vanity in American business, politics, and popular religion. It broadened the readership for a novelist accustomed to a comparatively small audience, and it confirmed him as one of the most gifted and serious writers of contemporary American fiction.

Biography

After spending his early childhood in New York City and on Long Island, William Gaddis attended a private boarding school in Connecticut for nine years. He then returned to Long Island to attend public school from grade eight through high school. He was accepted by Harvard in 1941 and stayed there until 1945 when he took a job as reader for *The New Yorker*. Gaddis left this position after one year in order to travel. In the years that followed, he visited Central America, the Caribbean, North Africa, and parts of Europe, all of which became settings in his first novel. He continued to write after returning to the United States and in 1955, with ten years of effort behind him, he published *The Recognitions*.

Within these broad outlines a few additional details are known despite Gaddis' extreme reluctance to discuss his life. Although he is sometimes seen at writers' conferences and occasionally does some teaching, he guards his privacy extremely well.

David Koenig and Steven Moore have made a number of important inferences about Gaddis' life. For example, the protagonist of *The Recognitions*, Wyatt, has a lonely and isolated childhood. His mother dies on an ocean voyage when he is very young, and his father gradually loses his sanity. When Wyatt is twelve, he suffers from a mysterious ailment that the doctors label *erythema grave*. They mutilate Wyatt's wasted body and send him home to die because they can find neither a cause nor a cure for his illness; unexpectedly, though, Wyatt recovers. Parallels to Gaddis' own childhood emerge. Apparently he was separated from his parents, at least while he attended a boarding school in Connecticut. He also contracted an illness that the doctors could not identify and therefore called *erythema grave*. Serious effects of the illness recurred in later years to cause further problems and to prevent the young Gaddis from being accepted into the army during World War II. Forced to remain in college, he began to write pieces for the Harvard *Lampoon* that anticipated the satirical, humorous, and critical tone of his novels. He soon became president of the *Lampoon*.

Gaddis was involved in an incident during his final year at Harvard that required the intervention of local police. Hardly a serious affair, the local newspapers, however, covered it and created embarrassing publicity for the administration. Gaddis was asked to resign and did so. The end of traditional academic success did not prevent him from acquiring knowledge. Through his travels—and more so through many years of research—Gaddis has constructed impressive works of fiction from a vast store of knowledge.

Analysis

Critics have placed William Gaddis in the tradition of experimental fiction, linking him closely to James Joyce and comparing him to contemporaries such as Thomas Pynchon. Gaddis himself has also indicated the influence of T. S. Eliot on his work, and indeed his books contain both novelistic and poetic structures. The novels employ only vestiges of traditional plots, which go in and out of focus as they are blurred by endless conversations, overpowered by erudite allusions and a multitude of characters, conflicts, and ambiguities. Like Joyce and Eliot, Gaddis uses myth to create a sense of timelessness— myths of Odysseus, the Grail Knight, the Fisher King, and Christ, along with parallels to the tales of St. Clement, Faust, and Peer Gynt. Using devices of both modern poetic sequences and modern antirealistic fiction, Gaddis unifies the diversity of parts through recurring images, phrases, and locations; a common tone; historical and literary echoes; and other nonchronological and nonsequential modes of organization. In *The Recognitions*, point of view is alternated to create tension between the first-person and third-person voices, and there are complicated jokes and symbolism deriving from the unexpected use of "I," "you," "he," and "she." In *JR*, the first-person perspective dominates through incessant talk, with very little relief or explanation in traditional third-person passages. As one reviewer wrote: "[Gaddis] wires his characters for sound and sends his story out on a continuous wave of noise—truncated dialogue, distracted monologue, the racket of TV sets, radios, telephones— from which chaos action, of a sort, eventually emerges."

All of Gaddis' work is about cacophony and euphony, fragmentation and integration, art and business, chaos and order. To a casual reader, *Carpenter's Gothic, JR*, and *The Recognitions* may appear only cacophonous, fragmented, and chaotic, for their formal experimentation is so dominant. To the reader prepared for the challenge of brilliant fiction, these novels illustrate how very accurate Henry James was in predicting the "elasticity" of the novel and its changing nature in the hands of great writers.

At its most fundamental level, *The Recognitions* is about every possible kind of recognition. The ultimate recognition is stated in the epigraph by Irenaeus, which translates as "Nothing empty nor without significance with God," but this ultimate recognition is nearly impossible to experience in a secular world where spiritual messages boom forth from the radio and television to become indistinguishable from commercials for soap powder and cereal.

The characters, major and minor, move toward, from, and around various recognitions. Some search for knowledge of how to perform their jobs, others search for knowledge of fraud, of ancestors, of love, self, truth, and sin. Wyatt, settling in New York City, moves sequentially through time and according to place to find his own recognition in Spain. His traditional path is crossed by the paths of many other characters who serve as his foils and reflections. Wyatt paints while Stanley composes music, Otto writes, and Esme loves. Wyatt, though, does more than paint; he forges the masterpieces of Fra Angelico and of Old Flemish painters such as Hugo van der Goes and Dierick Bouts. Thus, his fraudulent activity is reflected in others' fraudulent schemes. Frank Sinisterra, posing as a physician, is forced to operate on Wyatt's mother and inadvertently murders her. Frank is also a counterfeiter; Otto is a plagiarist; Benny is a liar; Big Anna masquerades as a woman, and Agnes Deigh, at a party, is unable to convince people that she is really a woman, not a man in drag; Herschel has no idea who he is (a "negative positivist," a "positive negativist," a "latent homosexual," or a "latent heterosexual"). In similar confusion, Wyatt is addressed as Stephen Asche, Estaban, the Reverend Gilbert Sullivan, and Christ arriving for the Second Coming.

As Wyatt matures from childhood to adulthood, his notions of emptiness and significance, of fraud and authenticity, undergo change. While his mother Camilla and his father are on an ocean voyage across the Atlantic, his mother has an appendicitis attack, is operated on by Sinisterra, and dies. Wyatt is reared by his father but essentially by his Aunt May. She is a fanatical Calvinist who teaches the talented boy that original sketches blaspheme God's original creation, so Wyatt eventually turns to copying from illustrated books. The distinctions between original work and forgery break down. When he is a young man, Wyatt becomes a partner with Rectall Brown, a shrewd art dealer who finds unsuspecting buyers for the forgeries that Wyatt produces. Wyatt is so convinced that "perfect" forgery has nothing to do with sinning, much less with breaking the law, that he has only scorn for the nineteenth century Romantics who prized originality above all else, often, he thinks, at the expense of quality. It takes many years of disappointments and betrayals for Wyatt to recognize that perfection of line and execution are empty and without significance. The first and crucial step of any great work of art must be the conceptualization behind it, the idea from which the painting derives; there is otherwise no meaningful distinction between the work of the artist and that of the craftsman. Wyatt's abnegation of any original conception implies abnegation of self, which in turn affects his efforts to communicate and to share with his wife Esther and his model Esme. Wyat's many failures are reflected—in bits and pieces—in the subplots of *The Recognitions*. Characters miss one another as their paths crisscross and they lose track of their appointments. They talk but no one listens, they make love but their partners do not remember, and finally, they are trapped within their useless and pretentious self-illusions.

The need for love, forgiveness, purification, and renewal emerges from this frantic activity motivated by greed and selfishness. Thus, Gaddis includes in the novel archetypal questers, priests, mourning women, arid settings, burials, dying and reviving figures, cathedrals, and keepers of the keys. These motifs bring to mind many mythic parallels, though it is hard not to think of specific parallels with Johann Wolfgang von Goethe's *Faust* (1808-1833) and Eliot's *The Waste Land* (1922) and *Four Quartets* (1943). Toward the end of his pilgrimage, as well as the end of the novel, Wyatt achieves his recognition of love and authenticity, yet Gaddis does not succumb to the temptation to finish with a conventional denouement but keeps the novel going. In this way, the form of *The Recognitions* reflects its theme, that truth is immutable but exceptionally well hidden. After Wyatt's success follow chapters of others' failures. Anselm castrates himself and Esme dies; Sinisterra is killed by an assassin and Stanley, while playing his music in a cathedral, is killed as the walls collapse.

Just as *The Recognitions* is rich in meaning, so it is rich in form. The forward movement through chronological time is poised against other combinations of time, primarily the juxtaposition of past and present. The immediate effect of juxtaposition is to interrupt and suspend time while the ultimate effect is to make all time seem simultaneous. For example, in Chapter II, Part II, Wyatt looks out the window at the evening sky as Rectall Brown talks. Brown begins speaking about ancient Greece and Rome but is interrupted by a description of the constellation Orion, by an advertisement for phoney gems, by instructions for passengers riding a bus, by a passage about Alexander the Great, by a quotation from an English travel book of the fourteenth century. The result is that the reader temporarily loses his orientation, but he need not lose orientation completely. Unity for these disparate time-periods is provided by a quality that is part of each passage—glittering beauty marred by a flaw or spurious detail. Thus, organization is based on concept, not on chronology.

Other nonchronological modes of organization include recurring patterns. Specific words become guides for the reader through difficult sections and also repeat the essential concepts of the novel. For example, "recognitions," "origin," "fished for," "design," "originality," and "fragment" can be found frequently. Larger anecdotes may also be repeated by different speakers, and opinions or metaphysical arguments may be repeated unknowingly or even stolen. The recurring images, words, and stories constitute an internal frame of reference that creates a unity apart from the plot.

In *The Recognitions*, it is possible, though not easy, to discover what activities Gaddis believes to be of enduring value. Deception and fraud are everywhere, but they cannot destroy the truth which is hidden beneath these layers of deception. A first-time reader of this novel will probably have an experience similar to that of first-time readers of Joyce's *Ulysses* (1922) in the years soon after its publication—before full-length guides extolled its merits and explained its obscurities. Like those readers of Joyce's masterpiece, readers of *The Recognitions* will be amply rewarded.

JR is also concerned with distinguishing between significant and insignificant activities, all of which take place in a more circumscribed landscape than that of *The Recognitions*. There are no transatlantic crossings and no trips to Central America, only the alternating between a suburb on Long Island and the city of Manhattan. Gaddis shifts his satirical eye to contemporary education through the experience of his protagonist, JR, who attends sixth grade in a school on Long Island. Amy Joubert, JR's social studies teacher, takes the class to visit the stock exchange, and JR is sufficiently impressed by it to interpret the lesson literally. He is fascinated by money and uses the investment of his class in one share of stock to build a corporate empire. Although his immense profits are only on paper, the effects of his transactions on countless others are both concrete and devastating.

Despite the centrality of this obnoxious child, JR remains a shadowy figure. The events he triggers and the people he sucks into his moneymaking whirlwind are more visible. Edward Bast, JR's music teacher and composer, Jack Gibbs, Thomas Eigen, and Shepperman are all artists of some kind, and their realm of activity is quite different from JR's. Bast is forever trying to finish his piece of music, even as he works reluctantly for JR in the Manhattan office that is broken down, cluttered, and chaotic. Thomas Eigen has been writing a play, and Gibbs has tried for most of his life to write an ambitious book, but he is always losing pages he has written. While some of Shepperman's paintings have been finished, they remain hidden from sight. The world of art is, however, at odds with the world of business. Bast wants nothing to do with his student's megalomania but proves to be no match for JR. The creative people cannot convince others to leave them alone to their paper, oil paints, and canvases, and as a result they are used and manipulated by those who serve as their liaison to others who buy, maintain, or publish their efforts.

The primary device for communication is not art but rather the telephone. The world that technology has created is efficient and mechanical since its purpose is to finish jobs so that money can be paid, at least symbolically on paper, and then be reinvested, again on paper. The artist is replaced by the businessman, and it is not even a flesh-and-blood businessman, but only his disembodied voice issuing orders out of a piece of plastic (JR disguises his voice so that he sounds older). The central "authority" is invisible, ubiquitous, and, at least while the conglomerate lasts, omniscient. The triumph of the telephone affords Gaddis endless opportunities for humor and irony, and the failure of art is accompanied by the failure of other means of communication— notably of love. As in *The Recognitions*, lovers miss each other, do not understand each other, and end their affairs or marriages unhappily.

The real tour de force of *JR* is its language. There is almost no third-person description to establish location and speaker and few authorial links or transitions between conversations or monologues. Originally, Gaddis did not even use quotation marks to set off one speaker from the next. *JR* is nearly one thousand pages of talk. The jargon, speech rhythms, and style of those in the educational establishment and in the stock market are perfectly re-created, but their language is a self-perpetuating system; regardless of their outpouring, the expressive power of words is obliterated by the sheer noise and verbiage. One early reviewer said of *JR* that "everything is insanely jammed together in this novel's closed atmosphere—there's no causality, no progression; and the frantic farcical momentum overlies the entropic unravelling of all 'systems.'" The words pile up as the structures of the culture collapse; the reader is faced with a formidable challenge in making his way through it all.

There can be no doubt that *JR*, probably even more than *The Recognitions*, poses serious difficulties for the reader. Despite them, and even perhaps because of them, *JR* is an extraordinary novel. Gaddis captures the dizzying pace, the language, and the absurdities of contemporary culture and mercilessly throws them back to his readers in a crazy, nonlinear kind of verisimilitude. The novel operates without causality, chronology, and the logical narrative devices upon which many readers depend. The cacophony of the characters and the lack of clarity are certainly meant to be disturbing.

In *Carpenter's Gothic*, this cultural cacophony runs headlong toward a global apocalypse. Again, there is the confused eruption of voices into the narrative and the forward spinning blur of events common to Gaddis' earlier fictions. Gaddis' third novel, however, is not only more focused and briefer, at 262 pages, but therefore the most readable of his works. Its story centers on Elizabeth Vorakers Booth and her husband Paul, renters of the ramshackle "Carpenter's Gothic" house, in which all of the action unfolds. Daughter of a minerals tycoon who committed suicide when his illegal business practices were exposed, Elizabeth married Paul Booth, a Vietnam veteran and carrier of Vorakers' bribes, after Paul lied in testifying before Congress.

All the novel's complexities unfold from these tangled business dealings. The Vorakers' estate is hopelessly ensnarled in lawsuits, manipulated by swarms of self-serving lawyers. Paul is suing or countersuing everyone in sight (including an airline, for an alleged loss of Liz's "marital services" after she was a passenger during a minor crash). Meanwhile, Paul's earlier testimony before Congress has landed him a job as "media consultant" for a Reverend Ude. Ude's fundamentalist television ministry, based in South Carolina, has mushroomed into an important political interest group, and Paul's meager pay from this group is the only thing keeping him and Liz from bankruptcy. Paul drunkenly schemes and rages at Liz, or at his morning newspaper; as in *JR*, the telephone intrudes with maddeningly insistent threats, deals, wrong numbers, and ads.

Events are intensified with the entry of McCandless, owner of the Carpenter's Gothic house. A sometime geologist, teacher, and writer, McCandless happens to have surveyed the same southeast African mineral fields on which the Vorakers company had built its fortunes. It also happens to be the same African territory in which Reverend Ude is now building his missions for a great "harvest of souls" expected during "the Rapture" or anticipated Second Coming of Christ. McCandless is being pursued by U.S. government agents for back taxes and for information about those African territories. He appears at the door one morning, a shambling and wary man, an incessant smoker and an alcoholic, but nevertheless an embodiment of romantic adventure to Liz, who promptly takes him to bed.

Events spin rapidly toward violence. During an unexpected visit, Liz's younger brother, Billy, hears McCandless' tirades against American foreign policy and promptly flies off to Africa—where he is killed when his airplane is gunned down by terrorists. The U.S. Congress has launched an investigation of Ude for bribing a senator to grant his ministry a coveted television license, a bribe that Paul carried. Ude has also managed to drown a young boy during baptismal rites in South Carolina's Pee Dee River. All of Liz and Paul's stored belongings, comprising her last links to family and tradition, have been auctioned off by a storage company in compensation for unpaid bills. Liz's behavior becomes increasingly erratic.

The apocalypse comes when all these events and forces collide. McCandless takes a payoff from the Central Intelligence Agency for his African papers and simply exits the novel, after Liz has refused to accompany him. She dies of a heart attack, the warning signs of which have been planted from the first chapter. Paul immediately files a claim to any of the Vorakers' inheritance that might have been paid to Billy and Liz, and he too simply exits the novel—notably, after using the same seduction ploy on Liz's best friend as he had originally used on Liz herself. In Africa, though, events truly explode: U.S. forces mobilize to guard various "national interests," and a real apocalypse looms as newspapers proclaim the upcoming use of a "10 K 'DEMO' BOMB OFF AFRICA COAST."

Liz Booth's heart attack symbolizes the absolute loss of empathy and love in such a cynical and careless world. Indeed, her death is further ironized when it is misinterpreted, and also proclaimed in the newspapers, as having taken place during a burglary. As with his earlier works, Gaddis' message involves this seemingly total loss of charitable and compassionate love in a civilization obsessed by success, as well as by the technologies for realizing it. Once more his satire targets the counterfeiting of values in American life, and the explosive force of mass society on feeling individuals.

The explosion of words that Gaddis re-creates is also a warning. As the efforts of painters, writers, musicians, and other artists are increasingly blocked, unappreciated, and exploited, those urges will be acknowledged by fewer and fewer people. Without an audience of listeners or viewers and without a segment of artists, there will be no possibilities for redemption from the chaos and mechanization. There will be neither sufficient introspection nor a medium through which any introspection can take concrete form. Gaddis' novels are humorous, clever, satiric, and innovative. They are also memorable and frightening reflections of contemporary culture and its values.

Miriam Fuchs

Bibliography
Gaddis, William. "The Art of Fiction, CI: William Gaddis." Interview by Zoltan Abadi-Nagy. *Paris Review* 105 (Winter, 1987): 54-89. An extensive interview with Gaddis, conducted during a 1986 visit to Budapest, Hungary. The author talks in detail about his sources, reputation, principal themes, and work-in-progress. He dispels a number of misconceptions, especially those linking his work to sources in Joyce, and discusses how the writer must ignore pressures of the literary marketplace.
Karl, Frederick R. *American Fictions, 1940-1980*. New York: Harper & Row, 1983. An important essay on Gaddis' place among contemporary writers such as Donald Barthelme and Thomas Pynchon, focusing in particular on Gaddis' satires of counterfeit art, fake sensibility, and empty values in American civilization. Includes useful discussions of Gaddis' narrative techniques, especially his development of scenes and characters in his first two novels.
Keuhl, John, and Steven Moore, eds. *In Recognition of William Gaddis*. Syracuse, N.Y.: Syracuse University Press, 1984. Gathers six previously published essays alongside seven new ones, altogether providing incisive disclosures of Gaddis' principal sources and his place among modernist and postmodernist writers. Particularly useful is David Koenig's discussion of Gaddis' early career and his sources for *The Recognitions*, and other essays on Gaddis' satire of the monetization of art and love in contemporary culture.
LeClair, Thomas. "William Gaddis, *JR*, and the Art of Excess." *Modern Fic-*

tion Studies 27 (Winter, 1981-1982): 587-600. An essay that links Gaddis' narrative practice, especially his excesses of dialogue and allusion, to the main thrust of his satire: the excesses of American culture.

Moore, Steven. *A Reader's Guide to William Gaddis's "The Recognitions."* Lincoln: University of Nebraska Press, 1982. An indispensable, line-by-line guidebook to Gaddis' difficult first novel, providing concise annotations of his extratextual allusions and quotations, as well as the novel's intratextual developments of character and events. Also includes a useful introductory essay and reprints three previously published but rare early pieces by Gaddis.

_____. *William Gaddis*. Boston: Twayne, 1989. The first full-length study of the writer's career and principal works, from *The Recognitions* through *Carpenter's Gothic*. An opening biographical chapter provides extensive information about his childhood, his education, his work, and his affiliations leading up to the first novel. A readable and critically incisive overview of Gaddis' satirical preoccupation with themes of failure, fraudulence, and ethical vanity in American life.

Review of Contemporary Fiction 2 (Summer, 1982). A special issue, one-half of which is devoted to Gaddis' work. Contains a rare though brief interview with the author, as well as seven original essays on *The Recognitions* and *JR*. Most of the essays concentrate on the bases of form in novels still regarded, in 1982, as too formless and sprawling.

ERNEST J. GAINES

Born: Oscar, Louisiana; January 15, 1933

Principal long fiction

Catherine Carmier, 1964; *Of Love and Dust*, 1967; *The Autobiography of Miss Jane Pittman*, 1971; *In My Father's House*, 1978; *A Gathering of Old Men*, 1983.

Other literary forms

Ernest J. Gaines published a collection of short stories, *Bloodline*, in 1968. One story from that collection, *A Long Day in November*, was published separately in a children's edition in 1971.

Achievements

For thirty years, Gaines has been a serious and committed writer of fiction. He has always worked slowly, frustratingly slowly to his admirers, but that is because of his great devotion to and respect for the craft of fiction. His five novels are all set in rural Louisiana, north of Baton Rouge: Gaines, like William Faulkner, has created a single world in which all his works are centered. Even though Gaines has written during a time of great racial turmoil and unrest, he has resisted becoming involved in political movements, feeling that he can best serve the cause of art and humanity by devoting himself to perfecting his craft. This does not mean that he has remained detached from political realities. Taken together, his novels cover the period of 1865 to 1980, reflecting the social movements which have affected black Americans during that time. Gaines has said again and again, however, that he is primarily interested in people; certainly it is in his depiction of people that his greatest strength lies. His focus is on the universals of life: love, pride, pity, hatred. He aspires thus not to have an immediate political impact with his writing but to move people emotionally. His supreme achievement in this regard is *The Autobiography of Miss Jane Pittman*. With its publication—and with the highly acclaimed television movie based on the novel—Gaines achieved the recognition he had long deserved.

Biography

From birth until age fifteen, Ernest J. Gaines lived in rural Louisiana with his parents. As a boy, he often worked in the plantation fields and spent much of his spare time with his aunt, Miss Augusteen Jefferson. He moved to Vallejo, California, in 1948 to live with his mother and stepfather, and he attended high school and junior college there before serving in the army.

After his military service, he earned a B.A. degree at San Francisco State College. On the basis of some stories written while he was a student there, he was awarded the Wallace Stegner Creative Writing Fellowship in 1958 for graduate study at Stanford University. Since that time, he has lived, impermanently, by his own testimony, in or near San Francisco, feeling that living elsewhere enables him to gain a perspective on his Southern material that would be unavailable to him were he to live in the South full-time. By making yearly trips back to Louisiana, where he holds a visiting professorship in creative writing at the University of Southwestern Louisiana in Lafayette, he retains contact with his native region.

Analysis

Before it became fashionable, Ernest J. Gaines was one Southern black writer who wrote about his native area. Although he has lived much of his life in California, he has never been able to write adequately about that region. He has tried to write two novels about the West but has failed to finish either of them. Thus, while he has physically left the South, he has never left emotionally. His ties remain with the South, and his works remain rooted there. When he first began reading seriously, Gaines gravitated toward those writers who wrote about the soil and the people who lived close to it, among them William Faulkner, John Steinbeck, Willa Cather, Ivan Turgenev. He was disappointed to discover that few black writers had dealt with the black rural Southern experience. (Richard Wright had begun his career by doing so, and his work weakened as he moved further from the South.) Thus, Gaines began his career with the conscious desire to fill a void. He felt that no one had written fiction about his people.

This fact helps explain why his novels always concentrate on rural settings and on the "folk" who inhabit them. One of the great strengths of his work is voice; the sound of the voice telling the story is central to its meaning. Among his works, *Of Love and Dust*, *The Autobiography of Miss Jane Pittman*, and all the stories in *Bloodline* are told in the first person by rural black characters. The voices of the storytellers, especially Miss Jane's, express the perspective not only of the individual speakers but also in some sense of the entire black community, and it is the community on which Gaines most often focuses his attention.

Louisiana society, especially from a racial perspective, is complicated. Not only blacks and whites live there, but also Creoles and Cajuns. Thus there are competing communities, and some of Gaines's more interesting characters find themselves caught between groups, forced to weigh competing demands in order to devise a course of action.

Several themes recur in the Gaines canon, and together they create the total effect of his work. Generally, he deals with the relationship between past and present and the possibility of change, both individual and social.

Using a broad historical canvas in his works, especially in *The Autobiography of Miss Jane Pittman*, Gaines treats the changes in race relations over time, but he is most interested in people, in whether and how they change as individuals. The issue of determinism and free will is therefore a central question in his work. Gaines has been very interested in and influenced by Greek tragedy, and in his fiction, a strain of environmental determinism is evident. In his works prior to and including *The Autobiography of Miss Jane Pittman*, a growing freedom on the part of his black characters can be seen, but the tension between fate and free will always underlies his works.

Some of Gaines's most admirable characters—for example, Marcus in *Of Love and Dust*, and Ned, Joe, and Jimmy in *The Autobiography of Miss Jane Pittman*—have the courage, pride, and dignity to fight for change. At the same time, however, Gaines reveres the old, who, while often resistant to change, embody the strength of the black people. In his work, one frequently finds tension between generations, a conflict between old and young which is reconciled only in the character of Miss Jane Pittman, who even in extreme old age retains the courage to fight for change.

Other recurring tensions and dichotomies are evident in Gaines's novels. Conflict often exists between men and women. Because of slavery, which denied them their manhood, black men feel forced to take extreme actions to attain or assert it, a theme most evident in *Of Love and Dust*, *The Autobiography of Miss Jane Pittman*, *A Gathering of Old Men* and the stories in *Bloodline*. Women, on the other hand, are often presented in Gaines's fiction as preservers and conservers. Each group embodies a strength, but Gaines suggests that wholeness comes about only when the peculiar strengths of the two sexes are united, again most clearly exemplified in Miss Jane and her relationship with the men in her life.

Among the male characters, a tension exists between fathers and sons. Treated explicitly in Gaines's fourth novel, *In My Father's House*, this theme is implicit throughout the canon. Though young men look to the older generation for models, there are few reliable examples for them to follow, and they find it difficult to take responsibility for their lives and for the lives of their loved ones.

Gaines's characters at their best seek freedom and dignity: some succeed, and some fail in their attempts to overcome both outer and inner obstacles. Viewed in sequence, Gaines's first three novels move from the almost total bleakness and determinism of *Catherine Carmier* to the triumph of *The Autobiography of Miss Jane Pittman*. *In My Father's House*, however, reflects a falling away of hope in both individual and social terms, perhaps corresponding to the diminution of expectations experienced in America during the late 1970's and early 1980's.

Gaines's first novel, *Catherine Carmier*, based on a work he wrote while an adolescent in Vallejo, has many of the characteristic weaknesses of a first novel and is more interesting for what it anticipates in Gaines's later career than for its intrinsic merits. Though it caused barely a ripple of interest when it was first published, the novel introduces many of the themes which Gaines treats more effectively in his mature fiction. The book is set in the country, near Bayonne, Louisiana, an area depicted as virtually a wasteland. Ownership of much of this region has devolved to the Cajuns, who appear throughout Gaines's novels as Snopes-like vermin, interested in owning the land only to exploit it. Like Faulkner, Gaines sees this kind of person as particularly modern, and the growing power of the Cajuns indicates a weakening of values and a loss of determination to live in right relationship to the land.

Onto the scene comes Jackson Bradley, a young black man born and reared in the area but (like Gaines himself) educated in California. Bradley is a hollow, rootless man, a man who does not know where he belongs. He has found the North and the West empty, with people living hurried, pointless lives, but he sees the South as equally empty. Feeling no link to a meaningful past and no hope for a productive future, Bradley is a deracinated modern man. He has returned to Louisiana to bid final farewell to his Aunt Charlotte, a representative of the older generation, and to her way of life.

While there and while trying to find a meaningful path for himself, Bradley meets and falls in love with Catherine Carmier. She, too, is living a blocked life, and he feels that if they can leave the area, they will be able to make a fulfilling life together. Catherine is the daughter of Raoul Carmier, in many ways the most interesting character in the novel. A Creole, he is caught between the races. Because of his black blood, he is not treated as the equal of whites, but because of his white blood, he considers blacks to be beneath him. He has a near incestuous relationship with Catherine, since after her birth his wife was unfaithful to him and he considers none of their subsequent children his. Feeling close only to Catherine, he forbids her to associate with any men, but especially with black men. A man of great pride and love of the land, Raoul is virtually the only man in the region to resist the encroachment of the Cajuns. His attitude isolates him all the more, which in turn makes him fanatically determined to hold to Catherine.

Despite her love for and loyalty to her father, Catherine senses the dead end her life has become and returns Bradley's love. Though she wants to leave with him, she is paralyzed by her love of her father and by her knowledge of what her leaving would do to him. This conflict climaxes with a brutal fight between Raoul and Bradley over Catherine, a fight that Bradley wins. Catherine, however, returns home to nurse her father. The novel ends ambiguously, with at least a hint that Catherine will return to Bradley, although the thrust of the book militates against that eventuality. Gaines implies that history and caste are a prison, a tomb. No change is possible for the characters because they cannot break out of the cages their lives have become. Love is the final victim. Catherine will continue living her narrow, unhealthy life, and

Jackson Bradley will continue wandering the earth, searching for something to fill his inner void.

Gaines's second novel, *Of Love and Dust*, was received much more enthusiastically than was *Catherine Carmier*; with it, he began to win the largely positive, respectful reviews which have continued to the present time. Like *Catherine Carmier*, *Of Love and Dust* is a story of frustrated love. The setting is the same: rural Louisiana, where the Cajuns are gradually assuming ownership and control of the land. *Of Love and Dust* is a substantial improvement over *Catherine Carmier*, however, in part because it is told in the first person by Jim Kelly, an observer of the central story. In this novel, one can see Gaines working toward the folk voice which became such an integral part of the achievement of *The Autobiography of Miss Jane Pittman*.

The plot of the novel concerns Marcus Payne, a young black man sentenced to prison for murder and then bonded out by a white plantation owner who wants him to work in his fields. Recognizing Marcus' rebelliousness and pride, the owner and his Cajun overseer, Sidney Bonbon, brutally attempt to break his spirit. This only makes Marcus more determined, and in revenge, he decides to seduce Louise, Bonbon's neglected wife. What begins, however, as simply a selfish and egocentric act of revenge on Marcus' part grows into a genuine though grotesque love. When he and Louise decide to run away together, Bonbon discovers them and kills Marcus. Even though he dies, Marcus, by resisting brutalizing circumstances, retains his pride and attempts to prove his manhood and dignity. His attempts begin in a self-centered way, but as his love for Louise grows, he grows in stature in the reader's eyes until he becomes a figure of heroic dimensions.

Through his use of a first-person narrator, Gaines creates a double perspective in the novel, including on the one hand the exploits of Marcus and on the other the black community's reactions to them. The narrator, Jim Kelly, is the straw boss at the plantation, a member of the black community but also accepted and trusted by the whites because of his dependability and his unwillingness to cause any problems. His initial reaction to Marcus— resentment and dislike of him as a troublemaker—represents the reaction of the community at large. The older members of the community never move beyond that attitude because they are committed to the old ways, to submission and accommodation. To his credit, however, Jim's attitude undergoes a transformation. As he observes Marcus, his resentment changes to sympathy and respect, for he comes to see Marcus as an example of black manhood which others would do well to emulate.

Marcus' death gives evidence of the strain of fate and determinism in this novel as well, yet because he dies with his pride and dignity intact, *Of Love and Dust* is more hopeful than *Catherine Carmier*. Gaines indicates that resistance is possible and, through the character of Jim Kelly, that change can occur. Kelly leaves the plantation at the end of the novel, no longer passively accepting what fate brings him but believing that he can act and shape his own life. Though Marcus is an apolitical character, like Jackson Bradley, it is suggested that others will later build on his actions to force social change on the South. *Of Love and Dust* is a major step forward beyond *Catherine Carmier* both artistically and thematically. Through his use of the folk voice, Gaines vivifies his story, and the novel suggests the real possibility of free action by his characters.

Without a doubt, *The Autobiography of Miss Jane Pittman* is Gaines's major contribution to American literature. Except for an introduction written by "the editor," it is told entirely in the first person by Miss Jane and covers approximately one hundred years, from the Civil War to the civil rights movement of the 1960's. Basing the novel on stories he heard while a child around his aunt, Augusteen Jefferson, and using the format of oral history made popular in recent decades, Gaines created a "folk autobiography" which tells the story of people who are not in the history books. While the work is the story of Miss Jane, she is merely an observer for a substantial portion of its length, and the story becomes that of black Americans from slavery to the present. Gaines's mastery of voice is especially important here, for Miss Jane's voice is the voice of her people.

From the very beginning of the novel, when Miss Jane is determined, even in the face of physical beatings, to keep the name a Union soldier gave her and refuses to be called Ticey, her slave name, to the end of the novel, when she leads her people to Bayonne in a demonstration against segregated facilities, she is courageous and in the best sense of the word "enduring," like Faulkner's Dilsey. In her character and story, many of the dichotomies that run through Gaines's work are unified. The differing roles of men and women are important elements in the book. Women preserve and sustain—a role symbolized by Miss Jane's longevity. Men, on the other hand, feel the need to assert their manhood in an active way. Three black men are especially important in Miss Jane's life, beginning with Ned, whom she rears from childhood after his mother is killed and who becomes in effect a "son" to her. Like Marcus Payne, Ned is a rebel, but his rebellion is concentrated in the political arena. Returning to Louisiana after the turn of the century, he attempts to lead his people to freedom. Though he is murdered by whites, his legacy and memory are carried on by Miss Jane and the people in the community. Later, in the 1960's, Jimmy Aaron, another young man who tries to encourage his people to effective political action, appears. Again the members of the older generation hang back, fearful of change and danger, but after Jimmy is killed, Jane unites old and young, past and present by her determination to go to Bayonne and carry on Jimmy's work. Thus Marcus' apolitical rebellion in *Of Love and Dust* has been transformed into political action. The third man in Jane's life is Joe Pittman, her husband. A horse-breaker, he is committed to asserting and proving his manhood through his work. Although he too dies, killed by a wild horse he was determined to break, Jane in her understanding and love of him, as well as in her affection for all her men, bridges the gap between man and woman. In her character, the opposites of old and young, past and present, and man and woman are reconciled.

Miss Jane's strength is finally the strength of the past, but it is directed toward the future. When Jimmy returns, he tells the people that he is nothing without their strength, referring not only to their physical numbers but also to the strength of their character as it has been forged by all the hardships they have undergone through history. Even though the people seem weak and fearful, the example of Miss Jane shows that they need not be. They can shake off the chains of bondage and determinism, assert their free spirit through direct action, and effect change. The change has only begun by the conclusion of *The Autobiography of Miss Jane Pittman*, but the pride and dignity of Miss Jane and all those she represents suggest that ultimately they will prevail.

Gaines's fourth novel, *In My Father's House*, was the first he had written in the third person since *Catherine Carmier*; the effect of its point of view is to distance the reader from the action and characters, creating an ironic perspective. Set during a dreary winter in 1970, in the period of disillusionment following the assassination of Martin Luther King, Jr., the novel suggests that the progress which was implicit in the ending of *The Autobiography of Miss Jane Pittman* was temporary at best, if not downright illusory. The atmosphere of the novel is one of frustration and stagnation.

Both the setting and the protagonist of *In My Father's House* are uncharacteristic for Gaines. Instead of using the rural settings so familiar from his other works, he sets his story in a small town. Rather than focusing on the common people, Gaines chooses as his protagonist Philip Martin, one of the leaders of the black community, a public figure, a minister who is considering running for Congress. A success by practically any measure and pridefully considering himself a *man*, Martin is brought low in the course of the novel. His illegitimate son, Robert X, a ghostlike man, appears and wordlessly accuses him. Robert is evidence that, by abandoning him, his siblings, and their mother many years previously, Martin in effect destroyed their lives. Having been a drinker and gambler, irresponsible, he tries to explain to his son that his earlier weakness was a legacy of slavery. Even though he seems to have surmounted that crippling legacy, his past rises up to haunt him and forces him to face his weakness. Martin wants to effect a reconciliation with his son and thus with his past, but Robert's suicide precludes that. *In My Father's House* makes explicit a concern which was only implicit in Gaines's earlier novels, the relationship between fathers and sons. No communication is possible here, and the failure is illustrative of a more general barrier between the generations. While in the earlier novels the young people led in the struggle for change and the older characters held back, here the situation is reversed. Martin and members of his generation are the leaders, while the young are for the most part sunk in cynicism, apathy, and hopelessness, or devoted to anarchic violence. If the hope of a people is in the young, or in a reconciliation of old and young, hope does not exist in this novel.

Hope does exist, however, in Gaines's *A Gathering of Old Men*, for which Gaines returns to his more characteristic rural setting. Here he returns as well to the optimism with which *The Autobiography of Miss Jane Pittman* ended. This time, as at the end of that novel and in *In My Father's House*, it is up to the old among the black community to lead the struggle for change, this time primarily because there are no young men left to lead. All of them have escaped to towns and cities that promise more of a future than does rural Louisiana.

In this small corner of Louisiana, however, as elsewhere in Gaines's fiction, Cajuns are encroaching on the land, replacing men with machines and even threatening to plow up the old graveyard where generations of blacks have been buried. When Beau Boutan, son of the powerful Cajun Fix Boutan, is shot to death in the quarters of Marshall plantation, where Marshall blacks have worked the land since the days of slavery, the old black men who have lived there all of their lives are faced with one last chance to stand up and be men. They stand up for the sake of Matthu, the only one of them who ever stood up before and thus the most logical suspect in the murder. They also stand up because of all the times in their past when they should have stood up but did not. They prove one last time that free action is possible when eighteen or more of them, all in their seventies and eighties, arm themselves with rifles of the same gauge used in the shooting and face down the white sheriff, Mapes, each in his turn claiming to be the killer.

As shut off as the quarters are from the rest of the world, it is easy to forget that the events of the novel take place as recently as the late 1970's. Beau Boutan's brother Gil, however, represents the change that has been taking place in the world outside Marshall. He has achieved gridiron fame at Louisiana State University by working side by side with Cal, a young black man. Youth confronts age when Gil returns home and tries to persuade his father not to ride in revenge against Beau's murderer, as everyone expects him to do. Gil represents the possibility of change from the white perspective. He convinces his father to let the law find and punish Beau's murderer, but he pays a heavy price when his father disowns him. He cannot stop other young Cajuns, led by Luke Will, who are not willing to change but would rather cling to the vigilantism of the old South.

In spite of their dignity and pride, the old men at Marshall risk looking rather silly because after all these years they stand ready for a battle that seems destined never to take place once Fix Boutan decides not to ride on Marshall. Sheriff Mapes taunts them with the knowledge that they have waited too late to take a stand. Ironically, they are ultimately able to maintain their dignity and reveal their growth in freedom by standing up to the one person who has been most valiant in her efforts to help them: Candy Marshall, niece of the landowner. In her effort to protect Matthu, who was largely responsible for rearing her after her parents died, Candy has gone so far as to try to take credit for the murder herself. What she fails to realize is that the days are long past when black men need the protection of a white woman. She is stunned to realize that she too has been living in the past and has been guilty of treating grown black men like children.

The novel does eventually end with a gunfight, because Luke Will and his men refuse to let the murder of a white man by a black one go unavenged. It is fitting that the two men who fall in the battle are Luke Will, the one who was most resistant to change, and Charlie Biggs, the real murderer, who, at fifty, finally proves his manhood by refusing to be beaten by Beau Boutan and then by returning to take the blame for the murder that he has committed. Charlie's body is treated like a sacred relic as each member of the black community, from the oldest to the youngest, touches it, hoping that some of the courage that Charlie found late in life will rub off. Apparently it already has.

With *A Gathering of Old Men*, Gaines returns to first-person narration, but this time the history is told one chapter at a time by various characters involved in or witnessing the action. His original plan was to have the narrator be the white newspaperman Lou Dimes, Candy's boyfriend. He found, however, that there was still much that a black man in Louisiana would not confide to a white man, even a sympathetic one, so he let the people tell their own story, with Dimes narrating an occasional chapter.

If *In My Father's House* represents a falling away of hope for human progress and perhaps also a falling away in artistry, one finds once again in *A Gathering of Old Men* evidence of the same genuine strengths that Gaines exhibited in *The Autobiography of Miss Jane Pittman*: a mastery of the folk voice, a concern for common people, a reverence for the everyday, a love of the land, and a powerful evocation of the strength, pride, and dignity people can develop by working on and living close to the soil.

Frank W. Shelton

Other major works

SHORT FICTION: *Bloodline*, 1968; *A Long Day in November*, 1971.

Bibliography

Gaines, Ernest J. "A Very Big Order: Reconstructing Identity." *Southern Review* 26 (Spring, 1990): 245-253. In this memoir, Gaines recalls his move from Louisiana to Vallejo, California, where he first had access to a public library but did not find there books about the South that he knew. He traces the movement in his writing back into his Southern past as he attempted to write for the African-American youth of the South the works that did not exist for him.

Gauden, Marcia, and Carl Wooton. "Talking with Ernest J. Gaines." *Callaloo* 11 (Spring, 1988): 229-243. In this interview, Gaines provides useful information about how his background influenced his art. He discusses his training as a writer, including the early lack of African-American models and the effects of his small-town upbringing. He also analyzes his use of point of view and his treatment of black men and women.

Hudson, Theodore R. "Ernest J. Gaines." In *The History of Southern Literature*. Edited by Louis D. Rubin, Jr., et al. Chapel Hill: University of North Carolina Press, 1985. This brief but concise entry in the section of this history of Southern literature entitled "The Recent South: 1951-82" gives an overview of the major themes, setting, and characters of Gaines's works through *In My Father's House*.

Laney, Ruth. "A Conversation with Ernest Gaines." *Southern Review* 10 (Winter, 1974): 1-14. In his clear and simple style, Gaines here discusses works, from Mark Twain's *The Adventures of Huckleberry Finn* (1884) to Ivan Turgenev's *Fathers and Sons* (1862), that influenced him, as well as members of his own family who gave shape to strong and enduring characters he has created. Included are his story of how *The Autobiography of Miss Jane Pittman* evolved and a frank celebration of his Louisiana roots.

Shelton, Frank W. "*In My Father's House*: Ernest Gaines After Jane Pittman." *Southern Review* 17 (Spring, 1981): 340-345. In his detailed analysis of *In My Father's House*, Shelton explores the relative neglect of the novel by reviewers, attributing their less than enthusiastic response in part to the distance achieved through a third-person narrator. Where Miss Jane Pittman symbolizes human survival, the more recent novel's Philip Martin symbolizes human failing and provides a vehicle for Gaines to explore two earlier themes: the nature of African-American manhood and the relationship between fathers and sons.

Stoelting, Winifred L. "Human Dignity and Pride in the Novels of Ernest Gaines." *College Language Association Journal* 14 (March, 1971): 340-358. Stoelting presents a detailed analysis of *Catherine Carmier* and *Of Love and Dust* in terms of the independence of the human spirit that allows their characters to survive and change.

MAVIS GALLANT

Born: Montreal, Canada; August 11, 1922

Principal long fiction
Green Water, Green Sky, 1959; *Its Image on the Mirror*, 1964; *A Fairly Good Time*, 1970; *The Pegnitz Junction*, 1973.

Other literary forms
Mavis Gallant's reputation rests more upon her short fiction than upon her novels. Of her more than one hundred published stories, the great majority have appeared in *The New Yorker*. Many of them have been collected in books, such as *The Other Paris* (1956); *My Heart Is Broken*, containing the novella *Its Image on the Mirror* (1964); *The End of the World and Other Stories* (1974); *From the Fifteenth District* (1979); *Home Truths* (1981); *Overhead in a Balloon* (1985); and *In Transit* (1988). Gallant has also written nonfiction; her long report on the case of an unfortunate French schoolteacher whose affair with a student led to her subsequent persecution and suicide became the introduction to *The Affair of Gabrielle Russier* (1971). She has also produced a substantial body of periodical essays, book reviews, and newspaper features and articles; some of these were collected in *Paris Notebooks: Essays and Reviews* (1986).

Achievements
Gallant's chief accomplishment has been to illuminate the physical and psychological displacements caused by World War II. Her recognition of the essential homelessness of the human spirit in the modern world gives her work an appeal on both sides of the Atlantic. Although she is often referred to as an expatriate Canadian writer—Gallant has lived in France since 1950—she transmutes the banalities of the life of the stranger abroad into metaphors of wandering in a confusing landscape, which is both another country and one's own heart. Recognition in Canada has come late to Gallant; she was awarded the Governor-General's Award in 1981 for her collection of stories *Home Truths*. In the same year, she was also made an Officer of the Order of Canada. Her papers are donated on an ongoing basis to the University of Toronto, where she has been writer-in-residence. She is considered by her peers to be the greatest Canadian writer of short fiction after Morley Callaghan.

Biography
Mavis Gallant was born in Montreal, Quebec, in 1922 of Canadian Scottish Protestant parents. Her early life in a city of diverse languages, religions, and

cultures gave her a sense of pluralism that permeates all her fiction. Her father died while she was still quite young, and her formative years were spent in a succession of seventeen different schools in both the United States and Canada, including one Roman Catholic convent school. Bilingual by the age of four, she recalls teachers asking her to entertain her classmates by speaking French for them. The hostility she felt directed at her because of her ability to call upon the magic of another language gave her a keen sense of the heartless cultural sideswiping that can be another, less pleasant outcome of the proximity of different cultures.

Perhaps because of her experience with so many different kinds of schools, Gallant chose not to attend college but returned instead to Montreal, intent on a writing career. Unable to find an opportunity to pursue her chosen vocation, she took a job with the National Film Board of Canada, working at first in the cutting room, editing documentary films. Finally, realizing she had little interest in or aptitude for such work, Gallant resumed her search for a writing job. This time, she was successful, being hired by the Montreal *Standard* in 1944 as a newspaper feature writer. Her story "With a Capital T," collected in *Home Truths*, is a good account of what it was like to be an intelligent, imaginative young woman grudgingly allowed by old newspapermen to fill in while the younger men were away at war.

Gallant had set herself the goal of being independent by the age of thirty and, in 1950, despite a chorus of dire warnings from her peers, she resigned her position with the *Standard* and, with a gift of five hundred dollars from her editor, went off to live in France. She has lived in Paris ever since and has long ago silenced those who doubted her ability to succeed on her own. In 1951, she published her first story with *The New Yorker*, "Madeline's Birthday." Gallant is rare among Canadian writers in that, beginning with her job on the *Standard*, she has always earned her living solely by her writing.

Gallant lives alone in an apartment in the fashionable Faubourg St. Germain district of the Left Bank. In the 1980's she abandoned long fiction in favor of short stories and essays; she maintains a keen interest in French social affairs and is often called upon to write about them, something she does with great tact and discretion. Preferring not to be tied to strict historical accuracy, she writes mostly from memory, although she continues to keep complete notebooks of her thoughts and observations. Her awareness of current literary trends in both North America and Europe is considerable, though she retains greatest fondness for those authors read during her youth: Anton Chekhov, Ivan Turgenev, Fyodor Dostoevski, Stendhal, Gustave Flaubert, and Marcel Proust.

Analysis

Because most of Gallant's works do not have conclusive endings, it is difficult to cite in traditional terms the theme or central idea governing her fiction. It may be more important to understand the point of reference from which she views her characters, most of whom are women, middle-class, and adrift in a confused sea of unmet expectations. Her view of her characters is almost always from without, classically dispassionate. A recurring image in her work is the mirror, which shows her protagonists with pitiless accuracy, faces they often do not recognize as their own, as in the case of "The Late-homecomer" in *From the Fifteenth District*. Despite the incoherence of the characters' lives, the world they inhabit is carefully and cleanly drawn, technically precise, perfect in detail. Her descriptions of a train station, a café, or a sitting room are exact as to proportion, color, and shape; in contrast, her characters are often indistinct except for their crippling flaws. This indistinctiveness is suggestive, however, never obscuring. Although her characters are emotionally confusing and unable to lift themselves out of the morass of indecision and compromise in which they are stranded, they evoke no pity, no sentiment other than a wistful compassion.

Gallant's concern with homelessness or displacement draws her to the strange amid the familiar. Rest stops—a café, a party, a day's outing—become symbols of the only kind of home her characters are ever likely to have. Anticipation is the rule; farther down the coast perhaps, or next season, or even tomorrow at a friend's, things will begin to come clear, problems will begin to resolve themselves. Gallant's figures are often people of little imagination, burdened with insufficient insight and strength of will to take control of their lives. Inevitably, they drift toward disasters, the consequences of which they foresee dimly, if at all. They live more on hope than by the efficacy of their own actions. The warning sounds they should heed in order to save themselves occur to them as echoes, as sounds of a past already too late to change. Gallant's sense of time is geometric rather than linear: lives collide and rearrange themselves like billiard balls subject to the tyranny of physics. Personal realities may be contemporaneous, but they never interpenetrate.

Often the sole correspondence between characters is a familial one, to which they give no more thought than to the color of their hair or to next Sunday's dinner. For Gallant, relationship by marriage or blood is almost certain to destroy whatever humanness could exist in the bonds between people. Many of her stories rehearse the chronicle of a thoughtless parent, usually a mother, spending her child's future to pay the debts of her own present, as if another's life were capital to be borrowed and squandered. "Going Ashore" in *The Other Paris* offers the flighty Mrs. Ellenger and her daughter, Emma, as an example of this kind of relationship. The spectacle of the shallow interests, selfishness, fraudulent friendships, and the conniving of people trying to live in grand style while on the thin edge of penury does not, as perhaps it might in the work of a more romantic writer, lead young people to throw off the tyranny of their foolish parents; instead, the children become more numbed by the constant movement, the maintenance of surface at the expense of substance. In consequence, the characters take refuge in an interior life contrived out of the rag ends of the only kind of existence they know. Rarely are Gallant's characters guilty of outrageously immoral actions: their small failings accrete to become an attitude, a way of life which denies personal responsibility while insisting that one is doing everything humanly possible to put things right.

In Gallant's fiction, few characters make good the occasional second chance. In her short story "The Ice Wagon Going Down the Street" in *Home Truths*, Peter and Sheilah Frazier are middle-class vagabonds lately returned from a posting in Hong Kong, out of which, as usual, they have made no profit, either material or spiritual. Their sole talisman of respectability is Sheilah's Balenciaga gown, which at times has been their ticket to some of the better parties. Peter has allowed one opportunity after another to slip through his fingers, while waiting for fate or chance or old friends to rescue him. He walks through the world in lordly fashion, unable to see himself as an aging do-nothing, a failure. Even a small inheritance becomes merely the occasion for a brief episode of happiness in Paris, while they imitate those of more substantial and lasting means. At one point, Sheilah's beauty and charm bring Peter a job offer with possibilities for making their fortune at last. Without comment, Gallant shows the couple having returned from that episode, sitting in Peter's sister's kitchen, as forlorn as ever, their sole emblem of prosperity a steamer trunk upended in the corner. The two sit holding hands across the table; there are no recriminations, no bitterness, only a sweetly elegiac sense of the loss of something undefined. Even this sense of loss becomes transmuted through naïve optimism into dreams which can only lead to disappointments, further failures. So it goes with most of Gallant's weary protagonists. Hope based upon false premises, action inappropriate to the situation, bad decisions, ineffective compromises—these take their toll upon the slowly dying, who puzzle over their distantly echoing pain.

Although Gallant's first novel, *Green Water, Green Sky*, is only 154 pages long, it spans some eleven years in the life of Florence McCarthy Harris, from her fifteenth to her twenty-sixth year. Like most of Gallant's protagonists, Flor is a halfhearted combatant against her own lingering dissolution. From Venice to Cannes to Paris, Flor drifts, allowing life simply to happen to her. Her mother, Bonnie McCarthy, is a witless pleasure seeker, a woman who strings her days together with no other end in view than making them an adornment, a strand of cheap, gaudy pearls. The novel's image of Flor comes variously from Bonnie; from Flor's cousin George Fairlee; from Wishart, her mother's sexless male companion; and lastly, from Bob Harris, her Jewish husband. Flor stands at the center of this square of mirrors, reflecting only what each gives back as its image of her. Her one serious attempt to take control of her fate is her marriage to Harris. Even in this, she is neutralized; her mother disapproves, not so much because Harris is a Jew, but because he understands how to make money, while Bonnie knows only how to spend it. Flor's attempts to make compromises between the contending forces in her life wear her down until she eventually takes refuge in madness— not the fine, burning madness of a striving consciousness strained beyond its capacity to reconcile the disparate contingencies of existence—but the attenuated surrender of presence in the world of the real.

In *Its Image on the Mirror*, her only long fiction set in Canada, Gallant turns her imagination to the effect of time on the lives of the Duncan sisters, Jean and Isobel. The action of the novella moves backward and forward, weaving a fabric of time in which the individual threads become muted, indistinct. Jean is now Jean Price, mother of four. Her sister is married to Alfredo, a Venezuelan doctor. Jean's life is ordered and sedate; Isobel's is chaotic and confused. The sisters arrive at their parents' cottage for a family reunion, and the past is revealed from Jean's point of view. Less favored than Isobel with beauty, grace, and wit, Jean has made the best of her gifts and is at peace with herself. Isobel has squandered her blessings and lived to see them become a mockery to her.

In her customary method, Gallant describes the surface of things with great precision; interior life is portrayed in relief, the subtle becoming visible by implication. The present is drawn out of Jean's memories of wartime Montreal and her humdrum existence of that time. By comparison, those days were Isobel's best. She led the more exciting life, involved in the shady business of procuring apartments for refugees at exorbitant rents. She always knew where to get cigarettes, whiskey, and nylons. She was in; Jean was out. Isobel's marriage to a South American doctor had seemed at the time romantic to the staid Duncans. In reality, they now find Alfredo to be short, unattractive, and boorish. The past again catches up with the present, bringing with it its full freight of disappointment. Gallant takes no sides; she is dispassionate, aloof, holding her characters up to the light so that the reader might better inspect them. In the end, Jean's father sums everything up in his observation that the salt does not taste as salty as it once did.

Shirley Perrigny, the protagonist of *A Fairly Good Time*, is a loser. She loses her first husband on their honeymoon and, by the end of the novel, she is losing her mind; in between, she loses just about everything else that gives meaning to life. She has married again, this time to Philippe, a hack writer of socially aware articles for a second-rate Paris periodical, *Le Miroir*. (The magazine devotes itself to such burning issues as the analysis of English nursery rhymes as the key to understanding the problems of a developing Africa.) Philippe is everything Shirley is not; he is neat, precise, fastidious, and dim. He is more married to his mother and sister than to his wife. Shirley accepts their combined slights as if she deserves them and finds all her efforts to accommodate Philippe's family turned against her. At one point, after her husband has left her to return home to his mother's to nurse his tender liver, Shirley cannot even get in to see him; his mother reduces their conversation to a whispered dismissal through a barely open door.

Shirley seems always to be confiding her secrets to the enemy. Chief among these is her own mother, who browbeats and humbugs Shirley through her caustic letters. Shirley befriends young Claudie Maurel, who has ordered a restaurant meal without the money to pay for it, and finds herself in the end an inexplicable object of scorn and ridicule to the entire Maurel family. Having forgotten to get money from Philippe before his departure, she goes to borrow some from her neighbor, a Greek lothario. She proceeds to go to bed with him not because she actively wants to but because she has nothing better to do. Her attempts to help her friend Renata simply add more mismanagement to a life already as confused as her own. In the end, a distraught and disintegrating Shirley, desperate for understanding, mistakes her own image in a mirror for that of a long-sought true companion. She walks joyfully toward the smiling girl.

The same spirit of futility informs Gallant's novella *The Pegnitz Junction*. Christine and Herbert have gone to Paris to enjoy an affair. Certain things, however, impinge on their fragile bliss: Christine is engaged to a theological student, and Herbert has brought along his little son, Bert. Christine remains faithful to her fiancé in her own way by reading Dietrich Bonhoeffer. Herbert tries unsuccessfully to nag her into his vision of the liberal pseudoparent. Little Bert enjoys sneaking a nighttime look at the naked, sleeping Christine and in general making a pest of himself. Gallant employs the return train journey to Strasbourg via Pegnitz as a metaphor for the predictable course of a life along the lines of its own antecedents. The narrative is interleaved with the stories of contingent characters. The complaints of an old woman with whom they share a compartment are rehearsed in her own italicized thoughts. Christine seems to be aware of these, and at times it is uncertain whether she is imagining them or reading the old woman's mind. At another point, Christine looks out the window at a group of people standing before the gates of an estate, and their story consequently unfolds. When the train is compelled to stop for rerouting, Christine takes notice of an elderly gentleman. His life is told in flashback, again as if occurring in Christine's consciousness. The trip itself is a series of delays, detours, and disappointments; hot drink vendors have coffee but no cups, sandwich hawkers have no sandwiches, the washrooms are locked, and the conductor orders the windows shut despite the heat. Everyone looks forward to Pegnitz; everyone is certain that a comfortable express train will be waiting there, and that there will be food and drink and a chance to freshen up. Their hopes, like their lives, are futile. No train is waiting, only more confusion, delay, and inconvenience. The entire trip has the quality of Christine's life: ill-planned and dependent upon others to give it direction. She is lost and will remain so.

Long fiction is not Gallant's métier. Her characteristically aloof, precisely rendered sketches of futile lives lose their bite if extended beyond the neat confines of the short story. Nevertheless, her handful of novels and novellas will repay study, for they work out at length her recurring themes.

Paul LaValley

Other major works

SHORT FICTION: *The Other Paris*, 1956; *My Heart Is Broken*, 1964; *The End of the World and Other Stories*, 1974; *From the Fifteenth District*, 1979; *Home Truths*, 1981; *Overhead in a Balloon*, 1985; *In Transit*, 1988.

NONFICTION: *The Affair of Gabrielle Russier*, 1971; *Paris Notebooks: Essays and Reviews*, 1986.

Bibliography

Besner, Neil K. *The Light of Imagination: Mavis Gallant's Fiction*. Vancouver: University of British Columbia Press, 1988. Covers the entire range of Gallant's writing over thirty-five years, and includes biographical details and critical analyses of her short and long fiction. Thorough and scholarly, as well as clearly written and absorbing.

Grant, Judith Skelton. "Mavis Gallant and Her Works." In *Canadian Writers and Their Works: Fiction Series*, edited by Robert Lecker, Jack David, and Ellen Quigley. Vol. 8. Toronto: ECW Press, 1989. In the "Gallant's Works" section, Grant concentrates on Gallant's short fiction as showing most successfully how Gallant's narrative technique and subject choices have evolved. A selected bibliography completes the essay.

Hancock, Geoff, ed. *Canadian Fiction Magazine* 28 (1978). This special issue, devoted to Gallant, is a thorough exploration of Gallant's works and personal concerns, containing interviews and essays by such major Canadian writers and critics as Robertson Davies and George Woodcock. Ending with an exhaustive bibliography, this issue is probably still the most useful Gallant compendium.

Hatch, Ronald. "Mavis Gallant and the Creation of Consciousness." In *The Canadian Novel*. Vol. 4 in *Present Tense: A Critical Anthology*, edited by John Moss. Toronto: NC Press, 1985. Hatch thoroughly discusses *Green Water, Green Sky, A Fairly Good Time*, and *The Pegnitz Junction*, exploring the thesis that storytelling is the vehicle through which Gallant's female characters define themselves.

Howells, Coral Ann. "Mavis Gallant: *Home Truths*." In *Private and Fictional Words: Canadian Women Novelists of the 1970's and 1980's*. London: Methuen, 1987. This chapter on Gallant's *Home Truths* is included in the context "Canadianness and women's fiction" that is Howells' central premise. Howells' impenetrable prose is a drawback, though her enthusiasm is unbounded. A bibliography of primary sources for each author discussed and an index are included.

Keefer, Janice Kulyk. *Reading Mavis Gallant*. Toronto: Oxford University Press, 1989. This timely book illuminates Gallant's concerns and grapples with the "problematic" aspects of much of her writing published between 1943 and 1988. Chapter notes and an index are included.

Twigg, Alan. "Mavis Gallant." In *Strong Voices: Conversations with Fifty Canadian Authors*. Madeira Park, British Columbia: Harbour, 1988. The nature of Canadians and Gallant's writing process are two major topics discussed in this lively 1981 interview with the expatriate Gallant.

JOHN GALSWORTHY

Born: Kingston Hill, England; August 14, 1867
Died: London, England; January 31, 1933

Principal long fiction

Jocelyn, 1898 (as John Sinjohn); *Villa Rubein*, 1900 (as John Sinjohn); *The Island Pharisees*, 1904; *The Man of Property*, 1906; *The Country House*, 1907; *Fraternity*, 1909; *The Patrician*, 1911; *The Dark Flower*, 1913; *The Little Man*, 1915; *The Freelands*, 1915; *Beyond*, 1917; *The Burning Spear*, 1919; *Saint's Progress*, 1919; *In Chancery*, 1920; *To Let*, 1921; *The Forsyte Saga*, 1922 (includes *The Man of Property*, "Indian Summer of a Forsyte," "Awakening," *In Chancery*, *To Let*); *The White Monkey*, 1924; *The Silver Spoon*, 1926; *Swan Song*, 1928; *A Modern Comedy*, 1929 (includes *The White Monkey, The Silver Spoon, Two Forsyte Interludes*, and *Swan Song*); *Maid in Waiting*, 1931; *Flowering Wilderness*, 1932; *Over the River*, 1933; *End of the Chapter*, 1934 (includes *Maid in Waiting, Flowering Wilderness*, and *Over the River*).

Other literary forms

John Galsworthy attempted and succeeded at writing in all major literary forms. His earlier short fiction is collected in *Caravan: The Assembled Tales of John Galsworthy* (1925); among the individual collections, some of the best known are *A Man of Devon* (1901), published under the pseudonym "John Sinjohn," *Five Tales* (1918), *Two Forsyte Interludes* (1927), and *On Forsyte 'Change* (1930). His plays made him, along with George Bernard Shaw, James M. Barrie, and Harley Granville-Barker, a leading figure in British drama during the early decades of the century. Galsworthy's most enduring plays include *The Silver Box* (1906), *Justice* (1910), *The Skin Game* (1920), and *Loyalties* (1922). Collections of Galsworthy's literary sketches and essays include *A Motley* (1910), *The Inn of Tranquility* (1912), and *Tatterdemalion* (1920). Galsworthy wrote poetry throughout his life, and the *Collected Poems of John Galsworthy* were published in 1934.

Achievements

Galsworthy was a writer who reaped the rewards of literary acclaim in his own time—and suffered the pangs that attend artists who prove truer to the tastes of the public than to an inner vision of personal potential. Galsworthy won the esteem of his countrymen with a play, *The Silver Box*, and a novel, *The Man of Property*, published in his *annus mirabilis*, 1906. From that time on, he was a major figure in the British literary establishment. Idealist, optimist, and activist, Galsworthy was a perennial champion of the underprivileged in his works. Women (especially unhappily married ones), children, prisoners, aliens, and animals (especially horses and dogs) engaged Galsworthy's sympathies. His literary indictments of the injustices forced upon these victims by an unfeeling society helped to arouse public support for his causes and frequently resulted in elimination of the abuses. After World War I, Galsworthy's crusading spirit was somewhat dampened. Despite his disillusionment, though, Galsworthy's conscience remained sensitive to inequities of all sorts.

Although popular as a writer of fiction and influential as a spokesman for humane, enlightened personal behavior and public policy, Galsworthy was not the sort of writer who changes the course of literature. His early works contain some powerful satire and some interesting experiments in probing and expressing his internal conflicts. By upbringing and inclination, however, Galsworthy was too "gentlemanly" to be comfortable with self-revelation or even with introspection. Thus, while the English novel was becoming increasingly psychological because of Joseph Conrad, Virginia Woolf, and D. H. Lawrence, Galsworthy continued in the nineteenth century tradition of Ivan Turgenev and Guy de Maupassant, carefully describing social phenomena and assessing their impact on private lives. Most of his characters are individualized representatives of particular social classes, whether the rural gentry, the aristocracy, the intelligentsia, or the London professional elite. He excelled at presenting the fashions, politics, manners, and phrases peculiar to certain milieus at certain times. In creating the Forsytes—and most notably Soames, "the man of property"—Galsworthy's talent transcended that of the memorialist or mere novelist of manners and provided England with a quintessential expression of the shrewd, rich, upright middle class of Victorian London, a group whose qualities subsequent generations found easy to mock, possible to admire, but difficult to love.

Biography

John Galsworthy, son and namesake of a solicitor, company director, and descendant of the Devonshire yeomanry, was born into the rich Victorian middle class he so accurately describes in *The Forsyte Saga*. His early years followed the prescribed pattern of that class. Having spent his childhood at a series of large, grand, ugly country houses outside of London, Galsworthy was graduated from Harrow School and New College, Oxford. Called to the bar in 1890, he commenced a languid practice of maritime law and traveled widely—to Canada, Australia, and the Far East. On returning to England, he committed an unpardonable breach of middle-class manners and morals: he openly became the lover, or more accurately husband *manqué*, of Ada, the unhappy wife of his cousin Major Galsworthy.

Having placed themselves beyond the pale, the lovers traveled abroad and in England and, with Ada's encouragement and assistance, Galsworthy began his literary career by writing books under the pen name "John Sinjohn." In 1905, after Ada's divorce, the Galsworthys were able to regularize their relationship, and, in 1906, public acclamation of *The Man of Property* and *The Silver Box* gave Galsworthy a secure place in the British literary establishment. Substantial resources permitted the Galsworthys to maintain London and country residences and to continue what was to be their lifelong habit of extensive traveling.

A kindly, courtly, almost hypersensitive person concerned throughout his life with altruistic ventures large and small, Galsworthy was distressed that his age and physical condition precluded active service in World War I. During these years, Galsworthy donated half or more of his large income to the war effort, wrote patriotic pieces, and for some time served as a masseur for the wounded at a hospital in France.

Friends observed that neither John nor Ada Galsworthy ever truly recovered from the war, and the last decade or so of Galsworthy's life was, beneath a smooth surface, not particularly happy. He had achieved all the trappings of success. Born rich, married to a woman he adored, he owned an elegant town house at Hampstead and an imposing country place at Bury, in Sussex. He was president of the International Association of Poets, Playwrights, Editors, Essayists and Novelists (PEN). The public honored him as a humanist and philanthropist, acknowledged him as one of the foremost British men of letters, and even—thanks to the nostalgic novels written during the 1920's which, along with *The Man of Property*, constitute *The Forsyte Saga* and its sequel *A Modern Comedy*—made him a best-selling author. Nevertheless, Galsworthy keenly felt that he had never made the most of his talent or fulfilled the promise of his early works.

Furthermore, though he was the sort of gentleman who found complaints and even unarticulated resentment "bad form," Galsworthy must have felt some unconscious hostility toward his wife, who, for all her devotion, was superficial, hypochondriacal, demanding, and possessive in the Forsyte way that Galsworthy found deplorable (at least in people other than Ada) and who, by obliging him to live life on her terms, was perhaps the principal force in the circumspection of his talents. He also felt anxious realizing that the intense, even claustrophobic bond of love that had joined him and Ada would eventually be severed by the death of one or the other. Ironically, in 1932, it became evident that the "stronger" of the two would not survive his "frail" companion. Galsworthy was stricken with an initially vague malaise that, though never satisfactorily diagnosed, was very likely a brain tumor. Galsworthy died at home in London on January 31, 1933, two months after having been awarded in absentia the Nobel Prize for Literature.

Analysis

John Galsworthy is one of those authors whose works are valued most highly by their contemporaries. Once placed in the first rank by such discriminating readers as Joseph Conrad, Edward Garnett, Gilbert Murray, and

E. V. Lucas (though Virginia Woolf despised him as a mere "materialist"), Galsworthy is now remembered as the workmanlike chronicler of the Forsyte family. Most of his other works are ignored. Changing fashions in literature do not suffice to explain this shift in critical esteem. Rather, the way Galsworthy chose to employ his talents—or the way his upbringing and personal situation obliged him to use them—guaranteed him the esteem of his peers but in large measure lost him the attention of posterity.

Galsworthy's literary strengths are impressive. His works are acutely observant and intensely sympathetic. In his novels, one finds carefully detailed presentations of the manners, codes, pastimes, and material surroundings of England's ruling classes as well as enlightened consideration of the diverse injustices these classes deliberately and inadvertently inflicted on those below them. Temperamentally inclined to support the "underdog"—whether an unhappily married woman, a poor workingman less honest than those in happier circumstances would like him to be, an ostracized German-born Londoner in wartime, or a badly treated horse—Galsworthy does not treat his characters as stereotypes of good or evil. Even when he is a partisan in one of the ethical dilemmas he presents (such as Soames Forsyte's sincerely enamoured but brutally proprietary attitude toward Irene, the woman who passively marries him but actively repents of that decision), he strives to show the mixture of good and bad, commendable and culpable, in all parties.

Galsworthy writes best when he deals with characters or situations from his own experience (for example, the various loves in *The Dark Flower*), comments on his own background or family history (as in the satirical group portrait of the Forsytes), or attempts to externalize the intricate course of motivations and ambivalences in his own mind (as does his study of Hilary Dallison, a prosperous writer suffering under the curse of "over-refinement," in *Fraternity*). Nevertheless, Galsworthy's reserve and stoicism, innate qualities further cultivated by his gentlemanly upbringing, made him increasingly unwilling to look within himself and write. His peripatetic existence and desire to grind out work for good causes must have made concentration on truly ambitious projects difficult. His wife's wishes and values, closer than he ever acknowledged to the more blighting aspects of Forsyteism, cut him off from many of the experiences and relationships that writers tend to find enriching. As a result, most of his carefully crafted literary works remain topical productions: he fails to confer suggestions of universality or living particularity on the social types and situations he describes, and thus, as novels of manners tend to do, his works seemed more profound and interesting to the age and society whose likenesses they reflect than they have to succeeding generations.

The first of the Forsyte novels, *The Man of Property*, is generally agreed to be Galsworthy's finest work, and the excellence of this book in great measure guaranteed that its less skillfully realized sequels and the peripheral Forsyte collections such as *Two Forsyte Interludes* and *On Forsyte 'Change* would attract and interest readers. If these social novels typify Galsworthy's achievement, two other works deserve mention, not for their continued popularity or complete artistic success but because they indicate the other avenues Galsworthy might have explored had he not directed his talent as he chose to do. *The Dark Flower*, one of Galsworthy's favorites among his works, displays his ability to handle emotional relationships; *Fraternity*, which he termed "more intimate than anything I've done . . . less *machinery* of story, less history, more life," is his most complex psychological study, a flawed but ambitious attempt at writing a "modern" novel.

In the spring of 1909, ensconced in the Devonshire countryside he loved, Galsworthy worked on the study of London life that would be *Fraternity*. The book's first title, however, was *Shadows*, a word that gives perhaps a clearer indication of the novel's ruling concern. In *Fraternity*, Galsworthy presents two adjacent but contrasting neighborhoods, elegant Campden Hill (where he and Ada then had their town residence) and disreputable Notting Hill Gate, and two sets of characters, the genteel, prosperous, enlightened Dallisons and their "shadows," the impoverished Hughs family.

Aware of the existence of their less fortunate brothers (Mrs. Hughs does household chores for Cecelia, wife of Stephen Dallison, and the Hughses' tenant models for Bianca, the artist wife of Hilary Dallison) and rationally convinced of the unity of mankind and the falseness of the divisions fostered by the class system, the Dallisons would like to take positive actions to help their "shadows" but find themselves unable to succeed at putting their theories into practice. Hilary in particular—like his creator Galsworthy a fortyish writer with a comfortable income and an uncomfortably sensitive conscience— is willing but unable to do some good. Discovering in one of many episodes of self-scrutiny that his benevolent intentions toward his wife's "little model" are far from disinterested and, worse yet, learning that the poor girl loves him, Hilary suffers a fit of repulsion. He is, as Catherine Dupre observes in *John Galsworthy: A Biography* (1976), "horrified by the prospect of any sort of union with someone whose difference of class and outlook would doom from the start their relationship." For Hilary and all the Dallisons, the common bond of shared humanity is ultimately less significant than the web of social life that separates the privileged from their "shadows," that permits observation without true empathy.

Galsworthy's friend Joseph Conrad was not alone in appraising *Fraternity* as "the book of a moralist." The great danger and difficulty of such a novel, Conrad argued to Galsworthy, is that its "negative method" of stressing a moral problem without prescribing a remedy leaves the reader dissatisfied: "It is impossible to read a book like that without asking oneself—what then?" In that sentence, Conrad characterizes a recurrent quality of Galsworthy's writing. Except in specific cases (and there were many of these—among them woman's suffrage, slaughterhouse reform, docking of horses' tails, vivisection, slum clearance, the condition of prisons, the state of zoos), Galsworthy tended to be a moralist without a gospel. His scrutiny of human behavior and social conditions detracted from the artistic success of his novels without providing anything but a sense of unease. Still, as Galsworthy explained to another critic of *Fraternity*, cultivating this awareness of moral problems is a step, albeit an oblique one, toward "sympathy between man and man."

The Dark Flower was one of Galsworthy's particular favorites among his novels. His professed intention in writing the book was to offer "a study (I hoped a true and a deep one) of Passion—that blind force which sweeps upon us out of the dark and turns us pretty well as it will." The book was taken by various readers, the most articulate among them being Sir Arthur Quiller-Couch, who reviewed it in *The Daily Mail*, as a case for free love, an assertion that commitment to a marriage should end when love ends. Interestingly, as Catherine Dupre suggests, the gist of *The Dark Flower* is something less general than either the authorial statement of purpose or the critical view would have it to be: it is an emotionally faithful representation of Galsworthy's own loves—most immediately, of his 1912 infatuation with a young actress and dancer named Margaret Morris.

The Dark Flower is divided into three parts, "Spring," "Summer," and "Autumn," each depicting a romantic experience in the life of the protagonist, Mark Lennan. Attracted to his tutor's wife in "Spring," the youthful Lennan is rejected and advised to find a woman of his own age. In "Summer," he meets and comes to love a beautiful, charming married woman, Olive Cramier, whose unyielding antipathy for the man to whom she has unwisely yoked herself obviously parallels Ada's revulsion for Major Galsworthy. Olive, the great love of Lennan's life, drowns; in "Autumn" he is happily but not passionately married to a wife of fifteen years, Sylvia, and infatuated with a lovely young girl, Nell. The middle-aged lover fondly hopes that he can retain Sylvia without giving up Nell. Like Ada in real life, Sylvia says she can be broad-minded but clearly demonstrates that she cannot. Lennan, like Galsworthy, accordingly sacrifices the more intense love for the long-standing one—in fact, his speeches and Nell's are, as Margaret Morris recalls in *My Galsworthy Story* (1967), accurate quotations of real-life dialogue. It is not surprising that having laid out his emotional autobiography, discreetly veiled though it may have been, and having been charged with promoting the sentimental and irresponsible sort of spiritual polygamy advocated by the very young Percy Bysshe Shelley, the reserved and dutiful Galsworthy was afterward reluctant to commit his deepest feelings to print.

The trilogy for which Galsworthy is principally known was launched with the publication of *The Man of Property* in 1906. Although Galsworthy thought at the time of continuing his satirical work and mentioned various possibilities in his letters to Conrad, not until 1917, when he returned to England from his stint of hospital service in France and began writing "The Indian Summer of a Forsyte," did Galsworthy resume the work that would be his magnum opus.

The Man of Property, the finest and fiercest of the Forsyte novels, combines portraiture of a whole gallery of Galsworthy's Victorian relations with a particular focus on one example of the tenacious Forsyte instinct for possession: Soames Forsyte's refusal to free his beautiful and intensely unhappy wife Irene from a marriage she sees as dead; Irene's affair with a "bohemian" (June Forsyte's fiancé Bosinney); and the grim but temporary victory of Soames over Irene, of Victorian convention over love. The triangular romance can be seen as symbolic or schematic—the two men, representing the possessive spirit and the creative temperament, both aspire in their different ways for Beauty—but it is also Galsworthy's thinly disguised account of Ada's tragic marriage with his cousin. The personal involvement results in what is least satisfactory about a fine book: Galsworthy's inability, despite an attempt to be philosophical, to moderate his extreme sympathy for Irene and his emotional if not rational assignment of total guilt to Soames, a man both sinned against and sinning.

The Man of Property begins with an "At Home" at the house of Old Jolyon, eldest of the Forsyte brothers and head of the family. At this gathering on June 15, 1886, a party honoring the engagement of old Jolyon's granddaughter June to the architect Philip Bosinney, the reader is privileged to observe "the highest efflorescence of the Forsytes." In the senior generation, the sons and daughters of "Superior Dosset" Forsyte, who had come from the country and founded the family's fortunes, are a variety of Victorian types, among them Aunt Ann, an ancient sybil tenaciously holding onto the life that remains to her; Jolyon, imperious and philosophical; Soames's father James, milder than Jolyon but even more single-minded in his devotion to the Forsyte principles of property and family; James's twin Swithin, an old pouter-pigeon of a bachelor whose hereditary prudence is tinged with antiquated dandyism; and Timothy, the youngest of the ten brothers and sisters and perhaps the Forsyte's Forsyte. He is a man whose caution and whose saving nature are so highly developed that he has retired early and placed all his resources in gilt-edged "Consols," retreating so successfully from the world's demands that even at his own house, the "Exchange," where Forsytes meet and gossip, his presence is felt more often than seen or heard.

The common bond that unites these superficially variegated characters and makes them representative of their whole class is described by young Jolyon, Galsworthy's mouthpiece in the novel: "A Forsyte takes a practical—one might say a common-sense—view of things, and a practical view of things is based fundamentally on a sense of property." The Forsytes, who know good things when they see them, who never give themselves or their possessions away, are the "better half" of England—the "cornerstones of convention."

The novel's principal demonstration of the Forsyte "sense of property" centers on the marriage of Soames, a prospering young solicitor, and the mysterious and lovely Irene. Troubled by his wife's chilly indifference to his strong and genuine love for her and the fine possessions which are his way of showing that feeling, Soames engages June's fiancé Bosinney to design and erect an impressive country house for him and Irene at Robin Hill, in the Surrey countryside outside of London. While building this house, a process which posits Bosinney's aesthetic scorn for base monetary matters against Soames's financial precision and passion for a bargain, the architect falls in love with Irene. She, seeing him as an emblem of all that her detested husband is not, reciprocates. The two of them betray their respective Forsytes and enter into a clandestine relationship.

These complicated circumstances pit Soames, determined to retain his property, against Irene, equally determined in her stubbornly passive way to be free of her enslaver. The outcome is tragedy. Bosinney, bankrupt because Soames has justly but vengefully sued him for overspending on the house, and crazed with jealousy and sorrow because Soames has forcibly exercised his conjugal rights, falls under a cab's wheels in a fog and is killed. As the novel ends, the errant Irene has returned to her prison-home, not out of inclination but because like a "bird that is shot and dying" she has nowhere else to fall. Young Jolyon, arriving with a message from his father, has one glimpse into the well-furnished hell that is Soames and Irene's abode before Soames slams the door shut in his face.

Galsworthy's friends and literary advisers Edward and Constance Garnett felt that this ending was unsuitable and wished for the telling defeat of Forsyteism that would be afforded by Irene and Bosinney succeeding in an elopement. Galsworthy, with better instincts, stuck to his "negative method" as a stronger means of arousing public feeling against the possessive passion he attacked. Still, if the crushing forces of property were allowed a victory, albeit a comfortless one, at the novel's end, Soames's triumph was to prove short-lived, though contemporary readers would have to wait eleven years to make the discovery. In "Indian Summer of a Forsyte," Old Jolyon, who has bought Robin Hill from Soames and lives there with his son and grandchildren, encounters Irene, now living on her own, and makes her a bequest that enables her to enjoy a comfortable independence.

In Chancery continues the conflict between the two hostile branches of the Forsyte clan. Soames, who feels the need of a child and heir to his property, is still in love with Irene and hopeful of regaining her. Young Jolyon, made Irene's trustee by his father's will, opposes Soames in his efforts and finds himself attracted by more than sympathy for the lovely, lonely woman. At length, Soames's persistent importunities drive Irene to elope with Jolyon. The infidelity gives Soames grounds for a divorce. Freed at last from any connection with the man she loathes, Irene marries Jolyon. Soames in his turn makes a convenient match with a pretty young Frenchwoman, Annette.

The novel ends with the birth of children to both couples.

To Let, the final volume of the trilogy, brings the family feud to a new generation. Fleur, daughter of Annette and Soames, and Jon, son of Irene and Jolyon, meet first by chance, then, mutually infatuated, by strategy. The cousins intend to marry but are dramatically separated by the dead hand of the past enmity. Jon goes off to America, where after some years he marries a Southern girl. Fleur, as passionately proprietary in her feeling for Jon as her father was toward Irene, believes that she has lost her bid for love and settles for a milder sort of happiness. She accepts the proposal of Michael Mont, the amiable, humorous, eminently civilized heir to a baronetcy.

The second Forsyte trilogy, *A Modern Comedy* (consisting of *The White Monkey, The Silver Spoon,* and *Swan Song*) centers on the adventures of the fashionable young Monts—Michael's stints in publishing and politics, Fleur's career as society hostess, femme fatale to a promising poet, canteen-keeper during the General Strike, mother, and most of all spoiled daughter to a fond yet wise father. In his love for his child, old Soames proves as selfless and giving as young Soames was possessive in his passion for Irene. Some twenty years after introducing Soames to the world, Galsworthy had come to admire, and at moments even to like, aspects of this gruff, practical, scrupulous incarnation of the possessive instinct, a character who as the years passed had usurped the place of Irene in the artist's imagination. Soames's death at the end of *Swan Song*—he succumbs to a blow on the head inflicted by a falling painting from which he saves Fleur—is at once an ironically appropriate end to the career of a man of property and a noble gesture of self-sacrifice.

When Galsworthy chose to terminate the life of Soames Forsyte, he symbolically presented the close of an age but also implicitly acknowledged the end of what was finest in his own literary career. However wide-ranging his talent might have been if possessed by another man, his personal temperament, training, and circumstances constrained it to a certain limited excellence. Galsworthy the artist was at his best depicting conflicts typical of the Victorian period, that consummate age of property, and relevant to his own life: the contradictory urges of artistic integrity and worldly wisdom, the foolish desire to possess beauty at war with the wise inclination to contemplate and appreciate it, the altruistic motto "do good" contending with the sanely middle-class imperative "be comfortable." Because he knew the overfurnished Victorian and post-Victorian world of the Forsytes and their kind from the inside, Galsworthy's best moral fables are credibly human as well, but when the old order he comprehended if never endorsed gave way to a new and unfathomable one, the novelist of principle dwindled to a kind of literary curator.

Peter W. Graham

Other major works

SHORT FICTION: *From the Four Winds*, 1897 (as John Sinjohn); *A Man of Devon*, 1901 (as John Sinjohn); *Five Tales*, 1918; *Captures*, 1923; *Caravan: The Assembled Tales of John Galsworthy*, 1925; *Two Forsyte Interludes*, 1927; *On Forsyte 'Change*, 1930; *Soames and the Flag*, 1930.

PLAYS: *The Silver Box*, 1906; *Joy*, 1907; *Strife*, 1909; *Justice*, 1910; *The Little Dream*, 1911; *The Eldest Son*, 1912; *The Pigeon*, 1912; *The Fugitive*, 1913; *The Mob*, 1915; *A Bit o'Love*, 1915; *The Little Man*, 1915; *The Foundations*, 1917; *Defeat*, 1920; *The Skin Game*, 1920; *A Family Man*, 1921; *The First and the Last*, 1921; *Hall-marked*, 1921; *Punch and Go*, 1921; *The Sun*, 1921; *Loyalties*, 1922; *Windows*, 1922; *The Forest*, 1924; *Old English*, 1924; *The Show*, 1925; *Escape*, 1926; *Exiled*, 1929; *The Roof*, 1929.

POETRY: *The Collected Poems of John Galsworthy*, 1934.

NONFICTION: *A Commentary*, 1908; *A Motley*, 1910; *The Inn of Tranquility*, 1912; *A Sheaf*, 1916; *Another Sheaf*, 1919; *Tatterdemalion*, 1920; *Castles in Spain*, 1927; *Candelabra*, 1932; *Letters from John Galsworthy, 1900-1932*, 1934 (Edward Garnett, editor).

MISCELLANEOUS: *The Works of John Galsworthy*, 1922-1936 (30 volumes).

Bibliography

Barker, Dudley. *The Man of Principle: A Biography of John Galsworthy*. New York: Stein & Day, 1969. Although not "scholarly" in the sense of being well documented, a well-written and objective account of Galsworthy's life and, to a lesser extent, of his literary work. Barker does discuss the writing of the works and the critical response to them, but his own brief, impressionistic responses to the literature are not particularly helpful. Includes a very abbreviated bibliography and an index.

Batchelor, John. *The Edwardian Novelists*. New York: St. Martin's Press, 1982. Begins by defining "Edwardian" literature and discusses Galsworthy in terms of his surprising similarities to D. H. Lawrence. *The Man of Property* and *Fraternity* are analyzed in detail, and the overall attitude toward Galsworthy is very positive. Contains an excellent bibliography of Edwardian fiction.

Dupre, Catherine. *John Galsworthy: A Biography*. New York: Coward, McCann & Geoghegan, 1976. A well-written and well-researched account of Galsworthy's life, relying heavily on letters and other primary sources. Also contains information about the writing of his literary works. Provides an excellent index, bibliographic notes, and several photographs.

Gindin, James. *John Galsworthy's Life and Art*. Ann Arbor: University of Michigan Press, 1987. Utilizing new sources, Gindin has written a masterful literary biography, particularly appropriate since Galsworthy's fiction is itself so closely tied to his personal life, social criticism, and historic times. Galsworthy moved from apprenticeship to being a "public edifice," but that image was tarnished and he became a "private edifice." This well-researched biography succeeds in relating Galsworthy's literary work to his life.

Mottram, Ralph H. *For Some We Loved: An Intimate Portrait of Ada and John Galsworthy.* London: Hutchinson University Library, 1956. This informal, undocumented account of Galsworthy's life, written by a personal friend of his, is anecdotal and laudatory. Mottram's focus is biographical, not critical, and he devotes little attention to Galsworthy's literary work. Contains a serviceable index.

Sternlicht, Sanford. *John Galsworthy.* Boston: Twayne, 1987. The most helpful critical volume on Galsworthy's literary and dramatic works despite being relatively brief. Four chapters are devoted to his novels, some of which, notably *A Modern Comedy*, are analyzed in some depth. His short stories, plays, and literary criticism are the subjects of three additional chapters. Provides a chronology, a biographical chapter, an excellent bibliography, including annotated secondary sources, and a helpful index.

JOHN GARDNER

Born: Batavia, New York; July 21, 1933
Died: Susquehanna, Pennsylvania; September 14, 1982

Principal long fiction

The Resurrection, 1966; *The Wreckage of Agathon*, 1970; *Grendel*, 1971; *The Sunlight Dialogues*, 1972; *Nickel Mountain: A Pastoral Novel*, 1973; *October Light*, 1976; *In the Suicide Mountains*, 1977; *Freddy's Book*, 1980; *Mickelsson's Ghosts*, 1982; *"Stillness" and "Shadows,"* 1986 (with Nicholas Delbanco).

Other literary forms

As a writer, John Gardner was as versatile as he was prolific. In addition to his novels, he published an epic poem (*Jason and Medeia*, 1973), two collections of short stories, four books for children, poetry, and reviews. During the early 1960's, when Gardner was a struggling assistant professor with a growing backlog of unpublished fiction and rejection slips, he turned to more academic pursuits. While some of this work is distinctly scholarly in nature, much of it is directed at a less specialized audience and is designed to make the literature more accessible and more understandable to the general reader or undergraduate student: thus Gardner's translations, or modernized versions, of medieval poetry, a textbook-anthology of fiction, a popular biography of Geoffrey Chaucer, his controversial attack on the contemporary arts and criticism, *On Moral Fiction* (published in 1978 but, like his Chaucer books, begun more than ten years earlier), and two books of advice for young writers, *On Becoming a Novelist* (1983) and *The Art of Fiction* (1984). Gardner also wrote a number of plays for National Public Radio's "Earplay" series and several opera librettos (one of which, *Rumpelstiltskin*, 1979, was professionally staged by the Opera Company of Philadelphia).

Achievements

At a time when the line between popular and innovative fiction is often considered, in critic Raymond Federman's word, "uncrossable," Gardner managed to make his mark in both camps. Although his first novel, *The Resurrection*, was indifferently received, his second, *The Wreckage of Agathon*, which deals with law and order in ancient Sparta, gained a small following as a result of its relevance to Vietnam and the Nixon Administration. *Grendel*, a parodic retelling of *Beowulf* (c. 1000) from the monster's point of view, was widely praised and in its paperback edition became *The Catcher in the Rye* (J. D. Salinger, 1951) of the early 1970's. Its success established Gardner's reputation as both an entertaining storyteller and an innovative parodist, a view that was confirmed by the publication of *The King's Indian:*

Stories and Tales in 1974. His next three novels all became best-sellers: *The Sunlight Dialogues*, *Nickel Mountain*, and *October Light*, which won the 1977 National Book Critics Circle award for fiction. Among his other awards and honors were a Woodrow Wilson fellowship (1955), a Danforth fellowship (1970-1973), an award from the National Endowment for the Arts (1972), a Guggenheim fellowship (1973-1974), an American Academy of Arts and Letters prize for fiction (1975), the Armstrong Prize for his radio play, *The Temptation Game* (1977), and the 1978 Lamport Foundation award for his essay "Moral Fiction."

Upon the publication of the full text of *On Moral Fiction* in 1978, Gardner became a center of literary attention. His plainspoken criticism of fashionable pessimism in the contemporary arts and his generally negative remarks concerning individual writers led to an appearance on the *Dick Cavett Show* in May, 1978, a cover story in *The New York Times Magazine* in August, 1979, a special issue of the journal *fiction international* devoted to the question of "moral" art, as well as the censure of those who saw Gardner as a reactionary and the praise of others who quickly adopted him as a spokesman for a more traditional approach to fiction.

Biography

John Champlin Gardner, Jr., was born on July 21, 1933, in the western New York community of Batavia, the setting of *The Resurrection*, *The Sunlight Dialogues*, and a number of short stories. Strongly influenced by his father, a farmer and lay preacher, and his mother, an English teacher, Gardner, nicknamed Bud (Welsh for poet), began writing stories when he was eight years old and reading his work aloud to the family in the evening. The death of his younger brother, Gilbert, in a farm accident on April 4, 1945, seems to have been the most formative event in Gardner's life. He felt responsible for his brother's death, which he has fictionalized in the story "Redemption" (1977), and as a result became deeply introspective. His mother has suggested that Gilbert's death may also account for her son's remarkable energy and productivity, as if he wished to live both his own life and his brother's. During his high school years, Gardner commuted to the Eastman School of Music in nearby Rochester where he took French horn lessons. He attended DePauw University for two years, majoring in chemistry, and then, following his marriage to Joan Patterson, a cousin, on June 6, 1953, transferred to Washington University where, under the tutelage of Jarvis Thurston, he began writing *Nickel Mountain*. From 1955 to 1958 Gardner attended the University of Iowa; at first he studied at the Writers Workshop (his M.A. thesis and Ph.D. dissertation were both creative rather than scholarly: one a collection of stories, the other a novel, "The Old Men") but later switched to the study of Anglo-Saxon and medieval literature under the guidance of John C. McGalliard.

Following his study at Iowa, Gardner held faculty appointments at various colleges and universities: Oberlin College (1958-1959); Chico State (1959-1962), where he coedited *MSS* and the student literary review *Selection*; San Francisco State, where he translated the alliterative *Morte d'Arthure* and the works of the Gawain-poet and began writing *The Resurrection*, *The Sunlight Dialogues*, and a study of Chaucer; Southern Illinois University (1965-1976), including visiting professorships at the University of Detroit (1970), Northwestern University (1973), and Bennington College (1975-1976), a sabbatical in England (1971), and a month-long tour of Japan for the United States Information Service (September-October 1974); Skidmore and Williams Colleges (1977); George Mason University (1977-1978); and, from 1978 until his death, the State University of New York at Binghamton, where he directed the writing program. Especially significant in Gardner's biography is the period from 1976 through 1978, when *October Light* won popular and critical acclaim. During that time, Gardner lectured on moral fiction at campuses across the country, and his opera *Rumpelstiltskin* premiered in Lexington, Kentucky. Then Gardner's life took a darker turn: the breakup of his first marriage; a plagiarism charge leveled against him for his Chaucer biography, a charge that for some reason made its way into the pages of *Newsweek* magazine; an operation (successful) for intestinal cancer; and the uproar over *On Moral Fiction*, as well as the often hostile reviews of *Freddy's Book* and *Mickelsson's Ghosts*. Until their amiable divorce in 1982, Gardner lived with his second wife, the poet L. M. (Liz) Rosenberg in Susquehanna, Pennsylvania, where he became active in the Laurel Street Theatre both as an actor and as a writer. He died in a motorcycle accident on September 14, 1982, a few days before he was to marry Susan Thornton of Rochester, New York. At the time of his death, Gardner had been working (as was his habit) on a variety of projects: operas, radio plays, a revival of his literary journal *MSS*, a television talk show on the arts, two books of advice for young writers (*On Becoming a Novelist* and *The Art of Fiction*), a translation of *Gilgamesh* (a poem which figures prominently in *The Sunlight Dialogues*), and the novel *Shadows*.

Analysis

John Gardner is a difficult writer to classify. He was alternately a realist and a fabulist, a novelist of ideas and a writer who maintained that characters and human situations are always more important than philosophy. He was, as well, an academically inclined new-fictionist whose work is formally innovative, stylistically extravagant, openly parodic, and highly allusive; yet, at the same time, he was an accessible, popular storyteller, one who some critics, in the wake of *On Moral Fiction*, have labeled a reactionary traditionalist. It is perhaps best to think of Gardner not as a writer who belongs to any one school but instead as a writer who, in terms of style, subject, and moral vision, mediates between the various extremes of innovation and tradition, freedom and order, individual and society. He employed the metafictionist's narrative tricks, for example, not to show that fiction—and, by extension, life—is mere artifice, meaningless play, but to put those tricks to some higher purpose. His fiction raises a familiar but still urgent question: How is man to act in a seemingly inhospitable world where chance and uncertainty appear to have rendered all traditional values worthless?

As different as his characters are in most outward aspects, they are similar in one important way: they are idealists who feel betrayed when their inherited vision of harmony and purpose crumbles beneath the weight of modern incoherence. Once betrayed, they abandon their childlike ideals and embrace the existentialist position that Gardner deplores for its rationalist assumptions and pessimistic moral relativism. His antidote to the modern malaise in general and Jean-Paul Sartre's "nausea" in particular is a twentieth century version of the heroic ideal: common heroes—fathers and husbands, farmers and professors, for example—who intuitively understand that whatever the odds against them, they must act as if they can protect those whom they love. Instead of pure and powerful knights dedicated to a holy quest, Gardner's heroes are confused, sometimes ridiculous figures who learn to overcome their feelings of betrayal and find their strength in love, memory, and forgiveness. Choosing to act responsibly, they achieve a certain measure of human dignity. In effect, the choice these characters face is a simple one: either to affirm "the buzzing blooming confusion" of life, as Gardner, quoting William James, calls it, or to deny it. Whereas the existentialist finds in that confusion meaningless abundance and historical discontinuity, Gardner posits meaningful variety and an interconnectedness that assumes value and makes the individual a part of, not apart from, the human and natural worlds in which he lives.

To find, or imagine, these connections is the role Gardner assigns to the artist. This view, propounded at length in *On Moral Fiction*, clearly puts Gardner at odds with other contemporary writers of innovative fiction who, he claims, too readily and uncritically accept the views of Sartre, Sigmund Freud, Ludwig Wittgenstein, and other twentieth century pessimists. Art, Gardner maintains, ought not merely to reflect life as it is but also should portray life as it should be. This does not mean that Gardner approves of simple-minded affirmations, for he carefully distinguishes "true" artists from those who simplify complex moral issues, as well as from those who, like William Gass, sidestep such issues entirely by creating "linguistic sculpture" in which only the "surface texture" is important.

Believing that art does indeed affect life and accepting Percy Bysshe Shelley's conception of the artist as legislator for all mankind, Gardner calls for a moral fiction that provides "valid models for imitation, eternal verities worth keeping in mind, and a benevolent vision of the possible" which will cause the reader to feel uneasy about his failings and limitations and stimulate him to act virtuously. Moral fiction, however, is not didactic; rather, it involves a search for truth. The author "gropes" for meaning in the act of writing and revising his story; then, by creating suspense, he devises for the reader a parallel experience. The meaning that author and reader discover in Gardner's work emphasizes the importance of rejecting existential isolation and accepting one's place in the human community, the "common herd" as Gardner calls it in one story. This meaning is not so much rational and intellectual as intuitive and emotional, less a specific message than a feeling—as is entirely appropriate in the case of a writer who defines fiction as "an enormously complex language."

Despite their very different settings—modern Batavia, New York, and ancient Sparta—Gardner's first two published novels, *The Resurrection* and *The Wreckage of Agathon*, share a number of common features—main characters who are professional philosophers, for example—and also share one common fault: both are overrich in the sense that they include too many undeveloped points which seem to lead nowhere and only tend to clutter the narrative.

The Resurrection is a fairly straightforward, realistic novel about the ways in which its main character, James Chandler, confronts the fact of death. His disease, leukemia, involves the mindless proliferation of lymph cells and so reflects the universe itself, which may be, as Chandler speculates, similarly chaotic and purposeless. Philosophy does not at first provide Chandler with a Boethian consolation because he, as a distinctly modern man, suspects that philosophy may be nothing more than a meaningless technique, a self-enclosed game. The novel thus raises the question of the purpose of philosophy, art, literature, and even medicine. Chandler's mother knows that the job of philosophers is to help people like her understand what their experiences and their world mean. Meaning, however, is precisely what contemporary philosophy generally denies and what Chandler wisely struggles to find. His breakthrough occurs when he realizes Immanuel Kant's fundamental error, the failure to see that moral and aesthetic affirmations are interconnected and need not—or should not—necessitate that the individual who makes the affirmation be entirely disinterested; that is, the affirmation may have—or should have—some practical application, some usefulness.

Sharing this knowledge becomes rather difficult for Chandler. His sympathetic and loving wife Marie is too practical-minded to understand him. Nineteen-year-old Viola Stacey, who, torn between cynicism and her childlike "hunger for absolute goodness," falls in love with Chandler, misinterprets his writing as an escape from reality precipitated by his intense physical suffering. More interesting is John Horne, who, like Chandler, is a terminal patient. According to Horne, a believer in legal technique, love is illusion and man a clown who acts but has no reason for acting the way he does. Like Viola, he assumes that art is an escape from life, or an "atonement" for one's failures and mistakes. Although he is interested in philosophy and acquainted with Chandler's published works, his endless prattling precludes Chandler's sharing the discovery with him. Yet Chandler does finally, if indirectly, communicate his vision. By putting it to some practical use (he dies trying to help Viola), Chandler finds what Horne never does: something or someone worth dying for, some vision worth affirming. "It was not the beauty of the world one must affirm," he suddenly understands, "but *the world*, the buzzing blooming confusion itself." Understanding that life is what drives man to art and philosophy, to fashion a life for himself and others that is ennobling and useful (realistically idealistic, Gardner seems to suggest), Chandler fights down his physical and philosophical nausea. His vision worth perpetuating, he lives on—is resurrected—in the memories of those whom he loved, and thus for whom he died.

Early in *The Resurrection*, Gardner quotes the British philosopher R. G. Collingwood: "history is a process . . . in which the things that are destroyed are brought into existence. Only it is easier to see their destruction than to see their construction, because it does not take long." Like Gardner, James Chandler affirms Collingwood's optimistic position, a position which the title character of *The Wreckage of Agathon* unwisely rejects. Insofar as he stands in opposition to the law-and-order society established in Sparta by the tyrant Lykourgus, the seer Agathon is an appealing figure. No system built solely upon reason, least of all one so inflexible as Sparta's, is adequate to the variety and complexity of life, Gardner implies, but this does not mean that the only alternative is the nihilism espoused by Agathon, who had "spent so much time seeing through men's lies he'd forgotten what plain truth looked like." Having once been a lover of truth and beauty, Agathon ("the good") now mocks them; choosing to embody "the absolute idea of *No*," he is the one who sees the wreckage that was, is, and will be, the one who dismisses all art and ideals as mere illusions.

Whereas Chandler learns to put his philosophy to some use, Agathon comes to value his ideas more highly than people. Unlike Chandler, who eventually accepts death, mutability, and human limitations and in this way transcends them, Agathon refuses to see wreckage as being part of life; for him it is the ultimate fact. The cause of Agathon's pessimism is not cosmic but personal; it is the result of his repeated betrayals of his friends, his wife, and lover. This is the knowledge that haunts Agathon, however much he tries to hide it behind his leering clown's mask, leading him to believe that to be alive is necessarily to be a threat to others. Although he dies of the plague, Agathon's real sickness is of the soul: the inability to believe in love and human dignity as actual possibilities. That they are real is clearly shown in the characters of his friend Dorkis, leader of the helot revolt, and his young disciple Demodokos, whose prison journal alternates with Agathon's (together they make up Gardner's novel). Demodokos, the "Peeker" to Agathon's "Seer," represents that childlike faith and goodness of heart which the disillusioned Seer has renounced. Patient, understanding (if not completely comprehending), and above all committed to others, the Peeker is the one who, for all his naïveté, or perhaps because of it, serves as Gardner's hero.

Agathon reappears in Gardner's next novel as the perversely likable narrator of *Grendel*, a retelling of *Beowulf* from the monster's distinctly modern point of view. In his 1970 essay, "Fulgentius's *Expositio Vergiliana Continentia*," Gardner argues that the *Beowulf*-poet used his three monsters as perversions of those virtues affirmed by Vergil in the *Aeneid* (c. 29-19 B.C.): valor, wisdom, and goodness (the proper use of things). Specifically, Grendel represents perverted wisdom; in Gardner's novel, he is the one who mistakenly chooses to believe in what he rationally knows and to reject what he intuitively feels. In both the epic and the novel, Grendel is an isoalato, a cosmic outlaw, but Gardner's monster is less a hulking beast than a shaggy Holden Caulfield (*The Catcher in the Rye*), a disillusioned and therefore cynical adolescent. Not simply a creature cursed by God, he is a detached Sartrean observer, a relativist for whom "balance" can be both "everything" and "nothing," and a comic ironist trapped within his own mocking point of view. For him the world is a meaningless accident, "wreckage." Although he finds the indignity of the men he observes humorous, he is less tolerant of the factitious patterns they use to make sense of their existence.

Grendel makes his chief mistake when, having become dissatisfied with what is, he goes to the Dragon for advice and guidance. The Dragon is a bored and weary existentialist who espouses the philosophy of Sartre's *Being and Nothingness* (1943). He tells the confused and terrified Grendel that values are merely things, all of which are worthless, and counsels fatalistic passivity in the face of a fragmented, purposeless world. Although Grendel becomes infected by the Dragon's nihilism, he still feels attracted to King Hrothgar's court poet, the Shaper, whose songs he believes are lies. Unlike the Dragon, who is the ultimate realist and materialist, the Shaper is a visionary who sings of the "projected possible" and an alchemist who transforms the base ore of barbarism into the gold of civilization. His songs bespeak hopefulness and, by means of what the Dragon scornfully terms the "gluey whine of connectedness," a dream of order. Moreover, his singing works: the Shaper's words first envision Hrothgar's splendid meadhall and then inspire the men to build it.

Grendel's ambivalence toward the Shaper also marks his attitude toward Wealtheow, the wife bestowed on Hrothgar by her brother in order to save his tribe from the king's army. Whereas Grendel gloats over man's indignity, Wealtheow, whose name means "holy servant of the common good," has the power to absolve it. She brings to Hrothgar's kingdom the illusion of timeless peace, an illusion that, like the Shaper's words, works. Although her "monstrous trick against reason" enrages Grendel, he too is affected by it, temporarily discontinuing his attacks and choosing not to commit "the ultimate act of nihilism," murdering the queen.

The Shaper (art), the queen (peace and love), and the hero Beowulf represent those values "beyond what's possible" that make human existence worthwhile. Interestingly, Gardner's Beowulf is, like Grendel, an isolato, and, in his fight with the monster, appears as a dragon—not Grendel's adviser but the celestial dragon that figures chiefly in Oriental religions. Where Grendel sees accident and waste, the hero finds purpose and regeneration. During their struggle, Beowulf forces Grendel to "sing walls," that is, to forgo his mocking cynicism and to take on the role of Shaper, the one who by his art shapes reality (what is) into an illusion or vision of what can or should be. Thus, Grendel is not simply defeated; he is transformed—his death a ritual dismemberment, a symbolic initiation and rebirth.

Although the novel affirms the heroic ideal, it nevertheless acknowledges the tragic view that informs its Anglo-Saxon source. The meadhall the Shaper sings into existence, to which the queen brings peace, and that Beowulf saves, is a symbol of what virtuous man can achieve, but it is also tangible evidence that art, love, and heroic action can defeat chaos for a time only and that, finally, the Dragon is right: "Things fade." Against this tragic awareness, to which the Dragon and Grendel passively acquiesce, Gardner posits the creative possibilities of human endeavor, especially art. It is, after all, as much the action (plot) of *Beowulf* as Beowulf's heroic act that defeats Gardner's Grendel and the monstrous values he represents. Gardner's alternative to Grendel's mindless universe and brute mechanics is implied in the novel's very structure. Its twelve chapters suggest not only Grendel's twelve-year war against Hrothgar and the twelve books of literary epics, but, as well, the symbol of universal harmony, the zodiac (each chapter of the novel is keyed to an astrological sign). *Grendel*, therefore, is not a postmodern parody of *Beowulf*; rather, it is a work in which parody is used to test the values presented in *Beowulf* (and its other sources: William Shakespeare, William Blake, John Milton, Samuel Beckett, Georges Sorel, Sartre, and others) to discover their usefulness in the modern world.

Like *Grendel*, *The Sunlight Dialogues* (which was written earlier) depends in part on Gardner's skillful interlacing of his literary sources: *Gilgamesh*, Sir Thomas Malory's *Le Morte d'Arthure* (1485), Dante, Herman Melville's *Moby Dick* (1851), William Faulkner, and A. Leo Oppenheim's *Ancient Mesopotamia: Portrait of a Dead Civilization* (1977). It appears to be, at first glance, part family chronicle, part mystery story, but beneath the surface realism, the reader finds elements of fantasy and myth. By an elaborate system of plots and subplots, each echoing the others, Gardner weaves together his eighty-odd characters into a densely textured whole that contrasts with his characters' sense of social and spiritual fragmentation. The main characters appear as isolatos—the marked children of Cain—and as prisoners trapped in cells of their own making. Some blindly strike out for absolute personal freedom (Millie Hodge, for example) while others passively accept the small measure of freedom to be had in the cage of their limitations (Millie's ex-husband, Will Hodge, Sr.). As adults living in a world "decayed to ambiguity," they are like one character's young daughter whose toys frustrate her "to tears of wrath." Their frustration leads not to tantrums but to cynical denial of all hope, all ideals, and all connections between self and other.

The modern condition is illustrated in the fate of the Hodge clan. Just as their farm, Stony Hill, is said to symbolize "virtues no longer found," the late Congressman represents the unity and sense of idealistic purpose missing in the Batavia of 1966. His qualities now appear in fragmented and diluted form in his five children: Will, Sr., a lawyer and toggler who can repair but not build; Ben, the weak-willed visionary; Art, Jr., the tinkerer; Ruth, the organizer; and Taggert, who inherits his father's genius, purity of heart, and pride, but not his luck. The failure of the Congressman's harmonious vision leads to the moral relativism of the Sunlight Man on the one hand and the reductive law-and-order morality of Batavia's Chief of Police, Fred Clumly, on the other.

The Sunlight Man is the Congressman's youngest child, the angelic Tag, transmogrified by misfortune into a forty-year-old devil. Badly disfigured by the fire that kills his two sons, he returns to his hometown in the shape of a Melvillean monomaniac. Having searched for love and truth but having found only betrayal and illusion, he claims that love and truth do not exist; having failed to heal his psychotic wife or protect his sons, he proclaims all actions absurd. His magic tricks are cynical jokes intended to expose all meanings as self-delusions. His four dialogues with the police chief serve the same purpose: to disillusion Clumly, representative of the Judaeo-Christian culture. Taking the Babylonian position, the Sunlight Man propounds the complete separation of spirit and matter, the feebleness and inconsequentiality of the individual human life, and the futility of the desire for fame and immortality. Personal responsibility, he says, means nothing more than remaining free to act out one's fated part. Although his dialogues are in fact monologues, it is significant that the Sunlight Man feels it necessary to make any gesture at all toward Clumly and that he finds some relief once he has made it. Similarly, his magic not only evidences his nihilism, but also serves to mask the fact that despite his monstrous appearance and philosophy, he is still human enough—vulnerable enough—to feel the need for fellowship and love.

It is this need that Clumly eventually comes to understand. Powerless to stop either the local or the national epidemic of senseless crimes and bewildered by a world that appears to be changing for the worse, the sixty-four-year-old police chief at first seizes upon the Sunlight Man as the embodiment of evil in the modern world. Slowly the molelike, ever-hungry Clumly abandons this Manichaean notion and begins to search for the complicated truth. Clumly strikes through the pasteboard mask and, unlike Melville's Ahab, or the Sunlight Man who is made in his image, finds not the abyss but Taggert Hodge.

Throughout the novel, Clumly feels a strong sense of personal responsibility for his town and all its citizens, but, at the same time, he finds no clear answer to his repeated question, "What's a man to do?" He understands that there is something wrong with the Sunlight Man's philosophy but is not able to articulate what it is; he realizes that in separating the world into actual and ideal, the Sunlight Man has limited the choices too narrowly, but he has no idea what the other choices might be. The conflict between head and heart affects Clumly profoundly and eventually costs him his job. Only at this point can he meet Taggert Hodge as "Fred Clumly, merely mortal." In the novel's final chapter, Clumly, speaking before a local audience, abandons the text of his hackneyed speech on "Law and Order" and delivers instead an impromptu and inspired sermon, or eulogy (Taggert having been killed by a policeman) that transforms the Sunlight Man into "one of our number." Ascending to a healing vision of pure sunlight, Clumly, "shocked to wisdom," spreads the gospel according to Gardner: man must try to do the best he possibly can; "that's the whole thing."

Although not published until 1973, *Nickel Mountain* was begun nearly twenty years earlier while Gardner was an undergraduate at Washington University. That parts of the novel originally appeared as self-contained short stories is evident in the work's episodic structure and unnecessary repetition of background material. Still, *Nickel Mountain* is one of Gardner's finest achievements, especially in the handling of characters and setting.

The novel's chief figure is the enormously fat, middle-aged bachelor Henry Soames, owner of a diner somewhere in the Catskill Mountains. Alternately sentimental and violent, Henry is a kind of inarticulate poet or priest whose hunger is not for the food he eats but for the love he has never experienced. Similarly, his Stop Off is less a run-down diner than a communal meeting place, a church where the light ("altar lamp") is always on and misfits are always welcome. Willard Freund and Callie Wells, for example, see in Henry the loving father neither has had. Longing to escape their loveless families and fulfill their adolescent dreams, they find shelter at the diner. Willard, however, chooses to follow his father's advice rather than act responsibly toward Callie, whom he has impregnated—a choice that, perversely, confirms Willard in his cynicism and colors his view of human nature. Betrayal comes early to sixteen-year-old Callie (Calliope: the muse of epic poetry) and, as with Willard, leaves its mark. When Henry fumblingly proposes marriage, she interprets her acceptance as an entirely selfish choice. Gardner's description of the wedding, however, shows that, whatever Callie's motivation, the ceremony serves as a communal celebration of those values she and

Henry unconsciously affirm and Willard mistakenly denies.

Henry's charity looms as large in the novel as his bulk and seems to extend to everyone but himself. When Simon Bale, a belligerently self-righteous Jehovah's Witness, loses his wife and his home, Henry naturally takes him in, but when Henry accidentally causes Bale to fall to his death, he turns suicidal. Henry's suicide-attempt takes a rather comical form—overeating—but his predicament is nevertheless serious. To accept Simon Bale's death as an accident, Henry believes, would be to admit that chance governs the universe and to forfeit all possibility of human dignity. This either/or approach precludes Henry's understanding of one fundamental point: that man is neither hero nor clown, savior nor devil, but a mixture of both; the best he can do is to hope and to act on the strength of that hope.

Henry's friend George Loomis understands Henry's predicament and understands too the flaw in his reasoning, but George is unable to act on this knowledge when he accidentally kills the Goat Lady. As foul-smelling as her goats and even more comically grotesque in appearance than Henry Soames, the Goat Lady passes through the area on her pilgrim's progress in search of her son, Buddy Blatt. Because the drought-stricken farmers turn this mindless creature into a symbol of hopefulness, George's lie—that he knows she is still alive and searching—keeps their illusion and hopes alive; in a sense, he saves his friends from despair, or so Callie believes. From Gardner's perspective, however, George's failure to explain what actually happened and to confess his guilt signals his having lost his place in the human community. That George has always been in danger of losing his humanity, and thus becoming a Grendel, is evident in the way he is described: an ankle smashed during the Korean War, a heart broken by a sixteen-year-old prostitute, an arm torn off by a corn binder, and his lonely existence in a house much too large for one man up on Crow Mountain.

In a key scene, George leaves the Soameses and returns to his house, where, having heard about a recent murder on nearby Nickel Mountain, he becomes terrified, expecting to find murderous thieves looting his "things." Only after he has crawled through the mud, searched the house, and put his rifle down, does he realize his absurdity. More shocking is the knowledge that had Henry Soames acted in precisely the same way, there would have been nothing absurd about it for Henry would have been acting for Callie and their son Jimmie.

It is true that Henry does appear ridiculous throughout much of *Nickel Mountain*; Gardner's purpose here is not to deny his dignity but to qualify it, to make human dignity a realizable ideal in a fictional world where the prevailing mood is one of comic reconciliation rather than existential despair. Against George Loomis' isolation and love of things, the novel counsels responsibility and charitable love. It is, as its subtitle attests, "A Pastoral Novel," in which the rural setting is used to affirm the value of community in the face of fragmentation and indifference. Gardner's pastoral simplifies the plight of modern man without becoming either simplistic or sentimental. Henry's Nickel Mountain represents freedom and clarity, but it also serves as a reminder of man's limitations and mortality. If the Christian virtues of faith, hope, and charity constitute one part of Gardner's approach to life, the other is, as one stoic character puts it, having the nerve to ride life down.

Gardner has called *Nickel Mountain* his "simplest" novel; *October Light*, also a pastoral of sorts, is a much more complex work—more varied in style and characters, at once funnier and yet more serious than *Nickel Mountain*. Most of *October Light* takes place on Prospect Mountain in Vermont, where seventy-two-year-old James L. Page and his eighty-year-old sister Sally Abbott are locked in "a battle of the bowels." James, the taciturn New England farmer, suffers from constipation as a result of having to eat his own cooking. A bigot, he simplifies right and wrong and rages against the valuelessness of modern life to the point of shotgunning Sally's television and locking her in her bedroom. James, however, is more than merely a comic buffoon; he is also a man burdened with guilt and oppressed by mortality—not only his own approaching end but also the accidental death of a young son, the suicides of his son Richard and his uncle Ira, and the passing away of his wife Ariah in bitter silence. Self-reliant in the worst sense, James is outwardly unemotional (except for his anger), distant from those around him and from his innermost feelings. Only when he realizes the degree to which he is responsible for Richard's death and the part Richard played in accidentally frightening his Uncle Horace (Sally's husband) to death, does James once again take his place in the natural world and the human community.

Sally, meanwhile, a self-appointed spokeswoman for all oppressed minorities, remains locked in her room where, having nothing to eat but apples, she suffers from loose bowels. A liberal in name if not in fact, she thinks of her stubborn refusal to leave her room as a protest against her tyrannical brother. She is encouraged in her "strike" by the paperback book she reads, *The Smugglers of Lost Souls' Rock*. Comprising nearly forty percent of the text of *October Light*, this novel-within-a-novel parodies the two kinds of fashionable literature assailed by Gardner in *On Moral Fiction*: the reflexive and the cynically didactic. Although Sally is not an especially discriminating reader, she does understand that *The Smugglers of Lost Souls' Rock* is trash— entertaining perhaps, but certainly not true. As she continues to read, however, the book, which she begins to see as a reflection of her situation, starts to exert its pernicious influence. Slowly Sally adopts its values and point of view as her own: its moral relativism, nihilistic violence, the acceptance of an accidental and therefore purposeless universe, and a casually superficial and irresponsible attitude toward human relationships. The subjects that are so weightlessly and artlessly handled in her paperback novel (suicide, for one) are substantive matters of concern in the "real" lives of James and Sally; but this is a point that Sally, caring less for the Pages to whom she is related than for the pages of her novel, does not understand.

In effect, *October Light* successfully dramatizes the argument of *On Moral Fiction*, that art provides its audience with models and therefore affects human behavior. Reading *The Smugglers of Lost Souls' Rock* leads Sally to devise and implement a plan to kill James; when the plan misfires and nearly results in the death of her niece, Sally, like the characters in her book, feels neither responsibility nor remorse. James is similarly affected by the violence he sees on television and, more particularly, by his Uncle Ira, who appears to have been more a monster than a man and certainly a poor model for James to pattern his own life after. The more James and Sally become like characters in what Gardner calls trivial or immoral fiction, playing out their inflexible parts as victimized woman locked in a tower or rugged New England farmer, the greater the danger that they will lose their humanity and become either caricatures or monsters. One such caricature in *The Smugglers of Lost Souls' Rock* dismisses all fiction, claiming that the trashiest "is all true" and "the noblest is all illusion." In their wiser moments, Sally and James know better; they understand that art is man's chief weapon in the battle against chaos and death (what James calls "gravity") and that the true artist is the one who paints "as if his pictures might check the decay—decay that . . . people hadn't yet glimpsed."

As in *Nickel Mountain*, Gardner's affirmation avoids sentimentality. Acknowledging the fact of death, acknowledging how easily the agreements that bind men together can be broken, he exposes the fragility of human existence. What makes his characters' lives even more difficult is the way in which their knowledge is, except for brief flashes of understanding, severely limited. Instead of the easy generalizations of trivial fiction, Gardner offers the complex and interrelated mysteries of Horace's death and Richard's suicide. Memory plays an especially important part in the novel; implying wordless connections between people and times, it is one effective antidote to Sally's "reasonable anger" and James's having stubbornly locked his heart against those he once loved. Another binding force is forgiveness—the willingness to forgive and to be forgiven—which absolves the individual of the intolerable burden of guilt without freeing him of all responsibility. James's son-in-law, Lewis Hicks, for example, can see all sides of an issue and so takes the one course open to men (as opposed to monsters): forgiving everyone. Lewis is the dutiful, ever-present handyman who stands ready to shore up everyone else's ruins, understanding them to be his own as well. Significantly, it is Lewis who first sees the October light that, while a sign of winter and therefore a reminder of death, has the power to transform the everyday world into a vision of radiant, magical beauty, a reminder of that life that is yet to be lived.

Many reviewers regarded *Freddy's Book* as one of the least satisfying of

Gardner's novels; certainly it is the most perplexing. Like *October Light*, it comprises two distinct stories, but in *Freddy's Book* the two are not interwoven (Gardner thought *October Light* was flawed for just that reason). The first part of *Freddy's Book* is sixty-four pages long and concerns Professor Jack Winesap's visit to Madison, Wisconsin, where he delivers a lecture on "The Psycho-Politics of the Late Welsh Fairy Tale: Fee, Fie, Foe—Revolution." Winesap, a psychohistorian, is a gregarious and sympathetic fellow who appears to accept the relativism and triviality of his age until his meeting with the Agaards makes plain to him the limitations of his easygoing rationalism.

Professor Sven Agaard is a self-righteous dogmatist; his son Freddy, the victim of a genetic disorder, is another in Gardner's long line of misfits: a sickly looking eight-foot monster dripping baby fat. The manuscript Freddy delivers to Winesap at midnight (*Freddy's Book*) comprises the one-hundred-and-eighty-page second part of Gardner's novel. Freddy's tale of sixteenth century Sweden, entitled "King Gustav & the Devil," is a dreadful bore—at least at first. Then the story begins to improve; the style becomes more controlled, the plot more compelling and more complex as Freddy begins to use his fiction-writing to explore the possibilities inherent in his story and, analogously, to explore alternatives to his own various confinements.

Many reviewers were puzzled by Gardner's decision to use the ending of Freddy's tale to conclude the larger novel, which, they felt, seemed broken in two. This narrative strategy is both understandable and effective once it is considered in the context of Gardner's "debate on fiction" with his friend, the novelist and critic William Gass. Gass contends that fiction is a self-enclosed and self-referential art object that does not point outside itself toward the world of men but back into "the world within the word." Gardner, on the other hand, maintains that fiction does extend beyod the page into the reader's real world, affecting the reader in various and usually indirect ways. In *Freddy's Book*, Gardner makes the reader think about what effect Freddy's manuscript has had on its midnight reader, Winesap.

Freddy's Book shares with *Grendel*, *The Sunlight Dialogues*, *Nickel Mountain*, and *October Light* the qualities that have made Gardner a significant as well as popular contemporary American novelist: the blend of realism and fantasy, narrative game-playing and serious purpose, and the interest in character which implies Gardner's interest in mankind. The reader finds characters such as Winesap and Freddy compelling because Gardner draws them honestly, and he draws them honestly because, in part, each represents a side of his own personality. He is as much Grendel as he is the Shaper, as much the anarchic Sunlight Man as the law-and-order police chief Clumly. Gardner sympathizes with those who show the world as it is, but ultimately he rejects their realism in favor of those heroes—poets, farmers and others—who choose to do what they can to transform the world into their vision of what it should be, those who, like Gardner, affirm the Shaper's "as if."

In the case of Peter J. Mickelsson, protagonist of Gardner's ninth and last novel, *Mickelsson's Ghosts*, the similarity between author and character is especially close: both are middle-aged, teach at the State University of New York at Binghamton, own farmhouses in Susquehanna, Pennsylvania, have two college-age children, marriages that end badly, difficulties with the Internal Revenue Service, and both find that their careers, like the rest of their lives, are in a state of decline. The very texture of the novel's 103-word opening sentence makes clear that "something, somewhere had gone wrong with (Mickelsson's) fix on reality." According to several influential reviewers, it was not only Mickelsson who had lost his fix; in the pages of *Esquire* and *Saturday Review*, for example, Gardner was venomously attacked for his carelessness, boring and pretentious pedantry, implausible language, and failure to resolve or even make sense of his numerous plots: love, ghost, murder, academic life, philosophy, marital stress, sex, environmental issues, and Mormonism. Whether these attacks were directed more against the author of *On Moral Fiction* than the author of *Mickelsson's Ghosts*, as Gardner believed, can only be conjectured. What is certain is that these reviews disturbed Gardner so deeply that for a time he considered giving up novel-writing altogether. Moreover, the hostility shown by reviewers James Wolcott, Robert K. Harris, and others is out of proportion of the novel's actual defects (in particular, the unconvincing last scene and Gardner's ill-advised attempts to deal openly with sex). Rather than being a "whopping piece of academic bull slinging" (Wolcott), *Mickelsson's Ghosts* is clearly Gardner's most ambitious work since *The Sunlight Dialogues*, the novel it most resembles both in scope and narrative power.

Mickelsson (who Gardner says is based on his friend, the poet James Dickey) is in most respects a familiar Gardner protagonist. Just as the novel follows no single course but instead branches out in many seemingly unrelated directions, so too is Mickelsson a man torn apart by his own inner conflicts. He fondly recalls the certainties and ideals of his past, yet at the same time he finds it easier to live in the present by adopting the cynical, existentially free position he abhors. Finding himself in a world that is at best trivial and at worst self-destructive, Mickelsson recoils from all sense of responsibility and from all human relationships (except the most sordid with a teenage prostitute). Having been betrayed by his wife, he himself becomes a betrayer. Mickelsson is, however, too much the good man, the man desirous of goodness and truth, unwilling to accept any rift between mind and body, thought and deed, to rest easy in his fallen state. Thus Mickelsson's many ghosts: those of the former owners of his farmhouse, the murderous Spragues; those from his past (wife, children, psychiatrist); the philosophical ghosts of Martin Luther, Friedrich Wilhelm Nietzsche, Wittgenstein, and others; and most importantly, the ghost of his better self.

By restoring his farmhouse, Mickelsson is in effect attempting his own moral restoration project. Before he can be freed of his ghosts, however, Mickelsson must first feel the need to confess his guilt (he is, among other things, responsible for a man's death)—to confess his guilt rather than to internalize it out of shame (as George Loomis does in *Nickel Mountain*) or to wallow in it as if values did not exist. Only then, through forgiveness, can he enjoy the saving grace of human community. Within the novel's murder-mystery plot, Mickelsson escapes from the murderous design of a fanatical colleague, Professor Lawler, a self-appointed avenging angel, only after making his act of faith in the form of a wholly irrational "psychic cry for help." Acknowledging his dependency on others and, later, accepting his place within the human community, Mickelsson becomes whole again. More than a novel about one man's redemption, *Mickelsson's Ghosts* is an exploration of the way in which the modern-world individual can truly find himself—the self, that he longs to be—and that discovery can only occur, Gardner believes, in the context of the individual's commitment to others and of their commitment to him.

The posthumously published novels *Stillness* and *Shadows* were drawn from the University of Rochester's extensive collection of the author's papers. *Stillness* appears as Gardner wrote it in the mid-1970's, in the form of a complete but unrevised draft which Gardner apparently never intended for publication, though he did mine it for two of his finest short stories, "Stillness" and "Redemption." Written as psychotherapy in an effort to save his failing first marriage, it is Gardner's most intimate and autobiographically revealing work. The main characters appear as thinly disguised versions of John and Joan Gardner. Martin Orrick, like Gardner nicknamed Buddy, is professor and novelist; he is stubborn, opinionated, unfaithful, and often drunk. Joan, his wife and cousin, is a musician who has given up her career in order to allow her husband to pursue his. Although she has reason to complain, she, too, has faults and must share responsibility for their marital difficulties. Both are, however, redeemed, in a sense, in that, as critical as they may be of each other outwardly, each is inwardly critical of himself or herself. The breakup of their marriage is handled with an intensity and sensitivity unusual in Gardner's fiction but not without the typically Gardnerian concern for seeing an isolated fact of domestic life as a sign of the universal decay which the novel's improbable happy ending serves only, ironically, to underscore.

Stillness evidences considerable promise; *Shadows*, on the other hand, suggests a certain pretentiousness on Gardner's part, given his remarks to interviewers on this work-in-progress. The published novel is nothing more than a patchwork toggled together by fellow novelist Nicholas Delbanco from the author's voluminous notes and drafts. Set in Carbondale, Illinois, the novel concerns Gardner's seriocomic, hard-boiled detective Gerald Craine, as he tries to find a murderer and protect a young Jewish student, Ellen Glass, who has come to him for help. Craine's search for the murderer becomes a search for truth. Delbanco's text makes clear what was to have been the novel's thematic center, Craine's discovery that he cannot protect Ellen, whom he has come to love. The published work, however, does not support Gardner's claim that *Shadows* would be his most experimental work in terms of technique as well as his most conservative in terms of values. That claim is nevertheless important, for much of Gardner's greatness as a novelist derives from the unresolved dialogue between the values he sought to affirm and the often postmodern ways he employed to test and often undermine those values.

Robert A. Morace

Other major works

SHORT FICTION: *The King's Indian: Stories and Tales*, 1974; *The Art of Living and Other Stories*, 1981.

PLAYS: *The Temptation Game*, 1977; *Death and the Maiden*, 1979; *Frankenstein*, 1979 (libretto); *Rumpelstiltskin*, 1979 (libretto); *William Wilson*, 1979 (libretto).

POETRY: *Jason and Medeia*, 1973; *Poems*, 1978.

NONFICTION: *The Construction of the Wakefield Cycle*, 1974; *The Construction of Christian Poetry in Old English*, 1975; *The Poetry of Chaucer*, 1977; *The Life & Times of Chaucer*, 1977; *On Moral Fiction*, 1978; *The Art of Fiction: Notes on Craft for Young Writers*, 1984.

CHILDREN'S LITERATURE: *Dragon, Dragon and Other Tales*, 1975; *Gudgekin the Thistle Girl and Other Tales*, 1976; *A Child's Bestiary*, 1977; *The King of the Hummingbirds and Other Tales*, 1977.

TRANSLATION: *Gilgamesh*, 1984 (with John Maier).

EDITED TEXTS: *The Forms of Fiction*, 1962 (edited with Lennis Dunlap); *The Complete Works of the Gawain-Poet*, 1965; *Papers on the Art and Age of Geoffrey Chaucer*, 1967 (edited with Nicholas Joost); *The Alliterative "Morte d'Arthure," "The Owl and the Nightingale," and Five Other Middle English Poems*, 1971.

Bibliography

Butts, Leonard. *The Novels of John Gardner: Making Life Art as a Moral Process*. Baton Rouge: Louisiana State University Press, 1988. Butts draws his argument from Gardner himself, specifically *On Moral Fiction* (that art is a moral process) and discusses the ten novels in pairs, focusing on the main characters as either artists or artist figures who to varying degrees succeed or fail in transforming themselves into Gardner's "true artist." As Butts defines it, moral fiction is not didactic but instead a matter of aesthetic wholeness.

Chavkin, Allan, ed. *Conversations with John Gardner*. Jackson: University Press of Mississippi, 1990. Reprints nineteen of the most important interviews (the majority from the crucial *On Moral Fiction* period) and publishes one new interview. Chavkin's introduction, which focuses on Gardner as he appears in these and his other numerous interviews, is especially noteworthy. The chronology updates the one in Howell.

Cowart, David. *Arches and Light: The Fiction of John Gardner*. Carbondale: Southern Illinois University Press, 1983. Discusses the published novels through *Mickelsson's Ghosts*, the two story collections, and the tales for children. As good as Cowart's intelligent and certainly readable chapters are, they suffer (as does so much Gardner criticism) insofar as they are concerned with validating Gardner's position on moral fiction as a valid alternative to existential despair.

Henderson, Jeff, ed. *Thor's Hammer: Essays on John Gardner*. Conway: University of Central Arkansas Press, 1985. Fifteen original essays of varying quality, including three on *Grendel*. The most important are John M. Howell's biographical essay, Robert A. Morace's on Gardner and his reviewers, Gregory Morris' discussion of Gardner and "plagiarism," Samuel Coale's on dreams, Leonard Butts's on *Mickelsson's Ghosts*, and Charles Johnson's "A Phenomenology of *On Moral Fiction*."

Howell, John M. *John Gardner: A Bibliographical Profile*. Carbondale: Southern Illinois University Press, 1980. Howell's detailed chronology and enumerative listing of works by Gardner (down to separate editions, printings, issues, and translations), as well as the afterword written by Gardner, make this an indispensable work for any Gardner student.

McWilliams, Dean. *John Gardner*. Boston: Twayne, 1990. McWilliams includes little biographical material, does not try to be at all comprehensive, yet has an interesting and certainly original thesis: that Gardner's fiction may be more fruitfully approached via Mikhail Bakhtin's theory of dialogism than via *On Moral Fiction*. Unfortunately, the chapters (on the novels and *Jason and Medeia*) tend to be rather introductory in approach and only rarely dialogical in focus.

Morace, Robert A. *John Gardner: An Annotated Secondary Bibliography*. New York: Garland, 1984. An especially thorough annotated listing of all known items (reviews, articles, significant mentions) about Gardner through 1983. The annotations of speeches and interviews are especially full (an especially useful fact given the number of interviews and speeches the loquacious as well as prolific Gardner gave). A concluding section updates Howell's *John Gardner: A Bibliographical Profile*.

Morace, Robert A., and Kathryn VanSpanckeren, eds. *John Gardner: Critical Perspectives*. Carbondale: Southern Illinois University Press, 1982. This first critical book on Gardner's work covers the full range of his literary endeavors, from his dissertation-novel "The Old Men" through his then most recent fictions, "Vlemk, The Box Painter" and *Freddy's Book*, with separate essays on his "epic poem" *Jason and Medeia*; *The King's Indian*:

Stories and Tales; his children's stories; libretti; pastoral novels; use of sources, parody, and embedding; and theory of moral fiction. The volume concludes with Gardner's afterword.

Morris Gregory L. *A World of Order and Light: The Fiction of John Gardner.* Athens: University of Georgia Press, 1984. Like Butts and Cowart, Morris works well within the moral fiction framework which Gardner himself established. Unlike Cowart, however, Morris emphasizes moral art as a process by which order is discovered rather than (as Cowart contends) made. More specifically the novels (including Gardner's dissertation novel "The Old Men") and two collections of short fiction are discussed in terms of Gardner's "luminous vision" and "magical landscapes."

HAMLIN GARLAND

Born: West Salem, Wisconsin; September 14, 1860
Died: Hollywood, California; March 4, 1940

Principal long fiction

A Member of the Third House, 1892; *Jason Edwards: An Average Man*, 1892; *A Little Norsk*, 1892; *A Spoil of Office*, 1892; *Rose of Dutcher's Coolly*, 1895; *The Spirit of Sweetwater*, 1898 (reissued as *Witch's Gold*, 1906); *Boy Life on the Prairie*, 1899; *The Eagle's Heart*, 1900; *Her Mountain Lover*, 1901; *The Captain of the Gray-Horse Troop*, 1902; *Hesper*, 1903; *The Light of the Star*, 1904; *The Tyranny of the Dark*, 1905; *The Long Trail*, 1907; *Money Magic*, 1907 (reissued as *Mart Haney's Mate*, 1922); *The Moccasin Ranch*, 1909; *Cavanagh, Forest Ranger*, 1910; *Victor Ollnee's Discipline*, 1911; *The Forester's Daughter*, 1914.

Other literary forms

Hamlin Garland published in nearly every literary form—short stories, biography, autobiography, essays, plays, and poems. Several of his short stories, such as "Under the Lion's Paw," "A Soldier's Return," and "A Branch Road," were much anthologized. His autobiographical quartet, *A Son of the Middle Border* (1917), *A Daughter of the Middle Border* (1921), *Trail-Makers of the Middle Border* (1926), and *Back-Trailers from the Middle Border* (1928), is a valuable recounting of life during the latter part of the nineteenth century through the early twentieth century. Garland also wrote about psychic phenomena in such books as *Forty Years of Psychic Research: A Plain Narrative of Fact* (1936).

Achievements

Garland was a pioneer in moving American literature from Romanticism to Realism. His early works of frontier life on the Middle Border (the Midwestern priarie states of Wisconsin, Iowa, Minnesota, Nebraska, and the Dakotas) made his reputation, and even today he is best known for his strongly regional, unpretentious pictures of the brutalizing life on the farms and in the isolated communities of the monotonous prairie lands.

Even though his reception as a writer did not afford him the financial rewards he sought, he was an active participant in the literary scene in Chicago and New York. He traveled widely in the United States and made the obligatory trip to Europe. He counted among his friends and acquaintances such literary giants as William Dean Howells, Mark Twain, George Bernard Shaw, and Rudyard Kipling, and such lesser lights as Bliss Carmen, Kate Wiggins, George Washington Cable, and Frank Norris (whom he regarded as a promising young writer).

While he published stories in magazines such as *The Arena, Circle,* and *Century,* he augmented his income by lecturing, often at the University of Chicago. He was instrumental in organizing and perpetuating literary clubs and organizations such as the National Institute of Arts and Letters, The MacDowell Club, The Players, and the Cliff Dwellers Club.

When his fiction-writing skills began to abate in his late middle age, Garland wrote plays, articles about psychic phenomena in magazines such as *Everybody's,* and his memoirs. The popular reception of his autobiographical quartet on the Middle Border region revived his confidence in his writing ability, and he won the Pulitzer Prize for the second of the quartet, *A Daughter of the Middle Border.*

Though he wrote several novels after his critically noteworthy Middle Border novel *Rose of Dutcher's Coolly,* they were mostly set in the Far West and dealt with cowboys, Indians, and Rangers; compared to his earlier work, they can be considered strictly commercial potboilers.

Primarily a gifted short-story writer, Garland had difficulty sustaining a narrative for the length of a novel. With the exception of *Rose of Dutcher's Coolly,* Garland is to be remembered more for what he accomplished as a writer of short stories and autobiography than for what he produced as a novelist. He was elected to the board of directors of the American Academy of Arts and Letters in 1918, and, in 1922, he won the Pulitzer Prize for Biography and Autobiography.

Biography

Hannibal Hamlin Garland's early years were spent on an Iowa farm. As soon as he was big enough to walk behind a plow, he spent long hours helping to plow the acres of land on his father's farm. After twelve years of springs, summers, and early falls working at the ceaseless toil of farming, Garland came to realize that education was the way out of a life of farm drudgery. He attended and was graduated from Cedar Valley Seminary. He next held a land claim in North Dakota for a year but mortgaged it to finance a trip to Boston where he intended to enroll in Boston University. Once in Boston, he was unable to attend the University but continued his education by reading voraciously in the Boston Public Library. He also began to write at that time.

His instincts for reform were ignited in Boston, where he joined the Anti-Poverty Society and, introduced to the work of Henry George, came to believe that the Single Tax Theory was a solution to many contemporary social problems. He eventually returned to North Dakota and began to see some of his stories, sketches, and propagandistic novels published. By 1894, he had formulated in a series of essays his theory of realism which he called "veritism."

He married Zulime Taft in 1899 and fathered two daughters (in 1904 and 1907). He continued to write, but by 1898 he had begun to feel that he had exhausted "the field in which [he] found *Main-Travelled Roads* and *Rose of*

Dutcher's Coolly." He believed that he had "lost perspective" on the life and characters of the Middle Border and had found new "creative strength" in the Colorado Hills, where he visited frequently.

By 1911, he believed that he had "done many things but nothing which now seems important." His various literary and cultural activites seemed to him to have been "time killers, diversions [adding] nothing to [his] reputation." At age fifty-two, he knew he had "but a slender and uncertain income." His home was mortgaged, his ranch unproductive, his health not particularly good, and he had "no confident expectation of increasing [his] fortune."

Then, after rejections from six editors, he finally sold *Son of the Middle Border* to *Collier's* magazine. His reputation was firmly established by 1918 with his election to the board of directors of the American Academy of Arts and Letters and then later with the Pulitzer Prize. In 1930, he built a home in Laughlin Park, Los Angeles, probably to be near his two married daughters. He died in 1940 of a cerebral hemorrhage.

Analysis

Hamlin Garland's theory of literature, detailed in his book *Crumbling Idols: Twelve Essays on Art* (1894), grew out of two concepts formulated early in his writing career: "that truth has a higher quality than beauty, and that to spread the reign of justice should everywhere be the design and intent of the artist." This theory of "veritism" obligated him to write stories early in his career that he said were "not always pleasant, but . . . [were] generally true, and always provoke thought."

Garland wrote about "truth" which, for the most part, he had himself experienced. The "justice" he sought to perpetuate was simplified by a reformer's zeal. As a result, he produced a series of didactic early novels which often retell his life experiences in thin disguise. Later on, when he began to view writing as a business, churning out books and shorter pieces that were intentionally "commercial," he wrote a series of safely inoffensive novels that were more romantic than realistic and that are consequently of little importance today.

In his first novel, *A Spoil of Office*, Garland set out to write propaganda, or social protest. In it, he achieved greater continuity of plot than in many subsequent books, he included fewer digressions, and he realized his indisputable though not lofty aim. *A Spoil of Office* is one of his better novels.

It is the story of a hired man, Bradley Talcott, who, inspired by political activist Ida Wilbur, decides to make something of himself, to become more than he is. He goes back to school, then on to law school, and becomes in succession a lawyer, an Iowa state legislator, and ultimately a congressman in Washington. He falls in love with and marries Ida, and together they work in the crusade for equal rights for everyone.

Garland showed in *A Spoil of Office* that corruption and inequality prevail in the legislative process. Prejudiced against the moneyed classes, Garland laid much of the injustice against the poor and average folk at the door of the well-to-do: Brad implies that the financially poorer legislators are the more honorable ones; that while living in a hovel is no more a guarantee of honesty than living in a brownstone is a "sure sign of a robber," it is a "tolerably safe inference."

Garland's own experiences and interests are reflected in Brad's fondness for oratory and Ida's alliances with various reform movements and organizations (the Grange, women's rights, the Farmers Alliance). In his youth, Garland had entertained the notion of an oratorical career; his reform activities under the influence of Benjamin O. Flowers, editor of the radical *The Arena* magazine, are well documented.

The "truth" of prairie living, its harshness and its prejudices, is seen in Garland's short novel of realistic incident, *A Little Norsk*. The story is about a Norwegian girl, Flaxen, adopted and reared by two bachelors. She grows up, well-loved by her adopted "father" and "uncle." When the two men find their paternal feelings changing to more romantic love, they wisely send her off to school. Flaxen, called so because of her blonde hair, meets and marries an irresponsible young man and soon bears him a child. The young man, hounded by gambling debts, flees them and his family; a drowning accident removes him permanently from Flaxen's life. She moves back with the older, fatherly bachelor, taking her baby daughter with her. The novel ends with the strong implication that she will marry the younger bachelor.

In spite of a contrived plot, the novel is a realistic portrayal of the harshness of life on the prairie. Garland desribes the blizzard that kills Flaxen's parents, conveying the terror which uncontrollable natural phenomena brought to the hapless prairie settlers. Although often romanticized for the benefit of those who had never experienced it, a blizzard on the isolated prairie was the harbinger of possible death. When a death occurs, as it does in *A Little Norsk*, there is the gruesome prospect of the dead bodies being attacked by hungry mice and even wolves—a prospect which Garland does not fail to dramatize.

Garland shows how Scandinavian women were treated by "native-born" American men when Flaxen occasionally encounters the village men who wink at her and pinch her. The two bachelors are aware that "the treatment that the Scandinavians' women git from the Yankees" is not nearly as respectful as that which Yankee women can expect. Ironically, Garland himself was probably guilty of such prejudices, because many of his fictional and autobiographical works reveal a condescending, patronizing attitude toward blacks, a disregard for hired hands (unless they are main characters, such as Brad Talcott), and an apparent dislike for aliens such as Germans, Scandinavians, and Jews. (In *Rose of Dutcher's Coolly*, a character says of another, "'he's a Jew, but he's not too much of a Jew.'") *A Little Norsk* thus documents both the harsh physical realities and the purely human harshness and prejudice of prairie life.

Garland's most sustained novel is *Rose of Dutcher's Coolly*. At the time of its publication in 1895, it was a most daring book, primarily because it treats rather openly the sexual misdemeanors of adolescents. To a modern reader, however, Garland's treatment of this subject will appear markedly restrained and even genteel, hardly in keeping with his resolve to tell the truth without evasion or prettification.

Rose, a motherless child, spends her infancy and early childhood with her father on their farm. She grows up hearing and seeing things that many children are never confronted with: the "mysterious processes of generation and birth" with a "terrifying power to stir and develop passions prematurely"; obscene words among the farm hands; "vulgar cackling of old women"; courtship, birth, and death. She goes to her father with all her questions and he, with sometimes blundering answers, manages to keep her from becoming too curious too soon. When the time comes in her teenage years when she can no longer hold her feelings in check, she, like other youngsters, experiments with sex. She tells her father, and he, by appealing to her love for him and his wish that she be a good girl, staves off further episodes.

Rose is interested in reading and writing, and a Doctor Thatcher who visits her school is so impressed by her that he promises to try to help her get into a college preparatory school. Though her father is reluctant, she is finally allowed to go. Once there, she—now a beautiful young woman—has many suitors but is not interested in them beyond friendship. She wishes for a life of intellectual activity and creative writing. Finishing the seminary, she goes to Chicago, again with her father's reluctant approval. There she meets and falls in love with Mason. After overcoming his disinclination to marry, Mason finally proposes to Rose.

Rose of Dutcher's Coolly has been called Garland's best novel. He dared to speak frankly about natural, common occurrences in a sincere, sensible way. This blunt approach was perhaps what shocked his first readers; apparently they were unprepared to face in print those things which they hardly talked about and then not in mixed company. Libraries ruled out the book, calling it "unsafe reading." Yet, even with these "realistic" elements, the book does not live up to its promise because Garland, as usual, romanticizes his "beautiful" heroine. Rose is nevertheless, a heroine fit to share the stage with Stephen Crane's Maggie and Theodore Dreiser's Sister Carrie.

One of Garland's most successful novels is a romanticized story of the Far West, *The Captain of the Gray-Horse Troop*. Captain George Curtis, surveying the mountainous land he has come to love, sums up the novel's plot elements when he says to his sister Jennie: "Yes, it's all here, Jennie . . . the wild country, the Indian, the gallant scout, and the tender maiden." Add the noble captain and the villainous ranchers, and the mix that makes the story is complete.

Unlike his earlier novels set in the Middle Border, *The Captain of the Gray-Horse Troop* is realistic primarily in the sense that it deals with a genuine problem (the encroachment on Indian lands and rights by avaricious whites). Intentionally or not, it also reveals the white's attitude of supriority in regard to the Indian. Curtis is a good and honorable man, yet he can say, having learned of a barbaric execution of an Indian: "It's a little difficult to eliminate violence from an inferior race when such cruelty is manifested in those we call their teachers." Earlier he remarks of the Indians that "these people have no inner resources. They lop down when their accustomed props are removed. They come from defective stock."

This "superiority" is reflected elsewhere throughout the novel: in the unintentionally ironic comment describing "a range of hills which separate the white man's country from the Tetong reservation," and in comments such as "A Mexican can't cook no more'n an Injun." Yet Garland has Captain Curtis, unaware of his own prejudice, remark about another character who is blatantly anti-Indian that she is "well-schooled in race hatred." Written in the stilted style more reminiscent of the genteel tradition than of the veritism Garland espoused in his earlier years, *The Captain of the Gray-Horse Troop* truthfully depicts relations between Indians and whites in the 1800's. Interestingly enough, all the white characters, even those who, like Curtis, want to help the Indians and thwart their persecutors, seem to believe that the Indians are at best very low on the social scale.

The significance of this novel today may well lie not in the story of one white man's attempt to secure justice for the oppressed Indians but rather in its revelation of the bigoted attitudes of whites toward nonwhites. In its time, the book sold very well, going into several editions. It ultimately sold nearly 100,000 copies, Garland's largest sale. (Thirty years after publication it was still selling.) It received better reviews than Garland had hoped for, even from critics who had condemned his earlier books.

Apparently it was the success of this book (which had been considered during the height of its popularity for a motion-picture production) that convinced Garland his earlier Middle Border stories would never bring him financial success. It is not difficult to understand why the remainder of his novels were like *The Captain of the Gray-Horse Troop*, though less successful.

Garland's subsequent literary output offers little that is memorable. His reputation in American literature rests primarily on his work as a short-story writer and autobiographer. An early realist, he also had a naturalistic bent. His earlier works, up to and including *Rose of Dutcher's Coolly*, show that man is controlled by the "outer constraints of environment and circumstance" as well as by the "inner constraints of instinct and passion." Garland used local color, not to caricature or make fun of his characters but to make his work more realistic and true to nature. The social elements he included helped provide the "significance" he felt all literature must have to survive. Certain impressionistic tendencies, seen in certain very subjective descriptions, indicate a concern for "individualism as the coloring element of a literature." His minor lapses into romantic sentimentality and genteel restraint (typified by his habit of referring to "legs" as "limbs") were in themselves evidence of this same individualism; his restraint demonstrated his personal reluctance to be unnecessarily graphic in describing certain aspects of life. Still he was forthright in delineating most of his subjects. Garland's early novels are, for the most part, fine examples of his veritistic theory.

American literature is indebted to Garland for the stronger realism and the wealth of social history he contributed. It is not difficult to applaud Garland's early novels. He set out to show truth in time, place, people, and incident. He sought to bring social significance to his work. He succeeded in several novels before succumbing to commercialism and the desire or need to be not only a good writer but also a financially successful one.

Jane L. Ball

Other major works

SHORT FICTION: *Main-Travelled Roads: Six Mississippi Valley Stories*, 1891; *Prairie Folks*, 1893; *Wayside Courtships*, 1897; *Other Main-Travelled Roads*, 1910; *They of the High Trails*, 1916; *The Book of the American Indian*, 1923.

PLAY: *Under the Wheel: A Modern Play in Six Scenes*, 1890.

POETRY: *Prairie Songs*, 1893.

NONFICTION: *Crumbling Idols: Twelve Essays on Art*, 1894; *Ulysses S. Grant: His Life and Character*, 1898; *Out-of-Door Americans*, 1901; *A Son of the Middle Border*, 1917; *A Daughter of the Middle Border*, 1921; *Trail-Makers of the Middle Border*, 1926; *The Westward March of American Settlement*, 1927; *Back-Trailers from the Middle Border*, 1928; *Roadside Meetings*, 1930; *Companions on the Trail: A Literary Chronicle*, 1931; *My Friendly Contemporaries: A Literary Log*, 1932; *Afternoon Neighbors*, 1934; *Joys of the Trail*, 1935; *Forty Years of Psychic Research: A Plain Narrative of Fact*, 1936.

Bibliography

Folsom, James K. *The American Western Novel.* New Haven, Conn.: College and University Press, 1966. Garland wrote from the point of view of a white man moving west to settle on what had been Native American lands. This book provides a provocative criticism of Garland's treatment of Native Americans.

Gish, Robert. *Hamlin Garland: The Far West.* Boise, Idaho: Boise State University, 1976. Garland wrote his best fiction before 1895, when he wrote stories concerning life on farms in the West. This book, designed for undergraduates, examines Garland's place among Western writers.

Holloway, Jean. *Hamlin Garland: A Biography.* Austin: University of Texas

Press, 1960. A standard biography, good for all students. Contains numerous photographs of Garland throughout his life and a chronology of his works.

McCullough, Joseph B. *Hamlin Garland.* Boston: Twayne, 1978. McCullough weaves analysis of Garland's major works with the story of his life. Provides an extensive bibliography of Garland's works, which consist mainly of short stories. Also lists a secondary bibliography with short annotations.

Pizer, Donald. *Hamlin Garland's Early Work and Career.* Berkeley: University of California Press, 1960. The best book available on Garland's life and work between 1884 and 1895. Suitable for all students.

GEORGE GARRETT

Born: Orlando, Florida; June 11, 1929

Principal long fiction

The Finished Man, 1959; *Which Ones Are the Enemy?*, 1961; *Do, Lord, Remember Me*, 1965; *Death of the Fox*, 1971; *The Magic Striptease*, 1973; *The Succession*, 1983; *Poison Pen*, 1986; *Entered from the Sun*, 1990.

Other literary forms

George Garrett has published several volumes of poems and collections of short stories. He has written plays, screenplays, and a biography of James Jones. He has also edited or coedited many books about literature.

Achievements

Garrett has served as poetry editor of the *Transatlantic Review*, coeditor of *The Hollins Critic*, and a contributing editor to *Contempora* and *Film Journal*. He has received a fellowship in poetry from *The Sewanee Review*, the Prix de Rome from the American Academy of Arts and Letters, a Ford Foundation grant, a Guggenheim grant, a grant from the National Endowment for the Arts, and an award in literature from the Academy and Institute for the Arts.

Biography

George Garrett was born in Orlando, Florida, in 1929, the son of George Palmer and Rosalie Roomer Garrett. He attended Sewanee Military Academy and the Hill School before entering Princeton University in 1947, from which he was graduated with a B.A. degree in 1952, the year in which he also married Susan Parrish Jackson. The couple would have three children: William, George, and Alice. Garrett served in the United States Army before returning to Princeton for his master's degree in 1956. In 1985, he was awarded a Ph.D. in literature from his alma mater.

Garrett has taught writing and literature and has served as writer-in-residence at Wesleyan University, Rice University, the University of Virginia, Princeton, Hollins College, the University of South Carolina, and the University of Michigan.

Analysis

George Garrett's career as novelist is divided into two stages, with distinct changes in style, subject material, and characterization coming at the beginning of his monumental Elizabethan trilogy. His early novels are essentially traditional American novels of the mid-twentieth century. They explore American life—mostly life in the South—with a mixture of smiling humor and serious concern about contemporary social issues. The characters of Garrett's early novels are people caught up in social and political troubles that threaten their senses of identity and self-worth. In these early novels, the press of a corrupting world intrudes upon deeply principled characters who sometimes buckle or break under the onslaught. Garrett's *Do, Lord, Remember Me* is a transitional novel. It retains his established technique of blending humorous and serious themes in a straightforward narrative line, but it points a new direction in its narrative voice. The story is told from the points of view of several of the novel's characters. Garrett had been experimenting with this device in his three previous volumes of short stories, and he carries the technique to full flower in his "Elizabethan" trilogy of novels: *Death of the Fox*, *The Succession*, and *Entered from the Sun*.

Garrett's first novel, *The Finished Man*, published in 1959, is a Southern political novel in the tradition of Robert Penn Warren's *All the King's Men* (1946). The central character, Mike Royle, is a man embroiled in the sins and deceits of a political system that is fearfully inhumane and racist, a system that is a travesty of Jeffersonian democracy. Royle works in the reelection campaign of an unprincipled senator whose cynical opportunism brings about his ultimate downfall. Also, Royle is witness to the failure of his father, a highly moral, charitable judge who is betrayed by his own vision and by corrupt politics around him. Royle hopes to learn about society and himself using these two failed lives as object lessons. What Royle actually learns is that the complexities of human motives are most often undiscoverable and that evil often seems to have a life and body of its own. At the end of the novel, Royle attempts to discover meaning through an inspection of the lives of his forebears. Here Garrett touches upon that American version of Shinto-ism that is a mainstay of the Southern novel. Much of *The Finished Man* is told by periodic flashbacks that enliven the psychological portraits of the main characters.

Do, Lord, Remember Me tells the story of evangelist Red Smalley and his perverse entourage of friends and lovers as they tour the South with their revival show, fleecing the rubes and causing noisy trouble. Garrett succinctly catalogs the misbehavior on the tent revival trail—the dramatically phony faith-healings, the sexual escapades of the brothers and sisters of the mad faith, and the sleazy magic tricks designed to bilk the naïve believers. Red Smalley is no comic stereotype preacher, however; he is a complex man pulled in opposite directions and pulled apart. He wants to be a true man of God, but he loves being a charlatan and a drunk. He believes his own propaganda from the makeshift pulpit, but he cannot bring himself to live the Faith that he prescribes for others. Smalley's revival crew, an ungodly collection of misfits, are similarly conflicted. They want to be what they cannot be, what they will not allow themselves to be.

This complex novel is told from several narrative points of view, with each of the main characters telling his own version of the novel's tumultuous events and interrelationships. Like Smalley, the other narrators are troubled by one overriding realization. They all are trying to escape the inescapable truth that forms the core of the novel: Human beings are inherently evil, and the institutions that they create and support are shot through with that evil.

In many ways *Do, Lord, Remember Me* is a testing ground for the large fictional techniques that pervade Garrett's Elizabethan cycle. The novel's choric narrative technique, the use of interior monologues, and the employment of various typography devices are expanded and supplemented in the three Elizabethan novels.

Garrett's first assumption about historical fiction is that a given historical period or event or character is locked in time; it has a definable beginning, middle, and end. Nevertheless, inside that static frame, he believes, the novelist may create a limitless theater for the individual and collective human imagination. In his essay, "Dreaming with Adam: Notes on Imaginary History," Garrett defines this imagination he is writing about: "The subject is the larger imagination, the possibility of imagining lives and spirits of other human beings, living and dead, without assaulting their essential and, anyway, ineffable mystery, to dream again in recapitulation the dream of Adam, knowing, as he did not until he awoke that it is true. . . . "

Death of the Fox, the first novel in Garrett's Elizabethan cycle, centers on the final days of the adventurer Sir Walter Ralegh as he contemplates his beheading. Ralegh was a poet, explorer, courtier, politician, and one of Queen Elizabeth's favorites. Ralegh's flamboyant personality dominates the novel. His story is told by Ralegh himself, James I, Henry Velverton, and others. These multiple narrations are blends of memory and imagination, so that interior monologues are bonded into recollections of historical events, people, and the familiar objects of everyday life. This blend allows the narration to travel back and forth in time and space, creating a fictional mosaic that finally combines into a portrait of the life and death of Ralegh. As Garrett portrays him, Ralegh was the embodiment of the spirit of the English Renaissance. He was a man who strove for moral and spiritual autonomy yet one who was swept into the intrigues of a complex political system that he could not understand or control.

Garrett's encyclopedic knowledge of the Elizabethan and Jacobean periods brings forth many fascinating details of Ralegh's times. In the novel are discussions of types of English beer, theaters, common utensils, clothing, food, manners, ships, household pests, illnesses, and myriad other incidentals of daily life. The cataloging of ordinary objects and concerns fastens the novel into a concrete reality that serves as the foundation for the actions and imaginings of the characters. Garrett's concentration on exact details of daily life illustrates a major theme in all of his fiction. He consistently turns to topical subjects to serve as kelson and ballast for his writing.

A dozen years after the appearance of *Death of the Fox*, Garrett published *The Succession*, a big novel that chronicles the last days of Queen Elizabeth and the succession of King James I to the throne of England. As in earlier novels, Garrett uses the multiple-narrator technique. Separate parts of the novel are told through the letters of Elizabeth and James, by a courtier, a priest, an actor who was involved in Essex's rebellion, and others of low and high caste.

As the novel begins, Elizabeth, now an old and dying woman, is contemplating her successor. She has kept James of Scotland dangling—and thereby has kept the armies of Scotland at bay. She has put down rebellion and imminent civil war with her intelligence and political cunning. On her deathbed, however, she is pondering larger issues. She concerns herself with the mysteries of mortality and immortality. The novel travels from idea to idea, from London to Scotland's castles and back, shuttling through time, as the narrators tell of their lives and their aspirations. As the novel ends, one of the speakers, a drunken plowman, shivering in the cold of a December night in 1602, says that he is "fearful of nothing, not past or future." Speaking into the dark, he wishes his dying queen a good night. Garrett's narrative voices create here what he has referred to as "simultaneity." He writes, "I was trying to deal in different ways with a variety of characters, some of whom really don't cause large things to happen in history but are a part of the whole picture."

In 1986, Garrett interrupted the Elizabethan cycle with the publication of the stinging satirical novel, *Poison Pen*. This novel is composed mostly of letters written by a failed academic, John Towne, who gives false names as signatures to his poison-pen letters. (This same John Towne is a character in Garrett's manuscript novel "Life with Kim Novak Is Hell," which has been in progress for thirty years.) Another level of fictional complexity is added: Towne's letters are collected and annotated by yet another failed academic, Lee Holmes, the "oldest Assistant Professor" at "Nameless College," a man who is desperate to publish something—just anything.

The bitter letters are addressed to various public figures and celebrities— Brooke Shields, Cheryl Tiegs, Barry Goldwater, and a dozen others. Now and then, author Garrett intrudes with direct commentary, most notably when he accuses a noted editor and writer of plagiarism, and in a long autobiographical letter to Christie Brinkley in which Garrett declares that he is the leading candidate for the "Tomb of the Unknown American Writer."

In praising the satirical bite of *Poison Pen*, Thomas Fleming in the *National Review* compares the novel to Alexander Pope's *The Dunciad* (1728-1743): "Like Pope Garrett is merciless on the pretensions of intellectual life . . . and like Pope, too, he combines a reactionary social vision with a relentless contempt for dullness."

Entered from the Sun, the third and concluding volume in the Elizabethan cycle, investigates the unsolved mystery of the death of famous poet and playwright Christopher Marlowe, who was killed in a pub brawl in 1593. In this novel, the fictional characters Joseph Hunnyman, an actor, and Captain Barfoot, a war-scarred soldier, are hired by unnamed people to uncover the intrigues behind Marlowe's murder. Hunnyman and Barfoot are joined by two other narrators, the beautiful widow Alysoun and an unsuccessful playwright, Cartwright.

The rare genius Marlowe was an enigmatic character in practically all ways. He may have been an outlawed Papist; he may have been a militant anti-Catholic, an atheist; and he may have been spying for Queen Elizabeth— or her enemies. In the course of the novel, Garrett shows that the Elizabethan Age was one of dramatic political intrigue, a time, as he puts it, when "half the people in England are spying on the other half." The narrators point out time and again that much of Elizabethan life was a life of illusion. Actor Hunnyman proposes, for example, that the drama of pretense, violence, and bombast sounding from the London stage serves as microcosm for English society at large. At the novel's end, the mystery is not solved; instead, it is deepened by the crosscurrents of illusion.

In his "Author's Farewell" at the conclusion of *Entered from the Sun*, Garrett writes of his feelings about the trilogy: "I hope that I shall always be able, for as long as I live, to go back to the Elizabethans for delight and instruction. I hope that I will not cease to visit that age and my old friends and enemies who live there. It seems that I could not even if I wanted to." In an interview with Judith Shulevitz, Garrett said that he was working on an American trilogy: "The first novel will describe the mounting of an opera at the 1893 World's Fair in Chicago; the second will measure the impact of Martin Luther King's assassination on a Florida town and the third will focus on 'a football game.'"

Charles Israel

Other major works

SHORT FICTION: *King of the Mountain*, 1958; *In the Briar Patch*, 1961; *Cold Ground Was My Bed Last Night*, 1964; *A Wreath for Garibaldi and Other Stories*, 1969; *An Evening Performance: New and Selected Stories*, 1985.

POETRY: *The Reverend Ghost*, 1957; *The Sleeping Gypsy and Other Poems*, 1958; *Abraham's Knife and Other Poems*, 1961; *For a Bitter Season: New and Selected Poems*, 1967; *Welcome to the Medicine Show: Postcards, Flashcards, Snapshots*, 1978; *Luck's Shining Child*, 1981; *The Collected Poems of George Garrett*, 1984.

PLAYS: *Sir Slob and the Princess: A Play for Children*, 1962; *Garden Spot, U.S.A.*, 1962; *Enchanted Ground*, 1982.

SCREENPLAYS: *The Young Lovers*, 1964; *The Playground*, 1965; *Frankenstein Meets the Space Monster*, 1966 (with R. H. W. Dillard and John Rodenbeck).

NONFICTION: *James Jones*, 1984; *Understanding Mary Lee Settle*, 1988.

EDITED TEXTS: *New Writing from Virginia*, 1963; *The Girl in the Black Raincoat*, 1966; *Man and the Movies*, 1967 (with W. R. Robinson); *New Writing in South Carolina*, 1971 (with William Peden); *The Sounder Few: Essays from "The Hollins Critic,"* 1971 (with R. H. W. Dillard and John Moore); *Film Scripts One, Two, Three, and Four*, 1971-1972 (with O. B. Hardison, Jr., and Jane Gelfman); *Craft So Hard to Learn*, 1972 (with John Graham); *The Writer's Voice*, 1973 (with John Graham); *Intro 5*, 1974 (with Walton Beacham); *The Botteghe Oscure Reader*, 1974 (with Katherine Garrison Biddle); *Intro 6: Life As We Know It*, 1974; *Intro 7: All of Us and None of You*, 1975; *Intro 8: The Liar's Craft*, 1977; *Intro 9: Close to Home*, 1979 (with Michael Mewshaw).

Bibliography

Dillard, R. H. W. "George Garrett." In *Dictionary of Literary Biography Yearbook: 1983*, edited by Jean W. Ross. Detroit: Gale Research, 1984. Dillard begins this article with an assessment of *The Succession* and with general comments on the other two volumes in the trilogy. The article ends with an enlightening interview with Garrett about his role as historical novelist.

_____. *Understanding George Garrett*. Columbia: University of South Carolina Press, 1989. The first book-length study of Garrett's work, this book is an excellent scholarly survey of Garrett's fiction and poetry, with extensive analyses of his major themes and techniques.

Rhodes, Jack Wright. "George Garrett." In *Dictionary of Literary Biography*. Vol. 2, *American Novelists Since World War II*, edited by Jeffrey Helterman and Richard Layman. Detroit: Gale Research, 1978. This biographical/critical/bibliographical essay is a thorough and informative discussion of Garrett's career as a writer, with emphasis on major themes in his novels and short stories.

Robinson, William R. "The Fiction of George Garrett." *Mill Mountain Review* 1 (1971): 39-41. Robinson places Garrett's early fiction in the rich traditions of Southern literature and examines the moral and spiritual dimensions of Garrett's fiction.

Spears, Monroe. "George Garrett and the Historical Novel." *Virginia Quarterly Review* 61 (Spring, 1985): 262-276. This essay investigates the major themes of the Elizabethan trilogy and assesses Garrett's place in the long tradition of historical fiction.

MRS. ELIZABETH GASKELL

Born: Chelsea, London, England; September 29, 1810
Died: Holybourne, England; November 12, 1865

Principal long fiction

Mary Barton, 1848; *Cranford*, 1851-1853; *Ruth*, 1853; *North and South*, 1854-1855; *Sylvia's Lovers*, 1863; *Cousin Phillis*, 1863-1864; *Wives and Daughters*, 1864-1866.

Other literary forms

The novels of Mrs. Elizabeth Gaskell appeared in serial form in journals such as *Household Words* and *All the Year Round* edited by Charles Dickens and *Cornhill Magazine* edited by William Makepeace Thackeray. During the years of novel-writing, she also published travel sketches, essays, and short stories. Her collections of stories which appeared in serial as well as hardcover form were *Lizzie Leigh and Other Tales* (1855); *Round the Sofa* (1859), containing also the separate tales inset in "My Lady Ludlow"; *Right at Last and Other Tales* (1860); *Lois the Witch and Other Tales* (1861); and *Cousin Phillis and Other Tales* (1865). Sketches of Manchester life appeared as *Life in Manchester* (1848) under the pseudonym "Cotton Mather Mills, Esq." A biography of Charlotte Brontë, still regarded as a standard source, appeared in 1856. The standard edition of Gaskell's work is the Knutsford edition (1906), which includes both fiction and nonfiction. *The Letters of Mrs. Gaskell* (1966), edited by Arthur Pollard and J. A. V. Chapple, accompany their *Mrs. Gaskell: Novelist and Biographer* (1965).

Achievements

The reputation of Mrs. Gaskell sank in the modernist reaction to Victorian literature in the post-World War I period, and she was relegated to the status of a second- or third-rate novelist, markedly inferior to Dickens, Thackeray, George Eliot, George Meredith, and Anthony Trollope, and even placed below Charles Kingsley and Wilkie Collins. With the reassessment of Victorian writers which has gone on since World War II, her reputation has risen, and the concerns of the feminist movement in the 1970's have led to such a revaluation that the scholar Patricia M. Spacks refers to her as "seriously underrated" in this century. Other writers about the women's movement, including Elaine Showalter, Jenni Calder, and Ellen Moers, have praised Mrs. Gaskell for detailing faithfully in her fiction the relation between women and marriage, the struggle for self-achievement, and the intermixture of women's careers and public history. The sense in her work of women of all classes as victims of economic and social restrictions has caused scholars to study her work and life more closely in the last decade. She has been elevated to the ranks of the major Victorian novelists.

Biography

Mrs. Elizabeth Gaskell's life was divided between the industrial Midlands of the North and London and rural Hampshire in the South of England, as was that of her heroine, Margaret Hale, in *North and South*. Her mother's family, the Hollands, substantial landowners, were established near Knutsford, Cheshire, which became the "Cranford" of her best-known work. Elizabeth Cleghorn Stevenson was born on September 29, 1810, at Chelsea-on-Thames, then just outside London, where the family had settled after a period in Scotland. Because of her mother's death, Elizabeth was taken to Knutsford, where she spent the next thirteen years in the care of her aunt, Mrs. Hannah Lumb. The years at Knutsford were very happy ones, and her affection for the town is indicated by the tales in *Cranford* about its inhabitants. Her brother, John, twelve years older, went into the merchant navy but simply disappeared on a voyage to the Far East in 1823, an event marked in Gaskell's fiction by various lost and recovered brothers.

Her father remarried, having two more children, and at fourteen Elizabeth was sent to Avonbank School in Stratford, which was kept by the Byerley sisters, her stepmother's aunts. It was a progressive school by Victorian standards of feminine education, serving Unitarian and other liberal religious groups. She left school at seventeen to tend her paralyzed father, the relationship between the two having been somewhat strained in the preceding years. From 1827 until his death in 1829, she faithfully nursed him, her dedication to the task bringing forth a grateful testimony from her stepmother. The experience furnished the basis for Margaret Hale's nursing of her critically ill mother.

The experience of Margaret in the fashionable home of her London relations appears to parallel the months spent by Elizabeth with her uncle, Swinton Holland, a banker, and her cousin, Henry Holland, a London physician. Following the fashion for educated and leisured Victorian women, she visited various places during the next few years: in and out of Knutsford (like her narrator, Mary Smith, in *Cranford*), two winters in Newcastle with a minister, William Turner (the model for the kindly Unitarian minister, Thurstan Benson, in *Ruth*), and his daughter, Anne, a visit to Manchester to Anne's sister, Mary, and a winter (1831) in Edinburgh with the intellectual and artistic company there. At Manchester, she met William Gaskell, assistant minister of Cross Street Unitarian Chapel, and their warm relationship eventuated in marriage at Knutsford in August, 1832. At her various residences in Manchester, to whose busy industrial life and brusque manners she had to adjust, Gaskell became the mother of four daughters and a son: Marianne, Margaret Emily, Florence, Julia, and William, whose death at the age of ten months caused her great sorrow and resulted in the writing of an idealized portrait of a boy, found in her novel *Ruth*.

Gaskell's husband, who became senior minister in 1854, had a solid reputation as a public speaker, teacher of English history and literature, editor of church publications, and preacher. Despite the uncomfortable weather and atmosphere of Manchester, it was a gathering place for well-educated Unitarians and other non-Anglicans, Cross Street Chapel being a center of lively discussion and numbering many self-made mill-owners among its members. It was also true, however, that class divisions between owners and mill-workers were strongly evident to Gaskell, whose character, Margaret Hale, wonders why two groups dependent upon each other regard their interests as opposed.

To understand Gaskell's preoccupation with social problems in her fiction, one must note her constant involvement in social welfare with Sunday and weekday schools for children of workers, her visits to working-class homes in the course of parish duties, and her concern for victims of the social system such as unwed mothers. The depression of 1839 to 1840, the Chartist movement aimed at gaining more political power for workers, the Factory Act of 1832 opposed by industrialists and widely evaded in its purpose of restricting hours of labor for women and children—all these conditions provided Gaskell with subject matter.

Gaskell's immediate impulse to write came from grief over her son's death, a decision which her husband hoped to channel constructively by encouraging her in her efforts. Her first attempt at a diary and further encouragement from publisher friends resulted in sketches about *Life in Manchester*, but this was a prelude to her first success as a novelist, *Mary Barton*. This novel presented the sufferings of the workers during labor unrest, the resistance of the mill-owners, the failure of parliament to respond to labor grievances, and the need for reconciliation. The book was praised by Friedrich Engels and Karl Marx, and condemned as unfair by the wealthy parishioners of Cross Street Chapel, a denouncement which led Gaskell to present what she considered an account more favorable to the industrialists in *North and South*.

The acclaim and damnation of *Mary Barton* made Gaskell rather visible among British intellectuals such as Thomas Carlyle, the social critic; Walter Savage Landor, the poet; Benjamin Jowett, the classicist; John Ruskin, the reformer of industrial ugliness; Charles Kingsley, author of *Alton Locke* (1850) and *Yeast* (1851) and a founder of Christian socialism; Antony Cooper, Earl of Shaftesbury, the prime mover of legislative reform in mid-Victorian England; and Dickens. Thus, Mrs. Gaskell joined the reforming group bent on altering the unsatisfactory living and working conditions among the laboring class in Britain.

Gaskell's friendship with Dickens inspired her to produce a story about an unmarried mother, "Lizzie Leigh," for Dickens' journal *Household Words* and created a writer-editor relationship that lasted more than a dozen years. Having become interested in the fate of the "fallen woman," she used, as the basis for her novel *Ruth* (first serialized and then published in 1853), the actual case of a sixteen-year-old female dressmaking apprentice who had been seduced, abandoned, and then imprisoned for theft in trying to keep herself alive. In the novel, a similar young girl is saved from a parallel disgrace by the intervention of a kindly minister and his sister and brought back to respectability and social usefulness by their tender concern. The presentation of Ruth's case, mild by modern standards, became almost instantly controversial, various prudish fathers refusing to allow their wives and daughters to read it, and even Gaskell kept the book from her own daughters. Gaskell had already interested herself in promoting emigration by unwed mothers to the colonies as a practical way of restoring their reputations and building new futures; the book was an outcome of her own concern, though Ruth is rehabilitated within the community rather than leaving it and must still suffer unfair stigmatization, precisely the kind which the novel itself received.

While visiting another reformer, James Kay-Shuttleworth, who promoted educational advancements for the workers, Gaskell met Charlotte Brontë, who had recently risen to prominence with *Jane Eyre* (1847); a strong friendship developed from this meeting and continued until Brontë's death in 1855. In fact, the riot of the working-men against their employer in *North and South* has similarities to a scene in Brontë's *Shirley*, which appeared six years before Gaskell's novel.

While *Ruth* was exciting controversy, *Cranford*, the work which for a long time overshadowed Gaskell's reputation as a social critic, created a nostalgic and melancholic mood. Yet even in this novel, Gaskell expresses a concern for lives that are close to poverty, genteel survivors of once lively and secure families. To please Dickens, in 1863 Gaskell added one more story to the collection for *All the Year Round*, his second magazine. Gaskell had by then established the parameters of her work: the creation of moving depictions of life under an industrializing social order; the alertness to social injustice; the longings for a more rural, innocent, and organic world of natural feelings and associations; and the melancholy strain of hopes unrealized because of social or financial constraints.

In *North and South*, written two years after *Cranford*, Gaskell made a determined effort to present the mill-owner, Thornton, as a man with integrity, initiative, and humanitarian concern for his workers, a sort of Samuel Greg who weathers the financial crisis both with the support of his wife, Margaret Hale, newly rich, and that of his workers, drawn to him by his philanthropy. Northern energy, brusque efficiency, and the rough democracy of industrialists sprung from the humble origins of their own workers are set against the arduous toil and isolation of Southern farm laborers and the class-consciousness of Southern workers, town-dwellers, and professional people. In the same year, Gaskell drew upon memories of Avonbank School for stories, which she inset in a frame story narrated by an aristocrat, Lady Ludlow. These appeared as "My Lady Ludlow," later added to and published as *Round the Sofa*. During these years, Gaskell also wrote various sketches, such as "Cumberland Sheep Shearers" with its Wordsworthian setting of rough toil among natural beauties, and Christmas stories, some with ghostly apparitions in the style of Dickens' own stories, which appeared in *Household Words*. Dickens' *Hard Times* (1854) provoked some anxiety in Gaskell since it dealt in part with union agitation and industrial unrest, as did *North and South*. What strained the relationship with Dickens, however, was the leisurely description and extended characterization in *North and South* together with difficulties of episodic compression for weekly publication in his journal. Though Dickens eventually came to appreciate the virtues of *North and South*, the editorial struggle over it induced Gaskell to look for publication elsewhere in more prestigious journals run on a monthly basis.

Upon the death of Charlotte Brontë in March, 1855, Gaskell undertook to write the authorized biography, using Brontë's words where possible but interpreting the facts somewhat freely. The biography, published in March, 1857, led to a continuing friendship with her new publisher, George Smith, Jr., whose firm, Smith, Elder, and Company, had been Brontë's publishers. Smith's support proved most helpful when questions of libelous statements in the biography necessitated apologies and vexatious changes in the third edition. Despite the partisanship evident in certain passages, the feeling for its subject and the general fairness in its presentation make it a good study of a writer by another writer.

Gaskell's work from 1858 to 1863 was uneven. She desired sales apparently to pay for increasing amounts of travel with her daughters, expenses of weddings for two of them, and new property. In Rome, in 1857, a new friend and major correspondent appeared, an American, Charles Eliot Norton, future president of Harvard University, who probably gave her information on Puritan New England to add to her lore of witchcraft and demonism which she drew on for the stories found in *Lois the Witch and Other Tales*. A trip to Heidelberg provided legendary matter for *Right at Last and Other Tales*. At this time, there was much interest in Great Britain in folklore materials and romantic wonders derived from ghostly and spiritual legends, and Gaskell among others, was willing to fictionalize this type of literature.

Writing in another contrary strain, Gaskell employed rural settings in her next two novels, *Sylvia's Lovers* and *Cousin Phillis*; the novel or novella following these two was *A Dark Day's Night*, intended to capture part of the market for intriguing mystery-and-suspense stories. As *Cousin Phillis* was winding up its serial publication in August, 1864, Gaskell started what some critics consider her major work, *Wives and Daughters*, an exploration of the role of women in Victorian intellectual and social life. It was never completed. Gaskell's unceasing activity, including essays for the *Sunday School Magazine*, was taking its physical toll. She had already had fainting spells. Hoping to retire to Holybourne, Hampshire, which she had used a decade earlier as

Margaret Hale's beloved home community, she had purchased a home there as a surprise for her husband. While spending a trial weekend with family and guests there, she suffered a sudden and fatal stroke on November 12, 1865. She was buried at Brook Street Chapel, Knutsford, where her husband was also buried in June, 1884.

Analysis

Despite her own creativity, which certainly had the support of her husband, Mrs. Gaskell, when questioned by a young writer, insisted that a woman's first duty was to husband and family. Friends recollected her carrying out her early career in the midst of household activities. Later, however, she often went traveling alone or with her daughters but—except for jaunts to a beloved vacation spot near Manchester—never with her husband. The traveling periods gave her isolation for writing, suggesting that her own practice ran counter to her advice.

Enid L. Duthie has found in Gaskell's fiction a strong interest in natural scenery, in country customs, crafts, and tales; a sympathy for conservative small towns, yet equally a concern for working men and women; a desire for practical knowledge to enhance living; a focus upon the family as the stable social unit where affections are close but able, on occasion, to extend to others in need; and an insistence that violence is futile, the human condition precarious, faith necessary. John McVeagh sees Gaskell as insisting that absolute judgments become meaningless when related to concrete human situations requiring compromise. In Gaskell's treatment of the laboring element, Jenni Calder sees her as avoiding the duality of other portrayers of working-class families—sympathetic yet condescending—and refers to Mrs. Gaskell as one of the few major Victorian writers showing marriage from a woman's viewpoint and not simply as an escape, a bid for social status, or a profitable contract. Gaskell has been praised for her concrete presentation of social milieus, in the spirit of seventeenth century Dutch genre painters, and her gift for recording the relationship between work and home and between husbands and wives is a special one. Patricia M. Spacks refers to a "steady integrity of observation" and "penetrating accuracy," especially as Gaskell draws, tacitly, the analogy between the plight of women in their dependency and that of workers in relation to their employers.

Gaskell's dilemma for a feminist such as Elaine Showalter lies in Victorian expectations of feminine domesticity and marriage as an end to intellectual creativity. Gaskell herself surmounted the problem, but her characters find it a difficult challenge. Spacks points out that Margaret Hale, Gaskell's greatest heroine, from *North and South*, tries to mediate between an impoverished working class which really does respect its own labor and an enlightened upper-class self-interest which enjoys emotional and cultural richness. In the end, however, Margaret must inherit property as a defense for her own introspective feeling and the diminution of her former social vitality. It is her way of surviving in a materialistic world.

The titular heroine of *Mary Barton* has a true lover, Jem Wilson, and a potential seducer, Henry Carson, son of a textile mill-owner. The love interest is established as the background for a social problem which Gaskell treats with historical accuracy. John Barton, Mary's father, aware of the sufferings of his fellow mill-workers during a lockout by the employers, is enraged by the death of the wife of his friend, Davenport, while the masters enjoy leisure, modernize their mills, and keep up profits by using scabs and decreasing wages when they reopen. Barton is hopeful that the workers will find redress for their grievances from a sympathetic parliament, to which the unionists will present the Chartist Petition. The charter is rejected, however, and the embittered workers are further incensed by Henry Carson's casual caricature of the striking workers which he passes around at a meeting of employers. He is selected as the target of assassination, Barton being chosen to murder him. Jem is accused of the murder, and Mary faces a conflict, since she can clear Jem only by exposing her father. Though Jem's acquittal makes this step unnecessary, the other workers shun him (a situation Gaskell borrowed from the true story of a former convict ostracized by those in the workplace), and he and Mary are forced to emigrate. Her father, still publicly innocent, confesses, somewhat implausibly, to Carson, Sr. and gains forgiveness. The solution to class conflict comes through mutual goodwill, recognition of wrongdoing, and restitution.

The heroine of *Ruth*, which takes issue with Victorian hostility toward the unmarried mother, is seduced among the romantic clouds and mountains of Wales. The idyllic moment turns to desperation when she is abandoned by her lover, Bellingham. A kindly, crippled Unitarian minister, Thurstan Benson, and his sister, Faith, take Ruth into their home and community, modeled on Knutsford, and deceive people about her condition to protect her reputation. The lie is the price of social respectability. Ruth's discreet conduct from this point on gains her admittance to the mill-owning Bradshaw family as companion to their daughter, Jemima. The electoral reforms of 1832 give Bellingham a chance to stand for political office, his reappearance in Ruth's life leading to a renewal of his interest in her and a new temptation for her to forgo her independence by accepting an offer of marriage. Her pride in her child, Leonard, makes Ruth reject Bellingham. Unfortunately, Bradshaw learns the truth about Ruth, and his self-righteous indignation leads him to repel Ruth and denounce his friend, Thurstan. Denied the opportunity for further cultural development in the Bradshaw family, Ruth must turn to nursing to establish her social usefulness. As a visiting nurse, her conscientious assistance during a typhoid epidemic brings the praise of the community.

Critics have said that Mrs. Gaskell, having made her point that unmarried mothers should be treated humanely so that their talents can be made productive, should have ended her novel. Unfortunately, three-volume publication, extended serialization, and a tendency toward melodrama fostered by Charles Dickens, led Gaskell to have Bradshaw's son forge a signature on some stocks entrusted to him by Thurstan. Bradshaw denounces his son, comes back ignominiously to the chapel worship he has furiously abandoned, and eventually breaks down and is reconciled to Thurstan, having repented of his harshness toward Ruth. Ruth, however, is not permitted to live since Gaskell apparently felt that her rehabilitation was not enough to gain sympathy. Wearied by constant care of the sick, Ruth falls sick while somewhat improbably tending her former lover, Bellingham. She dies possessing an aura of sanctity, and perhaps it was this martyrdom which Victorian critics found too much to accept.

In *North and South*, the protagonist Margaret Hale must adjust to life in industrial Darkshire (Derbyshire) after living in rural Hampshire, and, through her perceptions, Margaret guides the reader to a major issue: the way in which a money-oriented competitive society challenges a more leisured, socially stratified one. The abrasive confrontations of Margaret and John Thornton, a mill-owner being tutored in classics by Margaret's father, define the mutual incomprehension of North and South in England. Thornton wants to have a "wise despotism" over his workers; Margaret contends for understanding based upon common destiny in the mills. The question of authority is raised in another dimension in the Hale family's personal travail over the enforced exile of Margaret's brother, Frederick, because of charges, unwarranted, of inciting the crew of his naval vessel to mutiny. Through friendship with Bessy Higgins, a mill girl dying of a disease fostered by textile manufacturing, Margaret, the central consciousness of the novel, is able to observe the sufferings of the working class during a strike caused by union efforts to prevent wage cuts which the mill-owners justify because of American competition. The owners themselves, while cooperating in opposition to workers, fight one another for economic survival, according to Thornton, who sees an analogy with survival of the fittest. Though Margaret can see the closeness of working men and women in their common suffering, a riot, instigated without union approval by Nicholas Boucher, a weak agitator, against Irish scab labor, seriously compromises the position of the union in terms of its own self-discipline. The issue is posed whether coercive tactics to enlist worker support of unions can be justified when a weak leader can jeopardize legitimate demands. Margaret terminates the riot, in fact, by heroically intervening between Thornton and the rioters. She quite literally mediates between the two sides.

The difficulty of reconciliation is made evident, however, when Bessy's father, Nicholas Higgins, a unionist, argues that Christian forbearance will not answer the industrialists, though he admits that workers and employers might compromise if they could understand one another. The blacklisting of

Nicholas by other employers leads to Margaret's intervention, encouraging Thornton to rehire him, his own persistence equally helping to regain a job. Thornton realizes that employer responsibility must be broadened. The turmoil of the riot, in which Margaret must confront social disruption, has its counterpart in her own turmoil over the approaching death of her mother and the secret reappearance of her brother to be with their mother. Unfortunately, Frederick's departure from town involves a scuffle with a drunken informer which later requires that Margaret lie to protect Frederick. This lie, like that in *Ruth*, produces its painful outcome when Thornton, who has observed the scuffle, thinks that she is lying to protect a lover, thus causing further altercations. Margaret realizes, however, that her moral condemnation of manufacturers has been too harsh. Indeed, to an Oxford don, an old family friend who comes to her mother's funeral, she suggests that it would be well if intellectuals associated with manufacturers.

Margaret's opinions about the South as a preferable society also undergo change. She counsels Nicholas that his going to the South, when he is blacklisted, would lead to deadening toil, no real companionship, and intellectual decay because of the rural isolation. Visiting Helstone, her old home, Margaret encounters an old native superstition when a live cat is boiled to avert a curse. A meeting with her former lover, Lennox, confirms that Thornton is the more vital man. A fortunate inheritance from the Oxford don, Mr. Bell, enables Margaret to save Thornton, who is faced with mounting debts because of competition. He, too, has faced a moral dilemma: whether it is right to borrow money to keep himself afloat knowing that the lenders are at a strong risk. Thornton wishes to start again, seeking an opportunity for social interchange with his workers beyond the cash nexus. Margaret, now an heiress, helps Thornton stay afloat and marries him. Higgins, providentially having witnessed the scuffle, knows who Frederick really is. Thus, North and South are united, and Thornton turns into a philanthropist.

In *Wives and Daughters*, Gaskell explores the question of the middle-class woman seeking to define herself and her goals in an atmosphere uncongenial to intellectual independence. Molly Gibson, whose mother has died, must cope in her teens with the remarriage of her father, who has sought a wife as much to guide Molly as out of real love. Her father's new wife, Hyacinthe Kirkpatrick, is the epitome of the parasitical woman, a former governess previously married out of necessity and then forced back into supporting herself and her daughter, Cynthia, upon her husband's death. She has become a companion to the newly aristocratic Cumnor family, but, wanting comfort, she can achieve it only by marrying Gibson. Molly receives her moral education, in part, by seeing through her stepmother's artificial pretenses. Cynthia, shuffled off while her mother has pursued Gibson, comes to reside in the household and establishes a close friendship with Molly despite her moral skepticism and social opportunism. Thus, the daughters are contrasted, not in black and white, but as possible responses to the dependency of women.

Cynthia's mother tries to marry her to Osborne Hamley, eldest son of an old family, not knowing that he is already married, and that the child of the marriage has been kept secret for some time. The event has caused Hamley to fail in attaining his degree, and he returns home to mope, thus arousing the antagonism of his father, to whom he cannot acknowledge his liaison. Hamley finally dies, causing Mrs. Kirkpatrick to shift her sights for Cynthia to the second son, Roger. Molly meanwhile has naïvely pledged herself at sixteen to the odious Preston, a situation from which she is rescued by the more forthright Cynthia, who is in love with Roger but also the object of the affections of Walter Henderson, Gaskell's ideal of the practical, creative scientist, a new social type. Cynthia, socially ambitious, realizes that the Hamley family enjoys ancient honor but is materially threatened, and she transfers her affections to a superficial, weak, but socially prominent young man. Molly is left to marry Roger, but the problem remains as to whether she can forge for herself a free life with her husband's support. The life-styles of the two older women, Lady Harriet Cumnor and Mrs. Hamley, provide alternatives for her development. Lady Harriet is a realist about feminine hypocrisy as the price of dependency and wishes to challenge it, but Mrs. Hamley, despite her efforts to mother Molly, is emotionally sterile. Her death leaves Squire Hamley bereft and helplessly alienated from his infant grandson. The other, older men in the novel fare no better; Mr. Gibson suppresses his feelings about his wife to the point of emotional numbness, Lord Cumnor takes refuge in foolish snobbery, and even the younger Osborne painfully learns the price of romantic impulsiveness. The novel's probing analysis of the dilemma of femininity in a world guided by material values and restricted social consciousness, a world in which men too are caught by the inhibitions of social position and frozen into immobility, gives it peculiar power. It is an indication of what Gaskell could have accomplished if she had lived longer, and it shows her continuing effort to link broader social issues to very specific circumstances with careful attention to detail.

Roger E. Wiehe

Other major works

SHORT FICTION: *Lizzie Leigh and Other Tales*, 1855; *Round the Sofa*, 1859; *Right at Last and Other Tales*, 1860; *Lois the Witch and Other Tales*, 1861; *The Cage at Cranford*, 1863; *Cousin Phillis and Other Tales*, 1865.

NONFICTION: *Life in Manchester*, 1847 (as "Cotton Mather Mills, Esq."); *The Life of Charlotte Brontë*, 1857; *The Letters of Mrs. Gaskell*, 1966 (Arthur Pollard and J. A. V. Chapple, editors).

Bibliography

Craik, W. A. *Elizabeth Gaskell and the English Provincial Novel.* New York: Harper & Row, 1975. A major rehabilitation of Gaskell as an important novelist, comparing her with her contemporaries. Sets her five long fictions within the provincial novel tradition and demonstrates how she expanded the possibilities and universality of that tradition. A short bibliography and a chronology of major nineteenth century provincial novels are included.

Duthie, Enid. *The Themes of Elizabeth Gaskell.* Basingstoke, England: Macmillan, 1980. Despite their contrasting settings and plots, there is a unity of themes in all Gaskell's fiction. Her entire work and letters are drawn upon to reconstruct her imaginative world and the themes central to it. Contains a select bibliography and an index.

Easson, Angus. *Elizabeth Gaskell.* London: Routledge & Kegan Paul, 1979. Examines the relationship of all Gaskell's writings to her life and times, tracing the source of her fiction to her culture. A select bibliography and index are included.

Gerin, Winifred. *Elizabeth Gaskell.* New York: Oxford University Press, 1976. The first biography able to make use of the publication in 1966 of *The Letters of Mrs. Gaskell*, and still one of the best. Contains a select bibliography and an index.

Stoneman, Patsy. *Elizabeth Gaskell.* Brighton, England: Harvester Press, 1987. This feminist reading claims that previous accounts of Gaskell have seriously misread her and that the interaction of class and gender must be made central in any interpretation of her. A select bibliography and index are provided.

Wright, Edgar. *Mrs. Gaskell: The Basis for Re-assessment.* New York: Oxford University Press, 1965. Relates her novels closely to her personal development. Includes a bibliography and a chronological list of her publications.

WILLIAM H. GASS

Born: Fargo, North Dakota; July 30, 1924

Principal long fiction
Omensetter's Luck, 1966; *Willie Masters' Lonesome Wife*, 1968.

Other literary forms
Chiefly a writer of novels, William H. Gass is also the author of a book of short stories entitled *In the Heart of the Heart of the Country and Other Stories* (1968) and four volumes of essays about literature. In the chief of these, the collections entitled *Fiction and the Figures of Life* (1970) and *The World Within the Word: Essays* (1978), Gass illuminates his own work as a writer of fiction. He prefers novels, as his essay "Imaginary Borges and His Books" suggests, which render fictional worlds which are highly contrived metaphors for the real world. He values the kind of verbal experimentation, and the implications about human consciousness which lie behind it, characteristic of the fiction of Jorge Luis Borges, Gertrude Stein, and Robert Coover. Ultimately, Gass sees the fictional text as less a reflection of objective reality than an artifact created out of the consciousness of the author.

Achievements
While Gass is a highly individual writer, one whose work does not reflect the influence of his contemporaries, his fiction shares with work by authors such as John Barth, Donald Barthelme, and Thomas Pynchon an emphasis on the text as verbal construct. As his *On Being Blue: A Philosophical Inquiry* (1976) indicates, Gass believes that the words used to talk about a thing reveal the essence of the thing being talked about. His prose itself is highly rhythmic and reflexive, filled with images and allusions. The novels Gass has written, *Omensetter's Luck* and *Willie Masters' Lonesome Wife*, are as much meditations on the art of writing fiction as narratives about their title characters. His essays, often published in literary journals before their appearance in book form, are cogent statements of Gass's own thematic and technical preoccupations. They influence both other writers and general readers, not only in the way they read Gass's work but also in the way they read the fiction of his contemporaries.

Biography
While born in Fargo, North Dakota, on July 30, 1924, William Howard Gass was reared in Warren, Ohio. He attended Kenyon College and Ohio Wesleyan, served in the United States Navy during World War II, and returned to receive a degree from Kenyon in 1947. Gass came into contact with

John Crowe Ransom there, but his chief interest as a student was philosophy. He went on to do graduate work at Cornell University, and after writing a dissertation entitled "A Philosophical Investigation of Metaphor," he received his Ph.D. in 1954. He has taught at a number of colleges, beginning to publish fiction while teaching philosophy at Purdue University. Since 1969, Gass has been at Washington University in St. Louis, Missouri, where he is Distinguished University Professor in Humanities. He has received grants from the Rockefeller and Guggenheim Foundations.

Analysis

Examination of the stories collected in *In The Heart of the Heart of the Country and Other Stories* reveals the degree to which Gass's fiction reflects his emphasis as a critic on creation of an autonomous verbal construction. In the title story of the volume, for example, he uses recurring images, syntactic patterns, and subject matter to depict a rural community as perceived by a poet who has come to a small Indiana town to recover from a failed love affair. "In the Midwest, around the lower Lakes," the first-person narrator comments, "the sky in the winter is heavy and close, and it is a rare day, a day to remark on, when the sky lifts and allows the heart up. I am keeping count, and as I write this page, it is eleven days since I have seen the sun."

As is typical of all of Gass's work, the first-person narrator of "In the Heart of the Heart of the Country" controls the development of the narrative structure of the story. It is his story, and Gass works through him to reveal its meaning. The narrator's eye for detail is sharp: Nevertheless, he interprets it in terms of his own isolation and despair. "Lost in the corn rows, I remember feeling just another stalk, and thus this country takes me over in the way I occupy myself when I am well . . . completely—to the edge of both my house and body." This metaphor is central to the point of the story, for Gass demonstrates that his protagonist so fuses the data of his sensory experience and his subjective response to it that the two cannot be separated.

In this respect, he is typical of characters in Gass's longer fiction. In the novels, however, the narrative strategy is more complex than in the stories. Gass uses four different narrators in *Omensetter's Luck*, circling about the meaning of the life of Brackett Omensetter without ever entering into his consciousness. According to Henry Pimber, Omensetter's friend and landlord, he

> was a wide and happy man. . . . He knew the earth. He put his hands in water. He smelled the clean fir smell. He listened to the bees. And he laughed his deep, loud, wide and happy laugh whenever he could—which was often, long, and joyfully.

To the citizens of Gilean, a town on the Ohio River to which he comes around 1890, Brackett Omensetter is a mythic figure who is magically in touch with the natural world. That perception precipitates the emotional responses they have to him. It also precipitates a series of human tragedies.

Israbestis Tott, the first narrator Gass uses in *Omensetter's Luck*, functions like the narrator of "In the Heart of the Heart of the Country," in that he chronicles the history of a town. "Imagine growing up in a world," Tott comments at the start of the book, "where only generals and geniuses, empires and companies, had histories, not your own town or grandfather, house . . . none of the things you'd loved." Tott comes at the conflict at the center of Omensetter's story indirectly, not needing to explain to himself as he muses about the past that actually took place. He speaks from the perspective of old age. His Gilean is that of the reader's present, and he refers to Omensetter's life from the perspective of a survivor of the central action of the novel, which took place before the turn of the century.

Gass's use of Tott as his initial focus, and the placement of the action of the first section of *Omensetter's Luck* at an auction of the property of the late Lucy Pimber, enables him to suggest that the lack of vitality in Gilean derives from the community's inability to accept Brackett Omensetter. One of the items at auction is the cradle Omensetter and his wife used for their infant son Amos, and Tott wonders why Mrs. Pimber had it. She never had any children of her own. Her husband, Henry, the character Gass uses to narrate the second section of the novel, is ambivalent about Omensetter's strength and vitality. Both drawn to him and jealous of him, Pimber commits suicide by hanging himself from a tree deep in the woods. This death is the central element in the plot of the novel. Unsure of what has happened to Henry Pimber, the townspeople search for his body and speculate about the role Omensetter has played in his death.

Pimber is convinced that Omensetter is lucky beyond all deserving. On the rainy day on which he brings his family and household goods to Gilean in an open wagon, Omensetter miraculously escapes the rain. The house he rents from Pimber is subject to flooding, but the Ohio River avoids it while Omensetter's family lives there. Even when a fox falls into the well at the house, he is inclined to let nature take its course in confidence that things will work out. Angered by this attitude, Pimber shoots the fox in the well and wounds himself with a refracted shotgun pellet. Neither Dr. Orcutt's drugs nor Reverend Furber's prayers seem to affect the lockjaw Pimber develops, but Omensetter's beet poultice turns the trick. The experience becomes fraught with spiritual significance for Pimber. "It lay somewhere in the chance of being new. . . of living lucky, and of losing Henry Pimber." He sees Omensetter as a sign, as a secret indication of how he himself should live; unable to see that Omensetter is no more than a man like himself, Pimber hangs himself in despair about ever becoming the kind of person he believes Omensetter to be.

While Henry Pimber sees Omensetter as emblematic of positive elements, the Reverend Jethro Furber, the third of Gass's narrators in *Omensetter's*

Luck, sees him as the embodiment of moral evil. Furber is the most difficult to understand of the men Gass uses to narrate the story. His account comes so entirely from within his own consciousness that only the previous evidence of Tott and Pimber serves to put it in perspective. Furber sees Omensetter as a threat to his moral authority. Having coerced him into attending church one Sunday morning, Furber finds himself unable to preach effectively. Speaking to Matthew Watson, the blacksmith in Gilean, he suggests that Omensetter is an agent of Satan. "Listen Matthew, he was in the young corn walking and I said leave us Omensetter, leave us all. Oh I accursed him. I did. Yes, I said, you are of the dark ways, Omensetter, leave us all." When Henry Pimber disappears and foul play is suggested, Furber encourages the townspeople to suspect Omensetter of killing his landlord.

Obsessed by the sight of Omensetter and his pregnant wife Lucy bathing in a stream, Furber makes of the scene an icon of his own lust. He is gored by sexual fantasies, conceding to himself that there is more pleasure in dirty words than real experience, yet the unconstrained relationship of Brackett and Lucy Omensetter excites his jealousy. He titillates himself with words, those drawn from scripture as well as those describing sexual acts, and eventually produces a blasphemous mixture of elements suggesting a parallel between Omensetter, his wife, Lucy, and Furber himself and Adam, Eve, and Satan.

> Now there was in heaven, as you know, an angel, prince among them, Prince of Darkness. And he felt his wife drawn painfully from him, out of his holy body, fully half of himself, and given a place of dazzling splendor. How he hated it, and suffered his loss loudly.

Furber sees himself simultaneously as Adam and Satan; he both displaces Omensetter as the husband of Lucy/Eve and reveals the guilt he feels at this idea. Furber imagines that the sex act reunites the parts that God separated, reintegrating the masculine and feminine halves of His own personality, and he thereby suggests the roots of his own jealousy of Omensetter.

Gass provides the last chapters of *Omensetter's Luck* with an anonymous third-person narrator, one who stays largely outside the consciousness of Furber. The action of the plot develops with absolute clarity at this point. Omensetter comes to the minister with the news that he has located Henry Pimber's body deep in the snowy winter forest. He knows that Furber is trying to persuade others that he murdered Pimber, and he needs to clear his name. "A friend. I've spent my life spreading lies about you," Furber tells Omensetter tauntingly. Yet he does tell the search party the truth when they find Pimber's corpse. By this time, Furber is caught up in his own dark spiritual vision. "God was coming true, coming slowly to light like a message in lemon. And, what was the message? in yet another lingo? Truth is the father of lies; nothing survives; only the wicked can afford to be wise." Since his arrival in Gilean, Furber had tended a shady, walled garden attached to his church. With the graves of his predecessors in its four corners, the garden is an emblem straight from the fiction of Nathaniel Hawthorne or Herman Melville. Furber's dark vision has the same traditional literary source, but the people of Gilean see his words only as the ramblings of a madman. The Reverend Jethro Furber spends his final years in a mental institution.

Omensetter himself does not handle well the roles in which the people of Gilean have cast him. He is essentially a careless, happy man who is not deeply reflective about life. Cast as the embodiment of natural good by Henry Pimber and spiritual evil by Jethro Furber, he himself is unsure of his identity. For Omensetter, his arrival in Gilean was filled with the promise of a new life. "The trees were bare, I remember, and as we came down the hill we could see the tracks of the wagons glistening. You could see what your life would be." He is eager to prove that this promise was not a lie, and so he gambles on the life of his sick son Amos to see if the luck imputed to him by others will hold. "The infant lingered on alive, an outcome altogether outside science, Doctor Orcutt said, and Israbestis swore that Omensetter's luck would be a legend on the river—quite a while, he claimed—perhaps forever." Omensetter and his family leave Gilean, however, suggesting that his self-confidence has been permanently shaken by his experiences. With them, Gass suggests, goes all hope for vitality in the community.

In a fundamental sense, Omensetter, Furber, Pimber, and Tott are aspects of a single personality. They are the voices of human impulses competing for control. The multiple narrators of *Willie Masters' Lonesome Wife* are less clearly fragments of a single character, but they are equally strong symbol-making voices. Divided into four sections, each printed on paper of a different color, this novella is more overtly an experiment in narrative construction than *Omensetter's Luck*. It has little coherent plot at all, but there is plenty of action. The central character is Willie Masters' wife, a lonesome woman named Barbara who consoles herself with sexual encounters. "Well, I'm busty, passive, hairy, and will serve," she comments in the first, and blue-colored, section of the book. "Departure is my name. I travel, dream. I feel sometimes as if I *were* imagination (that spider goddess and thread-spinning muse)—imagination imagining itself imagine." While engaged in sexual intercourse with a bald man named Gelvin, "Busty Babs"—as her father called her—thinks about differences in the ways men and women think about sexuality. This is a topic to which Gass has returned time and again in his fiction; it fuels the speculations of the narrator of "In the Heart of the Heart of the Country" and the nearly pornographic fantasies of Furber in *Omensetter's Luck*.

Barbara Masters is a former stripper who danced professionally in a blue light. This explains, in part, the blue paper on which her thoughts are printed. She allows her mind to wander while Gelvin works out his fantasies on her body, and she imagines herself the author of a Russian play—printed in Gass's text on yellow paper to suggest its lurid nature—about a Russian named Ivan and his wife. Barbara casts herself in the role of the wife. The subject of the play is Ivan's reaction to evidence of his wife's infidelity, but the play soon gets overwhelmed by the footnotes providing a running commentary at the foot of each yellow page. The notes get longer, they are at times addressed to the reader of *Willie Masters' Lonesome Wife*, and eventually they swallow up the play. The text and notes do not match up, so the reader must choose whether to read the pages as printed or to work actively to construct a more coherent text.

Gass refers openly to the proposition that the reader is a collaborator in the section of *Willie Masters' Lonesome Wife* which is printed on red paper. The narrator here, perhaps still Barbara Masters, remarks,

> The muddy circle you see just before you and below you represents the ring left on a leaf of the manuscript by my coffee cup. Represents, I say, because, as you must surely realize, this book is many removes from anything I've set pen, hand, or cup to.

Like the play on yellow pages, this section contains simultaneous narratives. There is a dialogue about poetry and sexuality among characters named Leonora, Carlos, Angela, and Philippe; there is a running commentary on the art of writing—containing references to works by Henry David Thoreau, Henry James, and Thomas Hardy; and there is an interior monologue composed of random memories, supposedly events in the life of the narrator. In one sense, this technique re-creates the effect of a single human mind thinking simultaneously about several different subjects. In another, it is simply an elaborate parody of the method Gass uses in *Omensetter's Luck*. In a fictional text such as this one, all interpretations of significance are equally valid (or invalid), and there is ultimately nothing but a subjective reaction to be made out of the materials.

Gass addresses this fact in the final pages of the red section of the book. "You've been had," says the narrator, "haven't you, jocko? you sad sour stew-face sonofabitch. Really, did you read this far?" As Gass has made clear in his essays about literature, the essential nature of a literary text is the fact that it is made up of words. In the fourth section of *Willie Masters' Lonesome Wife*, printed on white paper and without the typographical variation to be found in the other sections of the book, the narrator identifies herself as a verbal construct.

> I am that lady language chose to make her playhouse of, and if you do not like me, if you find me dewlapped, scabby, wrinkled, old (and I've admitted as many pages as my age), well sir, I'm not like you, a loud rude noise and fart upon the town.

She is a new incarnation of the most traditional of muses, just as Willie Masters is a mask for the author William Gass himself.

Robert C. Petersen

Other major works

SHORT FICTION: *In the Heart of the Heart of the Country and Other Stories*, 1968.

NONFICTION: *Fiction and the Figures of Life*, 1970; *On Being Blue: A Philosophical Inquiry*, 1976; *The World Within the Word: Essays*, 1978; *The Habitations of the Word: Essays*, 1985.

Bibliography

Bradbury, Malcolm. *The Modern American Novel.* New York: Oxford University Press, 1983. Places Gass in the company of postmodern writers of the 1960's and 1970's. In discussing Gass's fiction and critical writing, Bradbury notes Gass's background in philosophy and that he is conscious of the "discrepancy between language and reality."

Hadella, Charlotte Byrd. "The Winter Wasteland of William Gass's *In the Heart of the Heart of the Country.*" *Critique: Studies in Modern Fiction* 30 (Fall, 1988): 49-57. Explores the connection between Gass's rejection of models as stiflers of imagination and his use of models in this work. Analyzes the narrator who is obsessed with models yet devoid of love. This essay stays with the content of this short-story collection but does little to relate this work to Gass's other fiction.

Hart, Paula. "William Gass." In *Contemporary Novelists*, edited by James Vinson. London: St. James Press, 1976. Hart discusses the difficulty in assessing Gass's writing, as the works "range from the purely imaginative to the imaginatively critical," and comments on his powerful images and "startling language." An appreciative piece of criticism that regards Gass as a vital literary presence.

Holloway, Watson L. *William Gass.* Boston: G. K. Hall, 1990. A formal study in which Holloway pays close attention to Gass's texts to "catch the music and intricacy of his work." Contains a valuable piece of criticism on *Omensetter's Luck.*

Saltzman, Arthur M. *The Fiction of William Gass: The Consolation of Language.* Carbondale: Southern Illinois University Press, 1986. A solid introduction to Gass's major works. Includes an interview with Gass.

GEORGE GISSING

Born: Wakefield, England; November 22, 1857
Died: St. Jean-Pied-de-Port, France; December 28, 1903

Principal long fiction

Workers in the Dawn, 1880; *The Unclassed*, 1884; *Isabel Clarendon*, 1886; *Demos*, 1886; *Thyrza*, 1887; *A Life's Morning*, 1888; *The Nether World*, 1889; *The Emancipated*, 1890; *New Grub Street*, 1891; *Denzil Quarrier*, 1892; *Born in Exile*, 1892; *The Odd Women*, 1893; *In the Year of Jubilee*, 1894; *Eve's Ransom*, 1895; *The Paying Guest*, 1895; *Sleeping Fires*, 1895; *The Whirlpool*, 1897; *The Town Traveller*, 1898; *The Crown of Life*, 1899; *Our Friend the Charlatan*, 1901; *The Private Papers of Henry Ryecroft*, 1903; *Veranilda*, 1904; *Will Warburton*, 1905.

Other literary forms

Though George Gissing will be remembered primarily as a novelist, he tried his hand at a variety of literary projects. In the 1890's especially, he found it profitable to write short stories; these were generally published in periodicals, but one volume—*Human Odds and Ends* (1898)—was published during his lifetime. Many of his other short stories, some from his early contributions to Chicago newspapers, have since been collected: *The House of Cobwebs* (1906), *Sins of the Fathers* (1924), *A Victim of Circumstances* (1927), and *Brownie* (1931). Gissing also wrote essays for a number of periodicals. *Notes on Social Democracy* (1968, with an introduction by Jacob Korg), reprints three articles he wrote for the *Pall Mall Gazette* in 1880. *Essays and Fiction* (1970, Pierre Coustillas, editor) prints nine prose works published for the first time. Late in his life, Gissing published *Charles Dickens: A Critical Study* (1898) and *By the Ionian Sea* (1901), his "notes of a ramble in southern Italy."

Achievements

During his lifetime, Gissing achieved neither the fame nor the fortune that he would have liked. His reputation, though it grew steadily, especially in the 1890's, was always overshadowed by the powerhouse writers of the late Victorian era. Gissing was nevertheless seriously reviewed and often applauded by the critics for his objective treatment of social conditions in England. After his death, his reputation was eclipsed for many years, and it is only in recent years that Gissing has begun to receive the reevaluation that is needed to determine his place in English literary history. The renewed academic attention, manifested by numerous new editions of his novels, critical biographies, full-length studies of his novels, and several volumes of his correspondence, suggests that Gissing's niche will soon become more firmly established than it ever has been.

Biography

Born on November 22, 1857, in Wakefield, Yorkshire, George Robert Gissing was the eldest of five children of Thomas Waller and Margaret Bedford Gissing. Thomas Gissing was a chemist in Wakefield and something of a religious skeptic whose extensive library provided the young George with convenient access to a variety of reading material. The early years of financial security and familial harmony were disrupted when Thomas Gissing died in December, 1870. George, only thirteen, and his two brothers were sent to Lindow Grove School at Alderley Edge, Cheshire. There, the young Gissing's studious habits gained for him the first of many academic accolades. His performance on the Oxford Local Examination in 1872 was especially encouraging, but financial circumstances made it necessary for him to attend Owens College in Manchester, where he had won free tuition for three sessions and where he continued with his academic success.

Gissing was not, however, enjoying the same success in his personal life. Living a lonely and studious life in Manchester, he fell in love with a young prostitute named Marianne Helen Harrison ("Nell"). With the zeal of the reformer, Gissing tried to save her from her profession and her penury, apparently not realizing at first that she was an alcoholic as well. Exhausting his own funds, the young Gissing stole miscellaneous property from his fellow students at Owens College. He was soon caught and the course of his life was radically altered, for he was forced to abandon all thoughts of an academic life. With the aid of friends, he sailed for the United States in the fall of 1876 and worked briefly as a high school teacher in Waltham, Massachusetts. Why he left Waltham, where he apparently enjoyed a reasonably good life, is not known, but in the spring of 1877 he moved to Chicago, where he tried to eke out an existence as a writer. Though he did publish his first work (a short story called "The Sins of the Fathers," in the Chicago *Tribune*, March 10, 1877), he was not well paid for his endeavors and left after only four months. He worked at odd jobs in New England and elsewhere, and then in the fall of 1877 he made his way to England. In London, he lived in near poverty, working sporadically as a tutor and drafting his first novels. Nell came to live with him, and in October, 1879, they were married. Despite Gissing's noble intention to reform her apparently self-destructive character, the marriage was not successful. A vivid fictionalized account of the sordidness of their married life is given in *Workers in the Dawn*, Gissing's first published novel. He lived a turbulent life with Nell until he put her in an invalids' home in January, 1882. Even after that, she gave him trouble, both financial and emotional, until she died in 1888.

The direction of Gissing's writings in the 1880's was influenced not only by his failed marriage but also by a number of other lifelong interests which were well established by the end of the decade: his friendship with the budding German writer Eduard Bertz, his reading of Auguste Comte, his unfailing compassion for the poverty of late Victorian England, his friendship with Frederic Harrison, who read his first novel and provided much-needed encouragement, and his friendship with Morley Roberts, who later became Gissing's first biographer with the thinly disguised *The Private Life of Henry Maitland* (1912). Not until 1886, with the publication of *Demos*, did Gissing gain moderate success with his writing. Buoyed by more favorable circumstances, especially the sense of freedom once Nell died, Gissing left for an extended tour of Europe in September, 1888. He also shifted the emphasis of his novels from the working class to the middle class, beginning in 1890 with *The Emancipated*.

The 1890's began auspiciously for Gissing's literary career, particularly with the publication of *New Grub Street* and *Born in Exile*. His personal life, however, was following a different course. On a trip to Italy in 1890, he noticed the first signs of the respiratory illness which would plague him the rest of his life. On February 25, 1891, he married Edith Underwood, a "workgirl," as he described her, with whom he was not in love. The marriage was a complete failure, despite the birth of two sons (Walter Leonard, born 1891, and Alfred Charles, born 1895). Gissing's literary success in the 1890's, as moderate as it was, was achieved in spite of his loveless marriage and domestic unrest. He persevered until September, 1897, when he permanently separated from his wife and went to Italy. In the summer of 1898, he met Gabrielle Fleury, a Frenchwoman who was the complete opposite of his two wives in her refined and cultured manner. Gissing was immediately attracted to her and would have legally married her had a divorce from Edith been possible. Instead, the two sanctified their relationship with each other in a private ceremony on May 7, 1899, in Rouen. Living in France under the most favorable circumstances of his entire life, Gissing continued to write, and in 1903 saw *The Private Papers of Henry Ryecroft*, his most popular work, go through three editions. His health, however, had been growing steadily worse, and his shortlived happiness came to an end when he died on December 28, 1903, of myocarditis at St. Jean-Pied-de-Port in France.

Analysis

In his personal life, George Gissing was a man of divided mind, and the biographical antitheses were paralleled by the literary and philosophical influences on his work. In private life, he gravitated toward Frederic Harrison's circle of intellectuals and sophisticated people; at the same time, he was drawn into marriages with psychologically, intellectually, and socially unsuitable women. He was attracted, on the one hand, to a scholarly career as a historian, philosopher, and classicist; on the other, he was drawn to journalism, hackwork, and lectures to workingmen's associations with an emphasis on social reform. Like many writers at the end of the nineteenth century, he was caught between the sociological realists with reform instincts and the adherents of an aesthetic movement with their emphasis on the attainment of ideal beauty. His sensuousness conflicted with his intellectual idealism; his desire for popularity and material success with his austere integrity as an artist.

Gissing's career as a novelist, at least until recently, has been assessed in the context of nineteenth century realism and naturalism. Certainly, the techniques employed in his novels, especially the early ones, owe much to the Victorian conventions that had become well established by the time of Gissing's first published novel. He was thoroughly acquainted with the work of Charles Dickens; his own novels are often sentimental, cautiously admonitory, and riddled with subplots. Gissing, however, never treated his subject matter as humorously as did Dickens in his early novels. Dickens' treatment of poverty, for example, is sometimes used for picturesque effects; Gissing saw poverty in a solemn manner, finding it both lamentable and execrable.

For other literary precedents, Gissing turned to the French and Russian writers, discovering in the French naturalists such as Émile Zola the pervasive effects of physical and social environments and finding in the Russian naturalistic psychologists the precise and complete analysis of character. Like Zola, he described the squalor of poverty, probed the psychology of sex (though with more reserve), and generally ended his novels in dismal defeat. Yet, unlike the naturalists, Gissing was not so much concerned with the particular details of the workshop, with conflicts between capital and labor, but with the whole atmosphere of poverty, especially the resultant loss of integrity on the part of those who struggle to go beyond and above it.

To divide Gissing's career into neat stages is not an easy task. For the purposes of an overview, however, it is convenient to look at three large, if not always distinct, groups of his novels. In the 1880's, beginning with *Workers in the Dawn* and ending. with *The Nether World*, Gissing was most often concerned with the lower class and social reform. In the first half of the 1890's, beginning with *The Emancipated*, Gissing turned to the middle class, examining the whole middle-class ethic and ranging his focal point from the tradesman to the "new woman." In the last half of the 1890's and until his death in 1903, Gissing's work was more varied, ranging from a historical romance to a travel book to reworkings of his early themes. In those last years, his works were not always successful, either commercially or critically, but that was the period of his most popular work, the semiautobiographical *The Private Papers of Henry Ryecroft*.

In an early and important reassessment of Gissing's career, Jacob Korg ("Division of Purpose in George Gissing," in *PMLA*, June, 1955) points out that the dichotomy between Gissing's artistic principles and his anger over

Victorian England's social problems is evident in five of his novels published in the 1880's: *Workers in the Dawn*, *The Unclassed*, *Demos*, *Thyrza*, and *The Nether World*. In each of these novels, Gissing the reformer contends with Gissing the artist; in none of them is the tension resolved satisfactorily.

Most of the material Gissing used in *Workers in the Dawn* can be found repeatedly in the other novels of the 1880's, and most of that material springs from his own experiences. Clearly, his early marriage to a girl from the slums underlined his interest in social themes throughout his life. In the late 1870's and 1880's, he had also become enthusiastic about the radical party, read Comte, promoted positivist doctrines, and spoke at various radicalist meetings. Between 1879 and 1880, Gissing began writing *Workers in the Dawn*, a novel of avowed social protest in which he serves, as he says in a letter of June 8, 1880, as "a mouthpiece of the advanced Radical party." Equally obvious in the novel, however, is the fact that George Gissing is perturbed about placing art in service to political and moral dogma. Arthur Goldring, the hero of the novel, is both a painter and a social reformer, but he is clearly upset with this duality in his life. Convinced that the aims of his two avocations are antithetical, he looks for consolation from Helen Norman, the woman he loves. Through the mouth of Helen, George Gissing propounds the ideas that he had gleaned from Percy Bysshe Shelley's *A Defence of Poetry* (1840)— most specifically that art is the true legislator of the moral order. Gissing, however, found it difficult to practice what he held to be intellectually valid; thus, the early Gissing, like Goldring, constantly found difficulty in accepting the tenet that art should not attempt to teach morality directly.

In *The Unclassed*, Gissing continued to struggle with the intricacies of the artist's world. The result, unfortunately, was a novel in which the fall of the two artist-figures is in one case oversimplified and in the other, muddled. Confused and worried about his own failings, Gissing attempted to analyze the artistic temperament and the forces operating against such a temperament by segmenting the artist into Julian Casti and Osmond Waymark. Casti's story is Gissing's attempt to depict an artist undone by an overriding sense of moral obligation to a shrewish and possessive woman, Harriet Smales, a character with clear similarities to Gissing's own wife Nell. Not until the last chapter is the physically debilitated and intellectually frustrated Casti convinced that his moral obligation to Harriet is futile. He leaves for the Isle of Wight, where he quietly spends his last days plaintively talking of the epic he will never write.

The portrait of Waymark is Gissing's attempt to counterbalance the oversimplified Casti. Waymark is a more complex figure, and his role as an artist is more thoroughly scrutinized by Gissing. Waymark is thwarted in his pursuit of art by a variety of causes: his aborted social consciousness, his vaguely defined ideological tenets, his relationship with women, and his pecuniary predicament. By the end of the novel, after a plethora of complications,

Waymark is neither a complete success nor a complete failure. His one published novel receives mediocre reviews, and Waymark himself shows little
concern either for its intrinsic value or for its critical reception. By placing
his artist-hero in the grips of consuming personal, political, and economic
woes, Gissing tries to suggest that art cannot flourish with integrity or purity.
The portrait of Waymark, however, is finally very muddled, for it is not clear
to which forces Waymark the artist succumbs. Questions about the role of
art in the political and moral order continued to dominate Gissing's thinking
in much the same way throughout the 1880's, and he entered the 1890's very
much in the middle of the two main currents of literary thought, drawn both
to the angry didacticism of the realists and naturalists and to the ivory towers
of the aesthetes.

In the 1890's, Gissing broadened the range of his novels and produced his
best work. At the beginning of the decade, he published *The Emancipated*,
the story of a young middle-class widow restricted by religious scruples until
she finds release in art. In *Denzil Quarrier*, Gissing tried his hand at a political
novel and produced one of his more popular works. In *Eve's Ransom*, a short
novel that was first serialized, he focused on the pangs of unrequited love.
In *Born in Exile*, Gissing examined the life of one born in the lower classes
who has the opportunity to rise to a higher socioeconomic level. In *The Odd
Women*, Gissing focused his attention on early feminists, making a careful
study of women who never marry but who must support themselves in a male-
dominated society.

The novel on which Gissing's reputation has most depended is *New Grub
Street*, his full-length study of the artist's role in society. From Jasper Milvain
to Whelpdale to Alfred Yule to Edwin Reardon to Harold Biffin, Gissing
offers a finely graduated hierarchy of the late nineteenth century artist. He
is particularly interested in characterizing the artist manqué and the forces
which have contributed to his failure. Unlike the earlier novels, however,
New Grub Street presents a wider-ranging understanding of the artist's
dilemma. It is no longer a simple case of idealized social reform versus an
even more idealized artistic purity. In keeping with his social interests of the
early 1890's, Gissing sees the factors operating against the artist arising more
from without than from within. He concentrates on two particularly potent
forces which militate against the artist and ultimately ensure his downfall.

The first force is the woman, and her influence on the artist is subtle,
pervasive, and lasting. Often sensitive and frequently lonely, the nascent
artists of Gissing's Grub Street are prime targets for the love of a good woman.
She appeals particularly to the psychologically insecure artist, promising a
lifetime of emotional stability. At the outset, she is a source of inspiration,
yet time and disillusionment reveal more distressing realities. It is the age-
old femme fatale who lures the artist away from his art into an emotionally
draining existence, thwarting his inclination and energy for production. It is

"the other woman" who instigates a complicated triangle with like results. It is the husband-hunting woman who tantalizes the frustrated artist with the attraction of domestic security, but soon she either stifles that inexplicable drive to write for the sake of writing or provides a marriage so socially disadvantageous that advancement is precluded.

Economics is the second, equally potent, force militating against the three failed artists (Reardon, Biffen, Yule) of *New Grub Street*. While the force of woman is chiefly felt on a psychological level, her destructive influence within the economic sphere is evident. After all, the necessity of supporting a wife and children increases the financial difficulties the artist must face. Monetary matters also prove a problem in and of themselves. An artist such as Biffen easily falls victim to the myth of so many struggling artists, convinced that poverty and hardship are essential in the experience of any would-be writer. In the portrait of Reardon, however, one quickly sees the artist at odds with real poverty, rarely an inspiration and usually a deterrent to his work.

Edwin Reardon is the novel's central character, and it is Reardon who is subjected to the greatest number of debilitating forces. When he is introduced, it is immediately clear that his marriage to Amy has entangled him in the finely woven web of woman. At the outset, Reardon is thirty-two, has been married two years, and has a ten-month-old child. None of his decisions, artistic or otherwise, can be wholly unaffected by this domestic responsibility. Gissing makes his viewpoint clear in the very first scene with Reardon and Amy. In this scene, largely a heated discussion over Reardon's approach to writing, Amy chides her husband for not compromising his artistic integrity and forcibly reminds him that "art must be practised as a trade, at all events in our time. This is the age of trade." Thus, in this one early scene, the two powerful influences of woman and commerce come together, and there is little doubt that they will take a heavy toll on Reardon the artist. Reardon's failure as an artist, both aesthetically and materially, runs in direct proportion to the failure of his marriage and the decline of his economic status.

Obviously lending itself to autobiographical interpretation, the artist-novel is the means by which the real-life writer works out—or fails to—his own aesthetic and personal conflicts. *New Grub Street*, like Gissing's earlier novels, has its share of autobiographical elements, but his analysis of his emotional and intellectual condition is far more perceptive. He has gained tighter control on the raw materials of the artist's world which are treated ambiguously in the early novels. The eleven years between *Workers in the Dawn* and *New Grub Street* were the training ground for an increased self-insight and a more encompassing, objective portraiture of the artist-figure and the gray areas with which he must cope.

The work Gissing produced in the last half of the 1890's has not generally contributed to his critical reputation. Part of his later years he spent on a variety of projects that are not especially characteristic of his overall career.

In 1898, he published *Charles Dickens: A Critical Study*. In 1901, he published *By the Ionian Sea*, a travel book about his experiences in Italy. He also worked on a historical novel which was never completed but published posthumously as *Veranilda* in 1904. The novels that Gissing published in his last years are for the most part undistinguished and often are reworkings of his earlier themes. *The Whirlpool* is a study of marriage in the "whirlpool" of modern life. *The Crown of Life* is his paean to the perfect marriage, significantly begun shortly after he met Gabrielle Fleury in 1898.

In 1900, Gissing did most of the writing of *The Private Papers of Henry Ryecroft*, though it was not published until 1903. The book is not really a novel. Pretending to be merely the book's editor, Gissing provides a short preface saying that he has come across the papers of his friend Ryecroft and has ordered them in an arbitrary way. There are four main sections, each labeled with one of the seasons, beginning with spring and ending with winter. The book is a mixture of autobiography and reverie, providing the author a platform on which he can discuss sundry subjects. Thus, there are memories of childhood, of poverty in London, of peaceful trips to Italy. There are descriptive sketches of rural scenes in England. There are short essays on philosophical ideas and terse confessions of various preferences, ranging from food to countries. The book provides delightful if not exciting reading and gives a memorable portrait of the aging author who has retired to the calmness of Exeter to ruminate.

When Gissing died in 1903, he left behind an impressive corpus, but the reputation he had at the time of his death did not continue to grow. By some, he was criticized as being too ponderous and undramatic, inclined to publish an analytical study rather than a dramatized story. By others, he was accused of being melodramatic, relying too exclusively on the contrivances of the Victorian "triple-decker." In more recent years, however, especially during the last two decades, Gissing has attracted more attention in academic circles. His seriousness as a novelist is slowly being recognized, both for his historic role in the heyday of English realism and for his integrity as an individual novelist.

David B. Eakin

Other major works
SHORT FICTION: *Human Odds and Ends*, 1897; *The House of Cobwebs*, 1906; *Sins of the Fathers*, 1924; *A Victim of Circumstances*, 1927; *Brownie*, 1931.

NONFICTION: *Charles Dickens: A Critical Study*, 1898; *By the Ionian Sea*, 1901; *The Immortal Dickens*, 1925; *Letters of George Gissing to Members of His Family*, 1927; *George Gissing and H. G. Wells: Their Friendship and Correspondence*, 1961; *The Letters of George Gissing to Eduard Bertz*, 1961;

George Gissing's Commonplace Book, 1962; *The Letters of George Gissing to Gabrielle Fleury*, 1964; *George Gissing: Essays and Fiction*, 1970; *The Diary of George Gissing, Novelist*, 1978.

Bibliography

Collie, Michael. *The Alien Art.* Hamden, Conn.: Anchor Books, 1979. Analyzes each of Gissing's main novels. Pays close attention to his style, noting that he avoids metaphor in his pursuit of realism. Unlike most of his contemporaries, Gissing responded more to Continental writers than to the English tradition. Contends that his novels should not be read as autobiographical, a position that is at odds with received opinion.

Coustillas, Pierre, and Colin Partridge, eds. *Gissing: The Critical Heritage.* London: Routledge & Kegan Paul, 1972. A very important research tool for the study of Gissing, containing a large selection of reviews dating from his own time to the late 1960's. Among the notable essays is a notice by the great Victorian critic George Saintsbury, who claimed that Gissing had an obsessional interest in attacking the social order, but who nevertheless liked Gissing because his writing was difficult to forget. Paul Elmer More argued that Gissing overcame the undue realism of his first novels. Gissing's study of the classics and philosophy tempered his overblown portrayal of society.

Grylls, David. *The Paradox of Gissing.* London: Allen & Unwin, 1986. Maintains that paradox is the key to reading Gissing properly. He was attracted to conflicting points of view on various topics, including women, social reform, poverty, and art. His novels express these contradictions, often by a sharp break in the middle. In *New Grub Street*, Gissing achieved an integration of diverse opinions.

Halperin, John. *Gissing: A Life in Books.* Oxford, England: Oxford University Press, 1982. The most comprehensive life of Gissing. Its dominant theme is that he wrote about his own life in his novels, and much of the book discusses Gissing's fiction from this point of view. Halperin does not confine himself to Gissing's life, devoting considerable attention to the critical reaction to Gissing after his death. Maintains that H. G. Wells launched a campaign of vilification against Gissing. Also includes a section that offers acidulous remarks of writers about Gissing.

Michaux, Jean-Pierre, ed. *George Gissing: Critical Essays.* New York: Barnes & Noble Books, 1981. This valuable anthology gives a good selection of twentieth century critics' discussions of Gissing. Includes an influential essay by Q. D. Leavis, who praised Gissing's portrayal of the misery of the Victorian world. His careful and realistic observations achieved their culmination in *New Grub Street*, which Leavis places among the outstanding English novels. An essay by George Orwell lauds Gissing's attack on respectability.

ELLEN GLASGOW

Born: Richmond, Virginia; April 22, 1873
Died: Richmond, Virginia; November 21, 1945

Principal long fiction

The Descendant, 1897; *Phases of an Inferior Planet*, 1898; *The Voice of the People*, 1900; *The Battle-Ground*, 1902; *The Deliverance*, 1904; *The Wheel of Life*, 1906; *The Ancient Law*, 1908; *The Romance of a Plain Man*, 1909; *The Miller of Old Church*, 1911; *Virginia*, 1913; *Life and Gabriella*, 1916; *The Builders*, 1919; *One Man in His Time*, 1922; *Barren Ground*, 1925; *The Romantic Comedians*, 1926; *They Stooped to Folly*, 1929; *The Sheltered Life*, 1932; *Vein of Iron*, 1935; *In This Our Life*, 1941.

Other literary forms

In addition to nineteen novels, Ellen Glasgow wrote a book of short stories, *The Shadowy Third and Other Stories* (1923); a book of poems, *The Freeman and Other Poems* (1902); a book on her views of fiction-writing (concerned primarily with her own works), *A Certain Measure* (1943); and an autobiography, *The Woman Within* (1954). She also wrote a number of articles on fiction for various periodicals and magazines. Her letters were published in 1958.

Achievements

Although Glasgow never felt that she had received the critical acclaim she deserved, or at least desired, she nevertheless played an important part in the development of Southern letters. A significant figure in the so-called Southern Renascence, she provided in her novels a new picture of the South, a region reluctantly ushered into the modern world. Against a sentimentalized view of the Old South, Glasgow advocated an acceptance of the inevitability of change.

Prior to 1925, Glasgow's critical reception was mixed—more positive than negative, but nothing that would mark her as a writer of the first rank. With *Barren Ground*, however, Glasgow's reputation began to grow with both critics and readers. That novel made the 1925 *Review of Review*'s list of twenty-five outstanding novels of the year. Represented also on the list for 1925 were Sinclair Lewis' *Arrowsmith*, Edith Wharton's *The Mother's Recompense*, Willa Cather's *The Professor's House*, and Sherwood Anderson's *Dark Laughter*. Glasgow's *The Sheltered Life* was a best-seller and greatly enhanced her reputation. *Vein of Iron* and *In This Our Life*, which received the Pulitzer Prize in 1942, helped to ensure her position as a writer of major significance.

"The chief end of the novel, as indeed of all literature," Glasgow wrote, is "to increase our understanding of life and heighten our consciousness." To this end she directed her artistic skills, writing with care and precision, for, as she also said, "The true novel . . . is, like poetry, an act of birth, not a device or invention."

Biography

Born in Richmond, Virginia, in 1873, Ellen Glasgow came from a combination of stern Scotch-Irish pioneers on her father's side and Tidewater, Virginia, aristocratic stock on her mother's side. Francis Glasgow was an ironworks executive, an occupation well suited to his Puritan temperament and character. Ellen Glasgow had little positive to say about her father. Her mother, on the other hand, was a cultivated, gracious, and humane woman. These divergent influences provided the crucible from which Glasgow's writings were to emerge.

The next to the youngest in a family of four sons and six daughters, Glasgow experienced a more-or-less lonely childhood, with Rebe, her younger sister, and Mammy Lizzie Jones, her black nurse, providing her only companionship. Because of fragile health and a nervous temperament that precluded adjustment to formal schooling, her isolation was increased, and most of her education came from her father's extensive library.

As a child, Glasgow admired the novels of Charles Dickens, Henry Fielding, and Jane Austen. From Dickens, she gained reinforcement for her already strong aversion to cruelty, and from the latter two, she learned that only honest writing can endure. Lesser novelists, she felt, lacked "the creative passion and the courage to offend, which is the essential note of great fiction."

Glasgow grew up in that period following the Civil War when, as she described it, the "prosperous and pleasure-loving" agrarians of the antebellum years were struggling for existence amid "the dark furies of Reconstruction." It was a conservative, even reactionary, time when, according to Glasgow, "being a rebel, even an intellectual one, was less exciting and more uncomfortable than it is nowadays." Rejecting the harsh Calvinism of her father and the bloodless social graces of Richmond society, she retreated even further into a life of the mind. Glasgow's growing sense of alienation and rebelliousness has been seen by critics as the wellspring of her literary vision.

By 1890, just one year after her hearing had begun to fade, Glasgow had produced some four hundred pages of a novel, *Sharp Realities* (unpublished). Putting that effort aside, she began writing *The Descendant* in 1891. Two years later, however, upon the death of her mother, with whom she had great affinity, she destroyed a good part of what she had written. Another two years passed before she returned to the novel and completed it. The following year, she made the first of numerous trips to Europe.

With the publication (anonymously) of *The Descendant* in 1897, Glasgow was launched on her prolific career, a career that saw novels appearing every two years or so. Writing became and remained her role in life, and she was ever mindful of the growth of her literary reputation, changing publishers when she felt it to her advantage and making sure that critics were fully aware of her books.

Presumably while on a trip to Europe in 1899, Glasgow fell in love with a married man, to whom she refers in her autobiography *The Woman Within* (1954) as Gerald B____ . A mystery man, Gerald B____ was described by Glasgow as an older man with a wife and children, a Wall Street man. There is some evidence, however, indicating that Gerald B____ was a physician. Another serious love affair was with Henry Watkins Anderson, a Richmond lawyer. He and Glasgow met in 1915, and were engaged in 1917. In July of the next year, Glasgow attempted suicide when she learned that Anderson, who was working with the Red Cross in the Balkan States, was attracted to Queen Marie of Romania. This turbulent love affair between Glasgow and Anderson was tacitly broken about 1920. In two novels, *The Builders* and *One Man in His Time*, Glasgow incorporated aspects of her relationship with Anderson.

As Glasgow began receiving the critical recognition for which she longed, her health began to fail. A heart condition worsened, and she died on November 21, 1945, in Richmond, Virginia.

Analysis

Turning away from a romanticized view of her own Virginia, Ellen Glasgow became a part of the revolt against the elegiac tradition of Southern letters. Although she rejected romance, she did not turn to realism; rather, she saw herself as a "verist": "The whole truth," she said, "must embrace the interior world as well as external appearances." In this sense, she strove for what she called "blood and irony"—blood because the South had grown thin and pale and was existing on borrowed ideas, copying rather than creating; and irony because it is the surest antidote to sentimental decay. Certain that life in the South was not as it had been pictured by previous writers, she produced a series of novels that recorded the social history of Virginia through three generations, picturing sympathetically the social and industrial revolution that was transforming the romantic South.

A central theme in this record is that of change—change brought about by the conflict between the declining agrarian regime and the rising industrial system. Arguing that such change must be accepted and even welcomed, Glasgow observed "For thirty years I have had a part in the American literary scene, either as a laborer in the vineyard or as a raven croaking on a bust of Pallas. In all these years I have found that the only permanent law in art, as in the social order, is the law of change."

In pursuing the theme of change, however, Glasgow was careful not to go to the extreme in her presentation of deterioration, feeling that "the literature that crawls too long in the mire will lose at last the power of standing erect."

In this respect, her works, unlike those of William Faulkner or Erskine Caldwell, lack shocking or sensational detail and maintain an almost Victorian sense of decorum. For example, when Dorinda in *Barren Ground* goes to the city, she is first approached by a fascinating lady clad in black who wants her to enter into a disreputable house. She is then rescued by a kindly doctor who gives her money to go back to Virginia and establish a dairy farm. This tendency toward propriety found in Glasgow's writing is explained in her plea to the novelist of the Southern Gothic school: "All I ask him to do is to deal as honestly with living tissues as he now deals with decay, to remind himself that the colors of putrescence have no greater validity for our age, or for any age, than . . . the cardinal virtues."

The theme of change gives a mythic quality to Glasgow's work. It is that quality that Henry Canby refers to when he says that Glasgow sees her world as always a departing and a becoming. Her instrument for this cutting away is her sense for tender and ironic tragedy, a tragedy that is, in the words of Canby, "a tragedy of frustration—the waste of life through maladjustment of man to his environment and environment to its men."

Often, too, Glasgow's works picture nobility cramped by prejudice, or beauty gone wrong through an inability to adjust to the real, or a good philosophy without premises in existing experience. A good example of the latter theme can be found in the character of John Fincastle in *Vein of Iron*. A man of deep thought, he is considered "as a dangerous skeptic, or as a man of simple faith, who believed that God is essence, not energy, and that blessedness, or the life of the spirit, is the only reality." Fincastle is a part of the constant change in the world, but he himself does not fully realize the implications of the dynamic society in which he lives. He sees nothing of any potential value in the machine age and is unable to reconcile his own philosophy to the reality of the times.

Although all of Glasgow's works contain a note of pessimism, there is also present a note of optimism. More often than not, this hope comes after a protagonist's contact with city life. Dorinda, for example, returns to Pedlar's Mill after her stay in the city, to start a successful farm and gain revenge from Jason. Then, too, there is Ada in *Vein of Iron*, who, with her cynical husband, returns to the manse that was once her home and, strengthened by the recovery of "that lost certainty of a continuing tradition," looks forward to a new beginning.

Perhaps, when compared with Faulkner or Thomas Wolfe, the theme of change, as treated by Glasgow, may seem somewhat sentimental; there is, however, a refreshing and heartening chord in her work that lends credence to the idea that the world is not destined to be one great naturalistic garbage can, but may perhaps be fertile enough for an occasional bed of flowers. At any rate, as Glasgow phrased it, "the true revolution may end in a ditch or in the shambles, but it must begin in the stars."

In *Virginia*, her first acknowledged masterpiece, Glasgow focuses on the Southern woman. "As an emblem," she writes of the Southern woman in *The Deliverance*, "she followed closely the mid-Victorian ideal, and though her sort was found everywhere in the Western world, it was in Virginia that she seemed to attain her finest and latest flowering." It would follow, then, that if Southern women attained their "finest and latest flowering" in Virginia, that also is where they would be most affected by the winds of social change that were sweeping over the South in the late nineteenth and early twentieth centuries. Bred and reared to tradition, they faced a new order that was both challenging and perplexing. While some held firmly to the pedestal on which they had been placed, others leaped from it and immersed themselves in the new world.

Virginia Pendleton, the heroine of *Virginia*, is, like her mother, the ideal Southern woman, the image of propriety and gentility. "Whenever I attempt to recall the actual writing of Virginia," Glasgow says in *A Certain Measure*,

and to recapture the mold in which the book was conceived, I find myself moving again in an imaginary world which was then more real to me than the world which I inhabited. I could not separate Virginia from her background, because she was an integral part of it, and it shared her validity. What she was, that background and atmosphere had helped to make her, and she, in turn, had intensified the life of the picture.

In Dinwiddie, Virginia, during the 1800's, Virginia has been reared as "the perfect flower of the Victorian ideal" and "logical result of an inordinate sense of duty, the crowning achievement of the code of beautiful behavior and the Episcopal Church." She has been taught that duty, devotion, and sacrifice are the lot of women and that husband and family must come before all else.

Virginia, educated at Miss Priscilla Battle's finishing school, the Dinwiddie Academy for Young Ladies, is indeed "finished," at least as far as any real purpose in life is concerned. The basis of her education was simply that "the less a girl knew about life, the better prepared she would be to contend with it." Thinking him an excellent choice for a husband, she marries Oliver Treadwell, son of an industrialist, and, bearing him three children, settles down to family life. Oliver, like his father, who had dominated Oliver's mother, exercises this same control over Virginia. A would-be dramatist, Oliver is unsuccessful as a serious playwright, but he does receive some financial return by writing claptrap for the New York stage. Although Virginia has become middle-aged and worn, Oliver has maintained the look of youth. Finding no understanding from Virginia, who is not equipped to give him any, he deserts her for Margaret Oldcastle, an actress. Not knowing how to fight for her husband's love, Virginia is left with her two daughters, whose independence and aggressiveness she cannot understand, and her devoted son, Harry. The purpose in life for which she and so many other Southern women had been prepared is gone. "Nothing but constancy was left to her," says Glasgow, "and constancy, when it has outlived its usefulness, is as barren as fortitude."

Virginia, in her minor tragedy, represents the ideal woman as victim of change, a change for which she has not been prepared and for which there is no effective antidote. One detects at least a small tear shed by Glasgow for the Virginias of the world. Once seen as ornaments of civilization and as restraints upon the more coarse natures of men, they now must replace self-sacrifice with an assertiveness that will be more in keeping with the changing social order. In that sense, Virginia points forward to *Barren Ground*.

Barren Ground marks Glasgow's emergence not only from a period of despondency regarding her social life, but also as a novelist who has moved without question from apprentice to master. Certainly her finest work to that time, *Barren Ground* was to Glasgow the best of all her novels. One of her country novels, it deals with that class of people often referred to as "poor whites." Glasgow herself refutes this appelation, preferring instead to call them "good people," a label that distinguishes them from the aristocratic "good families." Lineal descendants of the English yeoman farmer, these people were the ones who pushed the frontier westward. In this novel, they stand as a "buffer class between the opulent gentry and the hired labourers."

Dorinda Oakley, the heroine, is the offspring of a union of opposites: her father, Joshua, a landless man whose industry and good nature do not compensate for his ineffectuality; and her mother, Eudora, the daughter of a Presbyterian minister, with a religious mania of her own. This background, says Glasgow, has kept Dorinda's heart "in arms against life." More important, however, she has also inherited a kinship with the earth. This kinship enables her to make something positive out of "barren ground."

Dorinda falls in love with Jason Greylock, a young doctor, seeing in him the promise of something more than the grinding poverty she has known. They plan to marry, but Jason cannot go against his father's wishes, and he marries Geneva Ellgood instead. Pregnant by Jason, Dorinda flees to New York, where, after being struck by a taxi, she loses the baby. She works as a nurse for a Dr. Faraday until she learns that her father is dying. She returns home with enough money borrowed from Faraday to start a dairy farm. Back on the land, she becomes a tough-minded spinster and makes a success of the farm. Although she marries Nathan Pedlar, a storekeeper, she remains the head of the family. After his death in a train wreck, she is again alone, but happy, rearing Nathan's child by a previous marriage and managing the farm. Jason, in the meantime, has lost his wife by suicide and is forced to sell his farm to Dorinda. Because he is ill and an alcoholic, she unwillingly provides him with food and shelter. After a few months, he dies, and once more she is alone. When a local farmer asks Dorinda to marry him, she responds, "I am thankful to have finished with all that."

A tragic figure of sorts, Dorinda sees herself trapped by fate, "a straw in the wind, a leaf on a stream." Even so, she is not content to be simply a passive victim of that fate. Unlike Jason, who through his inherited weakness, succumbs to the forces that beset him, Dorinda looks upon the land as a symbol of that fate against which she must struggle. Hardened by adversity and with a deep instinct for survival, she refuses to surrender.

Although Dorinda's life may be compared to barren ground because it has been emotionally unfulfilled, it nevertheless is a successful life in that she does master herself and in turn masters the land. Just as the broom sedge must be burned off the land, so must romantic emotions be purged from Dorinda's soul. In giving her life to the land, she, in a sense, gains it back— and is thus, ironically, both victim and victor.

Following *Barren Ground*, Glasgow turned to the novel of manners with *The Romantic Comedians*. The first of a trilogy—the subsequent works being *They Stooped to Folly* and *The Sheltered Life*—this novel has been regarded by some critics as Glasgow's finest. After *Barren Ground*, Glasgow comments, a novel "which for three years had steeped my mind in the tragic life, the comic spirit, always restless when it is confined, began struggling against the bars of its cage." Because she never before had turned her hand to comedy of manners, *The Romantic Comedians* was written in the nature of an experiment.

The novel exhibits a high spirit of comedy with tragic overtones. "Tragedy and comedy were blood brothers" in Glasgow's image-making faculty, she writes, "but they were at war with each other, and had steadily refused to be reconciled." In *The Romantic Comedians*, says Blair Rouse, "we see people and their actions as participants in the follies of the comic genre; but we see, too, that a very slight shift of emphasis may reveal a tragic mask upon the actors."

Judge Gamaliel Bland Honeywell, the protagonist, "is a collective portrait of several Virginians of an older school," says Glasgow, "who are still unafraid to call themselves gentlemen." Living in Queenborough (Richmond, Virginia), he seeks female companionship after his wife of thirty-six years dies. At age sixty-five, he is expected to marry a former sweetheart, Amanda Lightfoot. Disdaining such expected decorum, however, he falls in love and marries Annabelle Upchurch, a young cousin of his wife. Annabelle marries him not so much for love, but rather, to heal the pain of being jilted by Angus Blount. As one might suspect in such a marriage, Annabelle is soon looking for greener pastures, finding them in Delaney Birdsong, with whom she goes to New York. Unable to win her back, the Judge, ill and disillusioned, believes that life holds nothing more for him. With the coming of spring, however, he looks upon his attractive young nurse and muses, "spring is here, and I am feeling almost as young as I felt last year."

Judge Honeywell, like many of Glasgow's women, is of another tradition. More than age separates him from Annabelle. While he is the target of some satiric jibes in the book and one finds it difficult to find much sincerity in him, he is, nevertheless, a victim of the same kind of romantic claptrap that dooms other Glasgow characters.

A refreshing book when contrasted with Glasgow's previous efforts, *The Romantic Comedians* displays the author's humanity as well as her humor. While she makes the reader laugh at the actions of the Judge and the other characters of the novel, she never lets them become completely ridiculous. Whatever else the Judge is, for example, he is a human being—and no one recognizes that more than Glasgow.

In *The Sheltered Life*, the last novel of her trilogy on manners, Glasgow employs two points of view—that of youth and that of age, in this case a young girl and an old man. Against the background of a "shallow and aimless society of happiness hunters," she presents more characters of Queenborough as they are revealed through the mind and emotions of Jenny Blair and her grandfather, General David Archbald.

Glasgow intended General Archbald as the central character in the novel— a character who "represents the tragedy, wherever it appears, of the civilized man in a world that is not civilized." General Archbald sees before him a changing world, a world that is passing him by. Thus, he holds to the social traditions of the nineteenth century, which have provided little shelter for him. He was never a man for his time. A sensitive person who had wanted to be a poet, he was ridiculed in his earlier years. Poetry had been his one love in life; it was lost before it could be realized. He married his wife only because of an accidental, overnight sleigh ride that, in tradition-bound Queenborough, demanded marriage to save appearances. A compassionate man, he gives up his desire to marry again after his wife dies in order not to disrupt the lives of his son's widow and her daughter Jenny.

Jenny, too, unknowingly is caught in the patterned existence of the Archbald heritage. A willful girl, she has been sheltered from the real world by culture and tradition and can see things only in terms of her own desires. At eighteen, she falls in love with an older married man, George Birdsong. George's wife, Eva, eventually finds them in each other's arms. Jenny flees the scene, only to learn later that Eva has killed George.

Eva Birdsong is another perfect image of Southern womanhood, beautiful and protected all her life. A celebrated belle prior to her marriage to George, she has striven to achieve a perfect marriage. Without children, she and George are thrown upon each other. Over the years, George has been a bit of a *roué* seeking pleasure where he could find it. In the end, Eva is left with the realization that what women "value most is something that doesn't exist."

When Jenny realizes what she has done, she flies to the General's understanding and sheltering arms, crying, "Oh, Grandfather, I didn't mean anything. . . . I didn't mean anything in the world." Ironically enough, she is right: she did not mean anything.

The Sheltered Life is more a tragicomedy than simply a comedy of manners.

It is also, perhaps, Glasgow's best work, the novel toward which its predecessors were pointed. Symbol, style, characterization, and rhythm all combine to make *The Sheltered Life* a poignant and penetrating illustration of the futility of clinging to a tradition that has lost its essential meaning.

Glasgow's goal in all of her writing is perhaps stated best in *A Certain Measure*, when she says in reference to her last novel, *In This Our Life*, that she was trying to show "the tragedy of a social system which lives, grows, and prospers by material standards alone." One can sense in such a statement a conservative regard for tradition; even though Glasgow and many of her characters struggled against a shallow romanticism, a yearning for a genuine tradition was never far from her own artistic vision. The land seems to be the single sustaining factor in all of Glasgow's novels—it was the land that gave rise to and nourished the so-called Southern tradition and that provides the "living pulse of endurance" to so many of her characters.

Wilton Eckley

Other major works

SHORT FICTION: *The Shadowy Third and Other Stories*, 1923; *The Collected Stories of Ellen Glasgow*, 1963.

POETRY: *The Freeman and Other Poems*, 1902.

NONFICTION: *A Certain Measure*, 1943; *The Woman Within*, 1954; *Letters of Ellen Glasgow*, 1958.

Bibliography

Godbold, E. Stanly, Jr. *Ellen Glasgow and the Woman Within.* Baton Rouge: Louisiana State University Press, 1972. The standard biography of Glasgow, although it has some weaknesses. Godbold gives only a cursory treatment of Glasgow's novels, but still paints a fascinating picture of both her social and private life.

Inge, M. Thomas, ed. *Ellen Glasgow: Centennial Essays.* Charlottesville: University Press of Virginia, 1976. Offers ten essays about Glasgow and her work. Six of these were read at the Centennial Symposium honoring Glasgow at Mary Baldwin College and the Richmond Public Library in Virginia in 1973.

McDowell, Frederick P. W. *Ellen Glasgow and the Ironic Art of Fiction.* Madison: University of Wisconsin Press, 1960. The first book analyzing Glasgow's writing. Still useful, offering insights into her writing within the context of her life story.

Raper, Julius Rowan. *From the Sunken Garden: The Fiction of Ellen Glasgow, 1916-1945.* Baton Rouge: Louisiana University Press, 1980. Raper offers criticism of ten of Glasgow's novels, including *One Man in His Time* and *Vein of Iron*, as well as an analysis of some of her short fiction. Also provides a bibliography and an index.

Thiébaux, Marcelle. *Ellen Glasgow*. New York: Frederick Ungar, 1982. Thiébaux offers extensive discussions of Glasgow's works but provides only a short biography which stresses Glasgow's divided personality and the pain that this caused her. Includes a good bibliography.

GAIL GODWIN

Born: Birmingham, Alabama; June 18, 1937

Principal long fiction

The Perfectionists, 1970; *Glass People*, 1972; *The Odd Woman*, 1974; *Violet Clay*, 1978; *A Mother and Two Daughters*, 1982; *The Finishing School*, 1985; *A Southern Family*, 1987; *Father Melancholy's Daughter*, 1991.

Other literary forms

In addition to her novels, Gail Godwin has published two collections of short fiction, *Dream Children* (1976) and *Mr. Bedford and the Muses* (1983). In the second collection, "Mr. Bedford" is a novella rather than a short story. Godwin is also a frequent reviewer of contemporary fiction for *The New York Times Book Review* and other publications. In 1985, she served as editor for *The Best American Short Stories*.

Achievements

Godwin has done much to broaden the scope of the contemporary woman's novel. While the struggles of women who seek both an independent life and a productive connection to others are central to her work, she strives in her novels and short fiction to place those efforts within a larger context, especially within the framework of modern theories of art and psychology. In 1971-1972, Godwin was a fellow of the Center for Advanced Studies, University of Illinois at Urbana-Champaign. Her other awards include a grant from the National Endowment for the Arts in 1974 and a Guggenheim Fellowship in 1975. Her story "Amanuensis" was included in the *Prize Stories, 1980: O. Henry Awards* collection.

Biography

Reared by her mother and her widowed grandmother in Asheville, North Carolina, Gail Godwin attended Peace Junior College in Raleigh, North Carolina, and was graduated in 1959 from the University of North Carolina at Chapel Hill (the alma mater of Asheville's other great native writer, Thomas Wolfe). Her B.A. was in journalism. After working as a reporter for the *Miami Herald*, she lived in London and worked with the United States Travel Service at the American Embassy. After returning to the United States, she took an M.A. (1968) and a Ph.D. (1971) in English at the University of Iowa, where she later served on the faculty of the Writers Workshop. She has been married twice, to *Miami Herald* photographer Douglas Kennedy and to British psychotherapist Ian Marshall. Her one-year marriage to Marshall is the basis for her first novel, *The Perfectionists*, as her early years with her mother and grandmother are for parts of *Glass People* and *The Odd Woman*. Her relationships with her father and her stepfather are also used in her fiction, especially in *Violet Clay* and *The Odd Woman*, respectively.

Analysis

Gail Godwin's novels (and her short fiction as well) all deal with several easily identifiable themes. First, and most often cited perhaps, is the theme of the modern woman, her dilemma in defining self and others in an era when the old frameworks and definitions have broken down, at least for the sort of women about whom Godwin writes. The conflict most often arises between the woman's work, usually an artistic pursuit of some kind, and her desire for security, love, and connection, most often through a relationship with a man. Thus, the theme of the woman struggling for identity divides into two separate thematic strands: her identity as artist and her identity as lover.

Another recurring theme in Godwin's work is, in many ways, the reverse of this quest for self-identity. Often, her characters long to penetrate the identities of the people around them; that is, they consciously seek to violate the human heart's sanctity, to use Nathaniel Hawthorne's description of such activity. Again, however, Godwin's perspective is definitively modern. These characters are all aware of the impossibility of coming to such knowledge in the almost mystical way that Hawthorne describes in "The Custom House" section of *The Scarlet Letter* (1850), and they are also conscious of the questionable morality of such invasions. Therefore, they seek lesser but more concrete knowledge and understanding by prying, by scrutinizing the objects the others possess or the words they write or say, words that the seeker will examine with total (or what he or she assumes to be total) awareness of the ironies and ambiguities involved in both the saying and their interpretation.

These divergent pursuits are most easily forged into a manageable aesthetic form through an artist figure; the role of the artist in relation to self, other, and art itself is, finally, Godwin's most important theme. Her main characters tend to be so self-consciously "artists," even when they are lawyers or psychiatrists or unemployed, that they make life itself into an art, which is to say that they view their own lives as artists view the canvas or the sheet of paper before them.

What makes Godwin an interesting and important figure in the world of contemporary fiction is the narrative technique by which she manages to develop and retell this essentially unchanging story. The noticeable and impressive growth in Godwin herself as an artist can be traced by examining the structural and technical variations in her telling of her stories. In the earlier novels, the distance between narrator and protagonist is less clearly defined. The overblown and romanticized version of the character sometimes seems to be an accurate representation of the narrator's perspective as well.

Beginning with *The Odd Woman*, however, and culminating in *A Southern Family*, Godwin makes that distance itself a matter of chief concern. Her narrators seem acutely aware of the responsibility involved in entering into the lives and souls of "others." The characters seem to move from being primarily concerned with personal happiness and security to doing true and constructive work that recognizes the dignity in whatever lives the artist consumes for the sake of the work and that acknowledges the limitations and fallibilities of the artist himself. These later characters, by having real and contructive work to do, manage to be less obsessed with their personal lives as objects of art; they also manage to find satisfaction in the art and the work itself, whether their personal lives are or are not so satisfying at any given moment.

The protagonists of *The Perfectionists* and *Glass People*, Dane Empson and Francesca Bolt, are both self-absorbed and frustrated in their relationships with their spouses. They are also the last of Godwin's protagonists to be married and unemployed. Not only are they unemployed, but also neither of them shows any desire for doing constructive, creative work. When these novels are read in the context of Godwin's later work, the conclusion that their shared lack of ambition and motivation is crucial to their discontent is inevitable.

Dane Empson has been married to John Empson, a psychologist, for ten months when they go on vacation with John's illegitimate son, Robin, and one of John's female patients, Penelope MacMahon. Although she worked as a journalist prior to her marriage—in fact, she met John when she covered a meeting at which he was the speaker—she no longer pursues her career. Her primary concerns are her relationship with John, in which she has begun to lose interest, and her efforts to become a mother to his son.

Thus, what Godwin does with this character, although it is done in a most unconventional way, is to have her confront the traditional roles and conflicts of the wife and mother. Dane fails in these roles, however, and she is most aware of that failure. She feels nothing, absolutely nothing, of the satisfaction and joy that the mythic versions of those roles provide.

The overt source of conflict in the story is Robin's total refusal to acknowledge Dane. He will not speak in her presence; he will not respond to her displays of affection; he will not compromise in any way in the small, daily struggles between parent and child.

He does, however, make demands on Dane, in both practical and emotional matters. She is expected to feed, clothe, and entertain him. She is also expected to nurture and soothe him while his father is thinking and writing in his journal. Because Godwin sets up the child as a double for the father, a point that John frequently reinforces by comparing himself to the child, the narrator suggests that Dane's real problem is John's refusal to acknowledge her.

Yet, Dane is guilty of expecting her husband to provide her with an identity to be acknowledged. She surreptitiously searches through his journal entries for clues as to what he sees when he looks at her, what he thinks when he thinks of her. When she does rebel, venturing outside the prescribed role that she has accepted with apparent willingness, she takes up with another frustrated wife, Polly Heykoop, who devotes herself to spying on her husband with his lovers, photographing their sexual encounters and compiling a scrapbook of the photos to present to him in their old age.

Dane's act in defiance of this utter decadence of domestic life is to beat the child, almost to kill him, in order to reassert her personal identity. Symbolically, she is also beating John, who, in her imagination, responds to her confession by ruining it. He points out that the action she takes in order to feel a powerful and private emotion is of necessity shared with the child and, by extension, with him. Because she cannot deny the truth of that observation and because she has available to her no other means of self-expression, she remains as self-absorbed and frustrated as she is at the novel's beginning.

Dane's counterpart in *Glass People*, Francesca Bolt, is even less involved in life. Wife to a successful attorney and politician who requires absolutely nothing of her expect that she be beautiful for him, Francesca has retreated from all human activity. She languishes in her bedroom, living for the alternate days when she tweezes the hairs from her legs one by one. At the instigation of Cameron, her husband, she undertakes a quest to discover a life for herself, a quest more dramatic and independent than that of Dane.

After a disappointing visit to her newly remarried and pregnant mother fails to allow Francesca to retreat into a former identity, she embarks upon a series of adventures, each eventually as unsuccessful as her visit home. She has an affair, a one-weekend liaison with a man she meets in the airport, but she romanticizes the encounter into much more than it is. When he does not reappear, she bravely tries to follow the plan the two of them laid to free her from Cameron's worshipful but manipulative grasp.

She rents a room in a cheap New York hotel and briefly takes a job as amanuensis to a bizarre woman named M. She even finds herself buoyed by the successful completion of the tasks she performs for her employer, the basic cleaning, shopping, and cooking chores she could not bring herself to do at home in California. After less than a week of being actively engaged in the world with nothing more than her own identity to define her, she collapses in a complete and devastating illness. She fears that all the fluids within her will leave her body and she will disappear.

Cameron appears, however, a *deus ex machina* in the best romantic tradition—the heroic man come to save the fallen beauty. The problem, as Francesca knows, is that he will save her for his own purposes, and her identity will be defined by those purposes. Still, despite this awareness, she cannot resist the comfort and ease of his salvation. That she is pregnant with the child of her lover seems only to increase Cameron's worshipful desire to hold and control her. As she moves around their beautiful apartment, decorated and maintained by Cameron, and eats plentifully of the food he prepares for her, secure in her knowledge that her husband will never let her get fat, Francesca thinks of the power she holds and of the possibilities for manipulating her husband with that power. She is the last of Godwin's protagonists to accept this traditional sort of power struggle as the best solution for her life.

Narratively, the problem with these novels is a matter of point of view. Because both are dominated by the perspectives of the protagonists, who have so constrained their lives as to have no outside viewpoints against which to test their own (except those of their spouses, whom they can only undermine as valid reference points), Godwin finds herself telling her stories without a reliable observer. Even in *Glass People*, where brief passages are given over to Cameron's point of view, the reader already so distrusts Cameron, from having seen him through his wife's eyes, that the narrator cannot give his view much credence.

The narrative voice, although it is a third-person voice, does not maintain enough distance between itself and the protagonists to convince the reader that the values of that character are not, in fact, the values being espoused by the novel. At the same time, however, the violent impotence of Dane Empson and the luxurious laziness of Francesca Bolt both carry a faintly distasteful flavor for most readers.

The perspective of Jane Clifford, the protagonist of *The Odd Woman*, marks a significant step forward for Godwin as a storyteller. First, her perspective is a much broader one than that of either of her predecessors. Jane works as a teacher of literature, and her work as a graduate student writing her dissertation on George Eliot, in addition to her current work— grading the exams for her just-finished course in visionary literature and preparing to teach a course on women in literature—is an integral part of the narrative.

Furthermore, Jane Clifford has a family, a background, that is richly developed and explored across several generations. Unlike Francesca's fruitless journey back home, Jane's similar trip, to the funeral of her grandmother, produces extended encounters with her memories of the grandmother, her mother, stepfather, sister, and brothers. Kate, mother of Francesca, spends most of her daughter's visit behind the closed door of her bedroom. Jane is involved in talks, reminiscences, and arguments that test her perspective constantly.

Jane also has friends, male and female, to whom she talks, in whom she confides. There is the male colleague with whom she trades confidences about sex and bathroom regularity; there is her old college friend Gerda, the editor of a feminist newspaper in Chicago; and there is Sonia Marx, her colleague at the university where she teaches and the woman who serves as the role model for what Jane wants to be—someone with a career, husband, and family, managing it all with every sign of ease and brilliance. Again, although Jane's point of view is the point of view of the novel, her constant encounters with these others broadens and modifies her view throughout.

Jane also has a lover, a married man, Gabriel Weeks, an art historian. In him, Jane finds an alternative to the cynical and jaded perspective she finds pervasive in the academic world. She gradually comes to realize, however, that the Gabriel she has found is a creature of her own making. She has imagined him and orchestrated their relationship in such a way as to provide herself with a view of the world that must come from within, must be made from oneself, if it is to have true value.

Here, Godwin begins to develop the ironic awareness of self as artist that is crucial to the success of her subject matter. Jane Clifford is painfully aware of her life as an object of art, with herself as the artist. She sees the scenes of her life as just that, scenes, and she manipulates both her own part and the parts of others. The problem is that such a life will never reach the state of natural grace and spontaneity that is Jane's primary goal.

Thus, she is more like Dane and Francesca than she would like to be. She does not find a way to overcome her frustrations with her need to rewrite the role she has been given or has voluntarily taken on. Unlike those predecessors, however, she does not capitulate. She takes actions that give her a chance for progress. She ends her affair; she takes an extension on her temporary appointment at the university, meaning that she will have productive work for another year; she confronts the demons of her past as represented by the family, Greta, and the actor who has been for half a century the arch villain of the family history.

Through these actions and confrontations, she learns that all truths may be artificial and self-imposed, but she also comes to believe in some purer, more absolute version of her own life that will be possible for her, if she acts to pursue it. Thus, despite Jane's own limitations, because Godwin equips her with such an acute sense of irony about herself as well as others, Jane is the first step toward a successful Godwin protagonist.

Interestingly enough, the promise of a truly successful Godwin woman made with Jane is realized in Violet Clay, whose story is the first that Godwin told from a first-person point of view. Although it might seem that first-person narration would lead to even greater self-absorption, this does not happen. Using the same principles that make *The Odd Woman* such a step forward, Godwin generated a plot in *Violet Clay* with a death. Jane keeps her job and her lover through most of her story, however, while, in addition to losing her uncle—her only living relative—Violet loses what Jane has been able to keep.

She is forced by these events of plot to confront the essentials of her character, to test the view of herself that she has created. While she probes into her uncle's past to make sense of his suicide, Violet learns much about herself as well and about how the artist manufactures both life and art, each feeding off the other. When she finally paints the painting that will set her on the road she has long aspired to travel, Violet uses some of the same material that her uncle failed to transform into the novel that he had struggled for decades to write.

Violet's success comes because she learns the limits of both life and art, partly through her uncle's example, his legacy to her, and partly through her own increasing ability to forget about "poor little me" and to enter into and learn from the struggles of those around her with compassion and respect. She learns that the artist must not and finally cannot both live and work successfully if she violates the integrity of the other, of the lives out of which her art and her own life are to be constructed.

If *Violet Clay* states an aesthetic credo, *A Mother and Two Daughters* puts that credo into action. In this novel, for the first time, Godwin is able to render a world of multiple viewpoints throughout the story; not coincidentally, it is her longest book to date as well as her most accomplished.

Nell Strickland and her two daughters, Lydia and Cate, are very different women. They, too, find themselves propelled into a plot generated by a death, in this case that of their husband and father. Each also finds herself continuing in the plot of her own life. Nell finds that she relishes the independence and privacy of her widowhood, and she also finds herself in love again before the novel concludes. Lydia, who is recently separated and eventually divorced from her husband and is mother to two teenage sons, returns to school, acquires a lover, and develops a career. Cate struggles with her own love life and the roller coaster of her career as a teacher of drama.

These women are the least self-conscious of all of Godwin's heroines, and their stories are the most straightforward and least manipulated among her works. Even so, the reader is always aware that each of the three women is shaping, in an increasingly conscious way, her life, constructing it so that it gives her the most satisfaction possible within the limitations of a "realistic" environment.

All three of these women also engage in a sustained relationship with a man during the course of the story. For Nell, it is the traditional relationship of marriage, but in her second marriage she is a different woman from the one she was in her first because of the time she spends alone and the things she learns about herself during that time. She is able to bring about a merging of the independent self and the attached self. Lydia and Cate also reach such an integration of these strands of their lives, but for them, traditional marriage is not the form that integration takes. Lydia and her lover, Stanley, live in a hard-won but precarious balance, together but unmarried, separate but irrevocably joined. He thinks at the novel's end, "You can still be independent and mine, at the same time. You are these two things now."

Cate, always more independent and free-spirited than her sister or her mother, has an even more unusual arrangement. She has designed a job to suit her, packaging classes and traveling to the places people want to have them taught, a sort of academic entrepreneur. She has also reached a stability in her relationship with Roger Jernigan after years of tension about how their feelings for each other could be formed into a pattern acceptable to them both. They are good visitors to each other.

The possibilities for marriage are not closed off for either sister, but the necessity of marriage does not exert its terrifying influence over them either. As Godwin goes into and out of the consciousnesses of these women and sometimes briefly into the points of view of the people who make up their worlds, she approaches a compassionate and respectful omniscience that would be unthinkable for the narrators of the earlier work.

In *The Finishing School*, the narrator is again a first-person voice, this time Justin Stokes, a forty-year-old actress remembering the summer she turned fourteen. Justin's preoccupations during that summer are typical of all of Godwin's characters' preoccupations. She has experienced loss: Her father and her beloved grandparents have died, and she, her mother, and her younger brother, Jem, have had to leave their Virginia home and move north to a newly created subdivision in Clove, New York. She develops a special relationship with an older woman, Ursula DeVane, who instructs her in the art of making one's life an artistic creation, lessons that feed into Justin's predisposition for the dramatic and her aspirations to the stage. Most important, however, Justin shares, with the characters from Jane Clifford onward in Godwin's work, a deep desire to come to terms with her own use of others' lives to construct her own, to make it what she needs it to be. In addition, Justin writes to thank Ursula for her contribution to the process of Justin's becoming the adult woman she wanted to be. Despite the fact that their relationship ends badly, Justin cannot overlook the crucial role that the relationship played in helping her through the most difficult summer of her childhood.

Godwin dedicates this sixth novel to "the Ursulas of this world, whoever they were—or weren't"; that dedication seems echoed by Justin's sentiments after remembering and making a story from her summer with Ursula. Justin says:

> I was able to be charmed and possessed by that woman. Such possessions are rare now. I mean by another person. The only thing I can rely on to possess me continually with that degree of ardor is my work. Most of the time I consider this a victory. Sometimes, however, it makes me a little sad. So here I am, in the middle of my own life. . . . And it has taken me this long to understand that I lose nothing by acknowledging her influence on me. . . . I know something of life's betrayals and stupidities myself. . . . I even know the necessity for making constant adjustments to your life story, so you can go on living in it. . . . But I also know something else that I didn't know then. As long as you can go on creating new roles for yourself, you are not vanquished.

In many ways Godwin's seventh novel, *A Southern Family*, is the aesthetic fruit of a challenge similar to the one her fictional alter ego raises at the end of *The Finishing School*. In *A Southern Family* Godwin creates for herself a new role as author/narrator, using for the first time in her novels the narrative strategy of multiple limited perspectives. She also appears to be moving toward a new role for the "typical" Godwin woman within her fictional world. The Godwin woman in *A Southern Family* is Clare Campion, the author's first novel protagonist to share her profession. In fact, Clare is a writer whose career, as rendered in this fiction, closely parallels Godwin's own. The "new" role Godwin carves out for Clare is that of secondary, rather than primary, character; thus, her challenge is to accept this new (and inevitably "lesser") status without losing the power to make art (stories) from her experience.

The plot of *A Southern Family* is generated by the death of Clare Campion's half brother Theo Quick in an incident that the police rule a murder-suicide. The story is presented from the perspectives of Clare, her best friend Julia Richardson, Clare's mother and her stepfather, her surviving half brother, Theo's ex-wife, and Sister Patrick, a beloved nun who has taught Clare and her brothers. (That Godwin's half brother Tommy Cole died in circumstances similar to those described in the novel further suggests the strongly autobiographical nature of *A Southern Family*.)

Perhaps the most significant achievement of the novel is Godwin's broadening of her narrative spectrum to include male characters, characters from a variety of social classes, characters with varying degrees of connection to the central action. There is no pretense of the omniscience that marks *A Mother and Two Daughters* here; the narrative in each section of the book is strictly limited to one or sometimes two perspectives.

A Southern Family opens up new narrative directions and a new approach to her "typical" protagonist for Godwin, but the novel also provides a clear culmination of other strands that are woven throughout the body of her fiction. The title makes clear that this is a family story, a Southern story— themes that have always been among the author's central concerns. The greater emphasis here on the family as a group, a unit, rather than on an individual's struggles reinforces the narrative decision Godwin makes.

A Southern Family also continues Godwin's exploration of people, particularly women, who tend to see their lives as performances, themselves as actors in a drama partly of their own making, partly a by-product of their environment and conditioning. Theo's action causes everyone in his family to reexamine his or her role in the Quick family drama, causes each individual whose consciousness the novel explores to evaluate the role he or she plays in the unfolding events before and after the momentary act that calls the foundations of family life into question. In addition to generating the story this novel tells, this profound examination of self-as-actor that takes place in *A Southern*

Family, read with full knowledge of the work that precedes it, is, in a sense, a reexamination of the author's body of work as well.

The author Gail Godwin has grown in much the same direction as her characters and narrators. The movement has been in the life-affirming direction of compromise, recognition of others, acceptance of responsibility for the self, and productive creativity. The life that gets affirmed is the well-made life, the one shaped out of the complexities and ambiguities of human experience. Godwin's novels speak clearly of the enormous difficulty of being a sensitive and thoughtful woman in today's world. They speak just as eloquently of what such women can make from those difficulties.

Jane Hill

Other major works
SHORT FICTION: *Dream Children*, 1976; *Mr. Bedford and the Muses*, 1983.
PLAYS: *The Last Lover*, 1975; *Journals of a Songmaker*, 1976; *Apollonia*, 1979.
ANTHOLOGY: *The Best American Short Stories*, 1985.

Bibliography
Cheney, Anne. "Gail Godwin and Her Novels." In *Southern Women Writers: The New Generation*, edited by Tonette Bond Inge. Tuscaloosa: University of Alabama Press, 1990. The most comprehensive overview of Godwin's career through *A Southern Family*. Emphasizes the autobiographical elements of the works, the contemporary love-hate relationship with the traditional South, and the evolving maturity of the author's vision. Factually interesting, the article's argumentative conclusions are less reliable and significant.
Frye, Joanna S. "Narrating the Self: The Autonomous Heroine in Gail Godwin's *Violet Clay*." *Contemporary Literature* 24 (Spring, 1983): 66-85. A strong and important article dealing with narrative technique in Godwin's fourth novel which has significant implications for her later works as well.
Gaston, Karen C. "'Beauty and the Beast' in Gail Godwin's *Glass People*." *Critique* 21 (1980): 94-102. Develops an interesting but flawed analogy using the novel and the fairy tale ("Sleeping Beauty" as well plays a part in the argument). The article's feminist thesis distorts to some extent the novel's plot and resolution.
Lorsch, Susan E. "Gail Godwin's *The Odd Woman*: Literature and the Retreat from Life." *Critique* 20 (1978): 21-32. Analyzes the novel's protagonist in terms of her use of literary interests as an escape from the realities of her life. Lorsch fails to deal with Jane Clifford's tendency to create her own stories in order, ultimately, to engage life, making this article's argument only partially valid.

Mickelson, Anne A. "Gail Godwin: Order and Accommodation." In *Reaching Out: Sensitivity and Order in Recent Fiction by Women*. Metuchen, N.J.: Scarecrow Press, 1979. Mickelson identifies with some accuracy the attitudes toward order in Godwin's work, primarily *The Odd Woman*, but then indicts those attitudes as inappropriate to contemporary women.

Rhodes, Carolyn. "Gail Godwin and the Ideal of Southern Womanhood." *Southern Quarterly* 21 (Summer, 1983): 55-66. Contains rather simplistic and limited readings of *The Odd Woman*, *Violet Clay*, and *A Mother and Two Daughters* in reference to Godwin's essay "The Southern Belle."

Smith, Marilyn J. "The Role of the South in the Novels of Gail Godwin." *Critique* 26 (1980): 103-110. Deals with the conflict in Godwin's protagonists between their impulse to flee the South and their need to hold onto certain Southern ideals. Smith argues that this conflict remains unresolved through *Violet Clay*.

WILLIAM GOLDING

Born: St. Columb Minor, Cornwall, England; September 19, 1911

Principal long fiction

Lord of the Flies, 1954; *The Inheritors*, 1955; *Pincher Martin*, 1956 (also known as *The Two Deaths of Christopher Martin*); *Free Fall*, 1959; *The Spire*, 1964; *The Pyramid*, 1967; *Darkness Visible*, 1979; *Rites of Passage*, 1980; *The Paper Men*, 1984; *Close Quarters*, 1987; *Fire Down Below*, 1989.

Other literary forms

William Golding's first and only book of poetry, entitled simply *Poems*, was published in 1934. "Envoy Extraordinary," a 1956 novella, was recast in 1958 in the form of a play, *The Brass Butterfly*; set in Roman times, *The Brass Butterfly* uses irony to examine the value of "modern" inventions. "Envoy Extraordinary" was published along with two other novellas, "The Scorpion God" and "Clonk Clonk," in a 1971 collection bearing the title *The Scorpion God*.

Golding has also produced nonfiction; his book reviews in *The Spectator* between 1960 and 1962 frequently took the form of personal essays. Many of his essays and autobiographical pieces were collected in *The Hot Gates and Other Occasional Pieces* (1965). *A Moving Target* (1982) is another set of essays; *An Egyptian Journal* (1985) is a travelogue. Golding has also given numerous interviews explaining his work; these have appeared in a variety of journals and magazines.

Achievements

Sir William Gerald Golding is without doubt one of the major British novelists of the post-World War II era. He has depicted in many different ways the anguish of modern man as he gropes for meaning and redemption in a world where the spiritual has been all but crushed by the material. His themes deal with guilt, responsibility, and salvation. He depicts the tension between individual fallenness and social advance, or, to put it differently, the cost of progress to the individual.

Golding portrays a period when the last vestiges of an optimistic belief in evolutionary progress have collapsed under the threat of nuclear destruction. In doing this, he has moved the classic British novel tradition forward both in stylistic and formal technique and in the opening up of a new, contemporary social and theological dialectic.

He is a Fellow of the Royal Society of Literature (elected in 1955), and in 1983 he received the Nobel Prize in Literature. He had won the James Tait Black Memorial Prize in 1979 for *Darkness Visible* and the Booker Prize in 1980 for *Rites of Passage*. He was knighted in 1989.

Biography

Born in the county of Cornwall in the southwest corner of England, the son of a rationalistic schoolmaster, William Golding had a relatively isolated childhood. Eventually his family moved to Marlborough, in Wiltshire, where he received his high school education at the local grammar school, while revisiting Cornwall frequently. He was graduated from Brasenose College, Oxford, in science and literature. The choice of arts over science was made at the university, but scientific interests and approaches can be easily discerned in his literary work. Each novel is, in a way, a new experiment set up to test a central hypothesis.

After the unsuccessful publication of a book of poetry in 1934, Golding moved to London and participated in fringe theater without achieving anything of significance. In 1939 he married Ann Brookfield and accepted a teaching post at Bishop Wordsworth's School, Salisbury, also in Wiltshire. Soon after the outbreak of war, he joined the Royal Navy, seeing extensive action against German warships, being adrift for three days in the English Channel, and participating in the Normandy landings.

After the war, he resumed teaching and tried writing novels. His first four were highly imitative and met only by editorial refusals. He then decided to write as he wanted, not as how he thought he ought. This shift in approach led to the immediate publication of *Lord of the Flies* in 1954; this work became almost at once a landmark on the British literary scene. Golding was able to follow this achievement with three more novels in the space of only five years, by which time paperback versions were being issued on both sides of the Atlantic. In 1961 he retired from teaching, becoming for two years a book reviewer with *The Spectator*, one of the leading British weekly cultural reviews. In *The Paper Men*, Golding depicts a novelist whose first novel turned out to be a gold mine for him—an autobiographical echo, no doubt.

After the publication of *The Pyramid* in 1967, when Golding was fifty-six years old, there came rather a long silence, and many people assumed that he had brought his career to a close. With the publication of *Darkness Visible* twelve years later, however, a steady stream of new novels emerged, including a trilogy. This second phase also marked the reception of various prizes, including the Nobel, and his being knighted, a comparatively rare honor for a novelist.

Golding has one son and one daughter. He and his wife returned to Cornwall to live in 1984.

Analysis

William Golding, like his older British contemporary Graham Greene, is a theological novelist: that is to say, his main thematic material focuses on particular theological concerns, in particular sin and guilt, innocence and its loss, individual responsibility and the possibility of atonement for mistakes made, and the need for spiritual revelation. Unlike Greene, however, he does not write out of a particular Christian, or even religious, belief system; the dialectic he sets up is neither specifically Catholic (like Greene's) nor Protestant. In fact, Golding's dialectic is set up in specific literary terms, in that it is with other works of literature that he argues, rather than with theological or philosophical positions per se. The texts with which he argues do represent such positions or make certain cultural assumptions of such positions; however, it is through literary technique that he argues—paralleling, echoing, deconstructing—rather than through narratorial didacticism.

Golding's achievement is a literary tour de force. The British novel has never contained theological dialectic easily, except at a superficial level, let alone a depiction of transcendence. Golding has accepted the nineteenth century novel tradition but has modified it extensively. Each novel represents a fresh attempt for him to refashion the language and the central consciousness of that tradition. Sometimes he has pushed it beyond the limits of orthodox mimetic realism, and hence some of his novels have been called fables, allegories, or myths. In general, however, his central thrust is to restate the conflict between individual man and his society in contemporary terms, and in doing this, to question at a fundamental level many cultural assumptions, and to point up the loss of moral and spiritual values in twentieth century Western civilization—an enterprise in which most nineteenth century novelists were similarly involved for their own time.

Golding's first and still most famous novel, *Lord of the Flies*, illustrates this thesis well. Although there is a whole tradition of island-castaway narratives, starting with one of the earliest novels in English literature, Daniel Defoe's *Robinson Crusoe* (1719), the text with which Golding clearly had in mind to argue was R. M. Ballantyne's *The Coral Island* (1858), written almost exactly one hundred years before Golding's. The names of Ballantyne's three schoolboy heroes (Ralph, Jack, and Peterkin) are taken over, with Peterkin becoming Simon (the biblical reversion being significant) and various episodes in Ballantyne being parodied by Golding—for example, the pig-sticking.

Ballantyne's yarn relied on the English public-school ethos that boys educated within a British Christian discipline would survive anything and in fact would be able to control their environment—in miniature, the whole British imperialistic enterprise of the nineteenth century. Most desert-island narratives do make the assumption that Western man can control his environment, assuming that he is moral, purposeful, and religious. Golding subverts all these suppositions: except for a very few among them, the abandoned schoolboys, significantly younger than Ballantyne's and more numerous (making a herd instinct possible), soon lose the veneer of the civilization they have acquired. Under Jack's leadership, they paint their faces, hunt pigs, and then start killing one another. They ritually murder Simon, the mystic, whose transcendental vision of the Lord of the Flies (a pig's head on a pole) is of the evil within. They also kill Piggy, the rationalist. The novel ends with the pack pursuing Ralph, the leader democratically elected at the beginning; the boys are prepared to burn the whole island to kill him.

Ironically, the final conflagration serves as a powerful signal for rescue (earlier watchfires having been pathetically inadequate), and, in a sudden reversal, an uncomprehending British naval officer lands on the beach, amazed at the mud-covered, dirty boys before him. Allegorically it might be thought that as this world ends in fire, a final divine intervention will come. Ironically, however, the adult world that the officer represents is also destroying itself as effectively, in a nuclear war. Salvation remains problematic and ambiguous.

What lifts the novel away from simple allegory is not only the ambiguities but also the dense poetic texture of its language. The description of Simon's death is often quoted as brilliantly heightened prose—the beauty of the imagery standing in stark contrast to the brutality of his slaying. Yet almost any passage yields its own metaphorical textures and suggestive symbolism. Golding's rich narrative descriptions serve to point up the poverty of the boys' language, which can only dwell on basics—food, defecation, fears and night terrors, killings. Golding's depiction of the children is immediately convincing. The adult intervention (the dead airman, the naval officer) is perhaps not quite so, being too clearly fabular. In general, however, the power of the novel derives from the tensions set up between the book's novelistic realism and its fabular and allegorical qualities. The theological dialectic of man's fallenness (not only the boys') and the paper-thin veneer of civilization emerges inexorably out of this genre tension.

The thinness of civilization forms the central thesis of Golding's second novel, *The Inheritors*. The immediate literary dialectic is set up with H. G. Wells's *The Outline of History: Being a Plain History of Life and Mankind* (1920), which propounds the typical social evolutionism common from the 1850's onward. At a more general level, Golding's novel might also be seen as an evolutionary version of John Milton's *Paradise Lost* (1667): Satan's temptation to Eve is a temptation to progress; the result is the fall. Just as Adam and Eve degrade themselves with drunken behavior, so do Golding's Neanderthal protagonists, Lok and Fa, when they stumble over the remains of *Homo sapiens*' cannibalistic "festivities."

Golding has subverted the Wellsian thesis that Neanderthals were totally inferior by depicting them as innocent, gentle, intuitive, playful, and loving. They stand in ironic contrast to the group of *Homo sapiens* who eventually annihilate them, except for a small baby whom they kidnap (again reversing a short story by Wells, where it is Neanderthals who kidnap a human baby). The humans experience terror, lust, rage, drunkenness, and murder, and their religion is propitiatory only. By contrast, the Neanderthals have a taboo against killing anything, and their reverence for Oa, the Earth Mother, is gentle and numinous in quality.

As in *Lord of the Flies*, the conclusion is formed by an ironic reversal—the reader suddenly sees from the humans' perspective. The last line reads, "He could not see if the line of darkness had an ending." It is a question Golding is posing: has the darkness of the human heart an end?

Golding's technique is remarkable in the novel: he succeeds in convincing the reader that primitive consciousness could have looked like this. He has had to choose language that conveys that consciousness, yet is articulate enough to engage one imaginatively so that one respects the Neanderthals. He explores the transition from intuition and pictorial thinking to analogous and metaphoric thought. The ironic treatment of *Homo sapiens* is done also through the limits of Neanderthal perceptions and consciousness. Unfortunately, humans, as fallen creatures, can supply all too easily the language for the evil that the Neanderthals lack.

Golding's third novel, *Pincher Martin* (first published in the United States as *The Two Deaths of Christopher Martin*), returns to the desert-island tradition. The immediate dialectic is perhaps with Robinson Crusoe, the sailor who single-handedly carves out an island home by the strength of his will aided by his faith. Pincher Martin is here the faithless antihero, although this is not immediately apparent. He, like Crusoe, appears to survive a wreck (Martin's destroyer is torpedoed during the war); he kicks off seaboots and swims to a lonely island-rock in the Atlantic. With tremendous strength of will, he appears to survive by eating raw shellfish, making rescue signals, forcing an enema into himself, and keeping sane and purposeful.

In the end, however, his sanity appears to disintegrate. Almost to the end it is quite possible to believe that Christopher Martin finally succumbs to madness and death only after a heroic, indeed Promethean, struggle against Fate and the elements. The last chapter, however, presents an even greater reversal than those in the first two novels, dispelling all of this as a false reading: Martin's drowned body is found washed up on a Scottish island with his seaboots still on his feet. In other words, the episode on the rock never actually took place. The reading of *Pincher Martin* thus becomes deliberately problematic in a theological sense. The rock must be an illusion, an effort of the will indeed, but an effort after physical death. Yet it is not that all of one's life flashes in front of one while one drowns, though that does happen with Martin's sordid memories of his lust, greed, and terror. It is more that the text is formed by Martin's ongoing dialectic with, or rather against, his destiny, which he sees as annihilation. An unnameable God is identified with the terror and darkness of the cellar of his childhood memories. His will, in its Promethean pride, is creating its own alternative. Theologically, this alternative can only be Purgatory or Hell, since it is clearly not heaven. Satan in *Paradise Lost* says, "Myself am Hell": strictly, this is Martin's position, since he refuses the purgatorial possibilities in the final revelation of God, with his mouthless cry of "I shit on your heaven!" God, in his compassion, strikes

Martin into annihilation with his "black lightning."

Golding's first three novels hardly suggested that he was writing from within any central tradition of the British novel. All three are highly original in plot, for all of their dialectic with existing texts, and in style and technique. In his next novel, *Free Fall*, Golding writes much more recognizably within the tradition of both the *Bildungsroman* (the novel of character formation) and the *Künstlerroman* (the novel of artistic development). Sammy Mountjoy, a famous artist, is investigating his past life, but with the question in mind, "When did I lose my freedom?" The question is not in itself necessarily theological, but Sammy's search is conducted in specifically theological categories.

It has been suggested that the literary dialectic is with Albert Camus' *La Chute* (1956; *The Fall*, 1957), a novella published some three years earlier. Camus' existentialism sees no possibility of redemption or regeneration once the question has been answered; his protagonist uses the question, in fact, to gain power over others by exploiting their guilt, so the whole search would seem inauthentic. Golding sees such a search as vital: his position seems to be that no man is born in sin, or fallen, but inevitably at some stage, each person chooses knowingly to sin. At that moment he falls and loses his freedom to choose. The only possibility of redemption is to recognize that moment, to turn from it, and to cry out, "Help me!"

This is Sammy's cry when he is locked up in a German prisoner-of-war camp and interrogated. His physical release from his cell is also a spiritual release, a moment of revelation described in Pentecostal terms of renewal and a new artistic vision. His moment of fall, which he discovers only near the end of the book (which is here culmination rather than reversal), was when he chose to seduce Beatrice (the name of Dante's beloved inspiration also), whatever the cost and despite a warning that "sooner or later the sacrifice is always regretted."

Other theological perspectives are introduced. Two of Sammy's teachers form an opposition: the rational, humanistic, likable Nick Shales and the religious, intense, but arrogant Miss Pringle. Sammy is caught in the middle, wanting to affirm the spiritual but drawn to the materialist. The dilemma goes back in the English novel to George Eliot. Though Golding cannot accept Eliot's moral agnosticism, he has to accept her inexorable moral law of cause and effect: Sammy's seduction of Beatrice has left her witless and insane. The scene in the prison cell is balanced by the scene in the mental institution. Redemption costs; the past remains. The fall may be arrested and even reversed, but only through self-knowledge and full confession.

In *Free Fall*, Golding chose for the first time to use first-person narrative. Before that he had adopted a third-person narrative technique that stayed very close to the consciousness of the protagonists. In *The Spire*, Golding could be said to have perfected this latter technique. Events are seen not only through the eyes of Dean Jocelin but also in his language and thought processes. As in

Henrik Ibsen's *Bygmester Solness* (1892; *The Master Builder*, 1893), Golding's protagonist has an obsessive drive to construct a church tower, or rather a spire on a tower, for his cathedral lacks both. (Inevitably one takes the cathedral to be Salisbury, whose medieval history is almost identical, although it is not named.) Ibsen's play deals with the motivation for such an obsession, the price to be paid, and the spiritual conflicts. Golding, however, is not so much in a dialectic situation with the Ibsen play as using it as his base, agreeing with Ibsen when the latter talks of "the power of ideals to kill." At the end of the novel, the spire has been built in the face of tremendous technical difficulties, but Jocelin lies dying, the caretaker and his wife have been killed, the master builder, Roger, is a broken man, and the whole life of the cathedral has been disrupted.

Thus Golding raises the question of cost again: What is the cost of progress? Is it progress? The power of the book is that these questions can be answered in many different ways, and each way searches out new richness from the text. The patterning of moral and theological structures allows for almost endless combinations. The novel can also be read in terms of the cost of art—the permanence of art witnessing to man's spirituality and vision, as against the Freudian view of art as sublimation and neurotic outlet, the price of civilization.

By staying very close to Jocelin's consciousness, the reader perceives only slowly, as he does, that much of his motivation and drive is not quite as visionary and spiritual as he first thinks. Freudian symbolism and imagery increasingly suggest sexual sublimation, especially centered on Goody Pangall, whom he calls "his daughter in God." In fact, much later one learns that he received his appointment only because his aunt was the king's mistress for a while. Jocelin manipulates people more and more consciously to get the building done and chooses, perhaps unconsciously at first, to ignore the damage to people, especially the four people he regards as his "pillars" to the spire. Ironically, he too is a pillar, and he damages himself, physically, emotionally, and spiritually (he is almost unable to pray by the end, and has no confessor). Yet despite all the false motives, the novel suggests powerfully that there really has been a true vision that has been effected, even if marred by man's fallenness and "total depravity," every part affected by the fall.

The language of *The Spire* is the most poetic that Golding has attempted. The density of imagery, recurring motifs, and symbolism both psychological and theological blend into marvelous rhythms of ecstasy and horror. The interweaving of inner monologue, dialogue, and narrative dissolves the traditional tight bounds of time and space of the novel form, to create an impassioned intensity where the theological dialectic takes place, not with another text, but within the levels of the moral, spiritual, and metaphoric consciousness of the text itself.

After the verbal pyrotechnics of *The Spire*, Golding's next novel, *The*

Pyramid, seems very flat, despite its title. It returns to *Free Fall* in its use of first-person narrative, to a modified form of its structure (flashbacks and memories to provide a personal pattern), and to contemporary social comedy, strongly echoing Anthony Trollope. The language is spare and unadorned, as perhaps befits the protagonist, Olly, who, unlike Sammy Mountjoy, has turned away from art and spirit to become *un homme moyen sensual*. His life has become a defense against love, but as a petit bourgeois he has been protected against Sammy's traumatic upbringing, and so one feels little sympathy for him. Theological and moral dialectic is muted, and the social commentary and comedy have been better done by other novelists, although a few critics have made out a case for a rather more complex structuring than is at first evident.

Perhaps the flatness of the book suggests that Golding had for the time being run out of impetus. Only two novellas were published in the next twelve years, and then, quite unexpectedly, *Darkness Visible* appeared. In some ways it echoes Charles Williams, the writer of a number of religious allegorical novels in the 1930's and 1940's. The reality of spiritual realms of light and darkness is made by Golding as explicitly as by Williams, especially in Matty, the "holy fool." Yet Golding never quite steps into allegory, any more than he did in his first novel. His awareness of good and evil takes on a concreteness that owes much to Joseph Conrad. Much of the feel of the novel is Dickensian, if not its structure: the grotesque serves to demonstrate the "foolishness of the wise," as with Charles Dickens.

The book divides into three parts centering on Matty, orphaned and hideously burned in the bombing of London during the war. At times he keeps a journal and thus moves the narrative into the first person. The second part, by contrast, focuses on Sophy, the sophisticated twin daughter of a professional chess-player (the rationalist), and overwhelmingly exposes the rootlessness and anomie of both contemporary youth culture and the post-1960's bourgeoisie (the children of Olly's generation). The third part concerns a bizarre kidnapping plot where Matty and Sophy nearly meet as adversaries; this is the "darkness visible" (the title coming from the hell of *Paradise Lost*). The end remains ambiguous. Golding attempts a reversal again: the kidnap has been partially successful. Matty has not been able to protect the victims, nor Sophy to complete her scheme, but still children are kidnapped.

Central themes emerge: childhood and innocence corrupted; singleness of purpose, which can be either for good or for evil (contrast also Milton's single and double darkness in *Comus*, 1634); and the foolishness of the world's wisdom. Entropy is a key word, and Golding, much more strongly than hitherto, comments on the decline of Great Britain. Above all, however, Golding's role as a novelist of transcendence is reemphasized: moments of revelation are the significant moments of knowledge. Unfortunately, revelation can come from dark powers as well as from those of the light. Ultimately, Golding's vision is Miltonic, as has been suggested. The theological dialectic is revealed as that between the children of light and the children of darkness.

When *Rites of Passage* followed *Darkness Visible* one year later, Golding had no intention of writing a trilogy (now called the Sea Trilogy). It was only later he realized that he had "left all those poor sods in the middle of the sea and needed to get them to Australia." The trilogy was well received, perhaps because the plot and themes are relatively straightforward and unambiguous, and the social comedy is more obvious than the theological dialectic. The trilogy fits well into the *Bildungsroman* tradition of Dickens' *Great Expectations* (1860-1861), in that it follows the education of a snob, Edmund Talbot, who, under the patronage of an aristocratic and influential godfather, is embarking on a political career by taking up an appointment in the new colony of New South Wales, Australia, in 1810. It is also enlivened by Golding's wide knowledge of sailing ships and life at sea; the trilogy is the fullest literary expression of this interest he has allowed himself.

The narrative proceeds leisurely in the first person as Edmund decides to keep a diary. In *Rites of Passage*, the plot focuses on the death of one of the passengers, a ridiculous young clergyman, the Reverend Robert James Colley. He is made the butt of everyone's fun, including that of the ordinary sailors. As the result of the shame of a joke, where he is made drunk and then engages in homosexual activities, he more or less wills himself to die. Captain Anderson covers up the incident—at which Edmund, for the first time, feels moral outrage and vows to expose the captain to his godfather when he can. The moral protest is vitiated, however, by Edmund's use of power and privilege.

In *Close Quarters*, Edmund's education continues. As conditions on board ship deteriorate, he increases in stature, losing his aristocratic bearing and becoming willing to mix socially. His relationship with Summers, the most morally aware of the ship's lieutenants, is good for him in particular. He also shows himself sensitive: he weeps at a woman's song, he falls in love (as opposed to the lust in *Rites of Passage*), and he admires Colley's written style (Colley, too, has left behind a journal). He suffers physically and shows courage. His falling in love is delightfully described, quite unselfconsciously. He learns, too, the limits of his power: the elements control everything. The speed of the ship runs down as weeds grow on its underside, reintroducing the entropy motif of *Darkness Visible*. He cannot prevent suicide or death. As the novel proceeds, the "ship of fools" motif of late medieval literature becomes very strong. Edmund is no more and no less a fool than the others.

Fire Down Below closes the trilogy as the ship docks in Sidney Cove, and Edmund is reunited happily with the young lady he met. The ending seems to be social comedy, until one realizes that Summers' fear, that a fire lit below decks to forge a metal band around a broken mast is still smoldering, is proved true. The anchored ship bursts into flame, and Summers is killed, having just been given promotion, partly through Edmund's efforts. Despite this tragedy, the ending is Dickensian, for the voyage has turned into a quest for love for Edmund, and love has helped mark his way with moral landmarks. Edmund has learned much, although at the end he has still far to go. The ending is perhaps the most mellow of all Golding's endings: if Australia is not "the new Jerusalem," it is not hell either, and if Edmund lacks spirituality, he is yet more than *un homme moyen sensual*.

The Paper Men is, like *Free Fall*, a *Künstlerroman*. The style is much more akin to that of twentieth century American confessional literature, especially Saul Bellow's. Golding's Wilfred Barclay could easily be a Henderson or a Herzog, with the same energetic, somewhat zany style, and with the themes of flight and pursuit in a frantic search for identity. Unusually for Golding, the novel seems to be repeating themes and structures, if not style, and perhaps for that reason has not made the same impact as his other novels. Wilfred's revelation of the transcendent in an ambiguous spiritual experience of Christ (or Pluto) marks the high point of the novel.

Although each Golding novel, with a few exceptions, has been a new "raid on the inarticulate," certain thematic and technical features have remained constant over the years. Golding's moral and didactic concerns have consistently sought theological grounding out of which to construct a critique of the lostness and fallenness of humankind, and specifically of contemporary Western civilization, with its spiritual bankruptcy. In this quest there is a line of continuity back to Eliot and Dickens in the English novel tradition. In his affirmation of the primacy of the spiritual over the material he echoes not only them but also, in different ways, Thomas Hardy and D. H. Lawrence. In his vision of the darkness of man's soul, unenlightened by any transcendent revelation, he follows Conrad.

He also seeks, as did E. M. Forster and Lawrence, to find a style that escapes the materiality of prose and attains to the revelatory transcendence of poetry. The result is usually dramatic, incarnational metaphors and motifs. The mode is usually confessional, almost Augustinian at times, coming from a single consciousness, though often with a sudden reversal at the end to sustain an ambiguous dialectic.

There is in Golding no articulated framework of beliefs: transcendence lies ultimately beyond the articulate. God is there, and revelation is not only possible but indeed necessary and salvific. Yet the revelation remains ambiguous, fleeting, and numinous, rather than normative. In the end, this often means that Golding's social critique, of the moral entropy of Britain in particular, comes over more powerfully than the darkness that is the refusal of the terror of believing in God.

David Barratt

Other major works

SHORT FICTION: *The Scorpion God*, 1971.

PLAYS: *The Brass Butterfly*, 1958; *Miss Pulkinhorn*, 1960 (radio play); *Break My Heart*, 1962 (radio play).

POETRY: *Poems*, 1934.

NONFICTION: *The Hot Gates and Other Occasional Pieces*, 1965; *A Moving Target*, 1982; *An Egyptian Journal*, 1985.

Bibliography

Biles, Jack, and Robert Evans, eds. *William Golding: Some Critical Considerations*. Lexington: University Press of Kentucky, 1978. This volume collects the proceedings of a symposium on aspects of Golding's earlier works. Includes a bibliography of critical writings.

Boyd, S. J. *The Novels of William Golding*. New York: St. Martin's Press, 1988. Provides a chapter on each of Golding's novels through *The Paper Men*, and includes a full bibliography.

Gindin, James. *William Golding*. Basingstoke, England: Macmillan, 1988. The novels are considered two by two; additional chapters examine themes in Golding's work and its critical reception. Provides a short bibliography.

Kinkead-Weekes, Mark, and Ian Gregor. *William Golding: A Critical Study*. New York: Harcourt, Brace & World, 1967. Still one of the standard critical accounts of Golding. Full analysis of the first five novels, showing imaginative development and interconnection. An added final chapter deals with three later novels.

Oldsey, Bernard S., and Stanley Weintraub. *The Art of William Golding*. Bloomington: Indiana University Press, 1965. Individual chapters devoted to Golding's first five novels and some of his other early writing. The emphasis is on the literary texts that form the Golding dialectic. A useful list of Golding's articles and reviews from *The Spectator* is appended.

Page, Norman, ed. *William Golding: Novels, 1954-1967*. New York: Macmillan, 1985. Part of the excellent Casebook series, this volume consists of an introductory survey, several general essays on Golding's earlier work, and eight pieces on specific novels through *The Pyramid*. Contains a very short bibliography.

N. V. M. GONZALEZ

Born: Romblon, Philippines; September 8, 1915

Principal long fiction
The Winds of April, 1940; *A Season of Grace*, 1956; *The Bamboo Dancers*, 1959.

Other literary forms
Although N. V. M. Gonzalez has traveled widely and has taught the craft of writing on several continents, his principal rapport has always been with the farmers and fishermen of his homeland. For such folk, social change over the centuries has been minimal, and their daily lives are attached to unvarying natural cycles. In each of his collections of short stories, Gonzalez has found a deceptively simple style appropriate to the tempo of frontier life and the peasant mind set. Many of his first stories in *Seven Hills Away* (1947) seem more like sketches, reproducing the quiet, sometimes desperate, static life-style of the Philippine *kainginero*. On the small islands of Romblon and Mindoro, south of Manila, the landless frontiersman regularly leaves the village barrio in search of land. The wilderness is his if he will clear it by slash-and-burn techniques; yet it can never be cultivated well enough, by these primitive means, to support a large population. The first and last stories in the collection establish an outward movement from a growing settlement by pioneers anxious to find one more uninhabited horizon. Even as the stress falls on small-scale self-reliance, however, the fulfillment of ancestral patterns in the process of pioneering becomes dramatically evident. The animistic minds of the *kaingineros* tell them that nature is unfriendly, but they meet each setback with a stoic lack of surprise and complaint. The style of these stories is stark.

In Gonzalez's next collection, *Children of the Ash-Covered Loam* (1954), the potential for melodrama and self-pity is further undercut by reliance on children and plain women as narrators or central characters. The women are long-suffering and resilient; their own bodies' rhythms have made them knowledgeable about the mysteries of nature. As for the children, they are in the midst of undergoing at firsthand the wonders of birth and death; the depletion of innocence which slowly drains away like so much baby fat; the gentle pace of experience. Contrasted with the enduring virtues of these ordinary people is the sophisticated lack of feeling in Mrs. Bilbao, failed wife and mother, in "Where's My Baby Now?" Too busy with city social obligations, she neglects her family.

A more elaborate contrast controls the 1963 collection, *Look, Stranger, on*

This Island Now, as the restless peasants' new horizon becomes the town of Buenavista, in Romblon, and later the commercial centers of the principal Philippine island, Luzon. Disconnected from nature, the townspeople suffer from loneliness and the tensions between their competing needs for companionship and privacy. At best, they achieve momentary consolations. Stories in the second half of the volume express the sense of exile among city-dwellers who have left the rural life-style behind but who have no traditions to guide them in their new life. In *Mindoro and Beyond* (1979), the five stories added to sixteen selected from previous volumes still waver between these poles: integrity, sustained with difficulty among the peasant poor, and the insecurity and corruption which befalls those who desert the land.

Achievements

The paradox of Gonzalez is that he has gained an international reputation for himself at a variety of intellectual centers, while identifying constantly with the uneducated but folk-wise peasant in the Philippines. His humor is far more subtle than that of Carlos Bulosan, for example, and his social criticism, though very real, is never doctrinaire, never polemical. For the pure portrait of the Filipino as frontier farmer—the dream of every landless tenant during centuries of oppression from Spanish overlords and now from estate holders who are his own countrymen—readers turn to the deceptively simple fiction of Gonzalez. Recognition of the honesty of these peasant images has made both the author and his work required presences in many lands. A 1949 Rockefeller Fellowship led to publication of his stories in a number of distinguished American "little magazines": *Sewanee Review*, *Hopkins Review*, *Pacific Spectator*, *Literary Review*, and *Short Story International*. Gonzalez's work has also appeared in such anthologies as *Stories from Many Lands* (1955), *Mentor Book of Modern Asian Literature* (1969), and *Asian-American Authors* (1972), and, in translation, in anthologies in Malaysia and West Germany.

His tight control of form, contrary to florid Malayan-Spanish traditions, his reliance on a narrative's ability to convey its own meaning without intrusion by the author, and especially his ability to find English constructions which, to the Filipino ear, retain resemblances to the native vernaculars of his characters: all these qualities have influenced numbers of younger writers, who occasionally refer to him as the Anton Chekhov or Ernest Hemingway of the Philippines. For his influence as a writer of fiction, as an essayist, and as a workshop director, he received the Republic Award of Merit (1954), the Republic Cultural Heritage Award (1960), and the Rizal Pro Patria Award (1961), thus fulfilling the earlier promise shown when, in 1940, his first novel won honorable mention in the Commonwealth Literary Awards contest, and, in 1941, his collection of stories, then called *Far Horizons*, shared first prize in the same annual contest.

Biography

Born in 1915 on one of the smaller mid-archipelago Philippine islands, Nestor Vicente Madali Gonzalez was taken as a child to the larger neighboring island of Mindoro by his father, who was a teacher. There, he spent his youth among farmers and fishermen, figures which have dominated his fiction ever since. After being graduated from the University of the Philippines, then in Manila, he turned to writing a newspaper column, as well as a novel and short tales about the people of Mindoro. He was one of the Veronicans, a group of young writers striving for stark and striking imagery. The authenticity of his fiction won him national attention just before Japanese Occupation forces landed on Luzon. When English was practically forbidden by the invaders, Gonzalez and others wrote in Tagalog but brought to the native language new techniques, themes, and theories as an alternative to formulas in conventional literature.

His chance for prominence came in 1947, when the Swallow Press in Denver published his prizewinning stories, *Seven Hills Away*. In 1949, a Rockefeller grant allowed him to visit several writing centers in the United States and to attend both Stanford and Bread Loaf workshops. On his return, he was appointed to the faculty of the state university, which had just been constructed in the temporary capital, Quezon City; there, he taught creative writing and comparative literature for eighteen years. During Carlos P. Romulo's presidency of the university, Gonzalez served as public relations assistant and speech writer to the former ambassador to the United Nations. Although he held no graduate degree, he was tenured on the basis of his distinguished contributions to the national culture as a novelist and short-story writer, as well as editor of the eclectic *Diliman Review* and consultant to Benipayo Press and to Bookmark, which risked nonprofit publication of Philippine literature in order to bring recognition and rewards to young writers. In 1964, he wrote in Rome and the Italian Alps on a second Rockefeller grant. In 1968, he held visiting professorships at both the University of Hong Kong and the University of California at Santa Barbara.

Beginning in 1969, Gonzalez was Professor of English, particularly Third World literature, at California State University in Hayward. In 1977, he served as visiting professor of Asian-American literature at the University of Washington, and in the summer of 1978, after a long absence, he briefly returned to the University of the Philippines as writer-in-residence. One result of that visit was the publication of *Mindoro and Beyond*, a retrospective volume drawn from four decades of his stories, which initiated the Philippine Writers' Series for the University of the Philippines Creative Writing Center. Gonzalez retired from university teaching in 1989.

Analysis

The superiority of N. V. M. Gonzalez's novels lies principally in their ability to provide social realism without submitting to sentimentality, at one extreme, or to any doctrinaire program of violent reform at the other. This same authenticity of character and situation acquits him of the charge of being a mere imitator, even though age-old struggles between peasant and proprietor, between barrio and city values, recur in his work. They do so not because of slavish adherence to literary formulas but because basic social patterns have persisted in Philippine culture for hundreds of years: it is to these patterns that Gonzalez is true, and in response to them that his vision has remained constant.

Even in his autobiographical first novel, *The Winds of April*, written in his youth, Gonzalez presents attitudes that reappear in his short stories and later novels: an attachment to the array of creatures on land and sea; a respect for the men and women whose lives depend on nature's whims and their own unflagging efforts; and a dream of surmounting these hazards without forgetting them, by moving to cities where opportunities for education and for writing about one's discoveries and their implications abound. At the same time that *The Winds of April* describes the aspirations of the author from birth to young manhood, it captures the hopes of a whole people on the verge of independence from the United States. Virtually all the copies of that novel, along with hopes for a smooth transition to national sovereignty, were destroyed during World War II.

What emerges in *A Season of Grace*, during postwar reconstruction, is a view less naïve but still based on the courage and determination of a people who find in hardship the same promise of life's renewal that the rich volcanic ash of their soil offers their labor. They do not arise abruptly, miraculously, like the phoenix from those ashes, but their right to stand erect is wholly and undeniably earned, if only gradually, painstakingly. The young married couple, Sabel and Doro, who leave the overworked plots of Tara-Poro and the fishing barrio at Alag to claim interior *kaingins* of their own on Mindoro, are in many ways like adult children. The cadences of Gonzalez's prose resemble rituals of survival, marked by seasons of seedtime, caretaking, and harvest. The action encompasses slightly more than one year's cycle in this couple's efforts to restore a wilderness to its garden state, although Gonzalez knows well that slash-and-burn techniques can destroy more than they cultivate. Petty officials requisition several intricately and meticulously woven mats from them. Their merchant landlord Epe Ruda maintains the rule that debts double if they are not repaid in time. Yet after the year covered in the novel, Sabel and Doro are not quite so impoverished as before and they have two male children; they are likely to endure and prevail.

The year has not been one completely filled with favors. Their friend Blas Marte, once debt-free, has become a sharecropper for a usurious rice merchant. Their own rice sack hangs empty for months, and there are nightmares, premonitions of death and disaster. Multitudes of rats attack their harvest, as greedily bent on taking what is not theirs as are the landlord, the treasurer, and his deputy. Even Sabel and her husband Doro come to blows occasionally, as a result of misunderstanding and exhaustion. She is the more resilient, gentle, contemplative, and naturally good-hearted. Doro is sometimes consumed by his own unending chores. When his wife is seriously ill, he is most concerned with how he will survive without her. He can be impatient, jealous without cause, more erratic than Sabel in growth toward maturity. Yet a contrast clearly is established between these two and their materialistic, childless landlord. The implied emphasis on their compliance rather than on bitter complaint is a sign, from the author, of a resignation nearly religious, an elemental act of faith. At the beginning of a new year, Sabel and Doro begin still another clearing; their infant lies nearby like a seedling, very much part of the stream of the life-force. What seemed a relentless cycle of trial, progress, and frustration has become a slow and painful spiral upward, a combination of change and continuity, of improvement gradual but sure.

The true polar opposite to the simple, instinctual peasant such as Doro is not his middle-class landlord but the *ilustrado*, the elitist intellectual portrayed in Gonzalez's *The Bamboo Dancers*. If the wilderness dominates *A Season of Grace*, wasteland imagery permeates the later novel. Ernie Rama is a sculptor who tries to conceal his lack of creativity by wandering through the world. Such is his nature that, wherever he goes on his study grant in the United States, he keeps a distance between himself and others, in order to avoid facing and confessing his own self-alienation. The stargazer at the Vermont writers' conference waves a message which Ernie avoids; the lonely United States Information Service girl in Kyoto whom he planned to meet, disappears; en route to Hiroshima, he is with an interpreter who stays mute; the Japanese switchboard operator and he are mutually unintelligible. Everyone remains a stranger, so quick is Ernie's passage among them, like someone running from an atomic cloudburst. Despite its scenes in Hiroshima, the novel is less about the unspeakable horror of nuclear war than it is about this deliberate detachment, this maintained silence which aggravates differences and helps cause war.

In his travels, Ernie avoids even his own countrymen, especially the elderly, lest they place some claim on his social conscience. He resembles the barren Fisher King from T. S. Eliot's *The Waste Land* (1922), who is doomed to sterility because of his lack of love, his inability to share. What Ernie fathers in an old acquaintance, Helen Reyes, who has turned to him for emotional warmth, is only a miscarriage. He is at best sexually ambivalent, actually preferring no intimacy under any circumstances with anyone. While Helen's American fiancé, Herb Lane, is involved in the accidental death of a Chinese girl in Taipeh, Ernie is characteristically removed from the scene by sickness. When Herb is murdered as a result of that death, Ernie can only offer abstract sympathy. Persuading Helen to escape to Macao, where perhaps she can purchase rare cosmetics, he contaminates her with his own self-indulgence. Even at the moment of near-drowning, while fishing back in the Philippines, when he cries out to be rescued, it is unclear whether he has learned the importance of others except to satisfy his own impulsive needs. To some extent, the people of Hiroshima, who think exclusively of their own suffering but not of those who were their victims in war, represent this same egocentrism, so opposed to the traditional sense of brotherhood among Filipinos.

The great subtlety of this novel lies in the author's strict dependence on a defective narrator, whose self-deception, contradictions, and confusions become evident through a recurring pattern of nonencounters, as well as through certain symbols. The principal symbol employed by Gonzalez is the national dance, the *tinikling*, in which the object is to maintain a rhythm of rapid movement that prevents the feet from ever being touched by the clash of poles. In the Philippines, the caste of "untouchables" is not the impoverished peasant but the elite leadership, on which society depends so much for patronage, but from which the masses more commonly have received indifference, cruelty, and betrayal of purpose.

In *The Bamboo Dancers*, as in his short stories and other novels, Gonzalez's characters are discovered rather than explained. They present themselves without comment from the author. Such subtlety and disciplined self-restraint keep Gonzalez's fiction far from the ordinary "literature of protest," which often disregards credibility or complexity of character in order to engage in extensive polemics. Perhaps Gonzalez's constant attentiveness to the manner of speech and even to silence owes much to his culture's reliance, for unobtrusive communication, on courteous consideration of others and on wordless body language. Gonzalez's craft is perfectly expressive of these Asian aspects of Philippine folkways.

Leonard Casper

Other major works
    SHORT FICTION: *Seven Hills Away*, 1947; *Children of the Ash-Covered Loam*, 1954; *Look, Stranger, on This Island Now*, 1963; *Mindoro and Beyond*, 1979.

Bibliography
Bernad, Miguel. *Bamboo and the Greenwood Tree*. Manila: Bookmark, 1961. Contrasts the simple nobility of Gonzalez's slash-and-burn farmers in *A Season of Grace* with the directionless elite in *The Bamboo Dancers*. Presents seven pages of the author's own comments on the latter novel.
Casper, Leonard. *New Writing from the Philippines: A Critique and Anthology*. Syracuse, N.Y.: Syracuse University Press, 1966. The chapter on Gonzalez defines the folk quality of pioneers south of Manila, conveyed through the language's severe formal restraint and the slow seasonal growth of these

simple farmers. The city-bred central character in *The Bamboo Dancers*, however, is self-centered and unproductive.

De Jesus, Edilberto, Jr. "On This Soil, in This Climate: Growth in the Novels of N. V. M. Gonzalez." In *Brown Heritage*, edited by Antonio G. Manuud. Quezon City: Ateneo de Manila, 1967. Presents a historian's perspective, demonstrating parallels between Philippine society and Gonzalez's novels as subsistence farming has become industrialized.

Gonzalez, N. V. M. *The Father and the Maid*. Quezon City: University of the Philippines, 1990. These lectures delivered on the author's return from years of teaching in California connect much of Philippine culture with Gonzalez's attempts to re-create that culture through fiction in Philippine English.

——————. *Kalutang: A Filipino in the World*. Manila: Kalikasan, 1990. A brief memoir of the author's development, comparable with the Hanunoo tribesman's beating two sticks together as he journeys to assure himself that body and soul have not separated.

Zuraek, Maria Elnora C. "N. V. M. Gonzalez' *A Season of Grace*." In *Essays on the Philippine Novel in English*, edited by Joseph A. Galdon. Quezon City: Ateneo de Manila, 1979. Comments on the two meanings of grace: a period of postponement or second chance and regeneration through sanctification by natural forces.

PAUL GOODMAN

Born: New York, New York; September, 9, 1911
Died: North Stratford, New Hampshire; August 2, 1972

Principal long fiction

The Grand Piano: Or, The Almanac of Alienation, 1942; *The State of Nature: A War*, 1946; *The Dead of Spring: After a War*, 1950; *Parents' Day*, 1951; *The Empire City*, 1959 (includes *The Grand Piano*, 1942, *The State of Nature*, 1946, *The Dead of Spring*, 1950, *The Holy Terror*); *Making Do*, 1963.

Other literary forms

By any standards, Goodman was a prolific writer. In addition to his novels, he wrote collections of poetry, several of which were privately printed. The most noteworthy are *The Lordly Hudson: Collected Poems* (1962); *Homespun of Oatmeal Gray* (1970); and the *Collected Poems* (1973). He also published ten plays between 1941 and 1970 and three books of literary criticism: *Kafka's Prayer* (1947); *The Structure of Literature* (1954); and *Speaking and Language: Defense of Poetry* (1971). Goodman also wrote a partial autobiography: *Five Years: Thoughts During a Useless Time* (1967). This list, however, represents only a fraction of his oeuvre, which includes more than thirty titles. In addition, he contributed regularly and served as film-review editor of the *Partisan Review* and as a television critic for *The New Republic*.

Achievements

Goodman more closely approximates the Renaissance man than does perhaps any other twentieth century American man of letters. A prolific writer in many genres—novels, poems, essays, dramas, short stories, literary criticism, the author of studies in psychotherapy, education, sociology, and community planning—Goodman has entries under twenty-one different categories in the catalogs of the New York Public Library. He was not discovered by the reading public until 1960 as a result of his book *Growing Up Absurd* (1960), a spirited attack on the values of mid-century America. Because Goodman wrote in such diverse forms, he is not easily categorized. He shares with many of his colleagues such as Saul Bellow, Philip Roth, and Bernard Malamud, a perspective that is distinctly Jewish: a feeling for alienation, a skeptical nature that is allied with visionary tendencies and a penchant for social justice. As a novelist, he is best remembered for *The Empire City*.

Biography

Paul Goodman was born in Greenwich Village, New York City, on September 9, 1911, to a family in financial straits so serious that his father deserted them soon after Paul's birth. Not surprisingly, many of Goodman's books deal with fatherless boys struggling to establish some sort of alliance both with adult males and with the society that surrounds them. The lonely boy excelled in school ("he made it difficult for us ordinary geniuses," one class-mate remarked). The years he spent at the College of the City of New York between 1927 and 1931 were formative ones in his intellectual growth. Here he came in contact with the legendary teacher/philosopher Morris Cohen, who found Goodman to be a willing student with an inquiring and skeptical mind. Thereafter, Goodman found outlets for his omnivorous interests, pub-lishing pieces on philosophy, short stories, cinema criticism, and poetry. Though considered a promising writer while still in his twenties, Goodman did not attract a wide audience. During the 1950's, in fact, he grew despondent over his lack of recognition; it was not until shortly before his fiftieth birthday that this reputation burgeoned.

"Too long a sacrifice makes a stone of the heart," remarked William Butler Yeats in a line that is appropriate to Goodman, who was often viewed by contemporaries as arrogant, distant, and hard, yet to his credit was coura-geous, committed to social good, and helpful to other writers. Complicating his life was his bisexuality, which he explored at length in his fiction. At a time when others were circumspect about such things, Goodman made little effort to conceal his sexual activities, being dismissed as a graduate student from the University of Chicago and later from other teaching positions. Very likely, his novel *Parents' Day* chronicles the difficulties his sexual activities created for him.

In 1942, Goodman's first novel, *The Grand Piano*, was published. This novel (Goodman referred to this book as an educational romance) focuses on the spiritual growth of a parentless eleven-year-old boy named Horatio Alger, who roams the streets of Manhattan, surviving by his wits, and defying all institutions, most notably the educational establishment. He is an "artful dodger" like Goodman himself, who also took pride in his street smarts. Goodman's fascination with psychotherapy—he became a lay analyst for the New York Gestalt Institute—permeates the later segments of his tetralogy, *The Empire City*. Despite his prolific output, Goodman was for most of his life as unsuccessful financially as his father had been, though he was a good deal more responsible. By his own contention, he lived below the poverty line—until 1960, he both boasted and lamented that he was as poor as any sharecropper.

Goodman's most difficult period occurred during the 1950's, at the height of his creative powers. His marriage was faltering, his daughter was ill, and his submissions were regularly rejected. Very likely, his outspoken views were considered alarming during the McCarthy era. In 1960, the shift in the coun-try's mood coincided with the publication of *Growing Up Absurd*, the book which earned Goodman recognition. His success, however, did little to rec-oncile him to those aspects of American culture he had been deploring; the

Vietnam War, so destructive of American morale, ironically established his credentials as a prophet to the young.

Success did not appreciably alter Goodman's life-style, though it did make him a sought-after lecturer. The reader who wishes to gain some appreciation of what that life-style was like is advised to read *Making Do*, as well as the now nearly unobtainable *Parents' Day* and the poetry. In 1967, Goodman's son Matthew was killed in a climbing accident, a grievous event that Goodman dealt with extensively in his poetry. Goodman died on August 2, 1972, at the age of sixty, leaving a wife and two daughters.

Analysis

"I have only one subject," wrote Paul Goodman, "the human beings I know in their man-made environments." All of Goodman's novels explore man in relation to the institutions that both reflect and shape his values. In Goodman's view, rather than abetting human development, institutions thwart aptitude and foster stupidity. From this base, Goodman argues passionately for a more humane society—one that would offer worthwhile goals, meaningful work, honest public speech, patriotism, and at the same time encourage healthy animal desire. Goodman indicts American culture for being unequal to all these aspirations.

In Goodman's works, society's failure leads the individual to attempt to create his own community—one that is scaled down and decentralized. The author is absorbed with the individual's wresting from the larger social order a more workable and personalized one—a community. In this endeavor, Goodman is not alone: in fact, he is engaged in a quintessentially American occupation, that of creating "a city upon a hill," however different from John Winthrop's ideal. Indeed, Nathaniel Hawthorne manifested a similar interest when he participated in the Brook Farm experiment. In fiction, Mark Twain's Huck Finn flees the larger society to find communion with Jim on the Mississippi. Both Jay Gatsby and Dick Diver among F. Scott Fitzgerald's characters create a community but are ultimately defeated by corrosive contact with the worst aspects of American materialism and illusion. A similar concern for community informs Goodman's writing, though his novels are typically urban; the sole exception, *Parents' Day*, is set in Upstate New York. In all of his novels, the protagonist and his friends strive to establish a workable, nourishing community but find themselves in constant danger of engulfment by the debased larger society.

As evidenced by the diversity of his interests, Goodman was an intellectual, keenly aware of his debt to Western traditions. His thought was shaped by Aristotle, Immanuel Kant, Thomas Hobbes, Franz Kafka, Martin Buber, and Wilhelm Reich. From Hobbes and Kant, Goodman derived material for his speculations on the social contract, by means of which man relinquished certain freedoms in order to achieve civilization. In Kafka, Goodman perceived a surrealist and comic spirit as well as the notion that writing was a form of prayer. One critic, Theodore Roszak, has identified a "coarse-grained Hasidic magic" about Goodman's work, presumably a reference to the author's search for transcendence in the mundane. Goodman may well have found Buber's idealized notion of human relations congenial—the effort to transform "I-It" relationships into "I-Thou" ones. Goodman's work as a lay therapist with the Gestalt Institute of New York no doubt reflected his interest in the psychosexual theories of Wilhelm Reich, which inform all of his writings. One detects this influence in the "therapy" sections of *The Empire City* (especially those in which Horatio woos Rosalind); in *Parents' Day*, where the teacher/narrator uses physical intimacy as an educational tool; and in *Making Do*, where Harold and Terry suffer from sexual deprivation. In all his novels, Goodman argues that personal contact should be communal and psychosexual. It may be disconcerting to the reader to discover that the narrator of *Making Do* is bisexual, and that the narrator/teacher of *Parents' Day* is engaged in homosexual liaisons with his adolescent students, but Goodman does not flinch from offering such revelations. Rather, he flaunts his protagonists' (and his own) sexuality—not always to good effect. The reader may well feel distracted when an author insists on toleration for his sexual preferences, may feel annoyed when asked to respond not to the event the artist is rendering but to the artist's challenge.

Though one must be cautious in identifying the narrator with the author, Goodman does not make much effort to conceal the autobiographical nature of much of his fiction. On the contrary, Goodman often addresses the reader in asides which prevent the normal suspension of disbelief. "This is no book/ Who touches this touches a man," boasted Walt Whitman as he artfully concealed himself, yet Goodman does not trouble to disguise himself. The narrators of *Making Do* and *Parents' Day* are interchangeable—both closely resembling the sort of intellectual Goodman was: a man of letters who was also a man of the streets.

At his best, Goodman is imaginative, profound, and witty. *The Empire City*, though uneven, is a neglected masterpiece. At his worst, Goodman becomes hortatory and shrill, as in *The Dead of Spring*, the third work in the tetralogy, or careless in his prose, as in *Making Do*.

The Empire City, Goodman's ambitious tetralogy, follows a cluster of characters who have become alienated not only from society but also from themselves. The first novel in the tetralogy, *The Grand Piano*, is subtitled "The Almanac of Alienation"; thus, Goodman announces that he will be exploring what Robert Frost called "inner weather"; he will be attempting a chronicle of the spirit as it unfolds in life. Given this aim, it should not be surprising if some of the book's passages do not yield themselves readily to analysis. Goodman, like his literary forebears, Kafka, André Gide, William Blake, and Rainer Maria Rilke, seems to be charting the ineffable and bidding his reader to follow.

The narrator of *The Grand Piano*, hardly distinguishable from Goodman himself, is often obtrusive in the manner of Henry Fielding. By mediating between character and reader, the narrator encourages the reader to regard the protagonists as friends, members of a community of which he or she is a part. These new friends are vital, larger than life, multitalented, heroic. Witness the name of the hero—Horatio Alger—based on the American writer who encouraged boys to lead virtuous lives full of heroic deeds.

The Alger tales dealt with the self-made man who succeeded in that great mecca of success, New York City. Goodman's Alger, however, is a street-smart guttersnipe who, having destroyed all records of his existence, revels in his outcast status. Untouched by social institutions, such as school, he is truly a self-made eleven-year-old youth. In the opening episode, he meets Mynheer Duyck Colijn. The critic Sherman Paul has observed that Mynheer is an exemplar of the cultured man. Like his Dutch forebears, Mynheer is a model of tolerance and civic virtue. If Horatio is alienated, Mynheer is the opposite. In their initial meeting, the cunning, sneering, artful dodger is pitted against the sophisticated, virtuous adult. Reading the latter's name as "Dick Collegian," however, suggests another aspect of his character: his innocence. His rationality and civic pride will be sorely tested by the outbreak of war.

Horatio has no parents, but is being reared, as Goodman was, by a brother and sister and, again like Goodman, is searching for a father. He settles on Eliphaz, a sort of Yiddish Daddy Warbucks but one who combines patriarchal wisdom with financial acumen. In Eliphaz, Goodman achieves the sort of fantastic realism that readers customarily associate with Charles Dickens. Eliphaz's presence creates some of the best scenes in the novel. This merchant prince represents the idealized spirit of early capitalism: he keeps a mysterious ledger containing only an accumulating number of zeros; he practices detachment by selling his own furniture, often while his family is still sitting on it; he idly places a price tag on his own son ("$84.95. $75 cash? Good! Sold!"). He is a man of culture who can spout Johann Wolfgang Goethe and Spinoza. Opposed to the anarchistic spirit of the Algers, who subsist on welfare, he impulsively sends them a grand piano, one that is so large that they are forced to sleep under it. Gnomically, he explains his gesture, which proceeds from mixed motives: "It's always worthwhile to hurl large gifts toward your adversary. Where is she going to put such an animal? How is she going to explain it to the relief investigator I'll send around tomorrow?" So wonderful a comic creation is Eliphaz that the reader can only regret his death at the opening of the second novel of the tetralogy. His place in literature has been usurped by the more impersonal Milo Minderbinder of Joseph Heller's *Catch-22* (1961), a similarly restless but more mindless spirit of capitalism.

Other members of the community include Horatio's family, Lothario/Lothair and Laura. Lothair, a follower of the anarchist Prince Petr Kropotkin, is a reformer who is vilified and persecuted by the state. As Sherman Paul comments, he is yet another side of Goodman himself—a reformer and educator. In this respect, he is also reminiscent of the protagonists of *Making Do* and *Parents' Day*. *The Grand Piano* proceeds toward a communal reconciliation which is partial at best; as in Richard Wagner's music, resolution is never far away but never quite arrives. Indeed, the climax of the novel has the characters attending a performance of Wagner's *Die Meistersinger*, which promises "an exulting community spirit," but as Horatio shrewdly observes, "It's all to be paid for at [Beckmesser's] expense. . . ." The survival of the larger society, as it does in fairy tales, hinges on the scapegoating of one of its members, hinges on projecting the dark side of the psyche into a villain who can then be defeated by a hero.

The novel ends with another musical contest, one involving the grand piano. Embedded in this section are hints of the Arthurian contest to secure the sword Excalibur. Lothair, who is a composer, performs beautifully and by rights should be declared the winner, but he is arrested and transported to jail—presumably a victim of scapegoating by a society preparing itself for war.

The second novel in the tetralogy, *The State of Nature* (1946), subtitled "A War," pursues Goodman's interest in the contact-point between the organism and its environment. The setting is now 1944. Horatio has grown to young manhood; his adopted father has, like Alfred Tennyson's King Arthur, died, leaving behind a world that has grown incomprehensible to him. In this book, the narrator discourses tirelessly (and, at times, tiresomely) on the subject of war, not only as a social reality but also as a spiritual phenomenon. Goodman viewed war as a debased form of the spiritual life which requires putting oneself in jeopardy. This novel is weaker than its predecessor, first because Goodman exhorts his reader rather than rendering his material into narrative, second because the author uses the war as a symbol but does not acknowledge the moral imperatives that made World War II a necessity.

The State of Nature explores the themes of putting oneself in danger and engaging in "a long drawn out losing fight"—both activities in which the social activist Goodman was experienced. In this book, the central figures pass from dissent to alienation. Horatio is shot at by overwrought National Guardsmen. Lothair broods in jail about the paradox that his ardent desire to serve society is unappreciated unless that service takes the form of fighting. Laura, the community planner and wife of Mynheer, has been ordered to undo her work: by means of camouflage, she is to transform a community of her design, a land of milk and honey, back into a desert. Lothair escapes, but, driven mad by social rejection (his name Lothario indicates he is a lover, but of humanity), he executes a plan to release the animals from the zoo. In the pandemonium created, little Gus, incestuous offspring of Arthur and his sister Emily (both children of Eliphaz) is killed. The zoo's curator happens to be Mynheer, who in contrast to Lothair is permitted to serve humanity but is fated to do so without conviction. He and his wife Laura, the reader is told, are "alienated from their natures." In his case, the result is that the connection between his intellect and his emotions is severed, rendering him impotent. In a scene reminiscent of Blake's prophetic books, Mynheer (intellect) is paralyzed by Emily's anguished cry (heart) concerning the sight of the tiger destroying little Gus. Lothair then leads Mynheer into the cage vacated by the tiger.

In this chapter, Goodman shifts emphasis from social concerns to psychological ones. Community needs must wait while individuals attempt to restore their shattered equilibrium. Emily, for example, is unable to save her son from the tiger; she is "frozen into action by her 'mixed desire.'" The death of her son, however, leads her to a primal cry that enables her to function once again. Her therapeutic experience (this section was conceived at the time of Goodman's developing interest in Gestalt therapy) becomes a paradigmatic model for others who also are experiencing their alienation from self. Social conditions only serve to enforce this alienation, as is revealed in the prophecy of Eliphaz which concludes the novel. In it, the dying capitalist foresees the advent of a consumer economy, mass conformity, and mass education, all resulting in "Asphyxiation"—a state in which the individual is unable to breathe freely or to experience his own vital desires. What has replaced human community he scornfully terms "Sociolatry."

The third novel in the tetralogy, *The Dead of Spring*, is subtitled "After a War." All must come to grips with the aftermath of war, must fight the long-drawn-out losing fight of the duration, as Eliphaz predicted. Lothair turns inward to his own pain, away from social concerns; Mynheer delivers a valediction on man combining elements of Prince Hamlet and Fritz Perls; the marriage between Emily and Lothair proves barren; the community spirit languishes. There is a brief interlude when Horatio meets Laura, but generally this is a gloomy period. Horatio discovers himself to be impotent, but is redeemed and taught to love by a young lad, whom Sherman Paul identifies as an aspect of Horatio's own submerged self—the youthful street arab Horatio had been in the opening novel. As is typical in a romance, the lovers overcome their vicissitudes—though here the impediments are largely of their own devising—and fall in love. As Horatio is about to become a father, however, he is arrested—forced, as it were, by parenthood into recognition of the social contract. Horatio is indicted, not for resisting the state as Lothair had been at the conclusion of *The Grand Piano*, but for refusing to adopt a stand, much like the lost souls in Hell's anteroom of Dante's *Inferno* (c. 1314). Horatio admits to his error but counters it with the information that he is in love; in comic fashion, the conflict is resolved, the charge is dropped.

This lighthearted respite provides comic relief from the chapters that precede it and the event which follows—the suicide of Laura. Her death serves as a sacrificial act, one that will redeem the community. Testaments to its effectiveness are the regenerations of Mynheer, Minetta (the social worker), and Horatio—each of whom begins finding ways to cope with the dilemma that results when one must choose between living within a mad society or the madness of living outside society. The dilemma is expressed, too, in the baseball game that follows, built as it is on a paradox: the participants "played in order to keep the ball alive, nevertheless desperately destroyed the play by bringing nearer the end of the game." Each copes with this paradox in his own fashion; each participates as an individual and as a teammate, but nothing can enjoin the game's end. To their common cry "Creator spirit, come," a combination of entreaty and sexual joke, a reply comes in the birth of St. Wayward. He is a restorer, a conservator of humanity's spirit, which has been abused by advancing civilization.

In the fourth and final novel of the series, *The Holy Terror*, Goodman promises a "register of reconciliation," and indeed, the principals move toward a harmony, what Blake would call experiencing their "joys and desires." Such chapter titles as "conversing," "dancing," "eating," "relaxing," and "wakening" reflect the social nature of their existence. Horatio and Rosalind dance in sexual joy, while Lothair finds fulfillment in his music. They undergo a kind of Gestalt therapy, a form of body mysticism. Each pursues self-awareness: Mynheer experiences primal consciousness by means of the Tao Te Ching; Lothair, the public man, discovers his repressed rage. In a poignant episode, Lothair, overcome by feelings of rage, hope, and love, is slain by his son Wayward in a scene rife with Oedipal implications. In killing his father, Wayward achieves manhood, and his exploits in Ireland, which later cap the book, offer an affirmative ending.

After Lothair's death, Horatio undergoes a form of madness which involves accepting the reality of the world as it is expressed by the now defunct newspaper, *The New York Herald Tribune*. The time is 1952. One symptom of Horatio's insanity is that he wishes to vote for General Eisenhower. Although this section is at times amusing, it seems inappropriate, more a symptom of the author's political outrage than a stage in the development of Horatio's personality. No effort is made by the author to imply that Horatio is seriously exploring conservative values; instead, Goodman sacrifices his character's credibility to parody topical theories of politics and education. Indeed, much of the final book reveals Goodman's flagging imagination. Events are related to one another only thematically rather than as the outgrowth of character. One such example involves the youthful cardplayers who appear as a foil for St. Wayward. The latter transcends and redeems the sordid world of boys, performing miracles in a way that suggests events in the Gospels. The boys, however, are only a convenience for the author, and they disappear from the novel. The Gospel parallel is reinforced in the next chapter, however, which is called "Good News" and deals with the discovery by Lefty Duyvendak, son of Mynheer and Laura, of an Edenic community where life is reasonable, joy permissible. As the novel nears its conclusion, the principals meet to reaffirm their sense of community, each announcing the "work that is at hand." The novel ends with a lyrical fantasy of St. Wayward freeing Ireland of its sexual repression. Horatio has the tetralogy's final word, entreating God for more life.

Since its publication in 1959, *The Empire City* has achieved a kind of cult status. Though at times obscure, it represents Goodman's most ambitious novelistic effort and clearly his best. His reputation as a novelist rests on this often impressive and imaginative work.

In *Making Do*, Goodman develops and amplifies themes he had earlier explored in *The Empire City*. "My only literary theme has been the community," he remarked in his journal *Five Years*. Once more, he returns to familiar themes: psychology, education, radical reform, and the efforts of the individual to satisfy natural desire in a repressive environment. *Making Do* is a less hopeful and exuberant novel than its predecessor: as *Communitatis* glosses *The Empire City*, so *Growing Up Absurd* clarifies *Making Do*. The titles of these latter works suggest the more circumscribed possibilities for achievement Goodman perceived in American life. Entitling his earlier work with New York's sobriquet the "Empire City" does suggest Goodman's hope: his vision of heroism and transcendence that has the capacity to stimulate the protagonists. "Making do," on the other hand, is far less optimistic, a diminished variation of the American credo—"making it"—that spurred an earlier generation of Jewish immigrants (among them Goodman's own father, perhaps). "Making do" implies less a remaking of the environment to render it worthy of its best citizens than an attempt to adjust and find comfort in a framework of truncated possibilities.

Unlike its predecessor, *Making Do* is not a fantasy imbued with the energy and spirit that such a form implies, but is a tale conceived in a realistic-naturalistic vein. As before, the novelist has a dual role as both narrator ("the tired man") and participant (Goodman appears by name in a cameo role). Once again, Goodman presents his characters as special friends, members of a community of which his persona is the guiding spirit. Other members include the saintly Harold, spiritual father to a gang of delinquent Puerto Ricans, and Jason, a graduate student in English with passionate convictions on education. Jason is writing a dissertation on Theodore Dreiser, an author who explored the tragic implications of the American dream. Another member of the group, Meg, has a generous sexual spirit and guilelessness which render her attractive, however undirected she appears. The narrator's friend, Roger, shares his commitment to their surroundings, as displayed in his eagerness to establish Vanderzee as a haven for artists. Finally, there is Terry, an inarticulate youth full of a kind of puppylike devotion to the community of friends.

The very qualities that make these individuals attractive also prove their undoing. Harold is mocked and abused by his hustler/lover Ramon, who eventually betrays his protector to the police. Jason expresses his rage (and probably Goodman's own) concerning educational textbooks by the impotent gesture of punching a textbook salesman. His dissertation is probably doomed for reasons that make a mockery of the notion of academia as a community of scholars. Meg's tolerant and nurturing sexual practices provide the police with a pretext for attacking the group; her innocence even permits her to cooperate with her persecutors. Terry, like Horatio, though lacking the street smarts and mental discipline to provide him with equilibrium, desperately embraces the notion of community. He is inarticulate, however, a primitive who relies on insight to the exclusion of cognitive thought; hence, he is unable to negotiate in a fallen world and is ultimately institutionalized. Unhappy though he is, the narrator, "the tired man," does cope successfully with the world—in large measure because he is sufficiently detached to achieve at least a modest success, satisfying his needs for love, work, and self-expression. As noted earlier, a character named Paul Goodman appears briefly in the novel, but the lineaments of the author's own life appear most fully in the character of the narrator.

The vicissitudes experienced by the community do not simply result from the larger society's victimization of the group (though that does exist); as in *The Empire City*, they result in large measure from weaknesses within the community. Harold has lost contact with his animal nature, as symbolized both by his impotence with Ramon and by his self-lacerating behavior at the race track, where he bets against his own selections. Meg is jealous of others' sexual pleasures; Jason is unwilling to act the responsible father; Terry is inarticulate unless he can be physically intimate. Presumably, for Goodman, Terry is the end-product of all that is distorted about American culture. The reader, however, may find that Joanna's attraction to him is rather implausible. "She did not see about her any other young man who was worthwhile," the narrator remarks. Hardly a very satisfactory explanation to justify her love affair with a promiscuous, bisexual, drug-addicted dropout on the verge of being institutionalized for schizophrenia. Even the founder of the community, Meg's former husband, Amos, is "insane," and threatens to kill his wife.

The setting of this novel is Vanderzee, a community directly across the river from New York City. For Goodman, everything Dutch has positive connotations (recall Mynheer of *The Empire City* or the collection of poems *The Lordly Hudson*). Vanderzee, however, having betrayed its origins, does not actualize its potential for community; the town is controlled by a venal police force and a narrow-minded mayor, both of whom endorse "community" but mean by it a life-denying, mind-numbing conformity. There is little difference in Goodman's eyes between the self-serving values of the Puerto Rican hustlers and those of the police force (a point Goodman had already made in *Growing Up Absurd*), so that when Ramon is arrested, Judas-like, he betrays the smaller community in order to gain entrance into the larger.

The novel ends on a mixed note. The narrator, "the tired man," has a glimmering vision of a transcendent love of country—an outgrowth, he explains, of erotic love. Harold and Meg find comfort in each other's arms, but Terry is institutionalized, the Puerto Rican youths are arrested, and Amos is left free but homeless.

As a novel, *Making Do* has occasional strengths and glaring weaknesses. Goodman, as ever, is a compelling writer, with trenchant insights into American culture and social life, but this book lacks the exuberant spirit and incandescent invention of *The Empire City*. A serious drawback of the book, as Richard Poirier observes, is that "its actions never [accumulate] the necessity that brings on subsequent actions. . . . The links between the events are largely external." *Making Do* is an interesting book, but not a good novel.

Goodman's novels have had a mixed reception. *Parents' Day* is largely forgotten, out of print and unavailable even in research libraries. *Making Do*, the most popular of his novels, is marred by serious flaws; it is best remembered for its vivid scenes of communal life in the 1960's. Goodman's reputation as a novelist rests on his tetralogy *The Empire City*, a work that will no doubt endure as a minor classic.

Stan Sulkes

Other major works

SHORT FICTION: *The Facts of Life*, 1945; *The Break-up of Our Camp and Other Stories*, 1949; *Our Visit to Niagara*, 1960; *Adam and His Works*, 1968.

POETRY: *The Lordly Hudson: Collected Poems*, 1962; *Hawkweed*, 1967; *Homespun of Oatmeal Gray*, 1970; *Collected Poems*, 1973.

PLAYS: *Stoplight*, 1941; *Faustina*, 1949; *Three Plays: The Young Disciple*, 1955; *Jonah*, 1965; *Tragedy and Comedy: Four Cubist Plays*, 1970.

NONFICTION: *Kafka's Prayer*, 1947; *Communitas*, 1947 (with Percival Goodman); *Gestalt Therapy: Excitement and Growth in the Human Personality*, 1951 (with Frederick S. Perls and Ralph Hefferline); *The Structure of Literature*, 1954; *Growing Up Absurd*, 1960; *The Community of Scholars*, 1962; *Utopian Essays and Practical Proposals*, 1962; *Compulsory Mis-Education*, 1964; *People or Personnel: Decentralizing and the Mixed System*, 1965; *Five Years: Thoughts During a Useless Time*, 1966; *Speaking and Language: Defense of Poetry*, 1971.

CHILDREN'S LITERATURE: *Childish Jokes: Crying Backstage*, 1951.

Bibliography

Gilman, Richard. Review of *The Empire City*, by Paul Goodman. *Commonweal* 70 (July 31, 1959): 401-402. This short article examines *The Empire City* as a part of the comic tradition of J. D. Salinger and Saul Bellow. Also cites Goodman's debt to Franz Kafka for his sense of the bizarre. Objects to the sermonizing quality of Goodman's fiction but notes that his characters are intended to teach us how to live.

Harrington, Michael. "On Paul Goodman." *Atlantic* 216 (August, 1965): 88-91. This short article is a general review of Goodman's work and a more intensive examination of his essays *People or Personnel.* Looks at Goodman as an existentialist critic of American life and as a philosopher of the student revolts of the 1960's, finding his belief in the goodness of human nature naïve.

McCaslin, Walt. "Absurdities of an Addled Society." Review of *Utopian Essays and Practical Proposals*, by Paul Goodman. *Saturday Review* 45 (February 17, 1962): 23-24. Notes the vigor and breadth of Goodman's critique of American life; he takes on everything from the superstitions of science to economics to cars. McCaslin suggests, however, that Goodman's existentialism is based on foggy thinking.

Ostriker, Alicia. "Paul Goodman." *Partisan Review* 43, no. 2 (1976): 286-295. Offers a good introduction to Goodman's poetry as part of the general tradition first of Walt Whitman, then of the Black Mountain poets and the Beat generation. Notes the vigor and explicitness of his political and sexual poetry but points out that his lack of metaphoric imagination and decorum makes his poetry "unpoetic" to some readers.

Paul, Sherman. "Paul Goodman's Mourning Labor: *The Empire City.*" Review of *The Empire City*, by Paul Goodman. *The Southern Review* 4, no. 4 (1968): 894-926. This meaty review is a book-by-book analysis of *The Empire City.* Examines its major themes of the education of a young man, looking especially at its themes dealing with war and at its position in the tradition of the philosophical novel.

NADINE GORDIMER

Born: Springs, South Africa; November 20, 1923

Principal long fiction

The Lying Days, 1953; *A World of Strangers*, 1958; *Occasion for Loving*, 1963; *The Late Bourgeois World*, 1966; *A Guest of Honour*, 1970; *The Conservationist*, 1974; *Burger's Daughter*, 1979; *July's People*, 1981; *A Sport of Nature*, 1987; *My Son's Story*, 1990.

Other literary forms

Nadine Gordimer is one of the twentieth century's greatest writers of short stories. Her first collection of stories, *Face to Face: Short Stories* (1949), was published in Johannesburg by Silver Leaf Books. Her first story published in *The New Yorker*, where most of her stories first appeared, was "A Watcher of the Dead" (June 9, 1951). Gordimer's first collection of stories to be published in the United States was *The Soft Voice of the Serpent and Other Stories* (1952). This collection was followed by *Six Feet of the Country* (1956), *Friday's Footprint and Other Stories* (1960), *Not for Publication and Other Stories* (1965), *Livingstone's Companions: Stories* (1971), and *A Soldier's Embrace* (1980). *Selected Stories*, from her first five volumes, was published in 1975. Gordimer has also written or edited several volumes of nonfiction, most notably *The Essential Gesture: Writing, Politics, and Places* (1988).

Achievements

Gordimer won the W. H. Smith and Son Prize in 1971 for *Friday's Footprint and Other Stories*. In 1973, she won the James Tait Black Memorial Prize for *A Guest of Honour*. *The Conservationist* was cowinner of the Booker Prize. Gordimer also has received the French international literary prize, the *Grand Aigle d'Or*. In the United States, it is for her stories that Gordimer is best known. As one reviewer wrote: "Gordimer is in the great mainstream of the short story—Maupassant, Chekhov, Turgenev, James, Hemingway, Porter." She has, however, received increased critical attention in the United States as an important novelist (*A Sport of Nature* became a Book-of-the-Month Club dual selection). She has been awarded honorary degrees from such American universities as Harvard and Yale (both in 1987) and the New School for Social Research (1988) as well as being awarded such European honors as the French Officier de l'Ordre des Arts et des Lettres (1986).

Biography

Nadine Gordimer spent her childhood in a gold-mining town near Johannesburg, South Africa. Her father, Isidore Gordimer, was a watchmaker, a Jew who had emigrated from a Baltic town to Africa when he was thirteen; her mother was born in England. In writing about her childhood, Gordimer refers to herself as "a bolter." She did not care for the convent school to which she was sent as a day student, and she frequently played hooky. When she did attend, she would sometimes walk out. The pressures of uniformity produced revulsion and rebellion in the child. She found herself imagining a school life that would be very different from the reality she knew.

Within Gordimer's environment, a white middle-class girl typically left school at about age fifteen and worked for a few years at a clerical job. Ideally, by her early twenties she would be found by the son of a family like her own and would then be ushered through her season of glory—the engagement party, the linen shower, the marriage, and the birth of the first child. There was no point in reading books; that would only impede the inevitable process by which the daughter was readied to fit the mold.

Gordimer, however, was an early reader and an early writer. By the age of nine, she was already writing; at fourteen, she won her first writing prize. She read the stories of Guy de Maupassant, Anton Chekhov, Somerset Maugham, D. H. Lawrence, and the Americans O. Henry, Katherine Anne Porter, and Eudora Welty. Reading these great artists of the short story refined her own story-writing, making her work more sophisticated. She found herself becoming increasingly interested in politics and the plight of black South Africans. Unlike other whites who rejected the white South African way of life, Gordimer did not launch into her writing career as a way to bring change. Already a writer, she could not help "falling, falling through the surface" of white South African life.

In her early twenties, Gordimer was greatly influenced by a young male friend. She has written that he did her the service of telling her how ignorant she was. He jeered at the way she was acquiring knowledge and at her "clumsy battle to chip my way out of shell after shell of readymade concepts." Further, she says, "It was through him, too, that I roused myself sufficiently to insist on going to the university." Since she was twenty-two at the time and still being supported by her father, her family did not appreciate her desire to attend the university.

Continuing to live at home, Gordimer commuted to Johannesburg and the University of the Witwatersrand. While at the university, she met the Afrikaans poet Uys Krige, a man who has broken free of his Afrikaans heritage, lived in France and Spain, and served with the International Brigade in the Spanish Civil War. He had a profound effect upon Gordimer. She had bolted from school; she was in the process of bolting from family, class, and the superficial values and culture of white South Africa. Uys Krige gave her a final push. She was free to be committed to honesty alone. When she began sending stories to England and the United States, they were well received.

Her course was set.

Despite her contempt for the social system and the economic exploitation that prevail in South Africa, Gordimer continues to make Johannesburg her home. She gave birth to and reared her children there. She is married to a Johannesburg industrialist. She and her husband frequently go abroad, to Europe, to North America, to other African countries. She has lectured at leading American universities such as Columbia, Harvard, and Michigan State, but she always returns to Johannesburg. She returns despite the censorship of and the prohibition against much of her writing. She returns despite the fact that an arbitrary government might prevent her from leaving again or might restrict her freedom in other ways. She returns because she has made commitments.

Analysis

To be personally liberated and to be South African is to be doomed to a continuing struggle between the desire for further freedom and development for oneself and the desire for the liberation of the oppressed masses. Both may be desired, but the question is whether both can be pursued effectually. South Africa is a nation in which a white legislature promulgates laws that make it impossible for the overwhelming majority of nonwhite persons to advance themselves. Apartheid, which in Afrikaans means "apartness," is the law of the land.

In her novels, Nadine Gordimer is engaged in an ongoing examination of the possible combinations of the private life and the public life. She has created a gallery of characters ranging from pure hedonists concerned only with their own pleasure to those who have committed their lives to bringing liberty, equality, and brotherhood to South Africa. Her most interesting characters are those who are wracked and torn by the struggle, those who both want to be themselves and yet find it impossible to take personal goals seriously in a society built on the exploitation of the black masses.

Some great writers have felt that in order to write freely they must live in a free country, writers such as James Joyce and Thomas Mann. During the 1920's, numerous American writers disgusted with American values chose to become expatriates. Other writers, such as the great Russians Fyodor Dostoevski, Leo Tolstoy, and Aleksandr Solzhenitsyn, have felt that nothing could be more oppressive to them than to be separated from their countrymen, however oppressive the government of their country might be. With her books banned, with some charge or other always dangling over her head, with her passport liable to be lifted at any time, Gordimer undoubtedly has been tempted to go into exile and live in a free country. She always, however, returns to Johannesburg from abroad. To her, the accident of being born in a particular place imposes obligations; having become a writer with an international reputation imposes special obligations. At the cost of the personal freedom and the very air of freedom that could be hers elsewhere, she remains in South Africa, living with frustration and danger, a witness to the power of compassion and hope.

A first novel is often a thinly veiled autobiography of the writer's childhood, adolescence, and coming of age. Gordimer's *The Lying Days* is of the type, but is nevertheless special. Full of innocence, tenderness, courage, and joy, it is an unusually mature celebration of a woman's coming of age. It is the story of Helen Shaw's growing up in a mining town not far from Johannesburg, the intoxication of her first love affairs, her days at the university, her immersion in the city's bohemian and radical circles, and finally her drawing back to protect herself from being swamped by values, attitudes, and goals that are not her own.

In her life at home, Helen Shaw is under the thumb of a mother who commands and dominates in the name of all that is conventional and trivial. The motivating force in the mother's life is her desire to guide her family through all the planned stops on the middle-class timetable: tea parties and dances, husband's promotions, the big vacation to Europe, and, most important, the molding of offspring to the community's notion of success. To celebrate these achievements and in all else to maintain an unruffled surface—such are the goals of Mrs. Shaw and the placid Mr. Shaw, who, important as he may be to the success of the gold-mining company, is completely submissive at home. As Helen comes to realize, both mother and father, their circle of acquaintances, and those in other similar circles are "insensitive to the real flow of life."

The whites of the mining towns have blacks in their midst as servants and are surrounded by "locations" where the black mine-workers and their familes are housed. Helen Shaw chooses a lover, Paul Clark, who has committed his professional and personal life to ameliorating the misery of blacks in the townships on the periphery of Johannesburg, on weekdays through his position in the government office dealing with native housing, on weekends through work for the black African Nationalist Congress.

Paul meets with frustration at every turn. His inability to get anything done that will have a lasting impact affects the quality of his relationship with Helen. He torments her in small ways, and she reciprocates. He feels ashamed and she feels ashamed, and they become aware of "a burned-out loneliness in the very center of one's love for the other." Helen, who had come to believe that the only way for a man to fulfill himself in South Africa was "to pit himself against the oppression of the Africans" and who had wanted to live with Paul "in the greatest possible intimacy" is compelled to leave him. His political commitments, which made him so attractive to Helen in the first place, have damaged their love irretrievably.

Helen decides to go to Europe. During the few days she spends at the port city, she meets Joel Aron, with whom she had become good friends in Atherton, the town where they grew up. Joel is off to try to make a life for himself in Israel. At first, Helen is envious of Joel; he's headed for a new life in a new country. She feels homeless. South Africa is like a battleground; she cannot join the whites, and the blacks do not want her. She does not want to end up like Paul, "with a leg and arm nailed to each side." In the course of her conversations with Joel, however, she succeeds in coming to a better understanding of her situation. She is not going to be tempted by exile and a new beginning. She accepts South Africa as home and the place to which she must return.

Toby Hood, the protagonist of *A World of Strangers*, has grown up in England in a family quite different from Helen Shaw's. Had Toby been a bolter from school and a rebel against bourgeois values his parents would have loved him all the more. His parents do not care about what other members of the upper-middle class think about them; they care about justice. Through his home there is a constant procession of victims of injustice who have come for aid from the Hoods. Thus, there has been bred into Toby "a horror of the freedom that is freedom only to be free" and a consciousness of the need to make every activity in which one engages an act of conscience. Toby, however, is not persuaded. His parents have not been successful in making him into a reformer and protester like themselves. Abstractions such as justice and socialism do not thrill him. Toby wants to live a life oblivious to the suffering in the world; what he feels most inclined to do is enjoy whatever is left of privilege.

Toby is sent to take over the management temporarily of the South African branch of the family-owned publishing company. Arriving in Johannesburg, he is determined to find his own interests and amusements, and not be channeled by the reformers back in England or distracted by the examples of man's inhumanity to man that will occur before his eyes. Indeed, it seems to Toby that those who would live private lives have become a hunted species, and he resents being hunted. Toby is confirmed in his desire to avoid being a do-gooder by his discovery of a talented black man who also insists upon living his own life, regardless of the condition of his people and his country. Toby marvels at the spirit and vitality of Steven Sitole. Steven refuses to allow the chaos and filth of the black townships and the hovels in which he sleeps either to deaden his spirit or inflame it to rage. He does what he does, seeking pleasure, satisfaction, or quick delight. He has no time for sorrow, pity, guilt, or even anger. He makes his money running an insurance racket, he gets into debt, he gets drunk, he laughs. He fleeces his own people and outwits whites. He is a new kind of man in the black townships; he is of them and not of them. The blacks who know him love him, and Toby Hood loves him as well.

Toby sees in Steven a brother. Drawn to him as if by a magnet at their first meeting, Toby goes into the townships with Steven, meets Steven's friends, gets drunk with him, and sleeps in the same hovels with him. What Steven can do with his life is so severely limited by white authority that he must live without hope or dignity; his life can only be a succession of gestures. That recognition by Toby illumines his own predicament. Steven was born into a South Africa that would not permit him "to come into his own; and what I believed should have been my own was destroyed before I was born heir to it."

Toby undergoes a transformation in the course of the novel. He has had the unusual experience of being able to enter alternately both black township life and the life of upper-crust Johannesburg. As much as he had thought that the privileged life was his natural base, he finds that life—for all its varied forms of recreation, luxury, freedom, and the outward good health of the rich—an empty, superficial existence. The rich, like Helen Shaw's middle-class mining-town family, are out of touch with "the real flow of life." Toby attempts a love affair with the most beautiful available woman among his circle of rich acquaintances. Primarily because the woman, Cecil Rowe, is incapable of expanding her concerns beyond herself, the affair comes to nothing more than a few perfunctory sexual encounters. On the other hand, Toby's relationship with Anna Louw, who is so different, is no more satisfying. She is a lawyer who is a former Communist and whose professional life is devoted to aiding blacks. Hers is anything but the self-centered life of Steven Sitole or Cecil Rowe; always sober, without embarrassment, she is unresponsive to the lure of euphoria. At the end of the novel, Cecil has accepted the marriage proposal of a wealthy businessman. Anna, too, is to begin a new phase. She has been arrested and is to be tried for treason. Anna is a prototype of the committed woman, the full development of whom in Gordimer's fiction does not occur until twenty years later, in *Burger's Daughter*.

Toby decides to stay in South Africa for a second year. His experiences with Cecil and the rich have made him reassess his conception of himself. As different as they are in character and personality, Toby has been greatly affected by both Steven and Anna, and the effect has been to make him care about the people of the townships. One of Gordimer's great accomplishments in this novel, as it is in her later work, is her rendering of township life. Toby also undergoes his transformation because Gordimer has made him think about what he has seen of township life on his sojourns with Steven. Life in the townships is more real than life among whites. There, the demands of life cannot be evaded through distractions; reality is right on the surface as well as below: "There is nothing for the frustrated man to do but grumble in the street; there was nothing for the deserted girl to do but sit on the step and wait for her bastard to be born; there was nothing to be done with the drunk but let him lie in the yard until he'd got over it." Among the whites, it is different. Frustrations can be forgotten through golf or horse racing, and trips to Europe take away the pain of broken love affairs.

In *A World of Strangers*, Gordimer has attempted to show a young man wholly bent on pursuing private concerns who, in the very process of pursuing those concerns, is changed into someone who cannot remain oblivious to South African injustice and unreason. To the extent that the reader can accept the change in Toby, the novel is successful.

Jessie Stilwell, the protagonist of *Occasion for Loving*, is a well-educated, freethinking socialist of the most enlightened, undogmatic kind. She might well have been arrested and tried for treason, but that would be in a different life from the one that fate has bestowed upon her. Her reality is her life as the mother of four children and a helpmate to Tom, a liberal history professor. She could be Helen Shaw fifteen years later, domesticated.

Jessie is content. Her husband, children, and home give continuity to her life; she is in touch with her past, and the future, in five-year blocks at least, seems predictable. She has room to develop; she can pick and choose goals for herself and pursue them to their conclusion. She is a total realist; she knows what is possible and what is not. She is at a point in her life when she will do nothing that is "wild and counter to herself." When someone else in the family causes discord, she will deal with it. Jessie has a son by a previous marriage who, in his adolescence, has become mildly disruptive. The task she wishes to devote herself to is repairing her relationship with him.

Jessie, however, cannot become absorbed in this duty because there are two new presences in her home. Against her better judgment, she has allowed her husband to invite to live with them a colleague and his young wife, Boaz and Ann Cohen. Boaz is a musicologist and is frequently away from Johannesburg to study the music and instruments of tribes. Ann is free to occupy her time as she wishes. What comes to dominate Ann's life is a love affair with a married black man, Gideon Shibalo. The difficulties and dangers of an interracial love affair are such that the lovers necessarily need the help of others. Thus, the affair between Ann and Gideon, whom Jessie and Tom like, intrudes upon the life of the Stilwells, and Jessie resents it.

Even when Jessie goes off with three of her children for a vacation by the sea, she must deal with Ann and Gideon, for they turn up at the remote cottage. Boaz has learned about his wife's affair, and Ann and Gideon decide to be with each other day and night; given South Africa's race laws, that means they must live an underground life. They appeal to Jessie to let them stay. Again, she resents the intrusion, but she yields to their need.

Boaz will not disavow Ann. His freedom to act in response to his wife's adultery is limited by his unwillingness to do anything that would harm a black man. Indeed, the affair itself may owe its birth to its interracial difficulties: "The basis of an exciting sympathy between two people is often some obstacle that lies long submerged in the life of one." After leading Gideon to believe that she was ready to go to Europe or some other African country with him, Ann leaves him, returns to Boaz, and the two, reunited, quickly leave South Africa. This action plunges Gideon into alcoholism.

Jessie's meditation on the affair makes clear the meaning Gordimer wants to convey. Race is a force even between lovers; personal lives are affected by society and politics. In South Africa, white privilege is a ubiquitous force; it provides Ann the freedom to go, denying Gideon the same freedom. White privilege is "a silver spoon clamped between your jaws and you might choke on it for all the chance there was of dislodging it." So long as there is no change in South Africa, "nothing could bring integrity to personal relationships." Had Jessie been more involved in the plot of the novel or even at the heart of its interest, the novel would have been more satisfying. Jessie, however, remains an objective observer and commentator. It is she with whom the reader identifies, yet not much happens to her; the events belong to Ann and Gideon.

Gordimer's fourth novel, *The Late Bourgeois World*, is her least successful. Brief and unconvincing, it is something of a parable, but it does not hit with the impact of the well-told parable. Too much has to be deduced. Without a knowledge of Gordimer's interests from her other works, the reader is hard pressed to see the meaning and coherence in this work. *The Late Bourgeois World* tells the story, with a great deal of indirection, of a Johannesburg woman whose marriage has broken up and who must take responsibility for a teenage son. Elizabeth Van Den Sandt, like Jessie Stilwell, does not have much feeling for the son of an ended marriage. Elizabeth's son, like Jessie's, is stowed in a boarding school. Elizabeth's having to bring her son the news that his father is dead by suicide is what gives the plot its impetus.

Max Van Den Sandt is the scion of one of Johannesburg's best families, but he rejects his heritage and white privilege. He marries Elizabeth, the medical-lab technician whom he has made pregnant. He joins the Communist Party, he participates in marches against the government, and, in the climax to his rebellion, he is arrested on a charge of sabotage. How much of what Max has done is gesture, though, and how much is the result of conviction? After serving fifteen months in prison, Max turns state's evidence and betrays his former colleagues. In return, he is released from prison. Then comes the suicide, which for Elizabeth provides the final answer; her former husband was a hollow man. It is possible to be a revolutionary without real conviction.

While allowing herself to indulge her contempt for Max, Elizabeth herself turns out to be unwilling to risk very much for the cause. She has the opportunity to respond positively to the plea of a young, handsome black activist for money to help pay for the defense of some of his friends who have been arrested, but Elizabeth equivocates and puts him off. The participation of whites from the middle class in the black revolution, Gordimer seems to suggest, is very unreliable. No matter how strong their sympathies appear to be, for whites the political struggle is not the imperative it is for blacks. The novel's title suggests another, complementary theme. Despite its staunch defense of its own privileges, the bourgeois world is falling apart. Families rupture too easily, children are shunted off for custodial care, commitments do not count. Elizabeth and Max are case histories.

Set in an invented nation in central Africa for which she has provided a detailed history and geography, *A Guest of Honour* is Gordimer's only novel that does not deal with South Africa. Still, the kinds of events depicted in this novel could very well occur in South Africa at some future time. With independence gained and a native government functioning in the place of the former British colonial administration, there are expectations of dramatic changes: civil rights will be respected, greater care will be taken in administering justice, natural resources will be used for the benefit of the people, the standard of living of the masses will improve. President Mweta believes that these legitimate expectations are being fulfilled in an orderly way and at a satisfactory rate. Edward Shinza, without whom independence might not yet have come, is dissatisfied. He believes that the country is no better off than it would have been under colonial rule. He is seeking a way to have an impact on the course of events. He may even be conspiring with the nation across the border. To Mweta, his former comrade Shinza is "a cobra in the house."

The novel's protagonist is Colonel James Bray, an Englishman who has been a district officer in the colonial administration. Bray is likable and loyal, a wholly sympathetic character. During the struggle for independence, he was of significant assistance to Mweta and Shinza. Now Mweta has invited Bray back to be an honored guest at Independence Day celebrations. Much to his chagrin, Bray discovers that while Mweta is covered with glory as the new nation's leader, Shinza, every bit Mweta's equal if not his better, has no role in governing the country and has not been invited to the celebrations; indeed, Shinza is living in obscurity in the bush. To Bray, this is an ominous sign.

President Mweta sends Colonel Bray on a mission to Gala, the district Bray formerly administered. He is to survey the district's educational needs. With Gala, Gordimer gives the first demonstration of her formidable knowledge of the life and people of rural Africa, of which she was to give further demonstrations in *July's People* and to a lesser extent in *The Conservationist*. With Gala, she has the opportunity to do a canvas of a whole province. She makes Bray pleased to be back in Gala and curious about what has happened in his absence. He knows the language, he likes the people, and he resonates sympathetically with the daily round of life. While in Gala, Bray will track down Shinza and get his viewpoint on the progress of the nation.

Shinza believes Mweta's principal concern is to consolidate his own power. He has no tolerance for dissent and is quite willing to use the police and torture to stifle it. Mweta allows foreign corporations to extract raw materials and export them rather than finding opportunities to make use of the country's natural wealth at home. Mweta will not allow any changes in the country that might give pause to these foreign interests. Shinza believes that Mweta's actions, taken together, make up a pattern of betrayal. While Shinza is trying to reassert himself by becoming a force within the trade-union movement, he also may be gathering a counterrevolutionary army, but his present intention is to attack Mweta through the unions and strikes.

Shinza comes onto center stage for the length of his impassioned speech on the ideals of the revolution at the congress of the People's Independent Party (P.I.P.), which has its factions but is still the only political party. Bray, who attends, cannot help but prefer the ideals of Shinza to the charisma and policies of accommodation of Mweta. In presenting the milieu of the party congress and in revealing the subtleties of motivations, alliances, and positions, Gordimer demonstrates a first-rate political intelligence. She has Shinza make use of his union support as the first phase in his scheme to dislodge Mweta; she has Mweta in turn capitalizing on the nationalistic fervor of the youth group within the P.I.P. to get them to attack strongholds of union supporters. Violence breaks out in Gala, and Bray is an accidental victim.

Bray, Shinza, and Mweta are new characters in Gordimer's gallery. She knows them and their social and political contexts exceedingly well. *A Guest of Honour* shows a prescience and knowledge that carry it to the top rank of political novels.

With *The Conservationist*, Gordimer turned back to South Africa. Again, she chose a male protagonist, Mehring, who bears no resemblance to anyone in her previous novels. Although this novel is of far larger scope, it is perhaps most similar to *The Late Bourgeois World*, for in both novels Gordimer attempts to delineate the life-style of a particular rung of white Johannesburg society. Mehring is a forty-nine-year-old industrialist and financier; he serves on several boards of directors. Given no other name, Mehring is admired and respected by everyone in his business and social circles, but it is clear that his life is essentially without meaning. He is deeply committed to nothing, not to ideology, country, or class, not to a sport, not to a single human being. He is quite the opposite of Colonel Bray.

Mehring has much more money than he needs. On impulse, he decides to buy a farm, very conveniently located only twenty-five miles from the city. Owning a farm will give him a feeling of being in contact with the land; it is something that is expected of a man of his station and wealth. The farm, however, complicates Mehring's life. He is unable to enjoy simple ownership; he must try to make the farm productive. He will practice conservation; he will see to it that buildings are repaired, fences mended, firebreaks cleared. The farm comes to occupy much more of his time and thought than he had intended. Nothing about the land, the weather, or the black people who live and work on the farm can be taken for granted. Something unexpected and unwanted is always occurring. A dead man is found on the property.

The dead man is black, and so the white police are not particularly concerned. Mehring expects them to remove the body and conduct an investigation, but they do neither. The unidentified body remains in a shallow, unmarked grave on Mehring's property. The presence of that body in the third pasture is troubling both to Mehring and to his black workers, although Mehring is never moved to do anything about it.

Much of the novel consists of Mehring's stream of consciousness. Along with the black man's body, another frequent presence in Mehring's consciousness is the woman with whom he has been having an affair. An attractive white liberal whose husband is away doing linguistic research in Australia, she has been drawn to Mehring because of his power; she is daring enough to taunt him and make light of that power. She is convinced that the reign of the white man in South Africa is nearing its end, yet she is a dilettante. When she gets into trouble with the authorities because of her associations with blacks, she wants to flee the country. She is humbled into asking Mehring to use his connections so that she can leave, and she sets herself up in London. Mehring, though, continues to think about her long after she has gone.

Mehring's relationship with this woman has been entirely superficial; when she is gone he thinks about her but does not really long for her. His relationships with his collegues and their families are also superficial. These connections are so meaningless to him that he reaches a point where he does not want either their invitations or their concern. On the few occasions each year when he has the company of his son, he has no real interest in overcoming the barriers between them. His son, like his lover, does not believe that apartheid and white privilege can survive for long. The son is contemptuous of what his father represents. He leaves South Africa to join his mother in New York rather than serve his term in the army. In his self-willed isolation, Mehring spends more of his time at the farm. Despite himself, as he discusses routine farm business with his black foreman, Jacobus, and as they deal with the emergencies caused by drought, fire, and flooding, Mehring finds himself feeling more and more respect for Jacobus.

Mehring spends New Year's Eve alone at the farm. As the new year approaches, he wanders across his moonlit field and settles with his bottle against the wall of a roofless, stone storehouse. He carries on a convivial conversation with old Jacobus. They talk about their children, the farm, cattle. They laugh a lot. They get along well. Jacobus, however, is not there. For Mehring, such easy, honest talk with a black can take place only in fantasy.

In the final chapter of the novel, the unidentified body in the third pasture is brought to the surface by flooding. The black workers, under Jacobus' direction, make a coffin, at last giving the man a proper burial. Mehring, in the meantime, is engaged in another of his faceless sexual encounters. He could be killed. If he is killed where will he be buried? Who are the real owners of the land to which he has title? Gordimer is suggesting that the unknown black man has more of a claim to the land than Mehring has. Mehring and his kind are going to meet ignoble ends. Their claim to the land of South Africa is so tenuous that their bodies will not even deserve burial.

There is little that is sympathetic about Mehring, which leaves Gordimer with the difficult task of keeping the reader interested in his activities. Once he begins to spend more time on the farm, his activities inevitably involve his black workers. Gordimer seizes the opportunity to render in some detail the life of their community. A few of them become minor characters of substance. Gordimer juxtaposes the flow of vital life in the black community with Mehring's isolation and decadence, and thereby saves the novel from being utterly unappealing.

Burger's Daughter is Gordimer's best novel. It is set between 1975 and 1977, as important changes are taking place in southern Africa but not yet in South Africa. The independence movements in Angola and Mozambique have succeeded. The Portuguese are in retreat, their colonial rule to be replaced by native governments. South Africa, however, remains firmly in the grip of the white minority. The white South African government will relinquish nothing.

Rosa Burger, the protagonist, is Gordimer's most fully achieved character. The hero of the novel, however, is Rosa's father, Lionel Burger. Just before he is to be sentenced to life imprisonment, Lionel Burger has the opportunity to address the court. He speaks for almost two hours. He explains why he and the Communist Party, of which he is a leader, have been driven to engage in the acts of sabotage for which he has been on trial. For thirty years, to no avail, he and South African Communists had struggled without resort to violence to gain civil rights and the franchise for the country's black majority. The great mass movement that is the African Nationalist Congress has been outlawed. In desperation, selected symbolic targets have been sabotaged. If such symbolic actions fail to move the white ruling class, there will be no further careful consideration of tactics. The only way to a new society will be through massive, cataclysmic violence.

Lionel Burger, in his childhood, was already sensitive to the unjust treatment of blacks. Later, as a medical student and doctor, he found it easier to accustom himself to the physical suffering of patients than to the subjection and humiliation forced upon blacks. He could not be silent and simply accept. He joined the Communist Party because he saw white and black members working side by side; there were people who practiced what they preached; there were white South Africans who did not deny the humanity of black South Africans. As a Communist, Lionel Burger came to accept the Marxist view of the dominance of economic relationships; thus, he perceived the oppression of blacks to be rooted in white South Africans' desire to maintain their economic advantages. Burger made a covenant with the victims.

Rosa Burger is very different from her father. She is also different from her mother, who was familiar with prison and who from young womanhood was known as a "real revolutionary." Both her father and her mother regard the family as totally united in their dedication to the struggle. Rosa, named in tribute to Rosa Luxemburg, the German revolutionary Marxist, knows that the family is not united. While her parents are free and active, she has no choice but to be extensions of them. Her mother has died, however, and, after three years of his life term, her father dies. When they are gone, Rosa does not take up their work. She is twenty-seven and has been in her parents' revolutionary circle since childhood. She has carried out numerous secret missions. Recently, she has pretended to be the fiancée of a prisoner in order to bring him messages. With the death of her father, she cannot deny that she is tired of such a life. She does not want to have anything more to do with the endangered and the maimed, with conspiracies and fugitives, with courts and prisons. Much more pointedly, *Burger's Daughter* deals with questions first considered in *A World of Strangers* and *Occasion for Loving*: To what extent must individual lives be governed by the dictates of time and place and circumstances not of the individual's choosing? Can a person ignore the facts and conditions that circumscribe his life and still live fully, or must a meaningful life necessarily be one that is integrated with the "real flow of life"? Despite his wealth and station, Mehring led a dismal life, because there was no such integration. Rosa Burger, though, is not devoid of redeeming qualities. She already has given much of herself.

Rosa chooses to escape. At first she escapes within the city of Johannesburg, in the tiny cottage of a rootless young white man, a graduate student of Italian literature who survives by working as a clerk to a bookmaker. Rosa and Conrad start out as lovers; after awhile they are more like siblings. Conrad, too, is struggling to be free, not of a revolutionary heritage but of his bourgeois heritage. Even after she is no longer with him, Rosa continues to talk to Conrad, silently.

Rosa decides to leave South Africa, but she cannot get a passport, because she is the daughter of Lionel Burger. Brandt Vermeulen is a cosmopolitan Boer, a new Afrikaner of a distinguished old Afrikaner family. He has studied politics at Leyden and Princeton and has spent time in Paris and New York. Vermeulen resembles Mehring, but he is rooted, more cultured, and more committed to the status quo. His solution for South Africa is to create separate nations for whites and blacks. Rosa goes to see him because he has friends in the Ministry of the Interior, which issues passports. Playing on the fact that he and Lionel Burger emerged from very similar backgrounds, Rosa succeeds in persuading him to use his influence to get her a passport.

The second part of this three-part novel takes place in Europe. Rosa goes to the French Riviera and looks up the woman who had been Lionel Burger's wife before he met Rosa's mother. The woman, who used to be known as Katya and who now is known as Madame Bagnelli, is delighted that Burger's daughter has come to stay with her. Rosa is welcomed by Madame Bagnelli's circle, consisting of unmarried couples, émigrés, homosexuals, persons formerly prominent in Paris, rootless persons for the most part. On the Riviera, life is easy, difference is distinction. Survival is not an issue. Politics seems a waste of time, revolution a form of craziness.

There is great empathy between Rosa and Madame Bagnelli. As Katya, the latter, years before, found it a relief to give up the role of revolutionary that was required of her as Burger's wife. She had not always been able to put private concerns aside; she had been considered a bourgeoise or even a traitor and was subjected to Party discipline. She has no regrets at leaving that part of her life. Rosa is encouraged about her own course. She allows herself the luxury of a love affair.

After a summer of love, Rosa and Bernard Chabalier make plans to live together in Paris, where he is a teacher at a lycée. Rosa visits London while Bernard makes arrangments in Paris. She attends a party for South African exiles and is filled with joy at meeting her black "brother," Baasie, who as a child had been taken into the Burger home but whom Rosa has not seen for twenty years. Rosa is shocked by Baasie's attitude; he is hostile and sullen.

That night in London, Rosa's sleep is broken by a phone call from Baasie. He is angry. He wants her to know that he did not have the life Burger's daughter had. He had been pushed back to the mud huts and tin shanties. His father was a revolutionary who also died in prison, driven to hang himself. No one knows of Isaac Vulindlela, but everyone talks about Lionel Burger. He hates hearing about Burger, the great man who suffered for the blacks. He knows plenty of blacks who have done as much as Burger, but they go unknown. He does not want to be her black brother, he tells Rosa.

Rosa goes back to South Africa. She does not want the soft life Bernard will provide for her in Paris. Defection is not possible. Suffering cannot be evaded. Back in Johannesburg, Rosa takes up the occupation for which she trained, physiotherapy. She also works for the revolution. As the novel ends late in 1977, Rosa is in prison. The authorities have solid evidence of unlawful acts.

In the brief *July's People* the end has come. Civil war rages; blacks are fighting whites. The whites have discipline, organization, knowledge, equipment. The blacks have will and numbers. They have the support of the rest of the continent, and the Russians and their Cuban allies are close at hand. Thousands of lives will be lost, but there can be no doubt about the eventual outcome. The artificial society based on apartheid is finished.

Bamford Smales is an architect, an upper-middle-class professional. His wife, Maureen, is, like Jessie Stilwell, an excellent helpmate, a strong, compassionate, intelligent woman. Before the uprisings, Bam and Maureen knew that unless whites, of their own volition, made significant reforms a conflagration was inevitable. They tried to show the way among their friends and neighbors, treating their male servant, July, with the utmost consideration. They did not, however, go so far as to break the ties with their community. They lived their lives within the pattern they found for their race and their class. Their liberal attitudes had no impact.

When the uprisings begin, the Smaleses flee their Johannesburg suburb. With their three young children, they drive six hundred kilometers in their recreational pickup truck to July's home village. Even though black-white relations are being turned upside down, July is still willing to oblige them; for fifteen years obliging the Smales family has been his life's purpose. Even after their dependence on him is clear, July continues to address Bam Smales as "master." He even moves his mother from her own hut so the Smales family can settle in it.

When they arrive in the village, the Smaleses are July's people. Over the course of a few weeks, relations change. July has been reunited with his wife and children, whom for fifteen years he has seen only on his vacations every other year. July becomes a presence among the people of his village. *They* become July's people, and his loyalty to the white family is eroded. That erosion occurs slowly through a number of ambiguous situations, for July has no political sensibility. As the relationship between the black servant and the white family loses its structure, July becomes less and less the servant and more and more the master of the family's fate.

When the Smales vehicle, the yellow "bakkie," first pulls into the village, there is no doubt concerning its ownership, but as July runs errands to the locked bakkie he comes to be the possessor of the keys to the vehicle. He does not know how to drive, but his young protégé Daniel does. July turns the keys over to Daniel, and they drive off to a store. After this, it is difficult for Bam Smales to claim sole ownership; and it is even more difficult once Daniel has taught July how to drive. Bam Smales has a shotgun. Although he tries to keep its hiding place a secret, the whole village seems to know where the gun is kept. When Ban discovers that the gun is gone, he is beside himself. The loss of the gun emasculates him. On his way to join the freedom fighters, Daniel has helped himself to the gun.

The family's future is completely uncertain. As the villagers begin to break the habit of deference to white skins, the Smaleses become nervous about their safety. They would leave, but they have nowhere to go. The predicament proves too much for Maureen. Sensing an opportunity to save herself, she runs off, frantically, leaving her husband and children. The Smaleses are victims of apartheid. When the tables are turned, as they surely must be, only a miracle will save whites from suffering what they made others suffer.

A Sport of Nature combines elements from several of Gordimer's earlier works. Like Helen in *The Lying Days*, Hillela Capran is a bolter, though not out of obvious rebelliousness. Rather, she is moved by the spirit of the moment in a more unthinking way. The family with whom she lives during her adolescence—her aunt Pauline, uncle Joe, and cousins Sasha and Carole—are similar to the Hoods of *A World of Strangers*, for they also are white liberals, trying ever to be ruled by acts of conscience rather than convenience, as Hillela's Aunt Olga and Uncle Arthur are.

Gordimer's early habit of distancing the reader from her characters is echoed in her treatment of Hillela. The first half of the book has Hillela spoken of mostly in the third person; she does not really come alive until after she meets Whaila Kgomani, a black revolutionary who becomes her first husband and the father of her child. His assassination changes the course of Hillela's life as she inherits his revolution.

Hillela's character has been regarded by many of Gordimer's readers as amoral and shocking, and even Gordimer has admitted that this creation fascinates her probably as much as anyone else. Yet, she does not back down from her portrayal of a revolutionary who accomplishes most of her goals through the use of her feminine wiles. *A Sport of Nature* may not be Gordimer's best book, but it is as thought-provoking as any of her earlier works. Its portrayal of the future, which includes a black African state installed in place of South Africa, has caused some critics to label the work weak and unbelievable.

Like all of Gordimer's novels, however, with the exception of *The Lying Days*, *A Sport of Nature* is didactic. From *A World of Strangers* on, Gordimer has probed moral and political questions with honesty and unfailing courage, never being dogmatic or predetermining outcomes, allowing vividly imagined characters and communities lives of their own. Her work does more than shed light on the predicament of South Africa; it deals in depth with the problems of individual identity, commitment and obligation, and justice. Gordimer is a novelist who clearly has a place in the great tradition of George Eliot, Dostoevski, Joseph Conrad, and Thomas Mann.

Paul Marx

Other major works

SHORT FICTION: *Face to Face: Short Stories*, 1949; *The Soft Voice of the Serpent and Other Stories*, 1952; *Six Feet of the Country*, 1956; *Friday's Footprint and Other Stories*, 1960; *Not for Publication and Other Stories*, 1965; *Livingstone's Companions: Stories*, 1971; *Selected Stories*, 1975; *A Soldier's Embrace*, 1980; *Something Out There*, 1984.

NONFICTION: *South African Writing Today*, 1967 (edited with Lionel Abrahams); *On the Mines*, 1973 (with David Goldblatt); *The Black Interpreters*, 1973; *Lifetimes Under Apartheid*, 1986 (with David Goldblatt); *The Essential Gesture: Writing, Politics, and Places*, 1988.

Bibliography

Clingman, Stephen. *The Novels of Nadine Gordimer: History from the Inside*. London: Allen & Unwin, 1986. Clingman interprets Gordimer's work within the context of history in general and the history of South Africa and

African literature in particular. Included are annotations to references within the chapters as well as a detailed bibliography that is divided into works by Gordimer, works about Gordimer, and South African history. An index is also included.

Cooke, John. *The Novels of Nadine Gordimer: Private Lives/Public Landscapes*. Baton Rouge: Louisiana State University Press, 1985. Cooke concentrates on developing the common themes that run throughout Gordimer's fiction. His bibliography includes "Primary Sources" (lists of Gordimer's canon by genre) and "Secondary Sources" (books and articles about Gordimer) and is followed by an index.

Haugh, Robert F. *Nadine Gordimer*. New York: Twayne, 1974. Part of Twayne's World Authors series, this text is divided into two parts. The first discusses Gordimer's short fiction and the second her novels. A useful chronology at the beginning of the book notes milestones in Gordimer's personal and professional life. Includes an index.

Heywood, Christopher. *Nadine Gordimer*. Windsor, England: Profile Books, 1983. This book is part of the Writers and Their Work series and provides literary criticism rather than biographical background. Heywood highlights Gordimer's place among African authors. A detailed bibliographical section provides a list of Gordimer's works as well as lists of works (such as bibliographies and critical essays) about Gordimer and about Africa and African literature.

Wade, Michael. *Nadine Gordimer*. London: Evans Bros., 1978. This text is from the Modern African Writers series, and Wade therefore presents his interpretation and literary criticism in the light of African literature. Includes a detailed bibliography and an index.

CAROLINE GORDON

Born: Todd County, Kentucky; October 6, 1895
Died: San Cristóbal de las Casas, Mexico; April 11, 1981

Principal long fiction

Penhally, 1931; *Aleck Maury, Sportsman*, 1934; *None Shall Look Back*, 1937; *The Garden of Adonis*, 1937; *Green Centuries*, 1941; *The Women on the Porch*, 1944; *The Strange Children*, 1951; *The Malefactors*, 1956; *The Glory of Hera*, 1972.

Other literary forms

Although Caroline Gordon was primarily a novelist, she wrote a number of superb short stories, several of which have been reprinted in anthologies for use in the classroom; "Old Red" is perhaps the best known, though "The Captive" and "The Last Day in the Field" have also received wide circulation. These and other of Gordon's stories were published originally in quality journals such as *Scribner's Review*, *Harper's*, *Sewanee Review*, and *Southern Review*, and have been reprinted in three collections, *The Forest of the South*, (1945); *Old Red and Other Stories* (1963); and *The Collected Stories of Caroline Gordon* (1981), with an introduction by Robert Penn Warren. Gordon lectured and published commentaries on the fiction of others, but she was not a literary critic in the usual sense; her interest was in setting forth and illustrating her theories about a method of writing fiction. These are contained in two works: *The House of Fiction: An Anthology of the Short Story* (1950, edited with Allen Tate), and *How to Read a Novel* (1957).

Achievements

Gordon's reputation was firmly established by the publication of her first novel, *Penhally*, particularly after it was reviewed by the English writer Ford Madox Ford in *Bookman*. Ford hailed Gordon as one of the important new novelists writing in America. The succession of novels and stories that followed *Penhally*, her marriage to the poet Allen Tate and her association with the Vanderbilt Agrarians, her lectures, and the short-story textbook *The House of Fiction* are all a measure of her significant contribution to the Southern Renaissance.

Gordon has been particularly admired for her craftsmanship, for the skill with which—in the tradition of Henry James, Joseph Conrad, and Ernest Hemingway—she is able to create impressions of life that are at once realistic and symbolic. Following her chief master, James, Gordon was a scholar of the novel, and her fiction emphasizes technique above plot and character, so much so, in fact, that with few exceptions, her books have never had popular appeal. *Aleck Maury, Sportsman* attracted an audience of hunters and fishermen, partly because of its subject, but also because the hero of the book is an appealing character. *None Shall Look Back* also attracted readers, particularly in the South, because of its evocation of the tragic heroism of the Civil War. *Green Centuries* dealt with material very popular in the 1930's, hardship on the frontier and conflicts between Indians and white settlers, though it lacks both the sentimentality and moralizing that often made such fiction popular. The remainder of Gordon's novels are demanding books that require of the reader alertness to symbolic meanings and close attention to the implications of technique. As a consequence of its special kind of excellence, Gordon's fiction appeals primarily to other writers and scholars of narrative craft. Many novelists and short-story writers, including Flannery O'Connor and Walker Percy, have acknowledged a debt to Caroline Gordon.

Biography

Caroline Gordon was born on a farm in Todd County, Kentucky, on October 6, 1895. Her mother, Nancy Meriwether, was a Kentuckian; her father, James Morris Gordon, was born in Louisa County, Virginia. In the 1880's, he moved west to Kentucky and became tutor to the Meriwether family. Later, he established a classical school for boys in Clarksville, Tennessee, to which his daughter was sent. This was the beginning of her lifelong interest in classical literature, an interest that was deepened during her college years when she studied Greek literature at Bethany College (earning a B.A. in 1916). After teaching high school for three years, Gordon took a job as reporter in Chattanooga from 1920 to 1924, an experience she said was of no help to her in learning to write fiction.

In 1924, Gordon married Allen Tate, poet, essayist, and author of an important novel, *The Fathers* (1938). She had met Tate through Robert Penn Warren, who lived on a neighboring farm in Kentucky, and her marriage signaled the beginning of an important change not only in her personal life but also in her career as a novelist, for despite the fact that Tate was primarily a poet, he was also a perceptive critic of the novel and proved to be one of Gordon's most important early teachers. The Tates moved to New York the year of their marriage, and then, in 1928, went to France on money from Tate's Guggenheim Fellowship. There, a friendship with Ford Madox Ford that had begun in New York was reestablished, and Gordon offered her services to Ford as typist-secretary. The relationship with Ford was most fortunate for Gordon, because it was with Ford's help that she was able to complete her first novel, which later, through his review in *Bookman*, was called to the attention of important readers.

After *Penhally*'s critical success in 1931, Gordon was awarded a Guggenheim Fellowship and the Tates spent the next year in France. On their return, they settled near Clarksville, Tennessee, and it was there—in a house the Tates called Benfolly—that Gordon wrote her next four novels and a number of short stories. In 1939, the Tates moved to Princeton, New Jersey, and although there were to be protracted stays in other places—Sewanee, Tennessee, and Minneapolis—Princeton was to be Gordon's permanent home for many years. The Tates were divorced in 1959, and thereafter Gordon served as visiting writer at universities in different parts of the United States. In the early 1970's, she founded her own school of writing at the University of Dallas and taught there until shortly before her death. She died in Mexico on April 11, 1981, where she had gone to be near her daughter, Nancy.

One other event in Gordon's life deserves special mention: her conversion in 1947 to Roman Catholicism. That conversion was a significant factor in her artistic as well as her personal life, for not only did it influence her subsequent fiction, but also it could be seen in retrospect as the logical culmination of a lifelong quest for models of moral perfection.

Analysis

Caroline Gordon's theories of fiction and her debts to the writers who influenced her were spelled out in lectures that she gave at the University of Kansas and later published as *How to Read a Novel*, and in commentaries and appendices to *The House of Fiction*, an anthology of short stories she edited with Tate. In her theory and in her practice, she combined ideas from Aristotle and Dante, Gustave Flaubert, Henry James, Ford Madox Ford, and James Joyce. From the modern masters came the technique of closely rendered scenes, the disappearance of the author from her fiction by means of an impersonal style, and the use of what Gordon called natural symbolism. From Aristotle came certain "constants," particularly his definition of tragedy as an "action of a certain magnitude" and the division of the novel's action into two parts, complication and resolution, with the resolution embedded in the complication. By *action*, Gordon understood Aristotle to mean overt action; the hero of a novel, properly understood, was a person who acted, and Gordon went on to add that traditionally the hero always faced the same task: the overcoming of evil so that good might flourish. This is a limited view of the novelistic hero, but for understanding Gordon's fiction it is a useful definition; the heroes of all her novels, from *Penhally* to *The Glory of Hera*, can be understood in this light. The action of her novels invariably involves the facing of evil and an attempt by the hero to overcome it.

In her first novel, *Penhally*, evil is defined from an agrarian perspective, and here one sees Gordon's kinship with the Vanderbilt group, who published Peter Smith's *I'll Take My Stand* in 1930. "Penhally" is the name of a plantation house in Tennessee, built in 1826 and passed down through the Llewellyn family into modern times. The current master, however—Nicholas Llewellyn—regards the Penhally lands not as a trust to be handed down but as a commodity to be exploited for his own gain. Nicholas' younger brother, Chance, loves the land but is excluded from ownership and is deeply grieved when Nicholas sells it to a Northern woman who turns it into a hunt club for rich strangers. At the opening ceremony of the new club, Chance, taunted by Nicholas for his old-fashioned attitudes, shoots his brother to death. Although this final action is presented in the detached manner of an impartial observer, the irony bitterly underscores the point, as one brother must kill another in a vain attempt to destroy what is evil: the misuse and perversion of the land.

Gordon's second novel, influenced to some extent by Siegfried Sassoon's *The Memoirs of a Fox-Hunting Man* (1928), also drew on her memories of her father, the prototype of the novel's hero, Aleck Maury, Gordon's most engaging character. Maury is a hunter and fisherman of remarkable skill and devotion to his sport. Unlike Gordon's other novels, which are written in the third person and in a somewhat detached manner, *Aleck Maury, Sportsman* is told in the first person by Maury himself as he recounts his attempts to escape from the demands of his wife, his teaching duties, and, later, his daughter, so that he can devote himself to the delights of his beloved pastimes. Andrew Lytle has referred to Maury as a man "dislocated" by the economic and cultural ruin of the South after the Civil War, which takes a more solemn view than the novel itself warrants, for Maury is a comic version of the hero: a man who overcomes evil (that is, duty) in order that good (fishing and hunting) might flourish. In this, he is eminently and delightfully successful.

It is not surprising that *Aleck Maury, Sportsman* has been Gordon's most popular novel, for most of her novels present a tragic view of the human condition. Like F. Scott Fitzgerald, Gordon was at heart a traditional moralist, too intelligent to moralize and therefore in search of ways to establish moral values indirectly. Writing in the 1930's and 1940's, periods of disillusionment and rejection of traditional moral and religious beliefs—and herself, at the time, a nonbeliever—she had found in contrasting attitudes toward the land a way of dramatizing the conflict between good and evil. In her next novel, *None Shall Look Back*, Gordon located her moral ground on the Civil War battlefields and used actual historical personages, particularly Nathan Bedford Forrest, as exemplars of moral conduct and heroic action in the conflict between good and evil. Forrest, it might be said, represented a model or paradigm of heroic conduct, and by including him (an actual man who did act decisively and selflessly for a cause in which he believed) as a character in *None Shall Look Back*, Gordon could introduce into the novel a standard by which readers could judge the protagonist, Rives Allard, who fights and dies under Forrest's command, and his wife Lucy, who acts as the point-of-view character through whom one experiences the tragic death not only of Rives but also of the whole Southern cause. The distinguished historian of the novel, Walter Allen, complained in *The Modern Novel in Britain and the United States* (1964), that in *None Shall Look Back* Gordon failed to deal with the injustices of slavery. Such criticism misses the point. The novel is meant to be a tragic action, not a tract against slavery or racial prejudice. The Civil War happened, and people gave their lives for a cause in which they believed, a cause that they knew to be doomed. It is this quality of doom and sacrifice that *None Shall Look Back* movingly evokes.

Since Gordon was neither a rebel against nor a defender of the status quo, but, like William Faulkner, a traditionalist in the modern world, she needed a way of giving authority to traditional values. Agrarianism, as a way of life as well as a philosophy, commanded respect in Nashville and in other pockets of the country, but not in New York or London. What was needed was the kind of mythological underpinning that T. S. Eliot had given his traditional moral vision in *The Waste Land* (1922). In Gordon's next novel, *The Garden of Adonis*, she was able to provide—and from one of Eliot's sources—that mythological underpinning. The title as well as the general structure of the book came from Sir James G. Frazer's *The Golden Bough* (1922); to be certain that the reader made the connection, Gordon used in an epigraph Frazer's account of how women of ancient Adonis cults would grow and tend newly sprouted plants in baskets (that is, Gardens of Adonis) that, together with images of the dead god, would then be flung into the sea or into springs. Gordon omitted Frazer's description of the more violent practice of sacrificing a living victim in a newly planted field in the belief that his death would propitiate the corn spirit and his blood fatten the ears of corn. This omission was probably deliberate, for such descriptions standing at the head of the novel would have revealed too much too soon about the resolution of the action.

In Gordon's handling of the Adonis ritual, the sacrificial victim is a Tennessee planter named Ben Allard. With a young tenant, Allard has planted "on shares" a field of clover that becomes especially valuable when a severe drought ruins Allard's tobacco crop, for the clover survives the drought. The tenant, Ote Mortimer, becomes obsessed with winning the favors of a young woman, and in order to get money to marry her, attempts to harvest the immature clover. Allard plants himself in the way of Ote's team and Ote strikes him down and kills him. Although Ote is the instrument of Allard's death, it is clear that he is only acting symbolically for the commercial society which hems in and destroys the way of life Allard represents. This is made clear by the contrast between Allard's sense of honor and strict moral code and the promiscuity of his children and their attraction to purely material values. This moral laxness and lust for money, seen not only in Allard's family but also in the woman that Ote wants to marry, is responsible for raising Ote's hand against Allard. Allard's death, viewed in the limited perspective of naturalism, would seem a pointless and ironic sacrifice, but by giving her hero a mythological precursor, Gordon invites the reader to see him not as a hapless victim but rather as the embodiment of timeless values; for whether the world realizes it, Allard is a hero who stands up for what he believes, even gives his life in a heroic if unprofitable action.

Four years elapsed between the publication of *The Garden of Adonis* and *Green Centuries*, Gordon's next novel, and the reason for the delay is quite clear. *The Garden of Adonis* had been written quickly and published the same year as *None Shall Look Back*; it was a novel that came out of the author's direct experience of life in Kentucky and Tennessee in the 1930's. *Green Centuries* is a carefully researched historical novel about Southern colonials pushing their way west into the vast new territory of Kentucky and is filled with the kind of detail expected of the best historical fiction: authentic accounts of daily life, travel, husbandry, courting, hunting, and quaint speech-ways. One's first impression might be that in electing to write what appears to be another account of hardihood on the frontier, Gordon had abandoned her usual subject in favor of a themeless historical romance. An exciting book about war and Indian raids and authentic historical characters such as Daniel Boone, the great hunter, and famous Cherokee Indian chiefs, Atta Kulla Kulla and Dragging Canoe, the work fully deserved the Pulitzer Prize it was considered for but did not get. *Green Centuries* also reflects Gordon's abiding concern for the glory and tragic splendor of heroic action. There are two main heroes in this novel: a white hunter, Rion Outlaw, a fictional creation of the author, who embodies the qualities to be found in the historical Daniel Boone, and a character based on the Cherokee chief Dragging Canoe. Rion Outlaw, like his namesake Orion, the mythical hunter, leaves the Virginia colony after he participates in a raid on a government powder train and pushes into the west, where eventually he joins forces with settlers who have been attacked by the Cherokee Indians led by Dragging Canoe. When the stockade is attacked by Indians and Rion's beloved wife is killed, he is suddenly made aware both of his loss and of his irrepressible drive to continue westward, losing himself in the turning like the mythical Orion in the heavens.

Dragging Canoe, who led the attack against the settlers, is also heroic, for he has determined against the advice of older and wiser chiefs to fight the settlers rather than give up more Indian lands. Though his cause is doomed— Atta Kulla Kulla has been to London and knows the Indians are no match for the white man's "medicine"—Dragging Canoe dies fighting to preserve his nation and his way of life. Rion Outlaw and Dragging Canoe, though on opposite sides in the struggle over the Kentucky lands, are both presented sympathetically because Gordon is not interested in taking sides in the historical conflict; her interest, as usual, is in the exemplification of heroic virtue wherever it may be found.

There is a sense in which Gordon's return to an earlier and simpler time in American history can be seen as a retreat, for in order to make her case for heroism, she had to abandon the world of the present about which other writers, such as Eliot, Fitzgerald, and Hemingway, seemed to find more conducive to failure and despair than to heroic action. Gordon's next novel,

The Women on the Porch, is set in the contemporary world, where disillusionment is rife and atrophy of the will is a mark of virtue. Her hero is Jim Chapman, a deracinated intellectual and professor of history at a New York university, whose affair with his assistant, Edith Ross, drives his wife Catherine away from the city and back to her ancestral home in Tennessee. For a time, Chapman wallows in uncertainty and moral confusion, but then he follows Catherine west, and after a strange vision in the woods of Swan Quarter, in which Catherine's pioneer forebear appears, Chapman is reunited with his wife. This action, though small when measured against the heroic deeds of the past, is for him deeply meaningful, since it signifies a return to action and a breaking out of the locked-in sensibility that has paralyzed his will.

Between the writing of *The Women on the Porch* and her next novel, *The Strange Children*, Gordon's personal life underwent a profound change; she became a convert to Catholicism. Looking backward from the perspective of this new novel, it is possible to see, if not the inevitability of that conversion, at least the logic of it. For Gordon, the commitment to art and the religious impulse were closely connected; both are, in their different ways, quests for perfection. Prior to her conversion, perfection meant not only perfection of form and style but of moral action as well, but action conceived in secular terms. In *The Strange Children* and in her next two novels, *The Malefactors* and *The Glory of Hera*, heroic action becomes not merely brave and selfless action that ends in an otherwise pointless death, but also moral action so that evil might be overcome and good might flourish.

The protagonist of *The Strange Children* is a girl, Lucy Lewis, whose parents, Stephen and Sarah Lewis, are cultivated intellectuals living at Benfolly, a farm in Tennessee. Stephen Lewis is writing a book about the Civil War, and on the weekend during which the action of the novel takes place, the Lewises are visited by a curious group of people: Kevin Reardon, a very rich, recent convert to Catholicism who has undergone a dramatic religious experience; his pale, beautiful, but mad wife; and a friend, "Uncle" Tubby, who has been having an affair with Reardon's wife. The intrigue between the lovers, a moral crisis in Lucy's life (over a valuable crucifix she took from Reardon's room), and a spiritual crises through which Lucy's parents are passing, are brought together at the end of the novel when the lovers elope, Lucy returns the crucifix, and Stephen Lewis is forced to recognize the desert in which those without religious faith are forced to wander. Reardon knew of Tubby's affair with his wife and had tried to warn him of her madness, but Tubby had only laughed. The good man had acted with the aid of a divine presence, while evil flourished in the elopement of the mad lovers; yet the seeds of understanding are planted in the mind of Stephen Lewis, who at the end of the novel is given to see the barrenness of his past and the terrors of a future devoid of faith.

Thomas Claiborne, the protagonist of *The Malefactors*, Gordon's second "Catholic" novel, is in much the same state as Lewis at the end of *The Strange Children*, except that Claiborne is unaware of his spiritual emptiness. Like Isabelle Reardon, Claiborne is a poet who is also somewhat mad. He has periods during which he cannot write and hears a voice inside his head that makes critical comments about his conduct and state of mind. Claiborne lives on his wife's farm in Buck's County, Pennsylvania, and Vera Claiborne, a very rich woman, raises prize cattle. Like Tom Chapman of *The Women on the Porch*, Claiborne is a morally paralyzed intellectual, and like "Uncle" Tubby of *The Strange Children*, he becomes enamored of a woman poet, pursues her, and becomes involved in a sordid love affair that eventually drives him to seek guidance from a nun and, later, from a Catholic lay sister who operates a farm for Bowery derelicts. After a spiritual crisis in which he has frightening dreams, a drunken realization that only his wife truly loves him and that his mistress is interested only in furthering her own career, Claiborne, who had quarreled with his wife, is reunited with her at the upstate farm where she has gone to assist in the work with derelicts. The means by which Claiborne is brought to the threshold of what appears to be a religious conversion is a complicated series of actions involving insights, visions, accounts of miraculous conversions, and revelations about Vera's own early baptism into the Catholic faith. One can see how fully Gordon's own religious conversion made it possible to handle the tangled web of marital infidelity with much more complexity than she had in *The Women on the Porch*. The Church had given her the means to represent the triumph of goodness in a fallen world.

Some time after the publication of *The Malefactors*, Gordon began an ambitious project which she tentatively entitled *A Narrow Heart: The Portrait of a Woman*, a title which seemed to echo those of two works of which she was very fond: *A Simple Heart* (1877) by Flaubert and *The Portrait of a Lady* (1881) by James. As originally planned, the book was to have had a higher and a lower action, the higher one consisting of tales from Greek mythology, the lower one, the author's fictionalized autobiography. The plan eventually was abandoned, however, and only the higher action of *A Narrow Heart* was published, under the title *The Glory of Hera*.

In the manner of a realistic novel, *The Glory of Hera* retells the labors of Heracles, which may seem curious in a novelist for whom Christ became the greatest hero and Christian virtue a guide to virtuous living. For Gordon, however, Heracles was a great precursor of Christ, and in retelling the story of his labors—one might say, his miracles—she did homage to her early and abiding love of Greek mythology by suggesting the Christlike quality of its greatest hero.

When she died in 1981, Gordon was at work on another novel, the fictionalized autobiography that was to have made up the "lower action" of *A*

Narrow Heart. It is not known how close that work was to completion or how it might contribute to her future reputation. Currently, there is no doubt about her historical importance; her name always appears in lists of important writers of the Southern Renaissance. As to the literary quality of her fiction, that is a matter to be decided as such matters always are, by the winnowing process of time. Her earliest works—*Penhally*; *Aleck Maury, Sportsman*; *None Shall Look Back*; and *Green Centuries*—seem the best candidates for survival; her later novels, though technically more complex, demand imaginative participation in religious beliefs to which few readers are able or willing to respond. Gordon wrote against the grain of her time; while the major writers of the period, poets as well as novelists, depicted or implied the collapse of Western civilization and the invalidity of traditional values, she never lost faith in the possibility of redemption by heroic action. To some critics, this was a sign of her attachment to a vanished past and a refusal to confront contemporary realities. Gordon denied that she believed that the Southern past, or any past, was superior to the present; what she did believe, though, was that the present was nourished by the best of the past, not because of its pastness, but because it made life richer and more meaningful. Gordon was aware of the misconceptions about her fiction and of the growing indifference of readers to her later work, but she never veered from her belief in the importance of what she was doing. It was her conviction that, if she wrote well, her work would endure and that would continue to find its own appreciative audience.

W. J. Stuckey

Other major works

SHORT FICTION: *The Forest of the South*, 1945; *Old Red and Other Stories*, 1963; *The Collected Stories of Caroline Gordon*, 1981.

NONFICTION: *The House of Fiction: An Anthology of the Short Story*, 1950 (edited with Allen Tate); *How to Read a Novel*, 1957; *A Good Soldier: A Key to the Novels of Ford Madox Ford*, 1963.

Bibliography
Fraistat, Rose A. *Caroline Gordon as Novelist and Woman of Letters*. Baton Rouge: Louisiana State University Press, 1984. Fraistat examines Gordon's life in terms of her work, and places her in a historical context. A study by a modern Southern woman of letters looking at one from a previous generation.

Landess, Thomas H., ed. *The Short Fiction of Caroline Gordon: A Symposium*. Dallas, Tex.: University of Dallas Press, 1972. Offers a variety of critical views on Gordon's short stories, for which she was famous. Most useful for advanced students of Gordon.

McDowell, Frederick P. W. *Caroline Gordon.* Minneapolis: University of Minnesota Press, 1966. A short pamphlet that briefly describes Gordon's life and work. Useful for a quick overview that puts her work into its context. Contains a selected bibliography for further study.

Makowsky, Veronica A. *Caroline Gordon: A Biography.* New York: Oxford University Press, 1989. An excellent biography of Gordon, about whom little has been written. Good for all students.

Stuckey, William Joseph. *Caroline Gordon.* New York: Twayne, 1972. A very useful book for all students of Gordon. Stuckey offers a moderately detailed biography, along with analysis of Gordon's major works. Includes a primary and secondary bibliography.

SHIRLEY ANN GRAU

Born: New Orleans, Louisiana; July 9, 1929

Principal long fiction

The Hard Blue Sky, 1958; *The House on Coliseum Street*, 1961; *The Keepers of the House*, 1964; *The Condor Passes*, 1971; *Evidence of Love*, 1977.

Other literary forms

Although Shirley Ann Grau has written introductions and an occasional essay for magazines, two forms, the novel and the short story, have dominated her literary career. The enthusiastic reception that greeted her first collection of short stories, *The Black Prince and Other Stories* (1955), has assured her reputation in the genre. Scarcely any anthology of American short fiction excludes her work. In spite of her initial success critically, her second collection of stories, *The Wind Shifting West* (1973), was not so warmly received as the first.

Achievements

The most obvious testimony to Grau's success is the Pulitzer Prize for Fiction that she received in 1965 for *The Keepers of the House*. Significantly enough, the same novel appeared in condensed form in *Ladies' Home Journal*. Thus, one sees evidence of one of the distinguishing characteristics of much of Grau's fiction: the ability to appeal simultaneously to two often opposed audiences, the person looking for the "good read" and the literary sophisticate. Not many contemporary writers have published stories in both *McCall's* and *The New Yorker*. In her last novel, *Evidence of Love*, Grau seems to have made an attempt to shed any vestige of her image as a "housewife writer" or yet another Southern regionalist. While *Evidence of Love* is rather straightforward, even in its effective use of three overlapping narratives, it nevertheless makes few concessions to a reader looking for the conventional melodramatic staples of sex or violence. *Evidence of Love* also silences the critics who, after the disappointment of *The Condor Passes*, sought to dismiss Grau as a one-novel writer. The one recurring criticism of Grau's later work—that her characters seem bloodless—seems less relevant after the success of other novelists with similar ironic visions—Joan Didion, for example.

As is true of all but a handful of contemporary writers, Grau's achievement cannot yet be fully measured. Her last novel suggests that she has shifted her emphasis away from the engaging plot to the creation of a cool, ironic vision of psychological intensity. In this process, she has kept those elements of style—the brilliant sensory images, the directness of language, the complex heroine—that have given vitality to all of her work.

Biography

At the age of forty-five, Katherine Grau presented her dentist husband, Adolphe, with a baby girl. Although Shirley Ann Grau's parents were well into middle age, she has described her childhood as free of unhappiness or social alienation. Her Protestant family, with roots both in New England and the South, moved back and forth from Montgomery, Alabama, to New Orleans. Shirley Ann attended a girls' finishing school in the Alabama capital until her senior year, when she transferred to an accredited high school in New Orleans, the Ursuline Academy—the institution that one of her heroines remembers as a place to knit, chant, and crochet.

Grau's first experiences with writing came while attending Sophie Newcomb College in New Orleans. Her stories appeared in the campus literary magazine, *Carnival*. After she was graduated Phi Beta Kappa, Grau lived in New Orleans' French Quarter and abandoned her graduate studies for a writing career. Success came quickly. In 1955, her volume of short stories, *The Black Prince and Other Stories*, received exceptionally fine reviews and her work was compared favorably with that of other Southern writers such as Eudora Welty, Flannery O'Connor, and Carson McCullers.

In the same year, Grau married James K. Feibleman, a remarkable professor of philosophy at Tulane University. Many years her senior, Feibleman had risen to the chairmanship of his department even though he himself had attended college for only two months. He had published numerous books and was acquainted with such luminaries as William Faulkner. Grau successfully combined her roles as wife, mother of two sons and two daughters, and writer. She has described her life as a "conventional upper middle class" one, divided between summers on Martha's Vineyard and school years in New Orleans.

As she reared her children, Grau continued to write. Novels appeared in 1958 (*The Hard Blue Sky*) and 1961 (*The House on Coliseum Street*). While both works received considerable notice, it seemed as if Grau might be categorized as a regionalist who had mastered "local color." Her selection as the Pulitzer Prize winner for fiction in 1965, however, did much to squelch such categorization. *The Keepers of the House*, a novel that attracted attention for its candid treatment of racial themes, brought her national attention; in fact, President Lyndon Johnson appointed her to the Commission on Presidential Scholars in the same year. In spite of this recognition, the rhythm of Grau's life remained largely unchanged, and she did not rush to bring out her next novel. Instead, she taught creative writing at the University of New Orleans, wrote an occasional story, and gave birth to her fourth child. When her next novel, *The Condor Passes*, appeared in 1971, its sales surpassed the combined total of all her previous works. Its critical reception, however, was at best mixed. Since that time, Grau has published only a few more works, including a collection of short stories entitled *The Wind Shifting West*, a generally acclaimed novel, *Evidence of Love*, and another short-story collection, *Nine Women* (1985).

Analysis

Shirley Ann Grau shares a fate common to many contemporary writers not yet admitted to the pantheon. They are the object of a handful of critical studies, often short and incomplete, that make only a slight effort to detect what vision, if any, gives continuity to the writers' works. At first glance, Grau's novels do seem to defy any attempt to find even a connecting thread. Until the publication of *Evidence of Love*, the label of "Southern regionalist" gave some of Grau's reviewers comfort. Readers familiar only with her last three novels could not avoid the recurrence of semilegendary patriarchs in possession of great wealth. Revenge at one time or another consumes such heroines as Joan Mitchell in *The House on Coliseum Street* and Abigail Mason Tolliver in *The Keepers of the House*, but an equally strong woman such as Lucy Henley in *Evidence of Love* possesses no such motive. Alwyn Berland (in his essay "The Fiction of Shirley Ann Grau") suggests that Grau's heroines favor the hallucinatory to the real, tend to be passive, and have ambivalent responses to sex. Berland's observation is helpful, but the title of Grau's last novel, *Evidence of Love*, gives the clearest clue to the sometimes elusive vision that informs her fictional world. While most of her male characters mechanically pursue money, sex, power, or ironclad order, the heroines seek some evidence of love. Their failure to find it renders both sexes solitary, and their subsequent sense of futility and despair makes their money and power meaningless. What saves the novels from an almost Jamesian pessimism is the possibility of redemption and rebirth. Both Joan Mitchell and Abigail Tolliver are last seen in literal fetal positions, as if awaiting resurrection. Their possibly temporary withdrawal resembles that of the wives of the fishermen in *The Hard Blue Sky*, who passively await the passing of the hurricane that may or may not destroy them.

In the development of her vision, Grau reveals considerable technical skill. Her sense of place is compelling. Equally convincing are such dissimilar scenes as William Howland's atavistic incursion into Honey Island Swamp and Harold Evans' drift into suicide in his meager and bare house in Princeton. As Paul Schlueter (*Shirley Ann Grau*, 1981) points out, few novelists are as successful as Grau in manipulating sensory images, particularly the olfactory. Most satisfying technically is her ability to treat the melodramatic with a cool, analytical detachment. The embattled house that Abigail defends and keeps is above all else a house, not Tara or Sutpen's Hundred. While Edward Milton Henley in *Evidence of Love* is capable of grandiose, operatic gestures and appetites, Grau's sardonic humor and sense of irony keeps him in the orbit of the real. Grau steadfastly refuses to sentimentalize.

Grau's occasional limitations are perhaps most noticeable in characterization. At times her characters lack emotional depth; the rich are not inherently interesting. In spite of lurid, exotic pasts, characters such as the Old Man in *The Condor Passes* lack the complex humanity necessary to be convincing. Further, her characters' motivations are not always clear. Even the sympathetic reader is not entirely sure, for example, why it is that Abigail so intensely dislikes Margaret's children.

Prior to 1964, Grau published two novels that anticipated her technique and vision in *The Keepers of the House*. The first, *The Hard Blue Sky*, revealed her ability to capture the world of southern Louisiana in stunning detail. Her plot consists of two different but connected stories that take place on islands along the Gulf Coast. The first story concerns the youthful Annie Landry's affair with Inky D'Alfonso. When she ultimately marries Inky, Annie is able to leave the islands for what may be a better life in New Orleans. Annie bears little resemblance to Abigail Tolliver: she has neither the wealth, the sense of family tradition, nor the consuming desire for revenge that drives Abigail. It is the second story that contains the violence and the revenge motif that will appear in *The Keepers of the House*. Rival groups on two different islands attempt to burn one another out after the disappearance of young lovers from the opposing families. Neither story ends with a clear resolution. It is not clear whether Annie's marriage will be a success, nor does one know if the feud will end, especially since both factions are threatened by a hurricane. Thus, in her first novel, Grau struck what became a crucial and familiar note in her fiction: her characters are left in a state of uncertainty as they face potential harm or destruction.

Grau's second novel, *The House on Coliseum Street*, has a much sharper focus than does her first. Joan Mitchell, the protagonist, anticipates Abigail Tolliver in several significant ways. Her relationship with men is disastrous. She is engaged to a businessman named Fred Aleman, whose rather passionless demeanor leaves her vulnerable to a young college professor, Michael Kern; their passionate lovemaking leaves Joan pregnant. After an abortion and Michael's abandonment, a guilt-ridden Joan becomes obsessed with destroying him. She does so by exposing him to his college dean. Like Abigail, Joan brings down her antagonist, but more significantly, she may have destroyed herself emotionally in doing so. That, however, is only a possibility: *The House on Coliseum Street* ends with Joan, having forgotten her key, unable to enter her family house. She is last seen in a fetal position, just as one sees Abigail at the end of *The Keepers of the House*. The possibility of rebirth and redemption is not excluded. Thus, *The House on Coliseum Street*, like *The Hard Blue Sky*, served as a preparation for the greater achievement in *The Keepers of the House*. In both, Grau was able to find sensory images that render the physical world immediate. More important, these early novels introduced Grau's evolving vision of a world with little clear evidence of love or community.

Nearly twenty years after its publication, the reader can see more clearly the truth of Grau's own commentary on *The Keepers of the House*: "The novel is about the whole human plight of how do you cope with evil? Do you fight back? The people are living in the South but they're just people facing the eternal human problem. I wanted to show the alternation of love and evil, which has always fascinated me. And if there is a moral, it is the self-destructiveness of hatred." If Grau sees the novel's significance in general moral terms, its popularity nevertheless was rooted in its then explosive characterization of Southern racial attitudes. The novel's narrator, Abigail Tolliver, granddaughter of William Howland, who himself is one of the "keepers of the house," finds herself in almost complete isolation. She and her husband are getting a divorce, two of her children have been forced to go away to school for safety's sake, and she has alienated the citizenry of her hometown, Madison City. Her desolation, mythic in intensity, is tragically linked to the discovery that her grandfather had married his black housekeeper, Margaret Carmichael. While the white community could cavalierly accept a mere sexual liaison, even one that has produced three children, marriage gives legitimacy. Thus, the men of Madison City attempt to burn the Howland estate in retaliation. The discovery of her grandfather's clandestine marriage destroys Abigail's marriage with her amoral, politically ambitious husband. The novel's evil is therefore easy to locate, as is Abigail's vengeful, Medea-like response. She not only burns the cars of the men who come to destroy her house; she also exercises her option to destroy the entire community financially. Yet difficult questions remain when one recalls Grau's own assessment of her work. How convincingly is the love that alternates with evil portrayed? How strongly felt is her "moral"—the self-destructiveness of hate?

Grau will never be accused of sentimentalizing love. Characters rarely, for example, confuse love with sex. When Abigail loses her virginity, she says, "I found that it wasn't so hard . . . nor painful either. . . . There's only one night like that—ever—where you're filled with wonder and excitement for no other reason but the earth is beautiful and mysterious and your body is young and strong." Her courtship by and marriage to John Tolliver is presented just as dispassionately. Tolliver, like Stephen Henley in *Evidence of Love* and the Old Man in *The Condor Passes*, subordinates love to ambition. Grau's sexes mate; they rarely love. Neither does there seem to be affection between generations. Abigail bears four children, but they remain abstractions. More mysterious, more horrific is the relation between the black woman, Margaret, and the children she bears William Howland. Half-white herself, Margaret sends each child off at the age of eleven to be educated in the North. She refuses to see them thereafter. She is particularly hostile and unyielding toward her oldest daughter, Nina, who returns to the South with her black husband. A certain curiosity exists between these racially mixed children and their mother, but there is no evidence of love.

The possible exception to this bleak vision of human existence is the thirty-year relationship between William Howland and Margaret. After the death of his first wife and the marriage of his daughter, Howland discovers the eighteen-year-old Margaret Carmichael washing clothes at a spring. She comes to him as a housekeeper and ultimately marries him. Both William and Margaret are characterized by Grau in terms larger than life. Howland is heir to the frontier tradition, in which men wrenched a living, indeed an immense fortune from a hostile environment. Prior to meeting Margaret, he makes a solitary journey into the mystery and danger of Honey Island Swamp, where he at one point strips himself naked and submerges himself into the primordial slime. When he returns to find Margaret at the spring, she appears to him as if she "had folded herself into the earth." Her stride is "a primitive walk, effortless, unassuming, unconscious, old as the earth under her feet." Like gods, apparently, William and Margaret possess the strength, the indifference to violate the most sacrosanct of Southern codes. Yet their love, if it exists, is concealed. The only evidence Abigail ever sees of their love is a single embrace.

Until Abigail's epiphany at the novel's end, Margaret is the character most cognizant of evil, particularly the evil inherent in racism. Her own white father abandoned her black mother, who in turn leaves Margaret to search for her missing lover. Margaret further realizes that it is necessary to send her white-appearing children out of the South, a tragic gesture that Abigail alone understands. It is a sacrifice that ends in alienation between parent and child, between white and black.

Grau states that the moral of the novel is the self-destructiveness of hatred. Is she suggesting that the South is destroying itself with its racial hostility? The attack on the Howland farm clearly does not go without destructive retribution. The local bigots have cut their own throats, because Abigail Tolliver owns almost every business in town. Yet her revenge, just as it may be, seems miniscule compared with the sure election of a staunch segregationist as the next governor—the most far-reaching consequence of the exposure of William Howland's marriage. Of more visceral concern to the reader, though, is the effect of hatred on Abigail. Not only has she decided to destroy Madison City, but she also has chosen to terrorize Margaret's vengeful son, Robert, by threatening to reveal his black origins to his white California wife. Stripped of compassion, devoid of love, Abigail at the conclusion of the novel has not yet taken the step that transcends hate. Her fetal position as she lies weeping in her office offers a possibility of rebirth, but the overriding vision of the novel is one of utter alienation and despair.

In the thirteen years between the publication of Grau's best novels, *The Keepers of the House* and *Evidence of Love*, one other novel appeared. Ironically, *The Condor Passes* received the worst reviews while posting the highest sales of any of Grau's works. The novel, a family chronicle, depicts the ninety-five years of Thomas Henry Oliver, who during his long life has amassed a huge fortune through such nefarious enterprises as prostitution and bootlegging. The novel bears only superficial resemblance to *The Keepers of the House*. As Grau herself has suggested, it is not concerned with the primitive. Survival is no longer a question. Instead, the characters seek to find a sense of identity in the presence of vast wealth. The novel, however, is wedded thematically to Grau's other works in its despairing vision. One senses that the male figures may have gained the whole world but lost their own souls. The Old Man's daughters are more complex, but their attempts to find enduring love are frustrated. They each have one son, but one dies and the other becomes a priest. The family therefore awaits little more than its own extinction.

By contrast, *Evidence of Love* is one of Grau's most successful novels. It too is a family chronicle, but its construction is still tight and sharply focused. Again the wealthy patriarch appears, but Edward Milton Henley possesses a sense of irony and self-awareness denied to earlier Grau patriarchs. Set outside the South, *Evidence of Love* frees Grau from often invidious comparisons with William Faulkner and allows her to concentrate on what has been one of the central concerns of all her novels, the need for some sign of love.

While the novel traces the lives of four generations of the Henley family, the voices of Edward Henley, his son Stephen, and his daughter-in-law Lucy dominate the narrative. Paul Schlueter maintains that "no where is there any 'evidence of love.'" He sees each character "seeking his own form of satisfaction to the exclusion of others." What in fact gives focus to each of the three stories is the pursuit of some apparently reasonable alternative to love. Because he chooses to relate his story in a satirical, ironic mode, it is not always easy to locate in an exact way Edward's feelings. The evidence of paternal love, he tells the reader, is the wealth his father gave him. If his mother, who is both literally and figuratively distant, did not love him, she at least imparted to him a sense of propriety and morality—which Edward chooses to ignore. These parents were, he says, happy. Himself physically and emotionally transient, Edward rather cavalierly dispenses with wives and male lovers. Yet he never indulges in self-pity. "I prefer to see my life as a pageant. Or a processional. Like that wonderful march in *Aida*." Through the elder Henley, Grau presents her paradox. About this old man, who still dreams of recapturing the drug-induced paradise he once experienced in Mexico, there is a considerable vitality. Edward's audacity, his iconoclasm, his rather mordant humor do not diminish life. His suicide is neither cowardly nor tragic. His life has been long and in its way full—even without the presence of love.

Edward says of his son, "Stephen was quiet and totally self-contained." Stephen is a Gatsby stripped of illusion and romance. As a young man, he makes a detailed plan of his life, a schedule that he unflinchingly follows. His marriage to Lucy Evans is as rational, as free of either anguish or passion as is his commitment to the ministry without believing in God. Here is a potential monster, but Grau does not ask the reader to see him as such. He does at least have some awareness of his own condition. For Lucy, he says, "I felt a sudden flood of feeling . . . not lust, not love. Something deeper, something older, something asexually human. The sympathy of blood for blood, of aching chalky bone for aching chalky bone. . . . The visceral sympathy of acquired identity." If what Stephen feels for Lucy is only kinship, it perhaps explains why he is confused by the passionate intensity of his youngest son, Paul. Quite by chance, Paul discovers, he believes, the identity of Stephen's mother, the young Irish woman Edward had paid to bear him a son sixty years earlier. Stephen wonders, "Was the presence of blood so important to him? What strange evidence of love was this?" The inability of yet another generation of Henleys to understand—or love—another is thus assured. Given Stephen's emotional isolation, one senses the inevitability of Stephen dying alone. Even death cannot shake his detachment. There has been no exhilarating pageant. Knowing he is dying, Stephen thinks, "I hardly cared. It didn't matter. Nothing did."

Although they seek refuge in quite opposing activities, both Stephen and his father rather straightforwardly eschew love. With Lucy, Stephen's wife, the case is more ambiguous, more complex. As in her earlier novels, Grau gives her female character a roundness that her males often lack. When Lucy recalls the sexual pleasure and pain she experienced with her first husband, she remarks that "All that was evidence of love." Because Lucy does not indulge in irony, the reader accepts her assessment. Her openness to physical love is reinforced by her enthusiasm for the lushness of Florida, although Lucy has reservations: when Harold makes love to her, she thinks, "I don't like this. . . . I don't like having feelings I can't control." Perhaps the fear of feeling paradoxically allows her to live comfortably for thirty years with Stephen. After his death, she states that "Old women are supposed to quake with an excess of emotion—perhaps love—and start talking to animals and birds and flowers on the windowsill. I didn't." At times, she seems even more alienated than either her husband or her father-in-law. When her worried son Paul phones her, she thinks to herself that "Love between the generations was a burdensome chore." She hopes to be saved from such love. In her way, Lucy proves as evasive to the reader as she does to her son. Ironically, her last appearance in the novel proves in a perverse way to be evidence of love. She hands Edward Henley the Seconal he wants to end a life grown exceedingly tiresome. Lucy's ambiguous complicity in his death is an appropriate action to close Grau's best work. As Edward's voice dies out, it says, "The taste of paradise, the perfect union. It must be here, Here." Grau teases the reader into thought. Paradoxes abound. Indeed, the novel has presented little if any conventional evidence of love, but one senses the value of the lives presented. In its own characteristically ironic way, *Evidence of Love* is just that. The vision is bleak, but here is her most affirmative work.

John K. Saunders

Other major works
SHORT FICTION: *The Black Prince and Other Stories*, 1955; *The Wind Shifting West*, 1973; *Nine Women*, 1985.

Bibliography
Canfield, John. "Women Alone." Review of *Nine Women*, by Shirley Ann Grau. *Southern Review* 22 (Autumn, 1986): 904-906. Emphasizes the profound similarities between the seemingly very different lives of the lonely women in these short stories. This essay points out the unfairness of dismissing Grau as a merely regional writer.

Grau, Shirley Ann. "A Conversation with Shirley Ann Grau." Interview by John Canfield. *Southern Quarterly* 25 (Winter, 1987): 39-52. In this important interview, Grau speaks thoughtfully about her relationship to the Southern literary tradition. She also explains her concern with technique and concludes by defining the most important criterion for good writing: the power of the writer's thought.

Rohrberger, Mary. "Shirley Ann Grau and the Short Story." In *Women Writers of the Contemporary South*, edited by Peggy Whitman Prenshaw. Jackson: University Press of Mississippi, 1984. Beginning with Grau's earliest work, published when the writer was only nineteen, Rohrberger painstakingly traces the changes in Grau's work and art, as seen in over three decades of short fiction. Rohrberger believes that Grau is given too little credit for subtlety and proves her point with numerous examples.

Schlueter, Paul. *Shirley Ann Grau*. Boston: Twayne, 1981. Although admitting that the quality of Grau's work varies greatly, Schlueter insists that hostile critics, dismissing her as a regional writer, have failed to appreciate Grau's achievements, particularly her evocation of a sense of place, her creation of vivid characters, and her mastery of language. Includes full treatment of all Grau's works up to 1981, extensive notes, and an annotated bibliography.

Simpson, Lewis P. Introduction to *Three by Three: Masterworks of the Southern Gothic*, edited by Lewis P. Simpson. Atlanta: Peachtree, 1985. In his introductory essay to a volume containing works by Doris Betts and Mark Steadman, along with Grau's *The Black Prince and Other Stories*, Simpson discusses the Gothic tradition in American literature and its manifestations among Southern writers. A stimulating essay which helps to explain the mythic qualities of Grau's early works.

Wagner-Martin, Linda. "Shirley Ann Grau's Wise Fictions." In *Southern*

Women Writers: The New Generation, edited by Tonette Bond Inge. Tusca-loosa: University of Alabama Press, 1990. This essay is based on the assumption that a writer's "Southernness" can contribute either to superficiality and triviality or to the greatness which arises from a sense of the presence of the past. For Grau, Wagner-Martin argues, it has been a source of strength. Also devotes some space to the consideration of Grau as a woman writer, in comparison to other women writers, particularly those from the South.

ROBERT GRAVES

Born: Wimbledon, England; July 24, 1895
Died: Deyá, Majorca, Spain; December 7, 1985

Principal long fiction

My Head! My Head!, 1925; *No Decency Left*, 1932 (as Barbara Rich, with Laura Riding); *I, Claudius*, 1934; *Claudius the God and His Wife Messalina*, 1934; *"Antigua, Penny, Puce,"* 1936 (also known as *The Antigua Stamp*, 1937); *Count Belisarius*, 1938; *Sergeant Lamb of the Ninth*, 1940 (also known as *Sergeant Lamb's America*); *Proceed, Sergeant Lamb*, 1941; *The Story of Marie Powell, Wife to Mr. Milton*, 1943 (also known as *Wife to Mr. Milton, The Story of Marie Powell*); *The Golden Fleece*, 1944 (also known as *Hercules, My Shipmate*, 1945); *King Jesus*, 1946; *Watch the North Wind Rise*, 1949 (also known as *Seven Days in New Crete*); *The Islands of Unwisdom*, 1949 (also known as *The Isles of Unwisdom*); *Homer's Daughter*, 1955; *They Hanged My Saintly Billy*, 1957.

Other literary forms

Robert Graves considered himself primarily a poet. Beginning with *Over the Brazier* (1916) and ending with *New Collected Poems* (1977), he published more than fifty books of poetry. His poems during and for some years after World War I explored themes of fear and guilt, expressive of his experience of trench warfare in France. He later became more objective and philosophical. Since he developed his theory of the White Goddess in the 1940's, he wrote love poetry almost exclusively.

Graves also had more than fifty publications in the nonfiction category, including literary criticism, books about writing and language, an autobiography (*Goodbye to All That*, 1929), a biography of T. E. Lawrence (*Lawrence and the Arabs*, 1927), social commentaries and studies in Greek and Hebrew myths. In addition, he translated such writers as Suetonius, Homer, Hesiod, Lucius Apuleius, Lucan Pharsalia, and Manuel de Jesus Galvan. He had one volume of *Collected Short Stories* (1964).

Achievements

Graves was one of the most versatile writers of the twentieth century, known as an excellent poet but also as a mythologist, novelist, translator, lecturer, and persistent intellectual maverick. He has perhaps the clearest claim among twentieth century poets to be regarded as the inheritor of the romantic tradition, although he has purified his poetry of the kind of flowery elaboration that is often associated with Romanticism. He avoided fads and schools in poetry, perfecting a delicate craftsmanship generally outside the modern trends inspired by T. S. Eliot and Ezra Pound.

For the novel *I, Claudius*, Graves received the Hawthornden Prize, oldest of the famous British literary prizes, and the James Tait Black Memorial Prize, administered through the University of Edinburgh for the year's best novel. Collections of his poetry brought the Loines Award for Poetry (1958), the William Foyle Poetry Prize (1960), the Arts Council Poetry Award (1962), and the Queen's Gold Medal for Poetry (1968).

The White Goddess: A Historical Grammar of Poetic Myth (1948) and Grave's other studies in mythology, particularly *The Greek Myths* (1955, 2 volumes), *Hebrew Myths: The Book of Genesis* (1964, with Raphael Patai), and *The Nazarene Gospel Restored* (1953, with Joshua Podro), together with his novels based on myth, have undoubtedly had a subtle and pervasive influence on modern literature. He was a prominent spokesman for the view that women and matriarchal values were much more prominent in the ancient world than once realized and that civilization has suffered from the overthrow of women as social and spiritual leaders. The demotion of women from their former prominence, Graves said, is recorded and rationalized in Hebrew texts and classical Greek mythology.

Biography

Robert Graves was born in Wimbledon (outside of London) on July 24, 1895, to Alfred Percival Graves and Amalie von Ranke Graves. His father was an inspector of schools, a Gaelic scholar, and a writer of poetry of a conventional sort. His mother was German, descended from Leopold von Ranke, whom Graves has called the first modern historian. Graves had a conventional Victorian home and upbringing, with summer visits to German relatives. These included an aunt, Baronin von Aufsess, who lived in an imposing medieval castle in the Bavarian Alps.

Because his name was listed as R. von R. Graves, his obvious German connections became an embarrassment during his years at Charterhouse, a private boarding school for boys, during the period before World War I when anti-German sentiment was on the rise. He finally earned his classmates respect, however, by becoming a good boxer. He also became friends with George Mallory, a famous mountaineer who later died on Everest. Mallory interested Edward Marsh, patron of the contemporary Georgian school of poetry, in the poetry Graves was writing. Marsh encouraged Graves in his writing, but advised him to modernize his diction, which was forty years behind the time.

When World War I began, Graves joined the Royal Welsh Fusiliers and soon went to France as a nineteen-year-old officer. In his autobiography, written when he was thirty-five, he provides one of the best descriptions of trench warfare to come out of the war—a gritty, objective account of a soldier's daily life. He was badly wounded, however, both physically and mentally, by his war experiences. The autobiography, which followed a long siege of war neurasthenia during which his poetry was haunted by images of horror and guilt, was a conscious attempt to put that part of his life behind him forever. Graves continued to use his gift for narrating war experiences, however, in subsequent novels, such as *Count Belisarius*, the Sergeant Lamb novels, and the Claudius novels.

During the war, Graves married Nancy Nicholson, a young painter, socialist, and vehement feminist. They were in essential agreement about the ruinous effect of male domination in modern society. Graves, along with his wartime friend, the famous war poet Seigfried Sassoon, was already thoroughly disillusioned with war and the leaders of society who supported it.

Graves and his wife parted company in 1929 after a shattering domestic crisis involving the American poet, Laura Riding. Riding was Graves's companion for the next thirteen years. They established themselves in Déya, Majorca, published the critical magazine *Epilogue* on their own Seizin Press, and devoted themselves to writing both poetry and prose. Graves wrote his best historical novels during that period—the Claudius novels and *Count Belisarius*.

After Riding met and married the American poet Schuyler Jackson, Graves—during the Spanish Civil War, when British nationals were evacuated from Majorca—married Beryl Hodge. Graves returned to Majorca with his new wife, where he stayed until his death in 1985. Graves had eight children, four by Nancy Nicholson, four by his second wife.

During the 1940's, Graves became fascinated with mythology. While he was doing research for his novel about Jason and the Golden Fleece, he became engrossed in the ubiquitous presence of a great goddess, associated with the moon, the earth, and the underworld. She was not only the source of life and intuitive wisdom, but also, as Muse, the patron of the poets and musicians. She bound men both to the seasons of nature and the demands of the spirit.

When Graves discovered a similar pattern in Celtic folklore and literature, and correlated the findings of such anthropologists as Robert Briffault, J. J. Bachofen, James Frazer, Jane Harrison, Margaret Murray, and some of the recent discoveries in archaeology, he was convinced that the goddess cult once permeated the whole Western world. In this pattern of myth, as explained in *The White Goddess*, Graves found the unified vision he needed to animate his poetry and much of his subsequent prose for the rest of his life. It not only inspired some of the best love poetry of his time, but also led to some lively treatments of Greek and Hebrew myth in both fiction and nonfiction.

Analysis

The novels of Robert Graves are usually a curious combination of detective work in history, legend, or myth and a considerable gift for narration. He never claimed any particular ability to invent plots, but he could flesh out imaginatively the skeletal remains of adventures he discovered in the past.

Thus, the Emperor Claudius lives again as the gossipy information in Suetonius and other Roman chroniclers passes through Graves's shaping imagination. Sometimes, as in *King Jesus*, a traditional tale takes on a startling new dimension through an unconventional combination with other legendary material.

Graves's first attempt at converting ancient history or myth into fiction was a short novel about Elisha and Moses, somewhat inauspiciously entitled *My Head! My Head!* It was begun, as most of Graves's subsequent novels were, because the original accounts were somewhat mysterious, leaving much unsaid about what really happened and why. The novel elaborates on the biblical story of Elisha and the Shunamite woman (II Kings, Chapters 8-37) and, secondarily, through Elisha's narration, the career of Moses.

The novel demonstrates both Graves's tendency to explain miracles in naturalistic terms and his contrary fascination with a certain suprarational possibility for special persons. The writer's curious views on magic are not entirely consistent with his debunking of miracles. The inconsistency is quite noticeable here because of the omniscient point of view. In most later novels, Graves wisely used a first-person narrator, which makes seeming inconsistencies the peculiar bias of a persona, rather than of the author. Thus, *King Jesus* is told by a first century narrator who is neither Jewish nor Christian. In such a person, rational skepticism about specific miracles such as the virgin birth might well coexist with a general acceptance of magic.

In spite of its technical shortcomings, *My Head! My Head!* shows Graves's interest in a number of themes which would continue to concern him for the rest of his life: the changing relationships between men and women, the nature of the gods, the way in which knowledge of the past and of the future must depend upon an understanding of the present.

On those two occasions when Graves did not depend on mythological or historical sources for his fiction, the results were strange, satirical compositions, lucidly told, but somehow disquieting. The first of these, a collaboration with Laura Riding, appeared under a pseudonym as *No Decency Left* by "Barbara Rich." It is a satirical potpourri of events, drawing on such discordant elements as the rise of dictators, the man in the iron mask, the miraculous feeding of the multitude in the Bible, and comic-opera romance. The ideas in his fantasy may be attributable more to Riding than to Graves, though the attitudes displayed are quite consistent with Graves's views on the follies of men and the hidden strengths of women. The action occurs in one day, the twenty-first birthday of Barbara Rich, who decides that on this special day she is going to get everything she wants. She forthwith crashes high society, becomes incredibly rich, marries the heir to the throne, feeds a multitude of hungry unemployed people by invading the zoo and arranging for the slaughter and cooking of zoo animals, captures the Communists who try to take over the country when the old king dies, and becomes a dictator in her own almost-bloodless revolution.

If the tone of this outrageous fable were lighter and its protagonist more lovable, it could be converted into Hollywood farce or Gilbert and Sullivan operetta, but everyone in it is disagreeable. People are either uniformly stupid and cowardly or utterly unscrupulous. The book was probably written primarily to make money when Riding and Graves were short of cash. (Graves has always claimed that he wrote novels primarily to support himself while he wrote poetry.) It is obviously accidental that the novel, written in 1932, might seem to satirize the blanket powers given to Adolf Hitler by the Reichstag in 1933, or the famous love affair of King Edward with the commoner, Wallis Simpson, in 1936.

The view of the human animal, male or female, as vicious, with superior cleverness and ingenuity the mark of the female, also dominates Graves's novel *The Antigua Stamp*. The everlasting battle of the sexes is dramatized here as sibling rivalry that is never outgrown—a controversy over the ownership of an exceedingly valuable stamp. A long-standing sour feud between brother and sister ends with the latter's victory because she is by far the more clever and conniving of the two. *The Antigua Stamp* and *No Decency Left* are potboilers, though interesting for the eccentric attitudes they exhibit toward human character and social affairs. These biases concerning the essential stupidity and greed of men and the intelligence and ruthlessness of women emerge in a somewhat softened form in Graves's better novels.

Eight of Graves's novels are based, at least in part, upon historical characters and events. The first of these is still the best—*I, Claudius*, which is probably also the best known because of the sensitive portrayal of Claudius by Derek Jacoby in the BBC television series based on the Claudius novels. *Count Belisarius*, about the brilliant general to the Byzantine Emperor Justinian, is also a fascinating excursion into an exciting time, even though the character of Belisarius is not so clearly drawn as that of the stuttering Claudius.

Although *Count Belisarius* deserves more attention than it has received, the other historical novels appeal to a rather limited audience. The exception is the last, *They Hanged My Saintly Billy*, which Graves facetiously described in lurid terms: "My novel is full of sex, drink, incest, suicides, dope, horse racing, murder, scandalous legal procedure, cross-examinations, inquests and ends with a good public hanging—attended by 30,000 . . . Nobody can now call me a specialized writer.

The novel is hardly so shocking as this dust-jacket rhetoric implies. The case of Dr. William Palmer, convicted of poisoning his friend, John Parsons Cook, and executed in 1856, instigated a popular protest against capital punishment in Britain. The notorious case was rife with vague, unsubstantiated suspicions about Dr. Palmer's past and irrelevant disapproval of his taste for gambling and race horses. Moreover, supposed medical experts could never agree about the actual cause of Cook's death.

The novel's best feature is the technique by which Graves preserves the confusion and ambiguity of the case. Most of the novel consists of personal testimony from persons who had known Palmer. Thus, each speaker talks from his own biases and limited contact, some insisting that "he never had it in him to hurt a fly." Others reveal an incredibly callous schemer who takes out insurance on his brother's life, knowing him to be an alcoholic, then arranges that he drink himself to death. No sure conclusion is ever reached about the justice of the case.

As a member of the Royal Welsh Fusiliers during World War I, Graves became interested in the history of his regiment and discovered the makings of two novels in the career of Roger Lamb, who served in the Ninth Regiment during the American Revolution, but joined the Fusiliers after the surrender of General Burgoyne and the incarceration of the Ninth.

Graves is more chronicler than novelist in the two books about Roger Lamb, much of which are devoted to details of military life, curious anecdotes about the colonists, the Indians, the French Canadians, the fiascos and triumph of generals. Graves explains in his Foreword to *Sergeant Lamb's America* that this story is not "straight history," though he has invented no main characters. The reader has no way of knowing exactly how accurately he conveys the texture of life in the colonies. "All that readers of an historical novel can fairly ask from the author," Graves writes, "is an assurance that he has nowhere willfully falsified geography, chronology, or character, and that information contained in it is accurate enough to add without discount to their general stock of history." This is a statement to remember, perhaps, in connection with any of Graves's historical novels. Although Graves seemed to have no particular rancor against Americans, the books do reveal a very iconoclastic attitude toward the Founding Fathers. His view of such notables as Benedict Arnold, Major André, and George Washington at least challenges the American reader's preconceptions.

Sergeant Lamb, like Count Belisarius, seems a bit wooden for all his military ingenuity. The protagonist's on-and-off love affair with Kate Harlowe provides only a tenuous thread on which to hang the semblance of a plot. The novels seem to be a scholar's compilation of interesting anecdotes and factual data about the time. Of course, this unimpassioned tone could be defended as exactly appropriate, since the novels are ostensibly the memoirs of a much older Roger Lamb, written when he is a schoolmaster in Dublin. This cool, dispassionate tone is often typical of Graves's style, however, even when he is describing his own experience in warfare in his autobiography, *Goodbye to All That*.

The Islands of Unwisdom celebrates, or rather exposes in its pettiness and greed, an abortive sixteenth century Spanish expedition to colonize the Solomon Islands. The leader of the expedition, Don Alvaro de Mendaña y Castro, had discovered the islands many years before. He called them the

Isles of Soloman, thinking perhaps they were the location of the famous gold mines of the biblical King Solomon. The natives adorned themselves with gold. When the King of Spain finally gave permission for the expedition, therefore, a great many avaricious participants joined in the venture ostensibly devoted to Christianizing the heathen.

Though a few devout persons, such as the three priests and the chief pilot, tried to maintain the Christian charity of their mission, their feeble efforts were in vain. Practically all the islanders greeted the Spaniards with affection and open hospitality, but sooner or later, the senseless slaughter of innocents converted friends into enemies. The combined stupidity and violence of the military and of the three Barretos, Don Alvaro's brothers-in-law, insured disaster wherever they went. Moreover, Doña Ysabel Barreto, Don Alvaro's beautiful wife, was as proud and cruel as her arrogant brothers. Don Alvaro was devout but indecisive and unable to control the stubborn wills that surrounded him.

Graves uses the narrator, Don Andrés Serrano, an undersecretary to the general, to propose a theory to account for the superiority of the English over the Spanish in such situations. The English soldier could and often did do a sailor's work when help was needed on shipboard. The more rigid class structure of the Spanish, however, prevented a Spanish soldier from doing anything but fighting. During long and hazardous voyages, the Spanish soldier was idle and bored, while the Spanish sailor was overworked and resentful. When a new land was reached, the Spanish soldier felt impelled to demonstrate his function by killing enemies. If none existed, he soon created them.

Graves was particularly drawn to this sordid bit of history not so much because of the too-often-repeated folly of bringing civilization to the heathen by murdering them, but because of a truly unique feature of this historical event. After the death of her husband, Doña Ysabel achieved the command of a naval vessel—surely an unusual event in any age, and unprecedented in the sixteenth century. Doña Ysabel is not the conventional kind of heroine, to be sure, but a kind that Graves finds most fascinating—beautiful, cruel, and ruthless. This novel was published in the year following *The White Goddess*, and the reader who is familiar with that study may see an uncanny resemblance between Doña Ysabel and the moon goddess in her most sinister phase.

The Story of Marie Powell, Wife to Mr. Milton is also rooted in history, yet it echoes Graves's own views of feminine nature, as well as his antipathy to John Milton, both as a poet and as a man. That Milton did, indeed, have some marital problems is clear; they were the inspiration for his pamphlet arguing that incompatibility should be sufficient grounds for divorce, which was followed by his brilliant "Areopagitica" against censorship of the press. (Graves notes that in spite of the admitted wisdom of the latter, Milton himself became an official censor under Cromwell.)

In Graves's treatment, Milton is the epitome of the self-righteous, dominating male, drawn to the poetic, half-pagan rural England from which his
young wife emerges but determined in his arid Calvinism to squelch these
poetic yearnings in himself and his bride. Milton chooses head over heart,
always a mistake in a poet, from Graves's point of view. Though Milton
desires love, like any man, he has a preconceived set of rules that would
define and coerce love, which can only be freely given. He resolutely divorces
sexuality from pleasure, for example, knowing his wife only when trying to
impregnate her—in compliance, presumably, with God's orders.

Marie is the weakest of Graves's fictional women, a kind of dethroned
queen, a person of independent mind, doomed to mental and emotional
starvation in Milton's household. T. S. Matthews, in his autobiography *Jacks
or Better* (1977), makes the provocative suggestion that Graves poured his
frustration and resentment about the marriage of Laura Riding to Schuyler
Jackson into the book. It was written immediately after Graves fled to
England, bereft of his long-time companion. Matthews has considerable background for this opinion, since he and his wife were living in America with
the group (including Riding, Graves, Alan and Beryl Hodge, Schuyler and
Kit Jackson) when the fruit basket upset. Even though Graves and Riding
were not lovers at that time, according to James McKinley in his Introduction
to Graves's last book, Graves was profoundly shocked at what he may have
perceived as Riding's abdication from her proper role. Whether this explanation is valid or not, this novel seems to touch a more personal vein of
frustration, resentment, and sadness than his other historical novels.

Moreover, Graves indulges in a bit of romantic mysticism in this novel,
more characteristic of his poetic than his prose style. Marie Milton falls into
a three-day swoon during her third pregnancy, at the precise moment that
her secret "true love" is killed in Ireland. According to her own account, she
spends those three days with her beloved. When she awakens she knows that
her cousin, with whom she had fallen in love at the age of eleven, is dead.
The child she bears thereafter, her first son, looks like her cousin, not Milton,
and Marie is more peaceful than she has ever been. Perhaps this touch of
fantasy expresses more about Graves than about Marie Powell Milton, but
the author is careful to note in the epilogue that when Marie died giving birth
to a third daughter, the one son followed her to the grave shortly after.

Readers may find the style of this novel somewhat ponderous, but Graves
tries to adjust his diction to the times he writes about. He has deliberately
used some archaic, seventeenth century terms, for which he provides a glossary at the end; most of these words are easily understood in context.

If the pathetic Marie Milton shows the White Goddess in her pitiable
decline, one need only return to the powerful women in *Count Belisarius* to
see her in her glory. This is true, despite the fact that Graves had not yet
formulated his theory of the monomyth which he expressed in *The White*

Goddess. In retrospect, his fictional women suggest that the goddess haunted his psyche before he knew her name. In *Count Belisarius*, not one but two striking women demonstrate the strength of the female. These are the Empress Theodora, wife to Justinian, and Antonina, Belisarius' wife. Both had been carefully educated, pagan courtesans, but they acquired Christianity when it became possible to marry prominent Christians. They inevitably display more good sense than most of the men around them. More than once, Theodora saves Belesarius from the vindictive jealousy of Justinian, or convinces the negligent monarch that he should send some relief in troops or supplies to his champion on the frontier. When Belisarius' situation becomes desperate because he is almost always vastly outnumbered on the battlefield and short of supplies as well, Antonina sends a private letter to Empress Theodora, who manages, by flattery or guile, to cajole Justinian into at least some action not altogether disastrous.

Of the two prominent men in the novel, Justinian is the more carefully characterized, even though he is invariably presented in a negative light. After Theodora dies and Belisarius throws out Antonina, because of the emperor's campaign to discredit her virtue, nothing remains to protect Belisarius from Justinian's jealousy and fear. Like Samson shorn of his hair, Belisarius is imprisoned and blinded.

Belisarius, the central figure, is the least understandable in psychological terms. Though his exploits against the Persians and against the many tribes that threatened early Christendom are truly remarkable and well told, he himself seems larger than life in moral terms as well as in his undoubted military genius. He is seemingly incorruptible in a world riddled with intrigue and deception, and as such, almost too good to be true. The jealousy of Justinian is more understandable than Belisarius' unswerving loyalty, devotion, and piety. The reader never knows what preserves Belisarius from the corrupting influence of power and popular adulation.

Ultimately, the effect of the novel is ironic, in spite of the total absence of ambiguity in Belisarius' character. The irony rests in the observation that for all the lifelong efforts of one of history's military geniuses, his accomplishments mattered little, since they were so soon negated by Justinian's bad judgment after the death of his greatest general. All the drama and the pageantry of war cannot compensate for its futility and incredible waste and its glorification of destruction in the name of true religion.

For his portrait of Claudius, grandchild of Mark Antony and grand nephew of Octavius Augustus, Graves had rich sources of information on which to draw; perhaps that accounts for the greater depth and complexity Claudius seems to exhibit in comparison to Belisarius. Both *The Annals of Tacitus* (c. 119) and Suetonius' *Lives of the Caesars* (c. 120, a book that Graves translated from the Latin in 1957) contain much of the gossipy, possibly slanted history that fills Graves's *I, Claudius* and *Claudius the God*.

I, Claudius is a more successful novel than its sequel. It builds to a natural climax as the protagonist, who calls himself "the cripple, the stammerer, the fool of the family," is proclaimed emperor by riotous Roman soldiers after the assassination of Caligula. Claudius captures the sympathy of the reader in this novel as a survivor of a fifty-year reign of terror in which all the more likely prospects for promotion to emperor are eliminated by Livia, Augustus' wife, to assure the elevation of her son Tiberius to the throne. Claudius owes his survival mostly to his physical defects, which seemingly preclude his being considered for high office, and to a ready intelligence and wit which protect him somewhat from the cruelties of Caligula, who is the first to give him any role at all in government. The caprice of the troops in choosing the "fool of the family" as emperor is as great a surprise to Claudius as to anyone else. Presumably the terrified Claudius acquiesces to the whim of the military because the only other alternative is assassination along with the rest of Caligula's close relatives.

With *Claudius the God*, the reader can no longer cheer the innocent victim of the vicious intrigues of court life. Claudius now has power and, in some respects, wields it effectively and humanely. He acquires, however, many of the tastes and faults of his class. The man who, as a boy, fainted at bloodshed now has a taste for violent entertainment. The scholar who despised ostentatious show now invades Britain so he may have a glorious triumph on his return. Worse yet, the unassuming person who knew how to survive the formidable machinations of Livia now foolishly succumbs to younger women, as ruthless as Livia but without her intelligence and executive ability. He dies of poison administered by a faithless wife.

Graves seems to be making a case for the older Claudius as a kind of tragic hero, who has come to a realization of his own shortcomings as well as those of his contemporaries. He had once idealistically hoped for the return of the Republic, but in his later years he understands that he has actually made self-government less attractive, simply because his rule has been more benevolent than that of his predecessors, Tiberius and Caligula. He decides that the Rupublican dream will not arise until the country again suffers under an evil emperor. The government must be worse before it can be better.

Graves attributes to Claudius a rather improbable scheme of secluding his son from the temptations of court life by sending him to Britain, then letting his ambitious second wife secure the throne for her own son, Nero, whose cruelty and decadence Claudius foresees. In the debacle that will occur in the reign of Nero, Claudius hopes his own son can come back as a conquering hero and reestablish the Republic.

This rather fanciful scheme misfires because Claudius' son refuses to cooperate, confident that he can deal with his foster brother, Nero, himself. Actually, Claudius' son was assassinated after his father's death, presumably at Nero's orders.

This attempted explanation of Claudius' seeming gullibility in his last days is probably intended to lend dignity to his unfortunate decline into a rather foolish old age. Part of the problem with the second novel is simply the intractability of historical facts, which do not necessarily make the most effective plots. One of the usual requirements of the tragic hero is that he attain some measure of self-knowledge and that he is at least partially responsible for his own fall from greatness. Graves has tried to retain empathy for a well-intentioned, thoughtful man who foresaw and accepted his fate, to be murdered by his wife, as a means to a greater good. This attempt to salvage a fading protagonist is understandable, but not wholly successful.

As Graves's historical novels depend partially upon the intrinsic interest of a historical period, so do his novels based on myth depend upon an intrinsic interest in myth interpretation. Quite aside from the familiar story of Jason and the Argonauts, for example, *Hercules, My Shipmate* offers sometimes believable explanations of some of the common ideas found in myth. The centaurs, for example, were not half horse, half men, but a barbaric tribe whose totem animal was the horse. They wore horse's mane and worshiped a mare-headed mother goddess. Many of Jason's shipmates were demigods; that is, one parent was a deity. This convention has a nonsupernatural explanation as well: their births were traceable to the ancient custom of temple prostitutes or priests whose offspring were attributed to the god or goddess under whose auspices they were conceived.

This does not mean that all supernaturalism is rooted out of Graves's treatment of mythic material. Hercules has exaggerated powers analogous to those of Paul Bunyan, a parody of the Greek ideal of the hero, a man so strong he is dangerous to friend and foe as well. Nor does Graves eliminate all supernaturalism from his *King Jesus*, the most controversial of his novels, which fuses biblical myth with his own ideas about the ancient goddess cult.

King Jesus creates a new myth about Jesus—a Jesus who is literally the King of the Jews, or at least the proper inheritor of that title. He is inheritor as the grandson of King Herod (through a secret marriage between Mary and Antipater, Herod's son), but also because he is annointed by God's prophet, John the Baptist, which was the traditional Hebrew way of choosing a king. In the latter sense, Herod had less right to the throne than Jesus, since Herod derived his authority from the Romans, not from ancient Hebrew custom. Moreover, Jesus fulfills other expectations built into what Graves presents as ancient Hebrew ritual, such as a marriage to the inheritor of the land. Graves claims that ownership of the land was matrilinear, and that in order to become a king, a man must marry the youngest daughter of the hereditary line, in this case Mary, the sister of Martha and Lazarus. (Graves points out that this matrilinear descent accounts for Egyptian pharoahs marrying their sisters and King David marrying a woman from each of the tribes of Israel, in order to unify the tribes.)

Jesus is an ascetic, however, and refuses to cohabit with Mary. Moreover, one of his chief adversaries in the novel is the cult of the goddess, whose chief priestess is yet another Mary, called the Hairdresser—the character known in the bible as Mary Magdalene. It is no accident that the three vital women who attend Jesus in his crucifixion conveniently represent the Triple Goddess—Mary the mother, Mary the wife, and Mary the crone, who lays out the mythic hero in death. The irony of the situation is that in spite of consciously choosing the pattern of the Suffering Servant, described in Isaiah, and trying his best to overthrow the cult of the fertility goddess, Jesus nevertheless fulfills the role of the sacrificial hero in the goddess mythology. Though religious people may be offended by the liberties Graves has taken with a sacred story, those who are fascinated by the whole of the mythic heritage from the ancient world will appreciate this imaginative retelling.

If *King Jesus* is the most serious of Graves's treatments of the goddess mythology, the most lighthearted is *Watch the North Wind Rise*, a futuristic utopian novel in which the great goddess cult has been revived in Crete (its stronghold in the ancient world) as a social experiment. The protagonist is a time traveler, conjured into the future by a witch, in obedience to the goddess. He also serves a Pandora-like function, bringing unrest into a land made dull by continuous peace. Great art, after all, demands conflict, which this ideal land has left behind. The novel is entertaining as a satire of utopian ideas, but also provides an interesting exploration of the relationship between an artist (the protagonist) and his muse (the goddess).

Graves's last novel on a mythic theme, *Homer's Daughter*, borrows heavily from the *Odyssey* (c. 800 B. C.) and from Samuel Butler's *The Authoress of of the "Odyssey"* (1897), which argues that the *Odyssey* must have been written by a woman. Graves's protagonist is the princess Nausicaa, who in the *Odyssey* befriended the shipwrecked Odysseus. In the novel, it is Nausicaa who endures many rude and insistent suitors as Penelope does in Homer's epic. A shipwrecked stranger rescues her in a manner attributed to Odysseus, by shooting the unwanted suitors and winning the fair lady for himself. She is the one who composes the *Odyssey*, incorporating her experience into the story.

In spite of the fact that Graves himself dismissed his fiction as a means of providing support for his writing of poetry, his best novels deserve to live on as imaginative treatments of history and myth. While he may not always have captured the "real" past, he has helped to make the past important in a time when many people have considered it irrelevant. He has shown how ancient symbol-systems may still capture the imagination of one of the most versatile writers of our time. He has also helped to overthrow the stereotype of women as weak in intelligence and will. This does not mean that Graves was particularly accurate in his perception of women, but his biases do offer a welcome antidote to the more insipid variety of fictional women. He must be partially responsible for the contemporary interest in mythology and the beginnings of civilization. Part of this is the result of his nonfiction works, such as *The White Goddess*, *The Greek Myths*, and *Hebrew Myths*, but his use of myth in popular novels has probably reached an even wider audience.

Katherine Snipes

Other major works

SHORT FICTION: *The Shout*, 1929; *¡Catacrok! Mostly Stories, Mostly Funny*, 1956; *Collected Short Stories*, 1964.

PLAY: *John Kemp's Wager: A Ballad Opera*, 1925.

POETRY: *Over the Brazier*, 1916; *Goliath and David*, 1916; *Fairies and Fusiliers*, 1917; *Treasure Box*, 1919; *Country Sentiment*, 1920; *The Pier-Glass*, 1921; *Whipperginny*, 1923; *The Feather Bed*, 1923; *Mock Beggar Hall*, 1924; *Welchman's Hose*, 1925; *The Marmosite's Miscellany*, 1925 (as John Doyle); *Poems: 1914-1926*, 1927; *Poems: 1914-1927*, 1927; *Poems: 1929*, 1929; *Ten Poems More*, 1930; *Poems: 1926-1930*, 1931; *To Whom Else?*, 1931; *Poems: 1930-1933*, 1933; *Collected Poems*, 1938; *No More Ghosts: Selected Poems*, 1940; *Work in Hand*, 1942 (with others); *Poems: 1938-1945*, 1946; *Collected Poems: 1914-1947*, 1948; *Poems and Satires: 1951*, 1951; *Poems: 1953*, 1953; *Collected Poems: 1955*, 1955; *Poems Selected by Himself*, 1957; *The Poems of Robert Graves Chosen By Himself*, 1958; *Collected Poems: 1959*, 1959; *The Penny Fiddle: Poems for Children*, 1960; *More Poems: 1961*, 1961; *Collected Poems*, 1961; *New Poems: 1962*, 1962; *The More Deserving Cases: Eighteen Old Poems for Reconsideration*, 1962; *Man Does, Woman Is*, 1964; *Ann at Highwood Hall: Poems for Children*, 1964; *Love Respelt*, 1965; *Seventeen Poems Missing from "Love Respelt,"* 1966; *Colophon to "Love Respelt,"* 1967; *Poems: 1965-1968*, 1968; *Poems About Love*, 1969; *Love Respelt Again*, 1969; *Beyond Giving: Poems*, 1969; *Poems: 1969-1970*, 1970; *Advice from a Mother*, 1970; *The Green-Sailed Vessel*, 1971; *Poems: Abridged for Dolls and Princes*, 1971; *Poems: 1970-1972*, 1972; *Deyá*, 1972 (with Paul Hogarth); *Timeless Meeting: Poems*, 1973; *At the Gate*, 1974; *Collected Poems: 1975*, 1975 (2 volumes); *New Collected Poems*, 1977.

NONFICTION: *On English Poetry*, 1922; *The Meaning of Dreams*, 1924; *Poetic Unreason and Other Studies*, 1925; *Contemporary Techniques of Poetry: A Political Analogy*, 1925; *Another Future of Poetry*, 1926; *Impenetrability: Or, The Proper Habit of English*, 1926; *The English Ballad: A Short Critical Survey*, 1927; *Lars Porsena: Or, The Future of Swearing and Improper Language*, 1927; *A Survey of Modernist Poetry*, 1927 (with Laura Riding); *Lawrence and the Arabs*, 1927 (also known as *Lawrence and the Arabian Adventure*, 1928); *A Pamphlet Against Anthologies*, 1928 (with Laura Riding, also known as *Against Anthologies*); *Mrs. Fisher: Or, The Future of Humour*, 1928; *Goodbye to All That: An Autobiography*, 1929; *T. E. Lawrence to His Biogra-*

pher Robert Graves, 1938; *The Long Week-End: A Social History of Great Britain, 1918-1938*, 1940 (with Alan Hodge); *The Reader over Your Shoulder: A Handbook for Writers of English Prose*, 1943 (with Alan Hodge); *The White Goddess: A Historical Grammar of Poetic Myth*, 1948; *The Common Asphodel: Collected Essays on Poetry, 1922-1949*, 1949; *Occupation: Writer*, 1950; *The Nazarene Gospel Restored*, 1953 (with Joshua Podro); *The Crowning Privilege: The Clark Lectures, 1954-1955*, 1955; *Adam's Rib and Other Anomalous Elements in the Hebrew Creation Myth: A New View*, 1955; *The Greek Myths*, 1955 (2 volumes); *Jesus in Rome: A Historical Conjecture*, 1957 (with Joshua Podro); *5 Pens in Hand*, 1958; *Greek Gods and Heroes*, 1960; *Oxford Addresses on Poetry*, 1962; *Nine Hundred Iron Chariots: The Twelfth Arthur Dehon Little Memorial Lecture*, 1963; *Hebrew Myths: The Book of Genesis*, 1964 (with Raphael Patai); *Majorca Observed*, 1965 (with Paul Hogarty); *Mammon and the Black Goddess*, 1965; *Poetic Craft and Principle*, 1967; *The Crane Bag and Other Disputed Subjects*, 1969; *On Poetry: Collected Talks and Essays*, 1969; *Difficult Questions, Easy Answers*, 1972.

CHILDREN'S LITERATURE: *The Big Green Book*, 1962; *The Siege and Fall of Troy*, 1962; *Two Wise Children*, 1966; *The Poor Boy Who Followed His Star*, 1968.

TRANSLATIONS: *Almost Forgotten Germany*, 1936 (by Georg Schwarz, trans. with Laura Riding); *The Transformation of Lucius, Otherwise Known as "The Golden Ass,"* 1950 (by Lucius Apuleius); *The Cross and the Sword*, 1954 (by Manuel de Jesús Galván); *Pharsalia: Dramatic Episodes of the Civil Wars*, 1956 (by Lucan); *Winter in Majorca*, 1956 (by George Sand); *The Twelve Ceasars*, 1957 (by Suetonius); *The Anger of Achilles: Homer's "Iliad,"* 1959; *The Rubáiyát of Omar Khayyám*, 1967.

EDITED TEXTS: *Oxford Poetry: 1921*, 1921 (edited with Alan Porter and Richard Hughes); *John Skelton: Laureate*, 1927; *The Less Familiar Nursery Rhymes*, 1927; *The Comedies of Terence*, 1962; *English and Scottish Ballads*, 1975.

MISCELLANEOUS: *Steps: Stories, Talks, Essays, Poems, Studies in History*, 1958; *Food for Centaurs: Stories, Talks, Critical Studies, Poems*, 1960; *Selected Poetry and Prose*, 1961.

Bibliography

Canary, Robert H. *Robert Graves.* Boston: Twayne, 1980. A good general introduction to Graves's work. Emphasizes Graves the poet, but also contains helpful information on his novels and literary criticism. Includes a chronology, notes, a selected bibliography, and an index.

Day, Douglas. *Swifter than Reason: The Poetry and Criticism of Robert Graves.* Chapel Hill: University of North Carolina Press, 1963. The first full-length study of Graves's poetry and criticism. Graves's work is examined chronologically in four major phases, concluding with his emerging concept of the "White Goddess." Includes a bibliography, secondary reading materials, and an index.

Keane, Patrick J. *A Wild Civility: Interactions in the Poetry and Thought of Robert Graves.* Columbia: University of Missouri Press, 1980. Critical and opinionated examination of Graves with preference for his early poems. Rambling discourse with emphasis placed on Graves's art, personality, and his poetic balance of precision and passion.

Seymour-Smith, Martin. *Robert Graves: His Life and Works.* New York: Paragon House, 1988. Intimate, fascinating glimpse of Graves the man. Seymour-Smith had known Graves since 1943 and has written extensively on him since 1956. An excellent introduction to Graves's remarkable life and literary career.

Snipes, Katherine. *Robert Graves.* New York: Frederick Ungar, 1979. A good introduction to Graves's general work. Devotes a number of chapters to his novels alone. Includes a chronology, an extensive bibliography, and notes.

HENRY GREEN
Henry Vincent Yorke

Born: Forthampton Court, England; October 29, 1905
Died: London, England; December 13, 1973

Principal long fiction
Blindness, 1926; *Living*, 1929; *Party Going*, 1939; *Caught*, 1943; *Loving*, 1945; *Back*, 1946; *Concluding*, 1948; *Nothing*, 1950; *Doting*, 1952.

Other literary forms
In addition to his novels, Henry Green published an autobiographical book, *Pack My Bag: A Self-Portrait* (1940), and several accounts of his World War II firefighting experiences: "A Rescue," "Mr. Jonas," and "Firefighting." Green's theories regarding writing are expressed in *Pack My Bag* and in his essays "The English Novel of the Future" and "A Novelist to His Readers," which can be found in *Contact* (1950) and *The Listener* (1950, 1951). From time to time, Green wrote book reviews on topics which interested him and personal essays ranging in subject from his friend and editor Edward Garnett to public school life in 1914.

Achievements
For a man who managed both business and literary careers, Green's achievements are remarkable. *Blindness*, published in 1926 when Green was twenty-one, announced the arrival of a novelist whose artistic poise was illustrated through narrative daring and an unusual sense of characterization. Successive novels continued to impress critics and reviewers, though some either misunderstood or disliked Green's highly individual technique. "Prose," Green stated in *Pack My Bag*, "should be a long intimacy between strangers with no direct appeal to what both may have known." He continued by writing that this intimacy should build slowly and encompass unexpressed feelings which "are not bounded by the associations common to place names or to persons with whom the reader is unexpectedly familiar." Friends and fellow writers such as Edward Garnett, V. S. Pritchett, W. H. Auden, Evelyn Waugh, Christopher Isherwood, and John Lehman recognized Green's talent. Several have published articles on his work. Although Green is less widely known in the United States, Terry Southern, Eudora Welty, and John Updike have paid homage to him in interviews and articles. As critical theory has developed to encompass precisely those narrative strategies articulated by Green in 1939, it seems likely that his literary stature, already assured, will increase.

Biography
Henry Green was born Henry Vincent Yorke at Forthampton Court, near

Tewkesbury, Gloucestershire, England, on October 29, 1905. He was the third son of a wealthy Midlands industrialist whose business concern, H. Pontifex and Sons, Green was later to manage. Like others of his social class, Green was sent away to school when he was quite young, in his case before he was seven. At twelve, he went to Eton and from there to Oxford, where he studied with C. S. Lewis.

While at Eton, Green began writing *Blindness*, whose self-conscious, awkward, dilettantish, yet introspective protagonist, John Haye, is a self-portrait. Like Haye, Green was a member of an art society, an avid reader, a self-styled aesthete. By the time he arrived at Oxford, however, already somewhat of a celebrity because *Blindness* was about to be published, Green was beginning to question his privileged position and his right to an inherited fortune. This dilemma led him to leave Oxford at the end of his second year without taking a degree. As he reports in *Pack My Bag*, he went to Birmingham "to work in a factory with my wet podgy hands." Far from feeling superior to the laboring class, Green found these working people full of life and humor. His experiences among them inspired *Living*, published in 1929.

That same year, Green married Mary Adelaide Biddulph, with whom he had a son, Sebastian, born in 1934. From 1931 to 1938, Green continued to build his business career and wrote *Party Going*, a reflection of his London social circle. War rumblings in 1939 moved Green to join the Auxiliary Fire Service, in which he served during World War II. The war years proved to be productive for Green; not only did he write *Pack My Bag*, a sort of autobiography published in 1940, but also three unique war novels: *Caught*, *Loving*, and *Back*.

The war's conclusion returned Green to the directorship of his business and a busy decade of writing (during his lunch hour and after dinner every night). In the 1950's, Green began refining his theories of communication and art, which he published in essay form, delivered in a series of British Broadcasting Corporation (BBC) broadcasts, and restated in three interviews. While on a cruise to South Africa in 1958, Green decided to retire from business.

No one has been able to account for Green's almost total silence for the remainder of his life. Until his death on December 13, 1973, he published only "An Unfinished Novel" and "Firefighting." His sequel to *Pack My Bag* remains unfinished. With increasing deafness, Green withdrew more and more into the privacy of his home and family, leaving behind a literary legacy rich in its suggestiveness.

Analysis

The ambiguous nature of Henry Green's fiction has long piqued and captivated the attention of readers and critics alike, for his individual departures from conventional narrative technique separate him from the literary mainstream. A successful businessman independent of popular success, Green felt free to experiment with the form and theory of the novel. His novels speak directly to the reader with minimal interruption or interpretation; taking on lives of their own, they maintain their own shifting realities and sustain an uncanny sense of the present.

Evident in his novels as early as *Blindness* are characteristics that Green was to polish throughout his writing career: close attention to balance and symmetry, objectivity in character presentation, action developed through juxtaposed scenes, and remarkable re-creation of spoken English interspersed with lyrical descriptive passages. His singular treatment was given to classical themes. Fascinated by language and the human capacity to interpret, Green dramatized the problems of communication by having his characters misunderstand one another. He further complicated these problems of understanding by creating intentional verbal ambiguity, so that the reader might also be uncertain of the speaker's intent. Often talking at cross purposes, Green's characters, prompted by loneliness, search for love. Although their love objects may at times seem strange, ranging as they do from peacocks and a pig to houses and fantasies, they nevertheless reflect the range of human passion. In an atmosphere suggestive of social dissolution, Green's characters pursue the relative stability of love, which they often discover in unsuspected places.

Most of Green's solipsistic characters are neither intelligent, gifted, nor particularly beautiful. Often vain and fanciful, they reveal themselves to be profoundly human as they engage in conversations revelatory of their own preoccupations. Fascinated by what people communicate through both speech and evasion, Green sought to make dialogue the vehicle for his novels, refining his conversation and decreasing his descriptive passages until, in his last two novels, dialogue carries almost the entire weight. To avoid the static quality of conversation, he created brief scenes, shifting his reader's attention from one group of characters to another. His technique also produces an acute sense of the present, a sense emphasized by the "ing" ending of his novels' titles.

That Green's novels create their own sense of the present is only one of several important factors to be considered when reading his fiction. Above all, Green wanted his work to assume a life of its own, a life differing according to the reader, providing each one with a sense of connection until he or she is drawn into a "community of people." Green accomplishes this primarily by suggesting rather than stating. Time and place, motivation and reaction, action and resolution are often evoked rather than delineated. Behind the slight plots and often silly activities is an unstated social context which tacitly influences action. Green's characters are also created through indirection. By allowing them to inarticulately express their obsessions, fears, anxieties, or confusion, by having them avoid direct responses, by refusing to make authorial judgments, Green populates his novels with lifelike creations. Their humanness is mutely expressed in their search for love. Examining *Blindness*,

Loving, and *Nothing* with these ideas in mind, the reader can begin to understand Henry Green's elusive art.

When Green had a family friend read the manuscript of *Blindness*, he did not receive much praise. He was, however, encouraged to show his work to Edward Garnett, then a publisher's reader, who gave Green sound advice concerning narrative technique and character development. The result is a first novel remarkable primarily for its close attention to structure and its multidimensional characters. While taking a usual avenue for a first novel, Green proceeded to treat his subject with daring. His protagonist, John Haye, a sensitive upper-middle-class schoolboy who aspires to be a writer, is blinded in a freak accident. During the course of the novel, John comes to new terms with himself and his world, awakening in the end to a fresh appreciation of life.

With the theme of growth in mind, Green divided *Blindness* into three sections—"Caterpillar," "Chrysalis," and "Butterfly"—suggesting John's psychological metamorphosis. "Caterpillar," presented as John's diary, reflects his physical response to natural beauty, his passion for literature, and his concentrated ambition to write. Because he derives intense pleasure from visual stimuli, John's blindness seems especially cruel. In "Chrysalis," he reconsiders himself. Lying dormant in layers of a protective cocoon—his bandages, his blindness, his fantasies and self-pity, his stepmother's pity and worry, the physical safety of his inherited estate—John's creative life is threatened until he determines to break free of this smothering safety. He emerges in "Butterfly," scarred but acutely aware of the value of life.

The narrative passages of *Blindness* are lush, as exuberant as John's imagination, as soaring as his emotions. Echoing with poetic resonance, Green's descriptive passages in *Blindness* far outweigh the oblique dialogue. Nevertheless, there are signs of Green's later mastery of dialogue: speech patterns are distinct for each character. The language is spare, with internal monologues reflective of individual character. John's thoughts are full of wonder and pain, his stepmother's are busy with seemingly dissociated concerns. Both characters' thoughts, however, circuitously return to one subject: blindness. Where Green introduces rich visual images through John's eyes in the first portion of the novel, he later confines John's responses to those of touch and sound. Indeed, the novel ends in a cacophony of bells and traffic noises, affirming John's rebirth.

Green seems precocious in his handling of the symbolic value of blindness. This he does by indirectly comparing John's blindness with various metaphorical failures of vision. Mrs. Haye, John's horsey stepmother, is "blind" in a number of respects, lacking all aesthetic response and being completely unintellectual. Two other figures are also introduced to indicate forms of moral blindness: Joan Entwhistle and her father, an unfrocked minister. They epitomize the destructiveness of self-deception, a potential trap awaiting John.

Joan, a dirty, dreamy girl who vacillates between romanticizing her situation and luxuriating in its squalor, becomes an unlikely love interest for John, who re-creates her in his imagination and renames her June. Worse still is Joan's father, who wallows in gin and self-pity. Like John, he thinks of himself as a writer, but his only creation is his disastrous life. Ultimately, Reverend Entwhistle has entered a darkness far more profound than John's.

While blindness carries much of the novel's symbolic weight, other images are also alluded to by Green, images that continue to reappear throughout his career, often assuming symbolic value. References to birds, birds' songs, and patterns of birds' flights recur throughout his novels. In *Blindness*, birds provide an oblique comment on human situations. Flowers, particularly roses, are also recurring images in Green's fiction. Their value varying according to the novel, they generally connote love.

While the language and images of *Blindness* are vivid and memorable, it is the characters who are the novel's main strength. Green's impressive talent has created four main characters whose distinct speech and thought patterns and conflicting desires he has woven into a narrative tapestry with perspective, texture, density, and dimension. Arranged in contrasting couples—John and Mrs. Haye, Joan and Reverend Entwhistle—Green plays his characters against one another, in pairs and individually, using this arrangement to illustrate mutual misunderstandings. John and Joan, who have much in common, are first drawn together and then move apart. For purely selfish reasons, each tries to impose a fantasy on the other. John imaginatively re-creates Joan, raising her from a lowly social position. Joan, in turn, sees John as a means of escape, though in the end she prefers her fantasy to reality.

Mrs. Haye and the Reverend Entwhistle are also contrasting figures. The minister, capable of the kind of aesthetic response that John admires, has, however, succumbed to self-delusion. Significantly, the Reverend Entwhistle has scarred Joan. Mrs. Haye, on the other hand, wants to protect John. As guardian of his estate (Barwood), she sees it as her duty to manage his inheritance. When John rejects Barwood, indicating a changing social order, Mrs. Haye reluctantly supports the decision although this means abandoning a comfortable home and secure social role. Rough and tweedy, Mrs. Haye is a triumph of characterization as she awkwardly assumes a maternal role for which she is unfit. She is spared from caricature by Green's ability to portray her confused, rambling feelings through indirection.

Through three successive novels, Green continued to experiment with narrative technique and character development. In *Loving*, he achieved a balance that has continued to impress readers and critics. Skillfully arranging themes, images, symbols, and characters in the form of a fairy tale and placing them in neutral Ireland during the London Blitz, Green created what is considered to be his finest novel.

His setting, "the most celebrated eighteenth-century folly in Eire that had still to be burned down," is ideal for bringing together upper and lower classes and for elaborating favorite themes. Social dissolution, the search for love, and the inability to communicate are intensified by the distant war, which threatens and thus influences all of the characters. Most discomforting is the fact that the social order seems to have collapsed. From Raunce the footman's bold takeover of the butler's position to the mingling of the cook's nephew with the owner's granddaughters, the reader is presented with evidence of accelerating social change. Indeed, real power has gravitated to the servants, whose departure would mean disaster for the house and its owners, significantly named Tennant. Far from thinking of leaving, however, most of the servants are intent on pursuing their respective passions, all of which are forms of loving.

Green pays careful attention to balance, transition, and symbol in *Loving* as he encircles the lives of his characters. Beginning and ending with a love moan, having as its center a lost ring, and moving its main characters, Edith and Raunce, in a circular direction, this novel revolves around various love relationships. Thus, *Loving* is rich in extravagant description; only in *Concluding* does Green's language achieve equal visual opulence. The color and detail that Green accords his gilded setting underscores its anachronistic existence and lends a sense of high comedy to the human activities taking place. Suggestive images recur throughout the novel, serving as transitional devices and assuming symbolic power. This is especially true of the peacocks and doves which stride and flutter through the action, symbolizing pride and love.

Dialogue in *Loving* is as important as narrative description, with Green seeming at times to be showing off his celebrated ability to create colloquial language. Each of the servants has a particualr speech pattern, so peculiar that understanding can be a problem between them. Paddy, the single Irishman employed by the Tennants, speaks so unintelligibly that only Kate, who loves him, can understand what he says. Raunce, who acts as mediator between the servants and the Tennants, uses two different languages. Of course, the Tennants speak in the cultured tones of their class. Not surprisingly, Mrs. Tennant cannot understand what her servants are saying. Indeed, one of the high comic scenes of the novel occurs when she attempts to converse with her cook, who carries on about drains while Mrs. Tennant interrogates her about a ring.

The characters of *Loving* are to a large extent created by their language. Raunce is finely drawn, a complex of contradictory, even mysterious habits. He is a transparent manipulator who rudely asserts his authority over the other servants, and he is, apparently, a dutiful son who faithfully writes to his mother and sends money. A petty thief and would-be blackmailer, Raunce eventually becomes a father figure for a young servant and Edith's trembling lover. While Edith lacks the many facets of Raunce, she is fully realized as the most loving and beloved character in this novel. A dreamy girl believing in the power of love potions, she sheds her fantasies in favor of practical possibilities. Even minor characters achieve distinction in this novel; through wonderfully individualized conversations, Green dramatizes the manifold nature of loving.

Although he had consistently accorded dialogue a prominent role in all of his novels, Green came to believe that pure dialogue, with minimal authorial direction, would constitute the novel of the future. Accordingly, he wrote *Nothing* and *Doting*, which, while bearing familiar Green themes and characters, progress almost entirely through conversation. Again, the unelaborated social background is an important influence. In fact, it may have as much significance in *Nothing* as any other narrative component.

While *Nothing* seems to be about very little, involving as it does a love chase among selfish people, it nevertheless implies a great deal. To ignore the subtext of this novel is to miss Green's point, for although he might not have used the term, *Nothing* can be seen as a phenomenological novel, with subjective judgments excluded in order to show reality as it is. Revealed is a protean shield of manners concealing a moral vacuum, the ultimate hollowness of polite society. Green, however, withholds judgment even as he lends a comic ambience to his characters. Thus, whatever judgment is accorded to the themes and characters of this novel will be imposed only by the reader.

The themes of *Nothing* are on a continuum with those of *Blindness*. The social erosion marked by John Haye's departure from his estate is now complete in the almost classless society of the welfare state. Little remains of the upper-middle-class characters' inheritance except memory and the children of this once privileged class consider themselves lucky to have dull civil service jobs. Aware of the passing of time, Green's characters turn to one another. The result is a comedy of manners involving six characters—John Pomfret and his daughter Mary; Jane Weatherby and her son Philip; Liz Jennings, John's mistress; and Dick Abbot, Jane's escort—which provides an opportunity for Green to demonstrate his ability to write ambiguously frothy conversation which reveals the intellectual and emotional shallowness of his characters and the absurdity of their lives.

At the heart of this novel is Jane Weatherby, one of Green's most effective creations, who, having determined to marry John Pomfret, skillfully arranges the lives of other people in order to achieve her ends. A study in calculating graciousness, Jane manages to retain the admiration of friends and verbally dispatch her enemies in the same breath. Though her methods are suspect, they remain undetectable, her intent double-edged. Consequently, Jane wins her man, a prize of dubious value and yet one wholly satisfying to her. The ironic justice of these two characters winding up with each other is not lost on the reader.

While *Nothing* was not Green's last novel, it can be read as a final statement, for he extends his theory of the novel to its logical conclusion. This work exemplifies what Green called the "nonrepresentational novel," a novel "which can live in people who are alive" and "which can die." More than its predecesors, *Nothing* demands the conscious collaboration of its readers. Even with active participation in the novel's present, ambiguities abound. This is just as Green would have wished, because he wanted his novels to evoke a sense of life's texture, a texture he felt was fluctuating constantly. *Nothing*'s moral ambiguity, often cited as its principal flaw, is a significant part of this texture. Creating as it does a palpable sense of life's mutability, *Nothing* perfectly embodies Henry Green's oblique, distinctive approach to the art of fiction.

Karen Carmean

Other major work
NONFICTION: *Pack My Bag: A Self-Portrait*, 1940.

Bibliography
Bassoff, Bruce. *Toward Loving: The Poetics of the Novel and the Practice of Henry Green.* Columbia: University of South Carolina Press, 1975. This lengthy study offers a complex, important discussion of Green's theory of "non-representational fiction." His sparse prose, reaching its epitome in *Loving*, requires a reader to participate imaginatively in the creation of the fiction. Green's novels show how a postmodernist fiction writer avoids the evaluative, determining narrator at the center of realistic fiction.
Holmesland, Oddvar. *A Critical Introduction to Henry Green's Novels.* New York: St. Martin's Press, 1985. Defines Green's originality by stressing the similarity of his "dynamic visualization and the effect of film." The author studies the novels individually and chronologically to show Green's creation of verbal montages that reveal life's multiplicity and complexity. The "living vision" is Green's pastoral ideal of a spiritually aware person living in simple communion with the natural environment.
Mengham, Rod. *The Idiom of Time: The Writings of Henry Green.* New York: Cambridge University Press, 1982. Studies Green's novelistic development from his first novel in 1926, heavily influenced by Gertrude Stein, through his unfinished novel in 1959, which made him stop writing in fear that he was repeating himself. The author finds Green's sparse, evocative style marks him as a writer of the 1930's and 1940's but that universal themes of life and death link him to timeless writers such as Sophocles and William Shakespeare.
North, Michael. *Henry Green and the Writing of His Generation.* Charlottesville: University of Virginia Press, 1984. Explores the personal and thematic links between Green and his major literary contemporaries: Evelyn Waugh, Anthony Powell, Stephen Spender, and Christopher Isherwood.

The most important tie is a sense of alienation engendered by strong political ideologies such as Fascism and Communism. These writers explore the problem of asserting the identity of the individual self in a hostile social environment.

Odom, Keith C. *Henry Green.* Boston: Twayne, 1978. Provides a useful biographical-critical study for the beginning student. After introductions to Green's life, fictional theory, and characteristic style, offers a leisurely, insightful reading of each novel, concluding with an unpretentious estimate of his importance and influence.

Russell, John. *Henry Green: Nine Novels and an Unpacked Bag.* New Brunswick, N.J.: Rutgers University Press, 1960. An enthusiastic study of Green. Offers numerous examples of Green's stylistic puzzles, poetry, enigmas, and sleights-of-hand, paying special attention to his autobiography as a source of Green's philosophy of art and life. Though Green's vision is essentially pessimistic, Russell argues that his literary artistry offers the compensating pleasure of intellectual challenge.

Ryf, Robert. *Henry Green.* New York: Columbia University Press, 1967. This brief, energetic introduction to Green's novels reads them in chronological order to trace out his diagnosis of modern society's spiritual and moral ills. His characters continually find life an enigma, a walk along fog-shrouded paths where premonitions must suffice. The novels' techniques of ambiguity (elusive plotting, shifting narrative voice, impressionistic language) reflect the characters' plight of searching for meaning without a map to guide them.

Stokes, Edward. *The Novels of Henry Green.* New York: Macmillan, 1959. Makes a case that Green is an important twentieth century novelist whose works offer a transcendent yet objective view of life and whose prose increasingly displays a poet's attention to language. Concludes with high praise: Green's prose is as original, effective, and influential among British writers as William Faulkner's prose is among American writers. Organized by topics rather than by novels.

GRAHAM GREENE

Born: Berkhamsted, England; October 2, 1904
Died: Vevey, Switzerland; April 3, 1991

Principal long fiction

The Man Within, 1929; *The Name of Action*, 1930; *Rumour at Nightfall*, 1931; *Stamboul Train: An Entertainment*, 1932 (published in the United States as *Orient Express: An Entertainment*, 1933); *It's a Battlefield*, 1934; *England Made Me*, 1935; *A Gun for Sale: An Entertainment*, 1936 (published in the United States as *This Gun for Hire: An Entertainment*); *Brighton Rock*, 1938; *The Confidential Agent*, 1939; *The Power and the Glory*, 1940 (reissued as *The Labyrinthine Ways*); *The Ministry of Fear: An Entertainment*, 1943; *The Heart of the Matter*, 1948; *The Third Man: An Entertainment*, 1950; *The Third Man and The Fallen Idol*, 1950; *The End of the Affair*, 1951; *Loser Takes All: An Entertainment*, 1955; *The Quiet American*, 1955; *Our Man in Havana: An Entertainment*, 1958; *A Burnt-Out Case*, 1961; *The Comedians*, 1966; *Travels with My Aunt*, 1969; *The Honorary Consul*, 1973; *The Human Factor*, 1978; *Dr. Fischer of Geneva: Or, The Bomb Party*, 1980; *Monsignor Quixote*, 1982; *The Tenth Man*, 1985.

Other literary forms

In addition to his novels, Graham Greene published many collections of short stories, including *The Basement Room and Other Stories* (1935); *Nineteen Stories* (1947); *Twenty-one Stories* (1954), in which two stories from the previous collection were dropped and four added; *A Sense of Reality* (1963); *May We Borrow Your Husband? and Other Comedies of the Sexual Life* (1967); and *Collected Stories* (1972). He also wrote five plays: *The Living Room* (1953), *The Potting Shed* (1957), *The Complaisant Lover* (1959), *Carving a Statue* (1964), and *The Return of A. J. Raffles: An Edwardian Comedy in Three Acts* (1975). With the exception of his first published book, *Babbling April: Poems* (1925), he did not publish poetry except in two private printings, *After Two Years* (1949) and *For Christmas* (1950). He wrote some interesting travel books, two focusing on Africa, *Journey Without Maps: A Travel Book* (1936) and *In Search of a Character: Two African Journals* (1961), and one set in Mexico, *The Lawless Roads: A Mexican Journal* (1939). He published several books of essays and criticism, including *British Dramatists* (1942); *The Pleasure-Dome: Graham Greene on Film; Collected Film Criticism, 1935-40* (1972), edited by John Russell Taylor; *The Lost Childhood and Other Essays* (1951); *Essais Catholiques* (1953); and *Collected Essays* (1969). He also wrote a biography, *Lord Rochester's Monkey: Being the Life of John Wilmot, Second Earl of Rochester* (1974), and two autobiographical works, *A Sort of Life* (1971), carrying the reader up to Greene's first novel, and *Ways of Escape* (1980), bringing the reader up to the time of its writing. A biographical-autobiographical work, *Getting to Know the General: The Story of an Involvement* (1984), spotlights Greene's relationship with General Omar Torrijos of Panama. Finally, he also wrote four children's books: *The Little Train* (1946), *The Little Fire Engine* (1950), *The Little Horse Bus* (1952), and *The Little Steam Roller: A Story of Mystery and Detection* (1953).

Achievements

Though Greene wrote in so many genres, the novel is the form upon which his reputation will rest. His strengths in the genre are many. Like all novelists who are more than journeymen, he returns throughout his oeuvre to certain recurring themes. Another strength is his gift for playing the devil's advocate, the dynamics that occur when his character finds himself divided between loyalties. In Greene's first novel, *The Man Within*, that division was handled crudely, externalized in a boy's attraction to two different women; in later novels, the struggle is internalized. Sarah Miles of *The End of the Affair* is torn between her loyalty to God and her loyalty to her lover. Fowler of *The Quiet American* cannot decide whether he wants to eliminate Pyle for the good of Vietnam or to get his woman back from a rival. The characters are shaded in, rendered complex by internal division.

Greene's style has often been singled out for praise. He learned economy and precision while with *The Times* in London. More than anything else, he struggled for precision, "truth" as he called it, in form as well as in substance. Additionally, his experience as a film reviewer seems to have given him a feel for cinematic technique.

Because he was a remarkable self-critic, Greene overcame most of his early weaknesses. He corrected an early tendency to distrust autobiographical material, and he seemed to overcome his difficulty in portraying credible women. In his first twenty-four years as a novelist, he depicted perhaps only two or three complex women: Kate Farrant of *England Made Me*, Sarah Miles of *The End of the Affair*, and possibly Ida Arnold of *Brighton Rock*. His later novels and plays, however, feature a host of well-drawn women, certainly the best of whom is Aunt Augusta of *Travels with My Aunt*. If there is one weakness that mars some of Graham Greene's later novels, it is their prolixity. Too often in his late fiction, characters are merely mouthpieces for ideas.

What Greene's reputation will be a century hence is difficult to predict. Readers will certainly find in him more than a religious writer, more—at least—than a Catholic writer. They will find in him a writer who used for his thematic vehicles all the pressing issues of an era: the Vietnam War; Papa Doc Duvalier's tyranny over Haiti; the struggle between Communism and capitalism; apartheid in South Africa; poverty and oppression in Latin America. Will these issues seem too topical for posterity, or will they prove again that only by localizing one's story in the specifics of a time and place can one appeal to readers of another time, another place?

Biography

Graham Greene was born on October 2, 1904, in the town of Berkhamsted. The fourth of six children, he was not especially close to his father, perhaps because of his father's position as headmaster of Berkhamsted School, which Greene attended. Some of the boys took sadistic delight in his ambiguous position, and two in particular caused him such humiliation that they created in him an excessive desire to prove himself. Without them, he claimed, he might never have written a book.

Greene made several attempts at suicide during these unhappy years; he later insisted these were efforts to avoid boredom rather than to kill himself. At Oxford, he tried for a while to avoid boredom by getting intoxicated each day of an entire semester.

During these Oxford days, Greene met Vivien Dayrell-Browning, a young Catholic woman who had written to him of his error in a film review in referring to Catholic "worship" of the Virgin Mary. He inquired into the "subtle" and "unbelievable theology" out of interest in Vivien and concluded by becoming a Catholic in 1926. Greene married Vivien, and the couple had two children, a boy and a girl. He separated from his parents' family after the wedding and was scrupulous about guarding his own family's privacy.

In 1926, Greene moved from his first, unsalaried, position writing for the Nottingham *Journal* to the position of subeditor for *The Times* in London. There, he learned writing technique, pruning the clichés of reporters and condensing their stories without loss of meaning or effect. Moreover, he had mornings free to do his own writing. When, in 1928. Heinemann accepted Greene's first novel, *The Man Within*, for publication, Greene rashly quit *The Times* to make his living as a writer.

Greene's next two novels, *The Name of Action* and *Rumour at Nightfall*, failed, and he later suppressed them. Still, in trying to understand what went wrong with these works, he discovered that he had tried to omit the autobiographical entirely; as a result, the novels lacked life and truth. He would not make that mistake again.

In 1934, Greene took the first of a seemingly endless series of trips to other parts of the world. With his cousin Barbara, he walked without maps across the heart of Liberia. Recorded in his *Journey Without Maps*, this hazardous venture became a turning point in his life. He had once thought death desirable; in the desert, he became a passionate lover of life. He came even to accept the rats in his hut as part of life. Perhaps more important for his writing, he discovered in Liberia the archetypal basis for his earliest nightmares. The frightening creatures of those dreams were not originally evil beings but rather devils in the African sense of beings who control power.

Mankind, Greene came to believe, has corrupted these primitive realities and denied its inherited sense of supernatural evil, reducing it to the level of merely human evil. To do so is to forget "the finer taste, the finer pleasure, the finer terror on which we might have built." Greene had found the basis for themes that persistently made their way into his novels.

Greene began his great fiction with *Brighton Rock*, the publication of which, in 1938, followed a trip to Mexico that delighted him much less than the one to Africa. Nevertheless, his observations in Mexico provided the substance of what many consider his finest achievement, *The Power and the Glory*. For the reader interested in a genuine insight into the way Greene moves from fact to fiction, the travel book that emerged from the Mexican journey, *The Lawless Roads*, is very rewarding, showing for example how his fictional whiskey priest was an amalgam of four real-life priests.

With the outbreak of World War II, Greene was assigned to the Secret Intelligence Service, or MI6, as it was then called. The experience—including his work for the notorious spy, Kim Philby—gave him the material for several later works, including *Our Man in Havana* and *The Human Factor*, and nurtured in him that "virtue of disloyalty" which informs his novels.

Greene ceased his writing of explicitly religious novels with *The End of the Affair* in 1951 when people began to treat him as a guru. Although his novels continued to treat religious concerns, none—with the possible exception of *A Burnt-Out Case* in 1960—was a religious problem novel. Increasingly, Greene turned to political concern in novels such as *The Quiet American* and *The Comedians*, but these political concerns transcend the topical and speak more enduringly of human involvement.

In his later years, Greene slowed his production somewhat. He continued, however, to write two hundred words every morning, then corrected in great detail in the evening. His practice was to dictate his corrected manuscript into a tape recorder and send the tapes from his home in Antibes, on the French Riviera, to England, where they were typed and then returned. Greene also continued to indulge his taste for travel: He visited Fidel Castro in Cuba, Omar Torrijos in Panama, and Ho Chi Minh in Vietnam. A full catalog of his travels would be virtually endless. Despite the reductive label critics have applied to his settings—"Greeneland"—Greene's novels have more varied settings than those of almost any other novelist, and his settings are authentic. Greene died on April 3, 1991, at the age of eighty-six.

Analysis

In an address he called the "Virtue of Disloyalty," which he delivered at the University of Hamburg in 1969, Graham Greene contended that a writer is driven "to be a protestant in a Catholic society, a catholic in a Protestant one," or to be a Communist in a capitalist society and a capitalist in a Communist one. While loyalty confines one to accepted opinions, "disloyalty gives the novelist an extra dimension of understanding."

Whatever the reader may think of Greene's theory, it is helpful in explaining most of his own novels. From *The Man Within* in 1929, which justified a suicide in the face of Catholic morality's abhorrence for such an act, to *The Human Factor*, fifty years later, which comes close to justifying treason, Greene practiced this "virtue of disloyalty."

Most of Greene's obsessions originated in his childhood. Where did the desire to be "disloyal," to play devil's advocate arise? Certainly his serving in MI6 under the authority of Kim Philby was a factor. Greene admired the man in every way except for what appeared to be a personal drive for power. It was this characteristic of Philby that caused Greene finally to resign rather than accept a promotion and become part of Philby's intrigue. Yet Greene later came to see that the man served not himself but a cause, and all his former admiration of Philby returned. Greene continued his friendship even after Philby's treason. As he saw it, Philby had found a faith in Communism, and he would not junk it because it had been abused by Joseph Stalin any more than Catholics would junk a faith that had been abused by the Inquisitors or the Roman Curia.

Clearly, however, Greene's "disloyalty" or sympathy for the rebel did not originate here. It too must be traced to his childhood, to his isolation at school, where neither the students nor his headmaster father could treat him unambiguously; it can be traced also to his love of Robert Browning, who very early instilled in him an interest in the "dangerous edge of things," in "the honest thief, the tender murderer." It was an influence more lasting, Greene said, than any religious teaching. Religiously, though, Greene's fierce independence manifested itself when, upon conversion to Catholicism, he took the name Thomas, not after the Angelic doctor but after the doubter.

Brighton Rock was the first of Greene's novels to treat an explicitly religious theme. Moreover, in attempting to play devil's advocate for *Brighton Rock*'s protagonist, Pinkie, the author had chosen one of his most challenging tasks. He made this Catholic protagonist more vicious than he was to make any character in his entire canon, yet Greene demonstrated that Catholic moral law could not condemn Pinkie, could not finally know "the appalling strangeness of the mercy of God."

Pinkie takes over a protection-racket gang from his predecessor, Kite, and must immediately avenge Kite's murder by killing Fred Hale. This murder inspires him to commit a series of other murders necessary to cover his tracks. It also leads to Pinkie's marrying Rose, a potential witness against him, and finally to his attempt to induce Rose to commit suicide. When the police intervene, Pinkie takes his own life.

Vicious as he is, with his sadistic razor slashings, his murders to cover murders, and his cruelty to Rose, Pinkie's guilt is nevertheless extenuated, his amorality rendered somewhat understandable. Pinkie's conscience had not awakened because his imagination had not awakened: "The word murder conveyed no more to him than the word 'box,' 'collar,' 'giraffe'. . . . The imagination hadn't awoken. That was his strength. He couldn't see through other people's eyes, or feel with their nerves."

As with so many of Greene's characters, the explanation for Pinkie's self-destructive character lies in his lost childhood: "In the lost boyhood of Judas, Christ was betrayed." In a parody of William Wordsworth's "Ode: Intimations of Immortality," Greene said that Pinkie came into the world trailing something other than heavenly clouds of his own glory after him: "Hell lay about him in his infancy." Though Wordsworth might write of the archetypal child that "heaven lay about him in his infancy," Greene saw Pinkie in quite different terms: "Heaven was a word: hell was something he could trust." Pinkie's vivid memory of his father and mother having sexual intercourse in his presence has turned him from all pleasures of the flesh, tempting him for a while with thoughts of the celibate priesthood.

When Pinkie is seventeen, Kite becomes a surrogate father to him. Pinkie's lack of conscience, his unconcern for himself, his sadomasochistic tendencies, which early showed themselves as a substitute or thwarted sexual impulses, stand the youth in good stead for a new vocation that requires unflinching loyalty, razor slashings, and, if necessary, murder. His corruption is almost guaranteed. To say this is not to reduce the novel from a theological level to a sociological one on which environment has determined the boy's character. Rose survives somewhat the same circumstances. Pinkie's guilt is extenuated, never excused.

Pinkie, however, is not the only character in the novel on whose behalf Greene invoked his "virtue of disloyalty." Rose is a prefiguration of the unorthodox "saint" that Greene developed more subtly in his later novels, in the Mexican priest of *The Power and the Glory*, in Sarah Miles of *The End of the Affair*, and to some extent in Scobie of *The Heart of the Matter*. Like Scobie, Rose wills her damnation out of love. She is not so well drawn as Scobie, at times making her naïve goodness less credible than his, but she is motivated by selfless concern for another. When she refuses to reject Pinkie and when she chooses to commit suicide, Rose wants an afterlife with Pinkie. She would rather be damned with him than see him damned alone: Rose will show "them they couldn't pick and choose." This seems unconvincing, until one hears the old priest cite the actual case of Charles Peguy, who would rather have died in a state of sin than have believed that a single soul was damned. In her confession to the old priest, Rose learns of God's mercy and also of the "saintly" Peguy, who, like Rose, preferred to be damned rather than believing that another person had been.

One is asked, then, to be sympathetic both to a character who has willed her own damnation and to one who leads a life of thorough viciousness, to believe that the salvation of both is a real possibility. In asking for this sympathy, for this possibility, Greene is not doctrinaire. As an effective problem novelist, Greene makes no assertions, merely asks questions that enlarge one's understanding. Greene does not equate the Church with Rose's official moral teaching, suggesting that the old priest in this novel and Father Rank in *The Heart of the Matter* are as representative as the teachers of Rose and Pinkie. Still, the moral doctrine provided Greene with the material that he liked to stretch beyond its customary shape.

In *The Heart of the Matter*, Greene achieved the genuine tragedy that he came close to writing in many of his other novels. His protagonist, Major Scobie, is a virtuous man whose hamartia lies in an excess of pity. In Scobie, pity exceeds all bounds and becomes as vicious as Macbeth's ambition. His pity wrecks a marriage he had wanted to save, ruins a lover he had hoped to help, kills his closest friend—his "boy," Ali—and brings about his own moral corruption. Compared to Aristides the Just by one character and to the Old Testament's Daniel by another, Scobie becomes guilty of adultery, smuggling, treason, lies, sacrilege, and murder before he kills himself.

The latest edition of the novel restores to the story an early scene between the government spy, Wilson, and Louise Scobie. Greene had written it for the original, then withdrew it since he believed that, told as it was from Wilson's point of view, it broke Scobie's point of view prematurely. When this scene is restored, Louise is seen in a more sympathetic light, and one can no longer see Scobie as hunted to his death by Louise. Though the reader still likes Scobie and is tempted to exonerate him, it is difficult to read the restored text without seeing Scobie's excess of pity for what it is.

The novel's three final, anticlimactic scenes effectively serve to reduce the grandeur of Scobie's act of self sacrifice, showing the utter waste of his suicide and the fearful pride contained in his act. It is not that the final scenes make Scobie seem a lesser person. On the contrary, his wife and Helen are made to appear more unworthy of him: Louise with her unkind judgments about Scobie's taking money from Yusef when that very money was borrowed to send her to South Africa as she wanted; and Helen giving her body to Bagster immediately after Scobie's death. Nevertheless, the very criticism of these women makes Scobie's suicide more meaningless and even more effectively shows the arrogance of his action.

Scobie's suicide, then, is not meant to be seen as praiseworthy but rather as the result of a tragic flaw—pity. In this respect, it differs from Elizabeth's suicide in *The Man Within*. Still, though his suicide is presented as wrong, the final fault in a good man disintegrating spiritually, the reader is compelled to feel sympathy for Scobie. Louise's insistence on the Church's teaching that he has cut himself off from mercy annoys the reader. One is made to see Scobie through the eyes of Father Rank, who angrily responds to Louise that "the Church knows all the rules. But it doesn't know what goes on in a single human heart." In this novel's complex treatment of suicide, then, Greene does not use the "virtue of disloyalty" to justify Scobie's act, but rather "to comprehend sympathetically [a] dissident fellow."

The epigraph for *The Human Factor* is taken from Joseph Conrad: "I only know that he who forms a tie is lost. The germ of corruption has entered into his soul." Maurice Castle's soul is corrupted because a tie of gratitude exists between him and a Communist friend.

The Human Factor may, in part, have been suggested by Greene's friend and former superior in British Secret Intelligence, Kim Philby, although Greene had written 25,000 words of the novel before Philby's defection. When Philby wrote his story, *My Silent War* (1968), Greene put the novel aside for ten years. In any case, Greene anticipated the novel long before the Philby case in his 1930 story, "I Spy," in which a young boy watches his father being whisked off to Russia after the British have detected his spying.

The Human Factor was Greene's first espionage novel since *Our Man in Havana* in 1958. Greene's protagonist, Maurice Castle, works for the British Secret Service in London and has, the reader learns halfway through the novel, become a double agent. He has agreed to leak information to the Russians to help thwart "Uncle Remus," a plan devised by England, the United States, and South Africa to preserve apartheid, even to use nuclear weapons for the purpose if necessary. Castle has not become a Communist, will not support them in Europe, but owes a Communist friend a favor for helping his black wife, Sarah, escape from South Africa. Also, he owes his wife's people something better than apartheid.

Castle's spying is eventually discovered, and the Russians remove him from England. They try to make good their promise to have his wife and child follow, but British Secret Service makes it impossible for Sarah to take the boy when it learns that Sam is not Castle's boy, but the boy of an African who is still alive. The novel ends in bleak fashion when Maurice is permitted to phone from Moscow and learns that his family cannot come. He has escaped into a private prison.

The Human Factor exemplifies again the "virtue of disloyalty," but even more, it demonstrates that Greene does not merely flesh out a story to embody that disloyalty. Though he does everything to enlist the reader's sympathies for Castle, demonstrating his superiority to those for whom he works, Greene ultimately condemns his actions as he condemned Scobie's. As Scobie had been a victim of pity, Castle is a victim of gratitude. In chatting with his wife, Sarah, before she learns that he has been spying, Castle defends his gratitude, and his wife agrees it is a good thing "if it doesn't take you too far." Moreover, as Scobie had an excessive pity even as a boy, Maurice Castle had an exaggerated gratitude. At one point, he asks his mother whether he was a nervous child, and she tells him he always had an "exaggerated sense of gratitude for the least kindness." Once, she tells him, he gave away an expensive pen to a boy who had given him a chocolate bun. At novel's end, when Castle is isolated in Russia, Sarah asks him in a phone conversation how he is, and he recalls his mother's words about the fountain pen: "My mother wasn't far wrong." Like Scobie as well, Castle is the most appealing character in the book, and many a reader will think his defection justified.

The novels considered above are perhaps extreme examples of Greene's "virtue of disloyalty," but the same quality can be found in most of his novels. In his well-known *The Power and the Glory*, for example, Greene sets up a metaphorical conflict between the powers of God and the powers of atheism, yet it is his "disloyalty" that prevents the allegory from turning into a medieval morality play. The forces of good and the forces of evil are not so easily separated. Although his unnamed priest acquires a real holiness through suffering, the author depicts him as a much weaker man than his counterpart, the atheistic lieutenant. The latter is not only a strong man, but also a good man, who is selflessly devoted to the people. His anti-Catholicism has its origin in his boyhood memory of a Church that did not show a similar concern for its people. Perhaps Greene's fairness to Mexico's dusty rationalism, which he actually despised, can be seen by contrasting the novel with its film version. In John Ford's 1947 film, renamed *The Fugitive*, the viewer is given a hero, the priest, played by Henry Fonda, opposed by a corrupt lieutenant.

That writer's judgment, so firmly founded on "disloyalty," also helped Greene to overcome his tendency to anti-Americanism in *The Quiet American*. While Greene is critical of the naïve and destructive innocence of the young American, Pyle, he is even more critical of the English narrator, Fowler, who is cynically aloof. In the end, Greene's "disloyalty" permits him to show Vietnam suffering at the hands of any and all representatives of the Western world.

Greene's painstaking attempt to see the other side and to be as "disloyal" as possible to his own animated his fictional worlds and gave both him and his readers that "extra dimension of understanding."

Henry J. Donaghy

Other major works

SHORT FICTION: *The Basement Room and Other Stories*, 1935; *The Bear Fell Free*, 1935; *Twenty-four Stories*, 1939 (with James Laver and Sylvia Townsend Warner); *Nineteen Stories*, 1947; *Twenty-one Stories*, 1954; *A Visit to Morin*, 1959; *A Sense of Reality*, 1963; *May We Borrow Your Husband? and Other Comedies of the Sexual Life*, 1967; *Collected Stories*, 1972.

PLAYS: *The Living Room*, 1953; *The Potting Shed*, 1957; *The Complaisant Lover*, 1959; *Carving a Statue*, 1964; *The Return of A. J. Raffles: An Edwardian Comedy in Three Acts*, 1975.

POETRY: *Babbling April: Poems*, 1925; *After Two Years*, 1949; *For Christmas*, 1950.

NONFICTION: *Journey Without Maps: A Travel Book*, 1936; *The Lawless Roads: A Mexican Journal*, 1939 (reissued as *Another Mexico*); *British Dramatists*, 1942; *Why Do I Write? An Exchange of Views Between Elizabeth Bowen, Graham Greene, and V. S. Pritchett*, 1948; *The Lost Childhood and Other Essays*, 1951; *Essais Catholiques*, 1953 (Marcelle Sibon, translator); *In Search of a Character: Two African Journals*, 1961; *The Revenge: An Autobiographical Fragment*, 1963; *Victorian Detective Fiction*, 1966; *Collected Essays*, 1969; *A Sort of Life*, 1971; *The Pleasure Dome: The Collected Film Criticism, 1935-40, of Graham Greene*, 1972 (John Russell-Taylor, editor, published in the United States as *The Pleasure-Dome: Graham Greene on Film, Collected Film Criticism, 1935-40*); *Lord Rochester's Monkey: Being the Life of John Wilmot, Second Earl of Rochester*, 1974; *An Impossible Woman: The Memories of Dottoressa Moor of Capri*, 1975 (edited); *Ways of Escape*, 1980; *Getting to Know the General: The Story of an Involvement*, 1984.

CHILDREN'S LITERATURE: *The Little Train*, 1946; *The Little Fire Engine*, 1950 (published in the United States as *The Little Red Fire Engine*, 1952); *The Little Horse Bus*, 1952; *The Little Steam Roller: A Story of Mystery and Detection*, 1953.

ANTHOLOGY: *The Spy's Bedside Book: An Anthology*, 1957 (with Hugh Greene).

MISCELLANEOUS: *The Old School: Essays by Divers Hands*, 1934 (edited); *The Best of Saki*, 1950 (edited); *The Bodley Head Ford Madox Ford*, 1962, 1963 (edited, 4 volumes); *The Portable Graham Greene*, 1973 (Philip Stout Ford, editor).

Bibliography

De Vitis, A. A. *Graham Greene*. Rev. Ed. Boston: Twayne, 1986. This readable, well-organized treatment evaluates the different ways Greene seeks to embody his religious belief in his fiction. Establishes both the intellectual and the social setting in which he developed as a writer and includes detailed discussions of his novels, plays, and short stories. Places particular emphasis on publications after 1938 in which religious themes become clearly apparent. Includes a chronology, a selected bibliography, and an index.

Evans, Robert O., ed. *Graham Greene: Some Critical Considerations*. Lexington: University Press of Kentucky, 1963. This lively collection of fourteen critical essays offers a variety of approaches to Greene's novels along with frequent references to the "entertainments" and travel books. Topics include Greene's Catholicism, his similarities as a writer to François Mauriac, his intellectual background, and his accomplishments as a dramatist, short-story writer, and motion-picture critic. Includes a comprehensive bibliography of his works and the criticism of them published by 1963.

Kunkel, Francis. *The Labyrinthine Ways of Graham Greene*. New York:

Sheed & Ward, 1959. One of the earliest attempts to establish Greene's place in modern letters. Uses Greene's travel books and collected essays, novels, and plays to his themes and his ethical and theological preoccupations, as well as his characters and the way in which they respond to moral crises. Neither a book-by-book overview nor a chronological and biographical approach. Includes a primary bibliography.

Sherry, Norman. *The Life of Graham Greene*. New York: Viking Press, 1989. This is part one of what is certainly the most comprehensive, most authoritative account of Greene's life yet published, written with complete access to his papers and the full cooperation of family, friends, and the novelist himself. Leads the reader to 1939 to offer a rich account of the novelist's formative years, struggles, and experiences as a journalist. Includes a generous collection of photographs, a bibliography, and an index.

Turnell, Martin. *Graham Greene: A Critical Essay*. Grand Rapids, Mich.: Wm. B. Eerdmans, 1967. This brief study explores the factors which determine the quality of the religion in Greene's work from a Christian perspective. Discusses his novels and dramas, includes biographical background, and considers Greene's dilemma as a Christian writer along with François Mauriac and Jean Cayrol. A selected primary/secondary bibliography is included.

Wolfe, Peter. *Graham Greene the Entertainer*. Carbondale: Southern Illinois University Press, 1972. The first book-length treatment of Greene's "entertainments." Opens by discussing the varying critical approaches that his novels have received and then offers a readable, book-by-book analysis of each novel's characterization, plot, setting, themes, and style. Includes a selected primary/secondary bibliography and an index.

FREDERICK PHILIP GROVE
Felix Paul Greve

Born: Radomno, Poland; February 14, 1879
Died: Simcoe, Canada; August 19, 1948

Principal long fiction

Settlers of the Marsh, 1925; *A Search for America*, 1927; *Our Daily Bread*, 1928; *The Yoke of Life*, 1930; *Fruits of the Earth*, 1933; *Two Generations*, 1939; *The Master of the Mill*, 1944.

Other literary forms

Beyond the novel, Frederick Philip Grove has published travel sketches, represented by his first two published books, *Over Prairies Trails* (1922) and *The Turn of the Year* (1923). Actually narrative essays, the pieces detail Grove's weekly horse-and-carriage journeys between distant points of rural Manitoba. His other essays on a variety of topics appeared in Canadian periodicals and in the collection *It Needs to Be Said* (1929), and a much smaller number of short stories collected and edited by Desmond Pacey appeared under the title *Tales from the Margin* (1971).

In Search of Myself (1946), Grove's autobiography, contains a detailed account of his life before he arrived in Canada and of his struggles to achieve recognition as a writer. *Consider Her Ways* (1947), written at the time the autobiography was coming out but conceived much earlier, reflects Grove's long-standing scientific interests, as well as his familiarity with travel literature and with various models of the satiric fable. Grove casts his fable as a narrative communicated to a sympathetic scientist by a tribe of South American ants on an expedition to the north in search of further knowledge about humans. He cleverly satirizes Western civilization not only through the ants' discoveries and observations about the human society they find, but also through the behavior of the ants themselves, who engage in the same power struggles and exhibit the same vanity of species they impute to mankind. Although a curiosity in Grove's canon, *Consider Her Ways* displays a tighter structure than most of his more conventional writings as well as many of the same attitudes toward human behavior and history.

Achievements

Grove's fiction constitutes Canada's most distinguished contribution to the literature of frontier realism. His work presents an authentic image of pioneer life, particularly in the central Canadian provinces. As an immigrant to Canada, Grove was able to question the North American pioneering effort in a disturbing and often profound manner and to form a perspective unique among the major English realists. Almost all of his fiction in some way scrutinizes the value system of progress behind the frontier movement in Canada and the United States, with implications reaching far beyond the time in which a work was set or written. His portrayal of social change transcends the limits of most frontier realism, often approaching the resonance of Thomas Hardy or Ivan Turgenev.

Grove's writing, however, is not without flaws. Because he acquired English in a purely academic manner, his prose is too often turgid. Also, his plots often lack a logical development which makes events appear arbitrary. Nevertheless, most of his novels offer a careful delineation of settings and incidents; he also gives his reader many vivid and memorable characters and situations, informed always by a frankness of tone and attitude.

The peculiarly telescoped nature of Canadian literature—whereby the development of basically eighteenth century models into modernism, which occurred more rapidly than in England or the United States—is reflected in the intensity of Grove's writing and vision, an intensity which links him to the later Theodore Dreiser and even to John Steinbeck, and which dramatizes the romantic basis of a realism bent on escaping Romanticism. Grove's fiction, and particularly his three strongest novels—*Settlers of the Marsh*, *A Search for America*, and *Fruits of the Earth*—thus carries much interest and value for the literary historian, as well as for the general reader.

Biography

Frederick Philip Grove was born Felix Paul Greve on February 14, 1879, in Radomno, Poland—on what was then the border with Prussia. Grove's most effective fictions were a result of these first thirty years of his life. His parents were middle-class citizens of Hamburg, and he attended the University of Bonn for a few years before dropping out for financial reasons and embarking on a career as a free-lance writer and translator. Grove may have known André Gide and others in turn-of-the-century Paris literary circles, and he certainly did write and publish poetry, fiction, and even drama in addition to his literary criticism and extensive translation.

Grove's migration to North America, in 1909 or 1910, provided for him a new source of subject matter for his fiction. Whether he rode the rails as an itinerant workman, as he often said, is open to question. Most certainly he could have done so for only a year or two, and not for the much longer period suggested in *In Search of America* and reiterated in the autobiography. One can only speculate about his reasons for coming to America and for adopting so elaborate a disguise—of name, of parentage, even of the year of his birth. Perhaps he wished to transcend his modest social station, or to elude the law or creditors—Grove had spent a year in Bonn prison for fraud—or perhaps to escape a constraining marriage.

In 1912, Grove was hired as a public schoolteacher in rural Haskett, Manitoba, which was the first of several appointments in a rather unhappy career that would last fifteen years. In the summer of 1914, he married Catherine

Wiens, a teacher in a school where he had become principal. They had a daughter and a son. The daughter's death in 1927, when she was only eleven, climaxed a string of difficulties besetting Grove in the 1920's, difficulties caused by the backward and often intolerant communities in which he found himself employed, by his own ill temper and inflexibility toward the rural mentality, by overwork and chronic financial hardship, and, perhaps most of all, by the erratic and ultimately unencouraging response of publishers and readers to his books.

In the late 1920's, Grove's fortunes turned somewhat as he became championed by a small but loyal and influential group of Canadian writers and academics. Increasing critical recognition of his work led to two lecture tours in 1928, to a brief career in the publishing business from 1929 to 1931, and to Grove's receiving the prestigious Lorne Pierce Medal of the Royal Society of Canada in 1931. Meanwhile, Grove had left teaching and settled with his wife and son on a small farm near Simcoe, Ontario, where he lived until his death. While his writing never made him much money, it won him growing acclaim. He was elected to the Royal Society in 1941, received several honorary degrees, and was given a lifetime grant of one hundred dollars per month by the Canadian Writers Foundation in 1944. A stroke that year left him partly paralyzed. He died in 1948 after a lengthy illness.

Analysis

Among Frederick Grove's primary themes, the foremost is the issue of free will. Through his characters, Grove asks how much freedom anyone has in the face of often accidental but usually overwhelming pressures of instinct and environment. Even as he dramatizes the complexity and frustration wrought by such pressures, Grove seems, paradoxically, to celebrate the determination of his heroic figures to act as if such pressures hardly exist. Of almost equal importance to Grove's vision is the more existential question of where in time one ought to situate objectives. While he can admire the person who plans and looks toward the future, he often exposes the illusions attending such an orientation. His novels also involve themes that develop out of the distinction made between materialism and a more transcendental value system, a distinction that his characters frequently fail to identify. That Grove does not always favor his characters, even as he sympathizes with their search for an authentic New World, suggests the complex viewpoint and dilemma central to much of his writing.

After publishing his two books of travel sketches, Grove moved into book-length and explicitly fictional narrative, retaining this critical stance toward the efforts of pioneers to conquer the plains. Although the detailed accounting of nature continues in *Settlers of the Marsh*, Grove's sympathy with nature and his corresponding critique of man-in-nature are found in the novel's characterization and plotting. The pioneering enterprise is questioned through the depiction of Niels Lindstedt, a young Swede who emigrated to escape the perpetual poverty meted him in Europe and to build his own fortune through hard work. Niels outdoes his neighbors and succeeds handsomely: he saves money, clears land, and harvests a bounteous crop. His crowning achievement is the building of a great house, in which he plans to live with Ellen Amundsen. Out of the presumptuousness and naïveté of Niels's scheme, Grove constructs the complications of his novel.

A curiously antiromantic love triangle develops in the novel, which combines elements of Thomas Hardy and D. H. Lawrence with Gustave Flaubert. Niels is cast as impressionable and sexually vulnerable, not unlike Hardy's Jude or the young Paul Morel of *Sons and Lovers* (1913). Just as Paul turns to an older, more aggressive woman when the younger woman of his choice rebuffs his sexuality, so Niels falls prey to the seductiveness of Clara Vogel— whose first name significantly matches that of her counterpart in the Lawrence novel. Grove's Clara, unlike Lawrence's and like Arabella in *Jude the Obscure* (1896), knowingly takes advantage of his ignorance and inexperience in sex. The literary triangle is completed in Ellen's aversion to sex despite her affection for Niels; the complex psychology behind her refusal to marry him recalls the different but equally complex reasoning of Lawrence's Miriam and Sue Bridehead.

To a much greater degree than Hardy or Lawrence, Grove limits sympathy with his central character. Although the reader sees the novel's action almost exclusively from Niels's viewpoint, and although Niels's strengths are reported and his intentions are understandable, each of the two women in his life is given a position of equal validity to his, and Niels's inability, or unwillingness, to appreciate that position constitutes a grave weakness. Ellen's sexual problems stem from her having witnessed the brutal subjugation of her mother by her father—who forced sex on his wife when she was ill and pressured her to seek abortions when she was pregnant—and from having promised her mother she would avoid intimacy with a man. Ellen's telling Niels all of this, even as she insists she admires him and desperately needs his friendship, shocked many of the novel's first readers.

Unfortunately, Niels cannot bring himself to accept a purely friendly relationship with Ellen, or to wait for her to feel differently about him—although subsequent developments suggest waiting might not have gone unrewarded. Instead, he ignores her plea for friendship and largely avoids her. His assumption that he can control his own sexuality backfires in his going to town in search of pleasure, in his succumbing there to Clara, and in—to her astonishment—his remorsefully insisting that they marry.

Despite Clara's promiscuous past, it is mostly Niels's blindness to the dullness of farm life for a city woman and his refusal to free her that lead to Clara's actively seeking other men and to the climactic discovery scene in which Niels murders her. Just as Clara would not idealize sexuality, neither would she denigrate it, or try to compensate for it, as does Niels. His response to the compelling problems of Ellen and Clara reveal him to be more insensitive and more shackled by sex than either of them. Objections to the final reunion of Niels with a now-willing Ellen reflect readers' uneasiness with Niels's ultimately receiving rewards without acknowledging the legitimacy of the two women's claims against him. Aesthetically pleasing injustice in a more-or-less tragic plot thus gives way to the jarring injustice of a romantic finale.

The problems of the novel's ending are reinforced by Grove's portrayal of prairie women as victims of male stupidity and insensitivity. If Niels's friend Nelson enjoys a happy marriage because, unlike Niels, he pursues a simple, earthy type of women, Nelson is the exception. Otherwise, Grove surrounds Niels with consistently unhappy marriages, where the blame rests mostly on husbands whose wives are burdened with hard work, too many children, and too little sympathy. Grove finds the problem not to be so much marriage itself but specifically marriage between unequals to which the male pioneer aspires and in which the wife becomes simply another beast of burden subordinate to the husband's selfish ambitions. Grove ironically compounds the human toil of such selfishness in the case of Niels, who has a measure of sensitivity not shared by his fellow settlers. Niels mistakenly acts as if this sensitivity translates into completely good behavior. Having sought a land of freedom, Niels increasingly wonders if he is not, in fact, enslaved. Never, though, does he fully put together the puzzle of his failures. Through one of its gentlest members, Grove thus indicts a whole pioneer movement.

A Search for America proved to be much less offensive and much more popular to its first readers than *Settlers in the Marsh*; in fact, it became the most popular of Grove's books. Rather than a narrative of constriction, it offers a story of discovery, of an opening up to the positive possibilities of life in America. In Phil Brandon, the narrator and protagonist, Grove presents his true adventurer, who reveals the moral ambiguities of the feverish activity characterizing North America at the turn of the century. Until recently, readers saw the narrative as thinly disguised autobiography; certainly Grove encouraged this notion by inserting parts in *In Search of Myself*. So convincing are many of the novel's scenes and incidents that even now, after the serious inaccuracies in Grove's account of his early years have been exposed, one believes he must have experienced most of the encounters and difficulties Brandon describes.

The literary antecedents of this book are, on the one hand, *Walden* (1854) and *The Adventures of Huckleberry Finn* (1884), and, on the other, a string of later immigrant narratives, from Jacob Riis' affirmative autobiography, *The Making of an American* (1901), to the fictional and more skeptical *Rise of David Levinsky* (1917) by Abraham Cahan. How much of this immigrant writing Grove himself had read is unknown; Henry David Thoreau and Mark Twain he cites explicitly. To all of these he adds, as the narrative progresses, strains of Thomas Carlyle and Leo Tolstoy: he takes the injunction from *Sartor Resartus* (1835) about increasing the "fraction of Life" by lessening the denominator as the basis for his turnabout in the middle of his "search," and in the final section compares the magnificent hobo Ivan in *Anna Karénina* (1875-1877).

Phil Brandon is a young man from a wealthy Swedish family whose father's financial crisis drives him to Canada. From Toronto, where he finds work as a waiter, he moves to New York, as a door-to-door book salesman; to the Midwest, as a drifter on the Ohio River; and finally, to the Dakotas, where he works in the great wheat harvest. Although Grove cut his original manuscript in half, the published narrative is frequently rambling and episodic. Nevertheless, it continues to have a legitimate appeal.

The novel features the memorable episodes and characters for which Grove is known, from the cultured young European's encounter with the strange and raw people on his first train trip in the New World, from Montreal to Toronto, to Brandon's being tossed out of a Western town as a radical agitator trying to defend immigrants' property rights. Along the way he meets restaurant employees who cheat in various ways, the rich and the poor on whom publishers try to foist books, a riverman so taciturn Brandon mistakes him for a deaf-mute, a village doctor completely trusting of the down-and-out, a millionaire landowner fascinated by radical political talk, and many other notable figures.

In *Frederick Philip Grove* (1973), Margaret R. Stobie points to the dreamlike quality, as well as the double movement, of Brandon's quest. Grove extends his story beyond the limitations of immigrant initiation by moving Brandon from a geographical to a psychological quest, from seeking an America outside himself to finding those "American" values in himself which lead to a vocation. While the result for Brandon is the decision to become a teacher aiding the newly arrived immigrants, the meaning of this decision and the shift of objectives preceding it even speaks to readers solidly established in American society. Grove parallels this shift with the development of the distinction between the superficial America—represented in the novel's first two books by the petty fraud of business—and the "real" America promised in Book 3, when Brandon travels the countryside by himself, and in Book 4, when he reattaches himself to humanity. He becomes convinced that, his misadventures notwithstanding, there are "real Abe Lincolns" out there, worth seeking and worth cultivating.

Grove's narrator-protagonist comes to devalue "culture" in the European sense, as prefabricated and fragile, and to appreciate the need for developing one's personal culture. Grove's affinity with Thoreau and Twain, as well as with Henri Rousseau, shows especially in Brandon's discovery of a new relationship with nature, responding to the commonplace in nature. Nature suggests to Brandon not only the insignificance of the past—which his flight from

European artifice may have already taught him—but also the virtual irrelevance of the future, as he learns to concentrate more on his present situation and less on what it might be. Repeatedly, Brandon wonders at the nature of being, at where he is through no effort or intention. The novel's basic optimism is underlined by the possibility for positive unforeseen events, which softens the determinism of much social thinking in the novel. If the European immigrant's experience in the 1890's seems remote today, Grove's warnings about a culture mired in materialism and separated from its roots in nature still have force.

Continuing the ideological tendencies of Grove's earlier fiction *Fruits of the Earth* is not only his most satisfying and moving novel but also arguably one of the two or three finest works to come out of the American frontier tradition. Strictly speaking, it does not concern the frontier so much as the painful transition from pioneer to modern life on the prairie. Abe Spaulding represents one answer to Phil Brandon's search for the authentically Lincolnesque American. Grove describes Spaulding's experiences and development from 1900, when he arrives from Ontario to clear a piece of land near a remote Manitoba village, to the 1920's, when—in his fifties and having achieved patriarchal status among his neighbors—he wrestles with the moral dilemmas posed by community growth, related pressures of mass culture, and his own children's coming of age.

Grove divides his novel into two principal sections. The first traces Abe from his start as a young homesteader through his remarkable economic success, which culminates in his building a great house on the site of his beginning. Paralleling this ascent is his rise in the school district and the municipality, where he is respected for his sagacity and honesty and is ultimately elected reeve. Early in the narrative a conflict develops in Abe, by which feelings for his family—to a lesser extent for his wife, who is ill-suited for prairie life, and to a greater extent for his son Charlie, whose sensitivity Abe comes increasingly to value—detract from his sense of external success. Such success is superseded, in Abe's and the reader's minds, by the accidental death of Charlie midway through the novel.

Grove ascribes Spaulding's success largely to the preeminent strengths he brings to the challenge of homesteading. Repeatedly, the secondary characters and events testify to Abe's intelligence and shrewdness, of which his imposing physique is emblematic. He nurses the pioneer ambitions to escape a constricting life, represented by the small family farm he had sold, and to pursue what Grove terms "a clear proposition," unencumbered by complexity. Such a plan rests on the premise that such objectives are inherently good and satisfying, as well as obtainable. Abe soon begins to suspect the fallaciousness of his premise when other values detract from the satisfaction of his success. Grove significantly casts Abe's happiness in the past, so that he rarely experiences it except in memory. His growing property holdings are accompanied by a sense of diminishing economic returns and by a feeling of increasing enslavement by his acquisitions. Even as he builds the magnificent house, Abe feels powerless; house construction, like the prairie itself, is beyond his grasp. Like Hardy and many naturalists, Grove portrays his protagonist in rather unflattering terms against the backdrop of nature. Abe seems never very far ahead of the natural forces he tries to control, and therefore he is unable to enjoy any real repose.

All of these characteristics emerge in the novel's first part. Charlie's death, which coincides with Abe's greatest public triumphs, brings out a latent dissatisfaction with such triumphs. Abe sees in the death an ominous sign of his inability to capture what he has belatedly recognized as more valuable than material or external success. Charlie's death reinforces a depressing sense of fatality, of an irreversible and unmodifiable commitment to decisions made and courses taken many years earlier. Having attended increasingly to Charlie not only to atone but also to make up time he had believed he was losing, Abe retreats into himself once Charlie is gone.

The second part of the novel, entitled "The District," depicts various changes brought on by the postwar era. Against this background and despite his skepticism regarding "progress"—a skepticism explicitly echoed by Grove— Abe allows unscrupulous political enemies to rob him of power and to proceed to transform the district in the modern commercial spirit he despises. The novel's first part centered on the suspense of when and at what price Abe would realize fully the conflict of values in himself; in the second part, Grove turns the issue to whether, having recognized that conflict, Abe will succumb to a paralysis of will.

Abe, however, ultimately chooses to assert whatever limited influence he may have and to take a stand despite his awareness of his power's limits. Grove indicates that Abe's heroism comes from that awareness rather than from the skills which helped him fashion out his estate or the sensitivity brought out in his relationship to Charlie. Having learned that life's "clear propositions" tend to be elusive and fundamentally unsatisfying, Abe in the end rises from psychological and moral torpor to act with genuine courage.

Grove's artistic successes have helped extend frontier realism beyond the dimensions it is usually accorded. Like his more celebrated American counterparts, Grove marked the ambitions, hopes, and disappointments attending pioneer life around the turn of the century. He also marked the ways in which such universally destructive aspects of human behavior as greed, jealousy, and snobbery found their way into a frontier experience, which had promised escape from them.

Grove's novels came too late to put him in the forefront of frontier realists. Nevertheless, his novels' tardy appearance permitted a perspective of which the other frontier realists were rarely capable. Grove was able to capture not only the futility but also the ultimate immorality of much pioneer venturing.

His best fiction records the compromise of simple virtue and pleasure demanded by the misleading complex life on the prairie. This ethical perspective deepens as Grove follows his pioneers beyond World War I and even into the 1930's, where pioneer and modern notions of progress clash openly.

Significantly, Grove shows women and children suffering the consequences of commitments made solely by adult males. Yet, even the hardy pioneers in Grove's world sense the inherent limitations of the economic and social system .to which they commit themselves and their families. In depicting their failures, economic and moral, as inevitable, Grove is a pessimist, particularly as he assigns a measure of responsibility to the pioneers themselves. In continuing to insist, however, on the ability of man to recognize good and to act on that recognition, Grove avoided naturalistic determinism and offered a measure of hope to the twentieth century.

Bruce K. Martin

Other major works

SHORT FICTION: *Tales from the Margin: The Selected Short Stories of Frederick Philip Grove*, 1971 (Desmond Pacey, editor).

NONFICTION: *Over Prairie Trails*, 1922; *The Turn of the Year*, 1923; *It Needs to Be Said*, 1929; *In Search of Myself*, 1946; *The Letters of Frederick Philip Grove*, 1976 (Desmond Pacey, editor).

MISCELLANEOUS: *Consider Her Ways*, 1947.

Bibliography

Hjartarson, Paul, ed. *A Stranger to My Time: Essays by and About Frederick Philip Grove.* Edmonton, Alberta: NeWest Press, 1986. Divided into four sections, each concerned with a Grove persona, the figures of the Other, the Immigrant, Estrangement, and Posterity. Thoroughly updates the evaluation of Grove and his contribution to Canadian literature. An extensive, selected bibliography and an explicit index add to the book's value.

Pacey, Desmond, ed. *Frederick Philip Grove.* Toronto: Ryerson Press, 1970. Encompasses Pacey's own "Introduction," chronologically arranged critical essays by other authors, book review excerpts on Grove's novels, and a bibliography of Grove's entire canon. Reflects Pacey's skill at providing a useful overview.

Spettigue, Douglas O. *Frederick Philip Grove.* Toronto: Copp Clark, 1969. Spettigue, who has done the most to untangle the enigma of Grove's origins, arranges this scholarly, objective book around a consideration of the interdependence between Grove's personality and the themes and heroes of his novels. Notes and a bibliography enhance this important analysis.

Stobie, Margaret. *Frederick Philip Grove.* New York: Twayne, 1973. Stobie does as much as possible to discover Grove, the man, behind the central theme in his writing: man as social and natural being. Comprises an interwoven analysis of Grove's life and his writing, presenting new insights gleaned from unpublished material and from personal anecdotes of people who knew him. Emphasizes Grove's successes over his failures as a writer. A chronology, a selected bibliography, and an index contribute to the thoroughness of this admiring study.

Stuewe, Paul. "The Case of Frederick Philip Grove." In *Clearing the Ground: English-Canadian Literature After "Survival."* Toronto: Proper Tales Press, 1984. Stuewe bluntly dismisses Grove as an inept writer but acknowledges his nonliterary value as a chronicler of social and historic themes of the late nineteenth and early twentieth centuries.

Sutherland, Ronald, ed. "Thoughts on Five Writers: What Was Frederick Philip Grove?" In *The New Hero: Essays in Comparative Quebec/Canadian Literature.* Toronto: Macmillan, 1977. Sutherland calls this series of interesting linked essays, on the individualistic "new" hero emerging from Canadian literature, "para-literary." The section on Grove reflects Sutherland's fascination with Grove's enigmatic personality, and praises his writing as that of a literary naturalist, not a social realist. Notes and a thorough bibliography are included.

DASHIELL HAMMETT

Born: St. Mary's County, Maryland; May 27, 1894
Died: New York, New York; January 10, 1961

Principal long fiction

Red Harvest, 1927-1928 (serial), 1929; *The Dain Curse*, 1928-1929 (serial), 1929; *The Maltese Falcon*, 1929-1930 (serial), 1930; *The Glass Key*, 1930 (serial), 1931; *The Thin Man*, 1934.

Other literary forms

Dashiell Hammett first attracted critical attention as the author of short detective fiction published in *Smart Set* and *Black Mask* magazines as early as 1923. The best of his stories were narratives told in the first person by the nameless "Continental Op," a fat, balding operative working out of the San Francisco office of the Continental Detective Agency. The Continental Op is also the narrator and principal character of Hammett's first two novels, both of which were published in magazines before their appearance in book form. A number of his short stories were anthologized in *The Continental Op* (1945) and, after Hammett's death in 1961, *The Big Knockover* (1966).

Achievements

Together with his contemporary Raymond Chandler (1888-1959), Hammett is credited with defining the form, scope, and tone of the modern detective novel, a distinctly American genre that departs considerably from the earlier tradition inspired by the British. Chandler, although some six years Hammett's senior, did not in fact begin publishing detective fiction until 1933 and readily acknowledged the younger writer's prior claim. Together, both authors have exerted considerable influence upon later exponents of the detective genre, notably on Ross Macdonald, their most distinguished successor. Hammett's work in particular has served also as a stylistic model for many novelists working outside the detective genre, among them Ernest Hemingway and John O'Hara.

Unlike his predecessors in the mystery genre, Hammett adopted a starkly realistic, tough-minded tone in his works, sustaining an atmosphere in which questions outnumber answers and no one is to be trusted. Hammett's reputation ultimately rests on his creation of two characters who embody the moral ambiguities of the modern world: Sam Spade (*The Maltese Falcon*) and Nick Charles (*The Thin Man*). Widely popularized through film adaptations of the novels in which they appear, Spade and Charles are among the most famous American detectives, known even to those with little more than marginal interest in the mystery genre. Tough-minded if occasionally softhearted, both characters may be seen as particularized refinements of Hammett's Continental Op, professional detectives who remain true to their personal code of honor and skeptical with regard to everything and everyone else.

Partially because of declining health, Hammett wrote no novels after the age of forty. His reputation, however, was by that time secure; some fifty years later, his five novels remain landmarks of the genre, a model for future novelists and a formidable standard of comparison.

Biography

Samuel Dashiell Hammett was born in St. Mary's County, Maryland, on May 27, 1894, of an old but modest Roman Catholic family. Leaving high school at fourteen after less than a year of attendance, Hammett worked indifferently at a variety of odd jobs before signing on with the Pinkerton Detective Agency around the age of twenty. At last, it seemed he had found work that he enjoyed and could do well, with a dedication later reflected in the character and behavior of the Continental Op. With time out for service in World War I, from which he was demobilized as a sergeant, Hammett continued to serve Pinkerton with distinction until failing health caused him to consider other options. In 1921, he married Josephine Dolan, a nurse whom he had met during one of his recurring bouts with tuberculosis. The couple moved west to San Francisco where Hammett returned to work for Pinkerton, only to resign in frustration and disgust after an ironic incident in which his detective talents proved too great for his own good: assigned by Pinkerton to ship out on an Australian freighter in search of stolen gold believed to be hidden aboard, Hammett managed to find the missing gold in a smokestack during a cursory search just prior to departure, and was thus denied the anticipated voyage to Australia.

During such spare time as he could find, Hammett had been trying to prepare himself as a writer; upon leaving Pinkerton, he devoted himself increasingly to writing, eventually leaving his family (which by then included two daughters) and moving to a cheap furnished room where he could live and write. Fearing that he had little time left to live, he wrote at a determined pace; encouraged by his first successes, he gradually developed and refined the writing style that was to make him famous. His first story featuring the Continental Op appeared in October, 1923. Increasingly successful, Hammett soon progressed to the writing of longer stories that were in fact independent sections of novels, eventually published as *Red Harvest* and *The Dain Curse*. Both appeared as hardbound editions in 1929. The following year, Hammett achieved both critical recognition and financial independence with the publication of *The Maltese Falcon*, an unquestionably mature and groundbreaking work that sold at once to the film industry; John Houston's landmark 1941 version of *The Maltese Falcon* was the third Hollywood film to be drawn from Hammett's original novel.

In the year 1930, Hammett made the acquaintance of Lillian Hellman, eleven years his junior, who was to become the most important and influential woman in his life. Although they never married (each was unhappily married to someone else at the time of their first meeting), Hellman and Hammett remained together in an intense, often turbulent but intellectually rewarding relationship until Hammett's death some thirty years later at the age of sixty-six. *The Thin Man*, Hammett's next and last published novel (*The Glass Key* having already been written by the time he met Hellman), reflects the author's relationship with Hellman in the portrayal of Nick and Nora Charles, represented in the screen version and its sequels by William Powell and Myrna Loy.

Following the success of *The Thin Man* both as book and as film, Hammett moved to Hollywood, where he worked as a writer and script doctor on a variety of screen projects. He became increasingly involved in leftist politics and toward the end of the Depression became a member of the Communist Party. Hammett did not, however, consider his politics an impediment to patriotism; soon after the United States went to war, he was back in a sergeant's uniform, despite his advanced age and obviously declining health. Attached to the Signal Corps, he served three years in the Aleutians, where his duties included editing a daily newspaper for his fellow servicemen. By the end of the war, however, his health was more precarious than ever, undermined by years of recurrent tuberculosis and heavy drinking; after an alcoholic crisis in 1948, Hammett foreswore drinking for the remainder of his life. At the same time, his political past was coming back to haunt him; like his fictional characters, however, he remained loyal to his convictions and his friends, declining to testify against his fellow associates in the Communist Party and other political organizations. In 1951, Hammett spent five months in various prisons for contempt of court as a result of his refusal to testify; around the same time, government authorities determined that he was several years behind in the payment of his income tax. Unable to find work in Hollywood because of his political views, Hammett was further impoverished by the attachment of his remaining income for the payment of back taxes. Increasingly infirm, Hammett spent his last years in the care and company of Lillian Hellman. He died at Lenox Hill Hospital in New York City on January 10, 1961.

Analysis

Unlike most of their predecessors in the genre, Dashiell Hammett's detectives live and work, as did Hammett himself, in a world populated with actual criminals who violate the law for tangible personal gain. Significantly, Hammett did all of his creative writing during the years of Prohibition, when lawlessness was rampant and organized crime was rapidly gaining a foothold in the American social structure. Prohibition indeed functions prominently in all of Hammett's published work as background, atmosphere, and frequently as subject. In *Red Harvest*, Hammett's first novel, a loose confederacy of bootleggers, thieves, and hired killers has set up what appears to be a substitute government, replacing law and order with values of their own; the resulting Hobbesian chaos clearly reflects, however indirectly, Hammett's own developing political consciousness. There is little place in such a world for genteel detectives cast in the mold of Dorothy Sayers' Lord Peter Wimsey; accordingly, Hammett presents in the Continental Op and his successors the kind of detective who can deal routinely and effectively with hardened criminals. As Raymond Chandler observed, "Hammett gave murder back to the kind of people who commit it for reasons."

Within such an evil environment, the sleuth often becomes as devious and mendacious as those whom he is pursuing, remaining faithful nevertheless to a highly personal code of honor and justice. Sam Spade, perhaps the most intriguing of Hammett's literary creations, is so well attuned to the criminal mind that he often appears to be a criminal himself; he is known to have been involved romantically with his partner's wife and is thus a likely suspect after the man is murdered. Still, at the end of *The Maltese Falcon*, he persists in turning over to the authorities the thief and murderess Brigid O'Shaughnessy, despite an acknowledged mutual attraction. Ned Beaumont, the protagonist of *The Glass Key*, remains similarly incorruptible despite outward appearances to the contrary: a detective by temperament, if not by trade, Ned serves as friend and aide to the rising local politician Paul Madvig, involving himself deeply in political deals and trades; still, he persists in revealing a United States senator as the murderer of his own son and insists that the senator stand trial rather than commit suicide. The law of the land, however tarnished, remains a strong value in Hammett's novels, suggesting an abiding need for structure against the threat of anarchy.

With *The Thin Man*, Hammett moved in a new direction. For the first time, humor became a significant element in Hammett's fiction, infusing the novel with a lightness of tone that sets it quite apart from the almost documentary seriousness of *Red Harvest* and *The Glass Key*. Its protagonist, Nick Charles, has retired from the detective trade after his marriage to the rich and pretty Nora, some fifteen years his junior. Released from the need to work, he clearly prefers the carefree life of parties, travel, hotels, and round-the-clock drinking, all the while trading jokes and friendly banter with his attractive wife and other boon companions. Still, some habits die hard, and unpredicted events soon bring Nick's well honed detective instincts back into operation. Moving back and forth between speakeasies and his lavish hotel suite, getting shot at by enraged gangsters, Nick urbanely unravels the mystery until, to no one's real surprise, one of his many casual friends stands revealed as the culprit. It is no secret that Hammett, in his portrayal of the witty Nora and her relationship with Nick, was more than a little influenced by his own developing relationship with Lillian Hellman, who returned the favor in her several volumes of memoirs. Like Nick, Hammett at the time of *The Thin*

Man, was approaching middle age without the need to work, free at last to indulge his taste for parties and other carefree pursuits. *The Thin Man*, although certainly not planned as Hammett's final novel, is in a sense a fitting valedictory, an exuberant *tour de force* in which, ironically, the tensions contained in the earlier novels are finally released and perhaps dissipated. An additional irony exists within the book: Nick and Nora Charles may well be Hammett's best-known literary creations, perpetuated by the film version of the novel as well as by several sequels scripted in Hollywood by Hammett himself.

Hammett's first published novel, *Red Harvest*, originally serialized in *Black Mask*, delivers in ample portion the harsh realism promised in its title. Indeed, the high body count of *Red Harvest* may well have set a kind of record to be met or broken by later efforts in the detective genre. Hammett's intention, however, is not merely to shock the reader; seen in retrospect, *Red Harvest* emerges as a parable of civilization and its possible mutations.

Nowhere in *Red Harvest* are Hammett's intentions more evident than in his choice of location, a mythical, Western community called Personville, better-known as Poisonville. Some fifty years after the lawless days of the Wild West, Personville/Poisonville has yet to be tamed, even as outlaws have been replaced by gangsters with Eastern accents wearing snap-brim hats instead of Stetsons. The Op, sent to Personville at the request of one Donald Willsson, makes an appointment with him only to discover that he has been murdered before the planned meeting can take place. Undaunted, the Op proceeds to investigate Donald Willsson's murder, plunging deeper and deeper into the town's menacing and malevolent atmosphere. Among the more likely suspects is Willsson's father Elihu, the town boss, who may well have tried to put a stop to his son's muckraking activities as publisher of the local newspaper. Other suspects, however, are present in abundance, at least until they begin to kill off one another during internecine combat partially masterminded by the Op. The Op, it seems, is particularly skillful in setting the various criminal elements loose upon one another, paving the way for eventual martial law and relative peace, "a sweet-smelling and thornless bed of roses." In the process, however, he frequently faces criminal charges himself; at the same time, the authorities who are pressing the charges may well be as corrupt as the more obvious criminals. In such an environment, the closest thing to a moral imperative is the Op's own case-hardened sense of justice.

The major weakness of *Red Harvest* is a bewildering multiplicity of characters and actions; often, a new character will be introduced and established, only to be killed on the following page. The acts of violence, although symptomatic of social ills and not included for their own sake (as in the work of later hard-boiled mystery writers such as Mickey Spillane), are so numerous as to weary even the least squeamish of readers, although a number of scenes are especially effective; in one, the Op, watching a boxing match that he has helped to "unfix," stands helpless as the unexpected winner falls dead in the ring with a knife at the base of his neck.

Later in the same year, 1929, Hammett published *The Dain Curse*, another formerly serialized novel featuring the Op as narrator and main character. Less sophisticated in its presentation than *Red Harvest*, *The Dain Curse* is more severely hampered by a multiplicity of characters and plot twists, all turning around the possibility of a family "curse" brought on by incest. Despite some rather skillful and memorable characterizations, *The Dain Curse* is generally agreed to be Hammett's weakest and least effective novel. Significantly, it is the last of Hammett's novels to feature the Op and the last (until *The Thin Man*, a different sort of novel) to be narrated in the first person.

Hammett's third novel, *The Maltese Falcon*, narrated dispassionately in the third person, combines the narrative strengths of his earlier works with a far more developed sense of characterization. Its protagonist, Sam Spade, although enough like the Op to be his slightly younger brother, is a more fully realized character caught and portrayed in all his ambiguity. Clearly the "brains" of the Spade and Archer Agency, he is careful to turn over to Miles Archer the case of a young woman client in whose presence he senses trouble. When Archer, blinded by the woman's flattery, goes forth to his death, Spade is hardly surprised, nor does he take many pains to hide his recent affair with the woman who is now Archer's widow; Spade, meanwhile, has grown tired of Iva Archer and her advances. Himself under suspicion for Archer's murder, Spade delves deeper into the case, learning that the young woman has given a number of aliases and cover stories. Her real name, it appears, is Brigid O'Shaughnessy, and it is not long before Spade connects her to a ring of international thieves, each of whom seems to be competing with the others for possession of an ancient and priceless treasure known as the Maltese Falcon. Supposedly, the football-sized sculpted bird, encrusted with precious stones, has been stolen and repossessed numerous times in the four hundred years of its existence, having surfaced most recently in the hands of a Russian general.

Spade's quest eventually brings him in contact with most of the larcenous principals except for the general himself (who at the end of the novel is found to have substituted a worthless leaden counterfeit for the genuine article). Among the thieves are two particularly memorable characters, interpreted in the John Huston film by Sydney Greenstreet and Peter Lorre, respectively: Casper Gutman, an eloquent, grossly fat manipulator and adventurer, keeps trying to maneuver Spade into his confidence; meanwhile, the other, Joel Cairo, a blatant homosexual and member of the international underworld, repeatedly (and most unsuccessfully) tries to intimidate Spade with a handgun that Spade keeps taking away from him. In 1930, Hammett's frank portrayal of a homosexual was considered daring in the extreme; by 1941, it was possible for Huston to apply such a characterization to Gutman as well, whose homosexuality in the novel is little more than latent. The book, for example, mentions that Gutman is traveling with a grown daughter, but the daughter is never mentioned in the Huston film.

In both novel and film, Spade's character develops considerably as he attempts to deal simultaneously with the matters at hand and with his growing affection for the obviously perfidious Brigid O'Shaughnessy. In Brigid, it seems, Spade has at last met his proper match, a woman whose deviousness and native intelligence compare favorably with his own. In her presence, it is all too easy for Spade to forget the cloying advances of Iva Archer or even the tomboyish charms of his secretary Effie Perine; it is less easy, however, for him to forget the tightening web of circumstantial evidence in which he finds Brigid strongly enmeshed. After the coveted falcon has been revealed as a forgery, Spade confronts Brigid with evidence that she, and not her deceased cohort Floyd Thursby, fired the bullet that killed Miles Archer. For all Archer's weaknesses and Spade's personal contempt for the man, Spade remains true to the code that dictates arrest and prosecution for his partner's murderer. Explaining to an incredulous Brigid that he still thinks he loves her but cannot bring himself to trust her, he declares that he is sending her to jail and may or may not be waiting when she is freed. They are locked in an embrace when the police arrive to take her away.

Considerably more thoughtful and resonant than Hammett's earlier novels, *The Maltese Falcon* is his unquestioned masterpiece. The falcon itself, a contested piece of plunder that, in the novel, has occasioned theft and murder throughout recent history and which in its present form turns out to be a fake, is without doubt one of the strongest and best developed images in recent American fiction. Another equally effective device, absent from the Huston film, is the Flitcraft parable that Spade tells to Brigid early in their relationship as a way of explaining his behavior. Early in his career, he recalls, he was hired to find a Seattle resident named Flitcraft who had disappeared mysteriously one day during the lunch hour, leaving behind a wife and two children. Spade later learned that, during the lunch break, Flitcraft had glimpsed his own mortality after a narrow escape from a falling beam. "He felt like somebody had taken the lid off his life and let him look at the works." That same day, he abandoned his family, wandering for two years, after which he fashioned for himself in Spokane a professional and family life very much like the one he had left behind in Seattle. "But that's the part of it I always liked," Spade tells Brigid. "He adjusted himself to beams falling, and then no more of them fell, and he adjusted himself to them not falling." Predictably, Spade's narrative has little effect on Brigid; for the reader, however, it does much to explain Hammett's approach to Spade as character and his own developing sense of the novelist's art. During that stage of his career, Hammett moved from "looking at the works" (*Red Harvest*) to a mature sense of contingency in which one's own deeply held convictions are all that matter.

Acknowledged to have been Hammett's personal favorite among his five published novels, *The Glass Key* is the only one not to feature a trained detective as protagonist. A rather unlikely hero at first glance, Ned Beaumont is tubercular, an avid gambler without a regular job. His principal occupation is that of friend, conscience, and unofficial assistant to Paul Madvig, an amiable politician of forty-five who, one suspects, without Beaumont's help would have made even more mistakes than he already has. Himself the father of a grown daughter, Madvig is currently unmarried and in love with Janet Henry, daughter of an aristocratic and powerful United States senator. Janet has done little to encourage Madvig's attentions, and Beaumont, for his part, is determined to prevent his friend from making a fool of himself. Complications arise with the brutal murder of Taylor Henry, Janet's brother, who may or may not have been in love with Madvig's daughter Opal. As usual in Hammett's novels, there is an underworld connection; Taylor, it seems, was deeply in debt to a professional gambler at the time of his death.

As Madvig's loyal friend and aide, Beaumont sets out to discover the truth behind Taylor Henry's murder, displaying detective instincts worthy of Sam Spade or the Continental Op. Amid serious encounters with angry gangsters and corrupt police, Ned perseveres in his efforts to clear Madvig's name of suspicion in the murder, fully aware that he may well be a suspect himself. Meanwhile, to both Madvig's and Beaumont's consternation, Janet Henry appears to be falling in love with Beaumont, if only because he seems to be proof against her charms. As the action proceeds, it becomes increasingly clear to Beaumont that Taylor Henry could only have been killed by the senator, who has somehow prevailed upon Madvig to accept the burden of suspicion. When Beaumont finally confronts the senator with his suspicions, Henry admits to killing his son in a fit of anger and tampering with evidence at the scene of the crime; he asks only that Beaumont give him five minutes alone with his loaded revolver. Predictably, Beaumont refuses: "You'll take what's coming to you." Beaumont decides to leave town permanently, and, in a surprise twist at the end, he agrees to take Janet with him; the relationship awaiting them can only be surmised.

Like *The Maltese Falcon*, *The Glass Key* is a thoughtful and resonant novel, rich in memorable scenes and images. The glass key itself occurs in a dream that Janet has shortly after the start of her problematical relationship with Ned: she dreams that they arrive at a locked house piled high with food that they can see through the windows; yet when they open the door with a key found under the mat the house turns out to be filled with snakes as well. At the end of the novel, Janet reveals that she has not told Ned all of her dream: "the key was glass and shattered in our hands just as we got the door open, because the lock was stiff and we had to force it." Just as the Maltese Falcon dominates the book bearing its name, the glass key comes to symbolize the dangerous fragility of Janet's life and especially of her relationships with men—Paul Madvig, her father, and finally Ned Beaumont. Born to wealth and privilege, Janet is potentially dangerous to herself and others for reasons that Hammett suggests are outside her control; she does not share in her father's venality and is quite possibly a decent person beneath the veneer of her upbringing.

Not easily deceived, Ned Beaumont has been skeptical about the Henrys from the beginning; early in the book, he warns Paul against deeper involvement with either Janet or her father: "Read about it in the *Post*—one of the few aristocrats left in American politics. And his daughter's an aristocrat. That's why I'm warning you to sew your shirt on when you go to see them, or you'll come away without it, because to them you're a form of lower animal life and none of the rules apply." To Beaumont, the Henrys are thoughtless and dangerous, much like Tom and Daisy Buchanan as seen by Nick Carraway in F. Scott Fitzgerald's *The Great Gatsby* (1925). Janet, however, develops considerably during the course of the novel, and at the end there is just the barest chance that a change of scenery will allow her to work out a decent life in Ned Beaumont's company.

Fifth and last of Hammett's novels, *The Thin Man* is the only one to have been written during his acquaintance with Lillian Hellman, whose witty presence is reflected throughout the novel. Thanks to the successful film version and various sequels, *The Thin Man* is, next to *The Maltese Falcon*, the most famous of Hammett's novels; it is also the least typical.

The narrator and protagonist of *The Thin Man* is Nick Charles (born Charalambides and proud of his Greek extraction), a former detective in his early forties who has married the rich and beautiful Nora, nearly young enough to be his daughter. Contrary to popular belief, the novel's title refers not to Charles himself but to one Clyde Miller Wynant, suspected of various crimes throughout the novel until the end, when he is revealed to have been the real killer's first victim: Wynant, an inventor, is described as being tall and painfully thin; at the end of the novel, his bones are found buried with clothes cut to fit a much larger man. In the filmed sequel, however, the title presumably refers to the dapper detective himself.

Peopled with a cast of café-society characters in addition to the usual underworld types, *The Thin Man* is considerably lighter in tone and texture than Hammett's earlier novels. Nick Charles, although clearly descended from Beaumont, Spade, and the Op, is nearly a playboy by comparison, trading lighthearted jokes and double entendres with his wife and boon companions. Close parallels may be drawn between Charles and the author himself, who by the time of *The Thin Man*, had achieved sufficient material success to obviate his need to work. Lillian Hellman observes, however, that the actual writing of *The Thin Man* took place during a period of abstemious, almost monastic seclusion that differed sharply from Hammett's usual pattern of behavior during those years, as well as from the carefree life ascribed to Nick and Nora in the novel.

Most of the action of *The Thin Man* turns upon the certifiably eccentric personality of the title character, Clyde Wynant, a former client of Nick during his latter years as a detective. Among the featured characters are Wynant's former wife, son, and daughter, as well as his lawyer, Herbert Macaulay. In particular, the Wynants are memorable, deftly drawn characters, nearly as eccentric in their own ways as the missing *paterfamilias*. Wynant's son, Gilbert, about eighteen, is notable for his voracious reading and morbid curiosity concerning such matters as murder, cannibalism, and abnormal psychology. Dorothy Wynant, a year or two older than Gilbert, keeps trying to parlay a former girlhood crush on Nick Charles into something more serious. Their mother, known as Mimi Jorgensen, is a vain, treacherous woman cut from the same cloth as Brigid O'Shaughnessy of *The Maltese Falcon*; she too makes repeated claims upon Nick's reluctant attentions.

Throughout the novel, Mimi and her children coexist uneasily in a state of armed truce that occasionally erupts into open warfare, providing scenes of conflict between parent and child considered rather daring at the time. Among the featured characters, only Macaulay appears sane or even remotely sympathetic; yet it is he who ultimately stands accused of the financial double-dealing and multiple murders originally attributed to Wynant, not to mention the murder of Wynant himself.

Like Hammett's earlier novels, *The Thin Man* is realistic in its portrayal of urban life during Prohibition, when the criminal element was even more visible and overt in its actions than in later times. Despite the witty urbanity of his characters, Hammett harbors a few illusions concerning human nature. When Nora asks Nick at the end of the novel what will become of Mimi and her children, he replies, "Nothing new. They'll go on being Mimi and Dorothy and Gilbert just as you and I will go on being us and the Quinns will go on being the Quinns." The novel ends with Nora telling Nick that his explanation is "pretty unsatisfactory." Perhaps it is, Hammett implies, but that is the nature of life.

Partly because of failing health and the pressures of work in Hollywood, Hammett published no fiction after *The Thin Man*. His reputation thus rests on a small and somewhat uneven body of work, redeemed by frequent flashes of brilliance. Notable for their influence upon the work of Raymond Chandler, Ross Macdonald, and a host of lesser writers in the mystery genre, Hammett's novels have also exercised an immeasurable influence on novelists and filmmakers outside the genre.

David B. Parsell

Other major works

SHORT FICTION: *Secret Agent X-9*, 1934 (with Alex Raymond); *The Conti-*

nental Op, 1945; *The Return of the Continental Op*, 1945; *The Adventures of Sam Spade, and Other Stories*, 1945; *Hammett Homocides*, 1946; *Dead Yellow Women*, 1947; *Nightmare Town*, 1948; *The Creeping Siamese*, 1950; *Woman in the Dark*, 1951; *A Man Named Thin and Other Stories*, 1962; *The Big Knockover*, 1966.

Bibliography

Dooley, Dennis. *Dashiell Hammett*. New York: Frederick Ungar, 1984. A particularly useful study for those interested in Hammett's short fiction, which makes up half of this book. His major novels are also discussed in the context of his life and his works considered in the context of their times. Contains notes, a bibliography, and an index.

Gregory, Sinda. *Private Investigations: The Novels of Dashiell Hammett*. Carbondale: Southern Illinois University Press, 1985. The first chapter discusses Hammett, his Pinkerton experiences, and the hard-boiled detective genre. Subsequent chapters focus on each of his five major novels. Foreword by Francis M. Nevins, Jr. Includes a preface and a conclusion, notes, a bibliography, and an index.

Hamilton, Cynthia S. "Dashiell Hammett." In *Western and Hard-Boiled Detective Fiction: From High Noon to Midnight*. Iowa City: University of Iowa Press, 1987. In addition to this fresh insight into detective fiction from the historical and generic perspective of the American Western novel, this study includes three chapters on the study of formula literature. A bibliography and an index are included.

Johnson, Diane. *Dashiell Hammett: A Life*. New York: Fawcett Columbine, 1985. This paperback edition of the 1983 biography was very well received critically and is an excellent source for personal information about Hammett's life. Organized chronologically. Includes illustrations, a bibliography, notes, and an index.

Nolan, William F. *Hammett: A Life at the Edge*. New York: Congdon & Weed, 1983. This biography draws on Hammett's letters, interviews, memoirs, and public statements and attempts to organize a thematic discussion of Hammett the man. Contains illustrations, a bibliography, notes, and an index.

Symons, Julian. *Dashiell Hammett*. San Diego: Harcourt Brace Jovanovich, 1985. A good critical introduction to Hammett, his life and works. Many illustrations enliven this discussion of Hammett's short stories and major novels. Includes notes, a bibliography, and an index.

JAMES HANLEY

Born: Dublin, Ireland; September 3, 1901
Died: London, England; November 11, 1985

Principal long fiction

Drift, 1930; *Boy*, 1931; *Ebb and Flood*, 1932; *Captain Bottell*, 1933; *Resurrexit Dominus*, 1934; The Fury Chronicle (includes *The Furys*, 1935, *The Secret Journey*, 1936, *Our Time Is Gone*, 1940, *Winter Song*, 1950, *An End and a Beginning*, 1958); *Stoker Bush*, 1935; *Hollow Sea*, 1938; *The Ocean*, 1941; *No Directions*, 1943; *Sailor's Song*, 1943; *What Farrar Saw*, 1946; *Emily*, 1948; *The House in the Valley*, 1951; *The Closed Harbour*, 1952; *The Welsh Sonata: Variations on a Theme*, 1954; *Levine*, 1956; *Say Nothing*, 1962; *Another World*, 1972; *A Woman in the Sky*, 1973; *A Dream Journey*, 1976; *A Kingdom*, 1978.

Other literary forms

James Hanley was one of the most prolific of twentieth century writers. Apart from twenty-six novels and many volumes of short stories, he wrote a considerable number of plays for stage, radio, and television. *Say Nothing* (1963) is a successfully produced play based on his novel by the same name. *Plays One* (1968) includes his famous play "The Inner Journey," which was staged at the Lincoln Center, New York, to excellent critical reviews.

Hanley's *Broken Water: An Autobiographical Excursion* (1937) provides insights into his early life at sea and his determined efforts to become a writer. *Grey Children* (1931), subtitled *A Study in Humbug and Misery*, is a compassionate study of unemployment among miners in South Wales. *John Cowper Powys: A Man in the Corner* (1969) is a biographical and critical study of the English novelist whose *A Glastonbury Romance* (1932) is Hanley's favorite novel. In *Herman Melville: A Man in the Customs House* (1971), Hanley's own love for the sea enables him to present Melville from a refreshing new perspective. *Don Quixote Drowned* (1953) is a collection of essays, personal and literary. In one of these essays, Hanley includes a passage which describes himself as a "chunky realist and flounderer in off-Dreiserian prose, naïve and touchy about style." The volume also provides valuable information about some of the sources for Hanley's novels.

Achievements

Hanley is the neglected giant of modern literature. Around 1940, T. E. Lawrence found in Hanley's novels "a blistering vividness." E. M. Forster called him a novelist of distinction and originality. Henry Green considered him to be superior to Joseph Conrad. Herbert Read commented that Hanley was one of the most vigorous and impressive of contemporary writers. John

Cowper Powys called Hanley "a genius." C. P. Snow recognized Hanley's humanity, compassion, and sheer imaginative power. Henry Miller wrote an enthusiastic introduction to the third edition (1946) of Hanley's novel *No Directions*. Yet, in spite of this impressive roster of applause, Hanley has been assessed as "one of the most consistently praised and least-known novelists in the English speaking world."

In the 1930's and early 1940's, Hanley was at the height of his popularity because of his novels about the war and some of the early volumes of the Fury saga. By the 1950's, however, his popularity had declined and his reading public was a small cult group; he was practically unknown in the United States. Hanley is a complex writer who demands from the reader the same undivided attention he devoted to his carefully conceived and crafted novels and plays. Irving Howe points out in his brilliant review of Hanley's *A Dream Journey* that "Hanley's novels demand to be read slowly, in order to protect oneself from his relentlessness. It's like having your skin rubbed raw by a harsh wind, or like driving yourself to a rare pitch of truth by reflections— honest ones for a change—about the blunders of your life."

Hanley was not unduly concerned about the lack of a wider audience. He pursued his art with dedication and artistic integrity, he was uncompromising and unwilling to change his style to satisfy fluctuating fads and fashions of the literary world, and he survived completely through his writings. Maintaining such an authentic aesthetic individuality over a period of nearly sixty years was in itself a major achievement of James Hanley.

Biography

James Hanley was born on September 3, 1901, in Dublin, Ireland. Early in life, he moved with his family to Liverpool, England, where he grew up. Hanley's father, Edward Hanley, gave up a promising career in law for a life at sea, thereby grievously disappointing his mother; James Hanley was strongly counseled by his grandmother not to go to sea. The advice fell on deaf ears, however, and he left school at age fourteen and went to sea as a shipboy. Some of this experience undoubtedly provided him with the raw material for his novel *Boy*.

During Hanley's first transatlantic voyage, war broke out, and for two years he worked on troopships transporting soldiers across the Mediterranean to Salonika, Greece, and Gallipoli, Turkey. *Hollow Sea* draws upon this phase of his life and portrays the intensity of life on troopships during hazardous missions. At age sixteen, Hanley deserted his ship on a stopover in St. John, New Brunswick, Canada. He lied about his age, took on a name randomly selected from a telephone directory, and joined the Canadian army. After training in Canada and in England, he served in France. When he was discharged from the army and returned to England, he settled down with his parents in Liverpool.

In his autobiography he writes, "I had finished with the sea. I had finished with the army. I had had practically no education." He had seen the ugly and brutal face of war and survived the trauma. In Liverpool, he came across an old sailor friend to whom he had entrusted a letter to his mother with some money. The friend had taken the money and thrown away the letter, an incident that deeply affected Hanley. He made no more friends, and for the next ten years, he kept to himself like a hermit. He found a new personal meaning in the advice "never trust a friend," from August Strindberg's play *Bränea Tomten* (1907; *After the Fire: Or, The Burned Lot*). He took a job as a storeman on the railway and obsessively started on his self-education. He read voraciously during his spare time, studied French and Russian in evening classes, and indulged in his great passion for music as he struggled to play Bach and Beethoven with his small, rough, workingman's hands.

Hanley also wrote short stories and plays with dogged determination and collected a number of rejection slips. He was determined to write "until he was accepted" and completed a book titled "Soldier's Journal of the War." He was asked to burn it, however, because, as he put it in his autobiographical *Broken Water*, "it went a bit too far as a picture of the war." He completed his first novel, *Drift*, and, after being rejected by eighteen publishers, it was finally published in 1930, with the support of wordmaster Eric Partridge. Hanley received five pounds and no royalties in payment.

Hanley's next project was to write "the odyssey of a ship" with no human characters. He abandoned it and wrote the controversial novel *Boy*, which proved to be a major success. Hanley then commenced work on his major achievement, a five-volume saga of the Furys, a Liverpool family. The first volume was published in 1935 and the final volume in 1958. After publishing *Say Nothing* in 1962, Hanley abandoned the novel and wrote plays for the next ten years. In these plays, Hanley shows kinship with playwrights such as Harold Pinter, Samuel Beckett, and Strindberg. "I wrote plays for economic reasons," explained Hanley. "I even wrote under a pseudonym Patrick Shone, hoping it might change my luck." In 1972, Hanley returned to the novel form with the publication of *Another World*.

Hanley suffered considerable piracy of his works. Notable examples are *A Passion Before Death* (1930), which was reissued in the United States in a limited edition without any remuneration to Hanley, and the play *Say Nothing*, which ran for two months in New York with Hanley receiving no royalties.

When Hanley wrote, he preferred to be in total isolation. He neither read nor talked with people while creating. "It's like a prisoner being a writer," Hanley said, and Wales provided him with a stimulating kind of solitude. As for the writing of the novel itself, to him it was a "series of blind gropings in a dark tunnel." Character in a novel was the most important feature to him. If after the third chapter, the characters took over the telling of the story, Hanley knew that his novel was going well.

Hanley settled in London but always regretted leaving Wales. His loneliness increased after his wife of more than forty years died in 1980 (they had one son, Liam, an artist). Hanley died in London in 1985.

Analysis

Two themes dominate James Hanley's writings. The first concerns men at sea in ships. Hanley explored, in each succeeding novel, the strange love/hate relationship that men and women have for the sea. The sea with its violence and tranquillity, its many mysteries and its hypnotic powers over those who live and die by it, is orchestrated by him and becomes "the central experience of his novels." Hanley views the sea from the sailors' viewpoint, unlike Joseph Conrad, who saw the ship from the vantage point of an officer.

Hanley's second theme—often interrelated with the first—concerns men and women imprisoned in the web of poverty from which they have no desire to escape. They have created a world of deprivation for themselves and are terrified to come out of their self-imprisonment; within this confinement, they revolve and eke out their livelihood. Their despair leads them to weave private dreams, and their reluctance to realize their dreams returns them to despair. His characters, for the most part, are marginal people, the remnants of society, the debris of human life: outcasts, hobos, loners, strangers, broken men, women, and children. Hanley is their compassionate chronicler as he conducts a complex investigation into their lives and discovers poetry and drama in their bleak existence. With deep social concern, Hanley reveals how very much these marginal people matter: "the more insignificant a person is in this whirlpool of industrialized and civilized society, the more important he is for me." In making them touch our own wellsprings of compassion, Hanley achieved the hallmark of great literature; he moves readers emotionally.

The novel *Boy* has become a collector's item. In *Broken Water*, Hanley writes about seeing a boy in a Liverpool slum by the docks dragging a heavy cart "like a mule." The dull, vacant look on that boy's face profoundly touched Hanley and became the creative impulse for *Boy*. Also, in an autobiographical sketch titled "Oddfish," from *Don Quixote Drowned*, Hanley reports his sense of shock when he listened to an episode of a shipboy being thrown overboard because he had contracted a contagious disease. The memory of that tale remained with him to become an integral part of *Boy*. Furthermore, in the earlier Hanley story *The German Prisoner*, two mentally unbalanced British soldiers rape and brutalize a beautiful German boy. The passionate outrage against mindless violence coupled with a keen sense of social concern expressed in that story are also echoed in the novel.

Boy, because of its graphic descriptions of brutality, sadism, and homosexuality aboard a ship, was banned upon publication. *Boy* became a *cause célèbre*, and E. M. Forster came to Hanley's defense. William Faulkner called

Boy "a damn fine job. It springs up like a purifying cyclone, while most contemporary novels sound as if they were written by weaklings."

Boy is the brutal and tragic story of Arthur Fearon, a Liverpool schoolboy who has dreams of becoming a chemist. His sadistic father has more practical plans of having his son work on the docks to help liquidate family debts. He himself had a brutal job as a boy, and he cannot see a better life for his son. At the age of thirteen, Arthur is initiated into physical horrors by the gang on the dock. Arthur flees home and stows away in the coal bunker on a freighter going to Alexandria.

The boy's humiliating experiences, physical and sexual, on the freighter at the hands of almost everyone on board is the theme of *Boy*. A visit to a brothel in Alexandria, his initiation into manhood, is Arthur's one and only experience with beauty. The beauty of the girl soothes him, and "like a dark tapestry it covered his wounded thought, the spoliation, the degradation, the loneliness, the misery of his existence." From the encounter, he contracts syphilis and is shunned by all on the freighter. The ship's doctor wants Arthur to jump overboard and drown himself. Instead, however, the drunken captain gently invites Arthur to come to him by holding up his great coat, and, when Arthur responds unsuspectingly, the captain smothers him to death. The official report is: "Boy was lost overboard."

In spite of all the brutality that Arthur faces, he maintains a boyish idealism to the very end. He remains uncorrupted and thereby heightens the sense of tragedy. The novel's strong connotations of sexual urge and clinical descriptions make it a naturalistic work reminiscent of Stephen Crane's *Maggie: A Girl of the Streets* (1893). The epitome of Hanley's technique and style—the use of letters to keep the flow of narrative, the grinding minutiae of financial details, descriptions that often read like stage directions, the longing for the past and the future because the present is so unbearable, prose rising to poetic eloquence when describing ships and sea—*Boy* is a blueprint of the author's craftsmanship and sets the tone for his later novels.

Comprising 2,295 pages and five volumes, the Fury family chronicle (*The Furys, The Secret Journey, Our Time Is Gone, Winter Song, An End and a Beginning*) is Hanley's *magnum opus*. Set in Gelton, the fictional counterpart of Liverpool, the sequence of novels chronicles the saga of the Furys, a lower-class Liverpool Irish family. Based on references to British and world events, a period of sixteen years from 1911 to 1927 is covered in the novel sequence. In some of the volumes, the period covered is very brief, as in the final volume, *An End and a Beginning*, where the time frame is only three weeks.

Dennis Fury, a seaman, is the main character in the saga. It is his wife Fanny, however, who is the dominating force in the sequence. One of the most fully realized women in contemporary fiction, she is, as Edward Stokes points out in his study *The Novels of James Hanley* (1964), "both prosaic and legendary, at once middle-aged, dowdy, toil-worn, intensely respectable and bigoted housewife and a creature vital, passionate and a-moral as a heroine of Celtic myth." Fanny Fury holds both the novel and the Fury family together, and Hanley has fused into her something of the obsession of Lady Macbeth. Her son, Peter, whom she wants to be a priest against the wishes of the rest of her family, murders Anna Ragnar, the shrewd moneylender, and so splits the entire Fury family. Fanny uses all her efforts to bring the family together in a semblance of peace. The final novel in the sequence, *An End and a Beginning*, is devoted entirely to Peter Fury, and Hanley skillfully weaves the past and the present to maintain the narrative flow.

In anatomizing the intricacies of the family relationships within the Fury family, Hanley draws upon elements of Lawrentian brutality. Dennis Fury is pitted against his eighty-two-year-old father-in-law, Anthony Mangan, who is incapacitated; Fanny is pitted against her daughter Maureen's husband, John Kilkey, a devout pacifist; the whole family, with the exception of Fanny, is pitted against Peter, who is studying to be a priest at their expense; Fanny and Dennis themselves are locked in ferocious combat concerning a multitude of daily minutiae. Hanley's use of dialogue to reveal these hostilities is crisp, direct, and theatrical in the best sense of the term.

The imagery of a prison dominates the entire saga. To Peter, the seminary is a prison; to Dennis, his home is a prison and the sea is freedom; to Fanny the sea is a steel trap taking away her men, and her very desire to keep the family together imprisons her in her responsibilities; Anthony Mangan, paralyzed and mute, finds the chair in which he is strapped to be his prison physically and verbally; Peter Fury murders the moneylender and cries out that he is free from debt only to find himself behind prison bars. All the characters in the Fury chronicle are attempting to escape their prisons but find themselves in darker traps for doing so. Hanley has worked out his imagery of frustration, loneliness, and inability to communicate throughout the saga, and an entire study can be made about prison imagery in his novels. Hanley creates a scene, introduces his characters, gives readers an intense close-up, and reveals his characters through dialogue and intimate conversation. There are always passages of lyrical beauty whenever the sea or a ship is described. Letters, journals, and inner monologues are all used to tell the story and reveal insights into a variety of characters that populate the chronicle. There are a few noteworthy characters among the many found in the novels: John Kilkey, physically repulsive, is a man of deep principles and compassion and a pacifist; Brigid Mangan, Fanny's youngest sister, is a spinster and a devout Catholic strongly feeling her alienation in England and eager to return to her spiritual home, Ireland; Desmond Fury, the eldest son, is ambitious and deeply involved in Labour politics, and his wife, Sheila, has an adulterous affair with Peter Fury; Mrs. Anna Ragner, the sharp moneylender, enjoys having people in her grip and getting rich on poverty; Professor R. H. Titmouse, a self-appointed professor of anthropology, is a homosexual with a hysterical crush on Peter but acts at times as the voice of sanity when he tells Peter that people are merely sheep ready to be manipulated by politicians. These and a host of other characters give the Fury chronicle a deep richness and diversity of humanity.

The saga of the Furys, however, has not received a great deal of critical attention. It is a work that is original, sustained, and above all, as Edward Stokes maintains, a "compassionate penetration into the dreams and desperations, the illusions and longings of the characters" that move throughout this epic work.

The years between 1938 and 1943 were a peak period in Hanley's creativity. He wrote three significant novels about ships and sailors, against the backdrop of war: *Hollow Sea*, *The Ocean*, and *Sailor's Song*. The first is set within the time frame of a few weeks and is a story of a troopship. A former liner called *Helicon*, the vessel is painted gray and called *A10* and is involved in a war mission to transport fifteen hundred soldiers to a secret destination. To Captain Dunford, *A10* is "the personification of uncontrollable madness"; to the men in overcrowded holds with shortages of food and water, life aboard the *A10* is nasty, brutish, and uncertain. The ship bristles with tensions and the voyage becomes "a microcosm of a whole world at war." During the voyage, *A10* gets into a violent and bloody skirmish and is compelled to add another two hundred soldiers to its population. Without adequate hospital facilities, the men die, and the ship's captain refuses to bury them without proper authorization. *A10* becomes "a coffin ship" and pressures intensify. Some men capitalize on the tensions and shortages by carrying on a black market in food; others seek escape in fantasy, letting their minds conjure images of reaching home and reunion with their families.

Hanley characterizes vividly the various men on the ship, from the captain who is "imprisoned by his mission," and hence must be totally authoritative, to boatswain Vesuvius with an "eruption of pimples on his face." There is, however, a poetic quality to the novel that echoes the legend of the Flying Dutchman and the eerie atmosphere evoked by Samuel Taylor Coleridge in *The Rime of the Ancient Mariner* (1798). Edwin Muir felicitously noted this in his review of the novel: "*Hollow Sea*'s great virtue is that it is poetically conceived. We are always conscious that the events that Hanley is describing are part of a large pattern." *Hollow Sea* captures the hustle, the bustle, and the ceaseless throb of life aboard a troopship, and had it not been so long, it would have emerged as a great novel.

A tight, short, well-structured novel, *The Ocean* is a powerful study in survival. The entire action takes place in an open boat containing five men: Joseph Curtain, the sailor; Father Michaels, a priest; Gaunt, a middle-aged businessman, who worries about his missing wife, Kay; Stone, a middle-aged teacher; and twenty-year-old Benton. These are the survivors from the torpedoed ship *Aurora*. Hanley has endowed a timeless quality to his story by not giving it a local habitation or a specific time. The reader is constantly made aware of the loneliness and helplessness of these men in the midst of the vast empty sea, which is full of beauty and terror.

Joseph Curtain is the key character in the novel. He knows how to deal with the men and can operate on the whole spectrum of human emotions. There is a lean, spare athletic quality to Hanley's prose in *The Ocean*, an economy of word and style that is reminiscent of the best of Ernest Hemingway. It is remarkable that Hanley, who wrote the long, discursive *Hollow Sea*, could also write *The Ocean*: it is one of his very best.

The last of Hanley's sea novels, *Sailor's Song*, is set on a raft and concerns four men. The story, told with biblical simplicity and lyrical beauty, is the story of the delirious sailor, Manion, on the raft. Manion's name is a play on "any man." Carefully, through a series of broken images and shuttling back and forth through the corridors of time, Manion's tale—the sailor's song—is unfolded. Manion is the captive of the sea, hypnotized and held by it. Through his life, Hanley distills the strange umbilical feelings that sailors have for the sea and ships. Delirious, Manion remembers his past, particularly the time when he was without a ship and became restless looking for one, believing in a miracle that would result in his signing on another ship. Hanley was also to use this theme—of a sailor desperately looking for a home, a ship on which to sign—in his novel *The Closed Harbour*. After he has sung his song, told his story, John Manion drifts in his sleep to death. *Sailor's Song* is perhaps Hanley's most moving novel.

Continuing to master his primary themes of the sea and entrapment, Hanley's creative talents are not exhausted. *The Closed Harbour*, set in Marseilles, is Hanley's only novel with a non-English setting. It is a powerful and intense study of a French merchant captain, Marius, who is under a cloud of suspicion. He wants to get a ship but none is available. Hanley relentlessly probes Marius' mind, moving back and forth in a fascinating study of a haunted man. George Painter in reviewing the novel rightly pointed out that Marius "is a figure worthy of Melville, a fallen angel, a monument of man's grandeur in defeat." Felix Levine, of *Levine*, like Marius, is a man without a ship, but Felix is also a man without a country: he is the quintessential displaced person. Felix is a typical Hanley character, who obsessively dreams and weaves fantasies and begins to believe in them so passionately that dreams become his reality. The entire novel itself is a backward dream, and through a series of interior monologues, diaries, and letters, Hanley orchestrates all the subtle nuances that make up the dark despair of loneliness and hunger.

Hanley's 1976 novel, *A Dream Journey*, is the best introduction to Hanley. The story of Clem Stevens, an artist, and his wife, Lena, it is the single novel which distills all of Hanley's themes, styles, concerns, and characterizations. Clem and Lena both appeared earlier in Hanley's short novel *No Directions*. Since Hanley has said that novel writing is a "series of blind gropings in a long dark tunnel," it seems that he looked back at the tunnel where he had left the characters from *No Directions* and found that "they were not so limp" as he had thought they were and so he "gave each character an extra squeeze." In fact, the longest section in *A Dream Journey*, "Yesterday," is the entire text of *No Directions*.

The novel opens in typical Hanley fashion, "a monosyllabic session." The moment a thought appears in the mind of one of the characters, the scene accompanying that thought is conjured in the mind of that character. Everyone is on a dream journey, and dreaming becomes a metaphor for living for both Clem and his wife. They use their dreams to seek tranquillity from the harshness of life by "fondling memories" in their minds.

Clem suffers from depression and has not left his house in more than a year. He has painted a sixty-year-old woman on five canvases, reflecting a whole day in her life, "a whole language of exhaustion." Clem seems to do in painting what Hanley does with words. Yet, Clem is not a successful artist; his paintings sold to the butcher get him "free meat for a month." Lena is his encourager, but the days grind out in sheer monotony, and there is no communication between them. They turn to the past and, in their minds, go on dream journeys. Their small claustrophobic rooms imprison them. Lena thinks of leaving Clem, but "you don't just walk out on a person because he's second rate"; furthermore, "people don't escape from their own illusions, you just live with them." In a way, she enjoys Clem's dependence on her. When the final catastrophe happens—a fire and Clem's death as he attempts to rescue his paintings—it is a logical conclusion based on the characters' "realities." In *A Dream Journey*, Hanley brings to bear the maturity and careful artistry of his talents.

Readers who are familiar with Hanley's works find new meanings and subtle nuances in his writings with each rereading. Those who have the patience to approach and discover his fiction for the first time will be richly rewarded with a satisfying literary and emotional experience. His position as a major literary figure in the twentieth century is firmly established.

K. Bhaskara Rao

Other major works

SHORT FICTION: *The German Prisoner*, 1930; *A Passion Before Death*, 1930; *The Last Voyage*, 1931; *Men in Darkness: Five Stories*, 1931; *Stoker Haslett*, 1932; *Aria and Finale*, 1932; *Quartermaster Clausen*, 1934; *At Bay*, 1935; *Half an Eye: Sea Stories*, 1937; *People Are Curious*, 1938; *At Bay and Other Stories*, 1944; *Crilley and Other Stories*, 1945; *Selected Stories*, 1947; *A Walk in the Wilderness*, 1950; *Collected Stories*, 1953; *Darkness*, 1973; *What Farrar Saw and Other Stories*, 1984.

PLAYS: *Say Nothing*, 1963; *The Inner Journey*, 1965; *Plays One*, 1968.

NONFICTION: *Broken Water: An Autobiographical Excursion*, 1937; *Grey Children: A Study in Humbug and Misery*, 1937; *Between the Tides*, 1939; *Don Quixote Drowned*, 1953; *John Cowper Powys: A Man in the Corner*, 1969; *Herman Melville: A Man in the Customs House*, 1971.

Bibliography

Bryfonski, Dedria, ed. *Contemporary Literary Criticism*. Vol. 13. Detroit: Gale Research, 1980. Presents a sampling of book reviews, including those from *New Leader*, *Spectator*, and *The New York Times Book Review*, on Hanley's writings. The reviews reflect the praise Hanley has received for his work, as well as the acknowledgment that he does not get the recognition he deserves.

Desmond, Graham. Review of *A Kingdom*, by James Hanley. *Stand* 20, no. 1 (1978-1979): 50-52. Desmond discusses Hanley's work in general, which he calls "poetic fiction." In the commentary on *A Kingdom*, set in Wales, Desmond notes that the work is much less stylized and mannered than *The Welsh Sonata*. Compares *A Kingdom* to the work of Henry James but says that it falls short and that it would have been more successful had it been expanded.

Mathewson, Ruth. "Hanley's Palimpsest." *New Leader* (January 3, 1977): 17-18. Reviews *A Dream Journey*, noting that it is a good introduction to Hanley's work. Mathewson also briefly discusses Hanley's earlier novels and comments that *A Dream Journey* is a "palimpsest of earlier works."

Vinson, James, ed. *St. James Reference Guide to English Literature*. Chicago: St. James Press, 1985. Contains an excellent piece of criticism on Hanley by Edward Stokes. Cites the importance of Hanley's writing, which has been compared to that of Thomas Hardy and Fyodor Dostoevski. Notes, however, that Hanley's work is uneven and his characters lacking in popular appeal.